FRANCIS FRITH'S

COTSWOLD VILLAGES PHOTOGRAPHIC MEMORIES

THE FRANCIS FRITH COLLECTION

www.francisfrith.com

FRANCIS FRITH'S

COTSWOLD VILLAGES

PHOTOGRAPHIC MEMORIES

JUNE LEWIS-JONES is a professional writer. Her published works include some 22 books as well as a regular feature series for 'Cotswold Life' magazine over 30 years, on people and places, crafts and cookery, history and heritage. Her work for BBC radio ranges from a series of plays on historical events in the West Country to narrating a Radio 4 play dramatised from one of her books. She has given talks on Cotswold villages and appeared many times on television in connection with her writing and research. She was elected a Fellow of the Royal Society of Arts in 1974. June is Cotswold born and bred, with family roots dating back to medieval times in the area close to Cirencester where she has lived all her life.

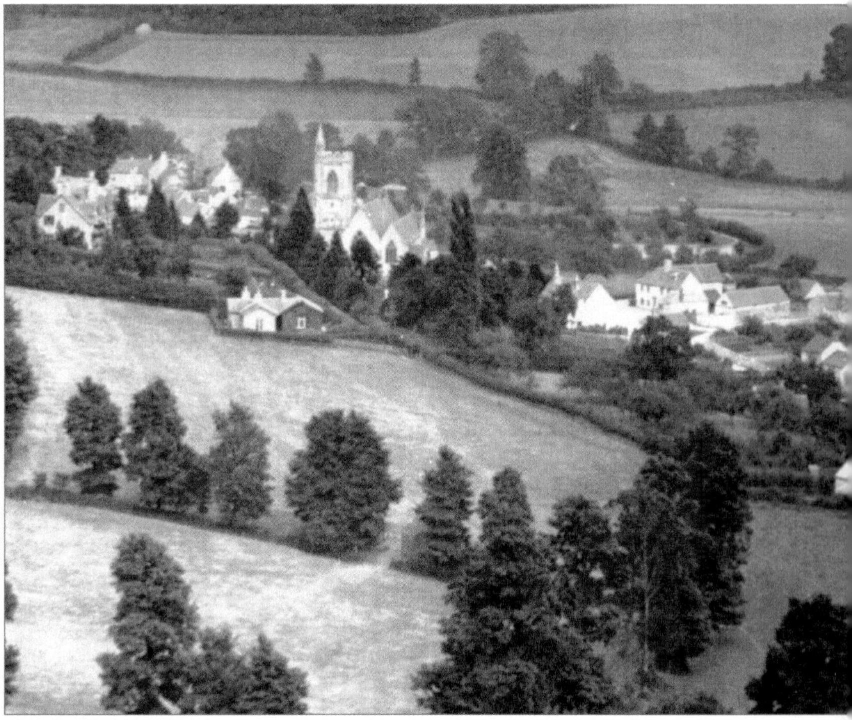

FRANCIS FRITH'S
PHOTOGRAPHIC MEMORIES

COTSWOLD VILLAGES

PHOTOGRAPHIC MEMORIES

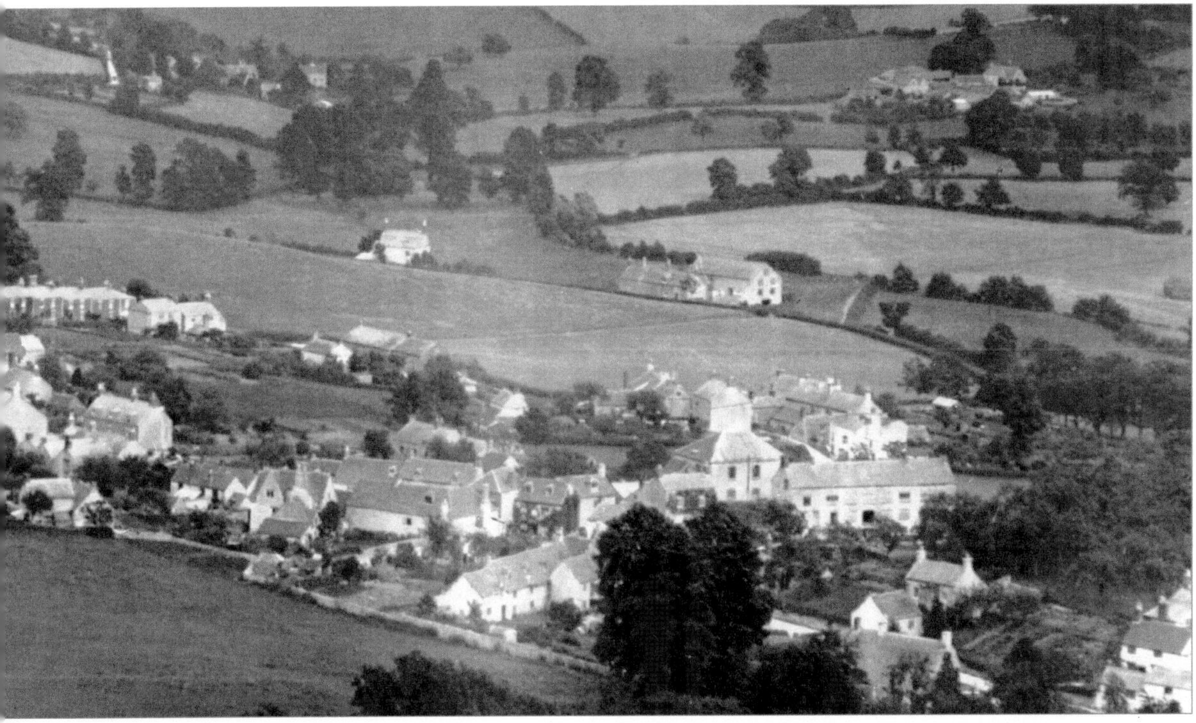

JUNE LEWIS-JONES

First published in hardback in the United Kingdom in 2005
by The Francis Frith Collection®
Hardback Edition ISBN 1-85937-645-2
Paperback Edition ISBN 978-1-84589-503-7

British Library Cataloguing in Publication Data

Cotswold Villages - Photographic Memories
June Lewis-Jones

The Francis Frith Collection
Frith's Barn, Teffont,
Salisbury, Wiltshire SP3 5QP
Tel: +44 (0) 1722 716 376
Email: info@francisfrith.co.uk
www.francisfrith.com

Printed and bound in Great Britain

Front Cover: **CHALFORD**, *The Village 1910* 62713t
Frontispiece: **ULEY**, *From Uley Bury 1900* 45539

The colour-tinting is for illustrative purposes only, and is not intended to be historically accurate

AS WITH ANY HISTORICAL DATABASE THE FRITH ARCHIVE IS CONSTANTLY BEING CORRECTED AND IMPROVED AND THE PUBLISHERS WOULD WELCOME INFORMATION ON OMISSIONS OR INACCURACIES

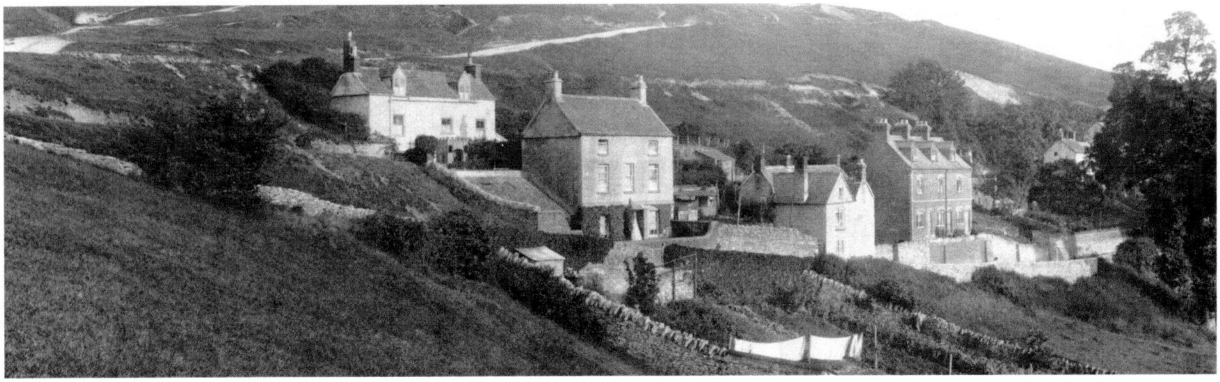

CONTENTS

For my husband, Ralph

FRANCIS FRITH

VICTORIAN PIONEER

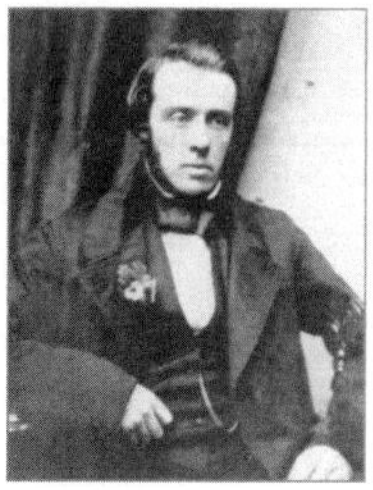

FRANCIS FRITH, founder of the world-famous photographic archive, was a complex and multi-talented man. A devout Quaker and a highly successful Victorian businessman, he was philosophical by nature and pioneering in outlook.

By 1855 he had already established a wholesale grocery business in Liverpool, and sold it for the astonishing sum of £200,000, which is the equivalent today of over £15,000,000. Now a very rich man, he was able to indulge his passion for travel. As a child he had pored over travel books written by early explorers, and his fancy and imagination had been stirred by family holidays to the sublime mountain regions of Wales and Scotland. 'What lands of spirit-stirring and enriching scenes and places!' he had written. He was to return to these scenes of grandeur in later years to 'recapture the thousands of vivid and tender memories', but with a different purpose. Now in his thirties, and captivated by the new science of photography, Frith set out on a series of pioneering journeys up the Nile and to the Near East that occupied him from 1856 until 1860.

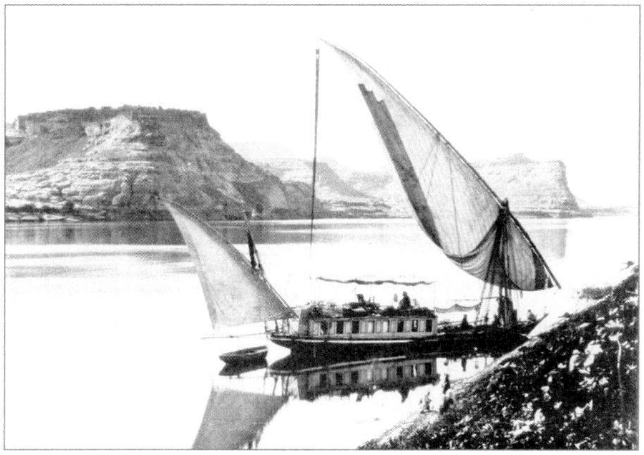

INTRIGUE AND EXPLORATION

These far-flung journeys were packed with intrigue and adventure. In his life story, written when he was sixty-three, Frith tells of being held captive by bandits, and of fighting 'an awful midnight battle to the very point of surrender with a deadly pack of hungry, wild dogs'. Wearing flowing Arab costume, Frith arrived at Akaba by camel sixty years before Lawrence of Arabia, where he encountered 'desert princes and rival sheikhs, blazing with jewel-hilted swords'.

He was the first photographer to venture beyond the sixth cataract of the Nile. Africa was still the mysterious 'Dark Continent', and Stanley and Livingstone's historic meeting was a decade into the future. The conditions for picture taking confound belief. He laboured for hours in his wicker dark-room in the sweltering heat of the desert, while the volatile chemicals fizzed dangerously in their trays. Back in London he exhibited his photographs and was 'rapturously cheered' by members of the Royal Society. His reputation as a photographer was made overnight.

VENTURE OF A LIFE-TIME

Characteristically, Frith quickly spotted the opportunity to create a new business as a specialist publisher of photographs. He lived in an era of immense and sometimes violent change.

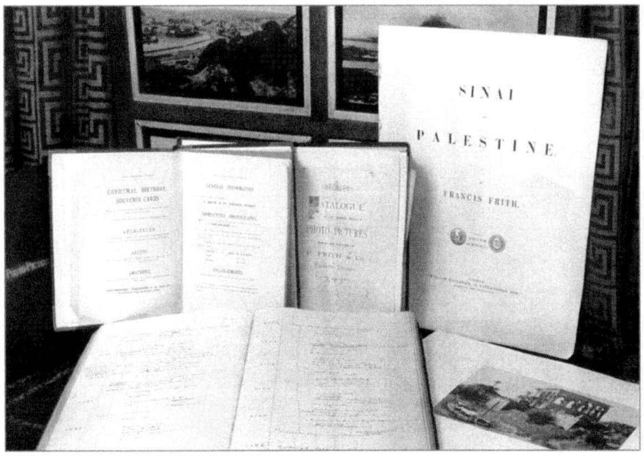

For the poor in the early part of Victoria's reign work was exhausting and the hours long, and people had precious little free time to enjoy themselves. Most had no transport other than a cart or gig at their disposal, and rarely travelled far beyond the boundaries of their own town or village. However, by the 1870s the railways had threaded their way across the country, and Bank Holidays and half-day Saturdays had been made obligatory by Act of Parliament. All of a sudden the working man and his family were able to enjoy days out and see a little more of the world.

With typical business acumen, Francis Frith foresaw that these new tourists would enjoy having souvenirs to commemorate their days out. In 1860 he married Mary Ann Rosling and set out on a new career: his aim was to photograph every city, town and village in Britain. For the next thirty years he travelled the country by train and by pony and trap, producing fine photographs of seaside resorts and beauty spots that were keenly bought by millions of Victorians. These prints were painstakingly pasted into family albums and pored over during the dark nights of winter, rekindling precious memories of summer excursions.

THE RISE OF FRITH & CO

Frith's studio was soon supplying retail shops all over the country. To meet the demand he gathered about him a small team of photographers, and published the work of independent artist-photographers of the calibre of Roger Fenton and Francis Bedford. In order to gain some understanding of the scale of Frith's business one only has to look at the catalogue issued by Frith & Co in 1886: it runs to some 670 pages, listing not only many thousands of views of the British Isles but also many photographs of most European countries, and China, Japan, the USA and Canada - note the sample page shown on page 9 from the hand-written Frith & Co ledgers recording the pictures. By 1890 Frith had created the greatest specialist photographic publishing company in the world, with over 2,000 sales outlets - more than the combined number that Boots and WH Smith have today! The picture on the next page shows the Frith & Co display board at Ingleton in the Yorkshire Dales (left of window). Beautifully constructed with a mahogany frame and gilt inserts, it could display up to a dozen local scenes.

POSTCARD BONANZA

The ever-popular holiday postcard we know today took many years to develop. In 1870 the Post Office issued the first plain cards, with a pre-printed stamp on one face. In 1894 they allowed other publishers' cards to be sent through the mail with an attached adhesive halfpenny stamp. Demand grew rapidly, and in 1895 a new size of postcard was permitted called the court card, but there was little room for illustration. In 1899, a year after Frith's death, a new card measuring 5.5 x 3.5 inches became the standard format, but it was not until 1902 that the divided back came into being, so that the address and message could be on one face and a full-size illustration on the other. Frith & Co were in the vanguard of postcard development: Frith's sons Eustace and Cyril continued their father's monumental task, expanding the number of views offered to the public and recording more and more places

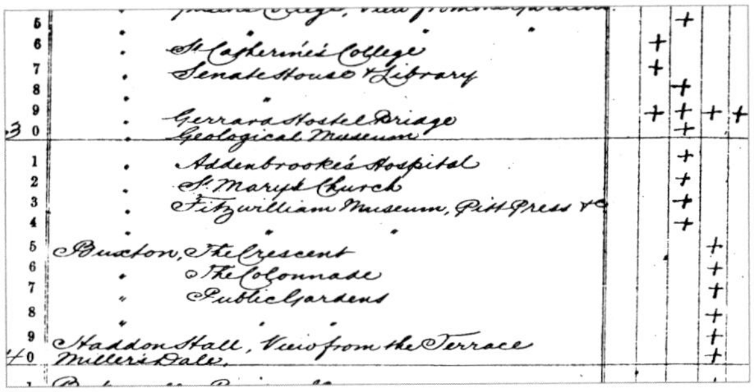
St Catherine's College
Senate House & Library
Gerrard Hostel Bridge
Geological Museum
Addenbrooke's Hospital
St Mary's Church
Fitzwilliam Museum, Pitt Press &c
Buxton, The Crescent
The Colonnade
Public Gardens
Haddon Hall, View from the Terrace
Millers Dale

in Britain, as the coasts and countryside were opened up to mass travel.

Francis Frith had died in 1898 at his villa in Cannes, his great project still growing. The archive he created continued in business for another seventy years. By 1970 it contained over a third of a million pictures showing 7,000 British towns and villages.

FRANCIS FRITH'S LEGACY

Frith's legacy to us today is of immense significance and value, for the magnificent archive of evocative photographs he created provides a unique record of change in the cities, towns and villages throughout Britain over a century and more. Frith and his fellow studio photographers revisited locations many times down the years to update their views, compiling for us an enthralling and colourful pageant of British life and character.

We are fortunate that Frith was dedicated to recording the minutiae of everyday life, for it is this sheer wealth of visual data, the painstaking chronicle of changes in dress, transport, street layouts, buildings, housing, engineering and landscape that captivates us so much today. His remarkable images offer us a powerful link with the past and with the lives of our ancestors.

THE VALUE OF THE ARCHIVE TODAY

Computers have now made it possible for Frith's many thousands of images to be accessed almost instantly. Frith's images are increasingly used as visual resources, by social historians, by researchers into genealogy and ancestry, by architects and town planners, and by teachers involved in local history projects.

In addition, the archive offers every one of us an opportunity to examine the places where we and our families have lived and worked down the years. Highly successful in Frith's own era, the archive is now, a century and more on, entering a new phase of popularity. Historians consider the Francis Frith Collection to be of prime national importance. It is the only archive of its kind remaining in private ownership. Francis Frith's archive is now housed in an historic timber barn in the beautiful village of Teffont in Wiltshire. Its founder would not recognize the archive office as it is today. In place of the many thousands of dusty boxes containing glass plate negatives and an all-pervading odour of photographic chemicals, there are now ranks of computer screens. He would be amazed to watch his images travelling round the world at unimaginable speeds through internet lines.

The archive's future is both bright and exciting. Francis Frith, with his unshakeable belief in making photographs available to the greatest number of people, would undoubtedly approve of what is being done today with his lifetime's work. His photographs depicting our shared past are now bringing pleasure and enlightenment to millions around the world a century and more after his death.

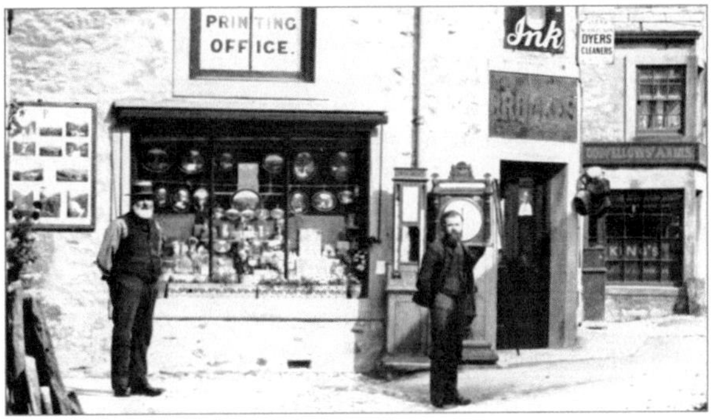

COTSWOLD VILLAGES

AN INTRODUCTION

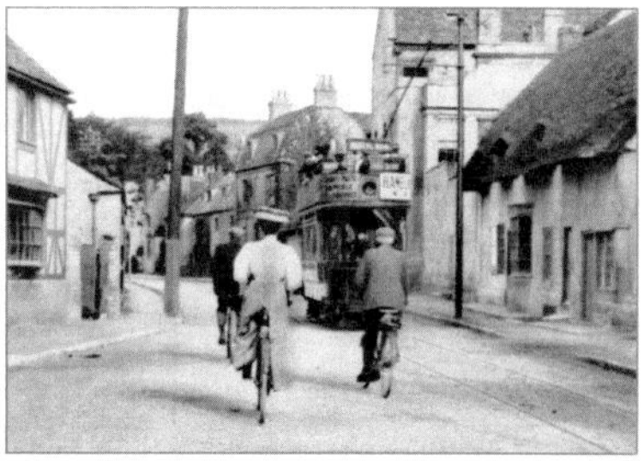

THE COTSWOLDS have long been designated an Area of Outstanding Natural Beauty, and the very name conjures up a picture of high rolling wolds and small river valleys, where honey-coloured stone buildings cluster in various sized settlements as part of the landscape. And this is where the homogeneity of the whole begins, because it is by using the native stone from under their feet that the first builders raised their humble cottages, their lords' and masters' manor houses, their Maker's churches and the monastic tithe barns. It can truly be said that the buildings grew out of the very land on which they stand. The patchwork of fields, the cottager's garden, the village street and the ancient churchyard - all are bound around by walls of the rough-hewn stone which time and climate encrust with grey and golden lichen. This is the over-riding picture of the Cotswolds that is close to the native heart and endears it to the visitor.

The topography is easy to define. From the west, its dominant steep scarp slope runs from Meon Hill in the north Cotswolds to just below the Stroud Valleys before undulating gradually down to Bath, for here the great mass of oolitic limestone was heaved up from ancient seas. Gentler slopes tilt across its breadth from this point to the east, where it peters out to the Oxfordshire plains. Definition of the Cotswold area is not so simple: it lies mainly in Gloucestershire, but unlike counties where planners draw demarcation lines governed by administrative policies, a region has no distinct boundaries - its character and characteristics define it. It is by this measure that some of the villages in this collection have been included, as a number belong properly to the vale under the escarpment, but they have an affinity with the hills; likewise, on the eastern edge, where there are even less definitive landscape features, it is the architectural and cultural ties to the Cotswolds that warrant their inclusion.

Villages themselves do not always fall into a neat category: Fairford and Lechlade, for instance, are strictly ancient market towns, but are little larger than villages and have village life communities, whereas Broadway and Bourton-on-the-Water trade like small towns, but still have village status. What they all have is the unifying character of the Cotswolds, and this is graphically illustrated in this collection of photographs, where the distinctive architecture is featured in diverse compositions.

There is no large urban sprawl in the

Cotswolds, just a handful of small market towns that have developed to meet modern day demands; neither is there any large-scale industrial area. But neither is there that kind of over-careful preservation that leads to stagnation, although such a unique area of natural beauty needs constant and careful conservation to maintain its character. Perhaps it is because Man started off by using the only two main natural resources to be found here: stone and water. Cotswold stone is the dominant feature in a style imposed by purpose rather than design; its distinctive features, steeply pitched roofs and gabled windows, were dictated by the need to carry the weight of heavy stone slates and to withstand the force of the elements on high and exposed hills and wolds.

The waters of the Cotswolds shaped the landscape into a series of valleys, with most of the main rivers that rise in the hills flowing south-east to feed the Thames. It is only in the Stroud valleys, where the water power was strong enough to drive the mills, that industry came - it was rooted from the Middle Ages to create a cloth-making centre of national importance. (The old mills have now been converted to other uses). It is by way of placing the villages in the context of the valleys in which they stand, or the ways they are topographically linked, that this collection of photographs can best illustrate the fact that even within such a homogenous entity as the Cotswolds, there is diversity and individual character throughout the region.

What is also of interest is how the economic structure laid the foundations for the shaping of the landscape over the last millennium. Following the Dissolution, the vast tracts of land over which monastic flocks of sheep roamed, their heavy white fleeces turning to gold in the market halls to swell the coffers of the great abbeys and monasteries, came under the ownership of enterprising wool merchants, who invested their wealth into rebuilding, endowing and beautifying the old churches of their parishes, leaving the Cotswolds a legacy of outstandingly fine medieval 'wool' churches. Local markets sprang up and expanded, creating a forum for trading in an even wider range of produce; the advent of the coaching era and the improvement in the road system spawned the increase in the number of inns and hostelries needed to cater for a new travelling public, and most of the inns in the Cotswolds can date their origins back to that period.

Within that general development arose two distinct social structures in the area we classify as the Stroud valleys and the valley villages of the central Cotswolds. In the industrialised Stroud area, it was a wealthy millocracy that sustained the economy; they built their big houses well away from noise and bustle of the mills that worked in the valley bottoms. In the central Cotswolds, the aristocracy set about developing agricultural land, around which a number of estate villages were built. Their passion for building grand mansions and landscaping their grounds left a rich heritage of architectural treasures and sweeping parklands.

This collection of old photographs captures a great deal of some of that diversity and certainly the essence of what is special about the Cotswolds.

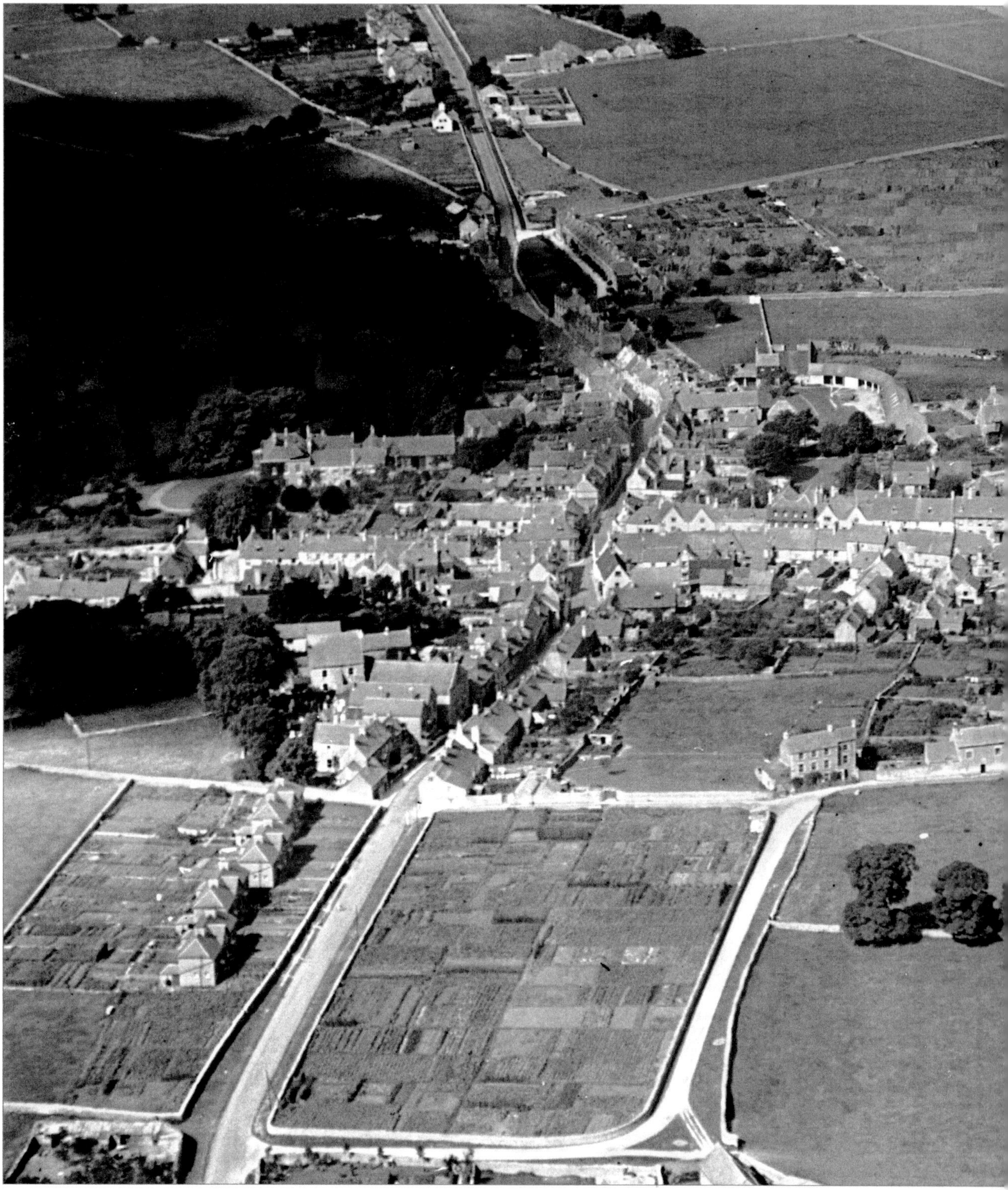

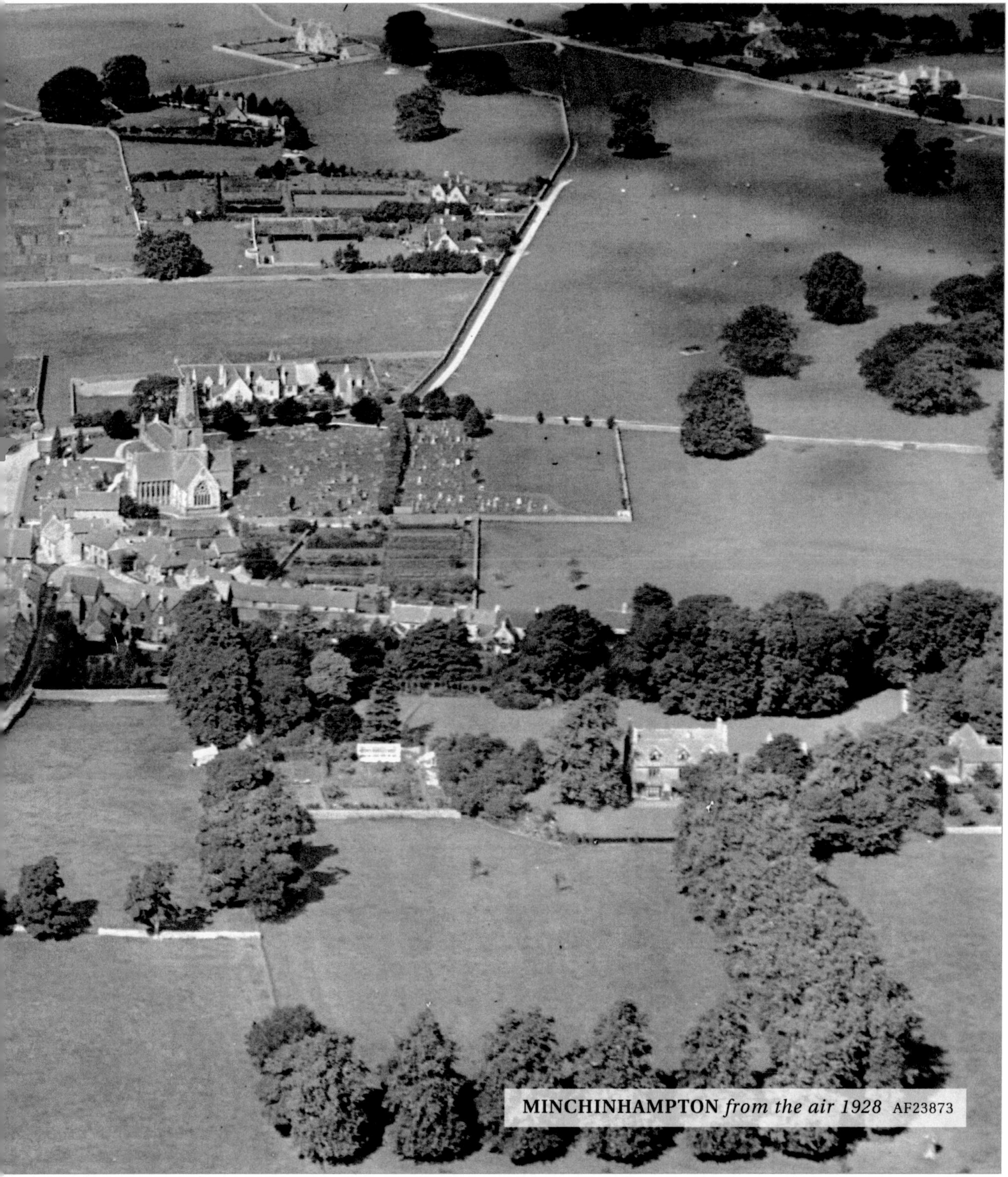

MINCHINHAMPTON *from the air 1928* AF23873

VALE AND HILL

THE VILLAGES featured in this section are a mix of those that belong to the hills of the north Cotswolds and of others that lie in the vale under the bluff of the escarpment. Bredon is included, as it is situated beside Bredon Hill, the largest of Cotswold's outliers, rising to almost 1,000 feet in the north-west. These villages may stand apart topographically, but they are unified by their origins and characteristics: all are built from the oolitic limestone, and are linked culturally by their tenacious hold on custom and heritage.

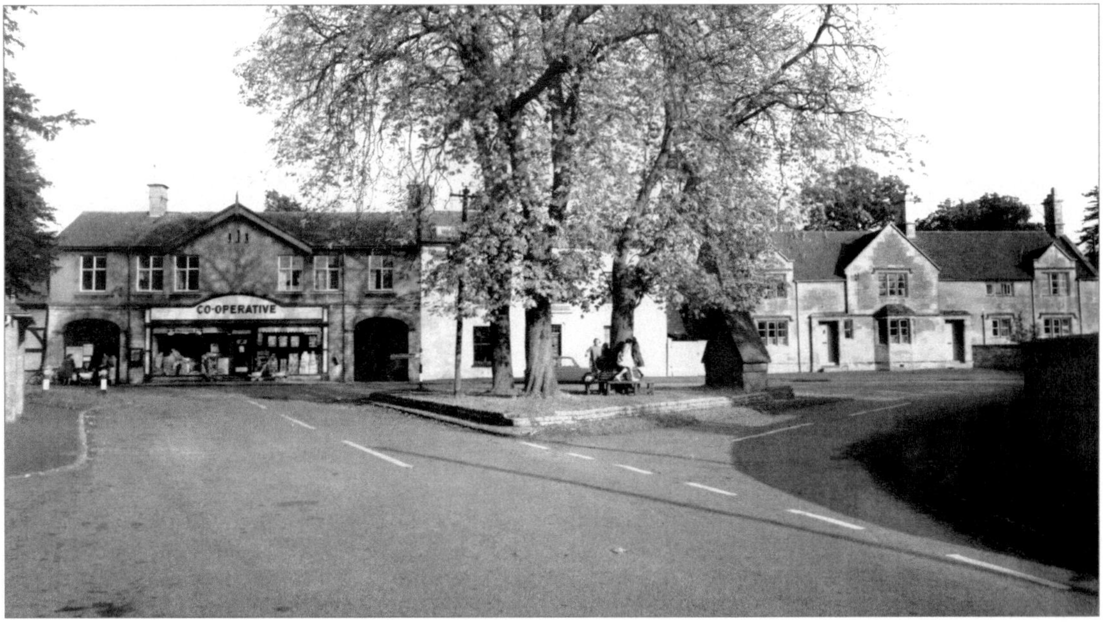

MICKLETON, *The Fountain c1960* M250008

At the northernmost tip of the Cotswolds, Mickleton lies just below the spur of the hills as they level out to Shakespeare's Warwickshire. It is a large village, showing its growth through the ages in the mixed architectural styles lining its broad streets.

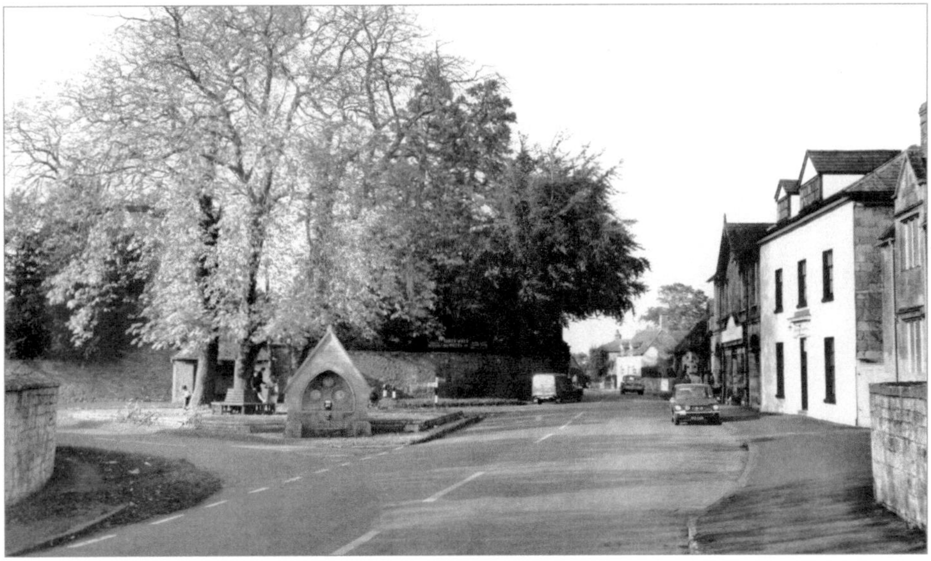

MICKLETON
The Fountain c1965
M250006

The gabled memorial fountain, with its arched niche containing medallion portraits and a coat of arms, is a central feature of the village, and a focal point for floral displays now that its original use as a public water supply is no longer the important amenity it was in 1875 when it was built.

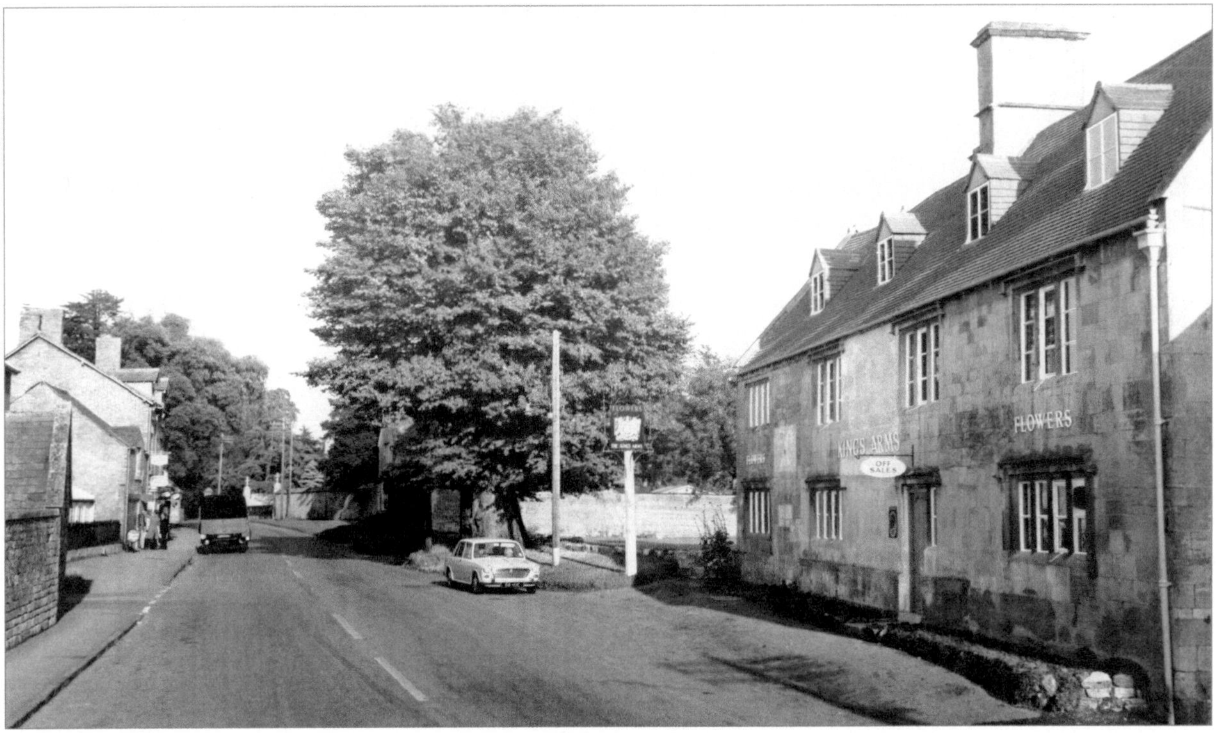

MICKLETON, *High Street and the Kings Arms c1960* M250005

This village must qualify for having had one of the most short-lived halts in railway history. Mickleton Halt, costing some £512 when it opened in 1937, with shelters, an oil hut, and paraffin vapour lighting on both platforms, was listed for closure in 1941. Motorists, however, have since made more than a brief halt at this attractive village.

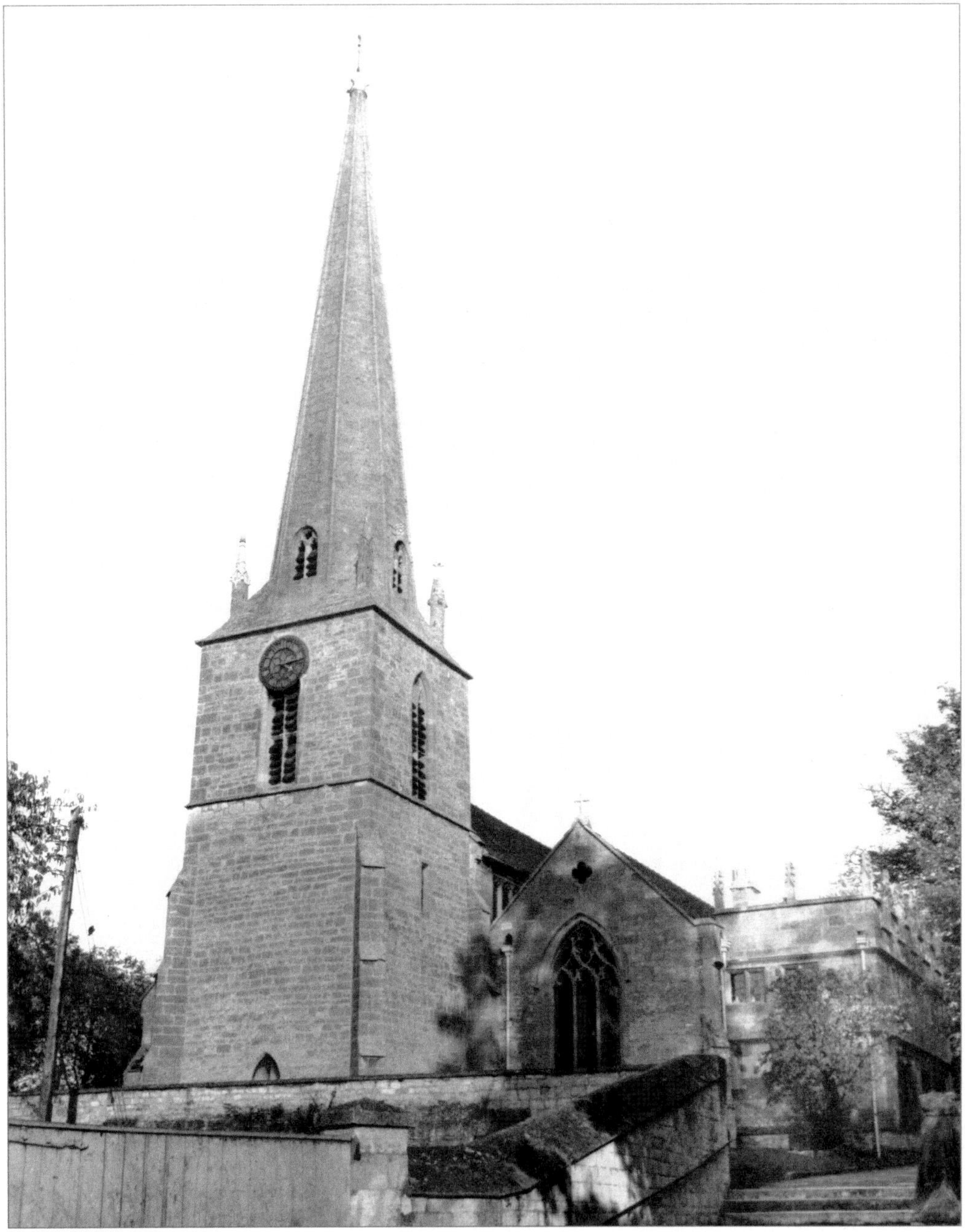

MICKLETON, *The Church c1960* M250009

The origin of the church of St Lawrence dates back to the 12th century; the tower and broached spire were added two centuries later. Inside are several memorials to the Graves family, who lived at Mickleton from Elizabethan times; Richard Graves (1715-1804) was acclaimed as one of the best writers and storytellers of his day, and featured his father in one of his novels, 'The Spiritual Quixote'.

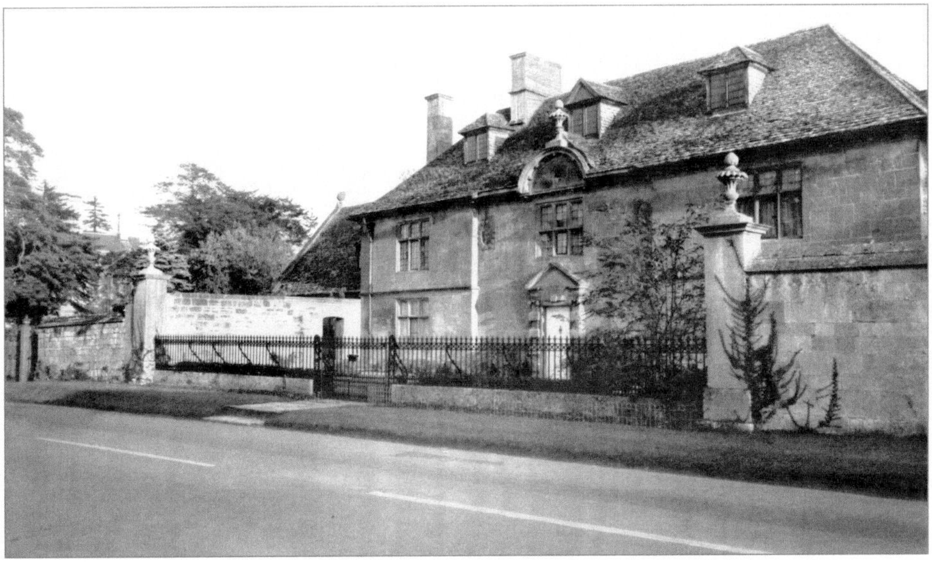

MICKLETON
Medford House c1960 M250011

Built in the later 1600s, this beautiful house has long been cited as a textbook example of the transition of the architectural style from traditional Tudor to Queen Anne classical, where the customary gables of the Cotswold style have given way to a hipped roof with dormer windows.

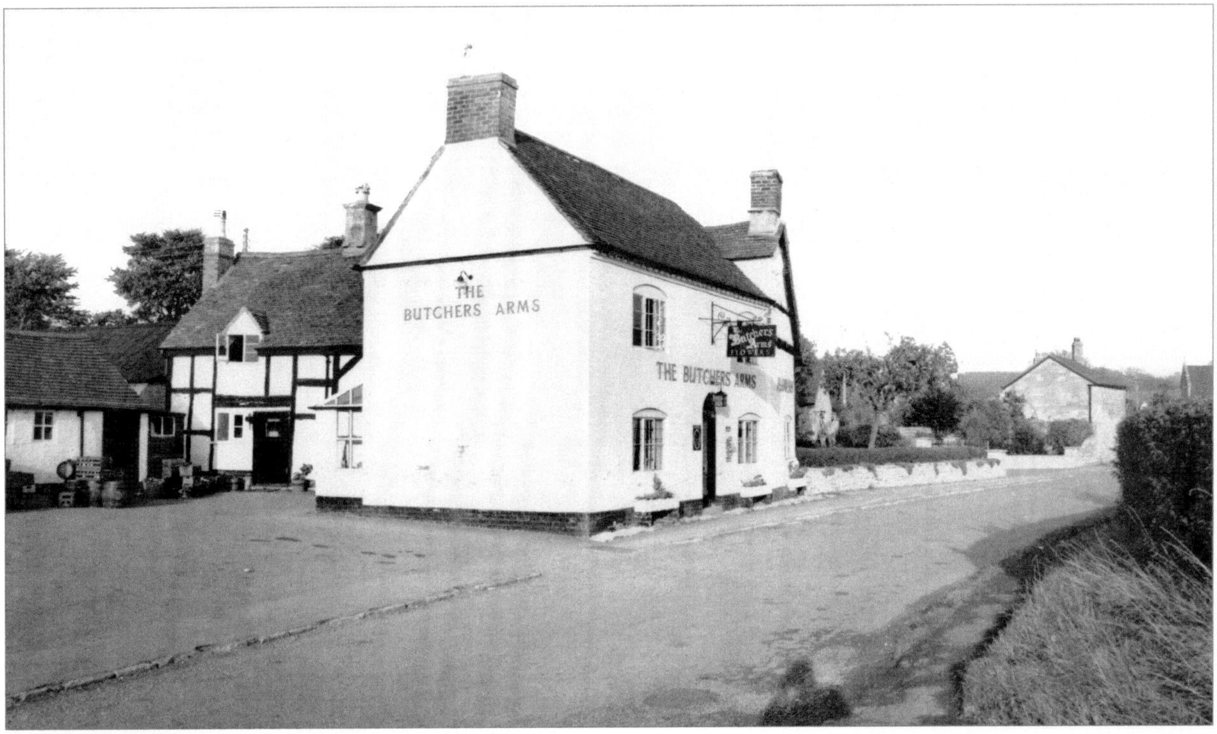

MICKLETON, *The Butchers Arms c1960* M250016

The black and white half-timbered frame of the building at the rear of the inn shows the influence of the Warwickshire Vale building methods on this Cotswold village.

BROADWAY
The Village 1899
44113

Early man came to this 'broad way' as the ancient ridgeway took him over the high wolds, and travellers have come to Broadway ever since. The charter granted by King Edgar is the earliest record of Broadway's existence; now the village features on every Cotswold tour. It was one of the first to be 'discovered' and restored at the end of the Victorian era, and has attracted artists, authors and visitors ever since. While trading like a small town, it remains in essence a village.

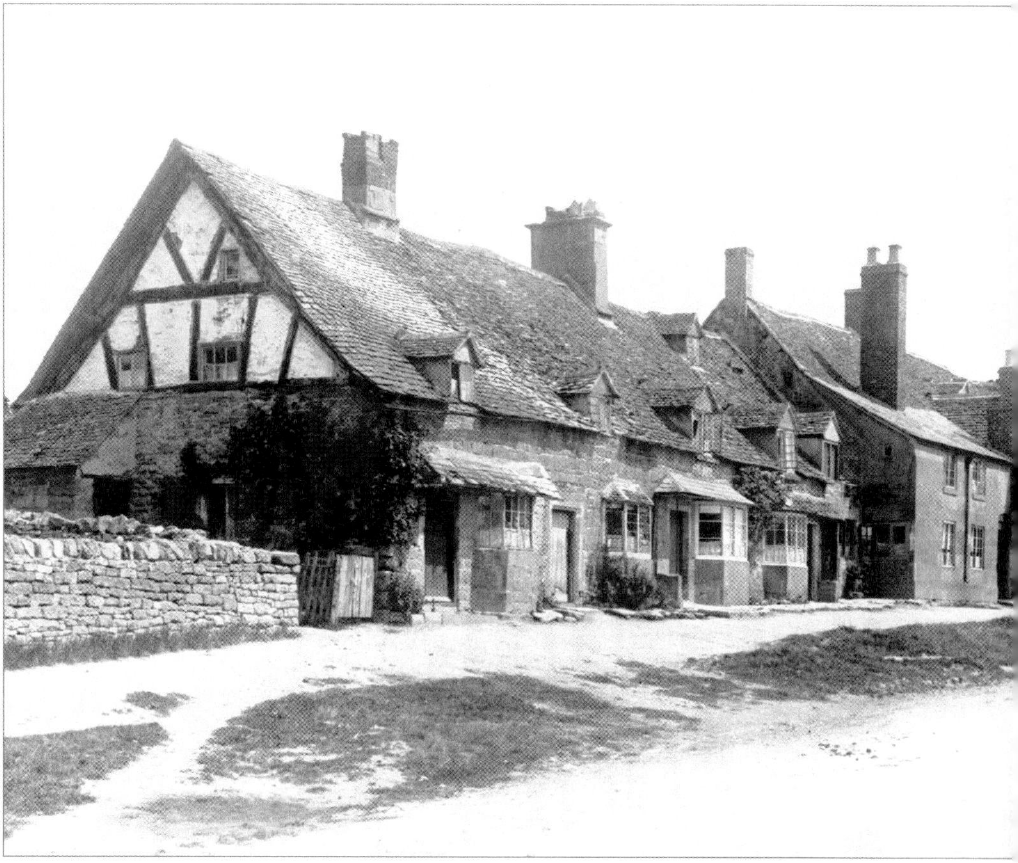

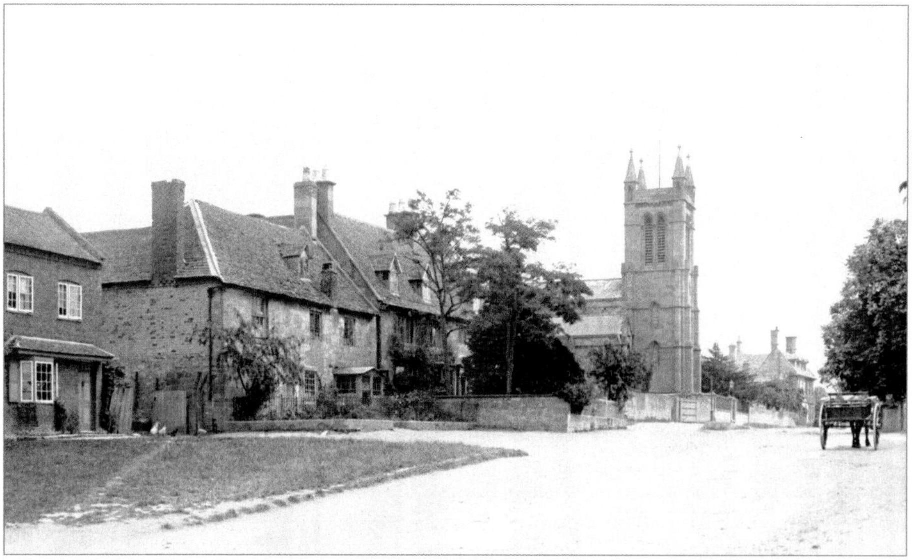

BROADWAY
The Village and the New Church 1899
44115

Broadway's oldest church lies about a mile to the south of the village on the Snowshill Road. The Victorians decided that St Eadburgh's, that had served the villagers for seven centuries, was too much of a trek, and built St Michael's, shown here, close to the village green.

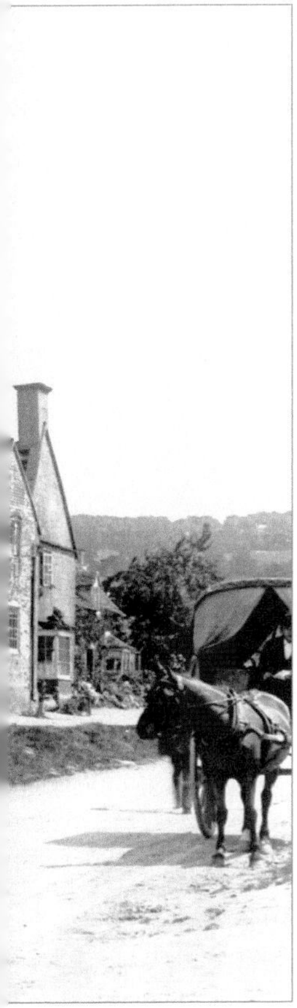

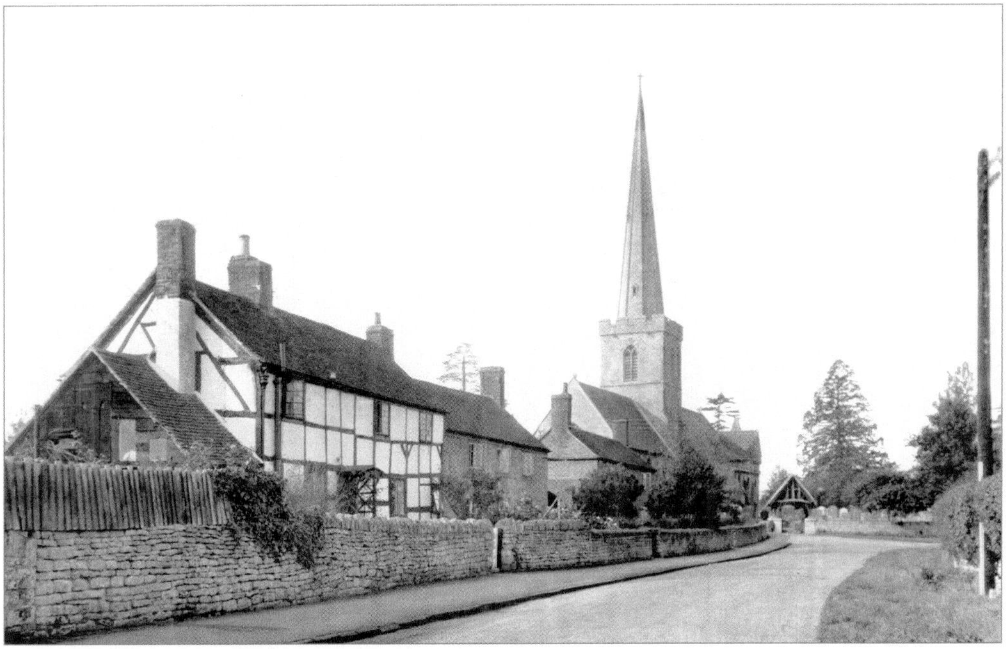

▲ **BREDON,** *St Giles's Church c1955* B423006

Bredon is one of the villages encircling Bredon Hill, which is an outlier of the Cotswolds, separated from the great oolitic limestone mass some time between the Ice Ages. Bredon holds faith with its ancient roots, with Cotswold stone buildings mixing happily with the timber and brick of the Vale in which it stands. Norman work is to be found in its church, mellow houses date back to Elizabeth I's day, and the village can boast one of the largest tithe barns in the kingdom - and a couple of its oldest inns.

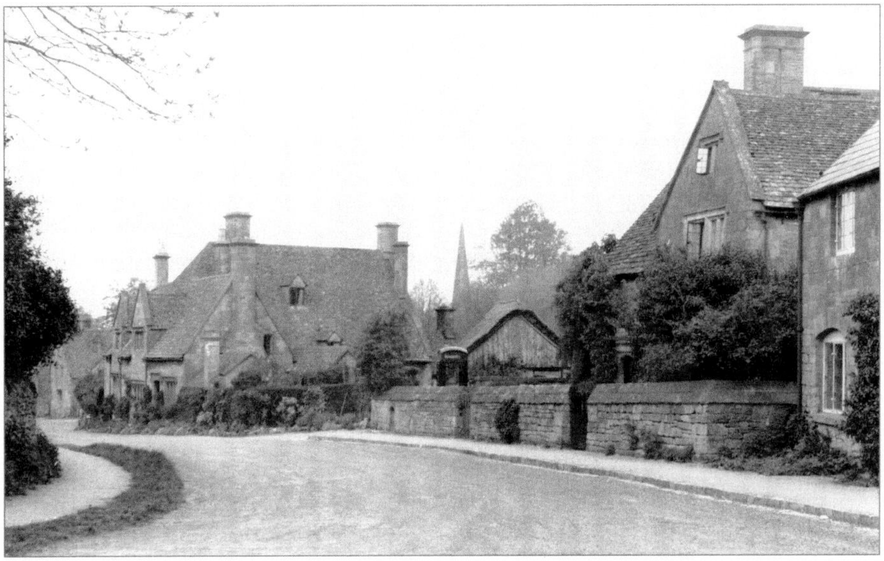

◄ **STANTON**
The Village c1960
S501005

Taking its name from the native stone (which in the native tongue is 'stan'), Stanton is quintessentially Cotswold; it owes much of its restoration work to the foresight of the architect Sir Philip Stott, who owned the estate from 1906 to 1937. Careful conservation has ensured that the classic character of this delightful little village has been maintained to this day.

▼ **BISHOPS CLEEVE,** *The Church and the Priory c1955* B531003

Considered to be one of the finest in Gloucestershire, the parish church has retained much of its 12th-century work, although the hand of successive centuries can be seen in its many treasures.

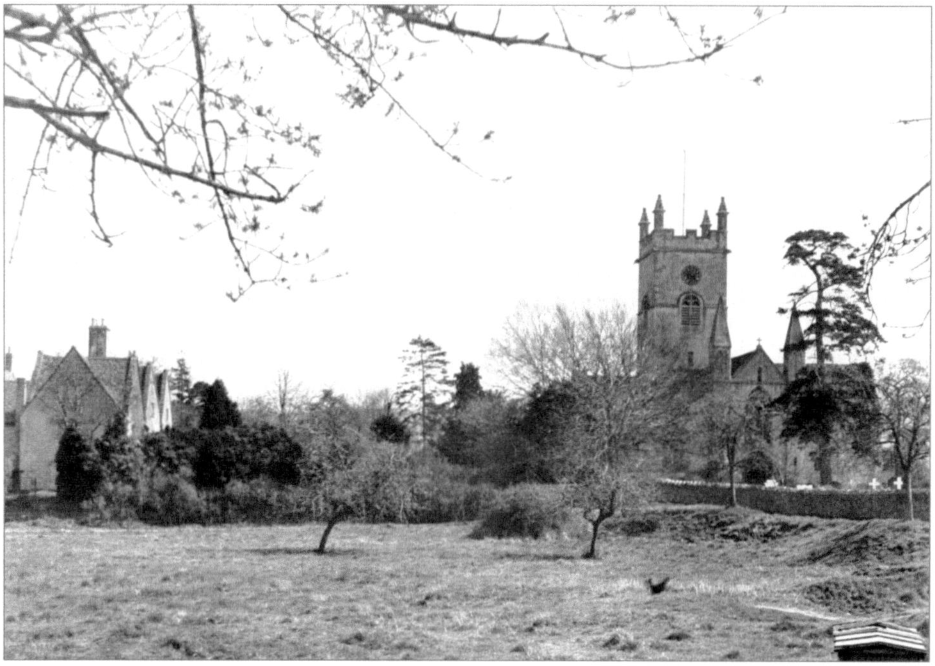

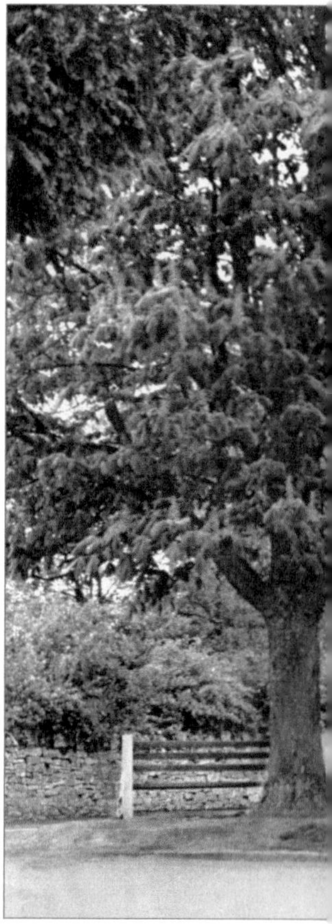

► **BISHOPS CLEEVE**
Station Road c1955
B531007

A bygone era of rail travel is perpetuated in the name of this road, photographed some five years before the village station closed. But thanks to the dedication of railway enthusiasts, the former trackbed has been re-laid through Bishops Cleeve, and passenger services are now operated by the Gloucestershire Warwickshire Railway south to Cheltenham Racecourse.

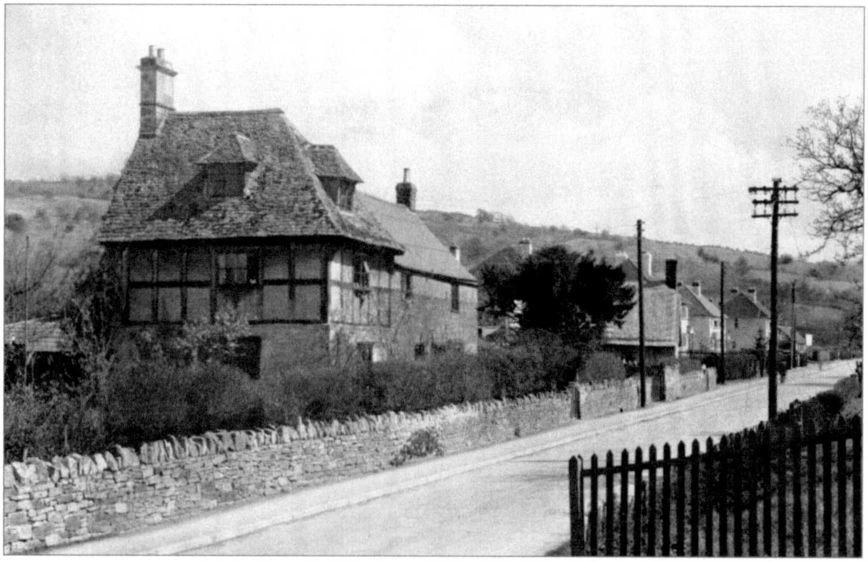

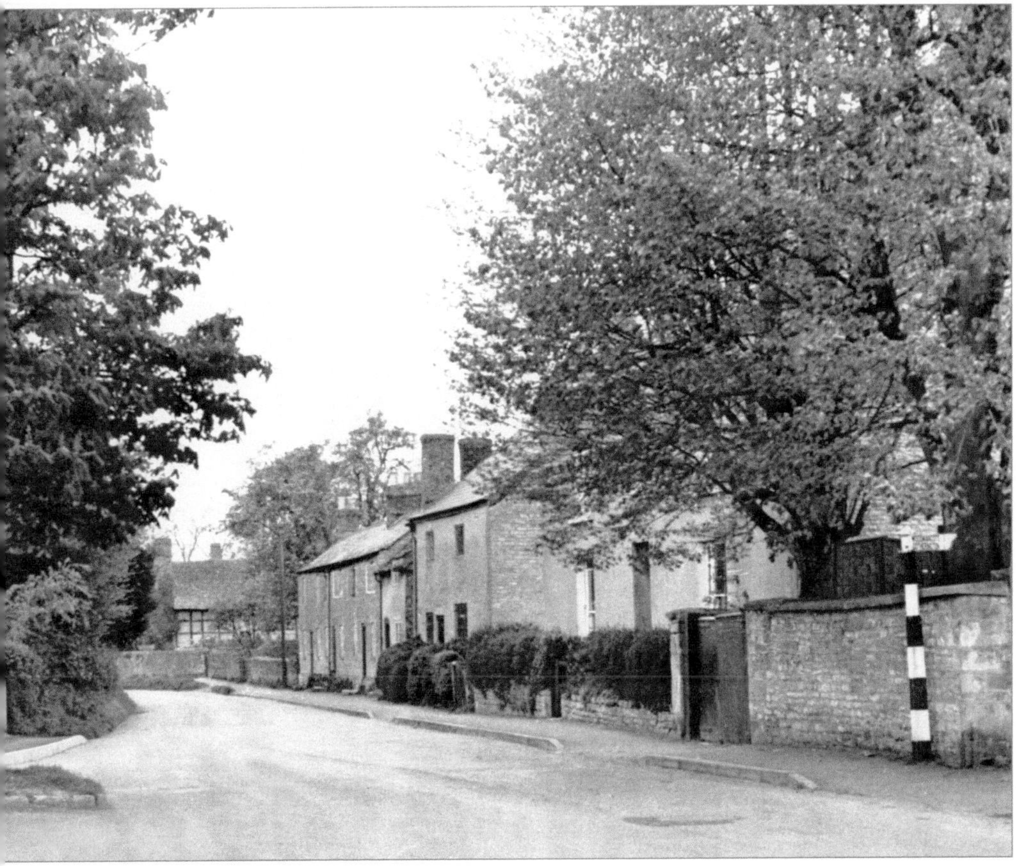

◄ **BISHOPS CLEEVE**
The Village c1960
B531020

The county historian, Samuel Rudder, writing in 1779, described the village as 'more than five miles in length and nearly of the same breadth'. After the agricultural depression, when the drift was away from the villages to the nearby towns for employment, Bishops Cleeve decreased in size, but it is now one of the largest villages in its own right in the Vale.

► **BISHOPS CLEEVE**
Cheltenham Road c1955 B531022

Originally known simply as Cleeve, this village gained its prefix at the time when it was owned by the Bishop of Worcester.
It is some three miles from Cheltenham, to which it is now linked since rapid development brought village and town closer together.

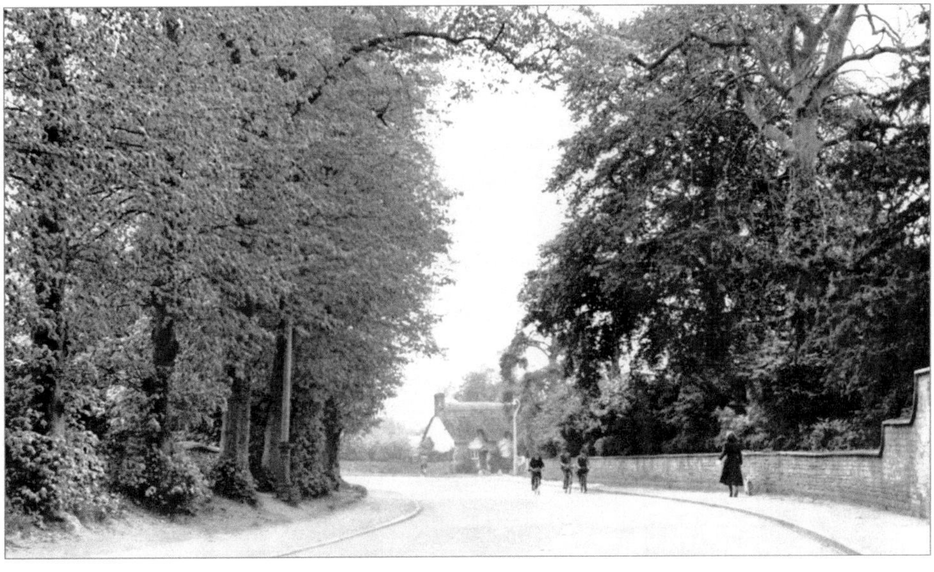

▼ BISHOPS CLEEVE, *From Cleeve Hill c1955* B531024

This village lies below the slope of Cleeve Hill. Once very small, it owes its considerable expansion to the move of Smiths Industries Aerospace and Defence Systems here to set up 'green field' factories during the Second World War. What was virtually a company village was built on adjacent land by the early 1940s for the employees' families; the Racecourse Garage - so named from the proximity to the famous Cheltenham Racecourse - and the Newlands Inn disappeared from the crossroads by the former Kayte Farm in the post-war development.

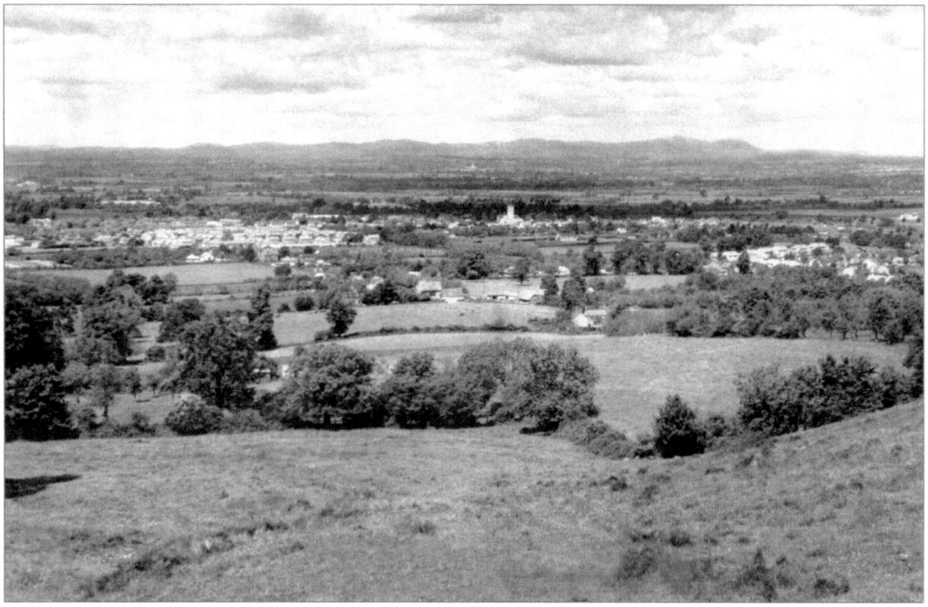

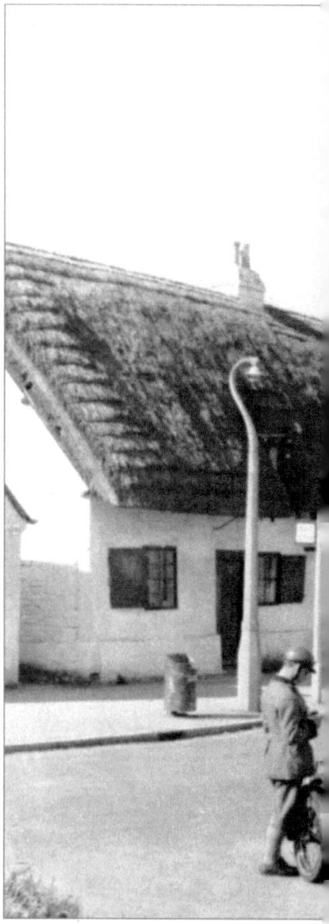

► BISHOPS CLEEVE
The Tithe Barn c1960 B531026

This is a fine old tithe barn. Its size indicates the former status of the produce belonging to the church that was stored there, harvested from land once owned by the bishopric of Worcester. This photograph was taken soon after the restoration of the barn and its conversion to a village hall; this was largely financed by the Smiths Company. The hall was officially opened by W S Morrison, Speaker of the House of Commons, in 1956. Still called the Village Hall, outwardly it remains today as it did 50 years ago. The farm buildings on the right behind the tithe barn have been replaced by a new supermarket accessed from the bypass.

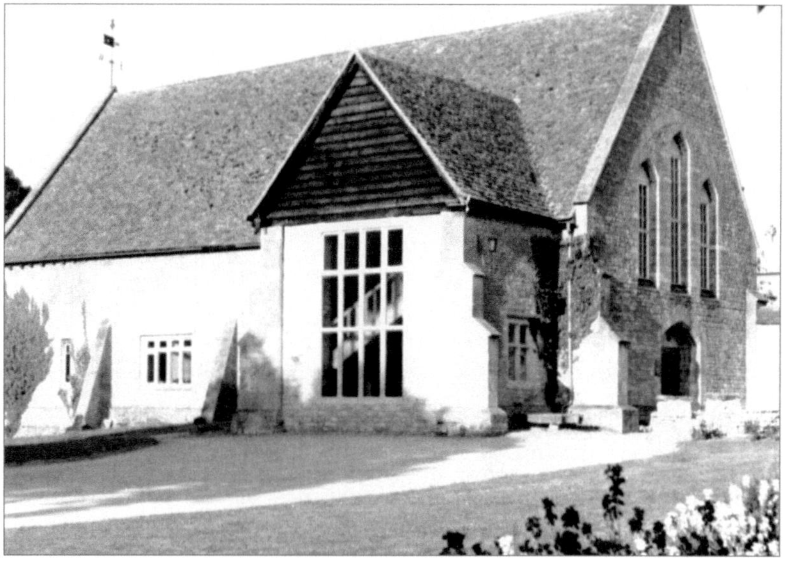

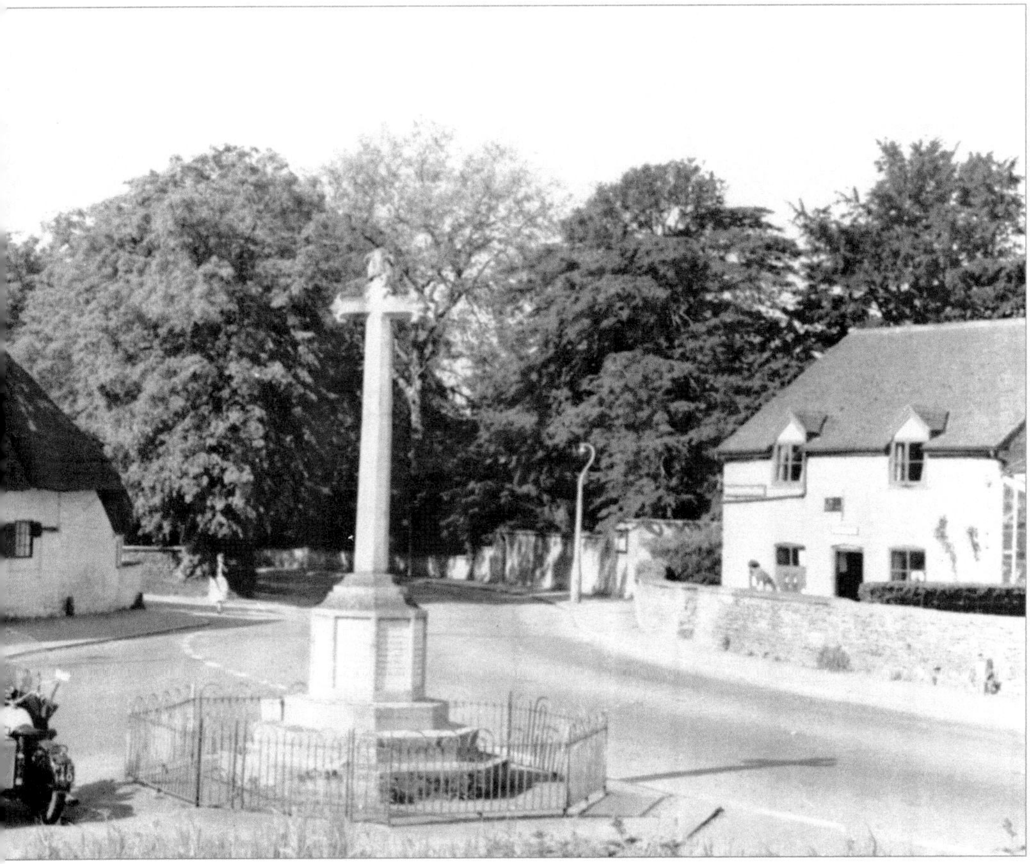

BISHOPS CLEEVE
The Kings Head, the War Memorial and the Post Office c1960
B531027

This view of the junction of Church Road and Cheltenham Road is still recognisable today - just. The war memorial was moved in the 1980s to the other end of Church Road to avoid damage by increased traffic to the supermarket. The King's Head survives with a new thatched roof, but when the post office moved further up Church Road the building shown here became a dwelling house. Some of the trees have disappeared - along with the motor-cycling AA patrol man!

CLEEVE HILL
c1960 C115032

The summit at 1083 feet is at the head of West Down at the southern point of Cleeve Common. The high plateau has been the gallops on which jockeys have put their horses through their paces since the days when Fred Archer and Black Tom Oliver raced into the history records in the 19th century.

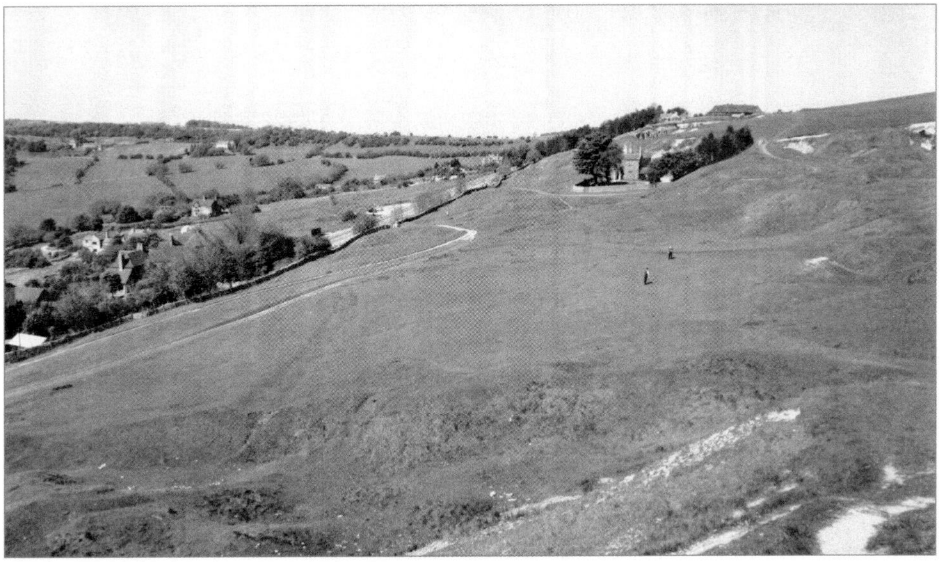

CLEEVE HILL
Courtaulds Convalescent Home c1960 C115022

Cleeve Hill, with its bracing air and superb views, was promoted as 'The Cotswolds Health Resort' in early Edwardian times - the Geisha Tea Rooms were advertising all-inclusive weekends for 10s 6d in 1903. The view of the convalescent home shown here is much the same, but it has now extended considerably into a modern nursing home open to all.

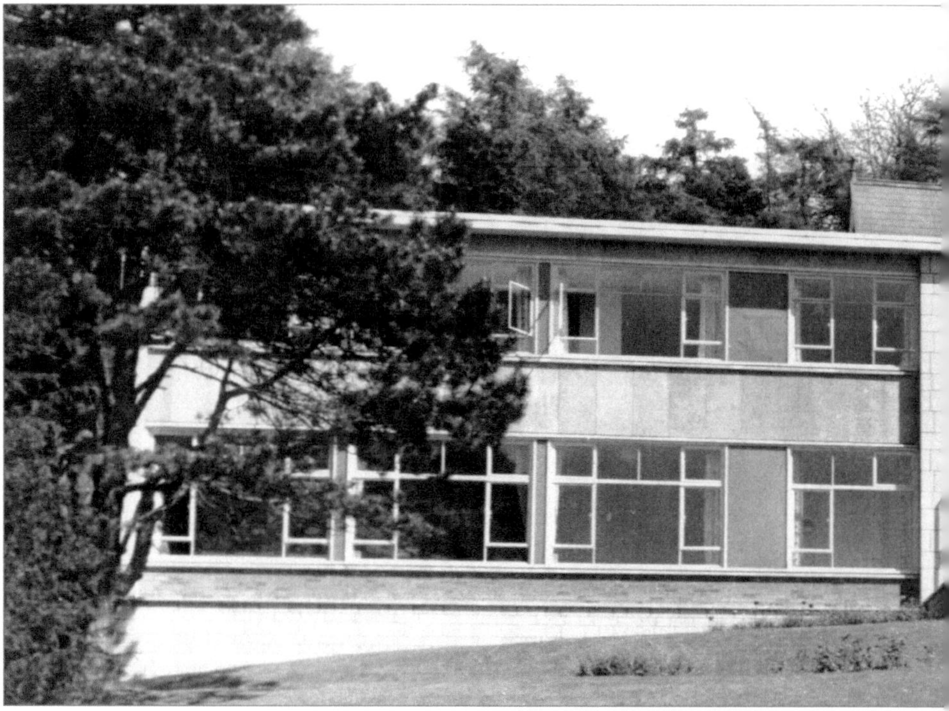

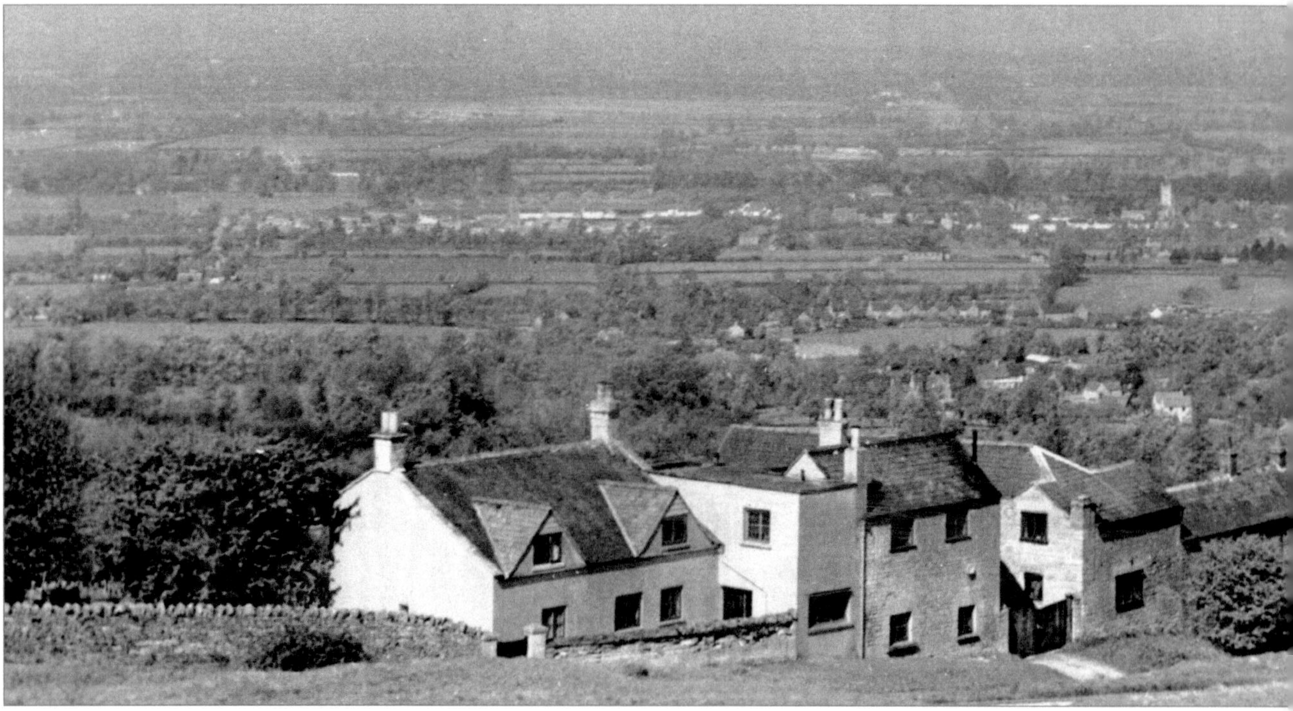

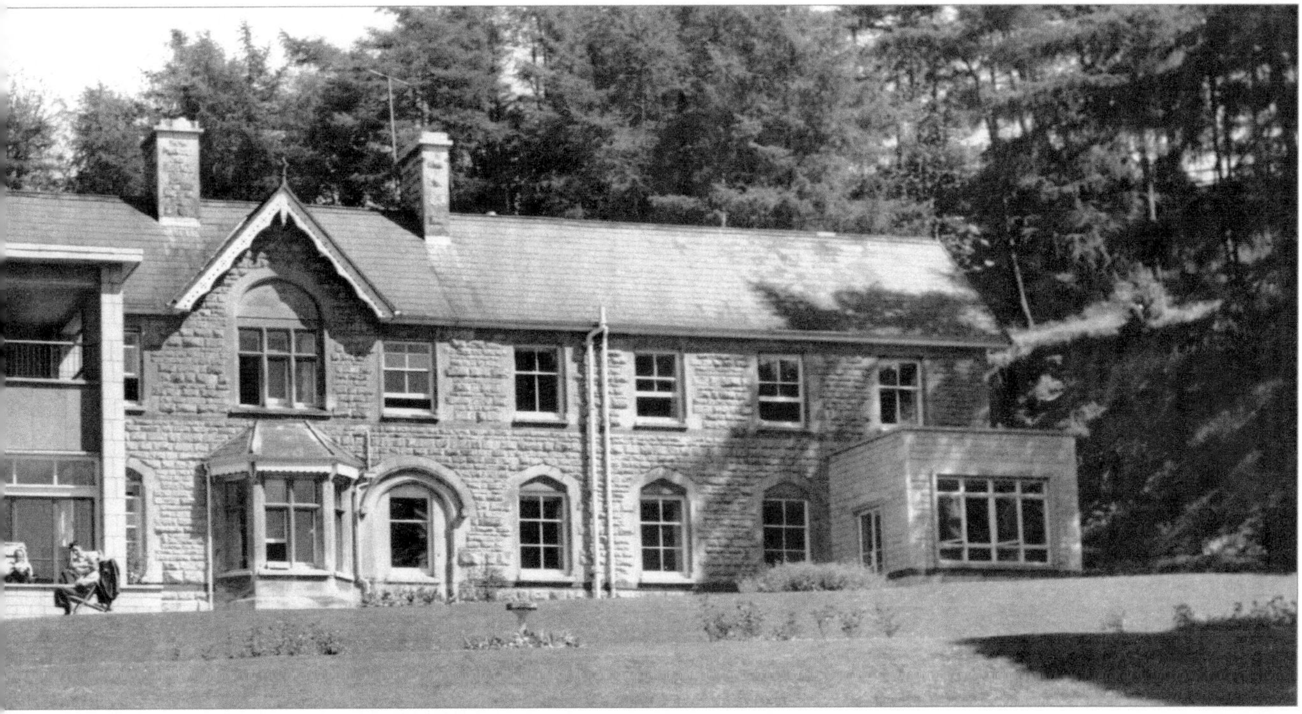

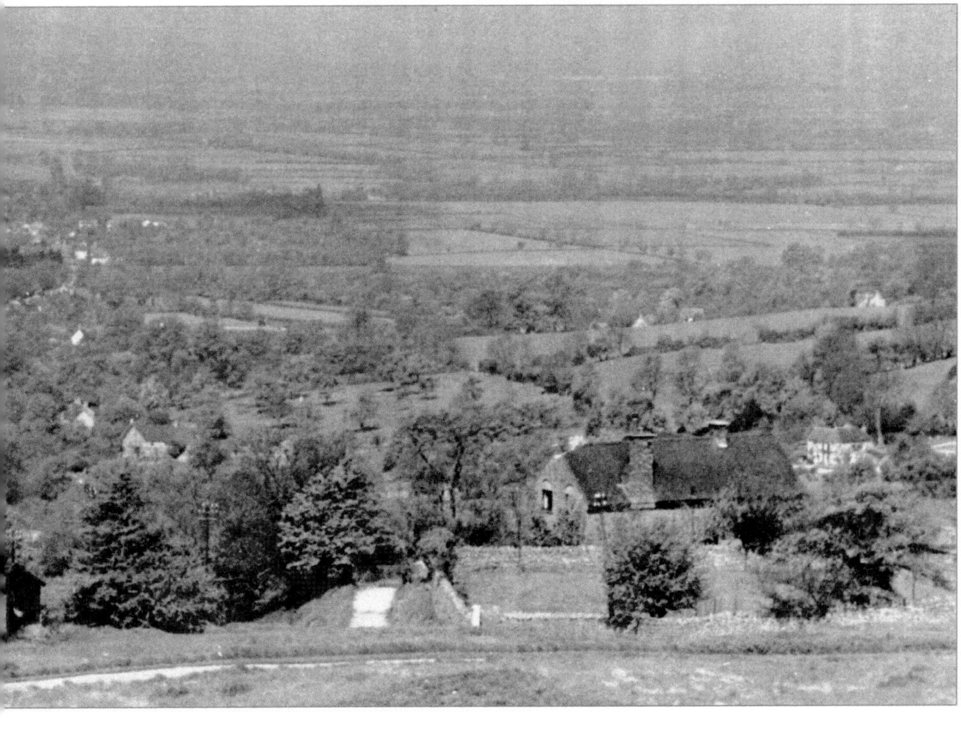

◄ **CLEEVE HILL**
Stockwell Lane c1955
C115019

The highest point of the Cotswolds is on Cleeve Common, which covers an area of some three square miles. It is a Site of Special Scientific Interest, scheduled as Grade I on account of its natural beauty.

CLEEVE HILL, *Nottingham Hill c1950* C115005

There are many hill forts that punctuate the western escarpment; the majority of them belong to the Iron Age, and date from about 600 BC. The one we see here on Nottingham Hill is one of the largest of its kind in the country at over 100 acres.

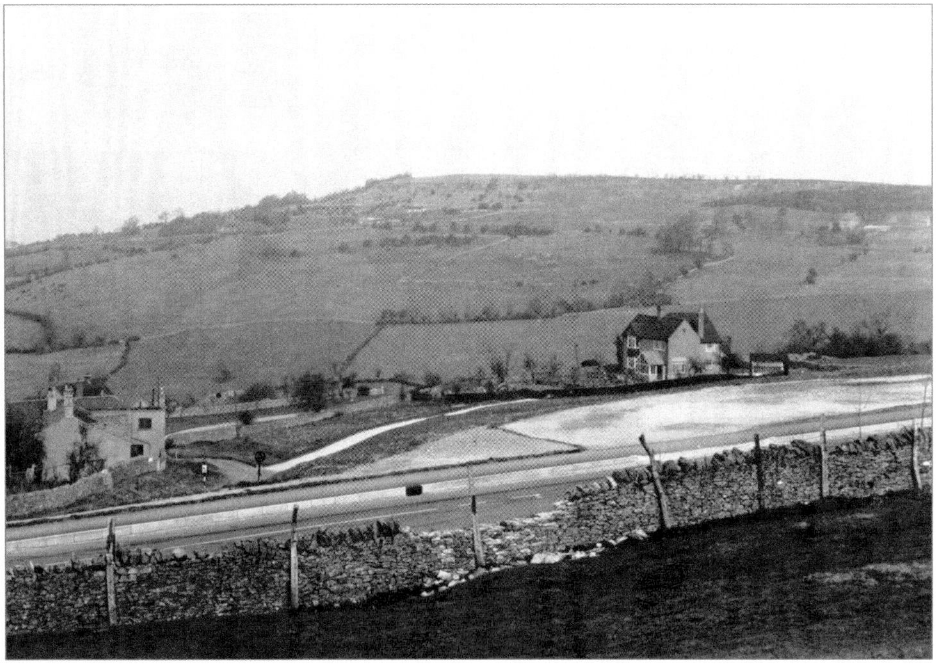

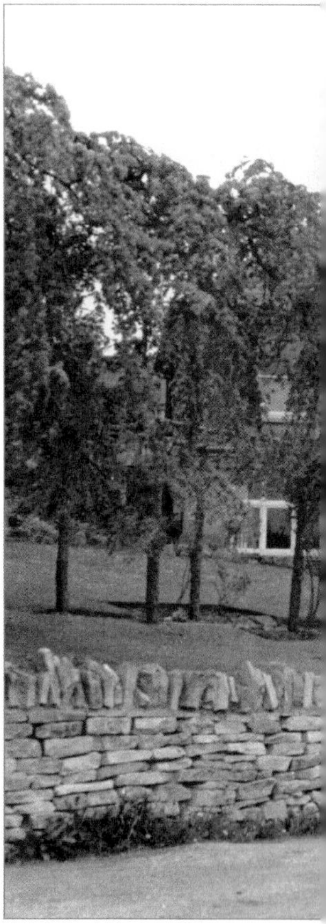

CLEEVE HILL
The Post Office c1940
C115002

Despite its steep position, Cleeve Hill has traded like any other village to supply local needs, and the advent of the 'Electric Tramway' in the early 1900s brought visitors from the town of Cheltenham below nearly to the top. From here they could post their view cards of Cleeve Hill.

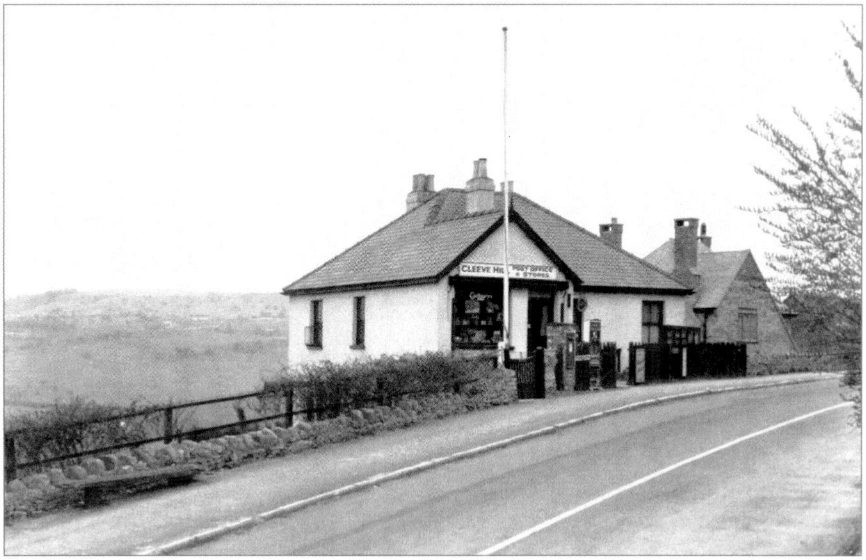

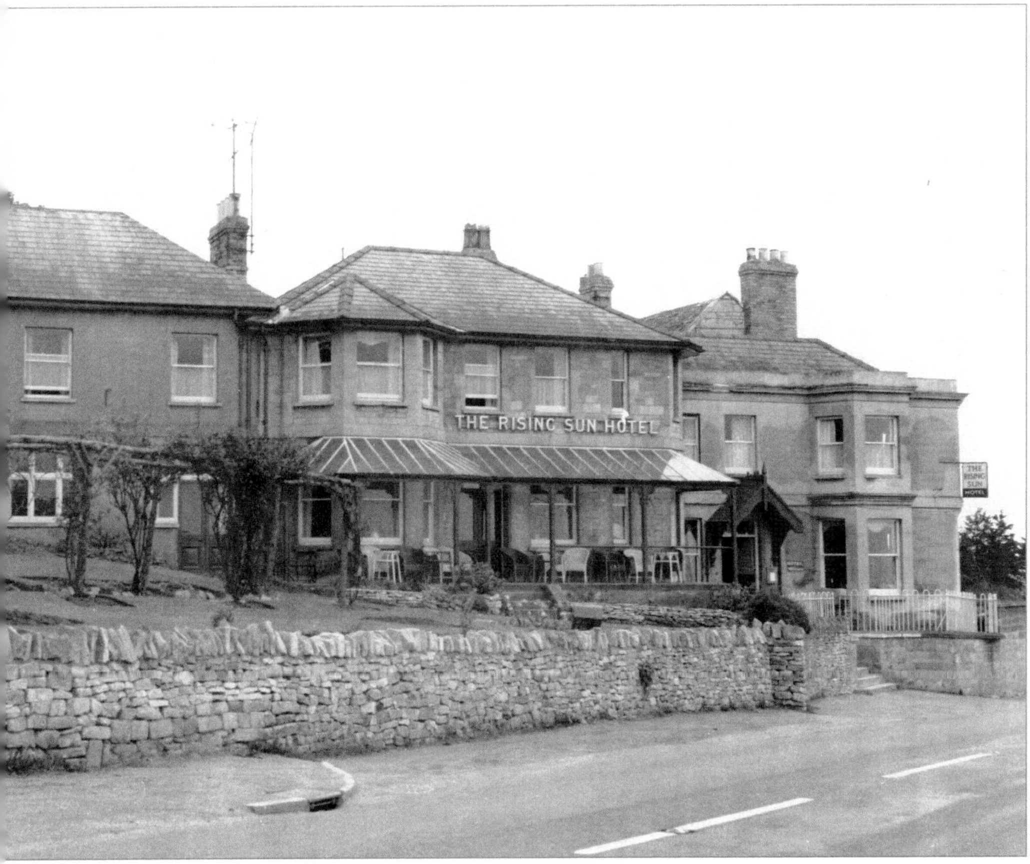

CLEEVE HILL
The Rising Sun Hotel c1960
C115044

The potential of catering for visitors to this 'breezy shoulder of the Cotswolds' (as one printer of view postcards described Cleeve Hill), was realised as soon as travellers could reach it by the new tramway. The same printer invested in a café on the hill which claimed to be capable of coping with 200 visitors 'at short notice', according to one of his cards posted from the hill in 1915.

PRESTBURY
High Street c1955
P112015

The King's Arms Inn, the black and white half-timbered building on the extreme left of this picture, was home to the legendary jockey, Fred Archer. Cheltenham leased the steeplechase course at Prestbury Park in 1823, and has achieved fame ever since for the race meetings held here under the title of Cheltenham Races.

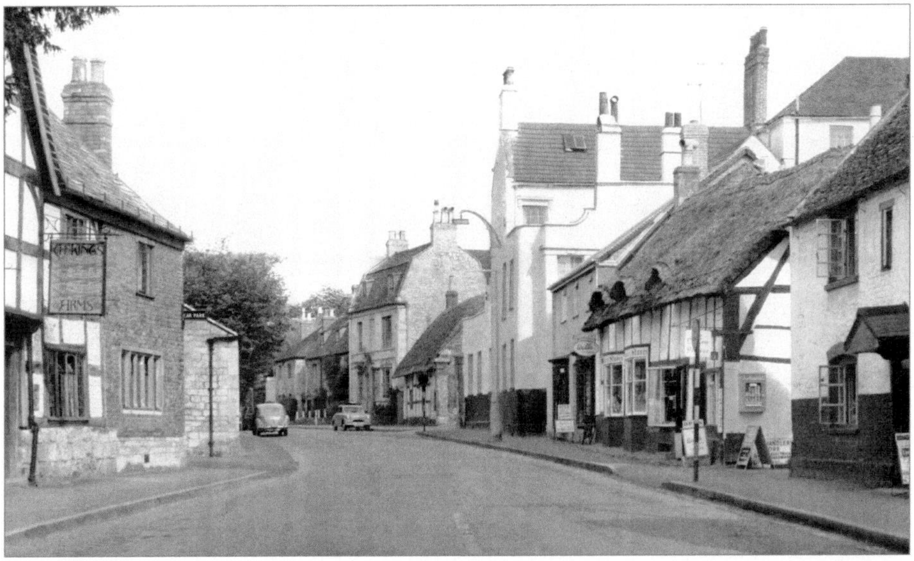

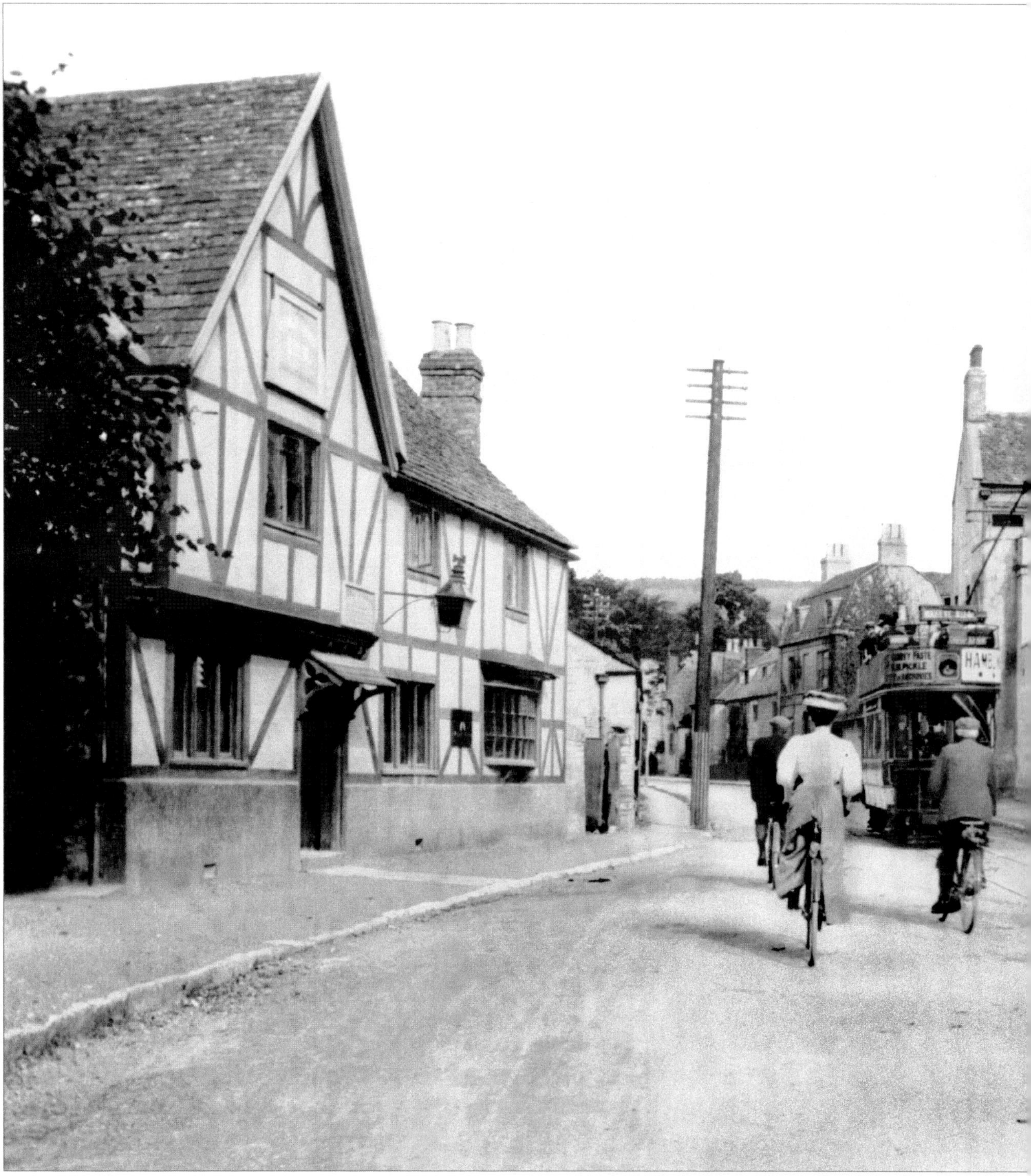

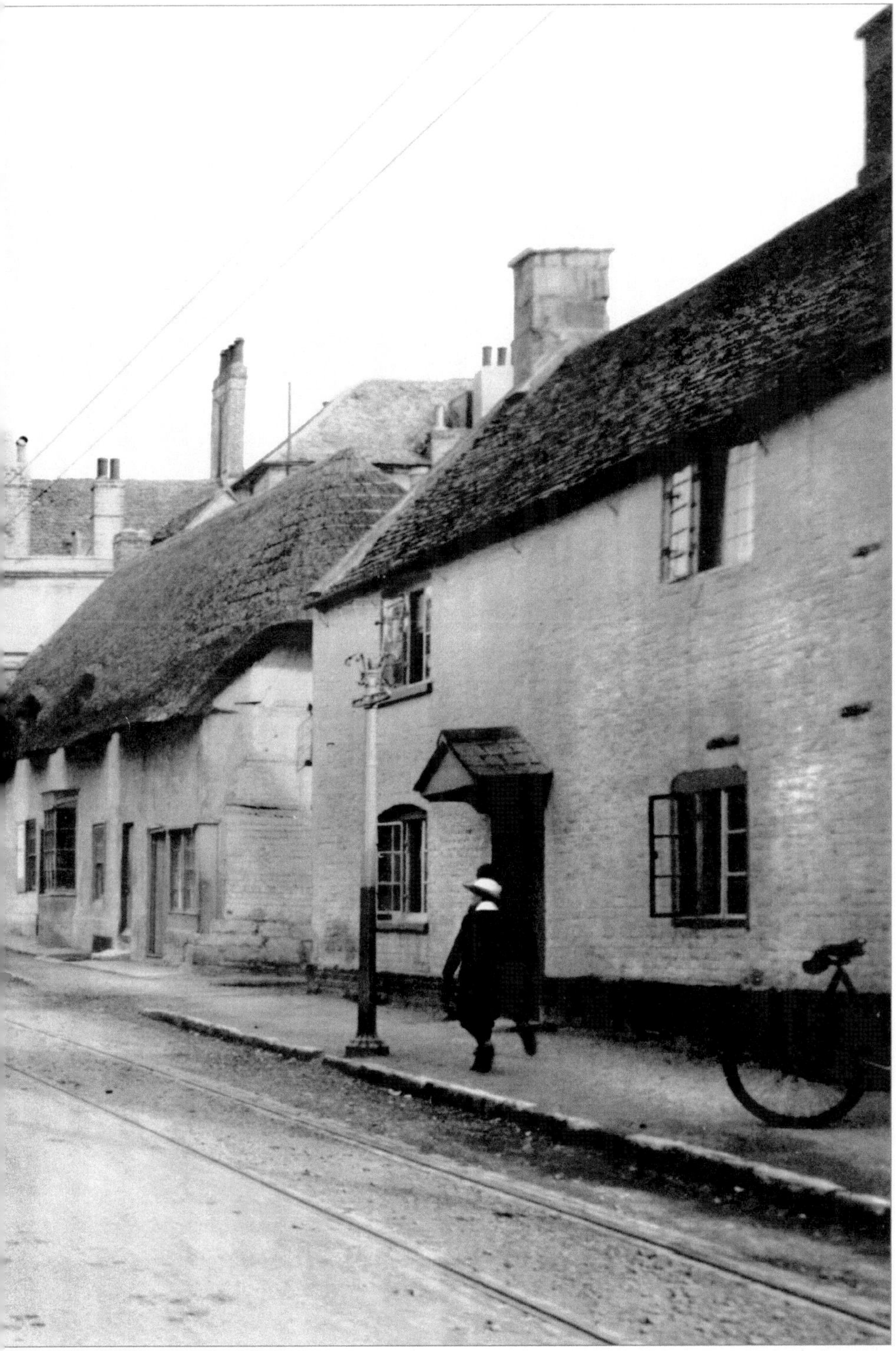

PRESTBURY
The Village 1907 59051

Prestbury lies under the great bluff of Cleeve Hill, the destination of the tram, not the only mode of Edwardian travel in this photograph! Prestbury is so close to Cheltenham that it is often mistaken as a suburb; but there is nothing suburban about it, for it has plenty of old-world charm and the identity of a long-established village in its own right, with roots firmly set down beyond Domesday.

PRESTBURY
Deep Street c1960
P112019

Prestbury is a strong contender for the title of the most haunted village in the country. One of its many ghosts, the Black Abbot, is reported to appear only three times a year - at Easter, All Saints' Day and Christmas - when it is said that he walks from the church (the tower of which can just be seen to the left of the rear of the Pharmacy in this picture) to Deep Street, where he knocks at the door of a 16th-century cottage before disappearing back into folklore.

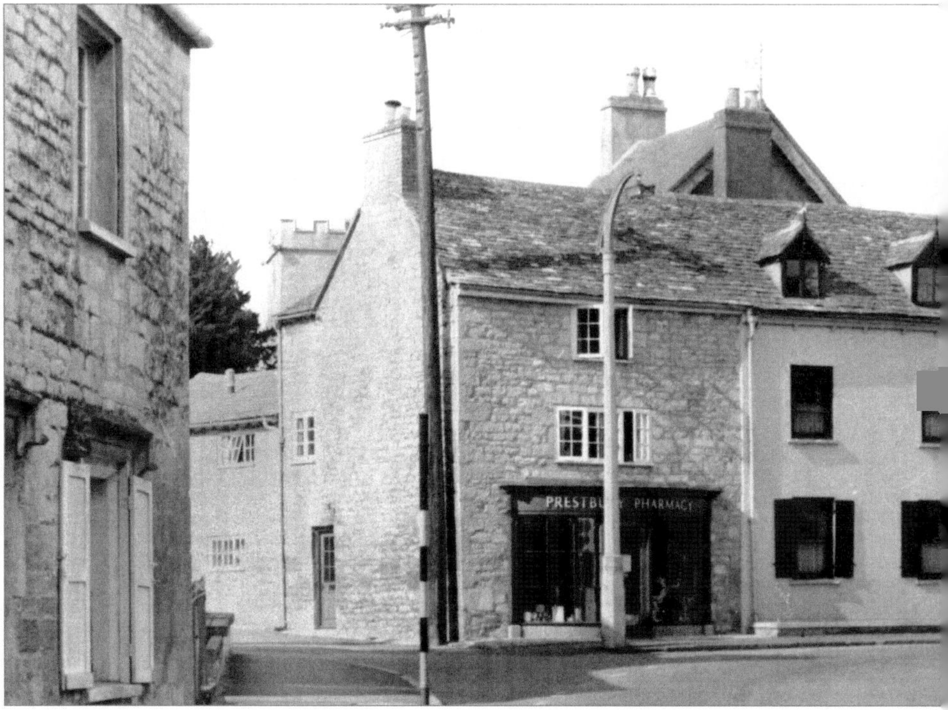

(far right) detail from
P112019

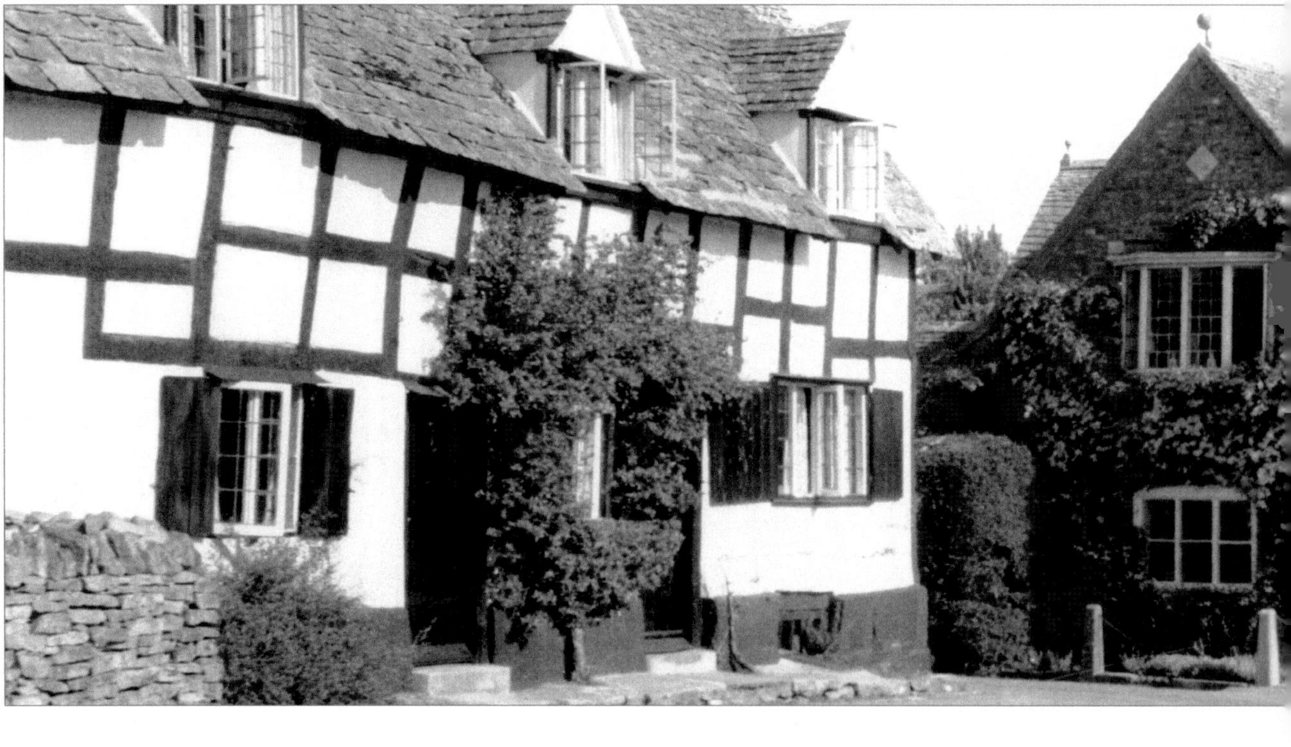

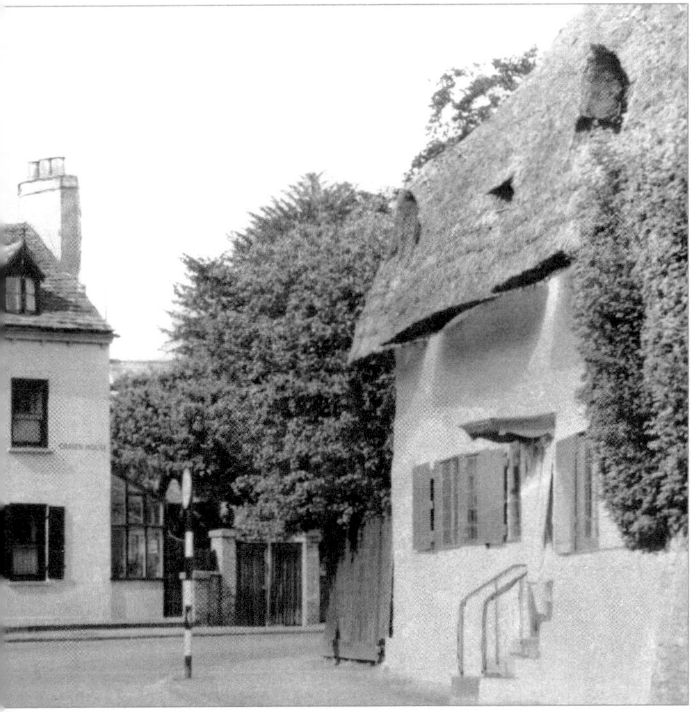

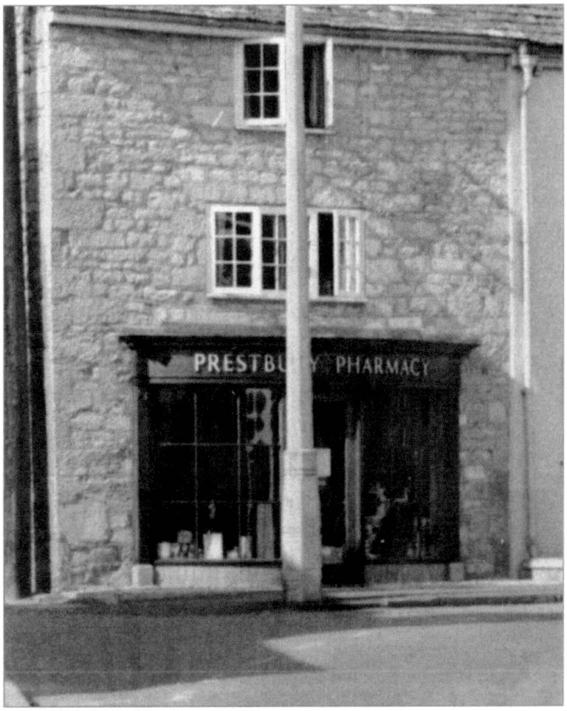

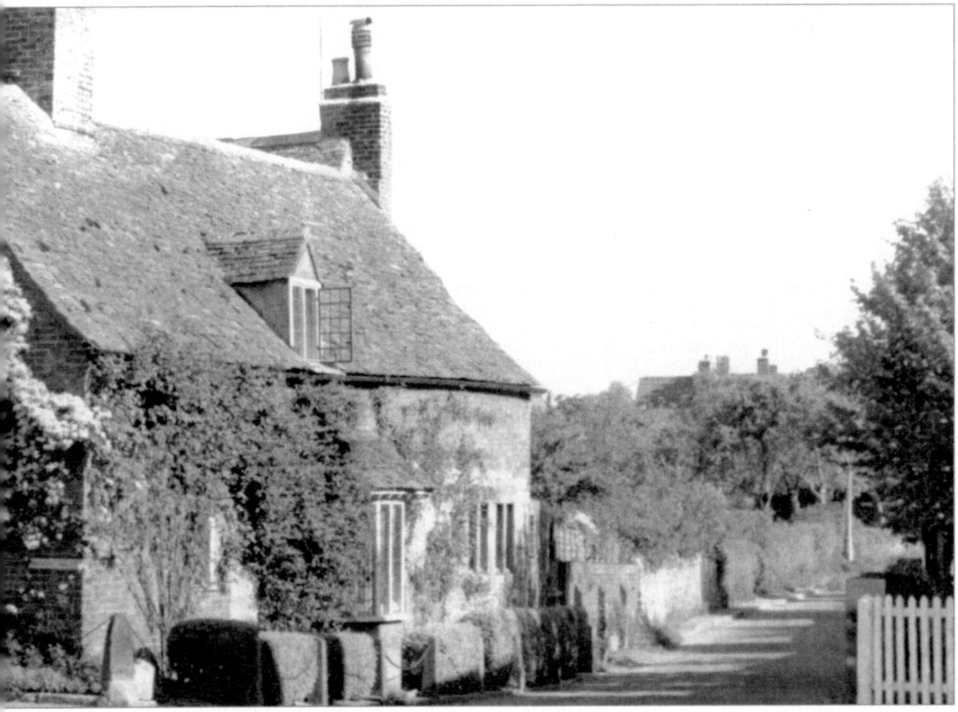

◄ **PRESTBURY**
The Burgage c1955
P112022

Burgage Street, once the main street of Prestbury, is thought to be where the annual fair and the weekly market were held - they originated from a charter granted in the 13th century.

THE STROUD VALLEYS

FIVE VALLEYS converge on the south-western scarp in which Stroud is the central town. The main river, the Frome, unlike the rest of the Cotswold rivers, does not follow the easterly flow towards the Thames, but takes a circuitous route to drain westwards to the mighty Severn. Collectively known as the Stroud Valley, it is the only area in the Cotswolds to develop into an identifiable industrial area. From early medieval times the powerful water force from the steep hill country was harnessed to drive millwheels, firstly for corn, then for the massive machinery and the copious supply needed in the cloth making trade. Individually, the valleys of Nailsworth, Chalford, Painswick, Stonehouse and Slad have villages that have been inextricably linked together by the woollen industry, but have developed their own identities within the broader context of the Cotswolds.

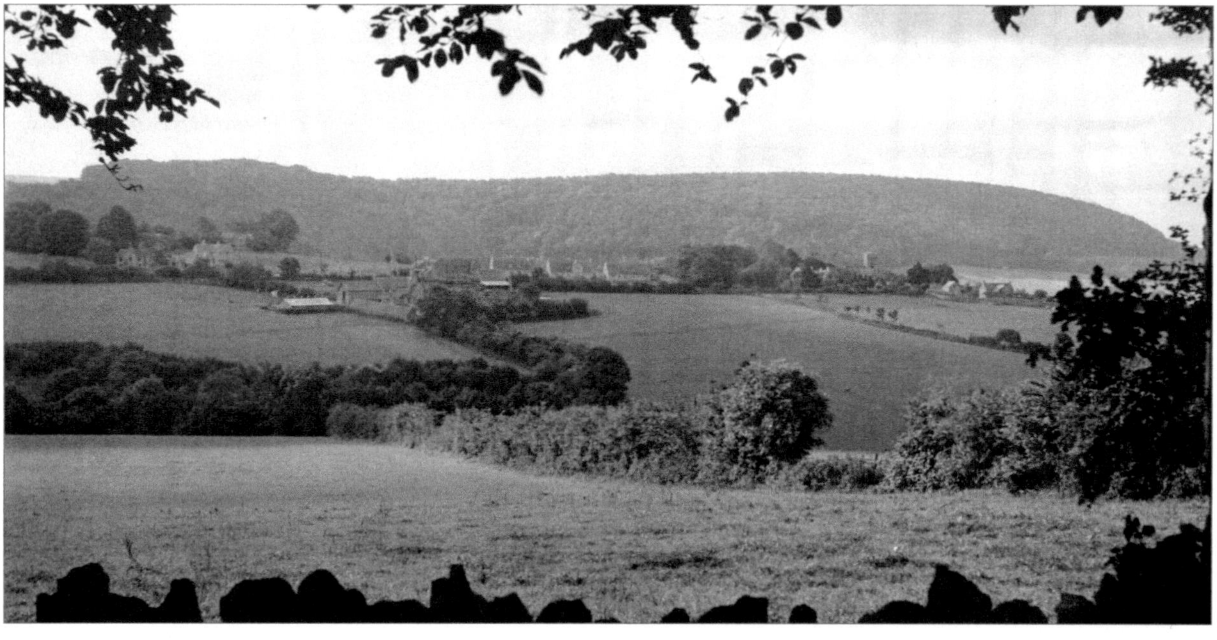

CRANHAM, *General View c1960* C179002

In his 'History of Gloucestershire', Samuel Rudder wrote of this area: 'Few landscapes are more truly picturesque or of greater variety than this'. Two centuries later, the same can still be said about this parish tucked into a deep hollow in the hills.

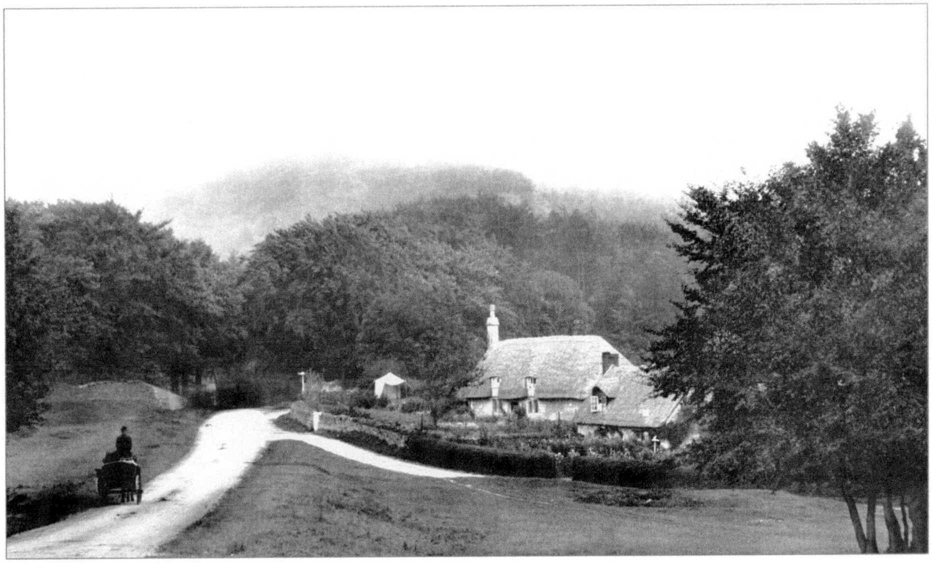

CRANHAM
The Beech Woods
1907 59066

The remnants of what was once a great beech forest still clothe the hills around the village. In this Edwardian scene the gentle pace of the pony-drawn cart adds to the idyllic mix of thatch and stone and little roads that lead in and out of the woods. Little wonder that it was a favoured spot visited by George III and his family while taking the waters at Cheltenham Spa.

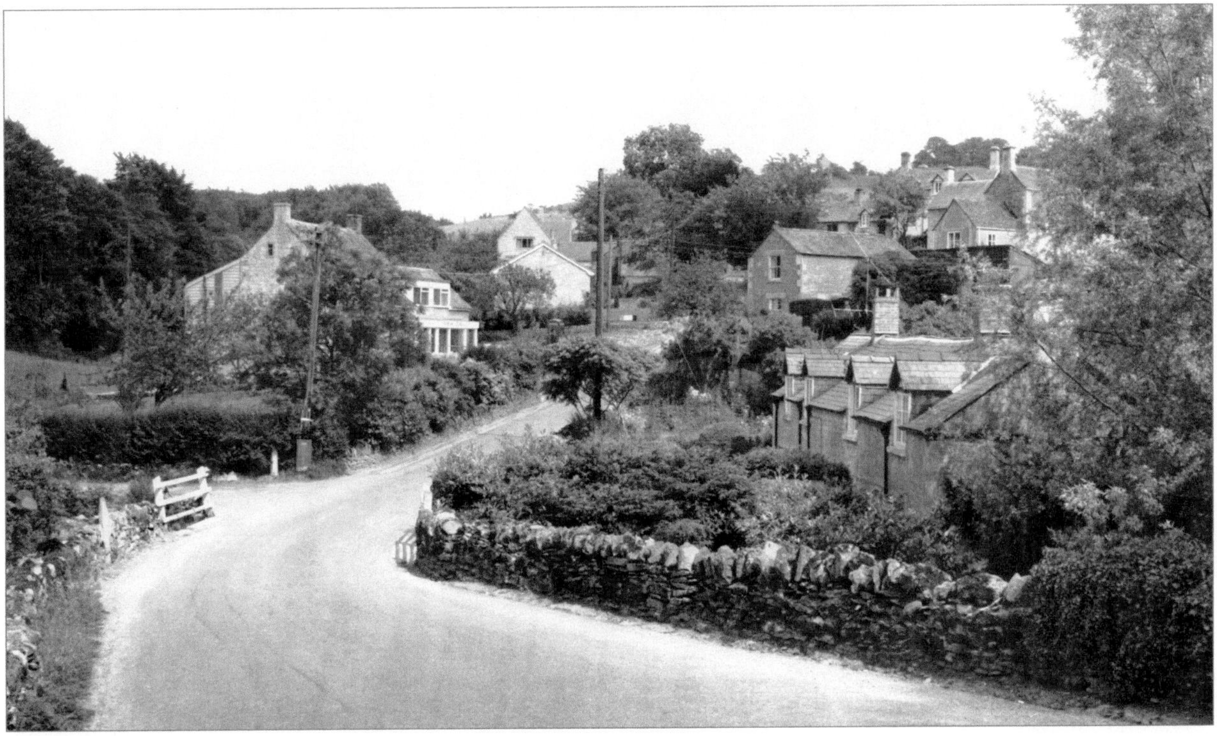

CRANHAM, *The Village c1960* C179061

All is not old at Cranham. As we can see in this picture, newer houses have enlarged the village, but it is still one of the beauty spots of the Cotswolds. Gustav Holst perpetuated the name of Cranham in the title of his music for the carol 'In the Bleak Midwinter'.

CRANHAM
The Old House
c1960 C179059

Justifying its name, The Old House in the middle of the village has the dates 1687 and 1727 carved on the lintel of the doorway. The house is built in traditional Cotswold style with its gables and mullioned windows.

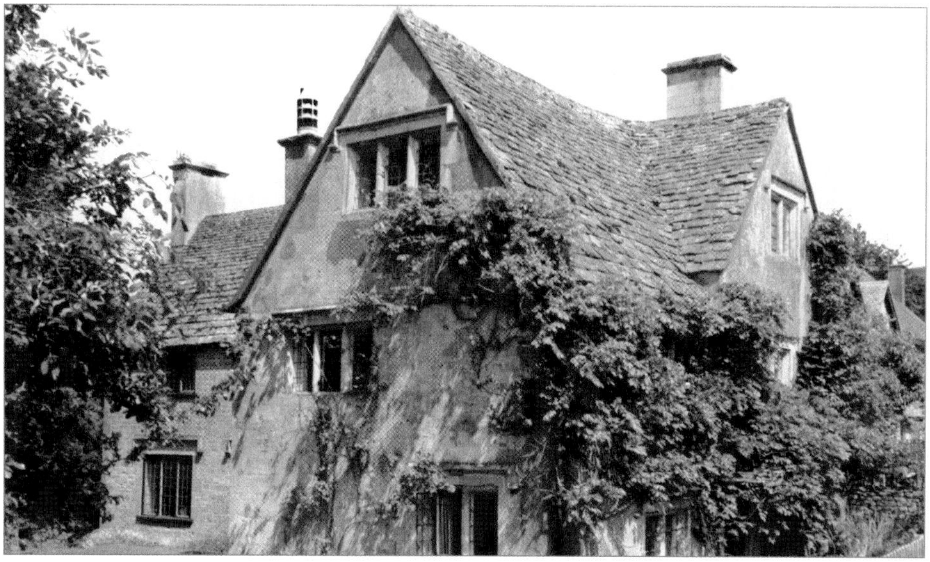

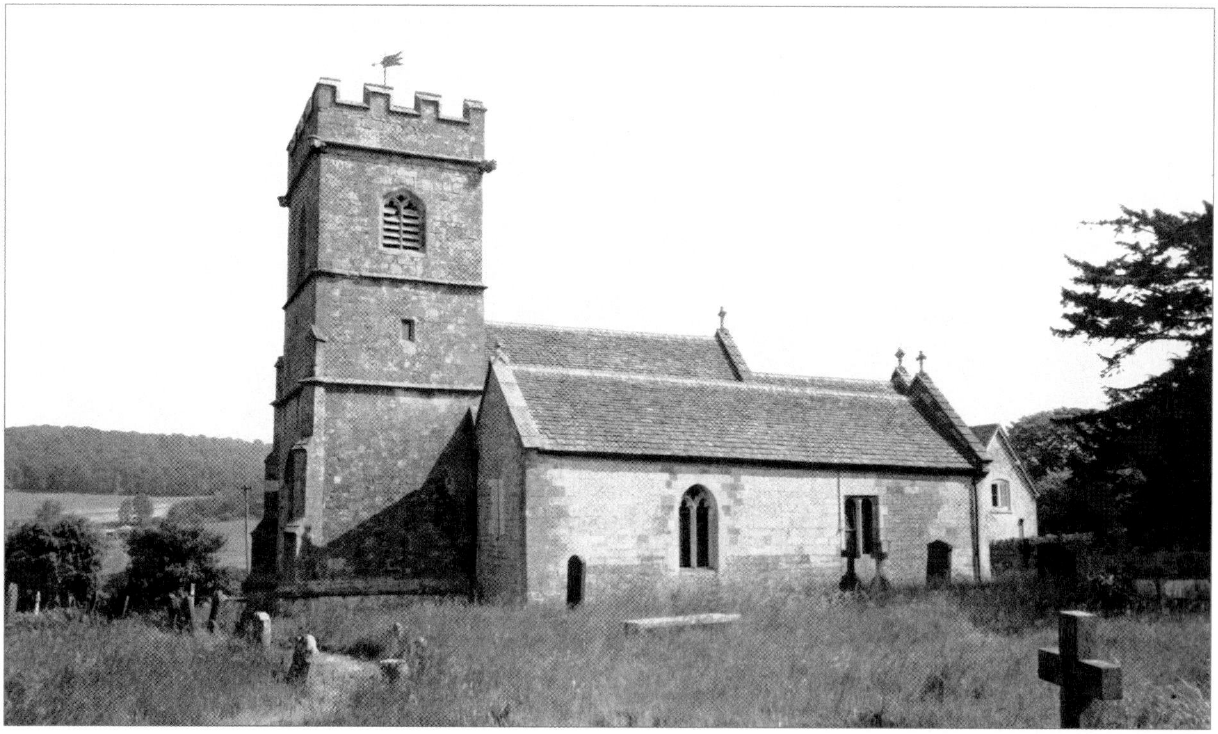

CRANHAM, *The Church c1960* C179054

Carvings of two pairs of sheep shears on the church tower are a reminder of the importance of wool in the Cotswold - and indeed the country's - economy at the time that this little church, dedicated to St James, was built in the 15th century. It was enlarged and restored at the end of the Victorian period.

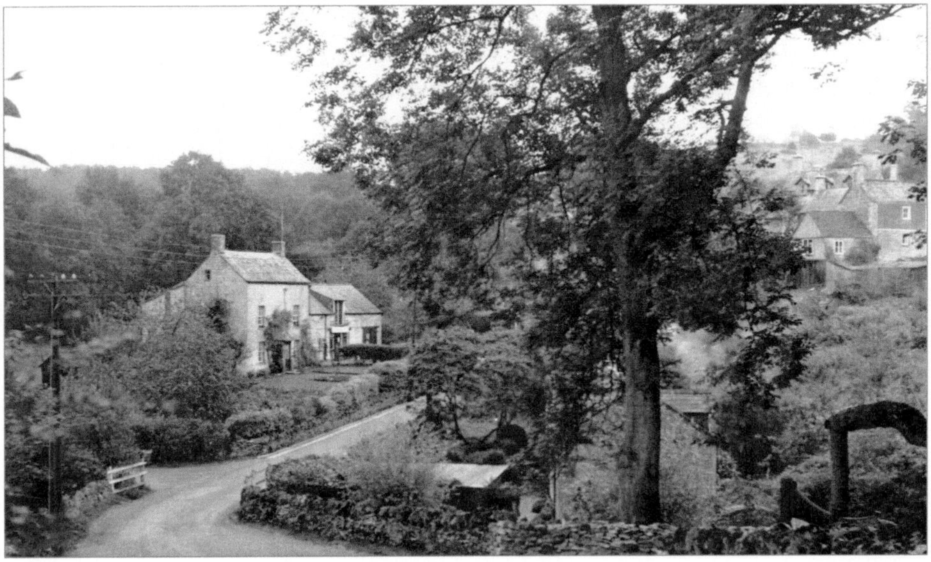

CRANHAM
The Village c1960
C179007

Local legend has it that it was at a house in Cranham, rather than at nearby Painswick, that Charles I slept and held his court on his way to and from the siege of Gloucester.

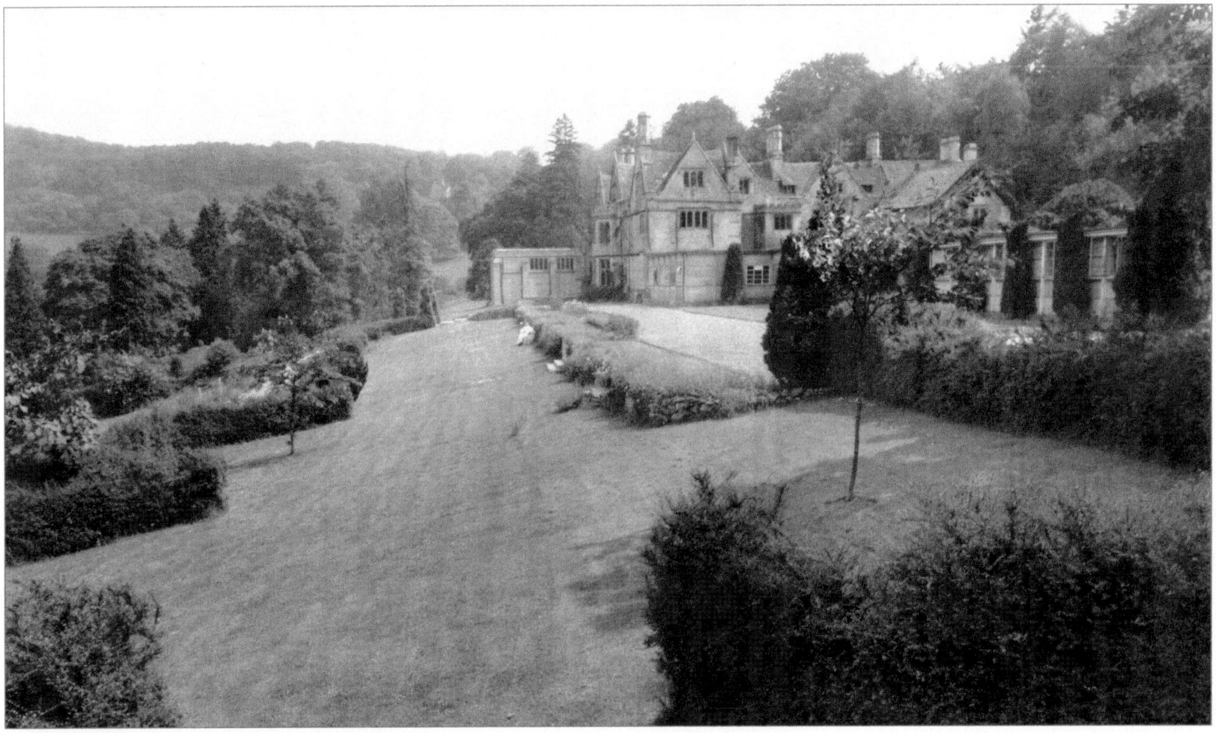

CRANHAM, *Prinknash Abbey, the Monastic Enclosure c1960* C179037

'It stands on a glorious but impracticable hill, in the midst of a little forest of beech and commanding Elysium', wrote Horace Walpole of Prinknash in 1774. It is here, to the old abbey, that Henry VIII came to hunt while paying court to Anne Boleyn.

▼ **CRANHAM,** *Prinknash Abbey, Model of the New Abbey c1960* C179025

Plans for a new abbey at Prinknash were drawn up in the 1930s when the Benedictine order of monks outgrew the old grange on the hillside, but these were modified over the years; the present abbey is in stark architectural contrast to the old house, which is now used as a retreat.

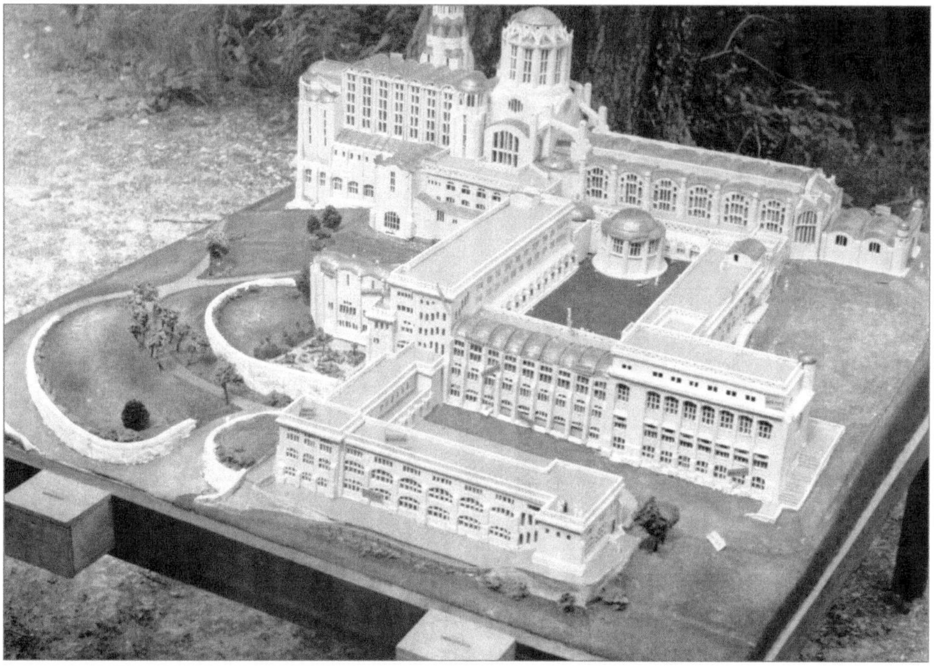

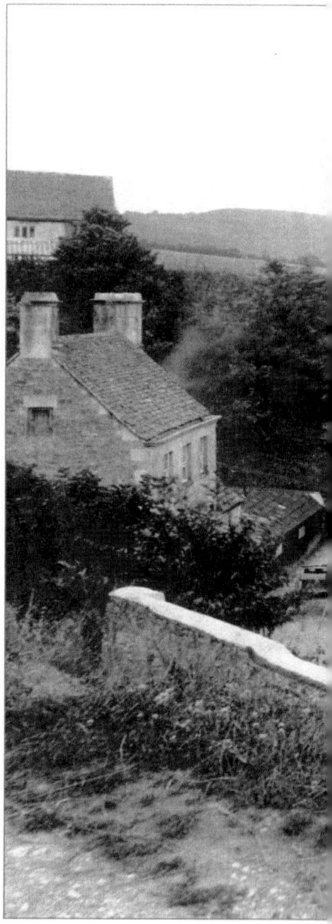

► **CRANHAM**
Prinknash Abbey, the Foundations of the New Abbey c1960 C179018

Building work on the new abbey was halted, initially because of the outbreak of the Second World War, and it was 1972 before it was completed. It was while digging the foundations for the new abbey that rich beds of clay were discovered, and from these the monks developed their now famous Prinknash pottery. Guided tours of the pottery are available, and the abbey grounds are open to the public with many attractions on offer.

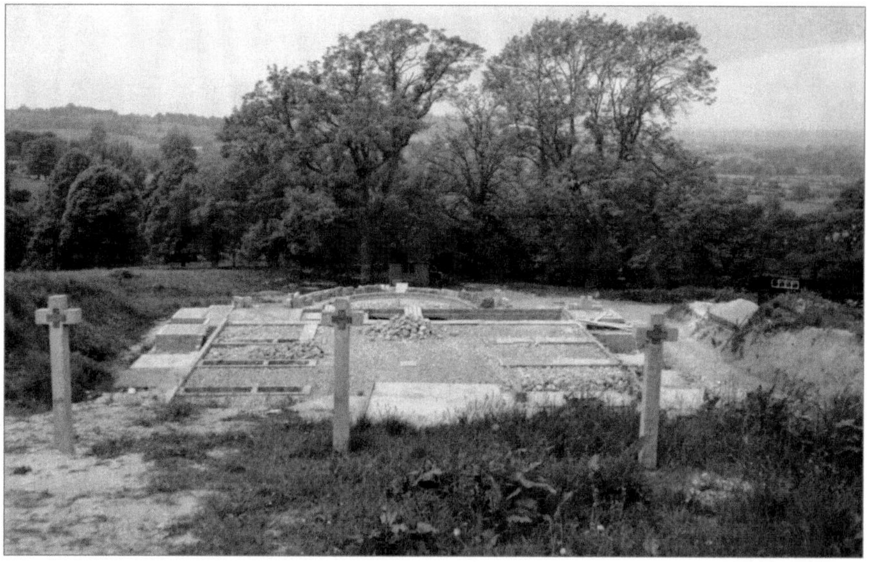

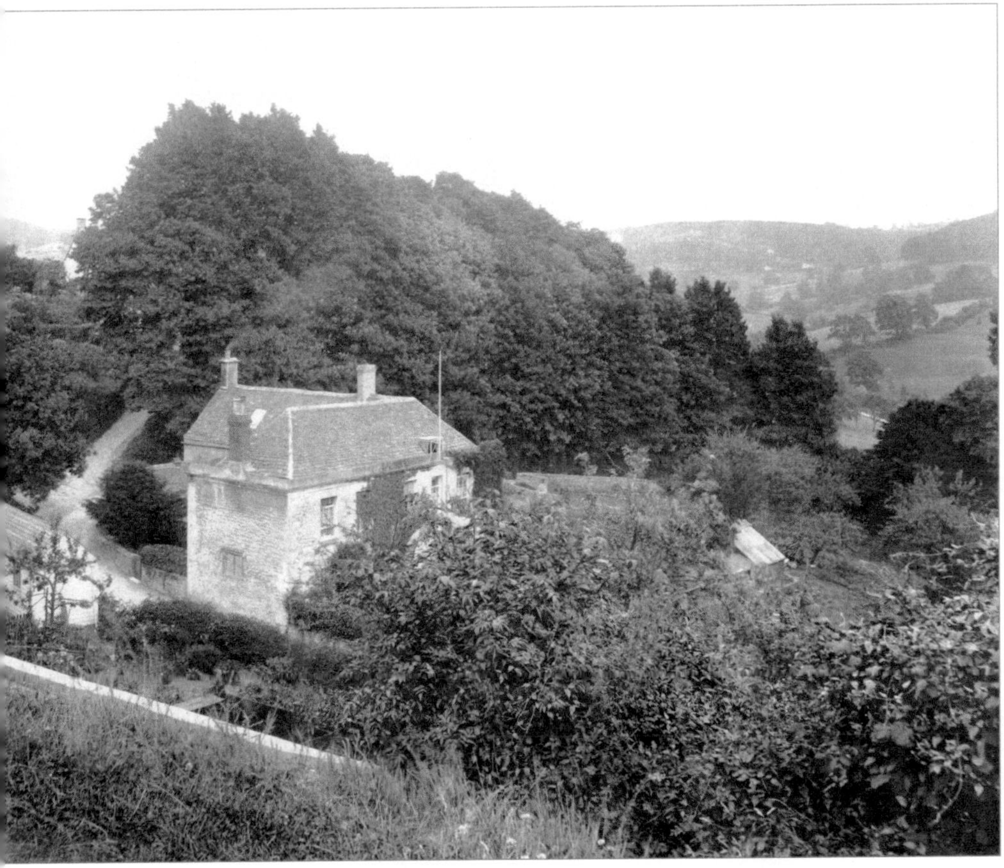

SLAD
Stean Bridge Lane 1910 62706

This is Laurie Lee's village of which he wrote so poetically, capturing life as lived in the valley villages between the wars in his evergreen classic, 'Cider with Rosie'. Little seems to have outwardly changed since the poet's schooldays when the village was, as he described it, a scattering of some twenty to thirty houses down the south-east slope of a valley. This photograph shows Steanbridge Lane, and in the centre is the house described by Laurie Lee: 'In the very sump of the valley wallowed the Squire's Big House - once a fine, though modest 16th-century manor, to which a Georgian façade had been added'.

BISLEY
High Street 1910
62697

Running north to south with closely built houses of all ages, the High Street of this quaintly composed village is set in a large parish rich in vernacular architecture, ancient burial barrows and tumps, and hoary old legends. Among its many curious treasures can be seen the village lock-up - a two-cell affair in George Street.

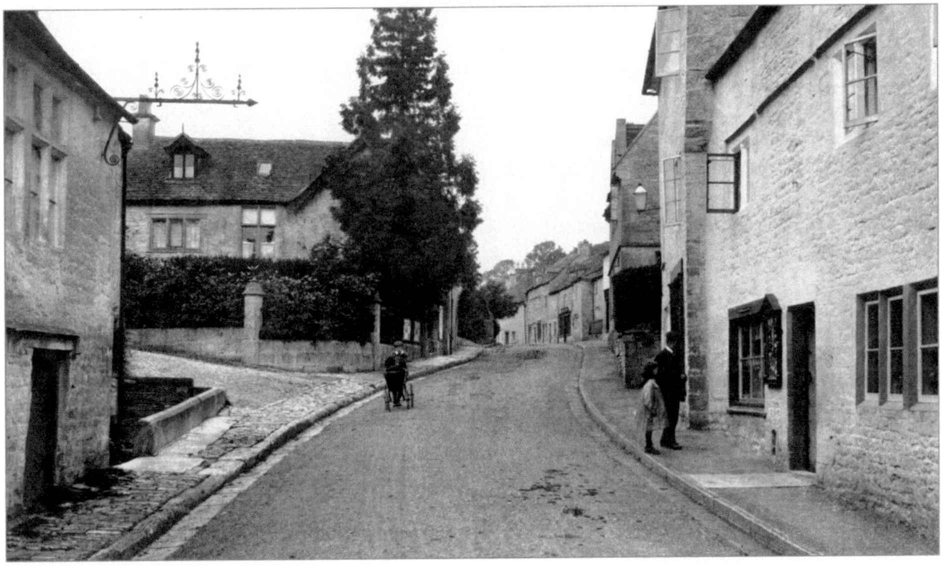

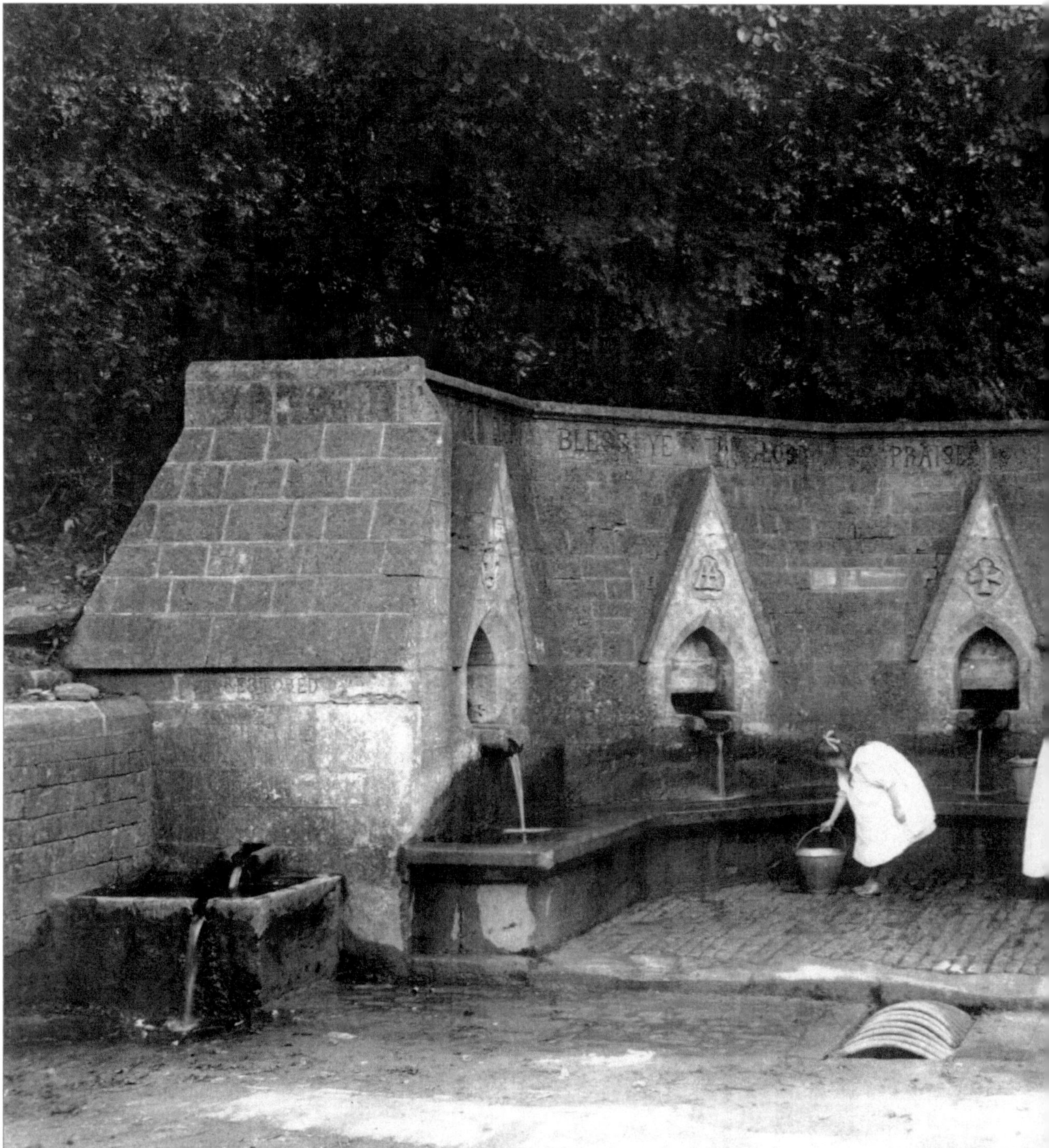
BLESS YE

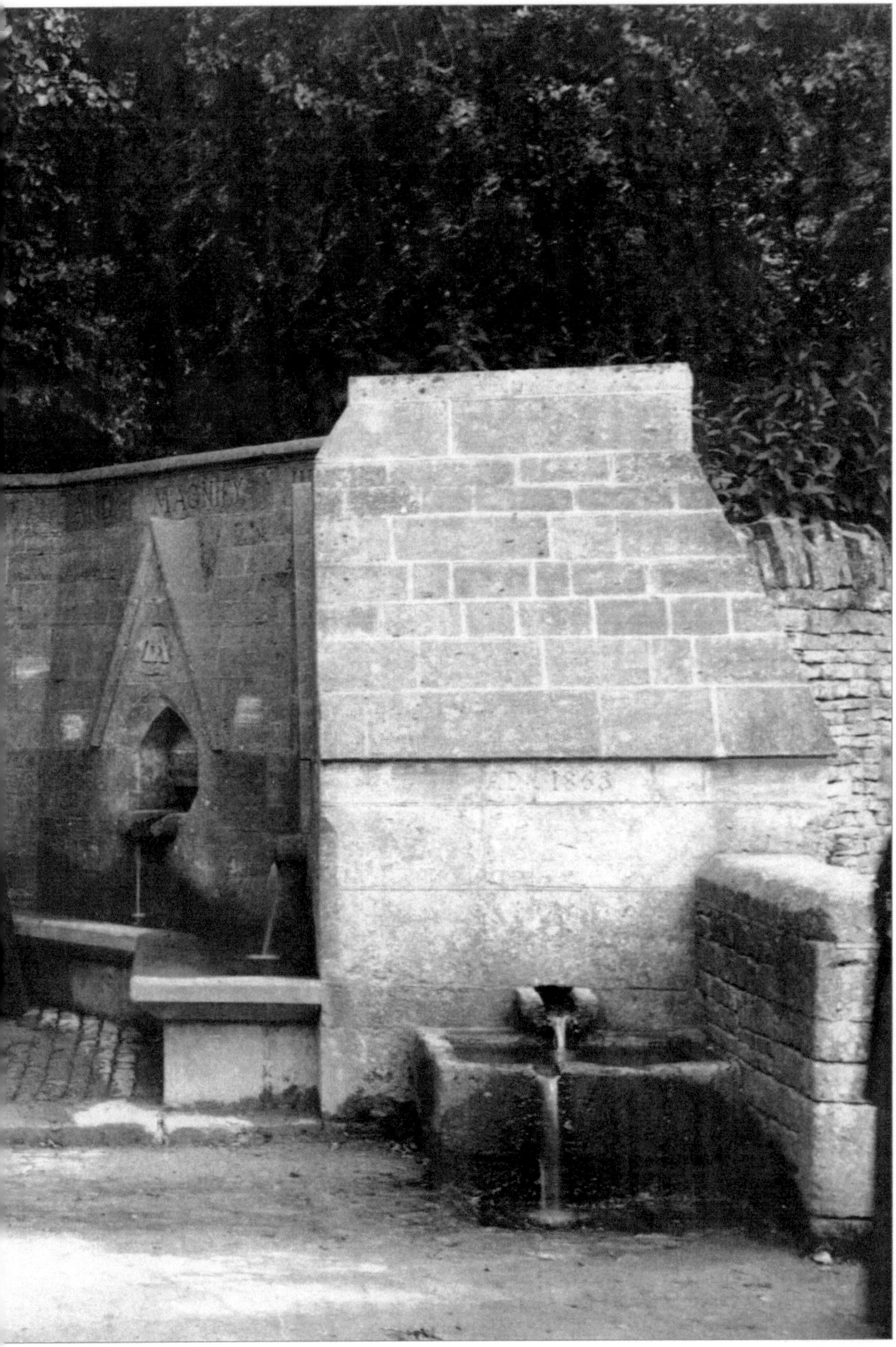

BISLEY
The Wells 1910 62696

Rural, rustic, practical and pretty are Bisley Wells. Five of the seven water chutes have gabled canopies, and were restored in 1863 for the Reverend Thomas Keble (brother of John Keble, the famous hymn writer and founder of the Oxford Movement). Dressing and blessing the wells on Ascension Day is a colourful village affair: the schoolchildren process through the street carrying garlands, and the wells are decorated with spring flowers.

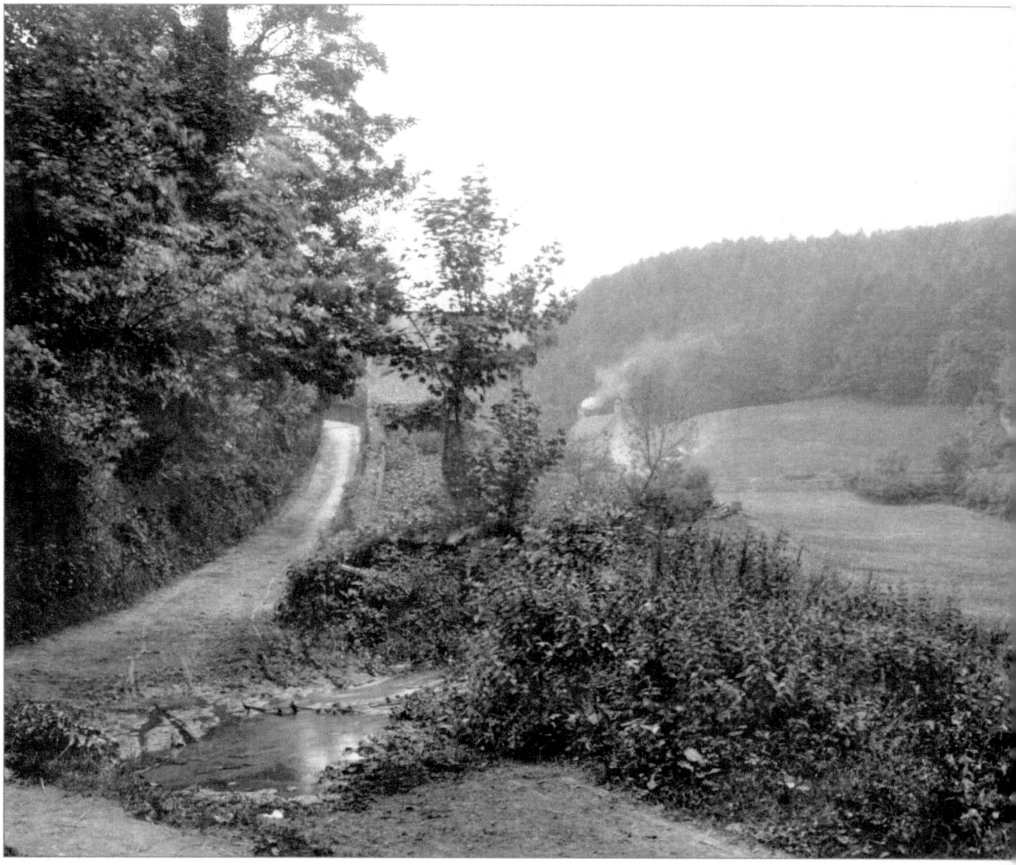

BUSSAGE
The Vale 1910
62703

This view captures the tranquillity of the Vale when Bussage was a small close-knit community reached by roads made for donkey carts and woodmen's wagons.

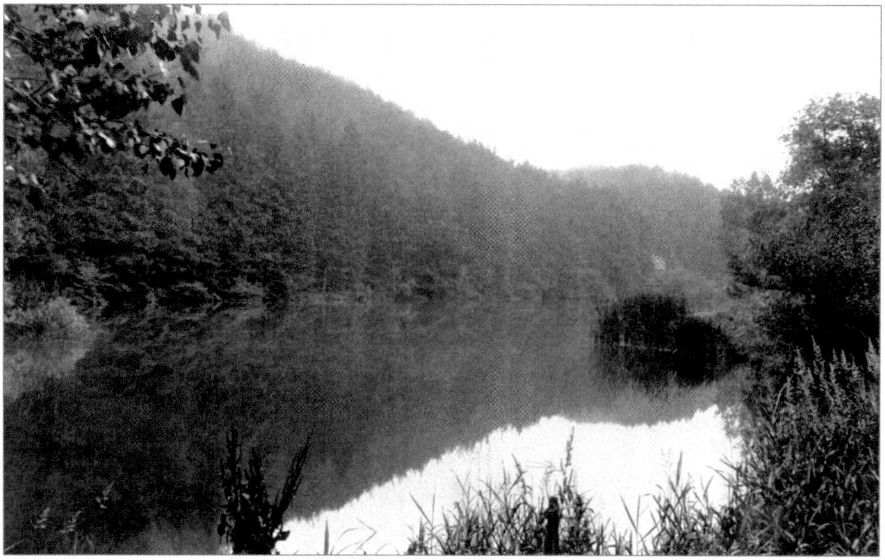

BUSSAGE
The Valley, Toadsmoor Lake 1910 62701

This picturesque spot in the Toadsmoor Valley, which runs up near Bisley, took on an almost alpine appearance in the days when winters were harsher and the lake became the skating rink for local folk. The building we can just glimpse in the distance between the trees (right) was the Woodman's Cottage - a handy refuge for any unfortunate skater who fell through the ice, who could be taken there for some neighbourly comfort and drying out.

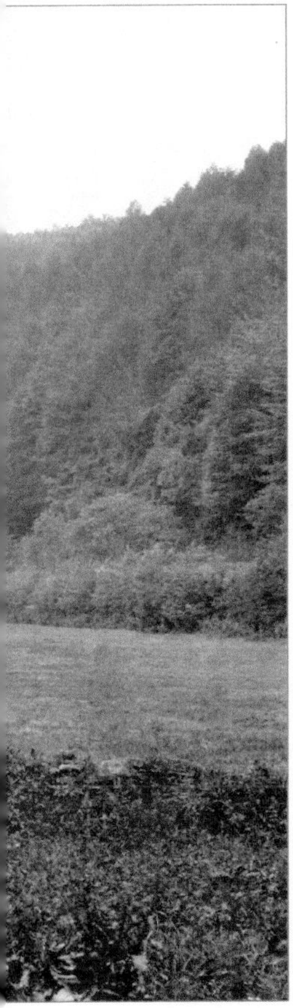

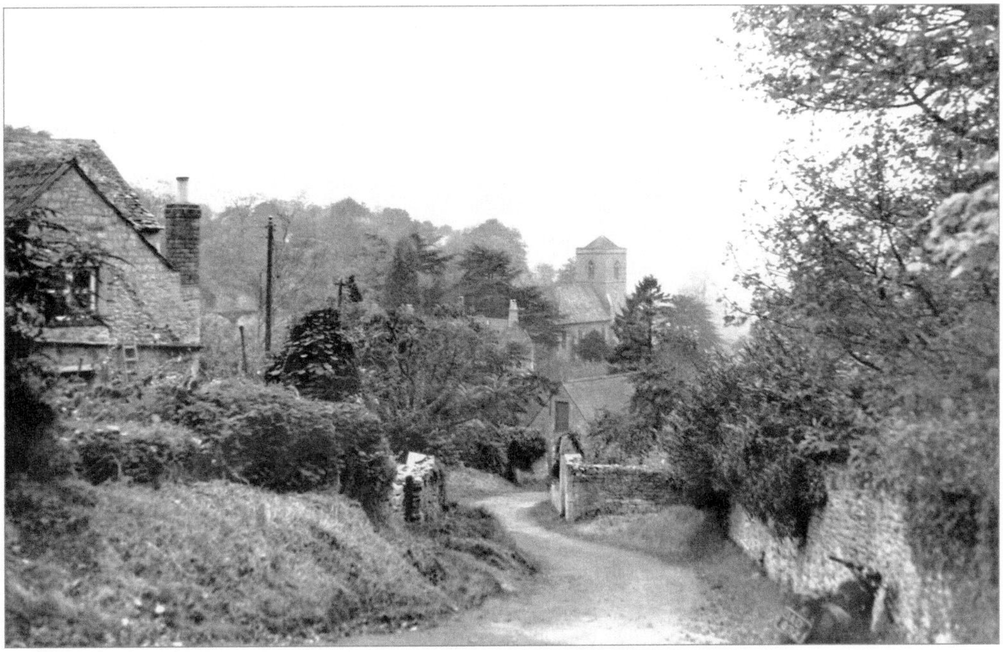

▲ **BUSSAGE,** *The Village c1955* B259026

The old village on its hill is centuries older than its parish church on an even steeper hill, seen here in the far background. St Michael's was built in 1846, mainly funded from subscriptions from undergraduates at Oxford University at the request of Thomas Keble who was vicar at Bisley, in whose extensive parish Bussage was until the late 19th century. The architect, J P Harrison, was regarded by some authorities as 'of no great note in his profession, but an Oxford man, a gentleman and a scholar'.

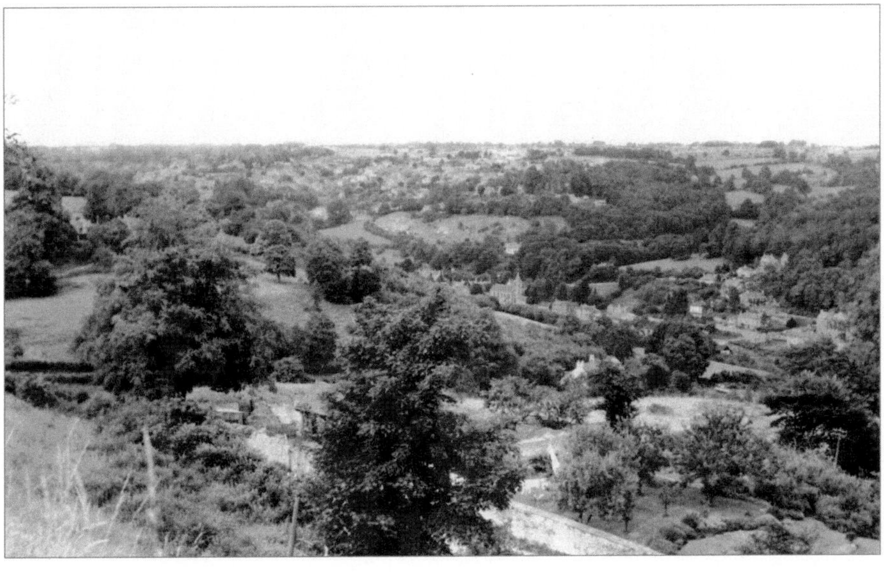

◄ **CHALFORD**
The Valley from the Hill c1960 C569014

Lovely at all times of the year, the Golden Valley where Chalford clings on its hillside is indeed glorious when autumn touches its many wooded steeps and slopes, dips and dells with a golden hand. Artists come in an attempt to catch the colour, and anglers come in their season to the River Frome that weaves its way through the valley.

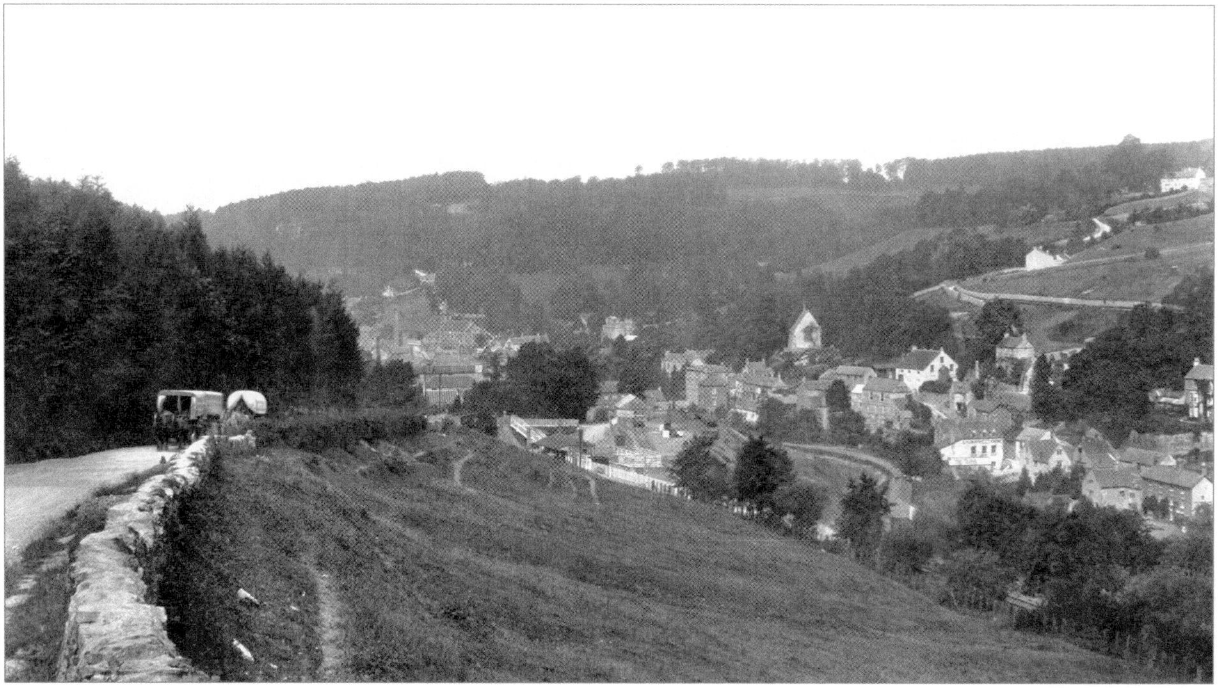

▲ **CHALFORD**
General View 1900 45587

Carriers' carts trundling their way along the stony steeps above the village were a familiar sight when this picture was taken, although transport by rail and canal had by then become established in the valley below.

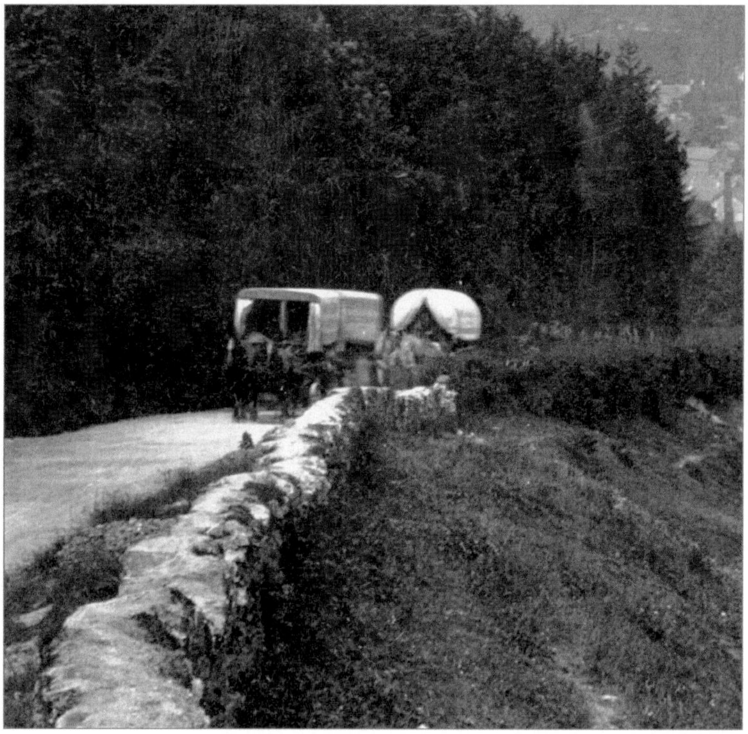

► *detail from* 45587

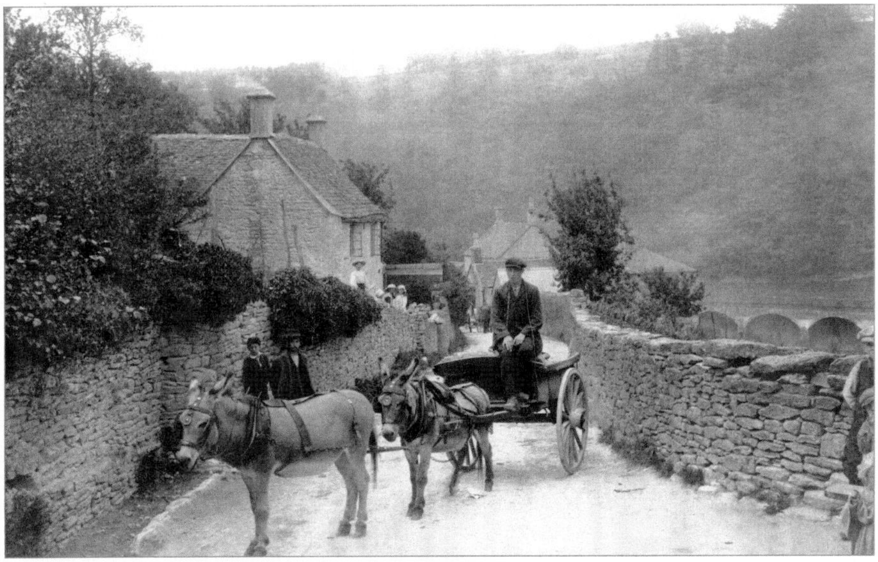

CHALFORD

The Village 1910 62713

Not for nothing was Chalford nicknamed Neddyshire: once it was only sure-footed donkeys that could traverse the precipitous roads leading through the village. Local people still affectionately recall the days of bread delivery by pony and trap, a twice-daily call from the milkman with his yoke and pails, a young Frankie Gardiner with his small donkey hung all around with big wicker panniers, and the immediate post-war treat of an ice cream from Sid Moseley's motorbike sidecar which he adapted as an ice chest.

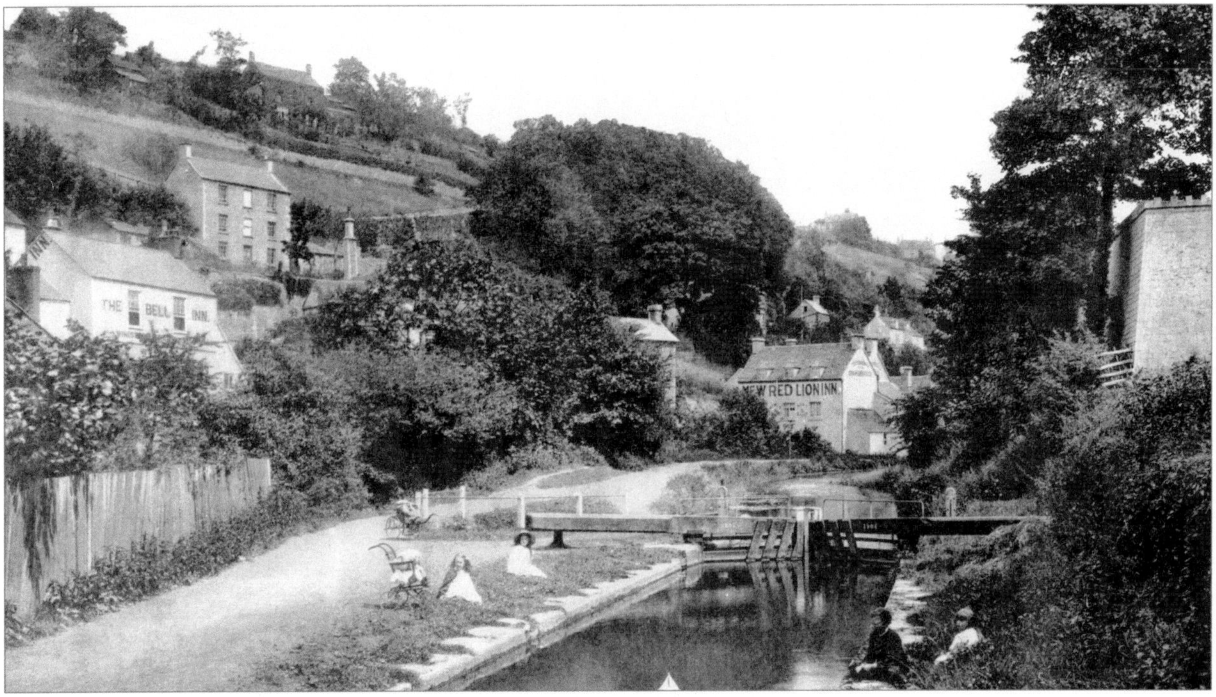

CHALFORD, *The Canal 1910* 62711

The Red Lion Inn shown here at the centre of the picture survives where others, such as the Bell (on the left) have not; public houses sprang up alongside the canal route which opened to great national acclaim in 1789. As the River Frome marked the boundary, the Red Lion was once in Minchinhampton parish, and the locals took advantage of the different pub closing time! The date 1904 on the beam marks the replacement of the lock gates here at Bell Lock.

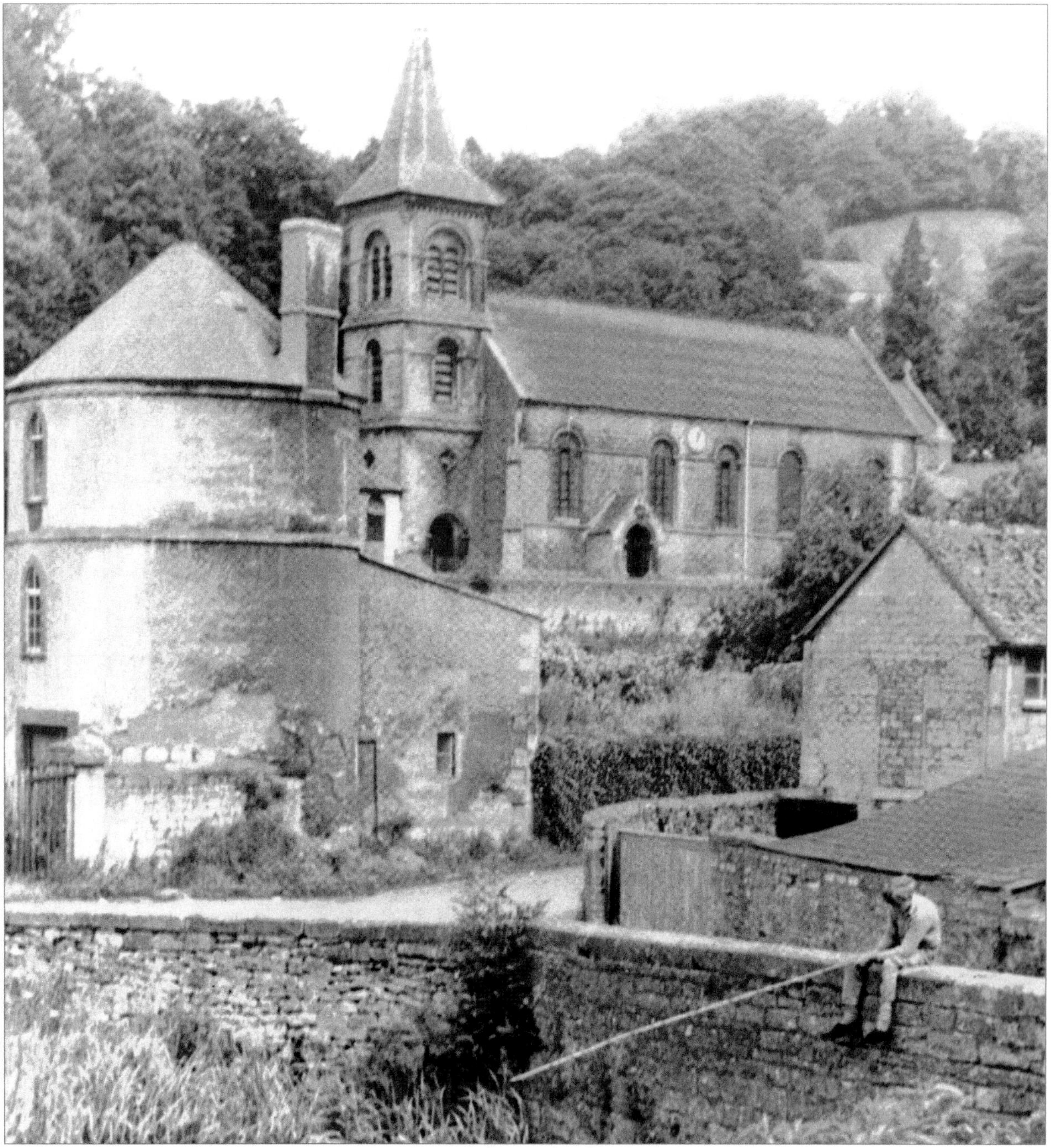

CHALFORD, *The Church and the Round Tower c1960* C569010

The round tower shown to the far left of the church is characteristic of the lengthman's (or maintenance man's) house to be found along the Thames and Severn Canal. Christ Church was built in 1724 and is interesting for its wealth of furnishings by the Cotswold members of the Arts and Crafts movement influenced by William Morris who settled in the valley.

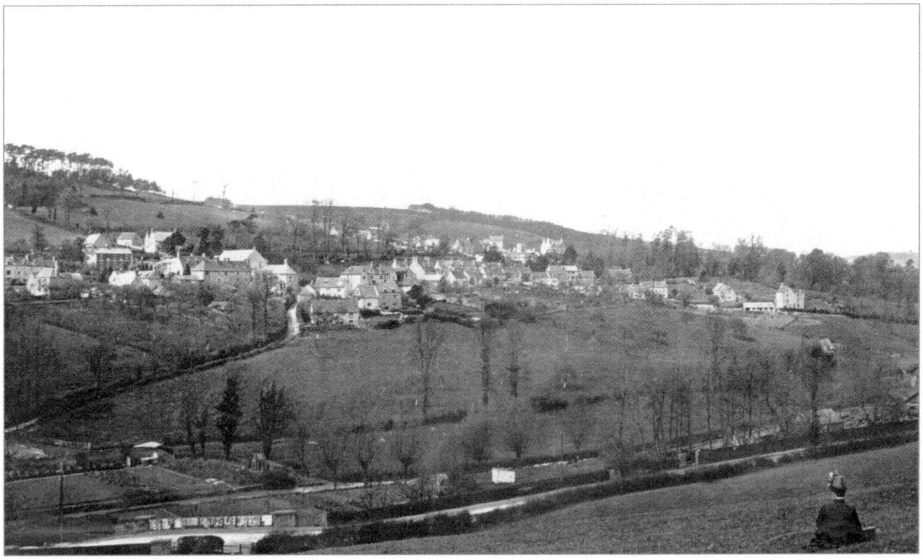

WOODCHESTER
The Village 1890
25173

As the 'chester' part of its name implies, Woodchester was a military post or station during the Roman occupation. Archaeological evidence of civil settlement here is the tessellated pavement discovered in the old churchyard, considered to be one of the finest of its kind in Europe. It is kept buried for its own preservation, and only uncovered for public viewing very occasionally.

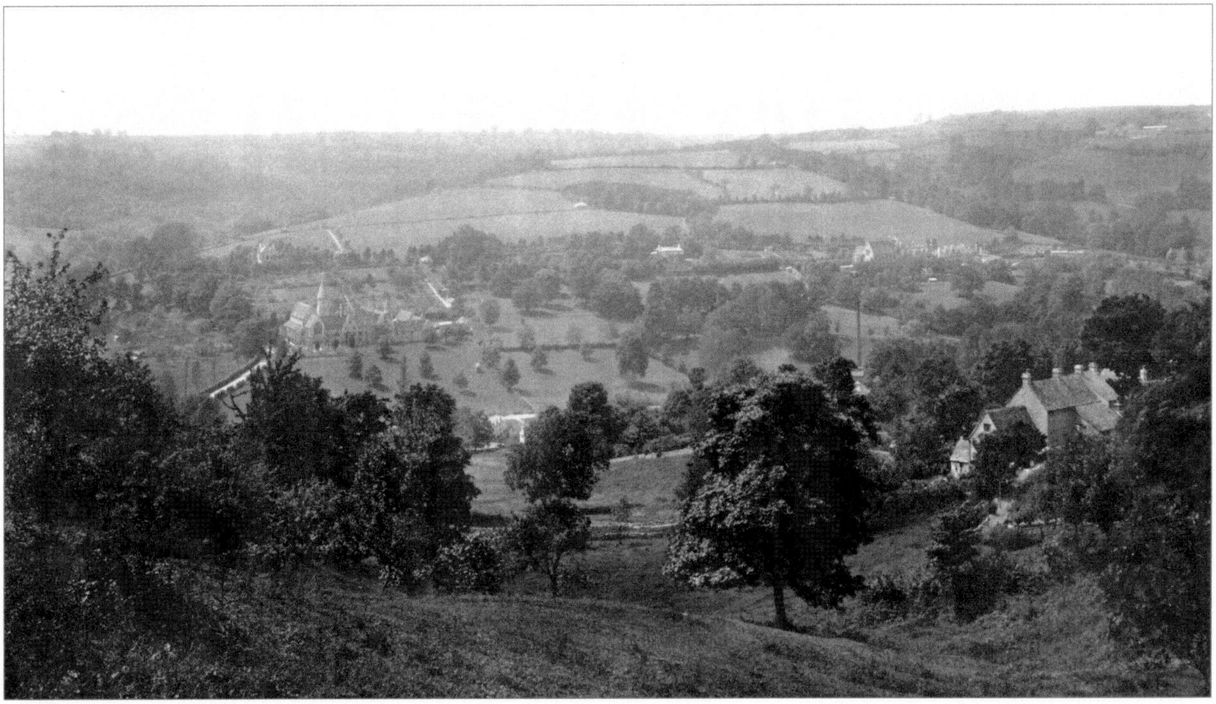

WOODCHESTER, *The Valley and the Monastery 1910* 62684

This view of the village on the side of the valley gives a glimpse on the left of the priory which William Leigh, who had just been converted to the Catholic faith, had built; the Dominicans moved into the priory in 1850. On the right of the picture is the Franciscan convent of the Poor Clares. Charles Francis Hansom was the architect of both these religious houses, after the trend-setting Pugin pulled out of the designing of the priory.

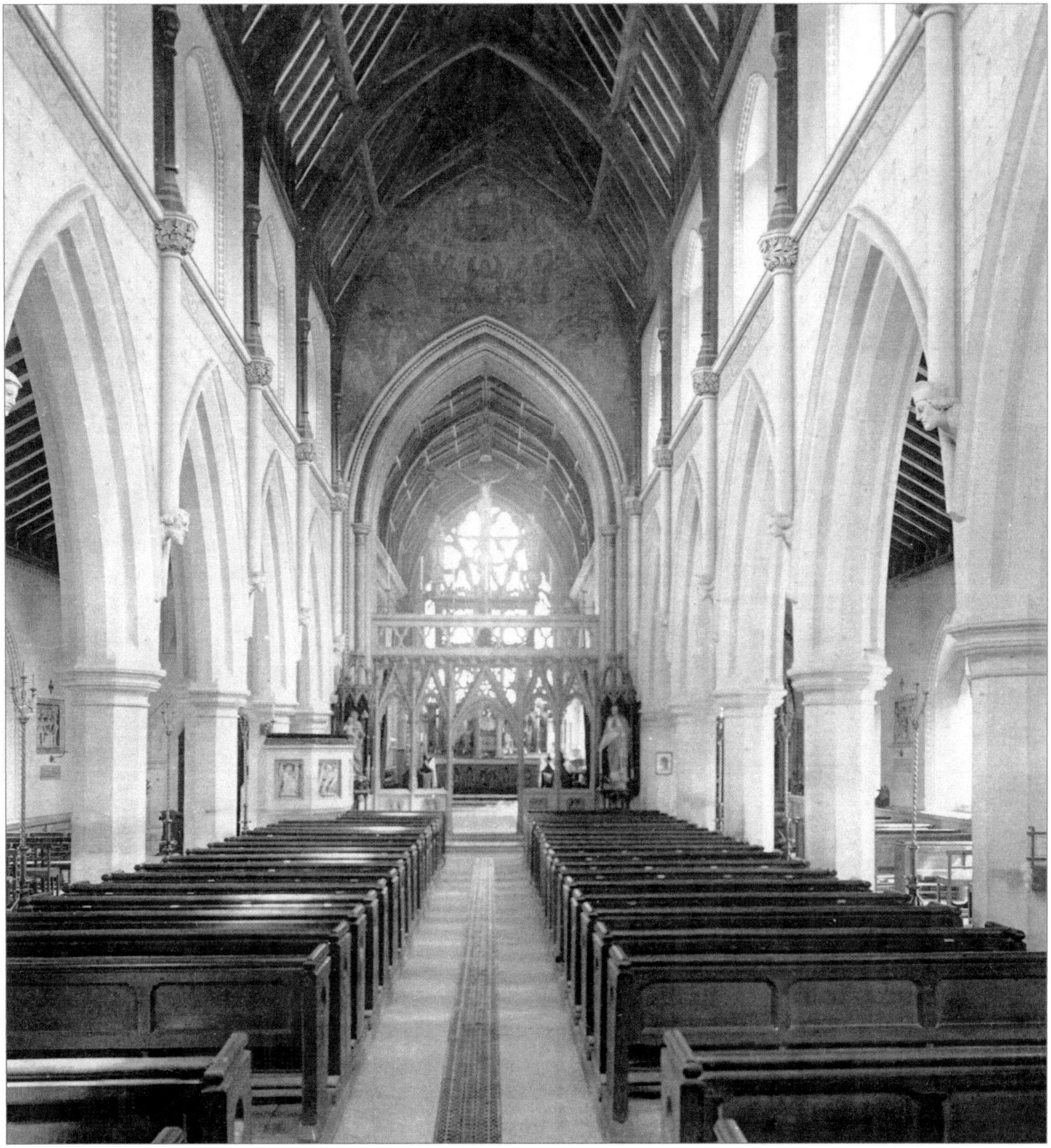

WOODCHESTER, *The Roman Catholic Church, the Interior 1890* 25179

Among its many memorials is an effigy of William Leigh, shown vested in the robe of a Knight of St Gregory and holding in his hands a model of the church he founded.

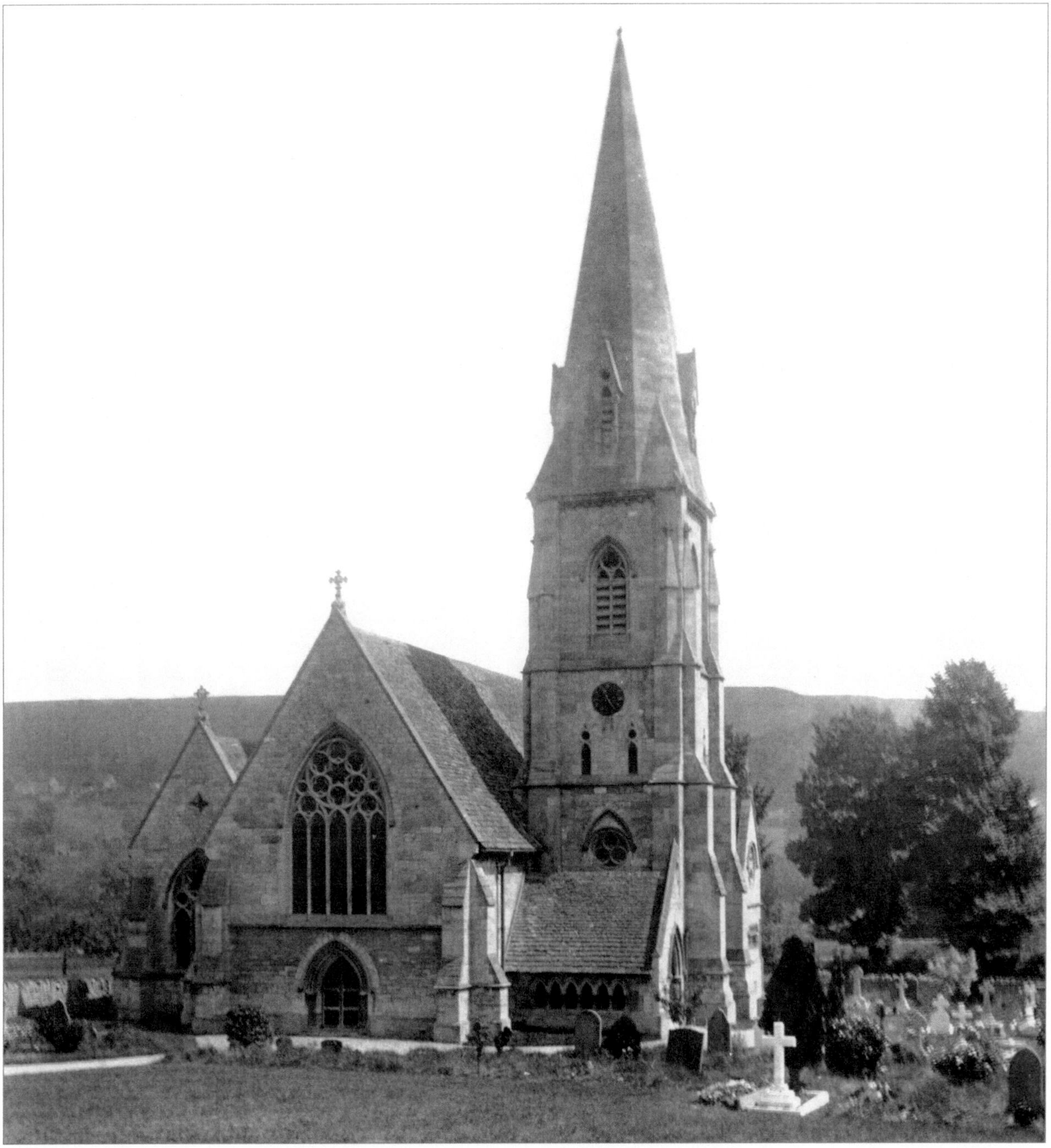

WOODCHESTER, *The Church 1900* 45593

The Priory Church of Our Lady of the Annunciation opened its doors soon after the old parish church of St Mary was abandoned. It is in the old churchyard, close to the site of the Roman pavement, that Sir Onesiphorus Paul, the great pioneer of prison reform, is buried.

WOODCHESTER
The Monastery c1960 W130005

A picture of perfect peace and tranquillity is shown here, but Woodchester was one of the places where riots broke out during the early 19th century industrial revolution when weavers and their families suffered extreme hardship. A century earlier, George III had visited the then prosperous mills at Woodchester.

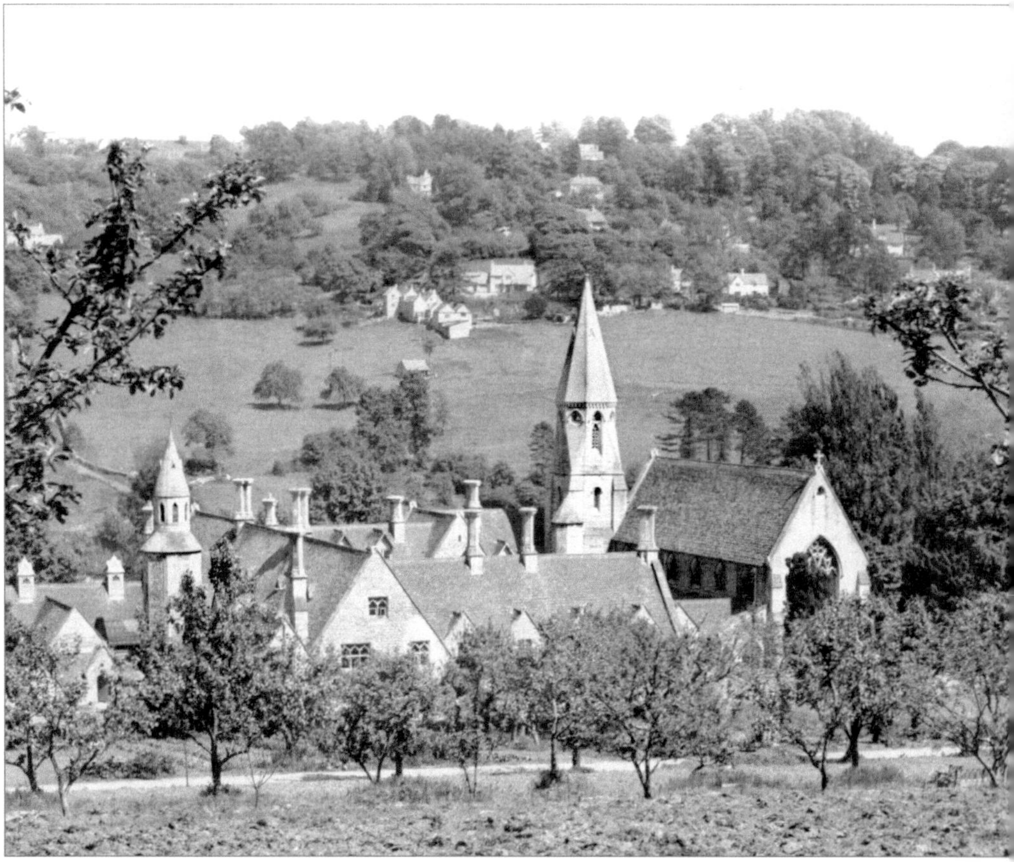

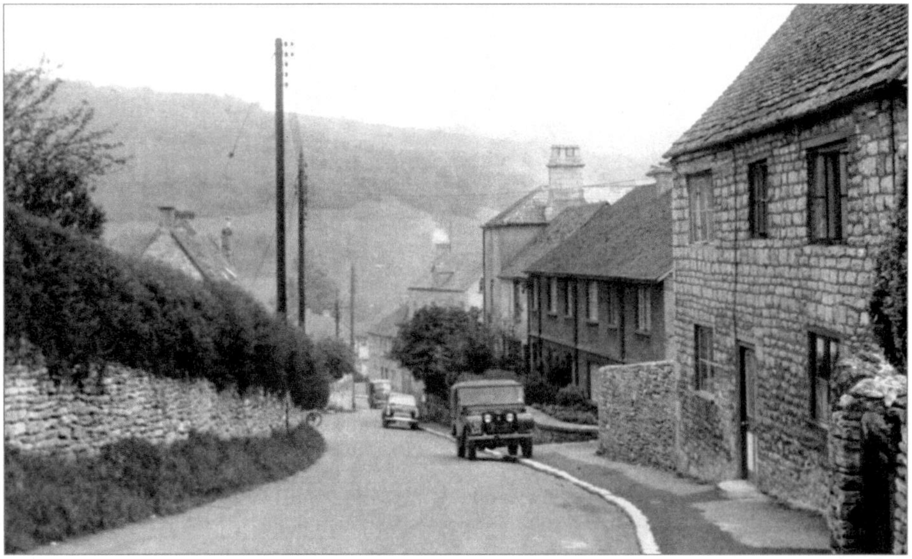

WOODCHESTER
The Village c1960
W130003

Beyond the terraced streets of the village is Woodchester Mansion, set in a remote valley and keeping its secrets within an unfinished masterpiece of Victorian architecture; mysteries and legends are locked into this fascinating place, which is open to the public on certain dates.

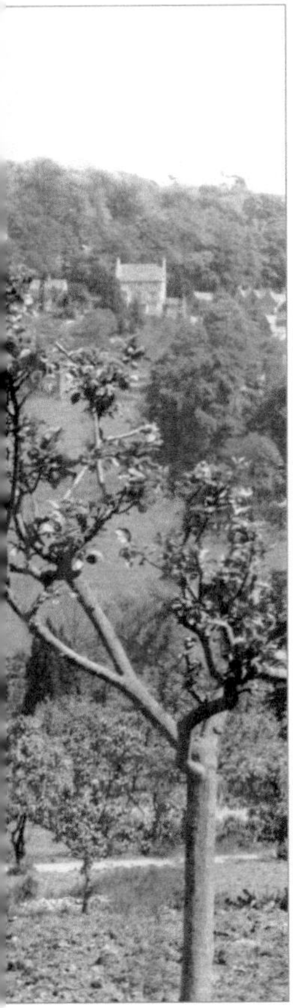

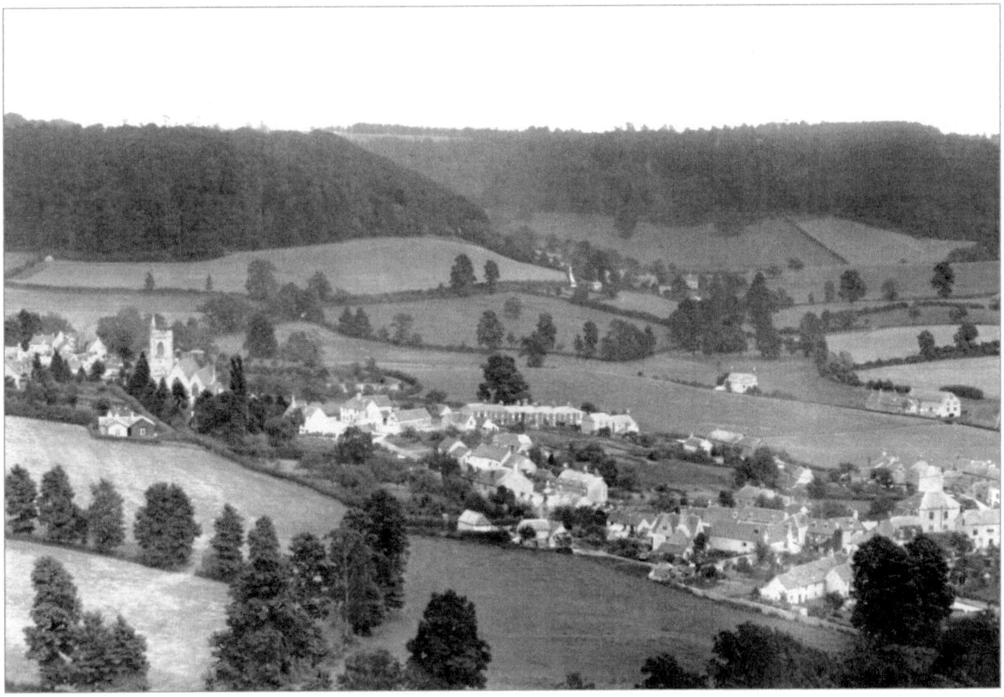

▲ **ULEY,** *From Uley Bury 1900* 45539

Uley Bury, from where this view was photographed, is acclaimed the most spectacular Iron Age hill-fort in the Cotswolds. Standing some 800ft up, rising in green terraces above the village, it affords panoramic views with the erosion caused by rivers and frost action during the Ice Ages evident in the isolation of the three peaks of Downham Hill, Cam Peak and Cam Long Down.

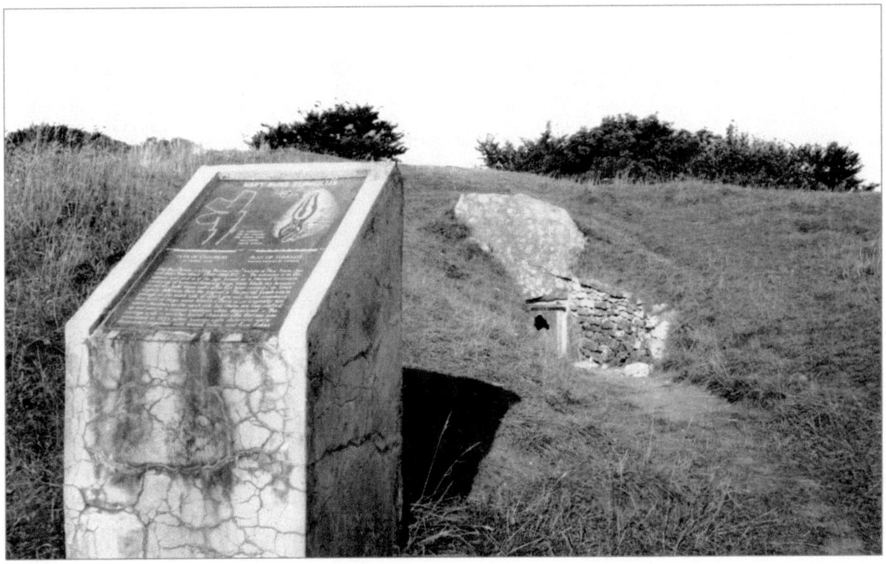

◄ **ULEY**
The Tumulus c1960 U3008

Generally known as Hetty Pegler's Tump, named after a local landowner (Tump being a Cotswold word to indicate a small hill or mound), this Neolithic long barrow a mile to the north of Uley is a scheduled Ancient Monument. Inside is a stone-lined gallery some 20ft long, with two side chambers leading off on the south side. A matching pair on the north side has long since collapsed.

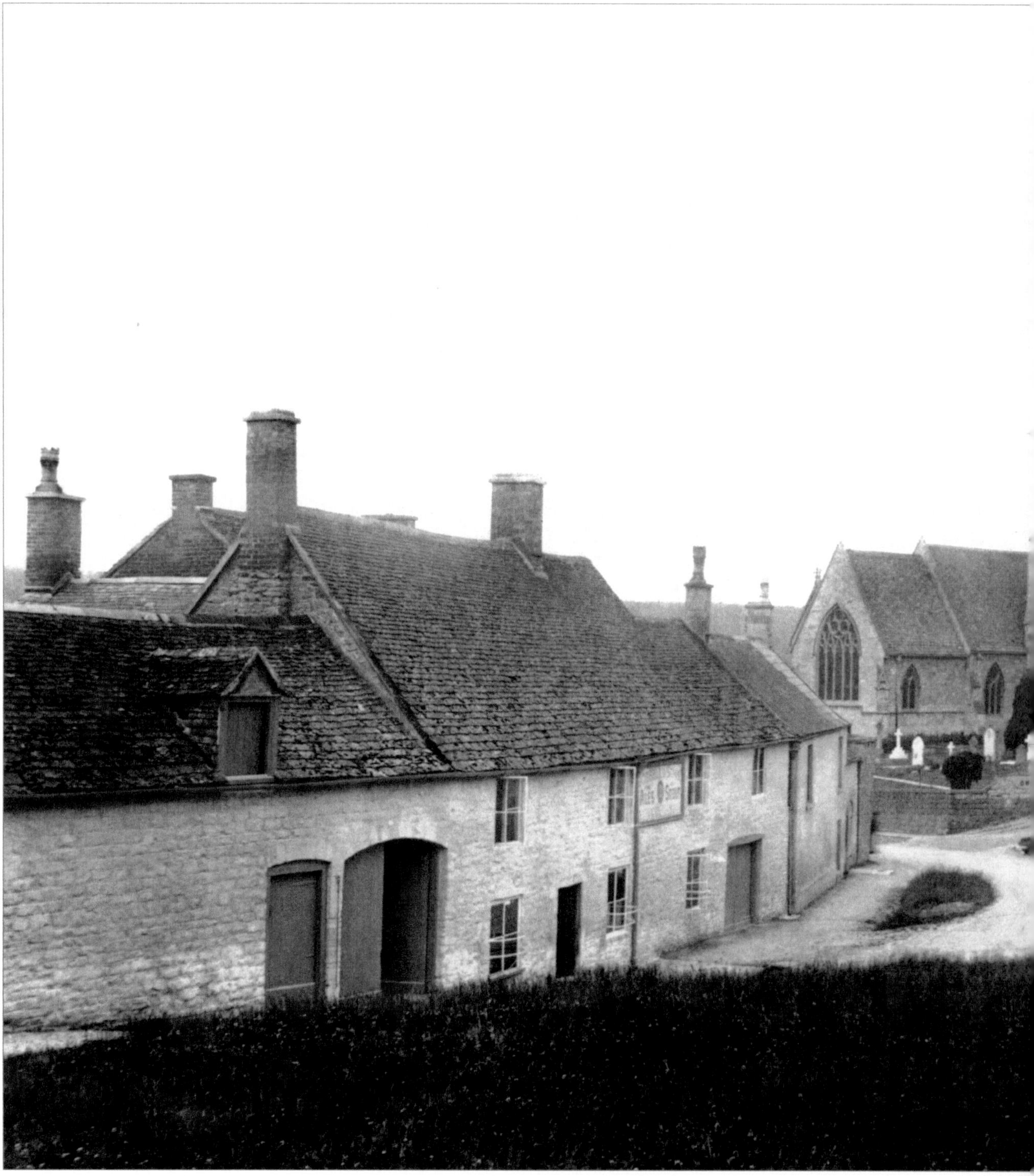

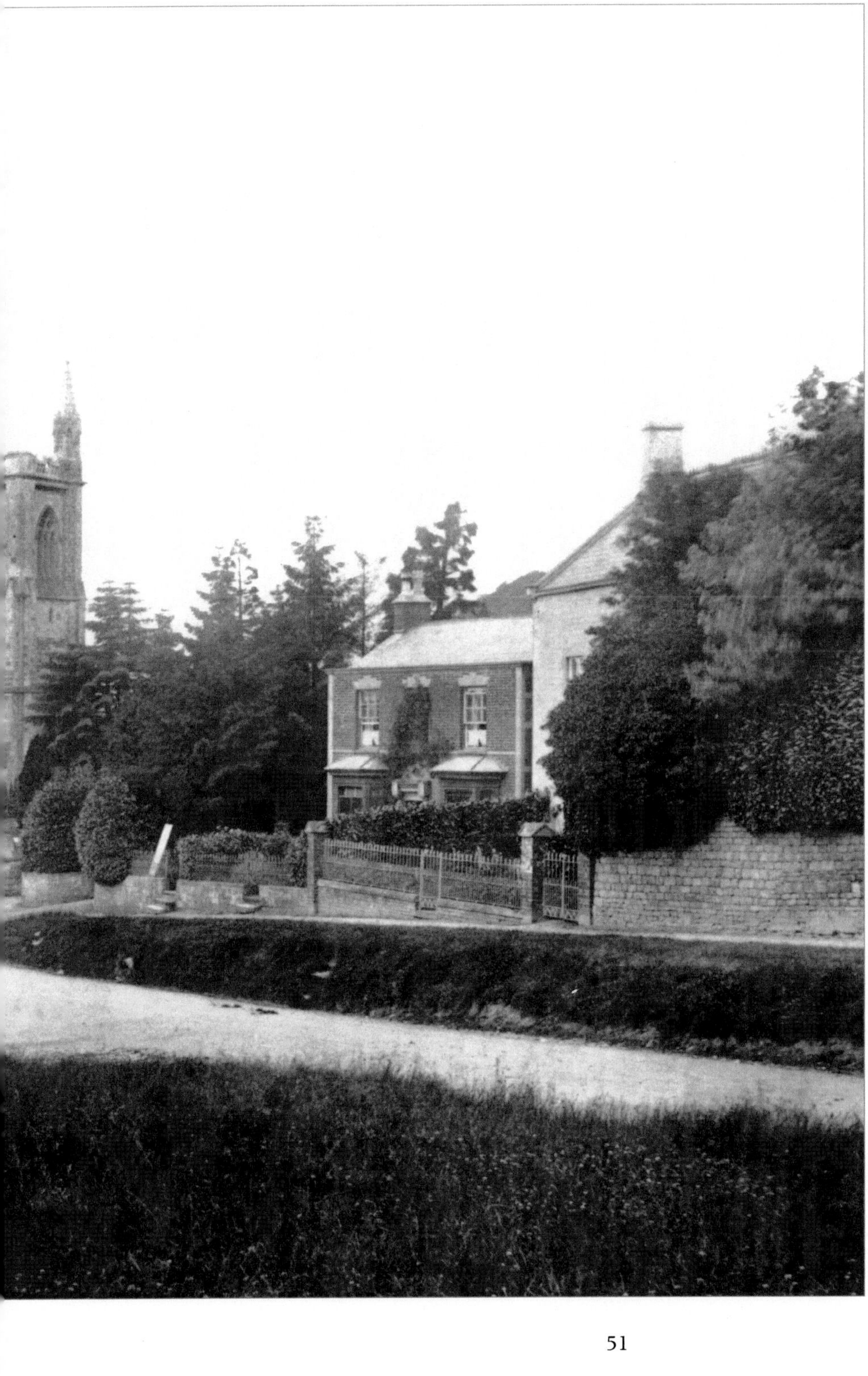

ULEY
The Green and the Church 1904 51953

The public house on the far left of this picture was served by the Stroud brewers Godsell & Sons, a household name from the mid 1850s after the family firm turned their 15th-century cloth mill into a brewery. A local ditty ran: 'Adam and Eve in Paradise and God sells beer!' (The Adam and Eve pub was in Paradise, a tiny hamlet near Painswick served by Godsells brewery).

▼ **ULEY,** *The Green and the Church c1965* U3010

The same scene as picture 51953 (page 51) is photographed from the same spot 60 years later. The only change is that the brewer now serving the Old Crown public house is Stroud Brewery, the successor to Godsell's, and a car and telegraph wires have made their appearance.

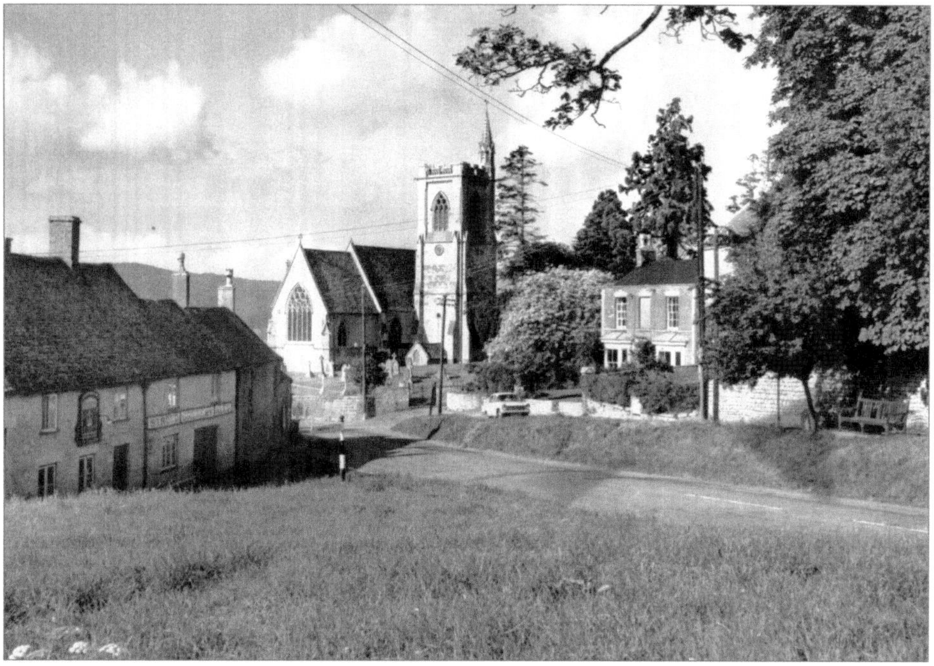

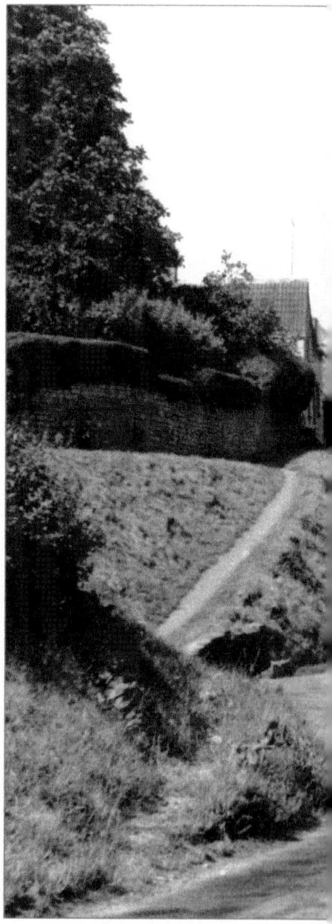

► **ULEY**
From the Church c1960
U3001

Twenty-nine local weavers were recorded working in what was then a small village in 1608, 19 of whom were specifically engaged in producing the broadcloth for which this area became famous. The villagers consequently suffered badly during the depression of the cloth making industry.

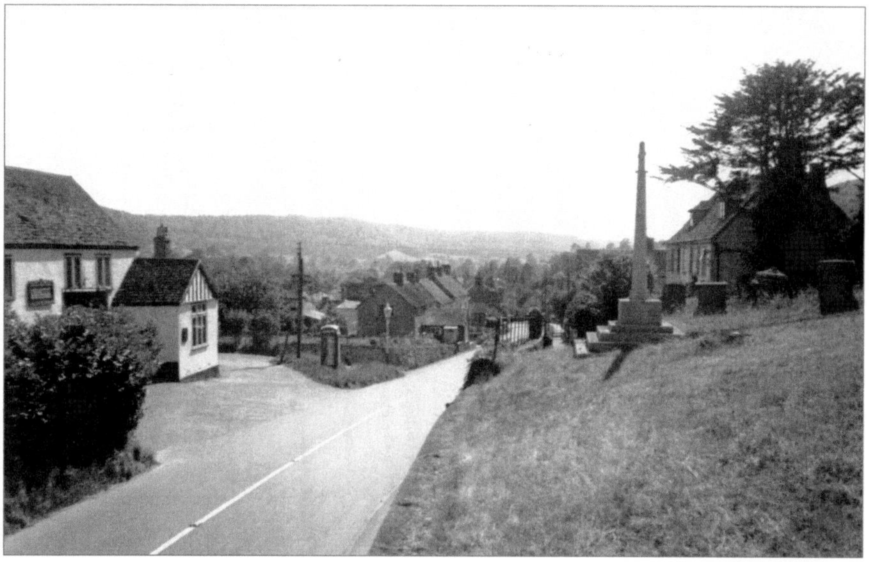

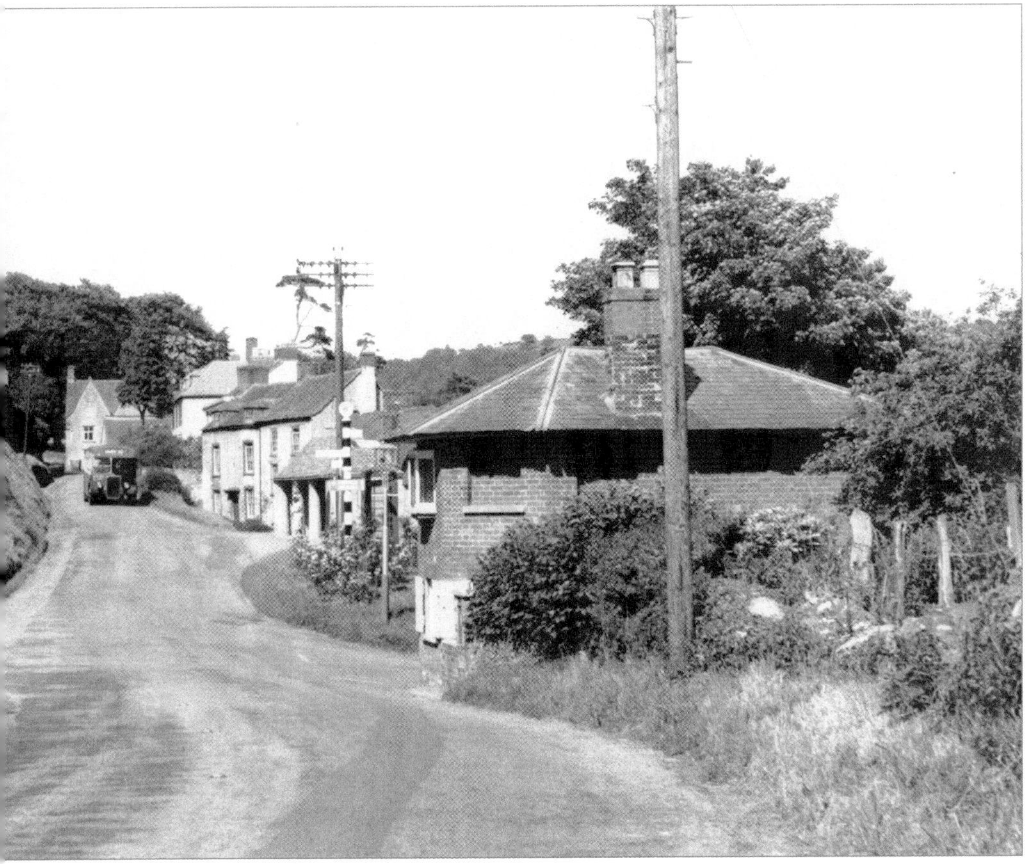

ULEY
The Village c1960
U3004

The hilly aspect of this village must have been a good test for the driving skills of the single-decker bus seen approaching in the background, while the old toll house (with a bricked in window) in the foreground is a reminder of earlier highway use.

ULEY
The View from Lampern Hill c1960 U3024

The landscape here is a fine example of the continuing denudation of the Cotswold Scarp; it is of great interest to geologists, as the outlying peaks and downs were once connected to the main hill mass.

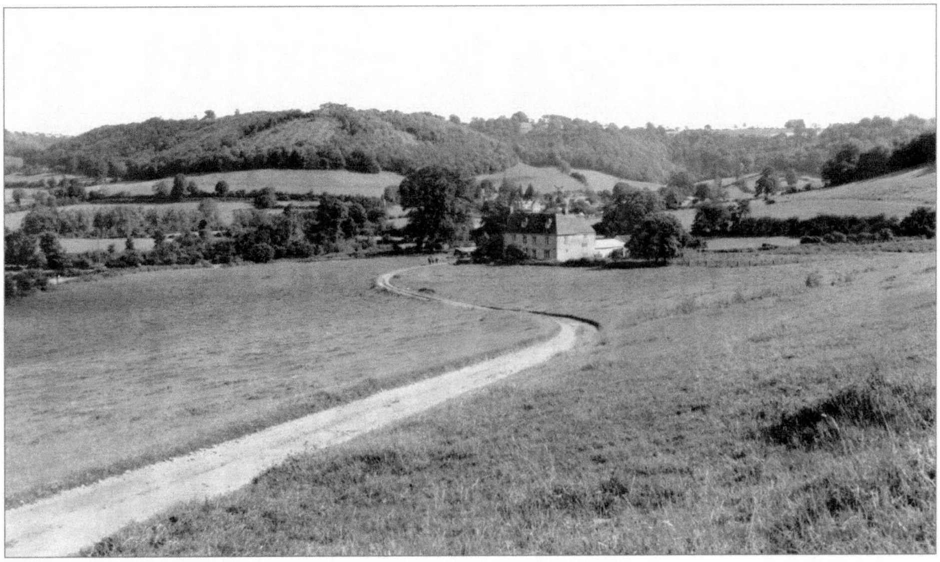

ULEY
The Green c1965 U3026

Several grand Georgian houses on the Green were probably built for the master clothiers who marketed the famous Uley Blue cloth, which was used for the superfine uniform of the British Navy.

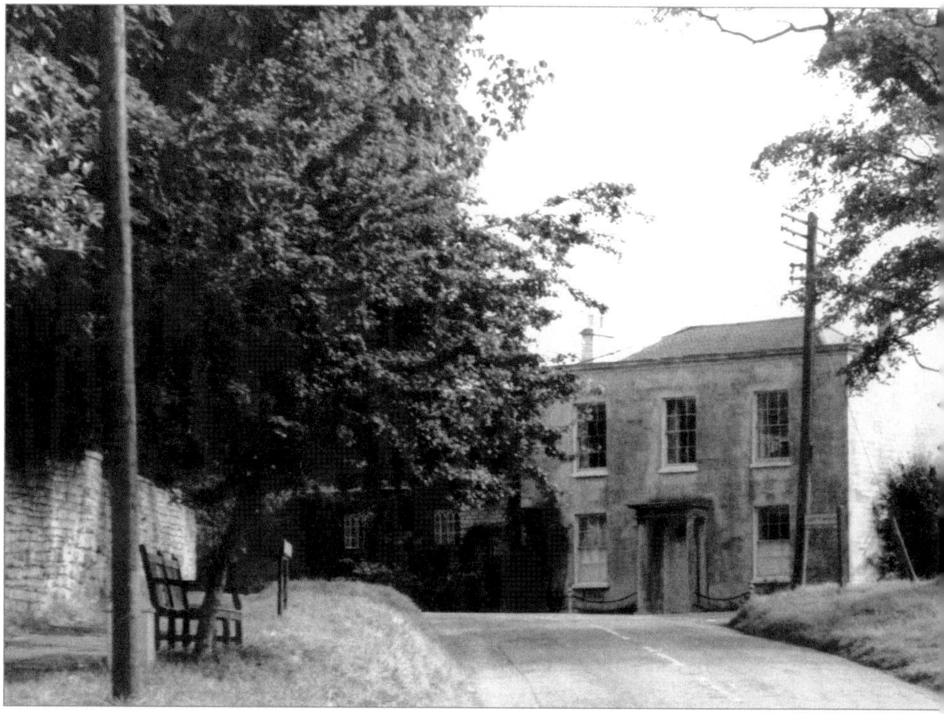

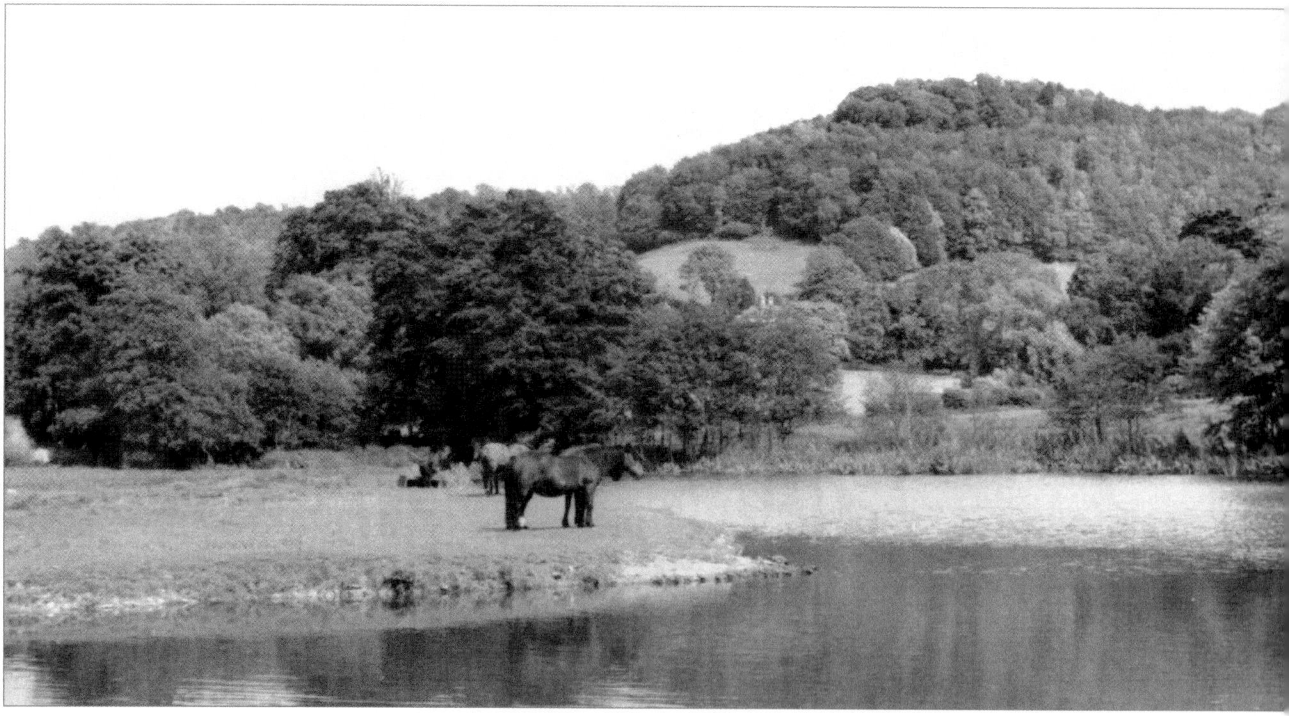

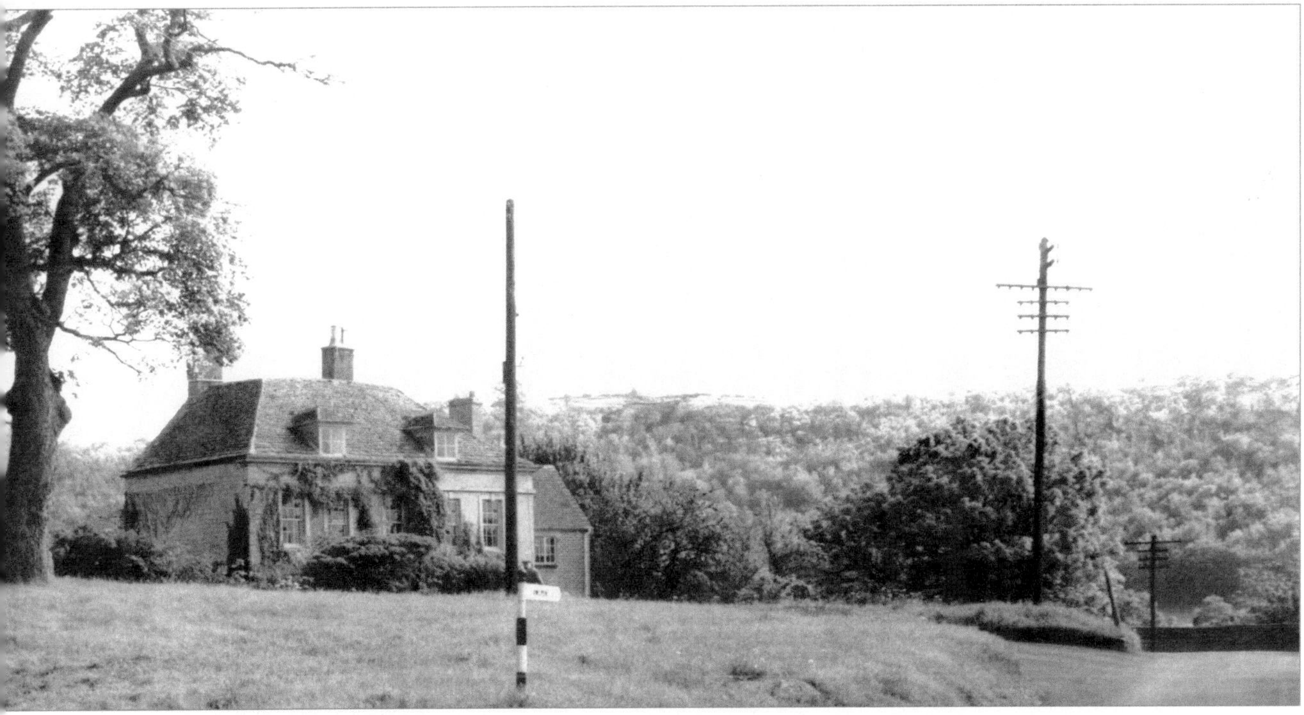

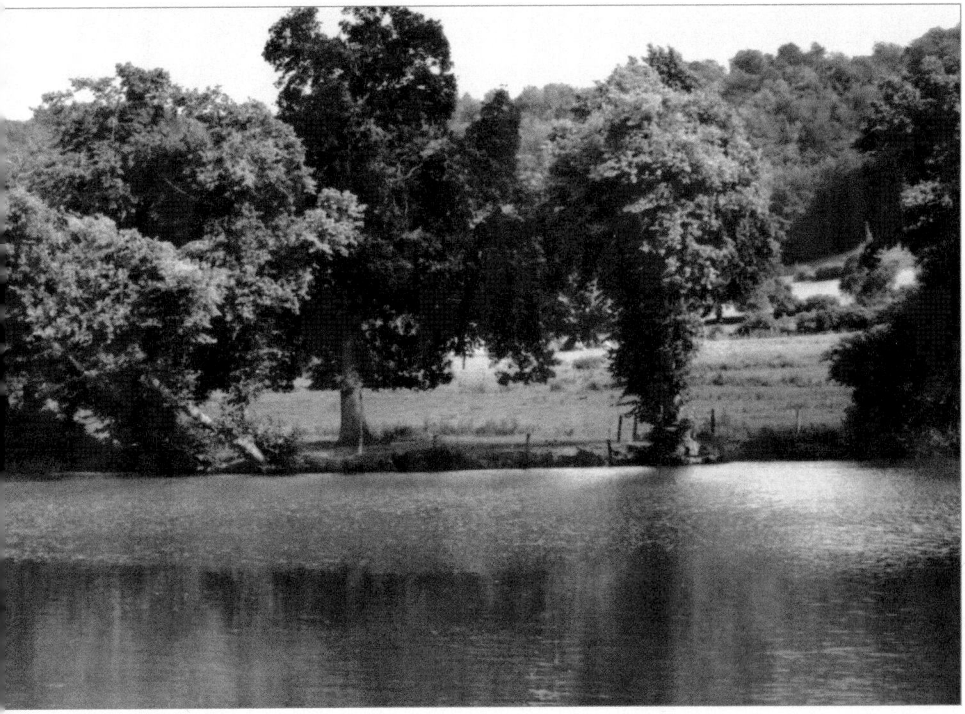

◄ **ULEY**
Stouts Hill Pond c1955
U3006

This tranquil scene would have not altered since Samuel Rudder, the eminent 18th-century historian, was born at Stout's Hill just outside the village of Uley. Rudder contributed a valuable chronicle of Gloucestershire history,and scholars have made use of it ever since.

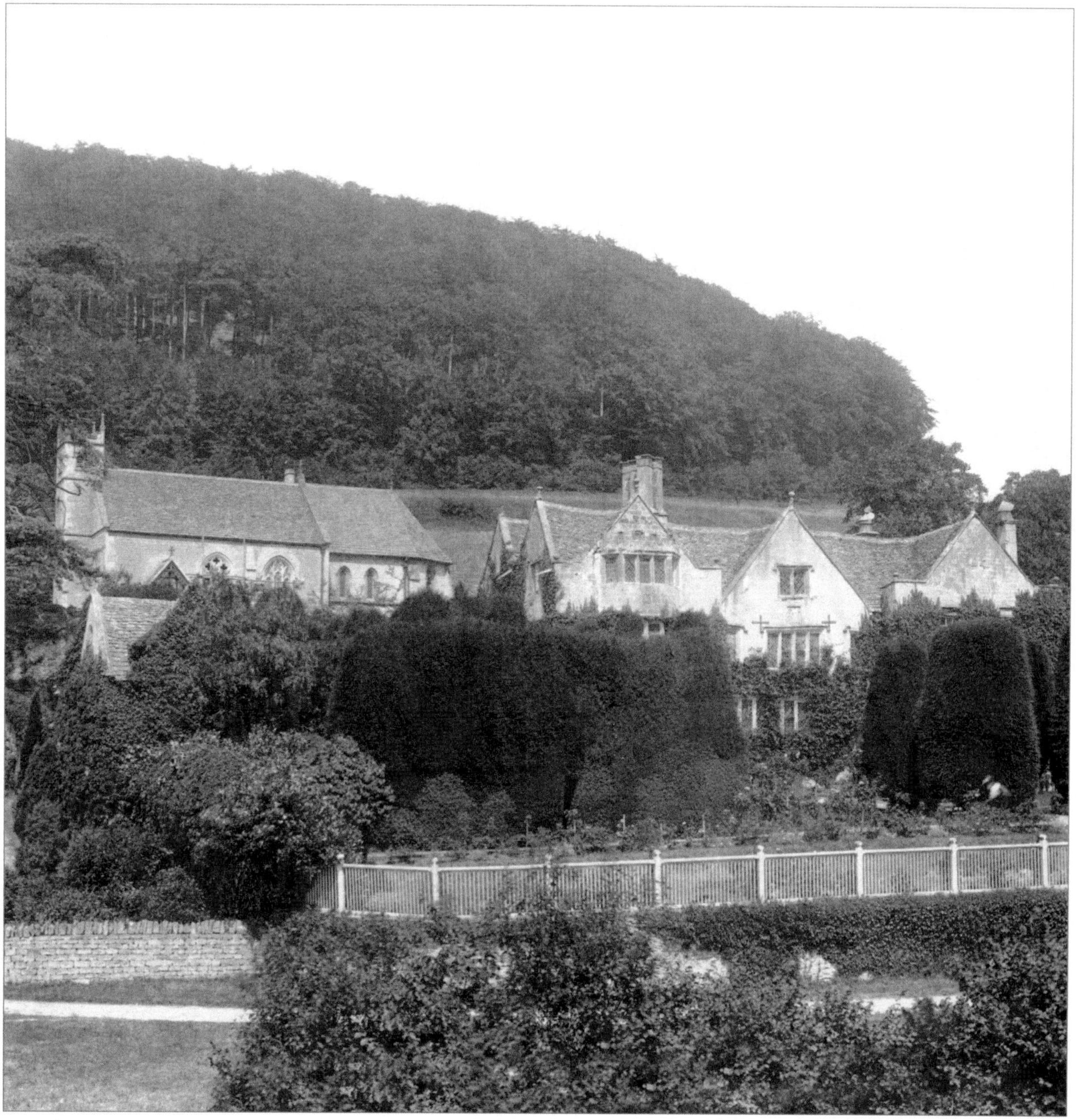

OWLPEN, *The Manor House and the Church 1900* 45543

This perfect composition of church, manor house, mill and barn could be the illustration from some medieval manuscript, so snugly does it tuck into a hollow in the wooded hillside. It comes somewhat as a surprise, then, to learn that the little church of the Holy Cross is mainly the result of a rebuilding programme carried out in the early 19th century. The Manor House does have its origins in the Middle Ages, however, and among its many treasured features are fireplaces in the Hall and Great Chamber from Tudor days. It is open to the public during the summer months.

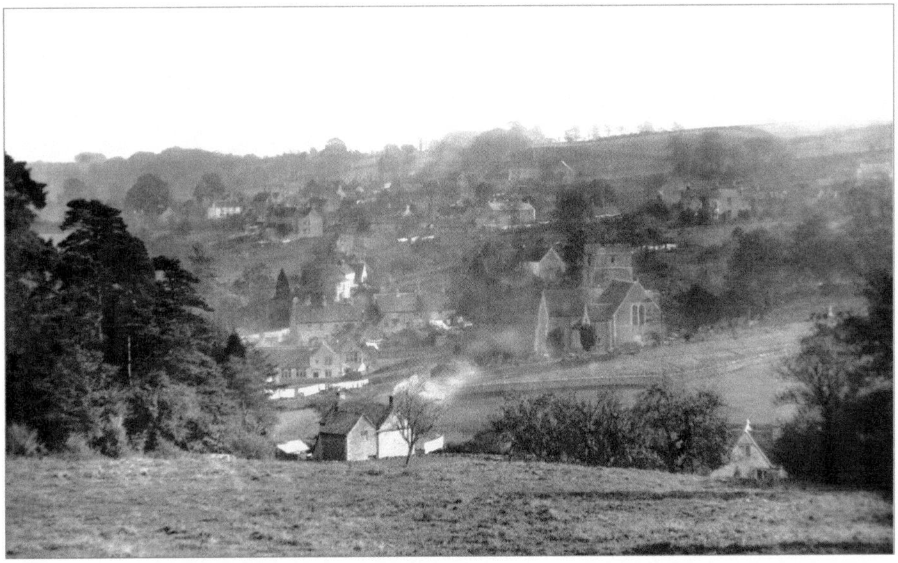

AVENING
General View 1904 53120

The village was held after the Norman Conquest by Queen Matilda, the wife of William I. It was she who had the church of the Holy Cross built; it is said that she built it as a penance of her sin in having the Saxon lord of the manor thrown into prison to languish until his death, after he had spurned her advances. On completion of the building of the church, Matilda gave a feast of 'pig's face' for the masons; the village has instituted the custom of the Pig Face Feast in recent years.

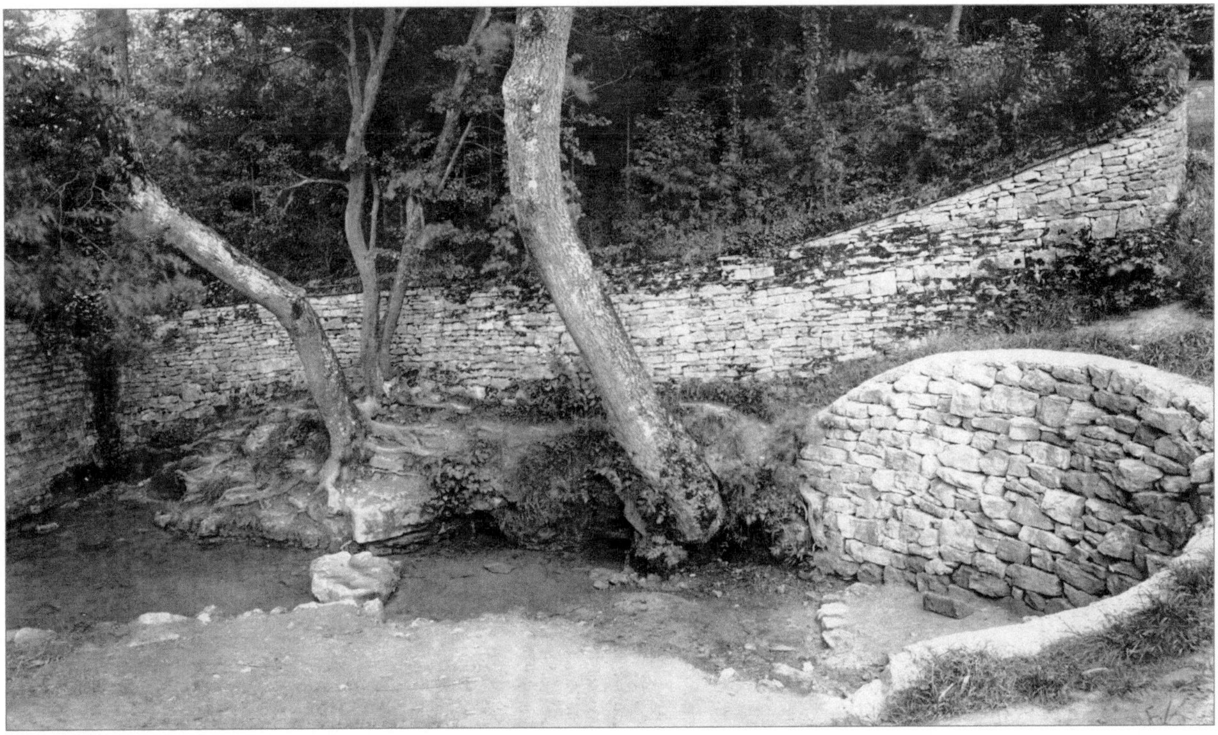

TARLTON, *The Source of the Thames 1901* 47305

There are a number of contenders for the exact source of the River Thames, but this picture shows a favoured spot, and one more picturesque and accessible than the inauspicious muddy patches put forward by some authorities.

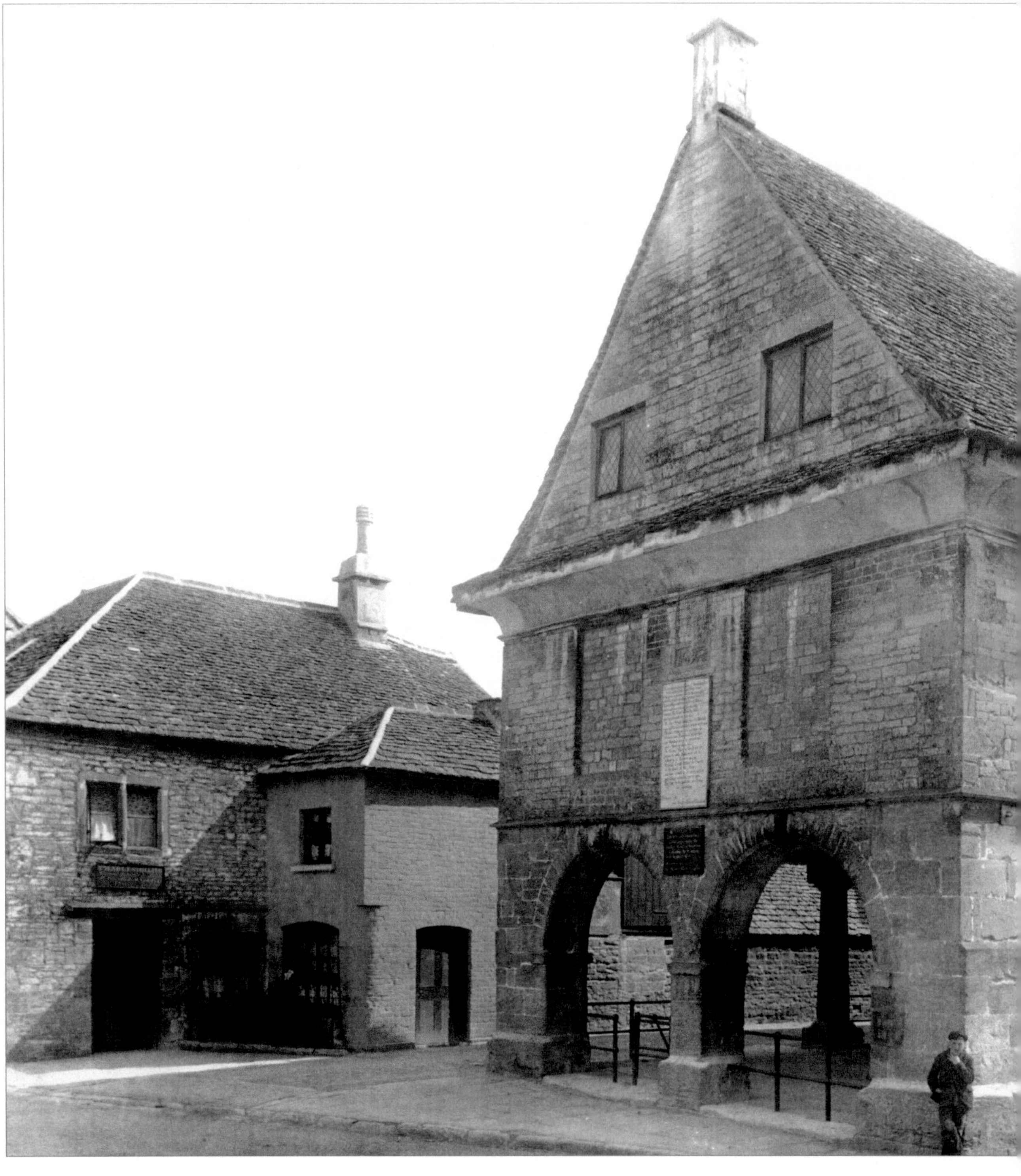

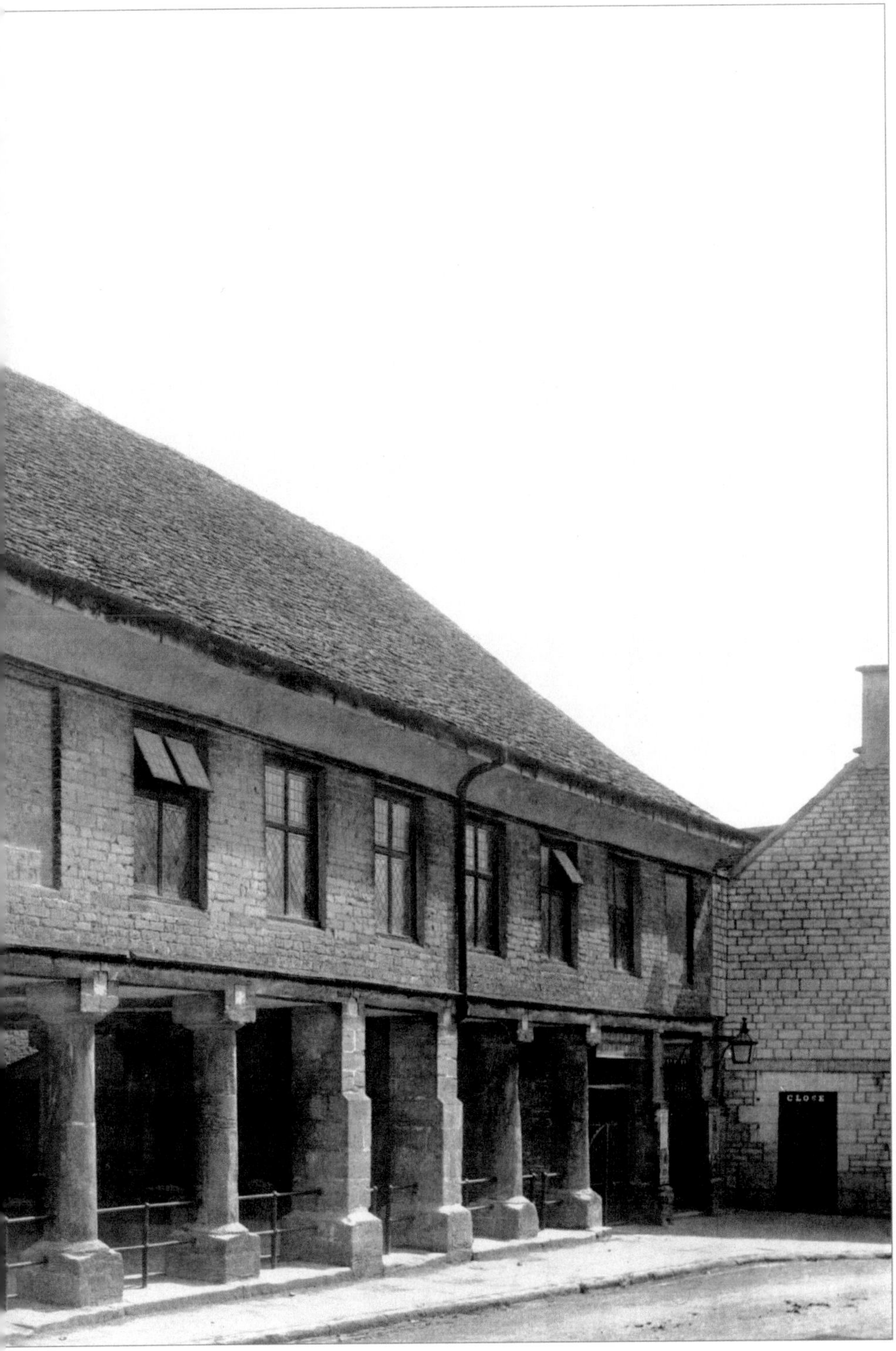

MINCHINHAMPTON
The Market House
1901 47348

Built in 1698, the Market House was used as a hall in which town business was transacted; it became a venue for entertainments after it had ceased its original function as a market centre. Mrs Siddons is said to have played here during the period between 1778 and 1782 when she was at Bath.

MINCHINHAMPTON
The Church Interior 1901
47352

Among the wealth of interesting features of Holy Trinity Church are its curious truncated spire - taken down to the present height in 1563 and crowned with a stone coronet - and the medieval south transept with its magnificent rose window, below which a knight and his wimple-hatted lady have rested for six centuries. The church seems to have attracted hunting parsons in their day. The Reverend William Cockin is said to have obtained the living in the 19th century by the toss of a coin while he was a dinner guest at Gatcombe House; a century later, the novelist Joanna Trollope recalls her grandfather, the Reverend Rex Hodson, delivering parish magazines on horseback and 'often taking communion services with his boots and spurs plainly visible below his cassock'.

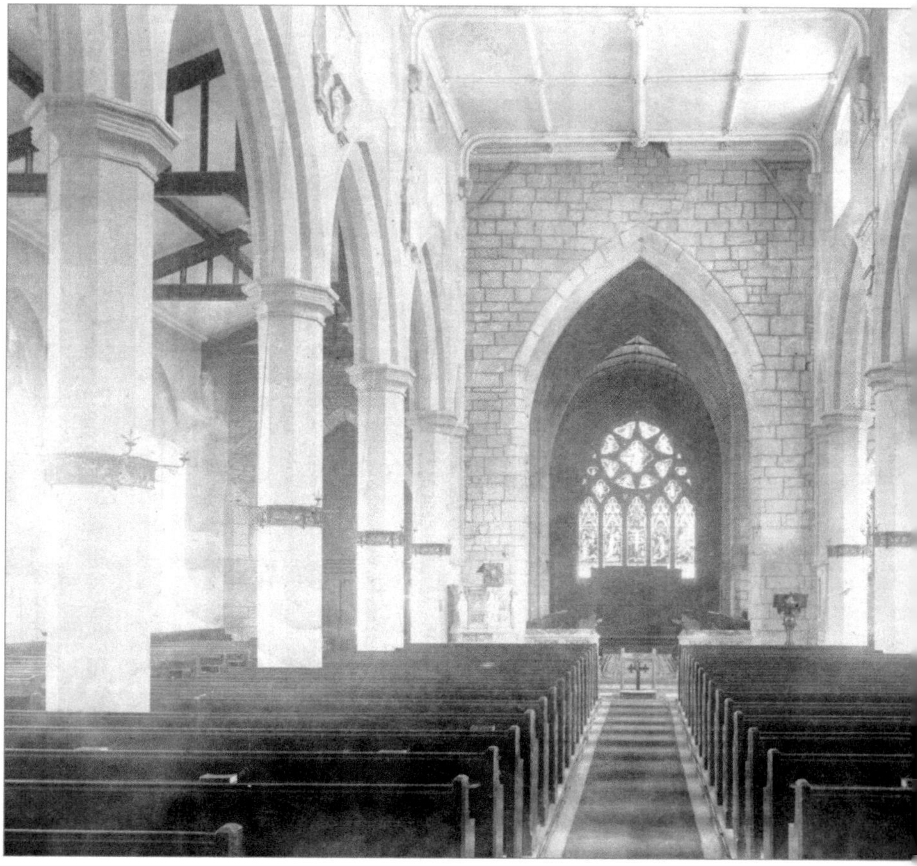

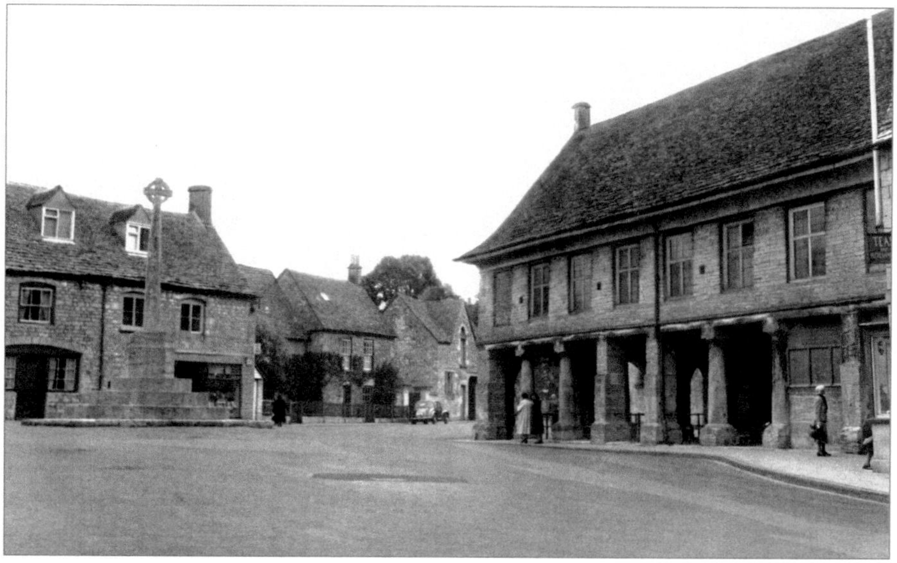

MINCHINHAMPTON
Market Square c1955
M83055

Records of the mid 18th century show that in the principal street 'almost all houses had pent-houses attached to them with movable standings placed in the street. In two large and one smaller market houses large quantities of butchers' meat, bacon, cheese and so on were brought for sale. Corn and wool were also sold and groups of cloth workers are to be seen making their purchases'.

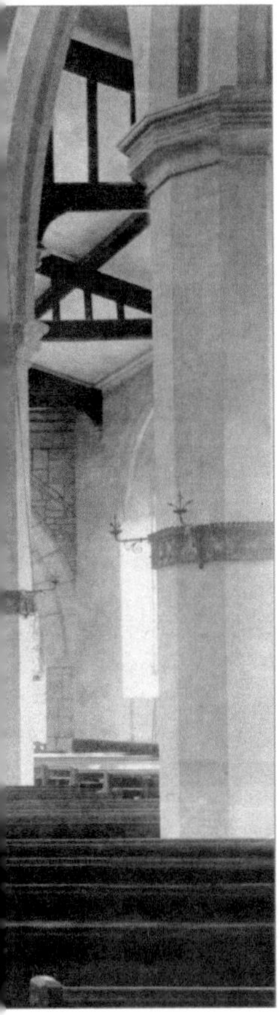

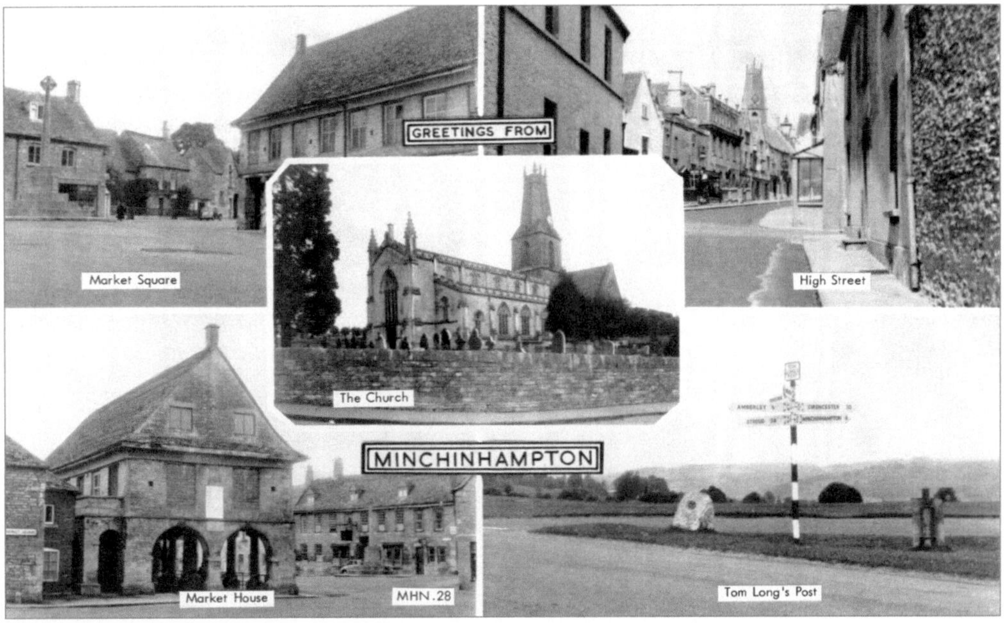

▲ **MINCHINHAMPTON,** *Composite Postcard c1955* M83028

Minchinhampton is situated on the high sweeping plateau between Nailsworth and Chalford, and its importance as a marketing centre is summed up in this description of about 1750: 'So great was the resort of this little town consisting of about 250 houses that there were twenty or more inns and public houses, many of them having large accommodation for horses'. Local legend has it that Tom Long's Post on the Common (bottom right) is so named after a highwayman who was buried at the crossroads so that his spirit would be confused as to which of the five roads to haunt.

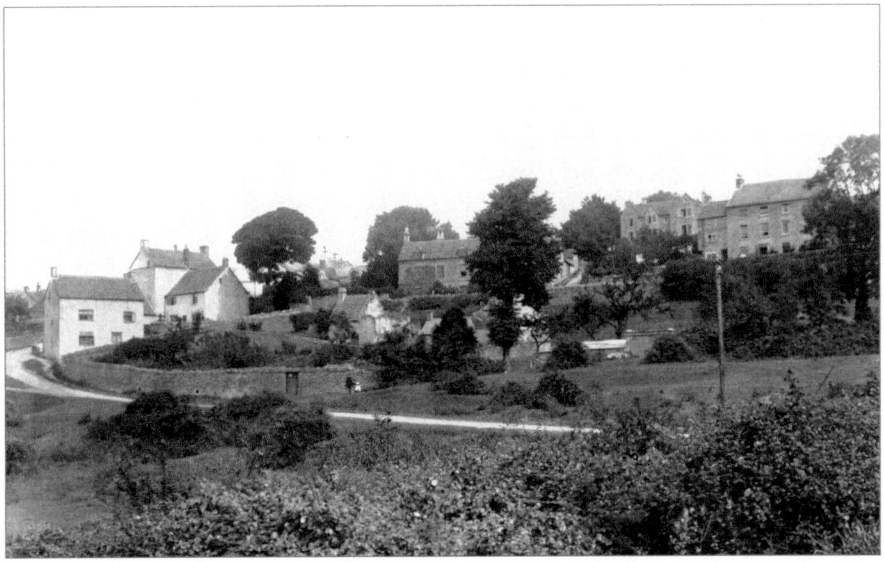

◄ **AMBERLEY**
Littleworth 1901 47356

'Such a fresh, free, breezy spot', wrote Mrs Craik of Amberley, which appears as Enderley in her novel 'John Halifax, Gentleman'. By any other name, the village would still be familiar to her today, although in this view of Littleworth the tumbledown cottage behind the man and little girl (just off centre left) has gone and new buildings fill the space there and close to the road on the right.

AMBERLEY
The Village 1901
47357

Like most of the villages in this area, Amberley played its part in the cloth making industry, but the larger houses built on the higher level of the steep hillside were well away from the clatter and bustle of the working mills in the valley below.

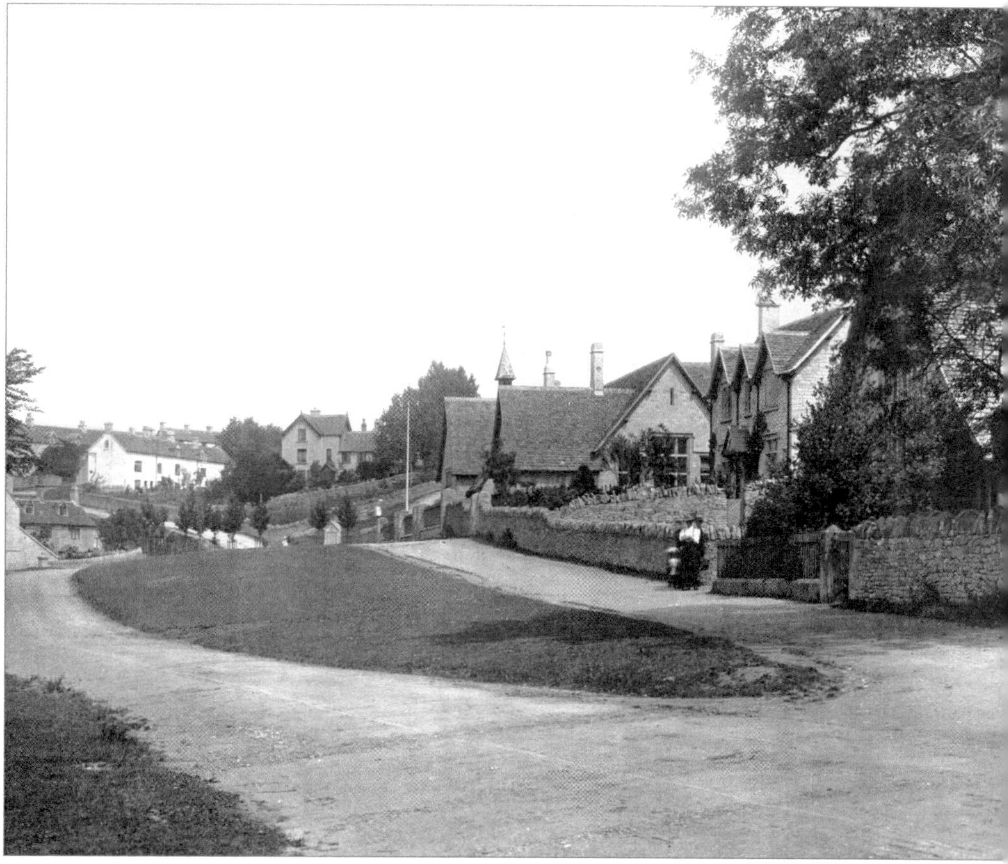

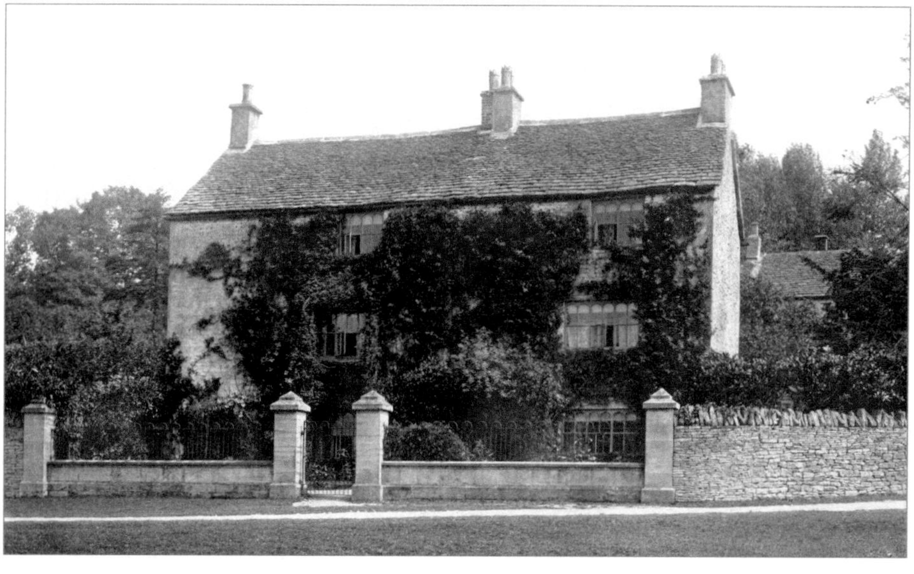

AMBERLEY
Rose Cottage 1901
47358

A beautiful example of 18th-century building, Rose Cottage attracts literary pilgrims to gaze at it on their way to Minchinhampton Common, for it was here that Mrs Craik set much of the action of her novel, 'John Halifax, Gentleman', published in 1857.

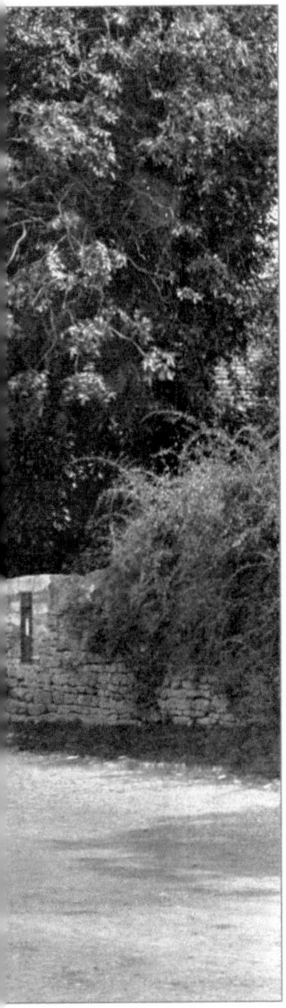

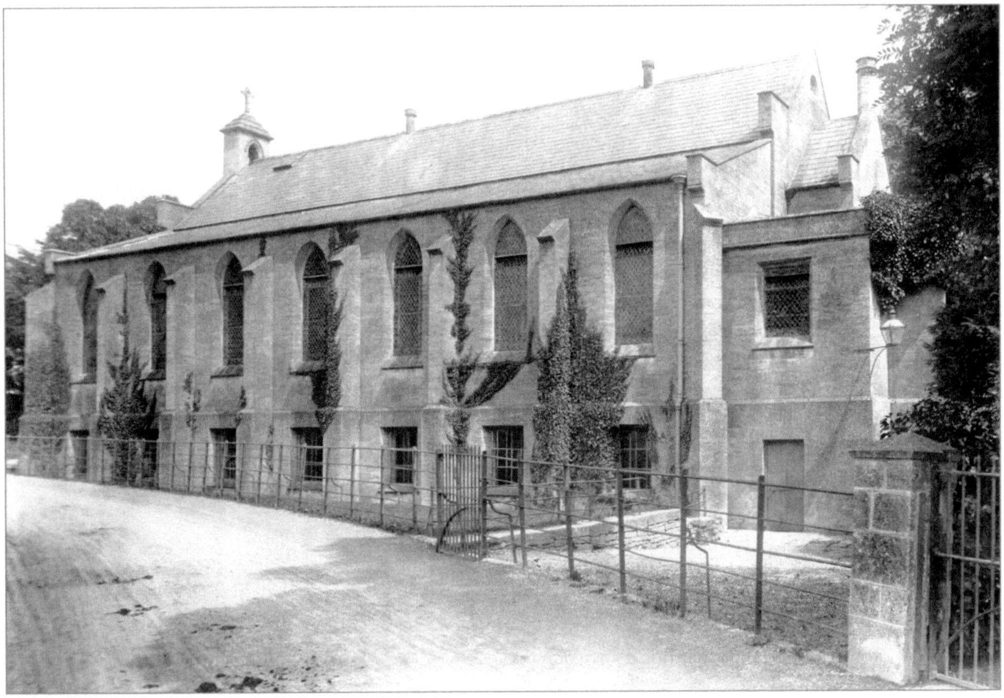

▲ **AMBERLEY,** *The Church 1901* 47359

This is an unusual style for a Cotswold village church; Holy Trinity was built in 1836 for David Ricardo, MP, with a church hall in the crypt.

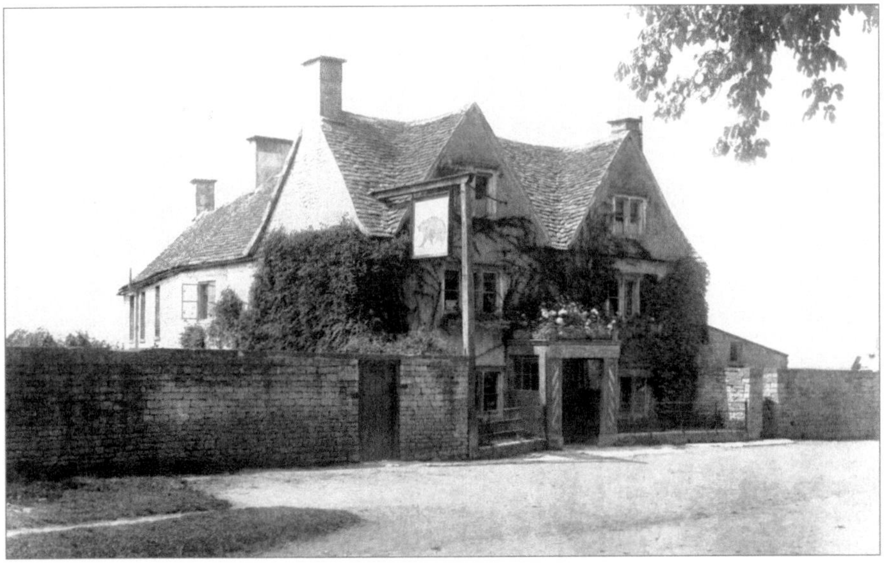

◄ **RODBOROUGH**
The Bear Hotel 1901
47360

This was a very welcome staging post for travellers and horses making the strenuous journey between Cirencester and Stroud by way of Minchinhampton Common. The Bear is recorded as an inn back in 1751.

RODBOROUGH, *The Common 1925* 77574

One of the commons that link neighbouring villages, Rodborough's was once greatly favoured by golfers and had a 9-hole course. On these uplands were found the embossed bronze bands from a wooden bucket - a rarity of ornamental metalwork to be unearthed from the Iron Age.

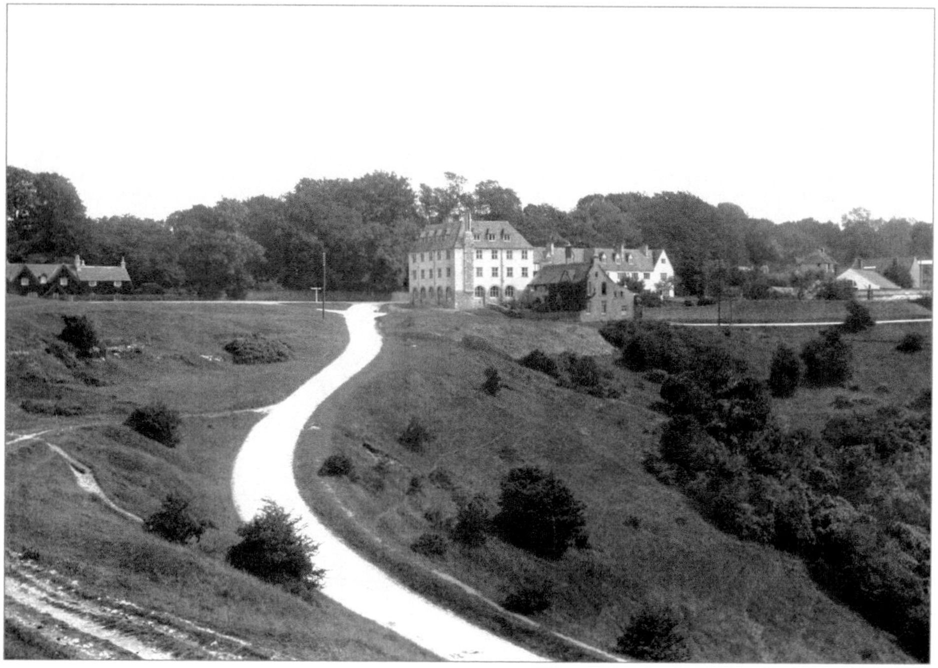

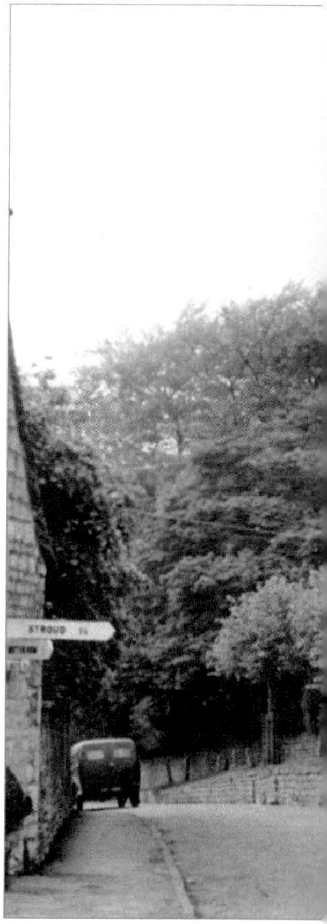

RODBOROUGH

The Fort c1955 R311003

The cattle holding centre stage in this picture look as though they are asserting their ancient rights for grazing on the common. The attraction of the wide spaces for recreation has brought motorists and walkers, golfers and picnickers to this area, particularly around the hillside of this scene, where the fort makes an impressive backdrop.

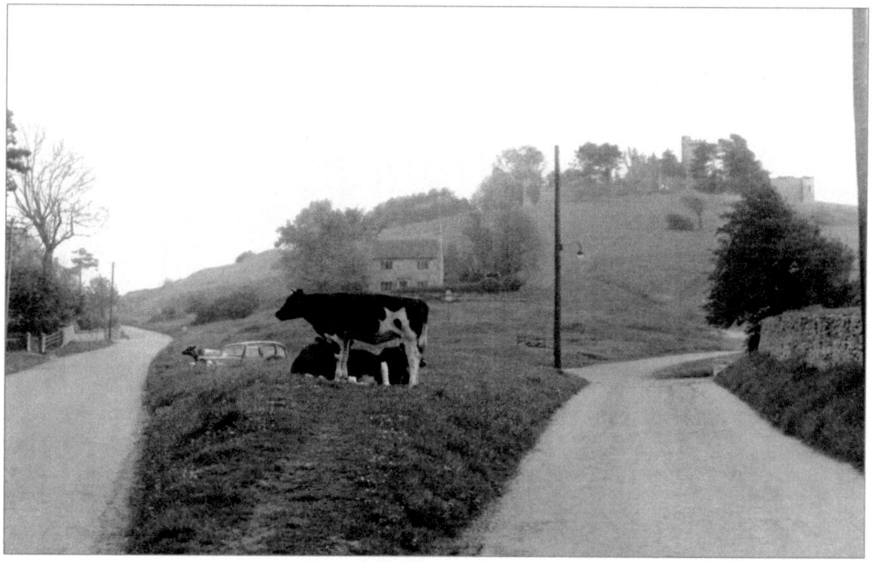

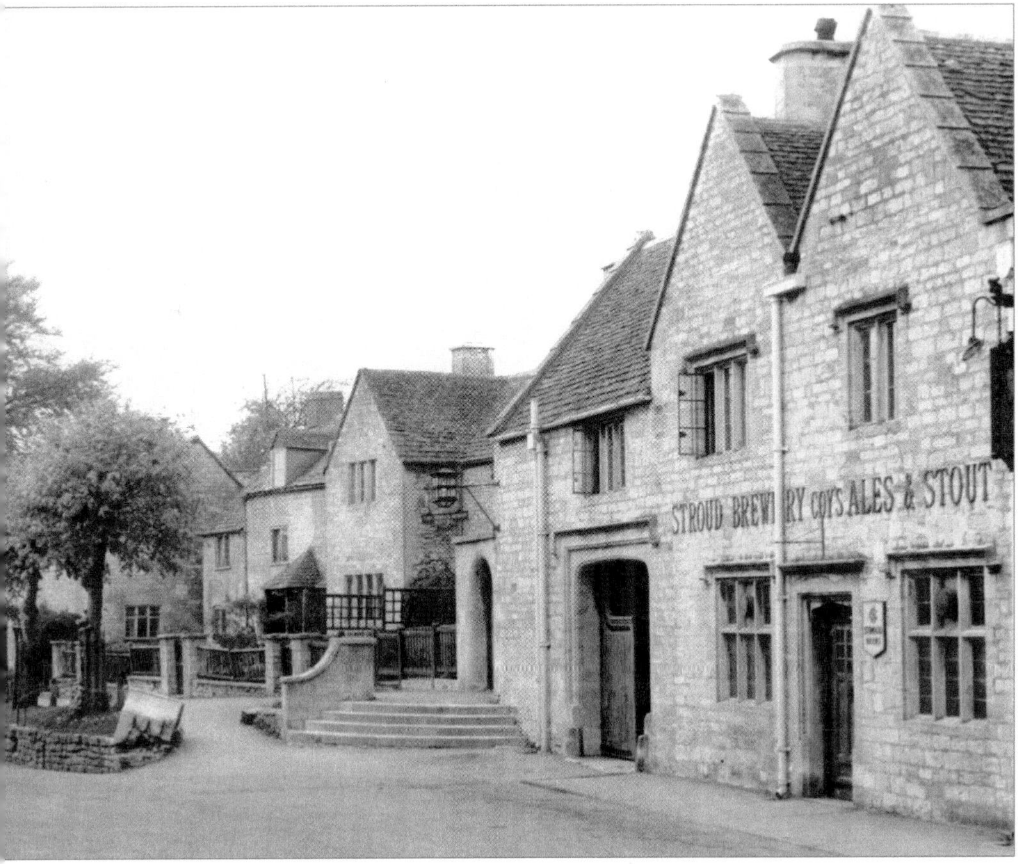

RODBOROUGH
The Village c1950
R311007

The large lettering of the Stroud Brewery across the façade takes precedence over the smaller hanging signs of the Prince Albert Hotel on this attractive corner. Benjamin Bucknell, the architect who designed Woodchester Park, was born in the village of Rodborough.

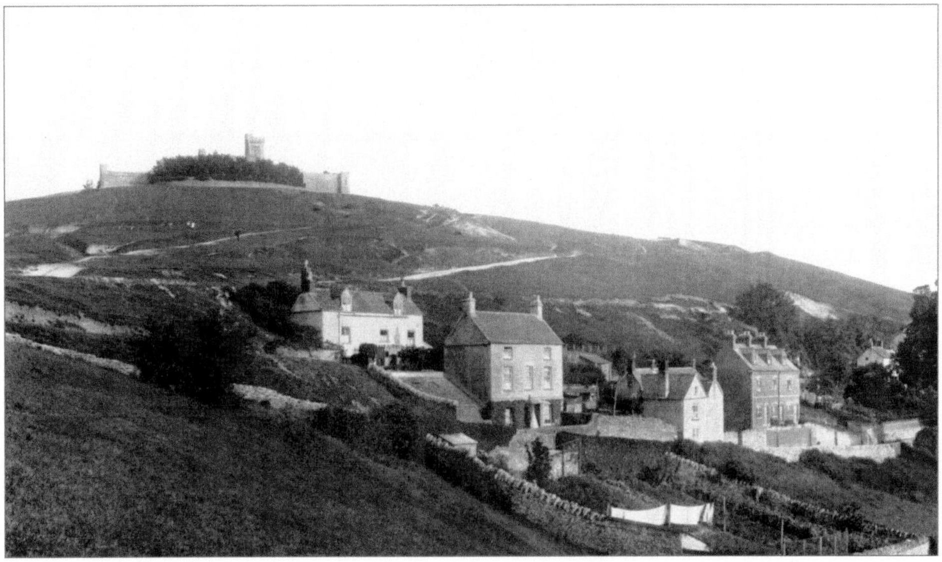

RODBOROUGH
The Fort 1900
45583

Belying its non-military origins, the outline of the fort succeeds in making a dramatic statement on the skyline of the common; it serves to highlight the domestic scene below, where each house has its walled enclosure with stone quarried from the hillside on which it stands.

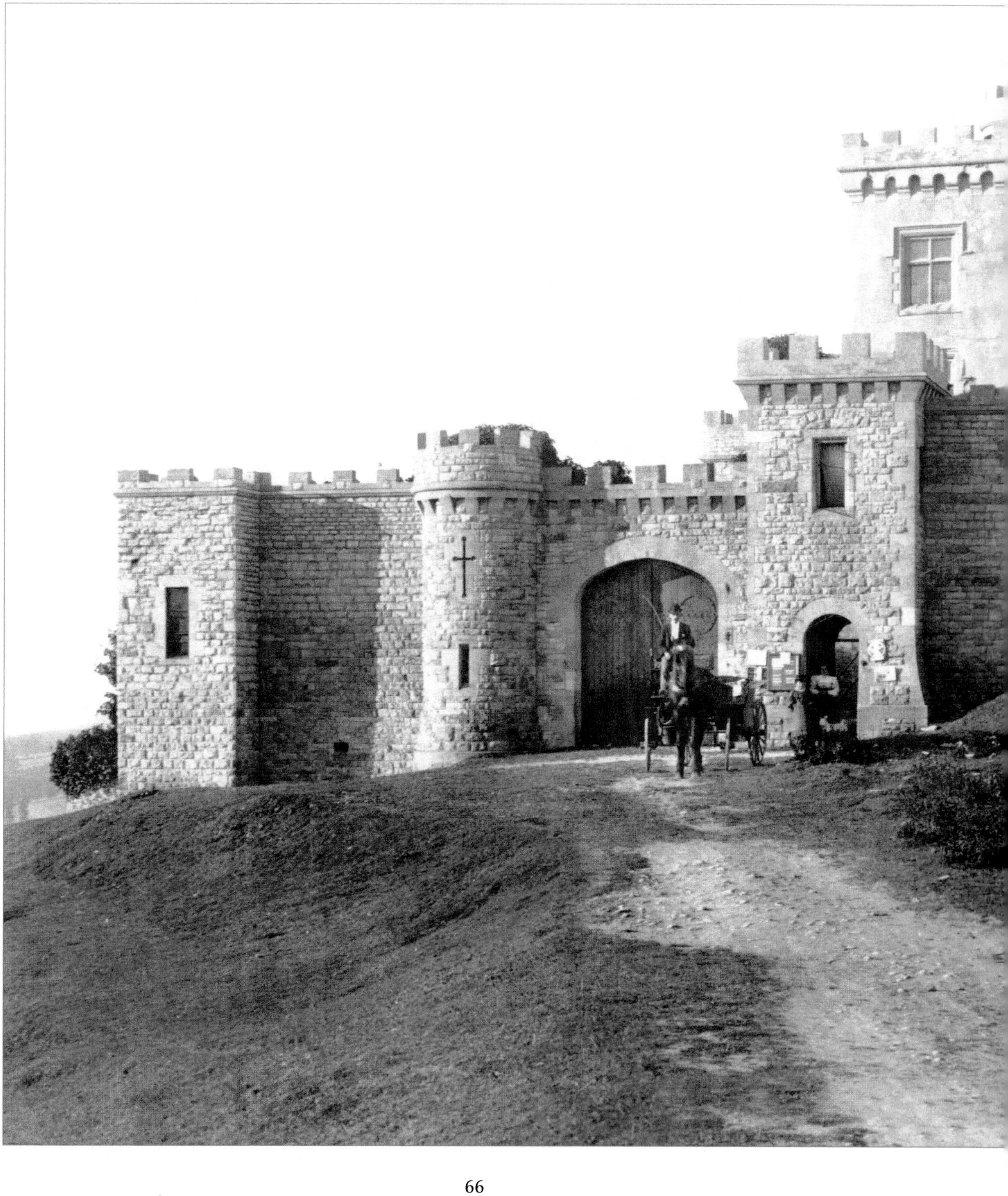

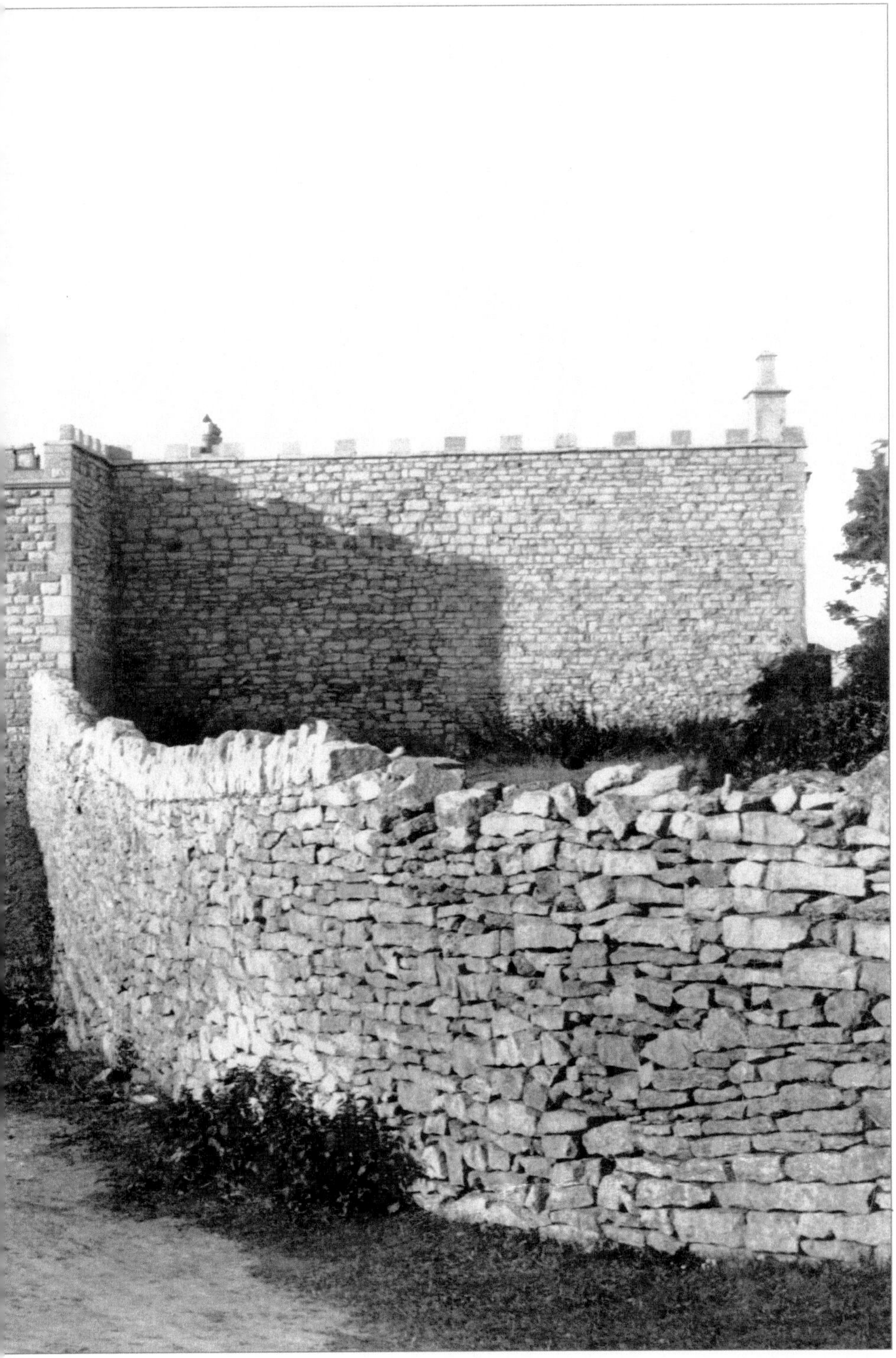

RODBOROUGH
The Fort 1900 45737

Typical of many 18th-century eccentric characters who made and lost fortunes with equal rapidity, George Hawker built Rodborough Fort in 1761 - with no water supply. It is a castellated showpiece making a conspicuous landmark to be seen for miles. It was rebuilt in 1870, and judging from what might well be postcards for sale on the entrance, was probably open to visitors. It is now part of a private residence.

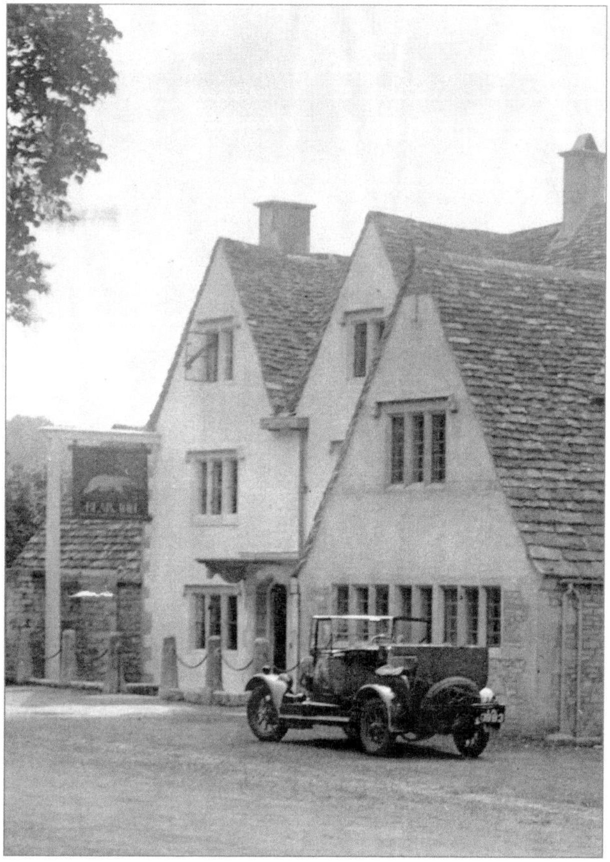

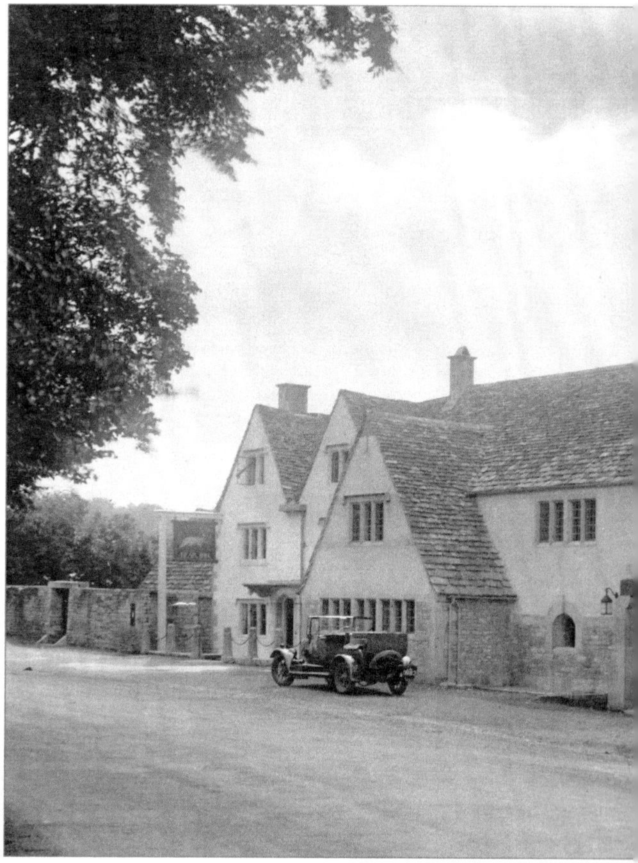

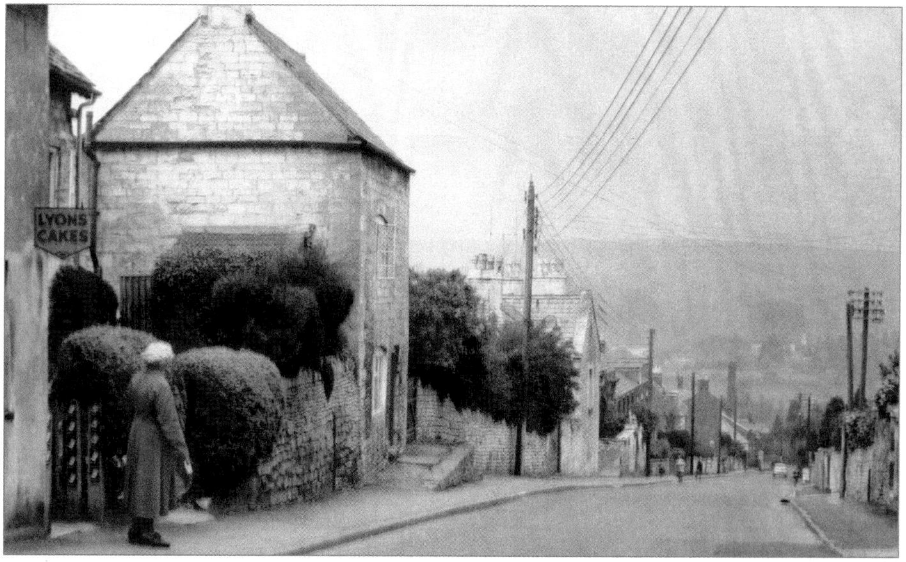

◄ **RODBOROUGH**

The Village c1955

R311008

One of Rodborough's most talented sons was Richard Clutterbuck, who lived here in the 17th century. Despite being blind, he is recorded as having 'made violins, bass viols, and citterns, and virginals with double jacks and other improvements of his own invention. He also taught music according to a scale of his own forming and cut his notes upon pieces of wood'.

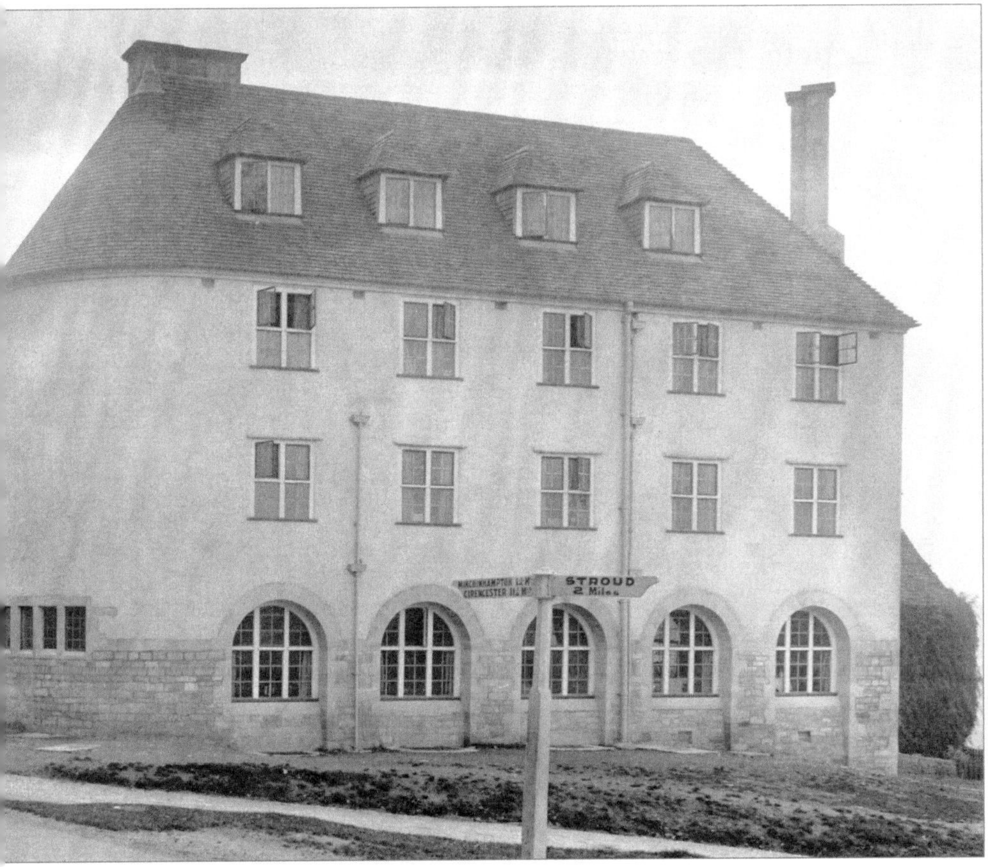

RODBOROUGH
The Common, the Bear Inn 1925
77576

Now known as the Bear of Rodborough, this has been a stopping place for centuries, and played an important part as a collecting point for carrier services in this area of steep hills. The bar, the oldest part of the Bear, is thought to date back at least 400 years, when the building was originally a farmhouse.

(far left) detail from
77576

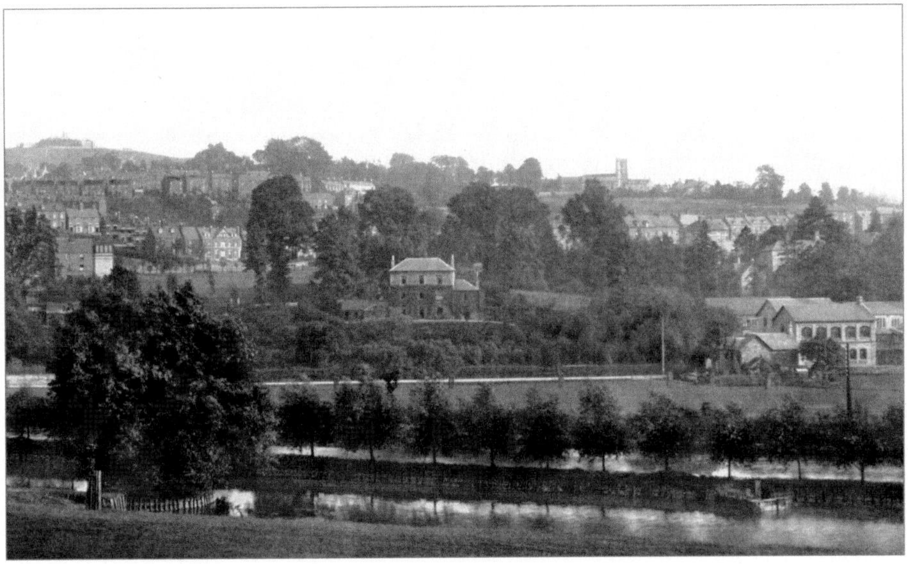

RODBOROUGH
Wallbridge 1900 45582

The scene here would once have been colourful with all the dyed cloth hung on its tenter racks. A painting in the Stroud Museum shows red, white, blue and yellow cloth drying in the field alongside Wallbridge Mill.

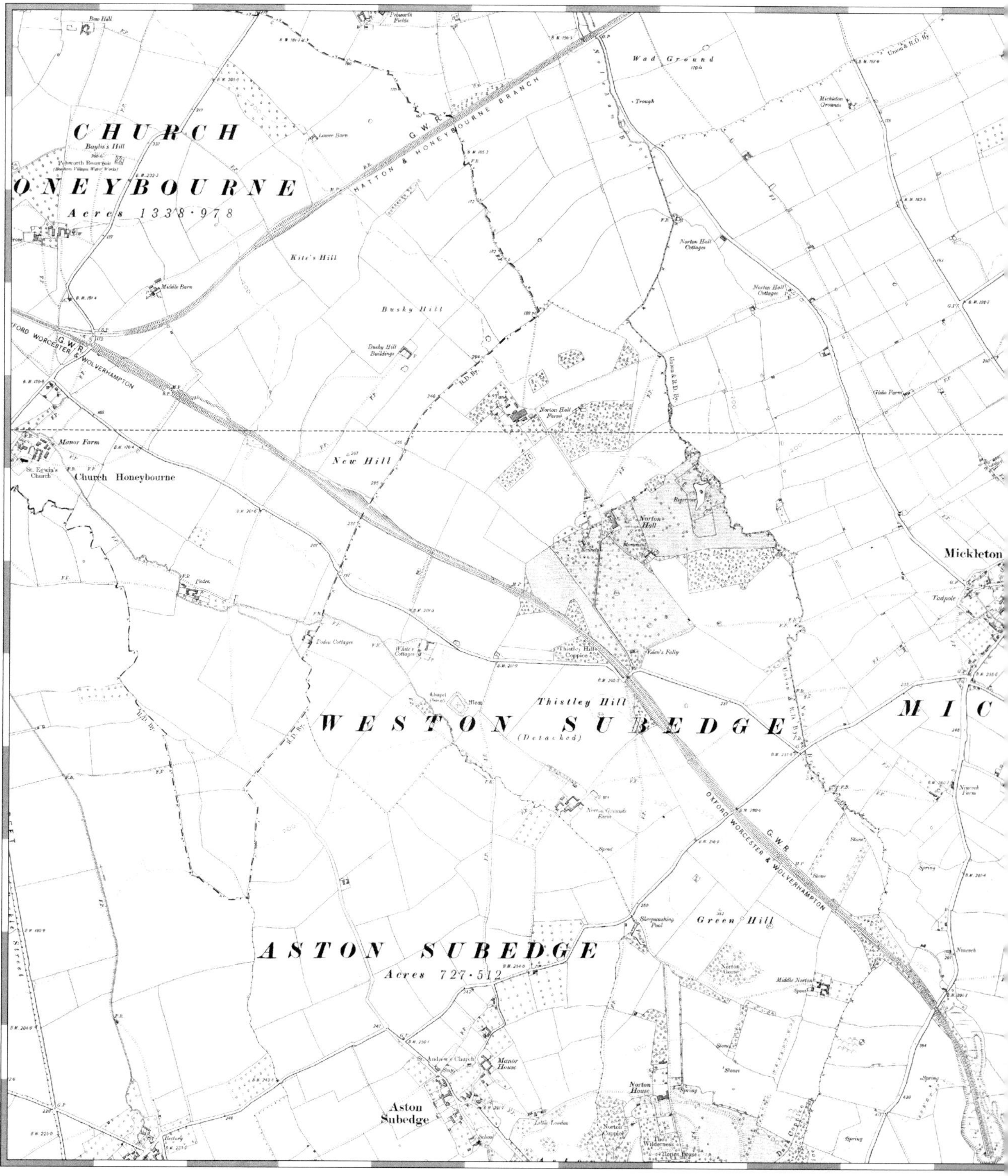
CHURCH
ONEYBOURNE
Acres 1338·978
Baylis's Hill
Pebworth Reservoir
Kite's Hill
Bushy Hill
Bushy Hill Buildings
Middle Barn
Lower Barn
G.W.R.
HATTON & HONEYBOURNE BRANCH
OXFORD WORCESTER & WOLVERHAMPTON
Wad Ground
Trough
Mickleton Grounds
Norton Hall Cottages
Glebe Farm
Norton Hall Farm
Manor Farm
St. Egwin's Church
Church Honeybourne
New Hill
Norton Hall
Poden
Poden Cottages
Thistley Hill Coppice
Eden's Folly
Mickleton
Tadpole
Chapel
Moat
Thistley Hill
WESTON SUBEDGE
(Detached)
Norton Grounds Farm
Nineveh Farm
Green Hill
Sheepwashing Pool
Norton Gorse
Middle Norton
ASTON SUBEDGE
Acres 727·512
St. Andrew's Church
Manor House
Norton House
Norton Coppice
Little London
The Wilderness
Aston Subedge
Rectory

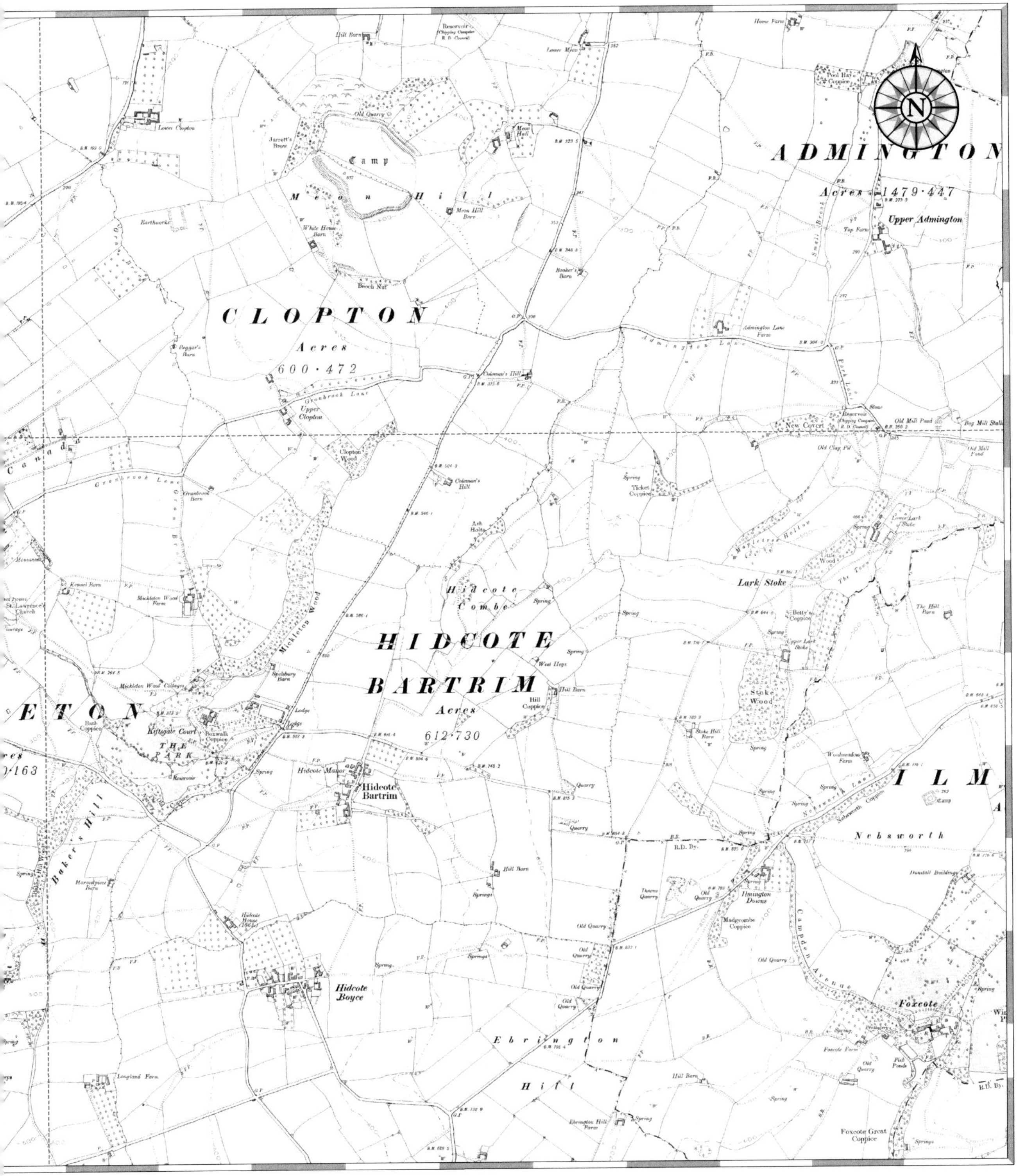
N
Lower Clopton
Jarrett's Brow
Old Quarry
Camp
Meon Hill
Meon Hall
Meon Hill Barn
White House Barn
Earthworks
Beech Nut
Booker's Barn
CLOPTON
Acres
600·472
Beggar's Barn
Coleman's Hill
Greenbrook Lane
Upper Clopton
Clopton Wood
Canal
Greenbrook Barn
Ash Holts
Hidcote Combe
HIDCOTE BARTRIM
Acres
612·730
Kennel Barn
Mickleton Wood Farm
Mickleton Wood
Mickleton Wood Cottages
Spelsbury Barn
ETON
Bath Coppice
Kiftsgate Court
Boxwalk Coppice
THE PARK
Reservoir
Lodge
Hidcote Manor
Hidcote Bartrim
West Hoys
Hill Barn
Hill Coppice
Baker's Hill
Hidcote House
Hidcote Boyce
Longland Farm
Ebrington Hill
Ebrington Hill Farm
ADMINGTON
Acres 1479·447
Upper Admington
Top Farm
Home Farm
Pool Hay Coppice
Small Brook
Admington Lane Farm
Admington Lane
New Covert
Old Clay Pit
Old Mill Pond
Bog Mill Stall
Ticket Coppice
Lark Stoke
Lower Lark Stoke
Upper Lark Stoke
Betty's Coppice
Stoke Wood
Stoke Hill Barn
The Hill Barn
Woodmeadow Farm
ILM
Nebsworth
R.D. By.
Ilmington Downs
Madgcombe Coppice
Campden Avenue
Dunstall Buildings
Foxcote
Foxcote Farm
Fish Ponds
Foxcote Great Coppice

THE CHURN VALLEY

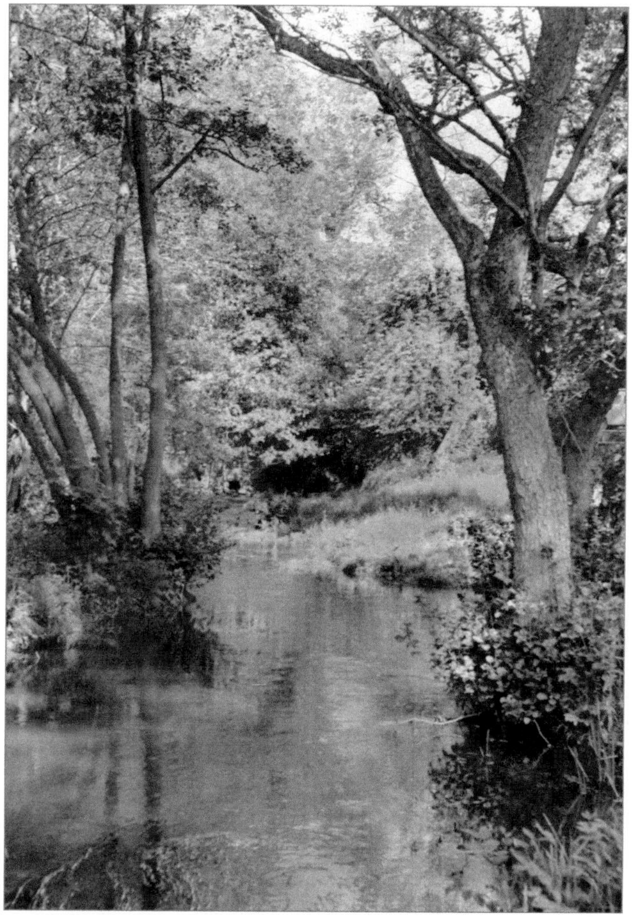

COLESBOURNE, *The River Churn c1960* C453013

The Churn is a tributary of the Thames, and rises at Seven Springs, which thus could be said to be the Thames's source. Along its meandering route it flows through the park at Colesbourne, home to Henry John Elwes (1846-1922), who created a fine garden and arboretum there; he has been regarded as the 'greatest lover of trees this country ever had', and the wonderful woodlands around the village consequently include some very rare trees.

ONE of the main rivers of the central wolds, the Churn is the longest and most inland tributary of the Thames, which itself comes into being within the valley. The actual source of the Thames has been in contention throughout the ages; the strongest contender for the title of its birthplace is at Seven Springs - the most distant source from London. The Regency town of Cheltenham, lying just below the western scarp line, is a mere four miles from Seven Springs, and the villages of the northern valley may well be considered to have been influenced by its proximity, while those in the lower reaches owe their charm to the rural aristocracy of the great landed estates around Cirencester. Here, at the ancient market town that grew over a millennium from the deserted ruins of Corinium, the second largest city after London in Roman Britain, the Churn appears in the old abbey grounds before dwindling to a small stream as it goes under the main London Road on its way to join the Thames at Cricklade over the county border in Wiltshire. In ancient times the letter 'c' was pronounced as 'ch', and this sound is retained in the name of the river Churn; however, the Cerney villages, taking their name from the river on which they stand, and Cirencester likewise, are pronounced as though spelt with an 's'; we can trace this sound change back to the Normans and their aversion to the 'ch' sound, which they changed to 'ts'.

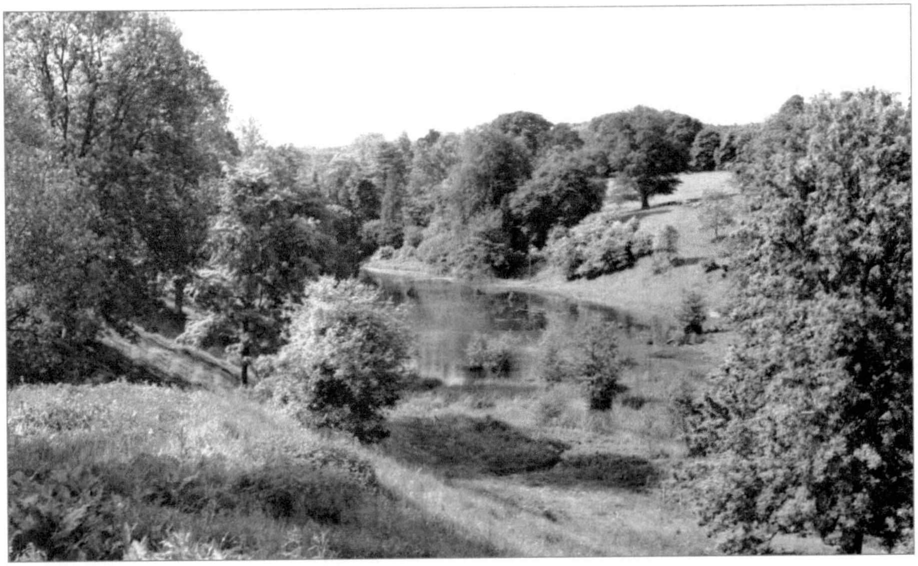

COLESBOURNE
The Lake c1960
C453003

Galanthophiles (as snowdrop enthusiasts are known!) pilgrimage to Colesbourne Park in early spring to marvel at the banks of snowdrops and other winter flowers along the lakeside and through the woodland. The collection was started by Henry John Elwes, who discovered his first specimen in 1874 while travelling in Turkey. Colesbourne now has a national collection of some 160 cultivars of snowdrop.

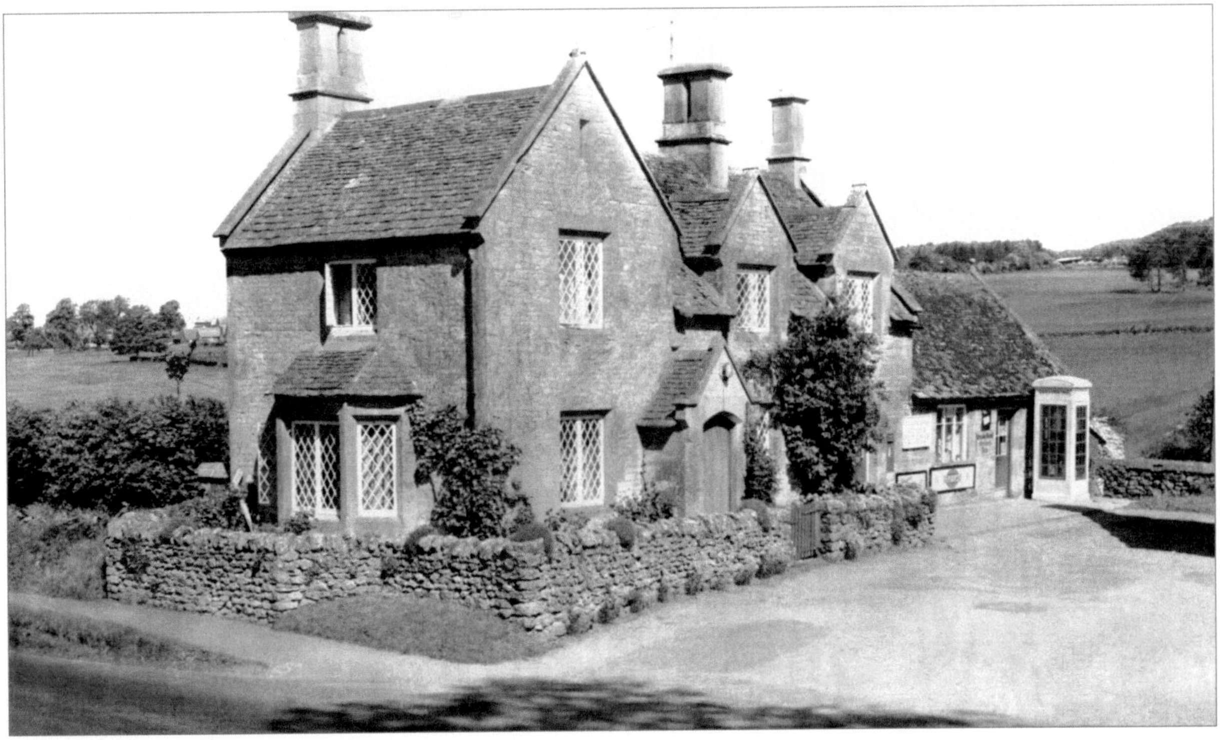

COLESBOURNE, *The Post Office c1960* C453005

This little group is a fine example of grand architecture on a small scale, typical of estate villages where uniformity in building style blends in so well with the landscape.

COLESBOURNE
The Colesbourne Inn c1960 C453006

This very popular wayside inn was built in 1827. The octagonal chimneys with moulded caps match those we can see on the post office (see C453005, page 73), but the frontage of the inn is built in quartz and tufa, giving it a more rugged appearance.

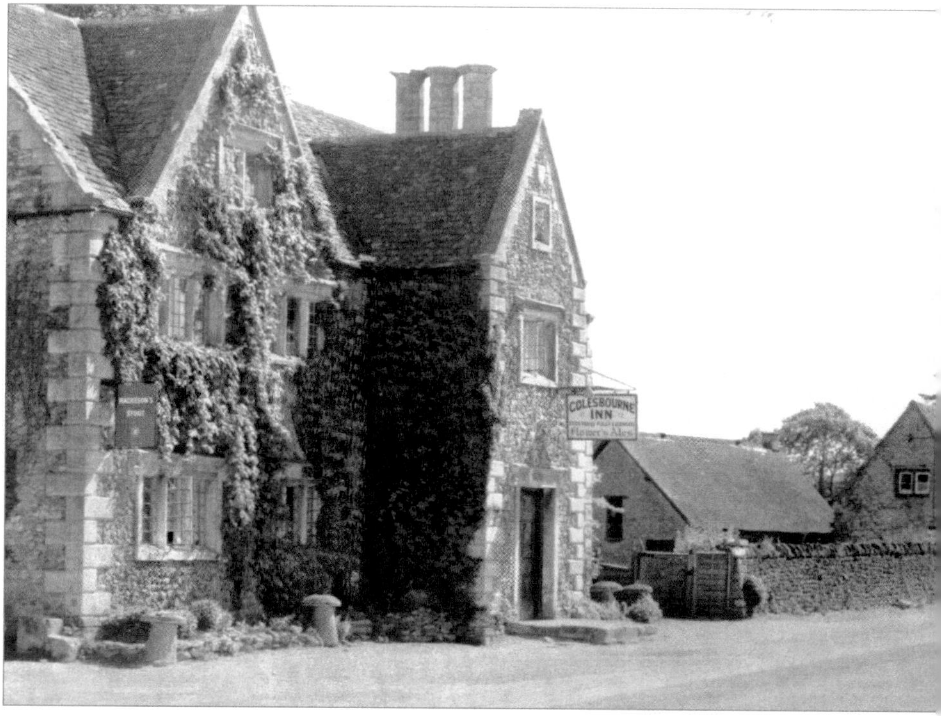

(far right) detail from C453006

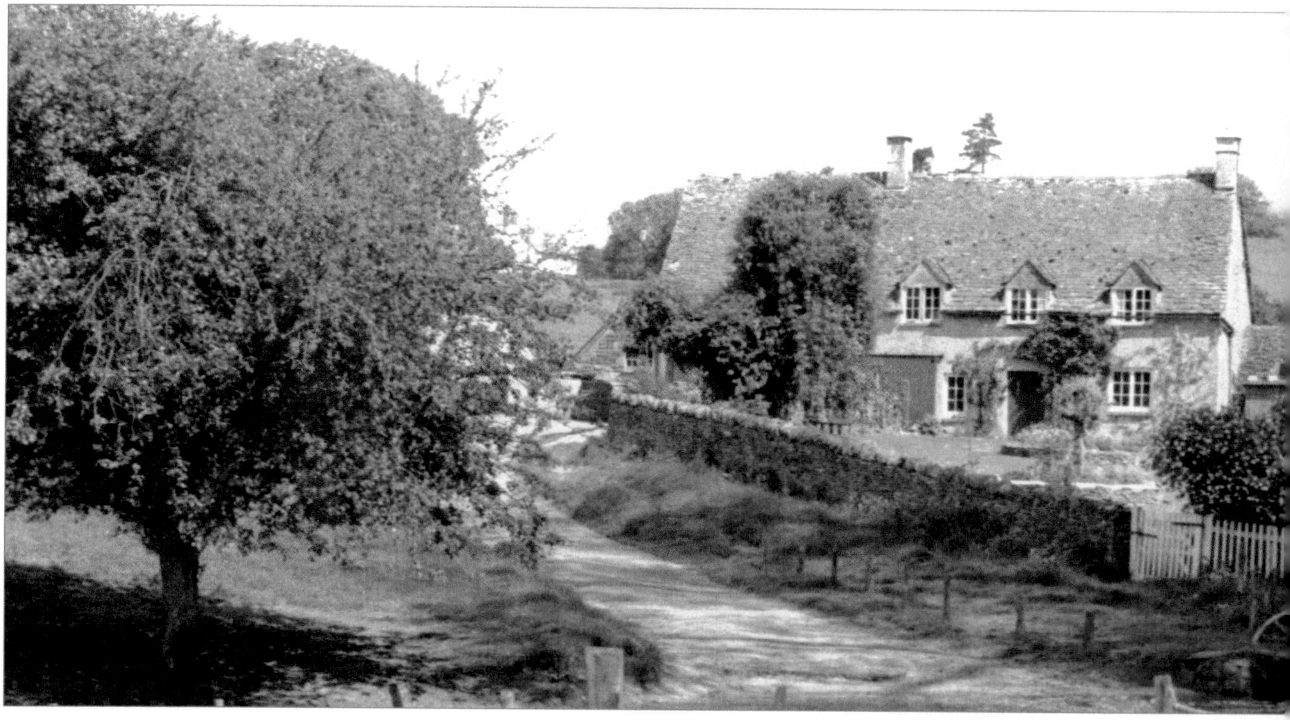

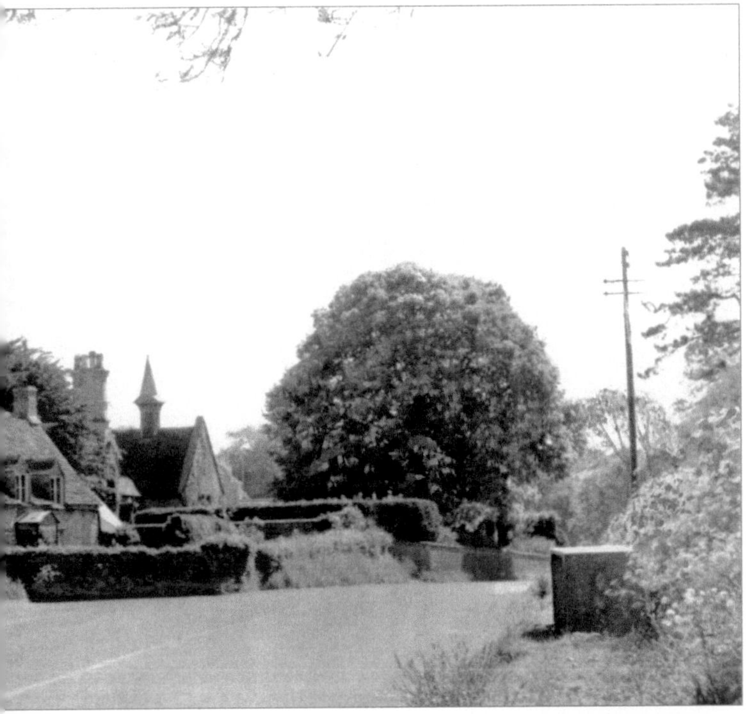

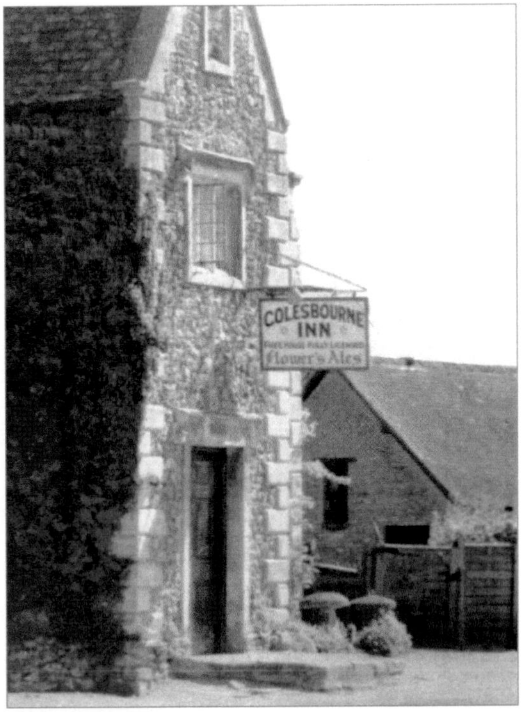

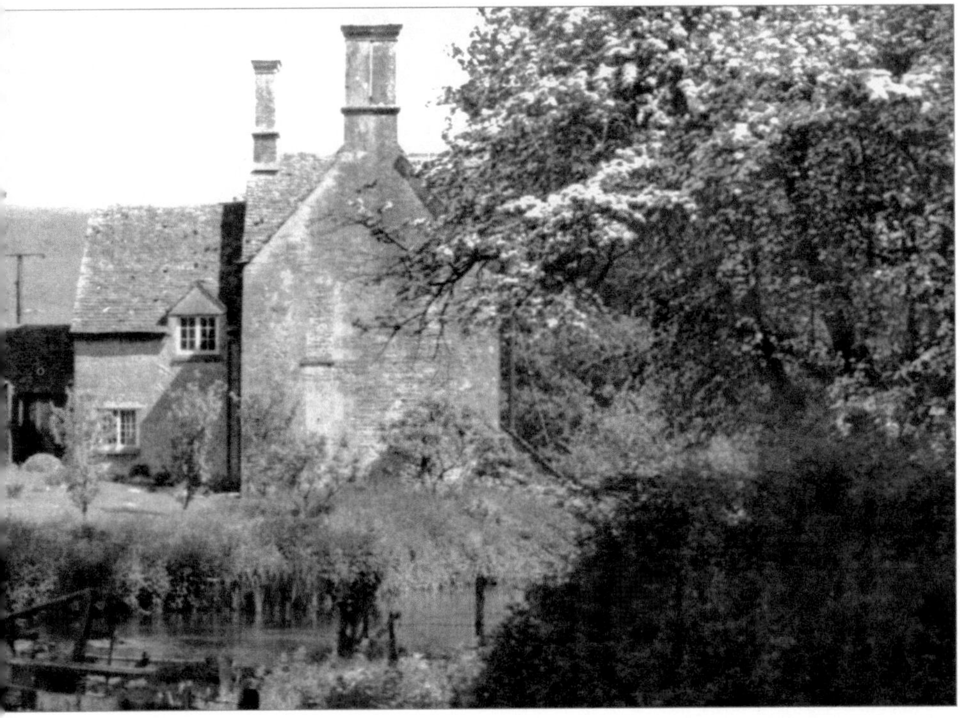

◄ **COLESBOURNE**
Lower Hilcot c1960
C453010

Houses at the hardly-a-hamlet Lower Hilcot still reflect the general style of Colesbourne. There is archaeological evidence that the parish has been inhabited since the Iron Age, and a Roman villa, considered to have been of some importance, was excavated by Samuel Lysons, a county historian in the late 18th century.

► **DUNTISBOURNE ABBOTS**
The Ford c1960
D161011

This watery way running through the village is where the stream was diverted to run along the road specifically to wash the wheels of carts and wagons and the feet of the horses.

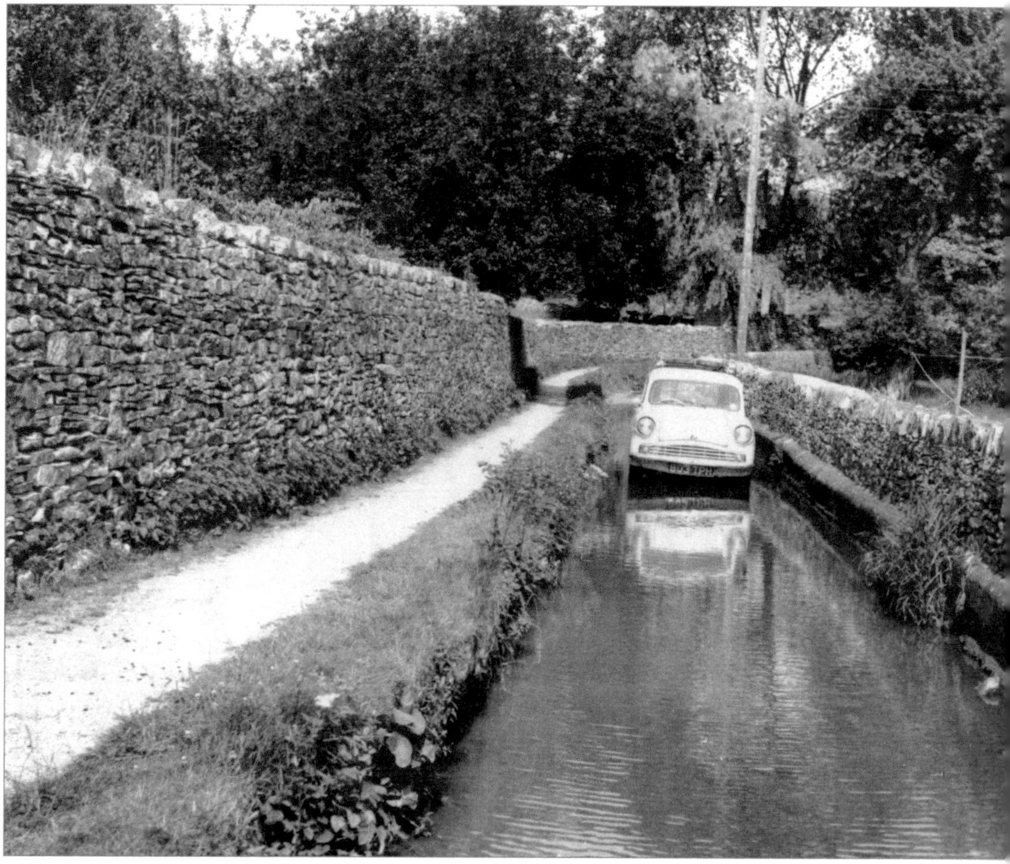

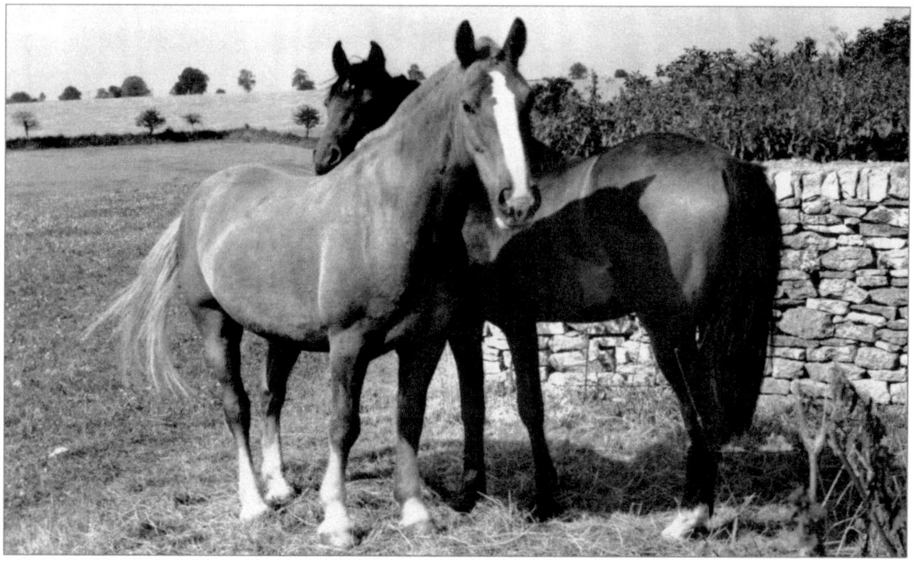

◄ **DUNTISBOURNE ABBOTS**
Grazing Horses c1960 D161007

The Duntisbournes (Abbots, Middle, Rouse and Leer) cluster in the dips and dells and cling to the slopes of these green hills, where horses and skylarks set them apart from the busy modern world beyond the valley.

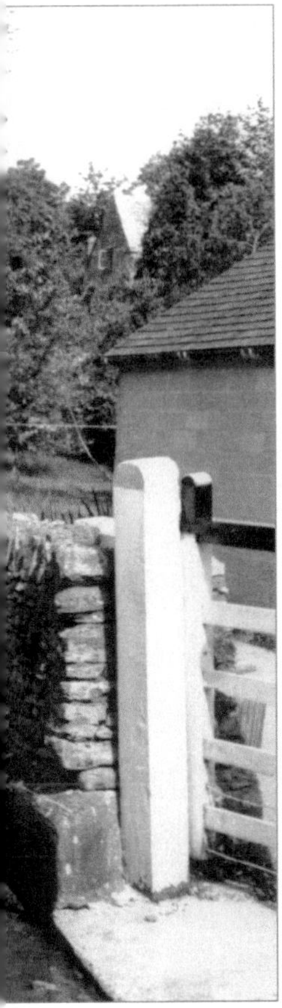

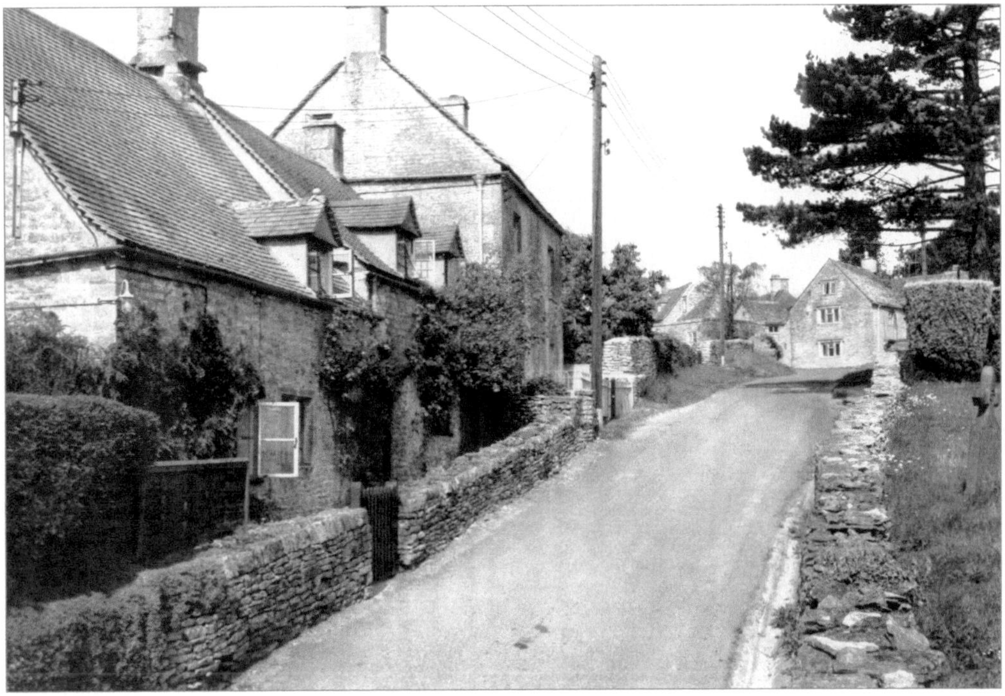

▲ **DUNTISBOURNE ABBOTS,** *The Village c1960* D161009

The largest of the Duntisbourne quartet reflects its former ownership by Gloucester Abbey in the name of the village and the dedication of its ancient church to St Peter, the same dedication as Gloucester's. Lying just a mile west of the old Roman Ermine Street, the village is full of charming old houses.

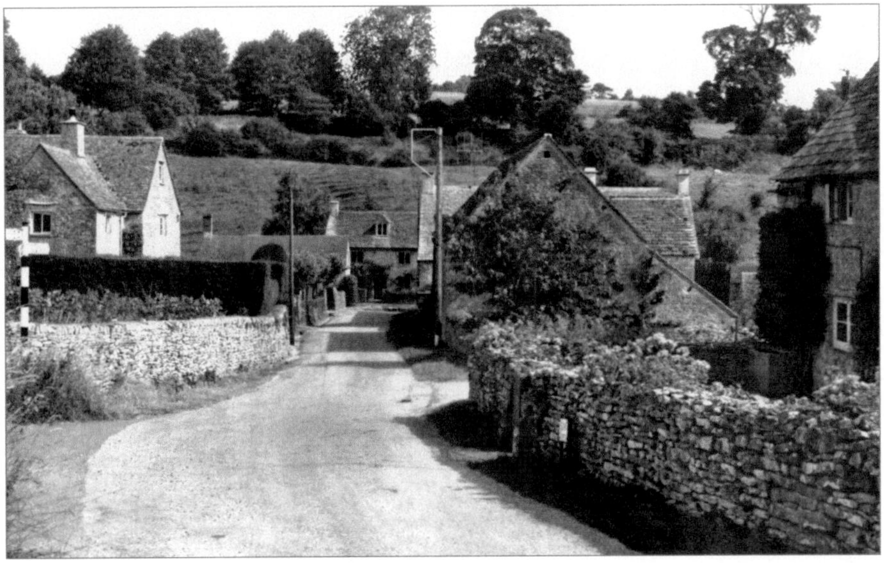

◄ **DUNTISBOURNE LEER**
The Village c1965
D245013

A hamlet of Duntisbourne Abbots, Leer was held by the Abbey of Lire in Normandy until 1416, after which date the manor was given to the great Augustinian abbey at Cirencester, some six miles away.

SOUTH CERNEY
The River Churn
c1960 S517009

The River Churn features attractively throughout the village of South Cerney, to which it gave its name - albeit in a slightly different form today from the previous 'Churney'. Here it is pictured flowing close by the building which belonged to Keith Harris, family butcher, in the sixties.

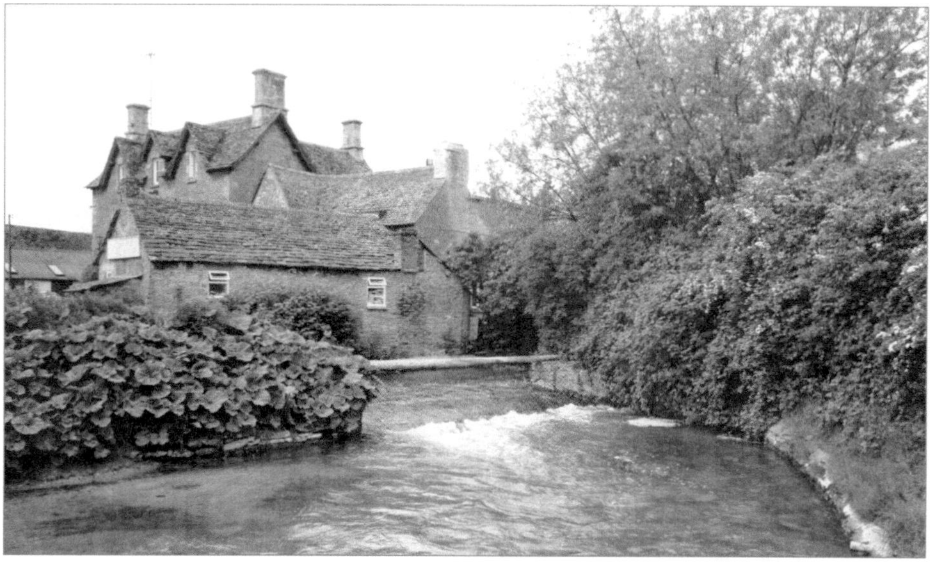

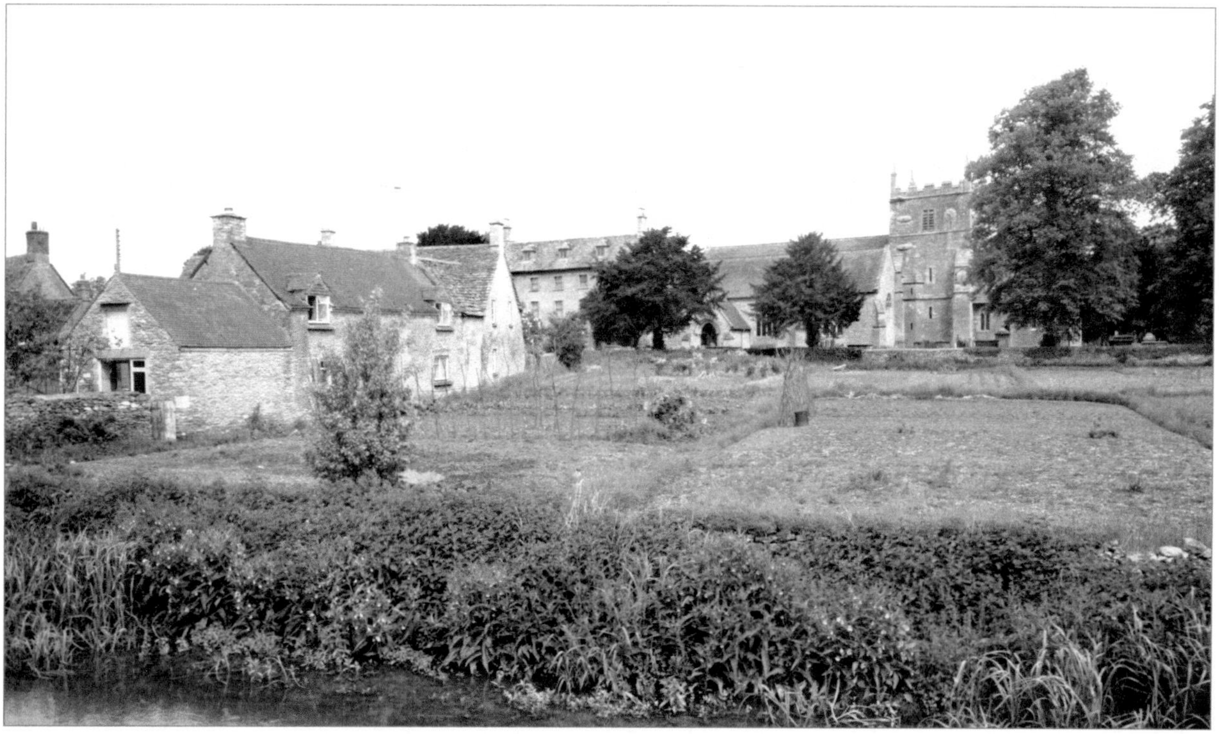

SOUTH CERNEY, *The Church c1960* S517008

Despite extensive expansion, South Cerney still retains its village heart. It was unusual for a place of its former size to have held three manors.

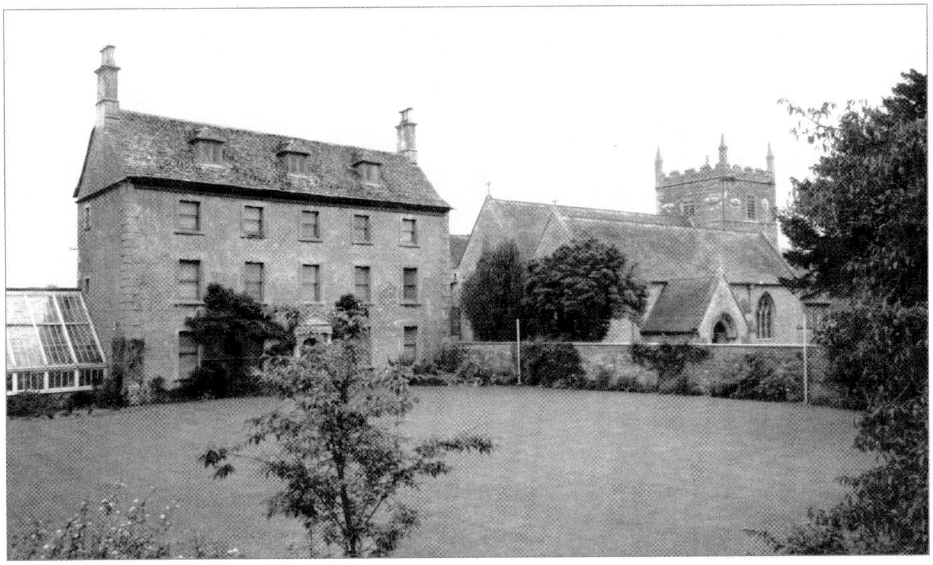

SOUTH CERNEY
The Manor and the Church c1965
S517001

Church Lane is a pretty cul-de-sac with several houses built in traditional style. The Manor House shown here is typical of the 18th-century plan with three storeys and five bays. It is the same date as The Old Vicarage. Atkyns Manor is a century older, and further to the east is Chapter Manor, whose origins are in the 18th century.

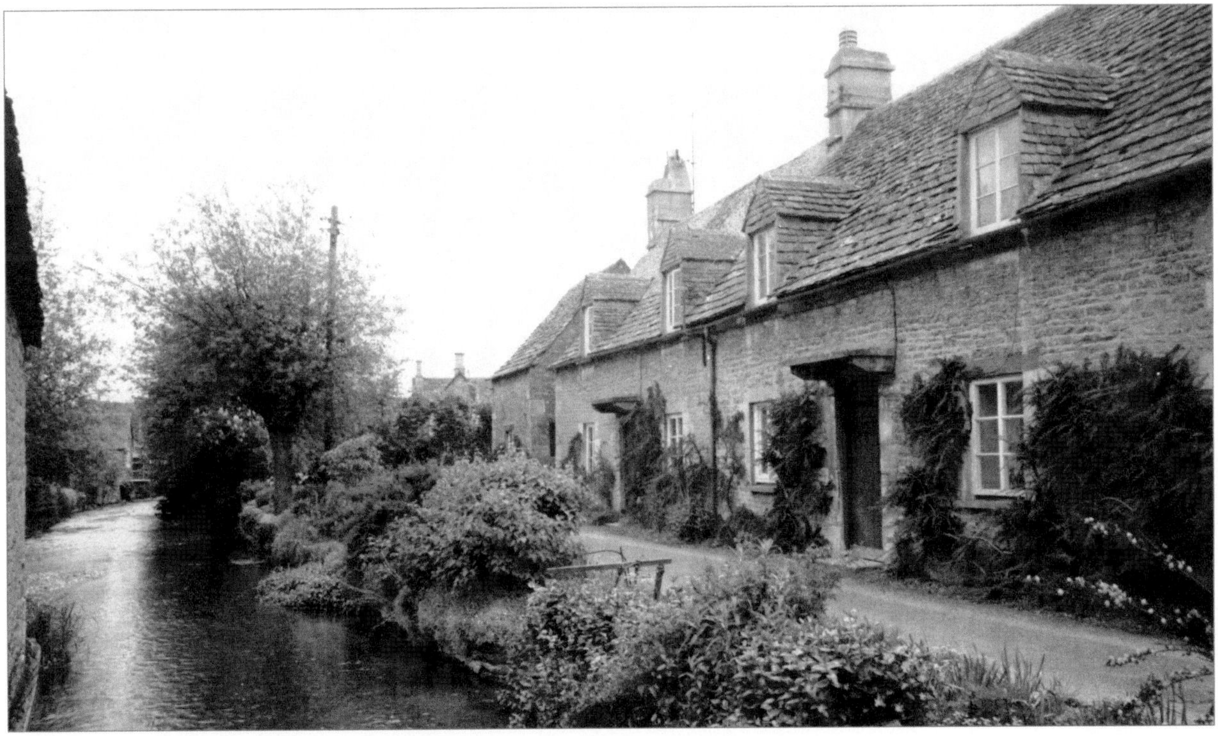

SOUTH CERNEY, *The Village c1965* S517007

South Cerney has some delightful street names, such as Bow Wow, close by the Old George Inn, and Upper Up, which now adjoins the village proper, but a reminder of the days when it was an outlying farming hamlet.

SOUTH CERNEY, *Silver Street c1960* S517005

Several houses in Silver Street date back to Elizabethan times. At the north end is Edwards College, built in Tudor-Gothic style as a home for clergy widows, founded by the will of Anne Edwards in 1834.

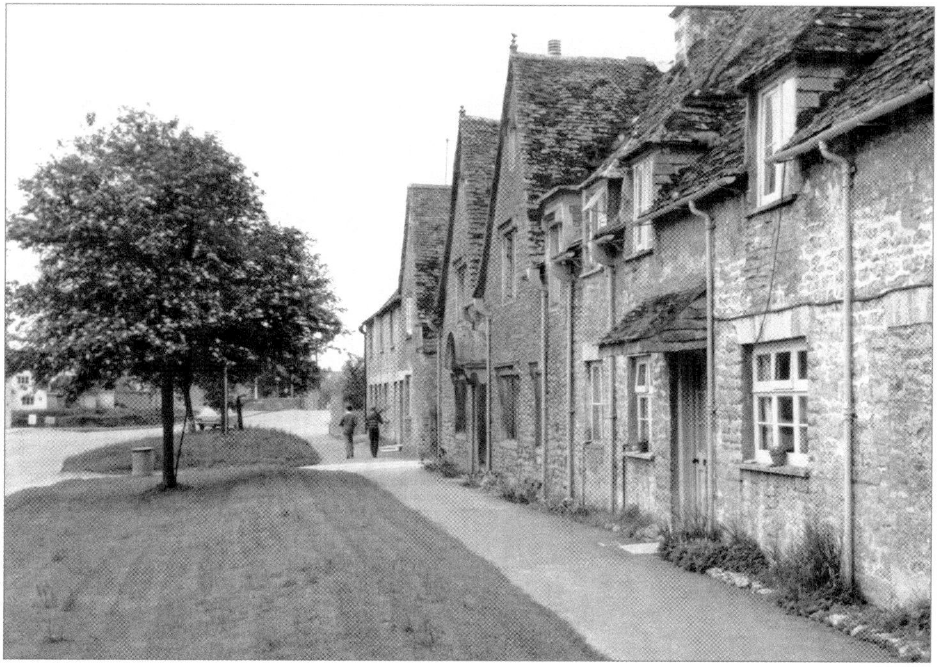

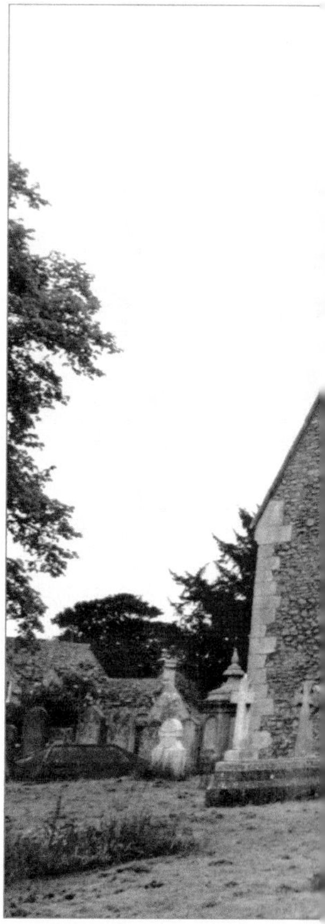

SOUTH CERNEY
The Memorial c1960
S517013

One of the two war memorial crosses in the village, this one stands at the corner of Broadway Lane. Memories of the Second World War are rekindled when anniversaries are commemorated at the nearby airfield.

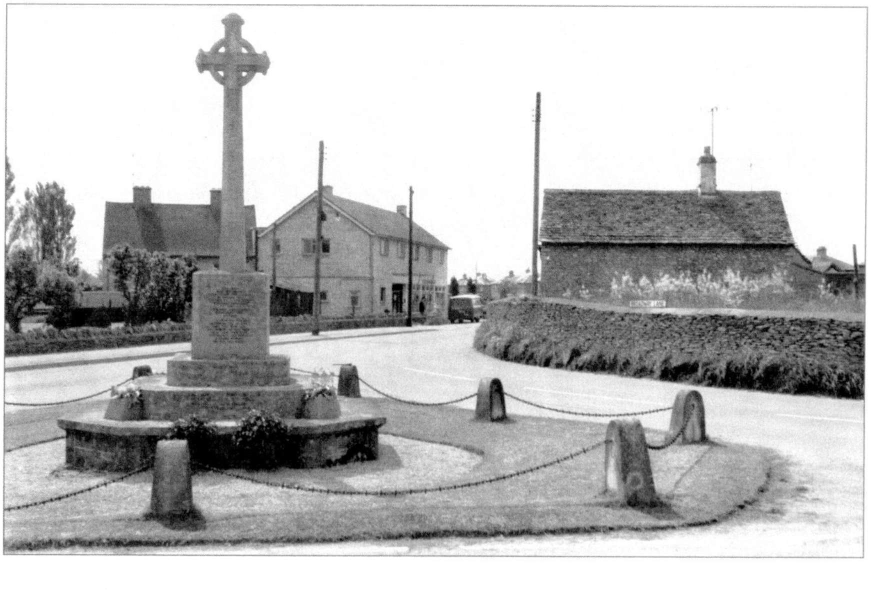

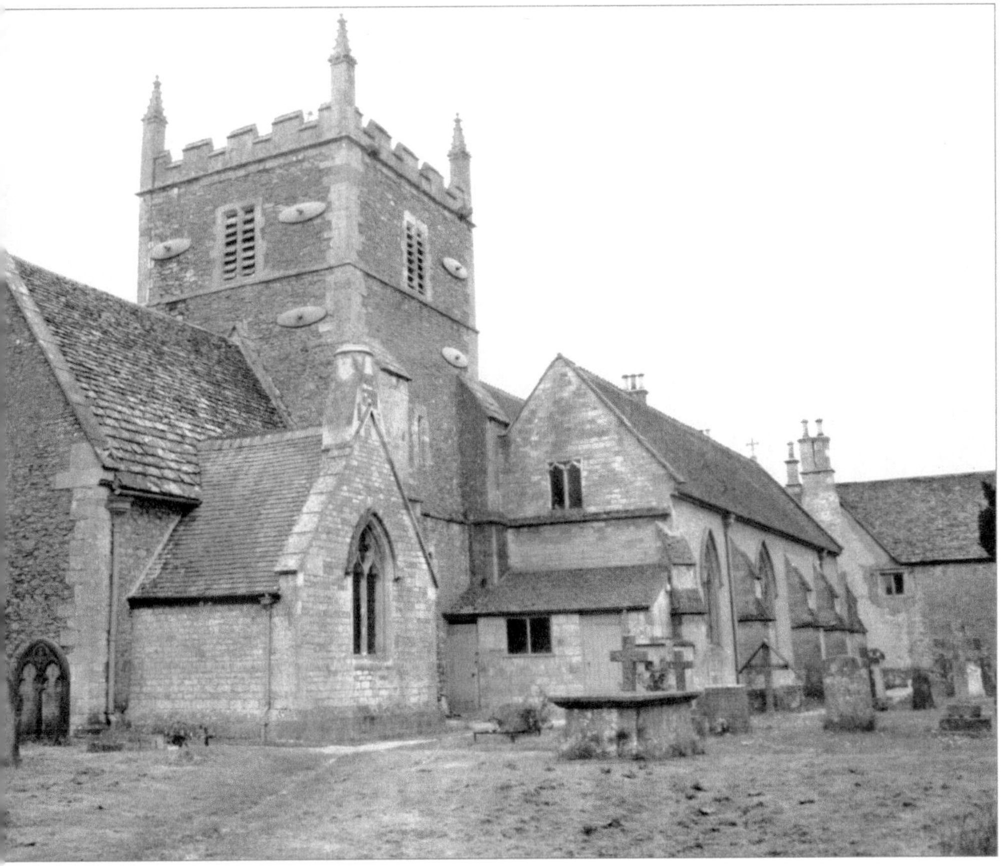

SOUTH CERNEY
All Hallows Church c1960 S517003

There is much Norman work to be seen in this spacious church, but it is the tympanum above the doorway that commands most attention - it is thought to have been sculpted in the early 12th century. One of the church's other treasures is the fragment of a wooden crucifix, which experts claim to be 'the earliest piece of wood carving in the country'.

SOUTH CERNEY
The Water Park c1960
S517011

Water has always featured large in this village at the southern end of the Churn. The Thames and Severn Canal came this way, and the route of the old towpath can still be walked for considerable sections; but it is the pits left by extensive gravel extraction that have been developed to make the Cotswold Water Park the largest in the country. Some 24 square miles of the 4,000 acres that constitute the Water Park are fully established at South Cerney, offering water sports, angling and sailing within a holiday and recreational centre.

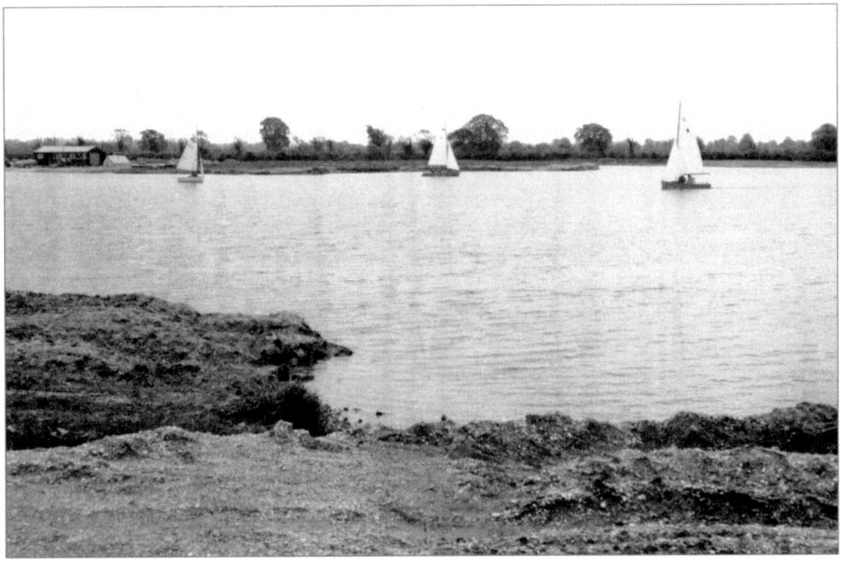

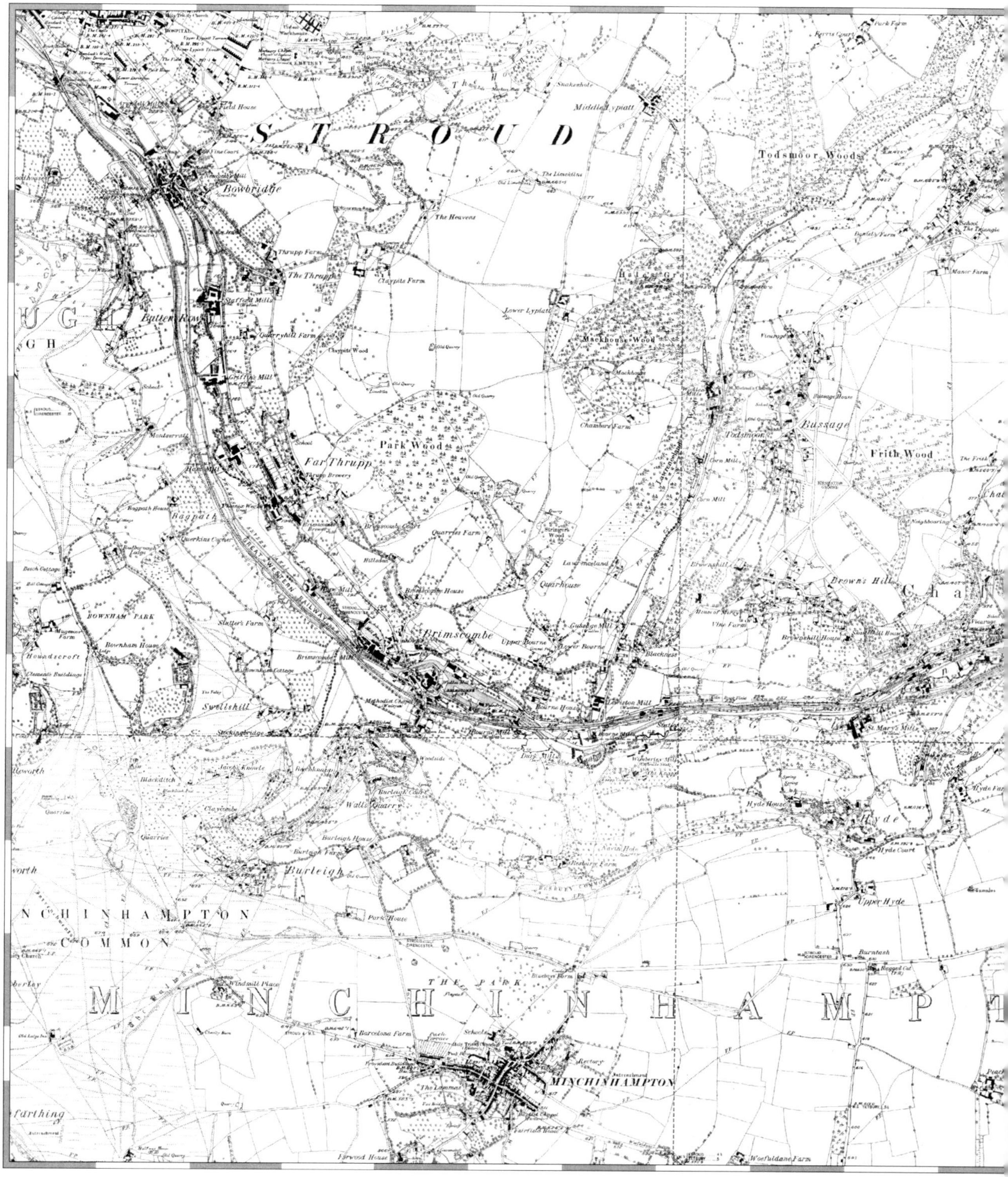
STROUD
Bowbridge
The Heavens
Middle Lypiatt
Todsmoor Woods
Thrupp Farm
The Thrupp
Claypits Farm
Lower Lypiatt
Mackhouse Wood
Stafford Mill
Butterrow
Quarryhill Farm
Claypits Wood
Griffin Mill
Chambers Farm
Bussage
Park Wood
Far Thrupp
Frith Wood
Thrupp Brewery
Ragpath House
Quarries Farm
Brown's Hill
BOWNHAM PARK
Slatter's Farm
Bownham House
Houndscroft
Brimscombe
Upper Bourne
Lower Bourne
Blackness
Swellshill
St Mary's Mills
Jacob's Knowle
Burleigh Court
Wall's Quarry
Hyde House
Hyde
Burleigh House
Burleigh
Hyde Court
Upper Hyde
MINCHINHAMPTON COMMON
Park House
Burnt Ash
Windmill Place
THE PARK
MINCHINHAMPTON
Barcelona Farm
Rectory
The Lammas
Forwood House
Woefuldane Farm

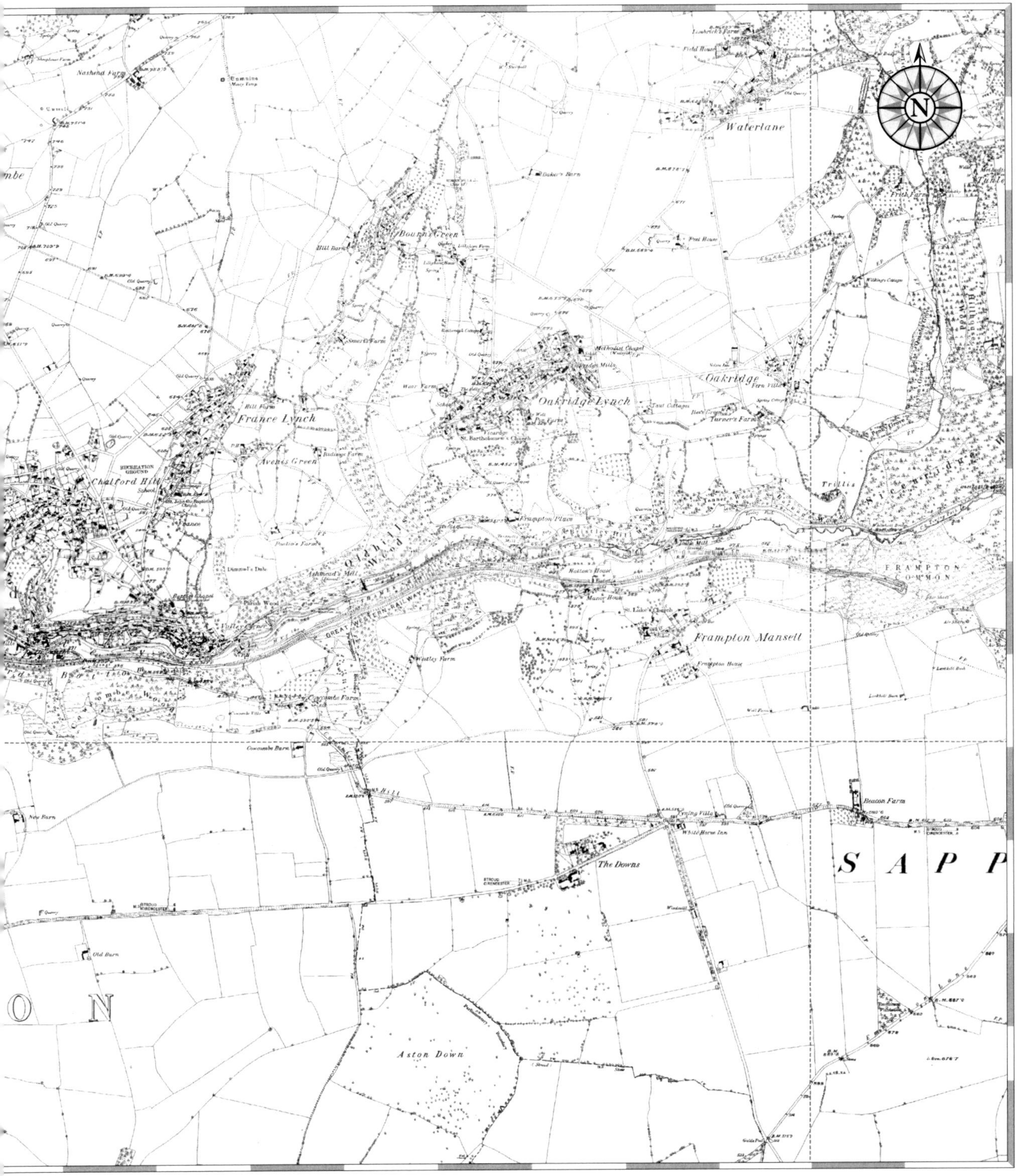
Nashend Farm
Waterlane
Baker's Barn
Hill Barn
Bournes Green
Methodist Chapel
Oakridge
Oakridge Lynch
France Lynch
Hill Farm
Avenis Green
RECREATION GROUND
Chalford Hill
School
St. Bartholomew's Church
Frampton Place
Trillis
FRAMPTON COMMON
Manor House
St. Luke's Church
Frampton Mansell
Frampton House
GREAT WESTERN RAILWAY
Westley Farm
Coccombe Farm
Coccombe Barn
New Barn
Old Quarry
Beacon Farm
White Horse Inn
The Downs
S A P P
Old Barn
O N
Aston Down
Frith Farm

THE COLN VALLEY

CONSISTENT in its Cotswold character, the Coln valley has a string of quite beautiful villages along the whole of its length. The river starts as a small stream springing from the high slopes on the east of Cleeve Hill, and goes under the name of the Clevely Brook until it reaches Withington, where it grows into maturity as the Coln. Much of its route as it flows south westwards to join the Thames at Lechlade is through wooded hill country, christening a triplet of villages on its way. At Bibury the Coln becomes a trout river in its own right, the crystal-clear water fed by sparkling springs; here trout are bred to stock other rivers throughout the kingdom. As a spectacular punctuation mark at the end of its valley, the Coln runs through the landscaped parkland at Fairford and weaves a watery ribbon at the foot of one of Cotswold's finest medieval churches. This church was built in the Age of the Golden Fleece on the backs of the sheep who once studded the hillsides in their thousands, and who created the wealth that turned tiny Saxon settlements into little market towns.

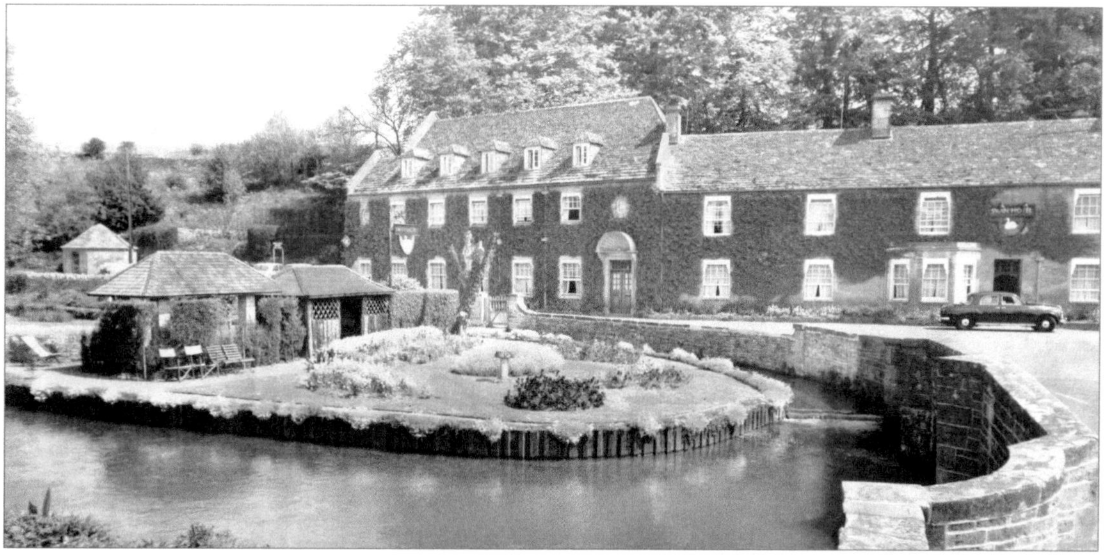

BIBURY, *The Swan Hotel c1960* B530008

William Morris described Bibury as the most beautiful village in England, and it has charmed visitors throughout the ages with its quintessential Cotswold character and composition. The Coln runs alongside the village street, where ducks waddle along the tops of low stone walls and spotted trout nose their way through the waving waterweeds. The Swan Hotel looks across its own island garden to one of the largest trout farms in the country. Parts of the hotel date back to 1640, and would have been known to the famous and infamous, royalty and riff-raff, in the heady days of Bibury Races, frequented in their day by Charles II and Nell Gwynne and George IV.

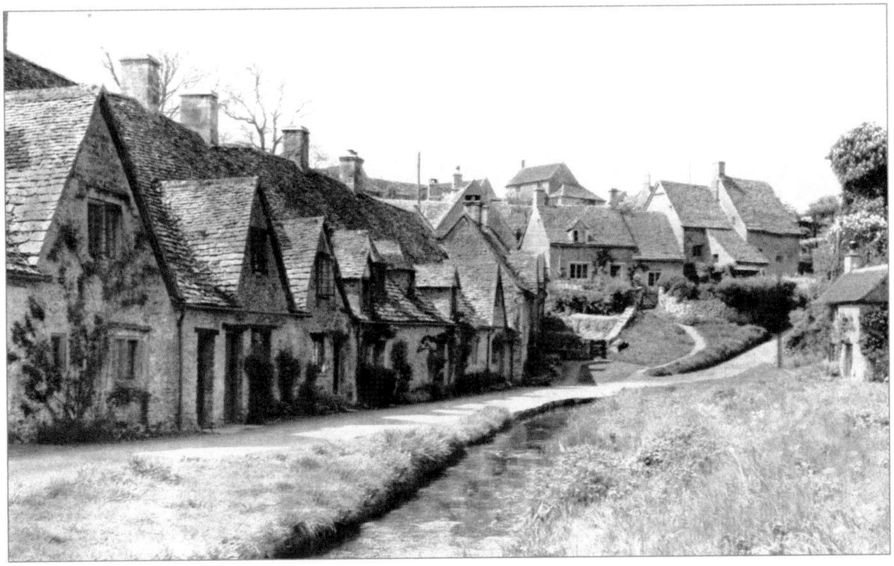

BIBURY
Arlington Row c1960
B530002

This is a story-book picture in Cotswold stone: the long row of higgledy-piggledy, steeply pitch roofed cottages is set against a backdrop of old trees. This is where the weavers lived in the 17th century who worked for Arlington Mill. The mill is reached by a footpath leading off to the right from this view and skirting Rack Isle, where the fulled cloth was hung to dry; it is now a wildfowl sanctuary, and forms part of the Arlington Row property held by the National Trust.

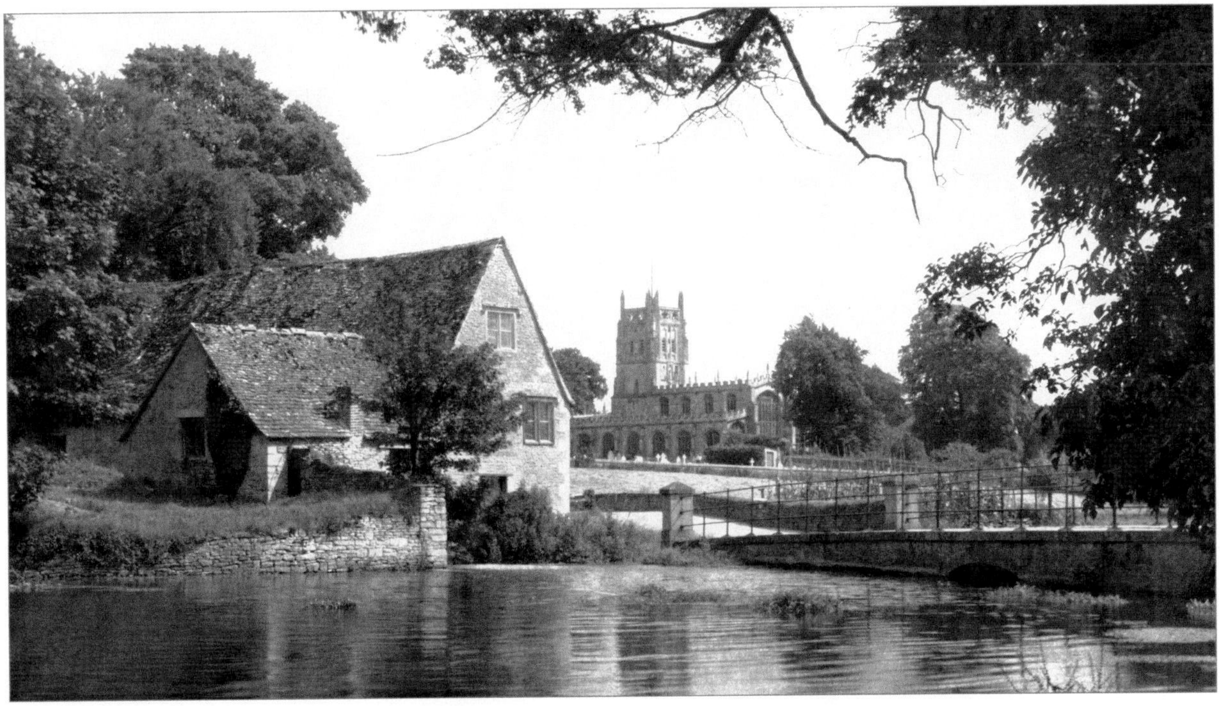

FAIRFORD, *The Church and the Mill c1955* F145001

Fairford Mill has been on this spot since Domesday - this one is the survivor of three that once worked in the parish. It dates back to Elizabethan times with later restoration, and presents an incomparable composition with St Mary's Church on the gentle rise in view. World-famous for its complete set of 28 medieval stained glass windows, St Mary's is one of the outstanding wool churches of the Cotswolds.

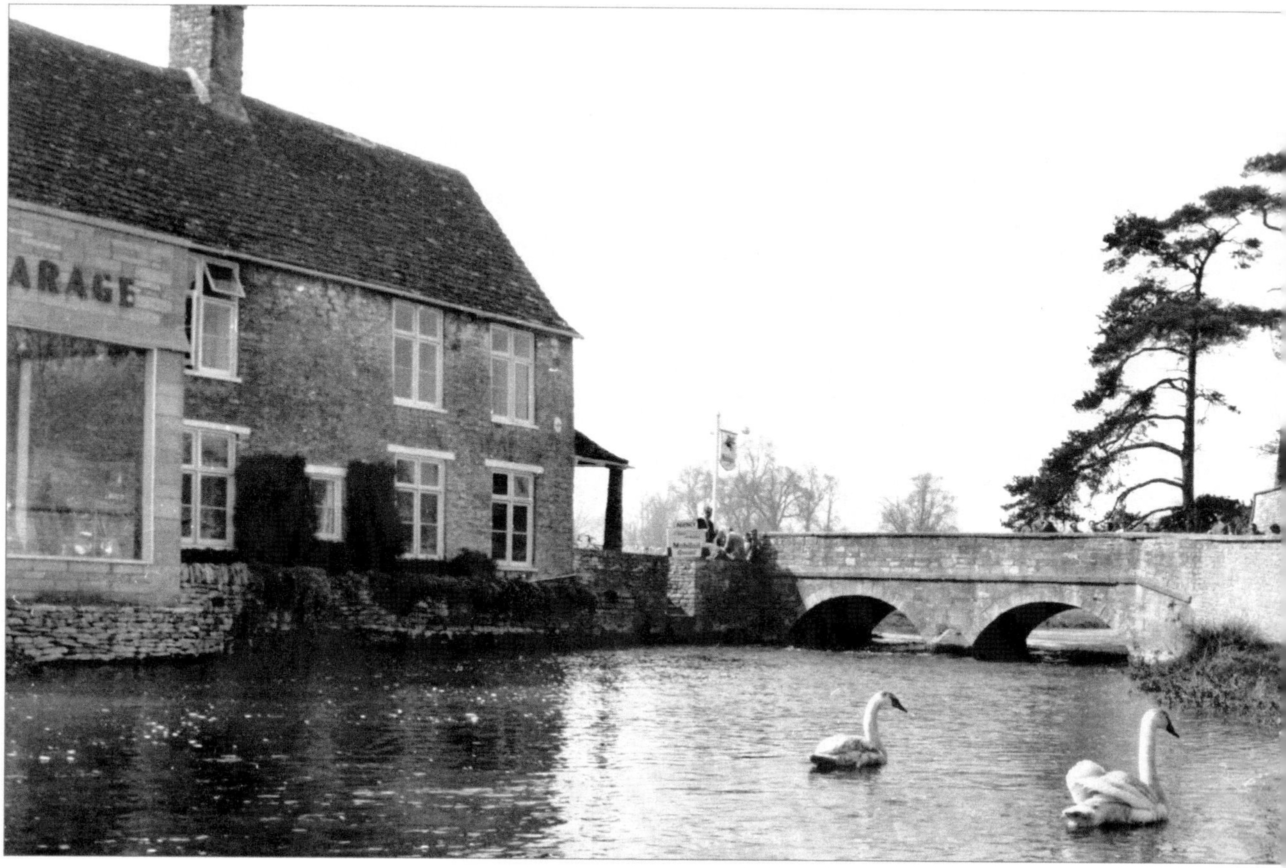

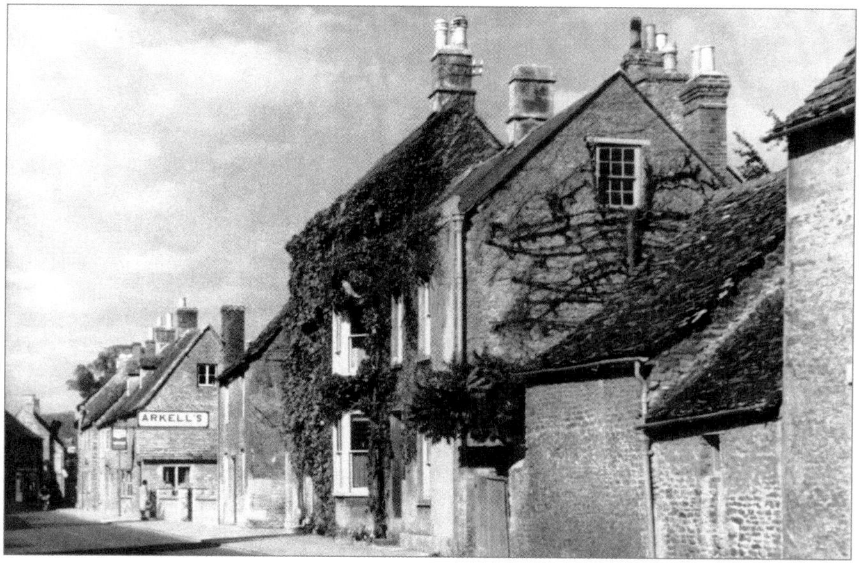

◄ **FAIRFORD**
London Street 1948
F145010

This scene has not changed over at least two centuries, except for the volume of traffic that passes along its narrow street - this is the main thoroughfare through Fairford. The White House, shown here clad in ivy, is a fine example of some of the small town's Georgian houses. The Plough beyond has survived as an inn, whereas the White Hart, seen on the far left, has not - it has been converted back to the small terrace of cottages from which it developed in the mid 15th century.

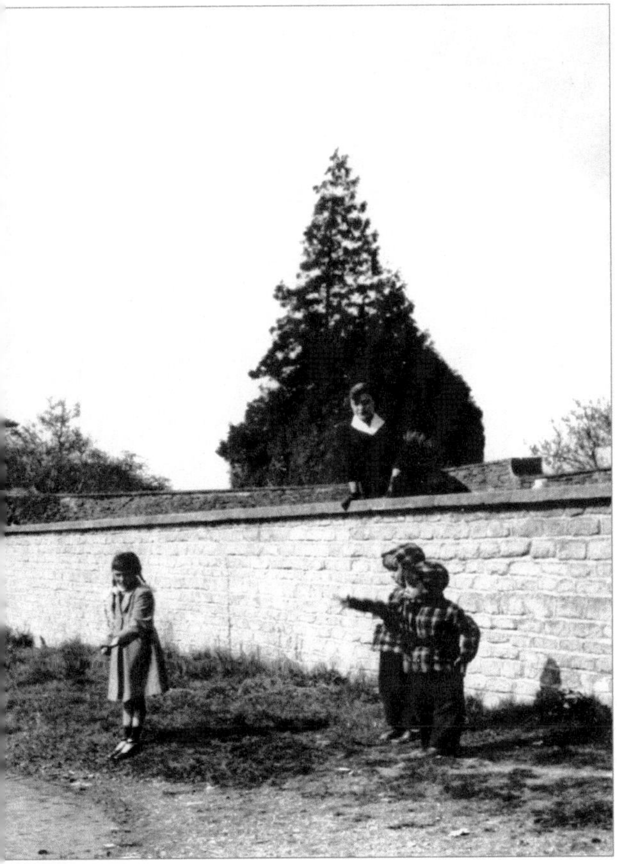

◄ **FAIRFORD**
The Bridge c1955 F145026

Fairford derives its name from the Saxon Fagranforda - the 'fair' ford, in this context meaning easy to cross where the Coln spread over the low-lying water meadows from this point to the mill. There has been a stone bridge carrying the main road through this ancient place since at least the 12th century. Busby's Garage on the left developed from Constable's carriage works when the motor superseded the horse; the site is now a small housing cul-de-sac. The bank on which the children are standing was the wheel wash where carters ran their wagons into the shallow water to stop the wooden wheels shrinking and to give the horses a chance to cool their feet.

▼ **FAIRFORD**
The Market Place c1958 F145024

Fairford was granted its first market charter by Henry II and flourished in the wool trade of the Middle Ages. The half-timbered building on the left (now the post office) originated as a chantry house for the church. It adjoins the long stretch of the Bull Hotel, which originated as a wool merchants' hall before becoming an important staging post in the heyday of the coaching era. It flanks the whole side of the Market Place. The High Street has an attractive mix of mainly 18th-century houses and shops. R W Bridges family grocer's shop (half of which is at the bottom right-hand side of this picture) was yet another inn, the Swan, with an even more ancient one time hostelry, the Cross Keys, further up the street and facing the church.

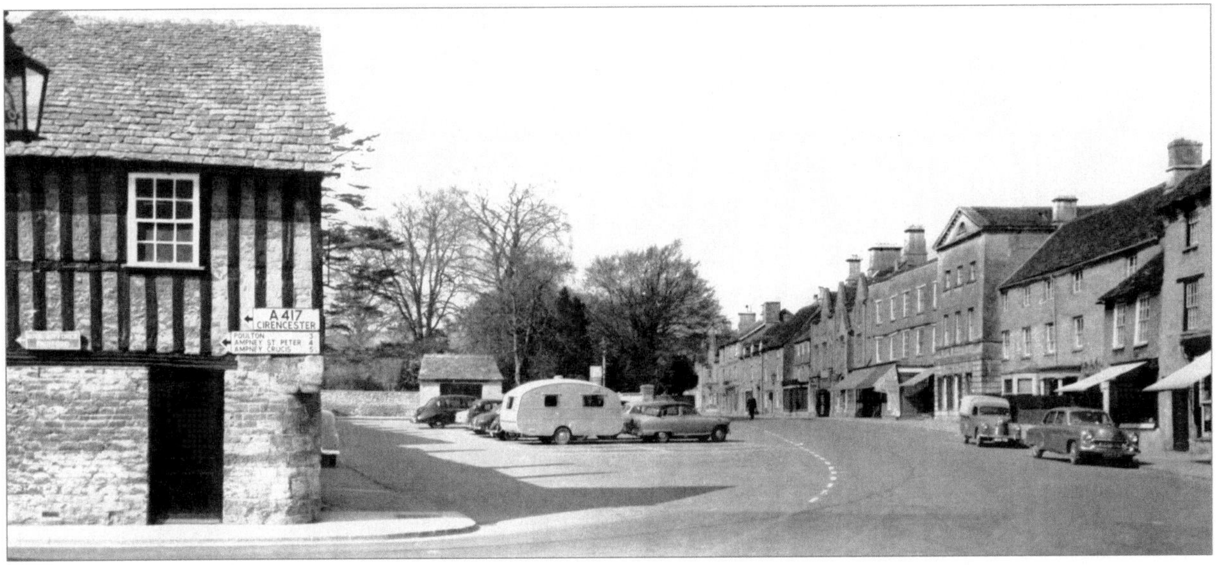

THE LEACH VALLEY

'Clear Coln and lively Leach go down from Cotswold's plain
At Lechlade linking hands come likewise to support
The mother of great Thames'

DRAYTON'S poetic description of these two small rivers that run almost parallel at their lower reaches would imply that the Leach is as lively as its neighbouring Coln is clear and bright: in fact, the Leach must be one of the most secretive of the Cotswolds rivers, and only makes a public appearance for any length of time at the village to which it gives its name. At Eastleach the river that once formed the boundary between the twin parishes of Turville and St Martin - or Bouthrop as it was anciently called - is spanned by one of the most picturesque clapper bridges in the country, and joins them together. From its rise near Northleach, a small market town built on the Cotswold wool trade, the Leach keeps to remote farmlands for most of its fairly short route, glancing by way of Southrop before joining the Thames at Lechlade.

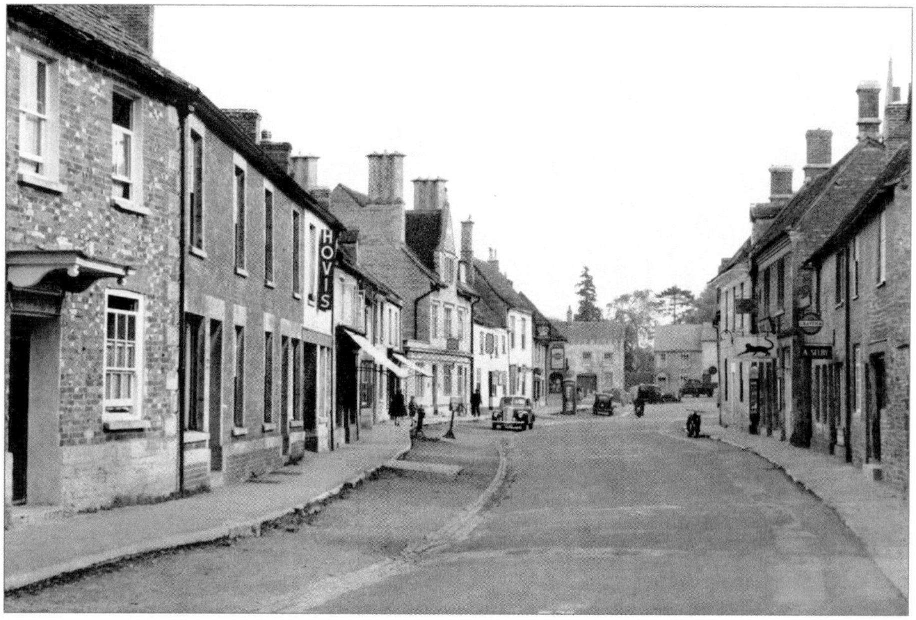

LECHLADE
High Street c1955
L147033

This is one of the three roads leading to the Market Place, shown at the far back of this view. The mix of shops and inns and residential houses in the High Street continues right through Lechlade, which grew up as a medieval market centre.

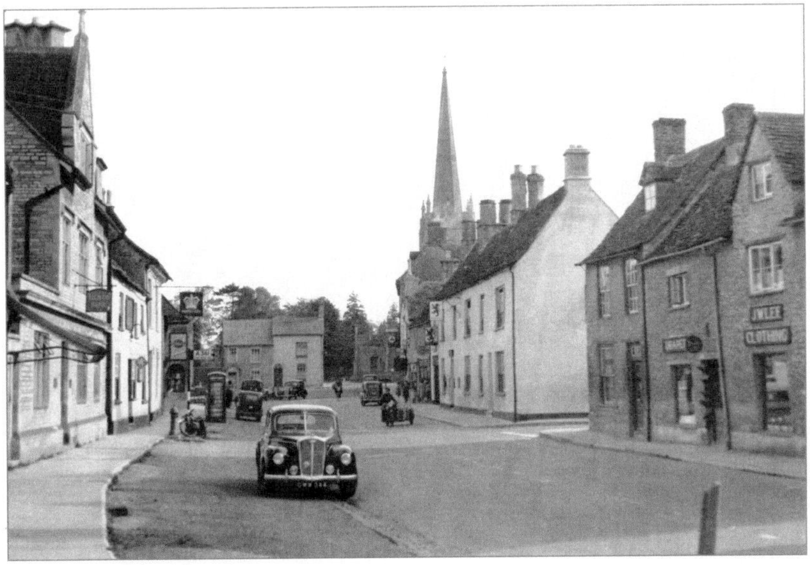

LECHLADE
High Street and the Church c1955 L147020

This view, taken further down the street, illustrates the important role it had as a posting stop in the coaching era: notice the close proximity of three substantial old hostelries. The Crown on the left faces the white plaster face of the Red Lion, and beyond it is the 300-year-old red brick New Inn, with its wide carriageway arch. The spire of the church of St Lawrence corners the Market Place, and inspired Shelley to pen his 'Stanzas to Lechlade Churchyard' in 1815. One of the cast iron water standpipes with its lion's head can be seen edging the pavement in front of the Crown Inn.

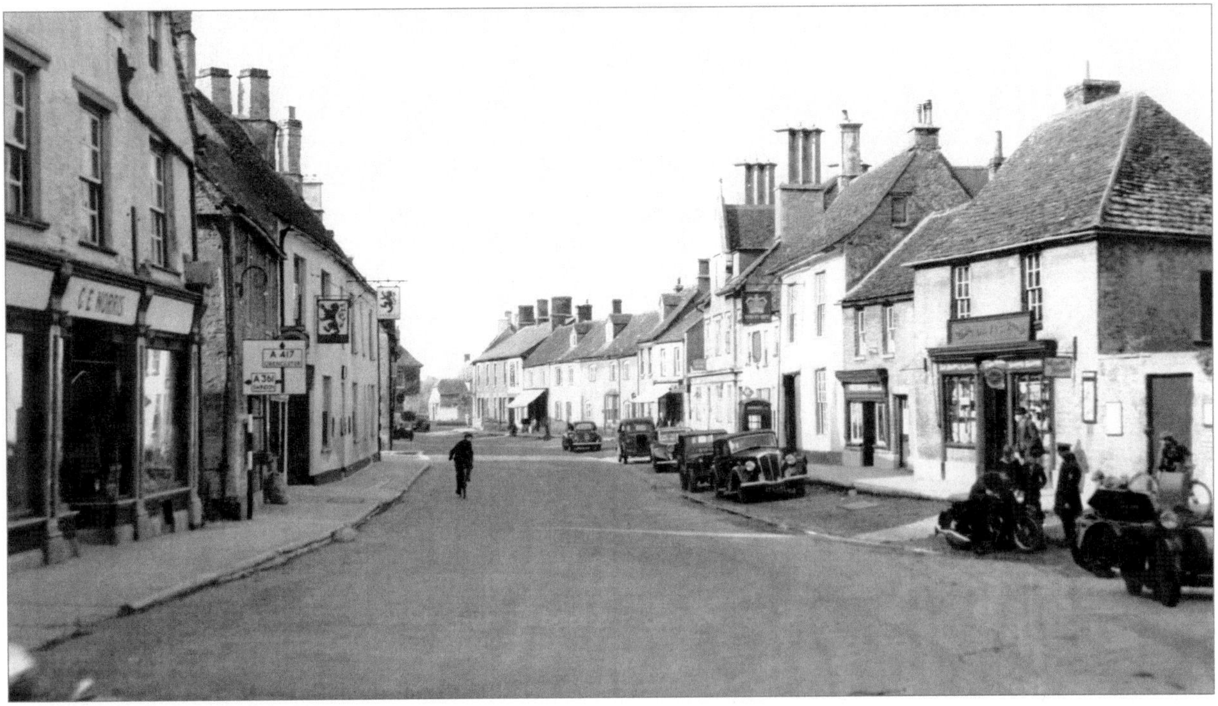

LECHLADE, *High Street c1955* L147025

We are looking back west from the Market Place, with Davis the chemist's and Stevens the baker's shops in ancient buildings on the right. Beyond them, the Crown, Lloyds Bank and Jenkins confectioner's are among the fine old houses leading to a glimpse of the white-washed front of the house in the far background. This was the old toll house at the turning to Little London - now a residential development, but once the winding route used by the Gloucester to London coaches.

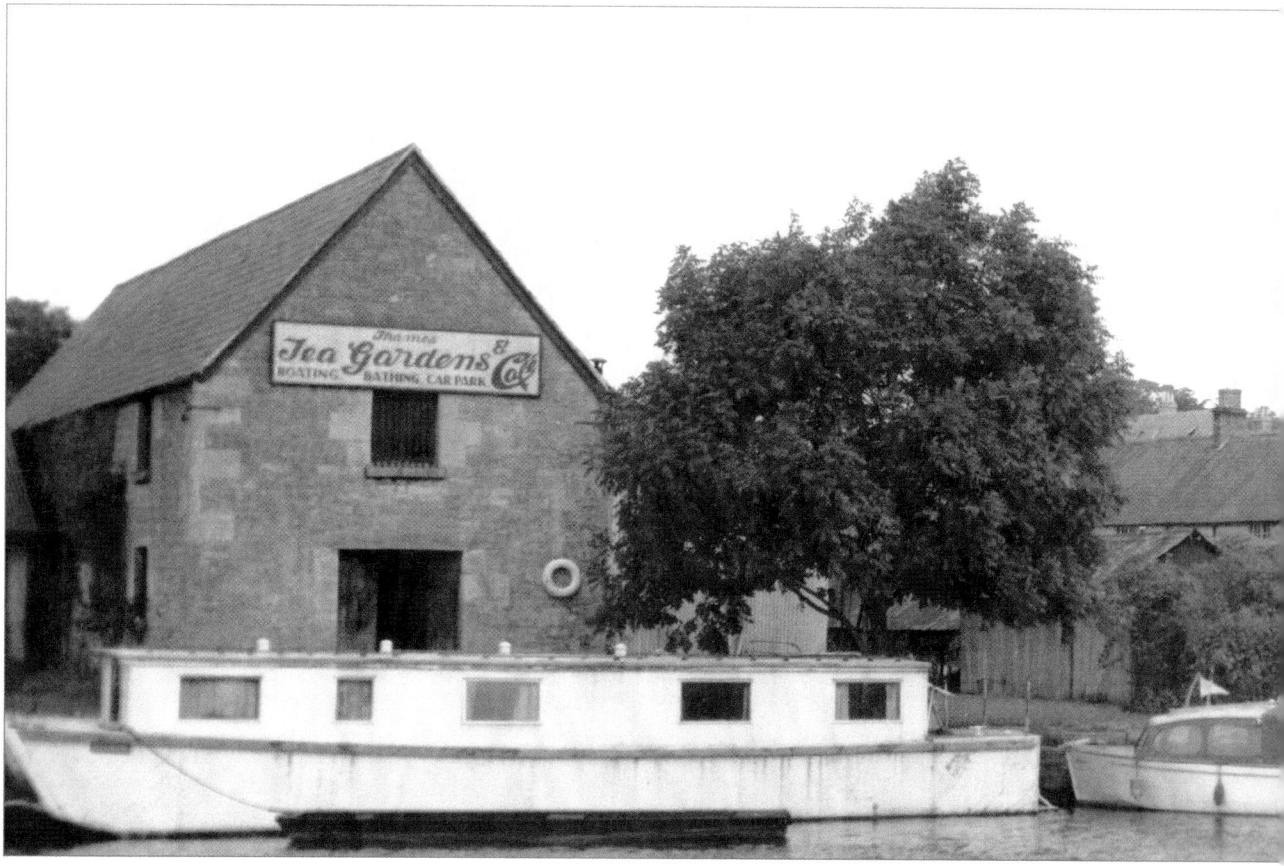

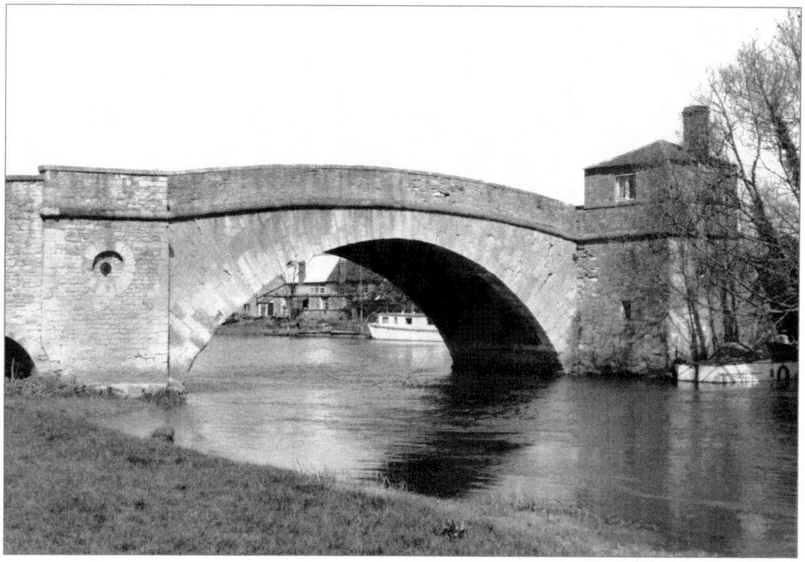

◄ **LECHLADE**
Halfpenny Bridge c1955
L147032

Spanning the Thames across the county boundaries of Gloucestershire and Wiltshire, this beautiful 18th-century bridge takes its name from the halfpenny toll. The squat square building on the right was the toll keeper's house. The towpath runs under the low arch on the left; once used by the bargees leading their horses, the path is now well trodden by walkers enjoying the riverside tranquillity further upstream to the old canal round house at Inglesham. Short boat trips now run along this stretch as part of the Thames and Severn Canal restoration programme.

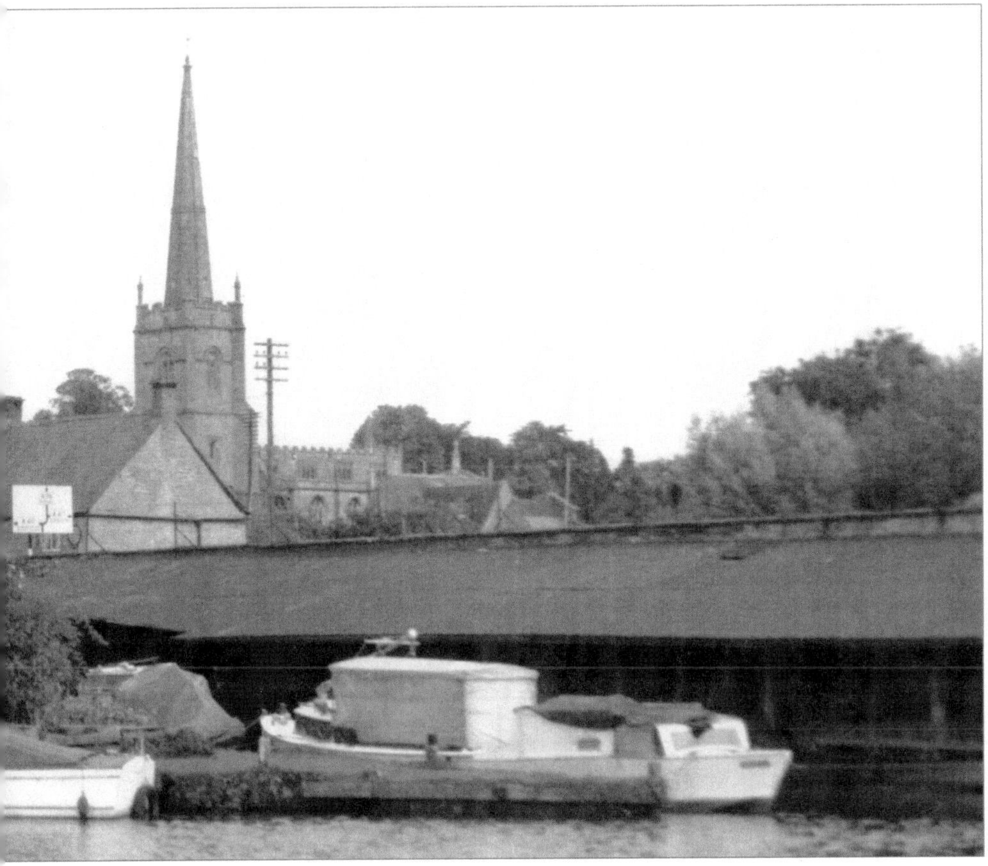

LECHLADE
The Thames Tea Gardens and Café c1955 L147023

As the highest navigable point on the Upper Thames, the river has shaped Lechlade's history throughout the centuries. The old wharf buildings seen here were once busy with barge traffic carrying corn and cheese, wool and stone down to Oxford and London. Since the decline in water transportation the old wharf became the centre for hiring boats and a recreational complex.

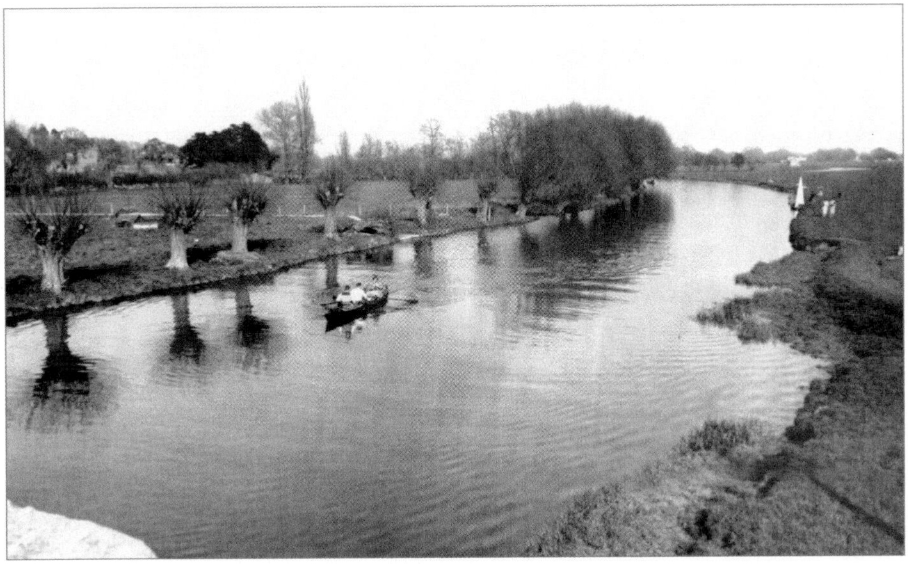

LECHLADE
The View from the Bridge c1960 L147048

We are looking downstream from Halfpenny Bridge along the water meadows towards St John's Lock, a stretch enjoyed by boaters, anglers and walkers.

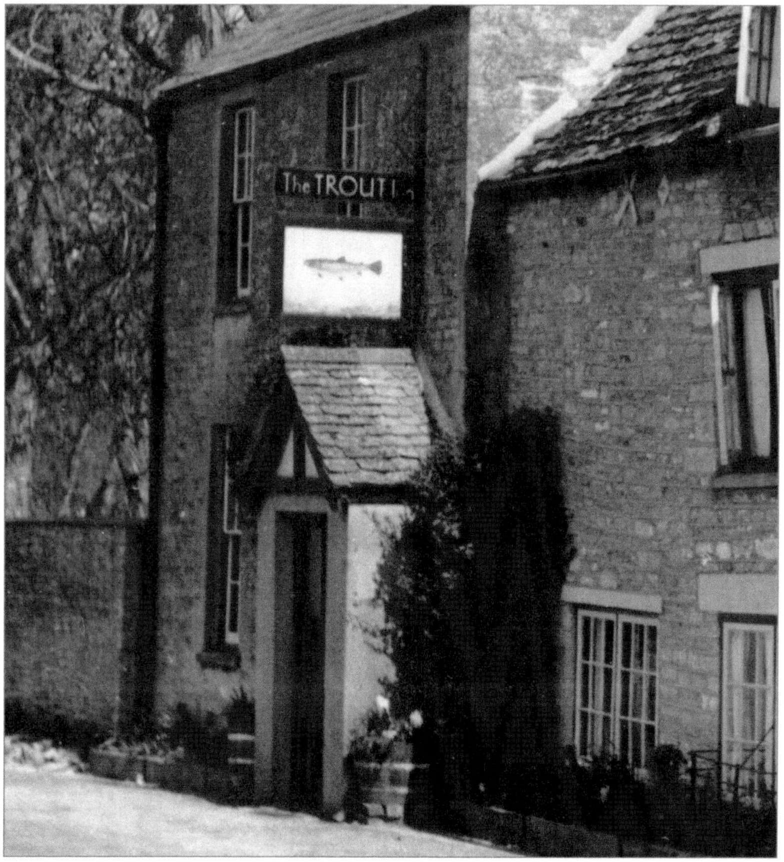

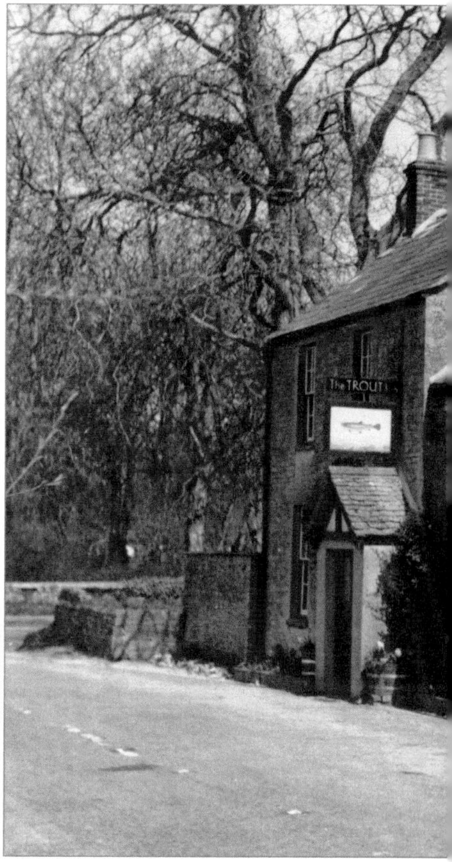

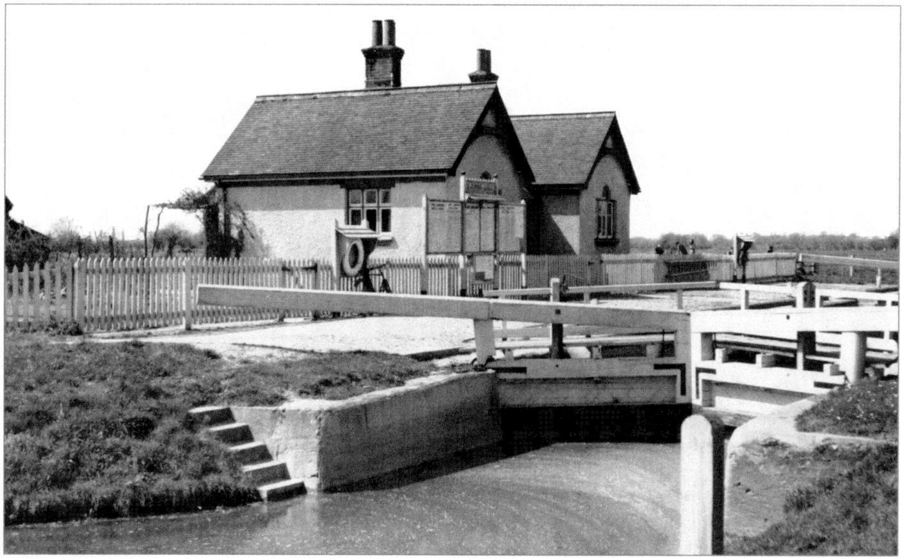

◄ **LECHLADE**
St John's Lock c1955
L147038

On the other side of the road from the old Trout Inn is the fascinating working of the lock marking the upper reaches of the Thames. The lock keeper's house is on the Oxfordshire side of the river, and Old Father Thames reclines in splendid stone effigy in front of the house - moved here for its own protection from its previous isolated spot at the source of the Thames.

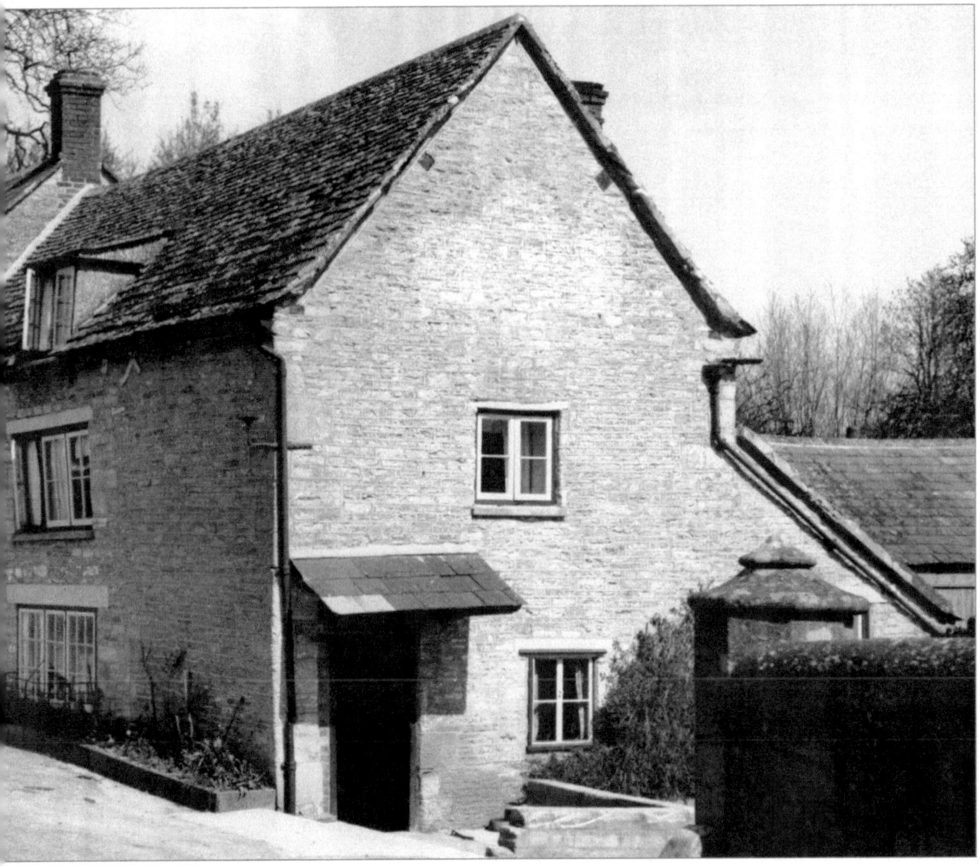

LECHLADE
The Trout Inn c1955
L147035

The original inn dates back to about 1220, when it was known as the Sign of St John the Baptist - it was part of the long demolished priory. The monks are reputed to have distilled their own Benedictine over the old fireplace in the Anglers Bar. The ancient fishing rights, granted to the brothers of the priory by Royal Charter, are vested in the landlord, who lets them out to an angling club. The inn is a popular venue for various functions; it is sited at a picturesque spot at the 13th-century St John's Bridge that spans the county boundary across the Thames on the road to Faringdon.

(far left) detail from
L147035

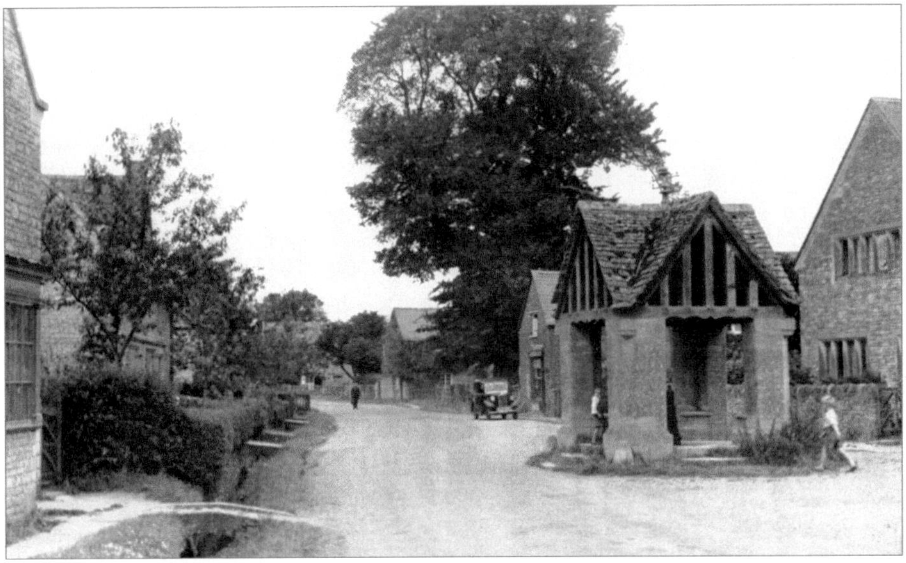

BUSCOT
The Village c1950
B886018

The next village downstream from Lechlade is little more than a hamlet. Buscot is a compact cluster of old Cotswold stone houses set in a model agricultural estate, with an enterprising and active community. Close by is Buscot Park, famous for its walled gardens, extensive grounds and lake, and the Faringdon art collection. It is open to the public under the National Trust.

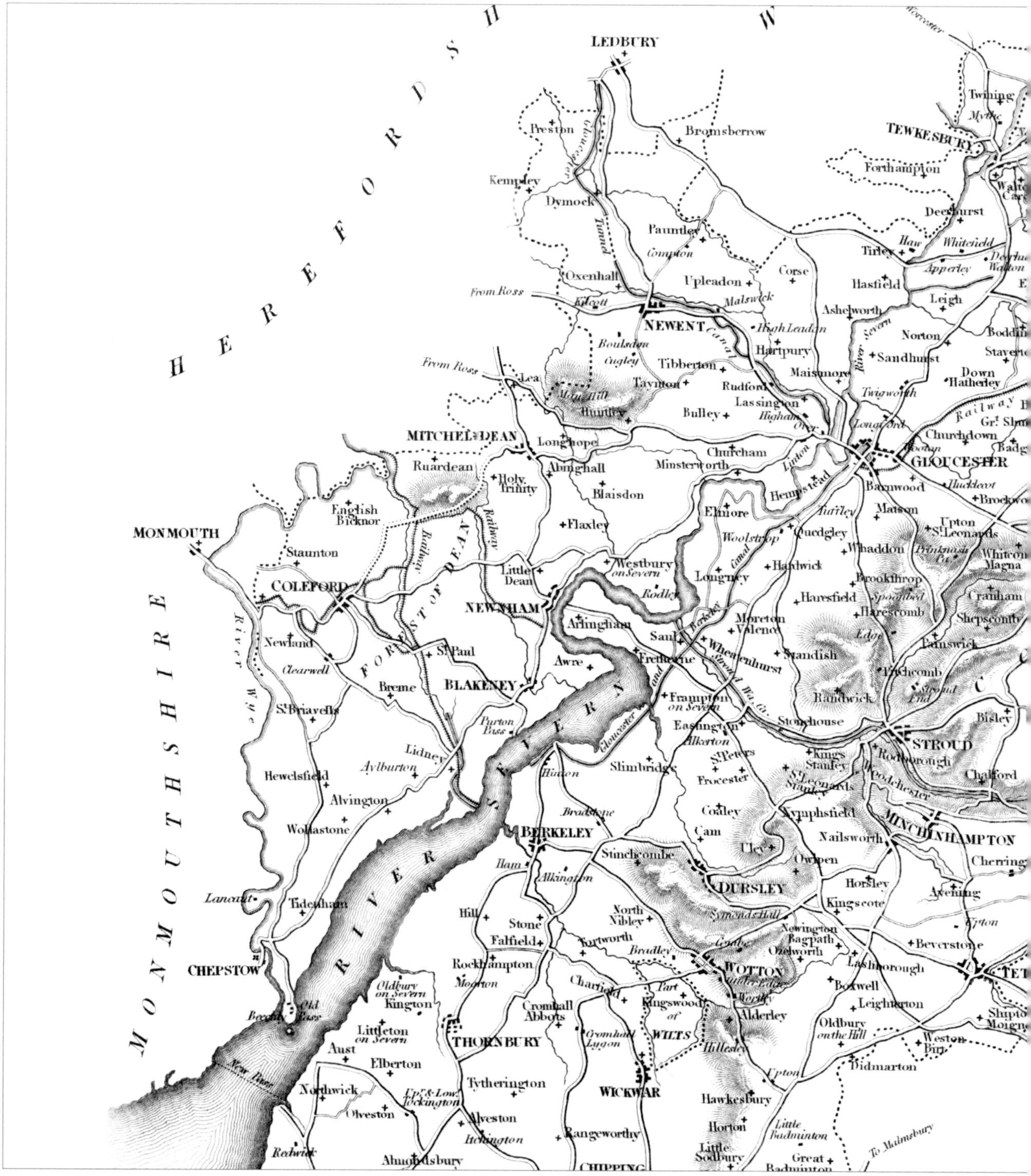
H E R E F O R D S H
W
M O N M O U T H S H I R E
LEDBURY
Preston
Bromsberrow
TEWKESBURY
Twining
Mythe
Forthampton
Kempley
Dymock
Pauntley
Compton
Deerhurst
Tirley
Haw
Whitefield
Apperley
Corse
Upleadon
Hasfield
Leigh
Oxenhall
From Ross
Kilcott
NEWENT
Malswick
Canal
Ashelworth
Norton
High Leadon
Hartpury
Sandhurst
Boulsdon
Cugley
Tibberton
Maisemore
River Severn
Down Hatherley
Taynton
Rudford
Lassington
Twigworth
Highnam
Huntley
Bulley
Over
Longford
Railway
Churchdown
MITCHEL DEAN
Longhope
Churcham
GLOUCESTER
Ruardean
Abinghall
Minsterworth
Linton
Holy Trinity
Blaisdon
Barnwood
Hucklecot
Brockworth
English Bicknor
Hempstead
Elmore
Tuffley
Matson
Upton St. Leonards
MONMOUTH
Flaxley
Woolstrop
Quedgeley
Staunton
Whaddon
Prinknash Pk.
Whitcomb Magna
Westbury on Severn
Little Dean
Longney
Hardwick
Brookthrop
COLEFORD
Rodley
Haresfield
Spoonbed
Cranham
NEWNHAM
Arlingham
Moreton Valence
Harescomb
Shepscomb
River Wye
Newland
Saul
Wheatenhurst
Standish
Edge
Painswick
St. Paul
Clearwell
Fretherne
Pitchcomb
Awre
Stroud Water
Breme
BLAKENEY
Randwick
Stroud End
FOREST OF DEAN
St. Briavells
Frampton on Severn
Purton Pass
Eastington
Stonehouse
Bisley
Alkerton
Gloucester and Berkeley Canal
Lidney
Kings Stanley
St. Peters
STROUD
Rodborough
Aylburton
Hewelsfield
Slimbridge
Frocester
St. Leonards Stanley
Chalford
Hinton
Woodchester
Alvington
Bradstone
Coaley
Nymphsfield
MINCHINHAMPTON
Wollastone
BERKELEY
Cam
Uley
Nailsworth
Stinchcombe
Owlpen
Cherrington
Ham
Alkington
DURSLEY
Horsley
Avening
Lancaut
Tidenham
Kingscote
Hill
Stone
North Nibley
Symonds Hall
Upton
Newington Bagpath
Ozelworth
Falfield
Tortworth
Bradley
Beverstone
Rockhampton
Morton
WOTTON under Edge
Lasborough
CHEPSTOW
Charfield
Boxwell
Oldbury on Severn
Kington
Cromhall Abbots
Part Kingswood of WILTS
Wortley
Leighterton
Alderley
Shipton Moigne
Beachley
Old Pass
Littleton on Severn
THORNBURY
Cromhall Lygon
Hillesley
Oldbury on the Hill
Weston Birt
Aust
Elberton
New Pass
Didmarton
Northwick
Up. & Low. Tockington
Tytherington
WICKWAR
Hawkesbury
Olveston
Alveston
Itchington
Horton
Little Badminton
Rangeworthy
Redwick
Almondsbury
Little Sodbury
Great Badminton
To Malmsbury
RIVER SEVERN

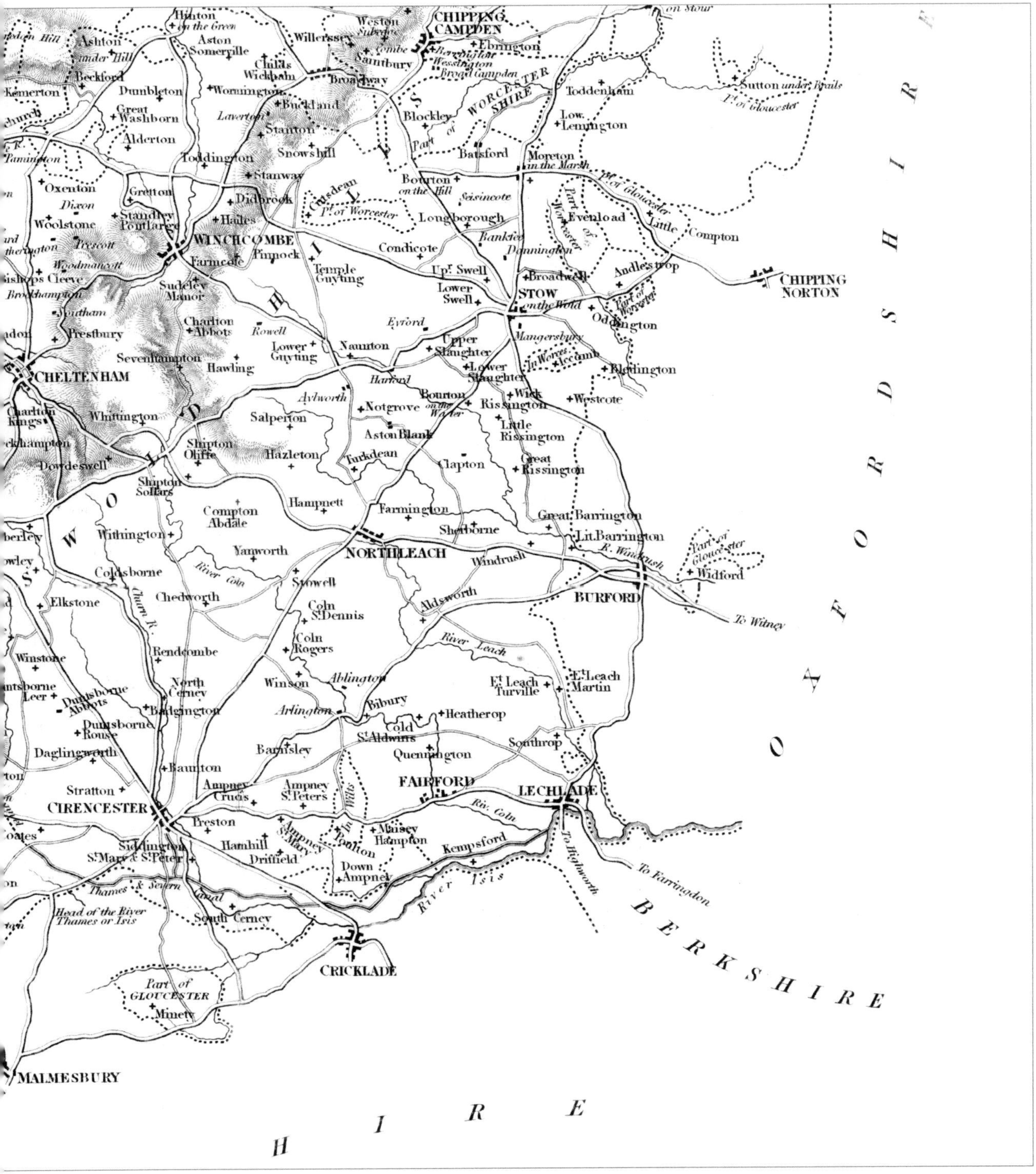

COUNTY MAP OF GLOUCESTERSHIRE *c1850*

ALONG THE WINDRUSH VALLEY

THE LARGEST of the Cotswold rivers, the Windrush runs for some thirty miles before entering the Thames in Oxfordshire. From its inauspicious beginnings in the wolds above Stanway, the Windrush is fed by the little tributaries of the Dikler, on which the Swells (Upper and Lower) stand, the Eye, which waters the Slaughters (Upper and Lower), and the Sherborne Brook, which gives its name to that delightful village also featured here. Bourton took its name and grew up on the fame of its water, by now widened into a miniature canal over which low footbridges link the village streets, which are edged by wide greens. Bourton-on-the-Water features on every tour of the Cotswolds, and it caters for its visitors accordingly. The layout of the village is uniquely demonstrated by the long-established model village. Built to a scale of one-ninth of the original and with the tiniest detail incorporated, this Lilliputian village in the garden of the Old New Inn is a veritable storybook in stone. After giving its name to one of the many villages it links, the Windrush glides gracefully alongside the lovely old town of Burford before adding its own romance in its final farewell to the Cotswolds as a haunting setting for memorable and mystical Minster Lovell.

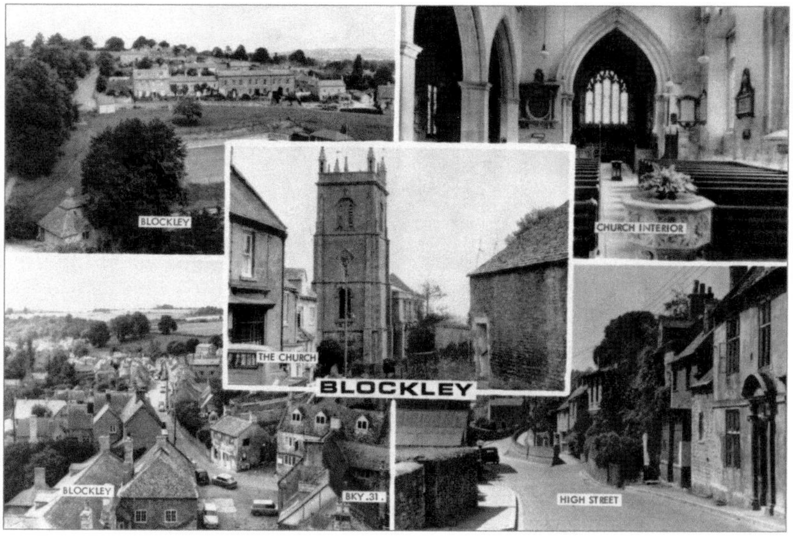

BLOCKLEY
Composite Postcard c1960
B528031

A large village, equidistant from Moreton in Marsh and Chipping Campden but not distant enough to develop into a market town itself, Blockley harnessed the water power of its deeply cleft valley early on in its history, and became famous as a silk throwing centre based on the Coventry ribbon trade in the aftermath of the woollen weaving depression. A hundred years ago, six mills employed some 600 people; today the buildings have been converted for other uses, and harmonise within the traditional village scene, the focal point of which is the Norman church with its 18th-century tower.

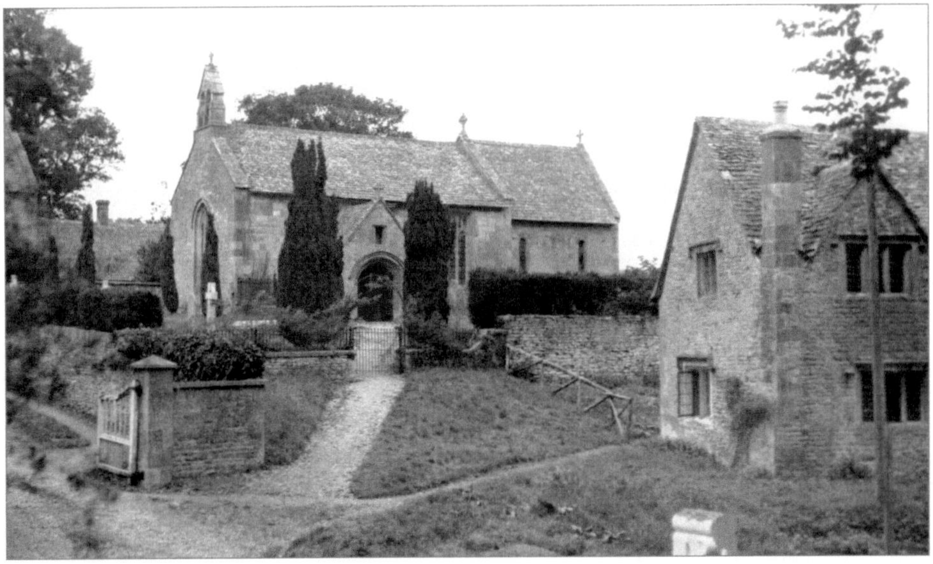

UPPER SWELL
St Mary's Church c1955 U56009

A corner of Old England in one of the greenest of Cotswold valleys is Upper Swell, its small church and manor house set on a rise above the rippling Dikler brook, which joins the Windrush further downstream. As with most Cotswold churches, St Mary's has Norman foundations.

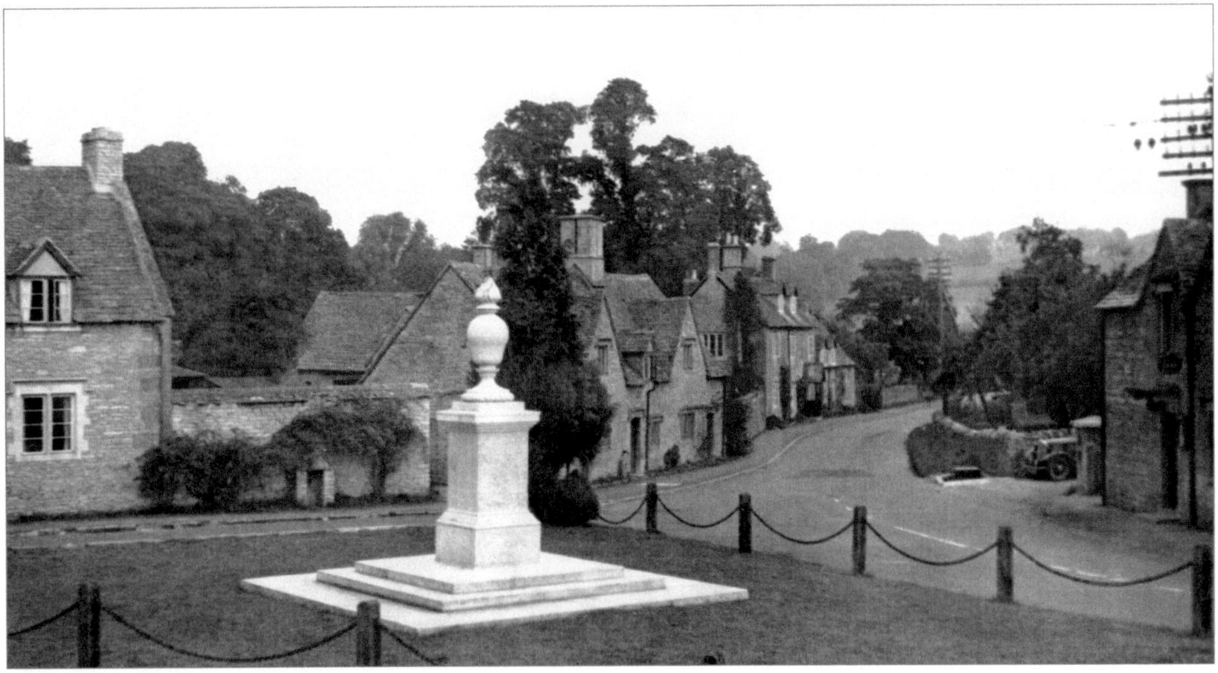

LOWER SWELL, *The Village c1955* L525011

The stone flaming urn of the war memorial, designed by Sir Edwin Lutyens, holds centre stage at the crossroads in this attractive village built exclusively in the native Cotswold stone. The oldest surviving houses date back to the 17th century. How different this quiet little place might have been had the potential been developed from the chalybeate spring, discovered in 1807 where the road leads out of the village to Stow, as inscribed on Spa Cottages with their distinctly exotic façade.

▼ **UPPER SLAUGHTER,** *Composite Postcard c1955* U44005

The twin villages of the Slaughters take their name from the 'slough' (or mire) of the little Eye stream on which they stand. It was at Upper Slaughter that a family called Slaughter lived in the 16th century, but the site of the origins of the village are more ancient, as evidenced by the castle mound, a raised grass-covered area above the stream. An evocative picture of life as a Cotswold parson was recorded in the diary of the Reverend Francis Witts (covering the period 1820-1852). His rectory home is now the Lords of the Manor Hotel.

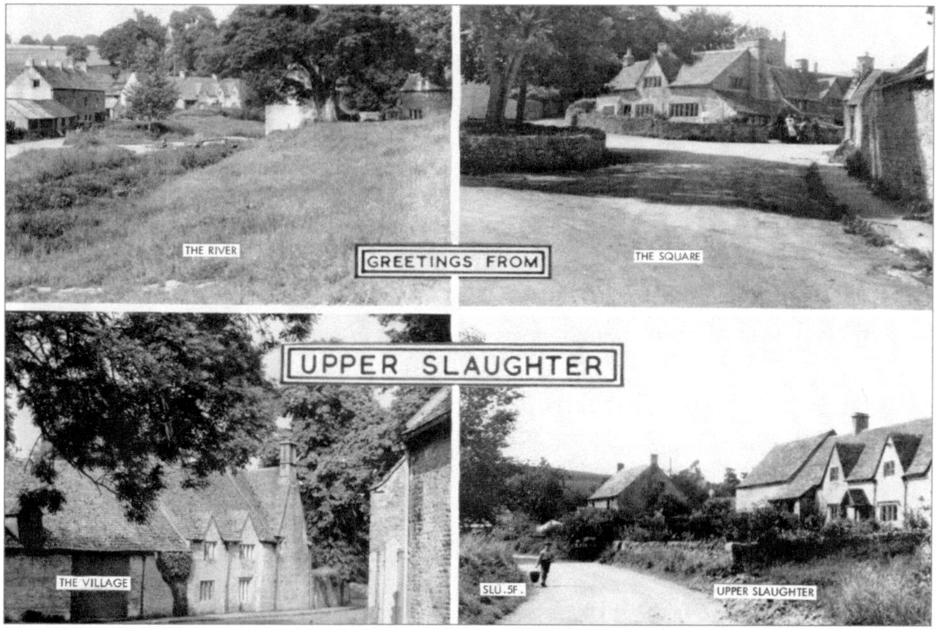

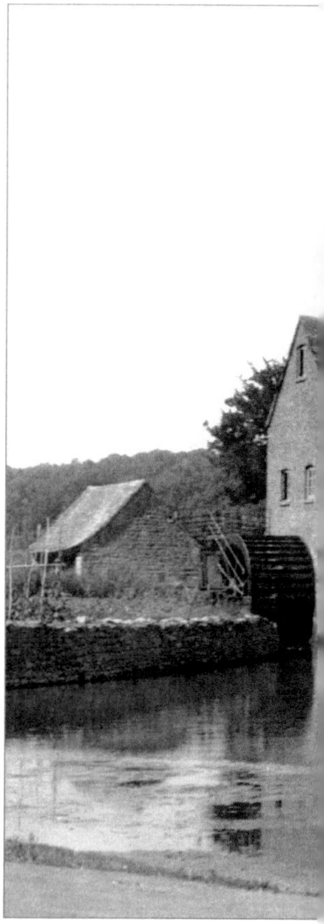

► **UPPER SLAUGHTER**
The Square c1960
U44004

It was Sir Edwin Lutyens who remodelled the village's open square and eight cottages in Edwardian times, but the little footbridges across the brook were in use some two centuries before that, and today's motorists take advantage of a shallow ford - but this is walking country, and walking is still the best way to appreciate the many facets of this village.

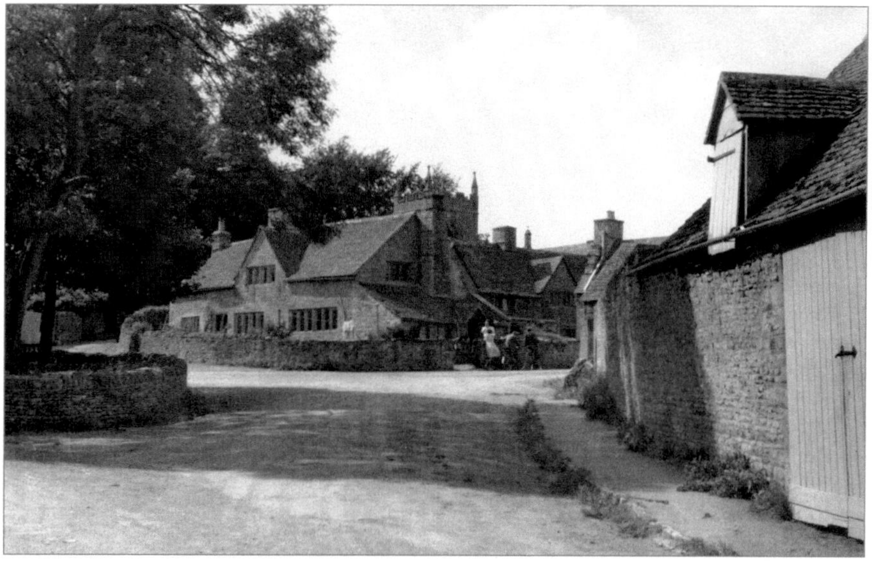

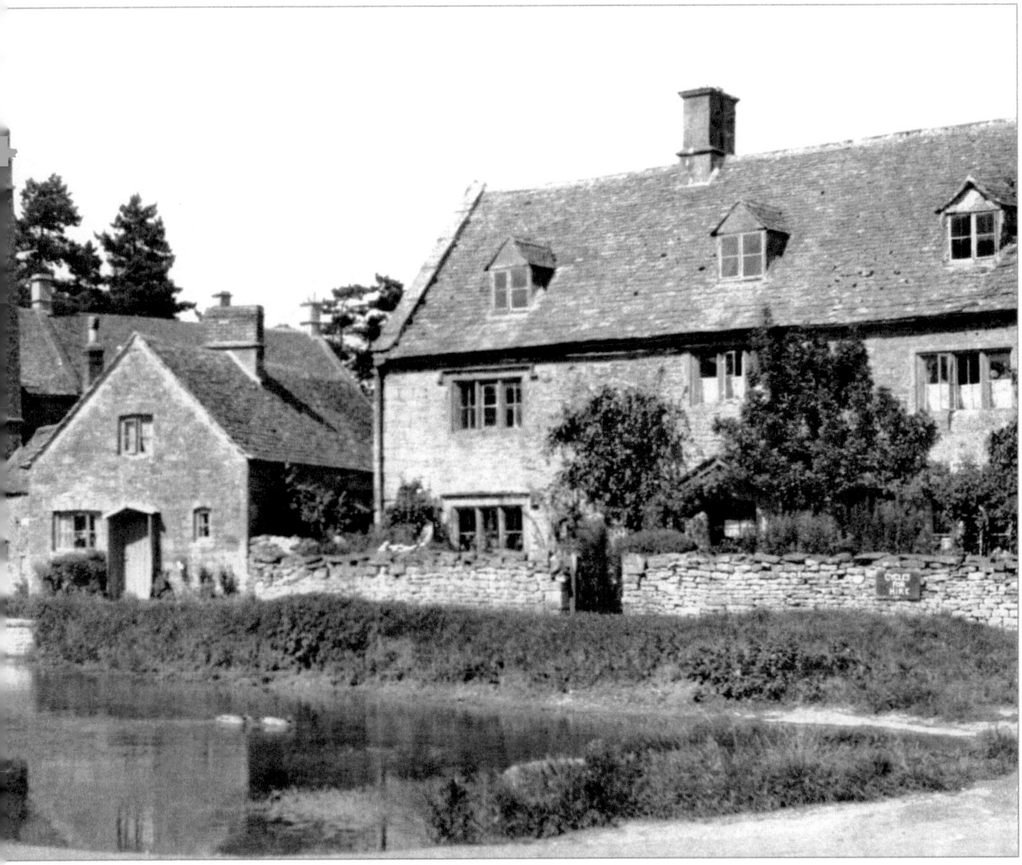

◄ **LOWER SLAUGHTER**
The Mill and the Pond c1950
L313008

Taking its name from its position downstream, this is the pretty sister of the twin Slaughters. As though to admire its own reflection, the tall brick chimney of the former corn mill (with its water wheel still in situ) has attracted photographers since the pioneering days of Francis Frith.

► **LOWER SLAUGHTER**
The Green c1955
L313007

Water weaves its magic through the fabric of this little village, and the fountain on the Green makes a focal point in the perfect picture; its design echoes the steeply pitched and gabled roofline of the old cottages.

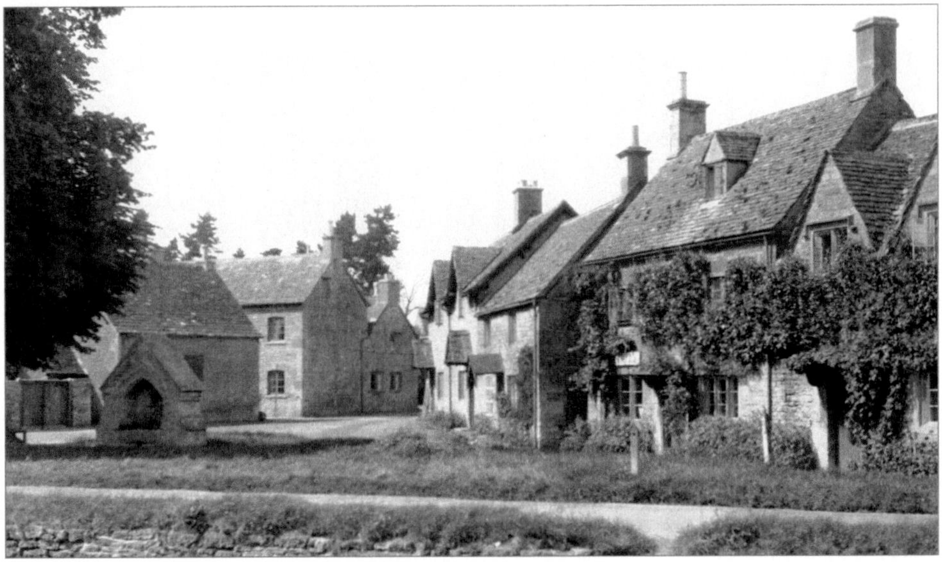

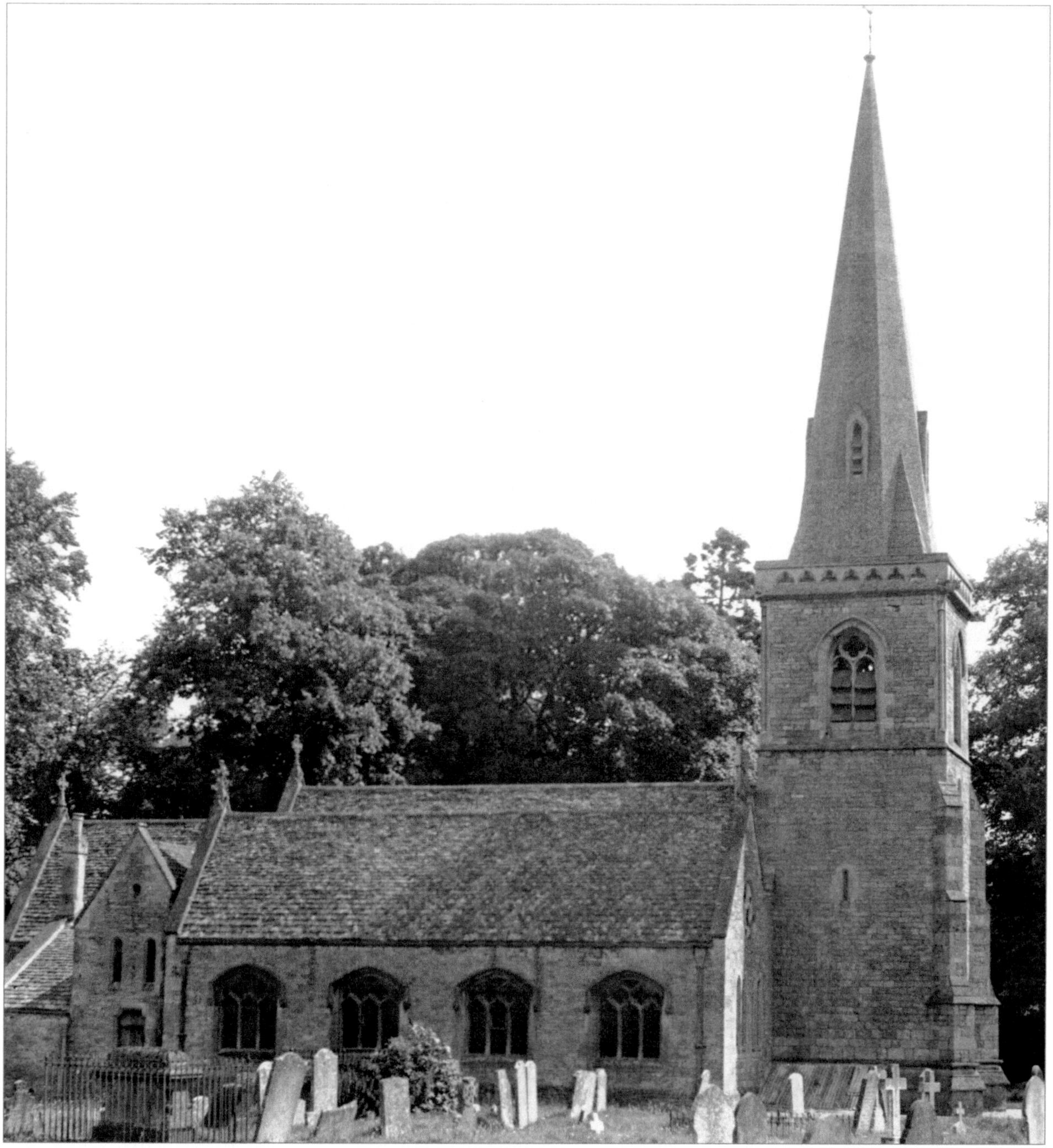

LOWER SLAUGHTER, *The Parish Church c1960* L313006

The parish church of St Mary was drastically restored in 1867; a century later the spire was topped in fibre-glass. But the whole composition still sits comfortably on its more ancient foundations close by the old manor house.

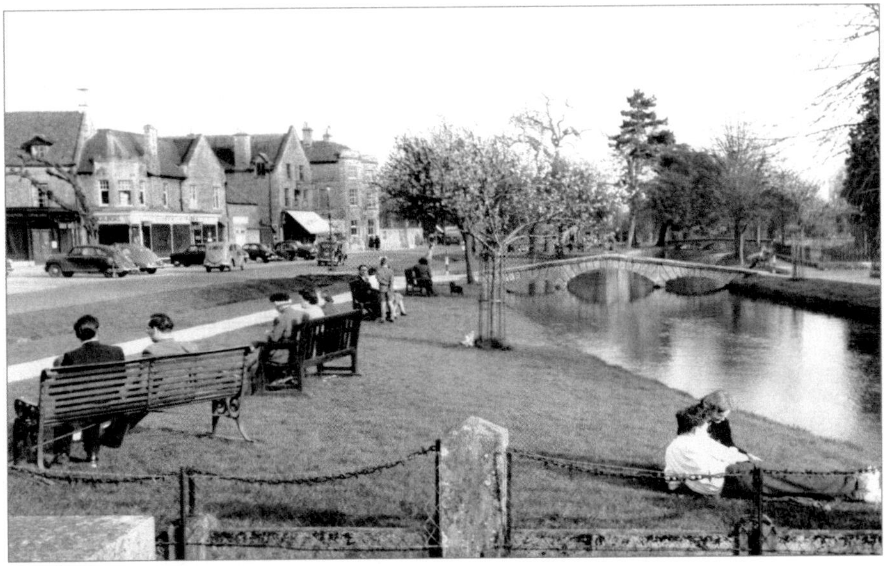

BOURTON-ON-THE-WATER
The View from the Memorial c1955 B392074

The low bridges over the river which flows through the centre of the village are its most familiar feature, and have given it the title of 'the Venice of the Cotswolds', although the county historian, Samuel Rudder equated it in the 18th century to a Dutch village. Irrespective to any such comparisons, Bourton on its Windrush waters is a tourist honey pot today, catering for its visitors accordingly, whilst still retaining its village identity.

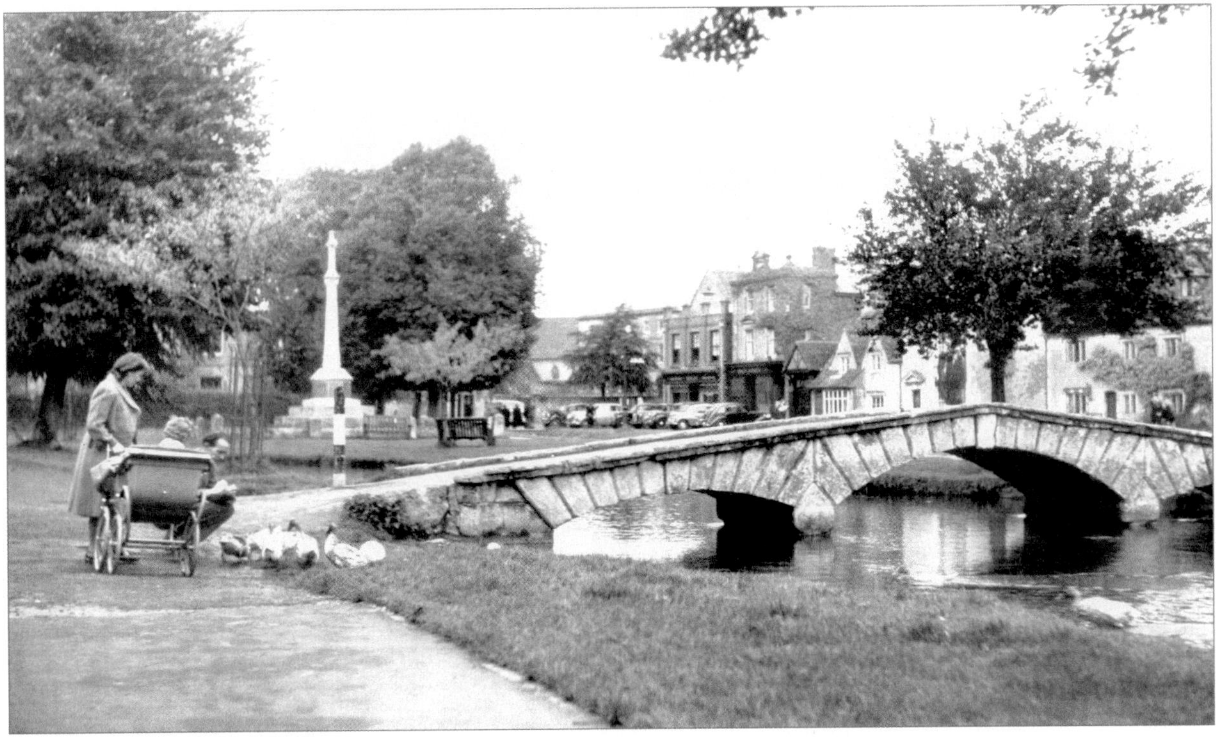

BOURTON-ON-THE-WATER, *Feeding the Ducks c1955* B392047

A settlement since the Iron Age, with the Romans and Anglo-Saxons leaving artefacts as evidence of their time at Bourton, the village uses its river as a focal point for such activities as setting the Christmas tree in it to spectacular effect, and playing an annual football match on August Bank Holiday Monday - a custom over a hundred years old.

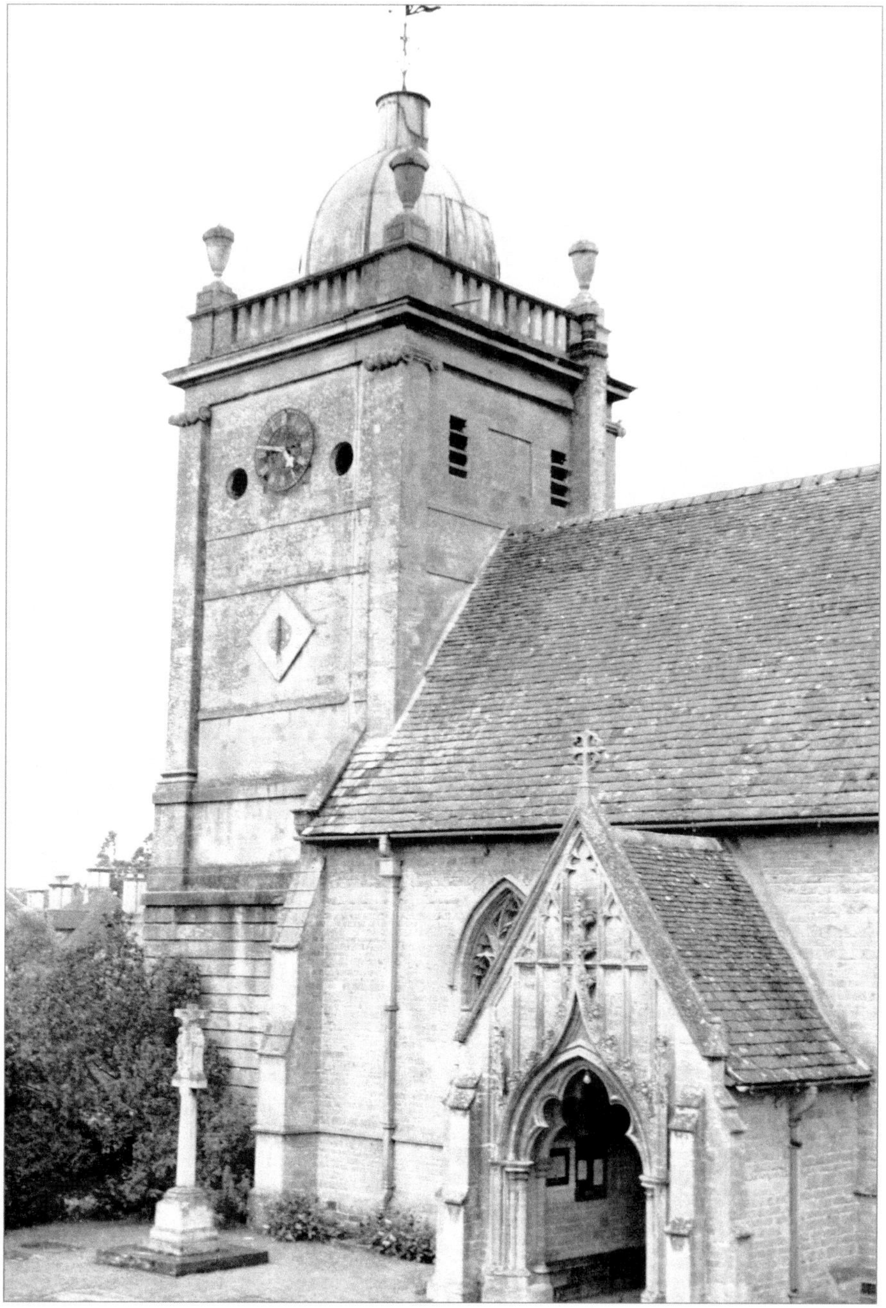

BOURTON-ON-THE-WATER, *St Lawrence's Church c1955* B392046

The hand of all ages has shaped the parish church we see today: rebuilt in Victorian times from a Norman church on Saxon foundations, St Lawrence's retained its late Georgian tower which has an unusual lead-covered dome. Inside there is a chancel and two windows dating from the 14th century.

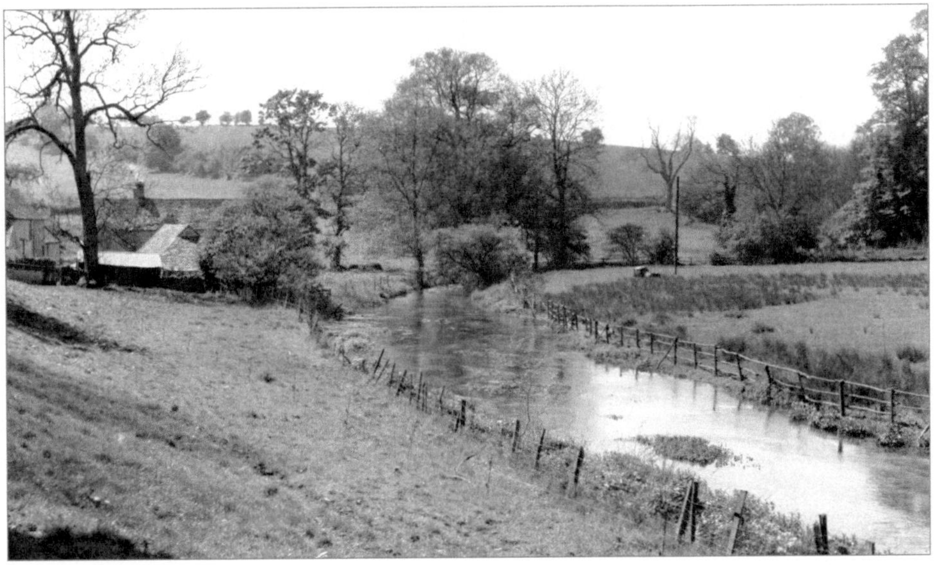

SHERBORNE
The Brook c1960
S762002

On the valley road between Northleach and Burford the village lies along the south bank of the peaceful little Sherborne Brook, from which it got its name.

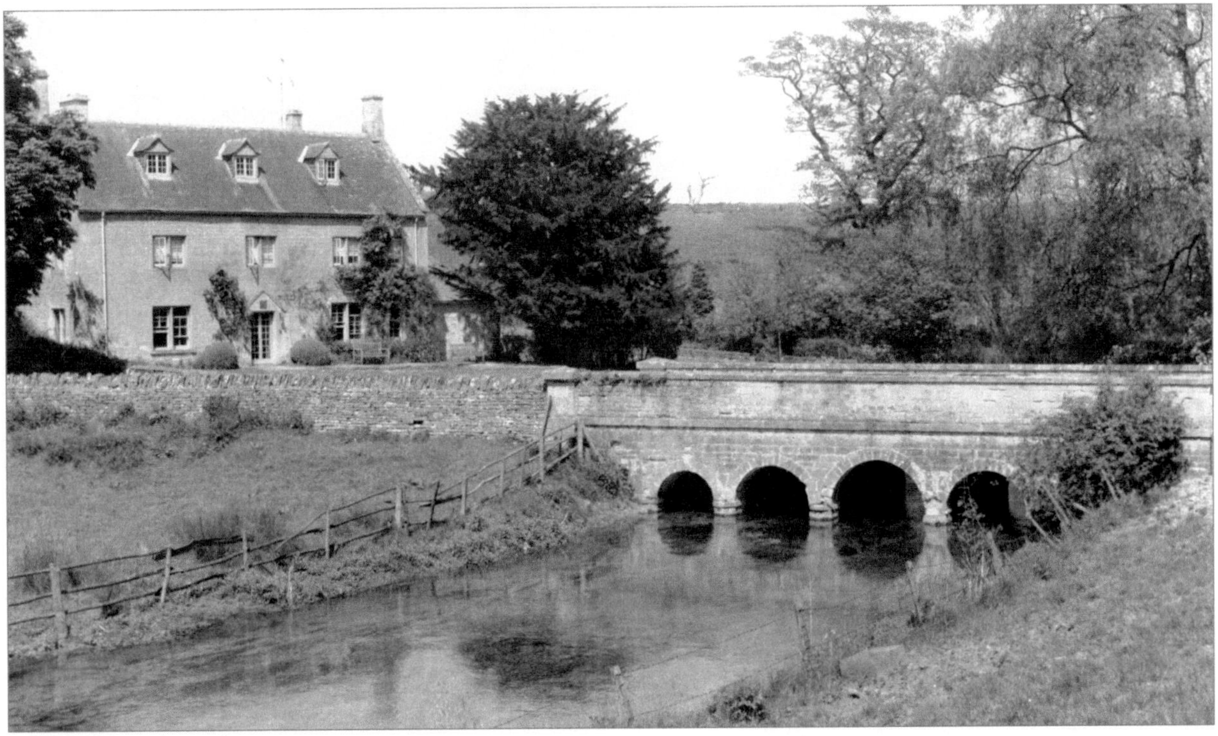

SHERBORNE, *The Bridge c1960* S762001

The road from the village leads to Lodge Park, some two miles away from the spot photographed here. Recently restored to its former 17th-century glory, the lodge was designed as a grandstand for Sir John Dutton, a friend of Oliver Cromwell, for viewing deer coursing in the extensive parkland.

SHERBORNE
The Village c1960
S762017

Sherborne Park separated the village into east and west ends back in the 14th century, but there is a uniformity throughout of well restored cottages, fronted by long well stocked gardens and bounded by traditional Cotswold dry stone walls.

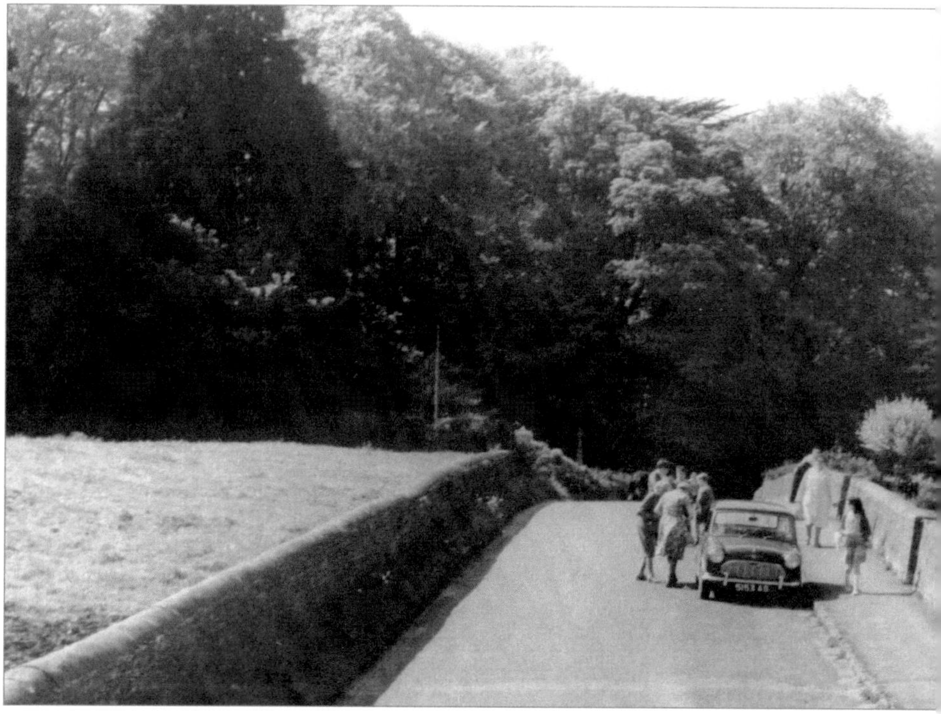

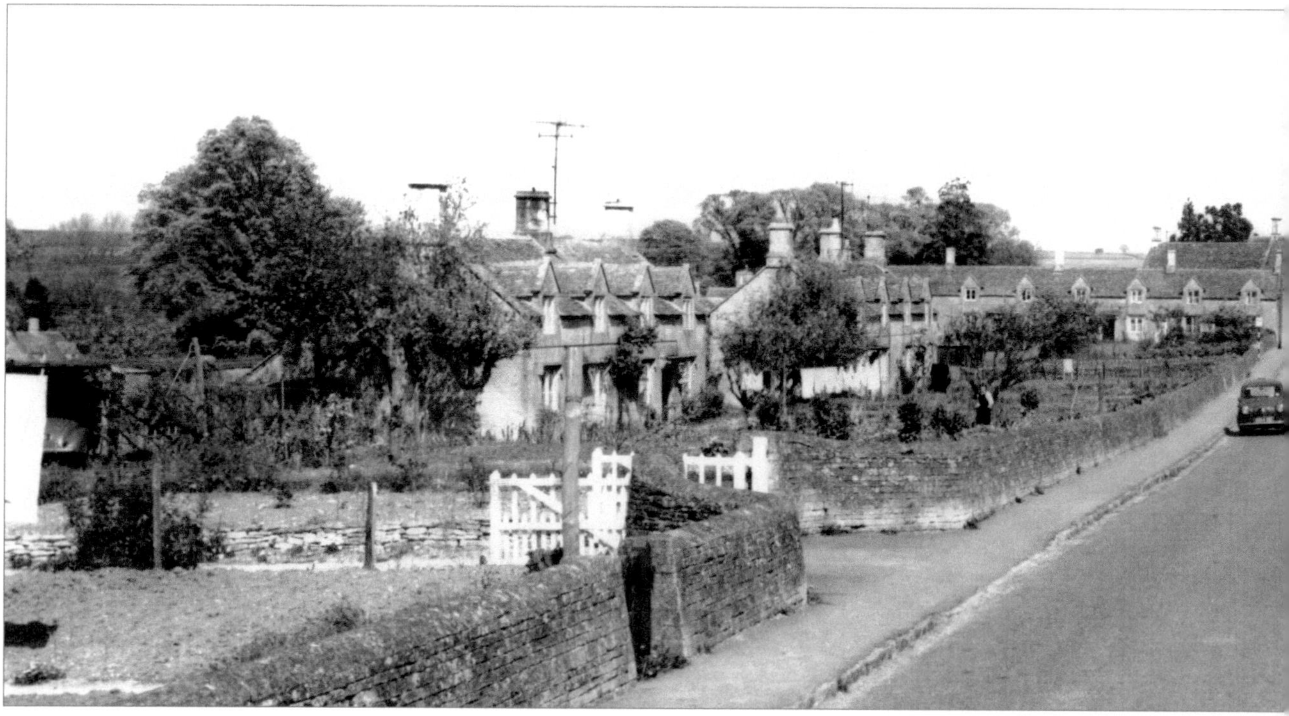

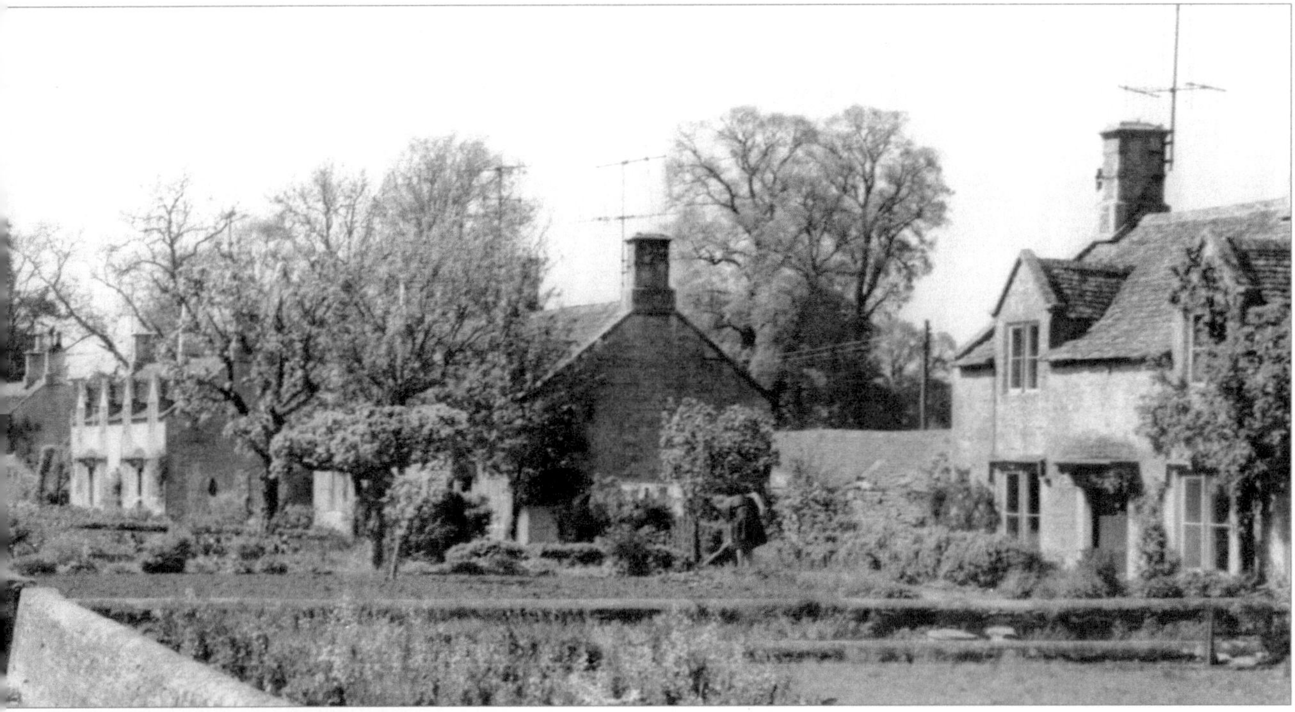

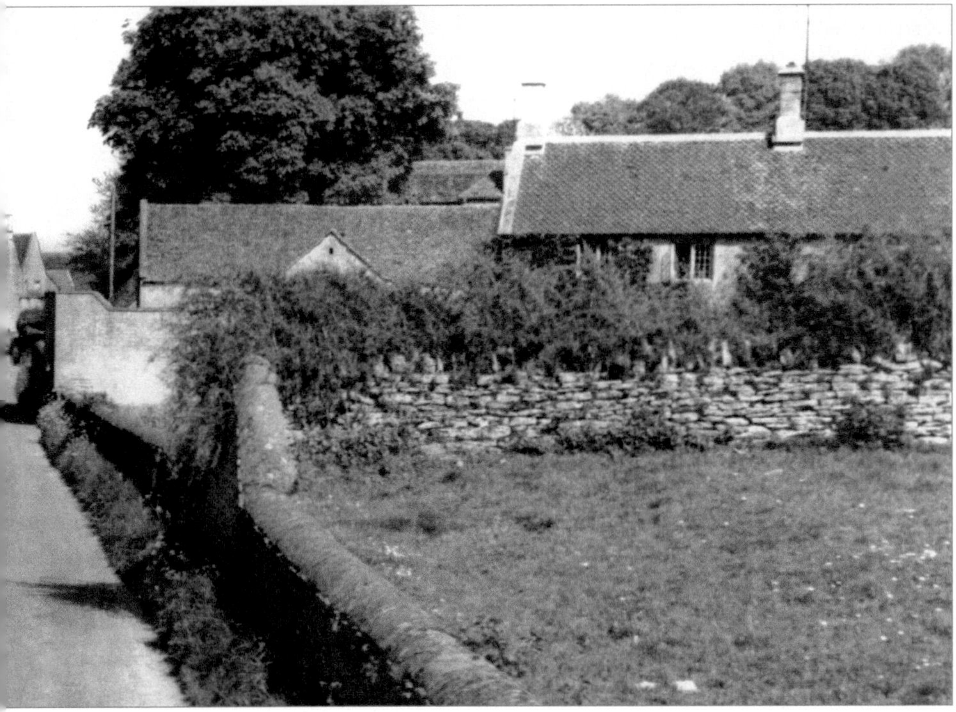

◄ **SHERBORNE**
The Village c1960
S762016

Architectural sleuths will find Number 88 Sherborne of particular interest, as features from the original Norman church have been incorporated in its building.

SHERBORNE
The Memorial c1960
S762018

This is a poignant reminder that even the smallest villages lost a number of sons in the world wars. One son of Sherborne, born in the 18th century, was James Bradley; he achieved fame as the father of modern astronomy, succeeding his friend Halley as Astronomer Royal.

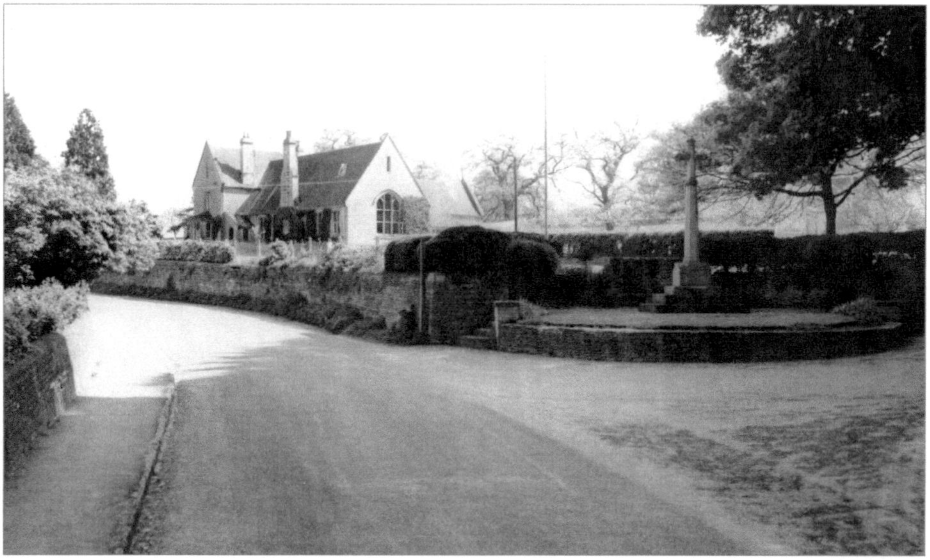

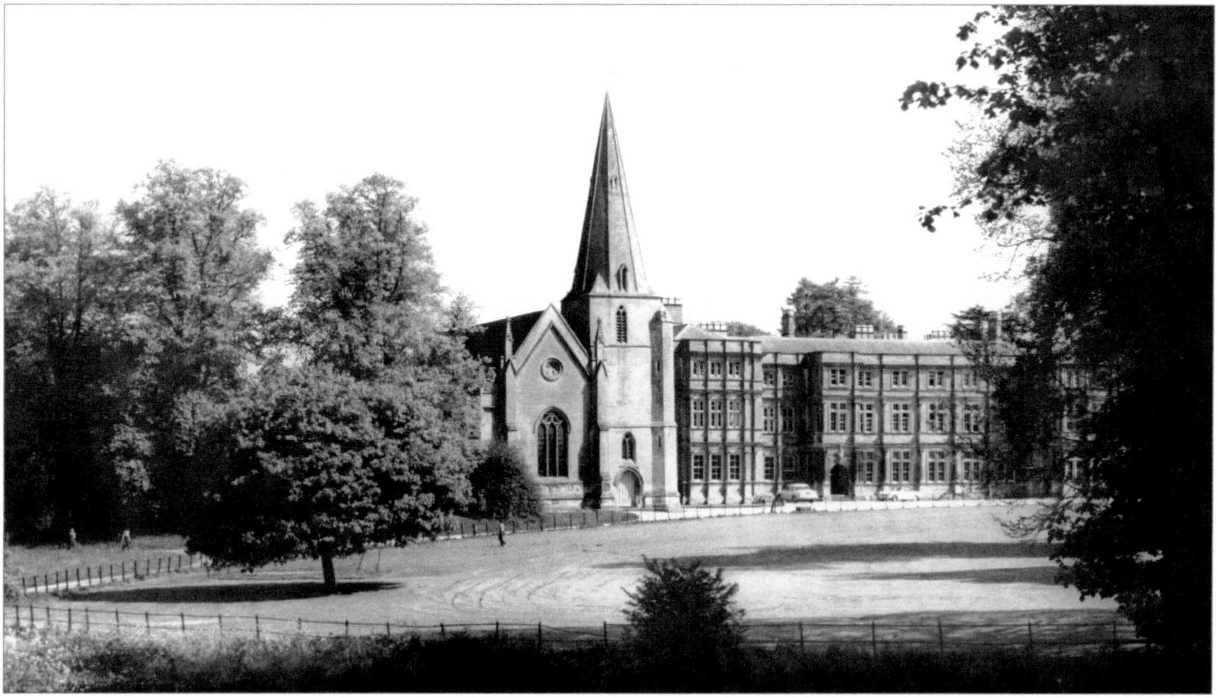

SHERBORNE, *The Church c1960* S762008

The tower and spire of the church of St Mary Magdalene have stood for over six centuries in a lovely parkland setting, although the church has been remodelled several times for successive lords of the manor, who lived in the adjoining Sherborne House. The façade of the mansion is the work of Valentine Strong, a local master mason, whose sons were principal masons in the building of St Paul's Cathedral under Sir Christopher Wren.

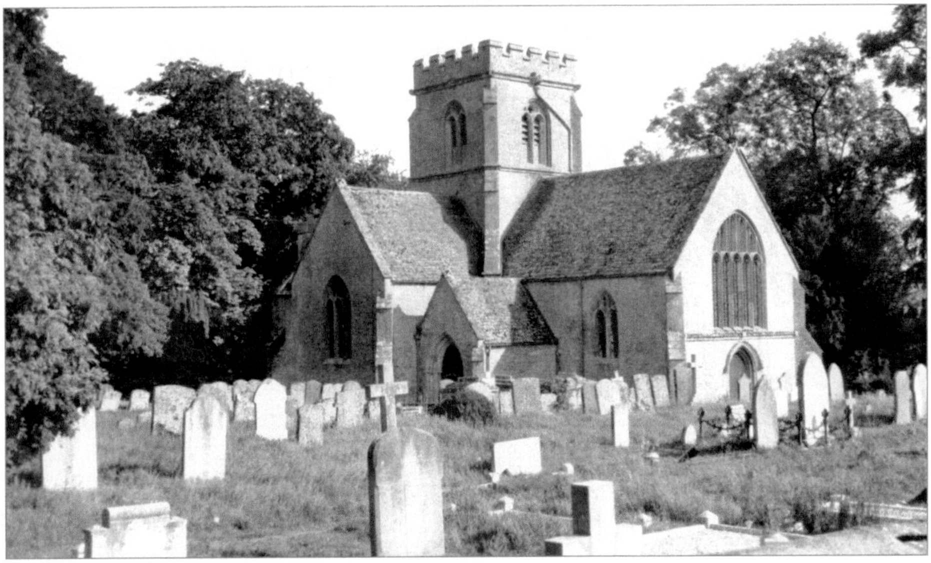

MINSTER LOVELL
The Church c1955
M161001

Minster Lovell is an enchanting village of stone and thatch with its church set above the River Windrush. An effigy of William Lovell, who built the church, is inside - he is shown in armour in what can only be described as a fine example of 15th-century artistry in alabaster.

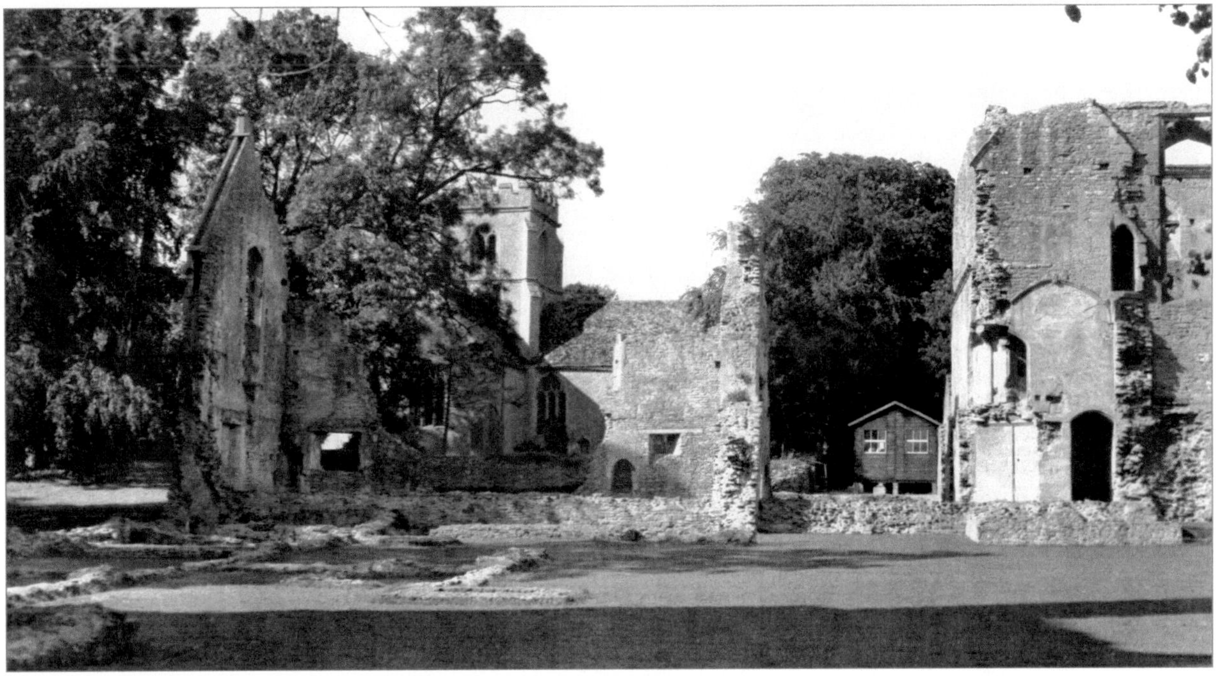

MINSTER LOVELL, *The Manor House Ruins c1955* M161002

Stately in ruin, the Manor House must have been splendid in its prime when it was the home of Francis, Lord Lovell, who sought refuge here after fighting for Lambert Simnel in the 15th century. Repairs to the house in 1708 revealed the skeletons of a man and his dog in a secret chamber - historians pieced together the mystery of Lord Lovell's disappearance, and concluded that the trusty servant who had hidden his master had met with an accident, leaving the young Lovell trapped to starve to death. A board showing the plan of the once magnificent mansion gives a fascinating interpretation of the site.

THE EASTERN EDGE OF EVENLODE AND UNDER THE FOREST

HILAIRE BELLOC and Edward Thomas were both inspired by the valley and villages of the Evenlode to write of their lyrical charms; it is on this eastern dip slope that the Cotswold hills and wolds level out into the plains of Oxfordshire under the shadow of the once great Forest of Wychwood. One of the five forests recorded in Domesday, Wychwood (Hwicca wuda) takes its name from the Hwicca to whom it was home before the Conquest. It was so stocked with deer in the Middle Ages that local poachers could live off more venison in a week than a London alderman could afford in a year. The enclosures of the late Georgian and early Victorian periods finally reduced the vast forest to sparsely wooded outcrops mere fragments of its former size, but still providing an attractive backdrop to the villages that perpetuate its name.

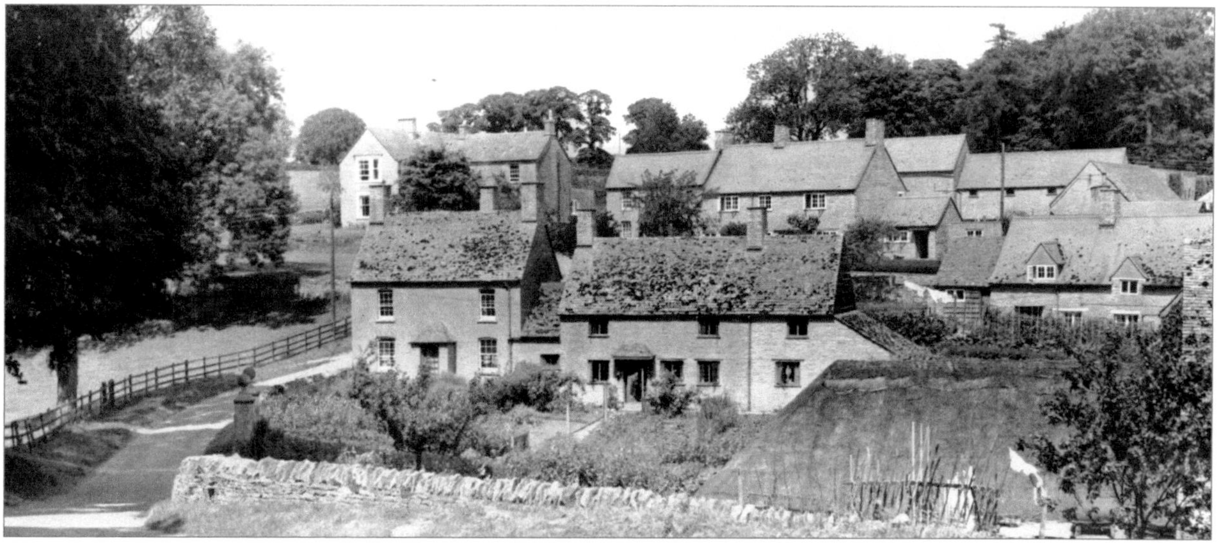

CORNWELL, ***The Village c1965*** C720049

Very much an estate village, Cornwell on the north-eastern periphery of the Cotswolds underwent full-scale modernisation of its cottages in the 1930s, when its American owner commissioned Sir Clough Williams-Ellis to create a model village.

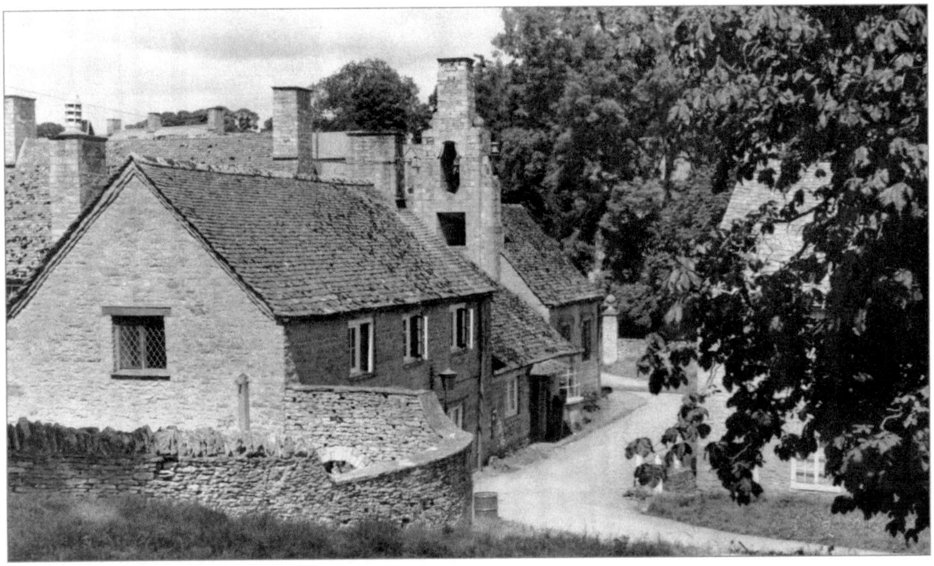

CORNWELL
The Village c1960
C720050

The parish church of this re-modelled village dates back to Norman times and has a 13th-century font. Its interesting chandeliers were designed by Sir Clough Williams-Ellis, who is best known for creating the famous Welsh village of Portmeirion.

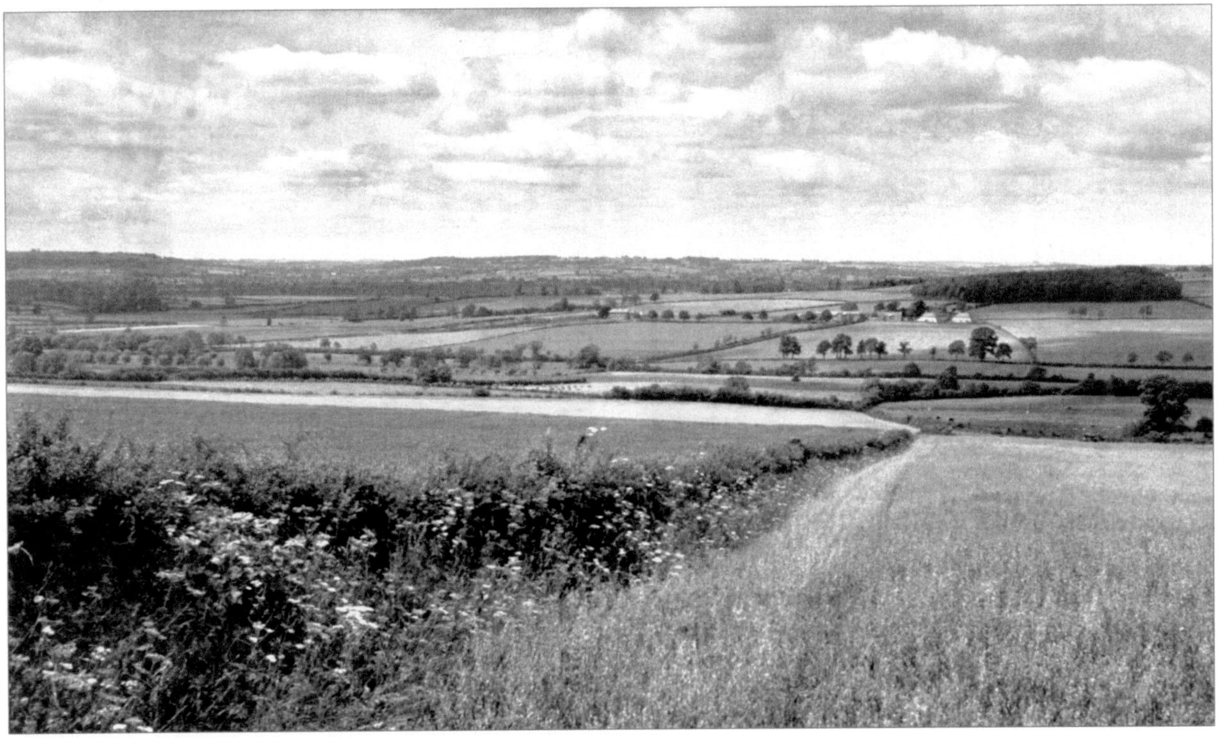

CHURCHILL, *The Cotswolds from the Village c1960* C290002

Hare coursing was a popular sport in this area of sweeping open spaces in the 1930s. The farming fraternity started the day's hunt with their greyhounds at the Chequers Inn at Churchill.

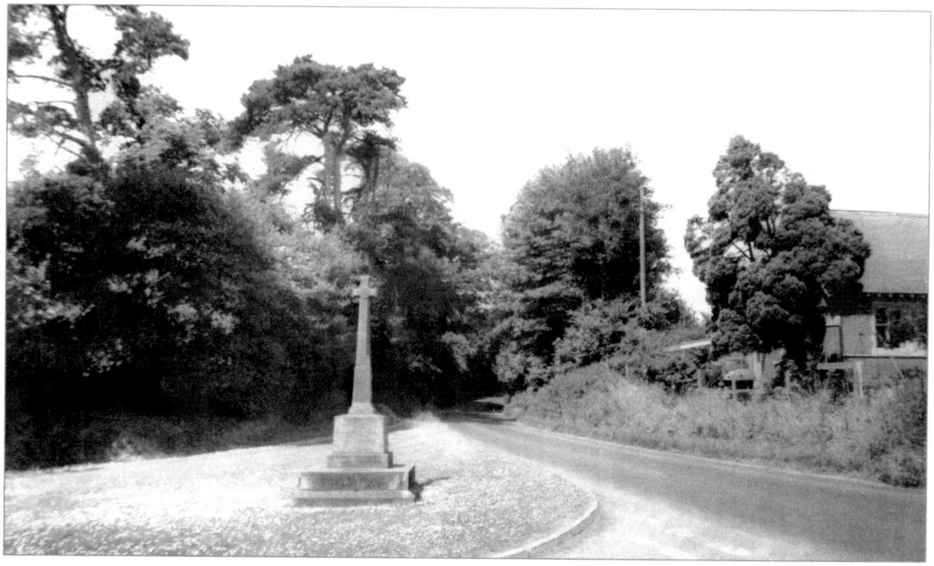

CHURCHILL
The Memorial c1960
C290005

The war memorial stands sentinel at the approach to this small village, which boasts many fine buildings. It is known today for its independent furniture workshops. The parish church was modelled on the Oxford buildings where Cotswold stone was used to full advantage. Inside the church is a memorial to William Smith, who was the founder of modern geology.

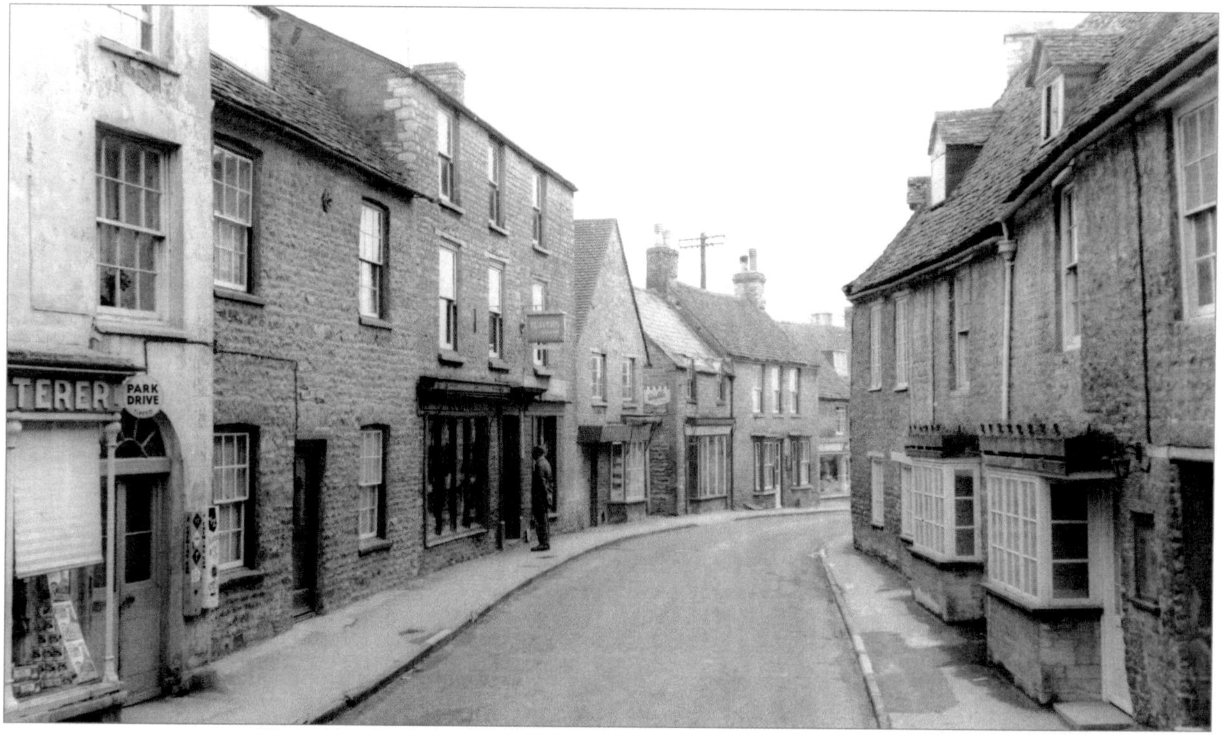

CHARLBURY, *Sheep Street c1965* C444025

One of Charlbury's treasured assets must be that it retains its delightful little country station. The coming of the railway must have been an enormous advantage for transporting livestock to and from its market; the importance of sheep in the rural economy can be traced in the naming of this street.

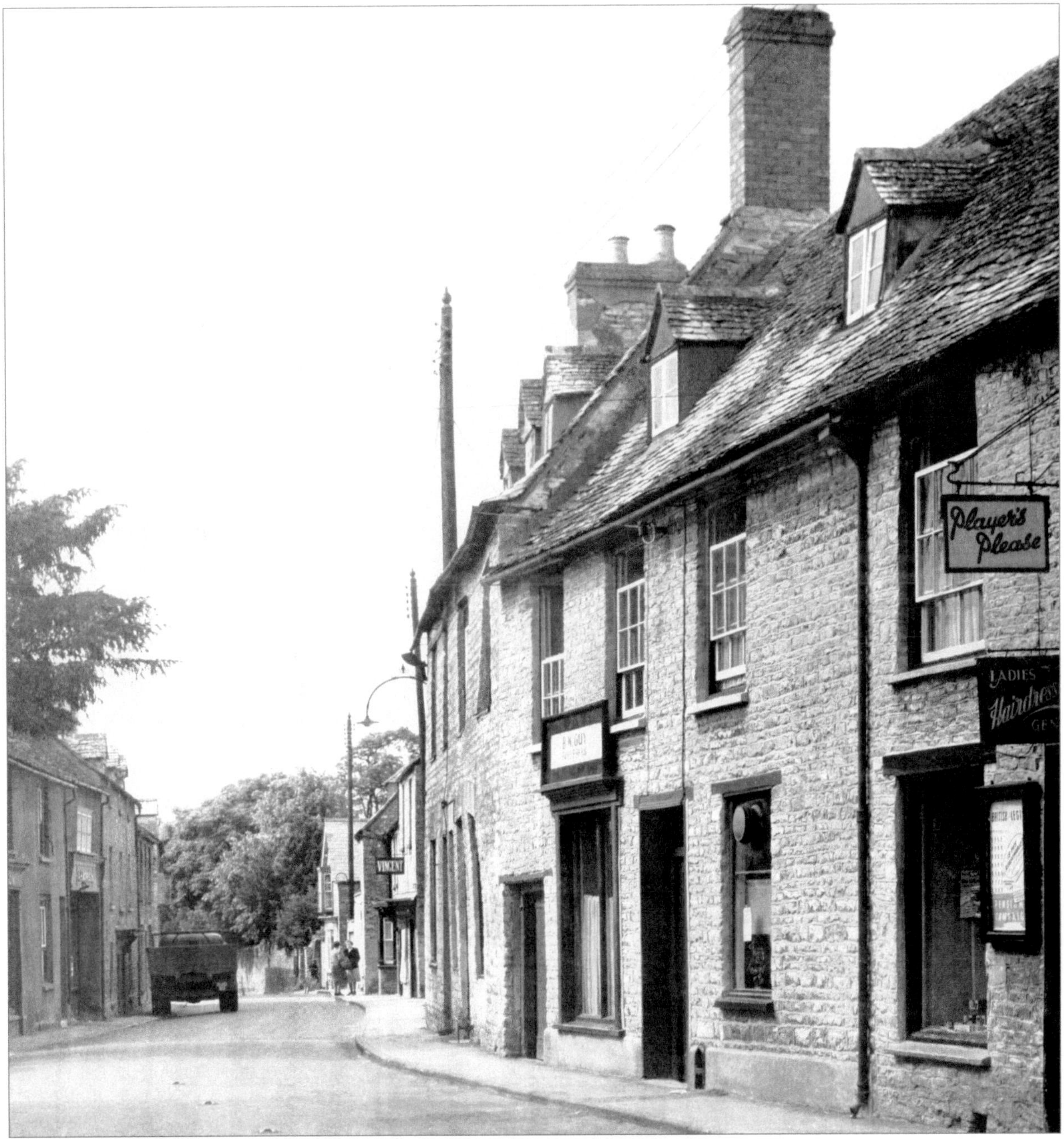

CHARLBURY, *Market Street c1955* C444001

The fact that Charlbury was a market centre, from which this street is named, gives some idea of the size of this large village. One of the most bizarre sales ever made here is that of a husband leading his wife in a halter to the market in 1843 and selling her for half a crown! It is recorded that the deal was celebrated between the vendor, the wife and the buyer in the 16th-century Bull Inn.

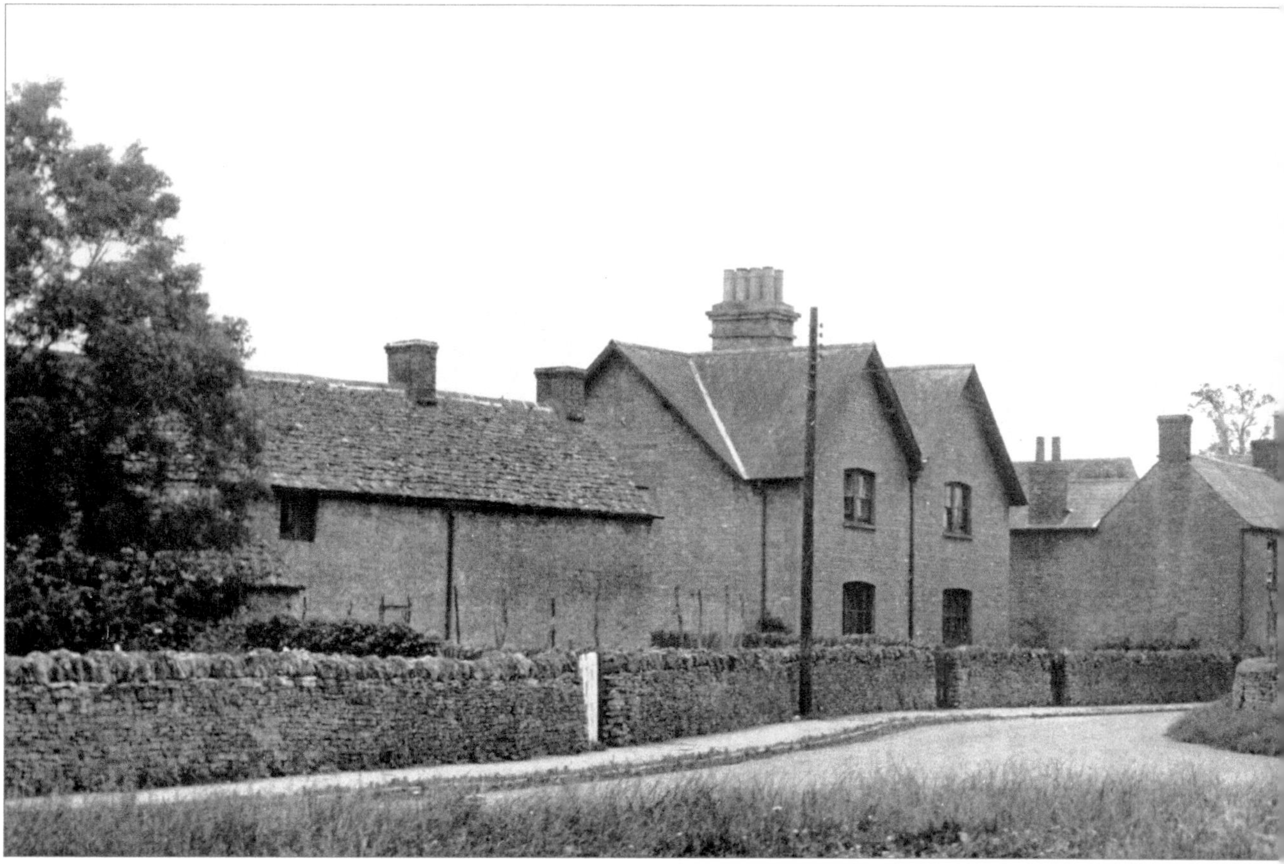

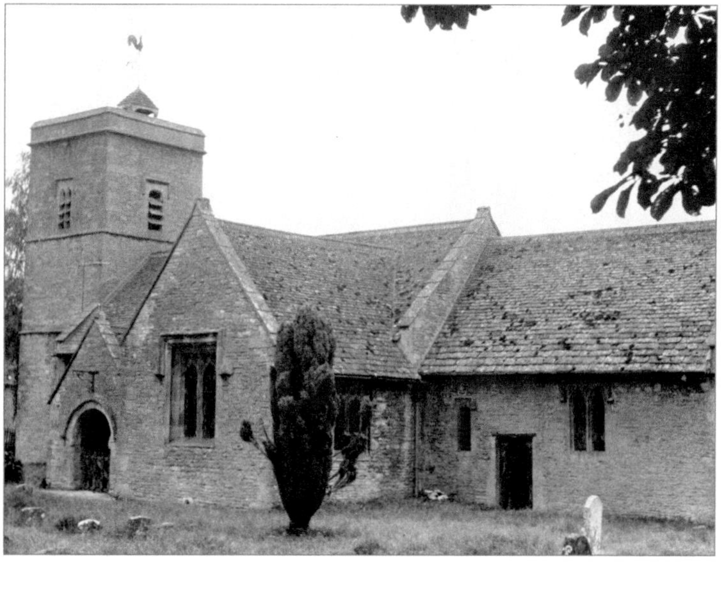

ASCOTT-UNDER-WYCHWOOD
The Church c1950 A140005

Midway between the ancient sites of two Norman motte and bailey castles at the extreme ends of the village, Holy Trinity Church is the topographical as well as the spiritual centre of Ascott; old stone houses are grouped round it on all sides. There are traces of all ages in its fabric and furnishings - but most striking is the tapestry covering the west door, which was worked by local people and depicts the village as it is today. Here, pictured with approaching a million stitches, is the parish at work and play, at church and home: the Scouts and Cubs and various clubs, the farms, the train that does not halt at Ascott Halt but can be heard rumbling its way past the village, the Morris dancers, and the Ascott Martyrs - a delightful commemoration of the small community.

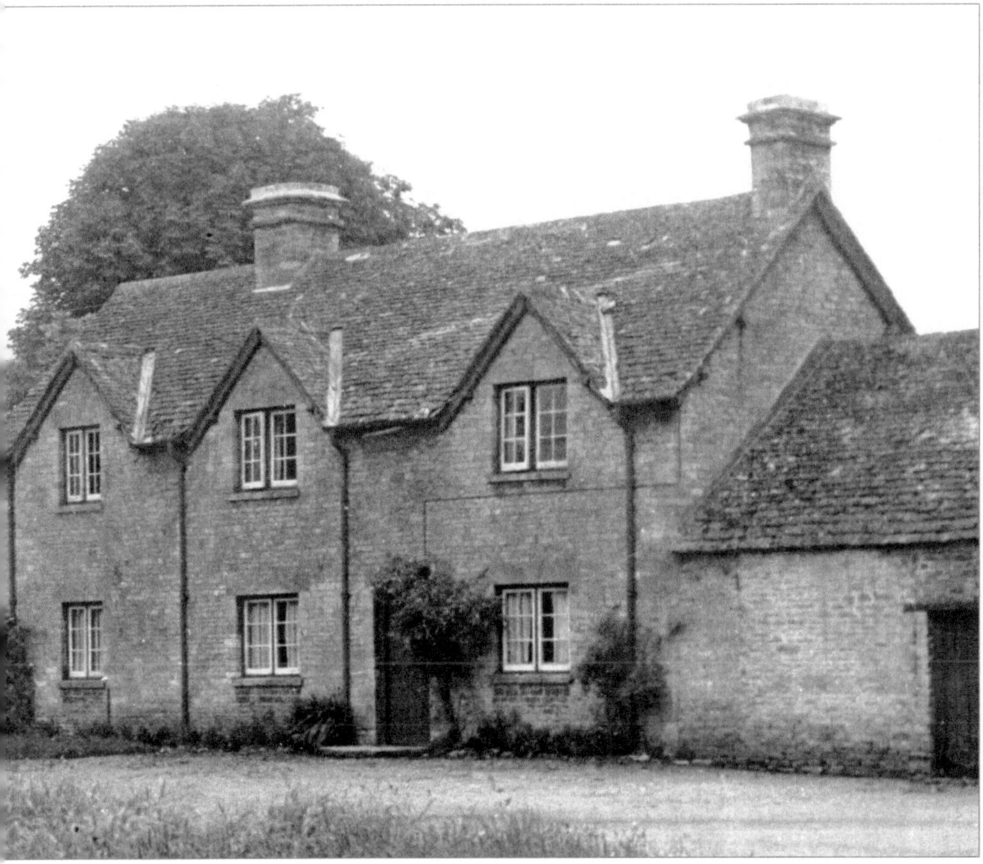

ASCOTT-UNDER-WYCHWOOD
The Green c1960
A140003

This scene is still instantly recognisable from the green, where seats encircle a shade giving tree. Behind the spot where the photographer must have stood is Windrush Valley School, founded in 1951, and the low building on the extreme right of the picture, next to the three-gabled house, is the Forge Garage - all indications of meeting the demands of an increased village population over the last few decades. At Domesday there were 26 people recorded here. The number had doubled by the 13th century, and the coming of the railway in 1853 brought new employment to the village that suffered, like many others, during the agricultural depression.

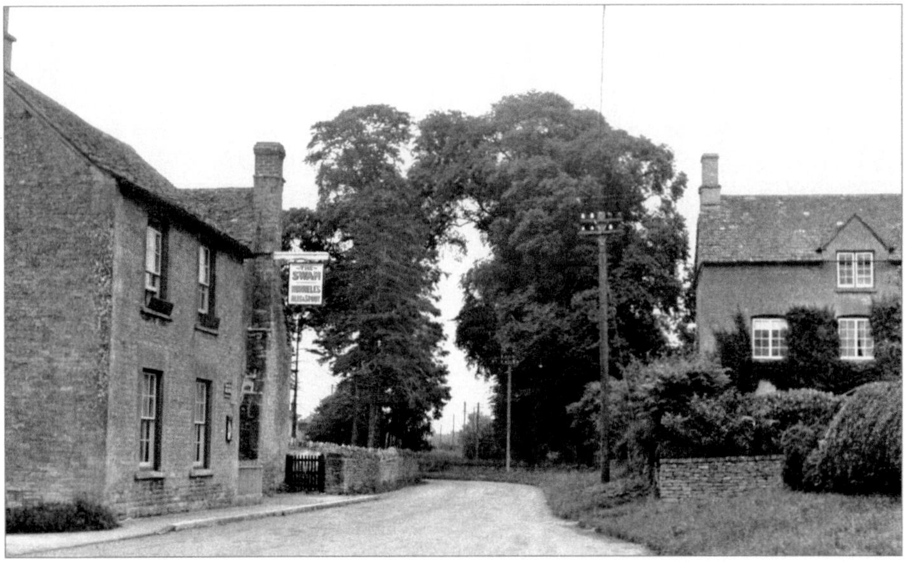

ASCOTT-UNDER-WYCHWOOD
The Swan c1950
A140008

Very much a village pub, the Swan has a beer garden at the back to cater for the local populace, who number around 500, and visitors who come this way to walk round this quiet spot. Beyond the Swan the road forks at the Green within sight of a railway level crossing.

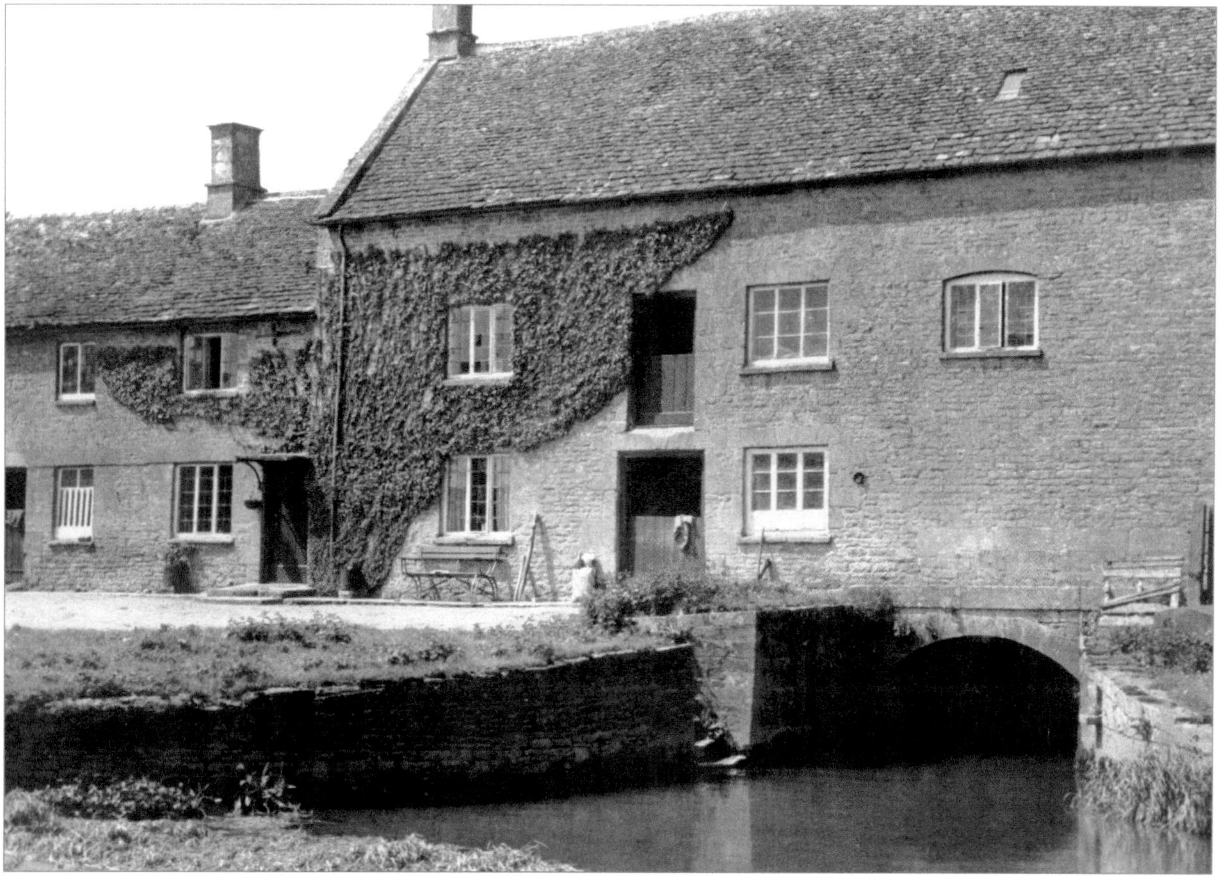

ASCOTT-UNDER-WYCHWOOD
Langley Mill c1950 A140011

The village had its own mill, Ascott Mill, at one time; Langley Mill, shown here, was outside the village, nudging the Shipton-under-Wychwood border - the River Evenlode marks the parish boundary. Although Langley is now a private residence, the mill machinery was dismantled and used for its original purpose elsewhere.

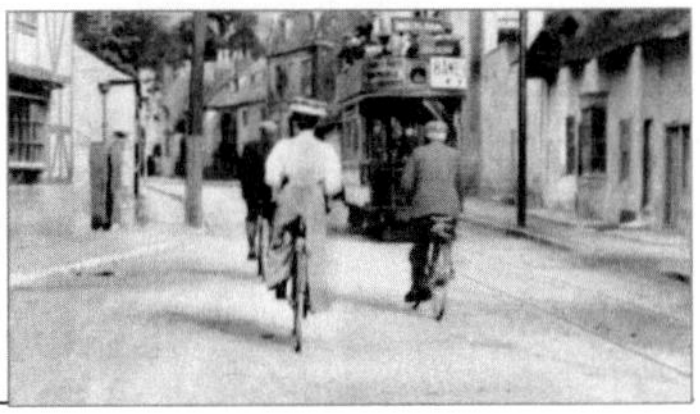

INDEX

FRITH PRODUCTS & SERVICES

Francis Frith would doubtless be pleased to know that the pioneering publishing venture he started in 1860 still continues today. Over a hundred and forty years later, The Francis Frith Collection continues in the same innovative tradition and is now one of the foremost publishers of vintage photographs in the world. Some of the current activities include:

INTERIOR DECORATION

Today Frith's photographs can be seen framed and as giant wall murals in thousands of pubs, restaurants, hotels, banks, retail stores and other public buildings throughout the country. In every case they enhance the unique local atmosphere of the places they depict and provide reminders of gentler days in an increasingly busy and frenetic world.

PRODUCT PROMOTIONS

Frith products are used by many major companies to promote the sales of their own products or to reinforce their own history and heritage. Frith promotions have been used by Hovis bread, Courage beers, Scots Porage Oats, Colman's mustard, Cadbury's foods, Mellow Birds coffee, Dunhill pipe tobacco, Guinness, and Bulmer's Cider.

GENEALOGY AND FAMILY HISTORY

As the interest in family history and roots grows world-wide, more and more people are turning to Frith's photographs of Great Britain for images of the towns, villages and streets where their ancestors lived; and, of course, photographs of the churches and chapels where their ancestors were christened, married and buried are an essential part of every genealogy tree and family album.

FRITH PRODUCTS

All Frith photographs are available Framed or just as Mounted Prints and Posters (size 23 x 16 inches). These may be ordered from the address below. Other products available are - Address Books, Calendars, Jigsaws, Canvas Prints, Postcards and local and prestige books.

THE INTERNET

Already ninety thousand Frith photographs can be viewed and purchased on the internet through the Frith websites and a myriad of partner sites.

For more detailed information on Frith products, look at this site:
www.francisfrith.com

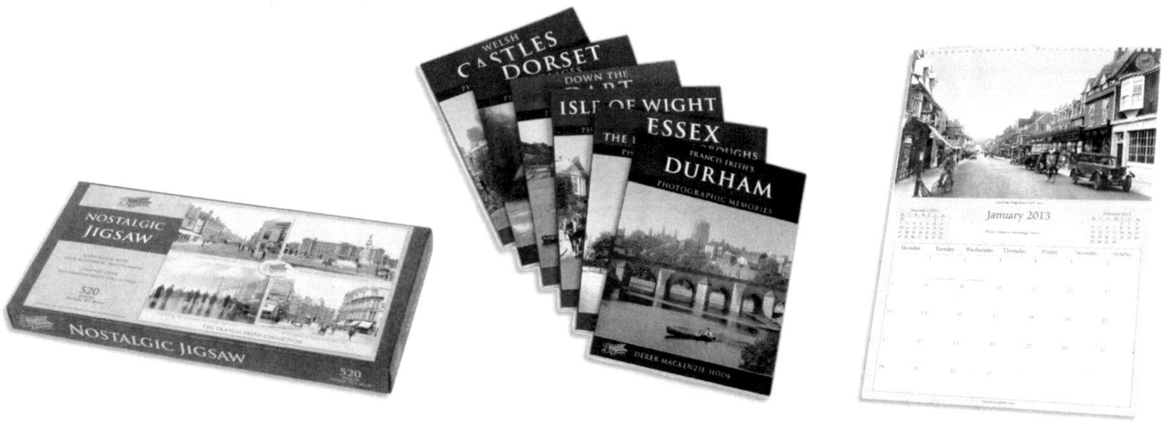

See the complete list of Frith Books at: www.francisfrith.com
This web site is regularly updated with the latest list of publications from The Francis Frith Collection. If you wish to buy books relating to another part of the country that your local bookshop does not stock, you may purchase on-line.

For further information, trade, or author enquiries please contact us at the address below:
The Francis Frith Collection, Unit 6, Oakley Business Park, Wylye Road, Dinton, Wiltshire SP3 5EU.
Tel: +44 (0)1722 716 376 Fax: +44 (0)1722 716 881 Email: sales@francisfrith.co.uk

See Frith products on the internet at www.francisfrith.com

Free Print - see overleaf

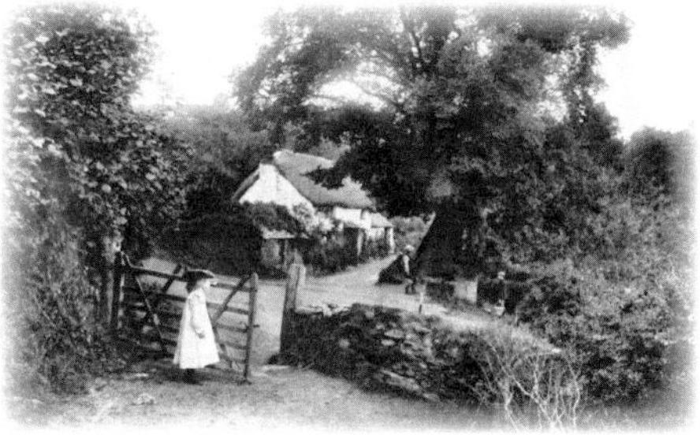

Can you help us with information about any of the Frith photographs in this book?

We are gradually compiling an historical record for each of the photographs in the Frith archive. It is always fascinating to find out the names of the people shown in the pictures, as well as insights into the shops, buildings and other features depicted.

If you recognize anyone in the photographs in this book, or if you have information not already included in the author's caption, do let us know. We would love to hear from you, and will try to publish it in future books or articles.

An Invitation from The Francis Frith Collection to Share Your Memories

The 'Share Your Memories' feature of our website allows members of the public to add personal memories relating to the places featured in our photographs, or comment on others already added. Seeing a place from your past can rekindle forgotten or long held memories. Why not visit the website, find photographs of places you know well and add YOUR story for others to read and enjoy? We would love to hear from you!

www.francisfrith.com/memories

Our production team

Frith books are produced by a small dedicated team at offices near Salisbury. Most have worked with the Frith Collection for many years. All have in common one quality: they have a passion for the Frith Collection.

Frith Books and Gifts

We have a wide range of books and gifts available on our website utilising our photographic archive, many of which can be individually personalised.

www.francisfrith.com

FF013033

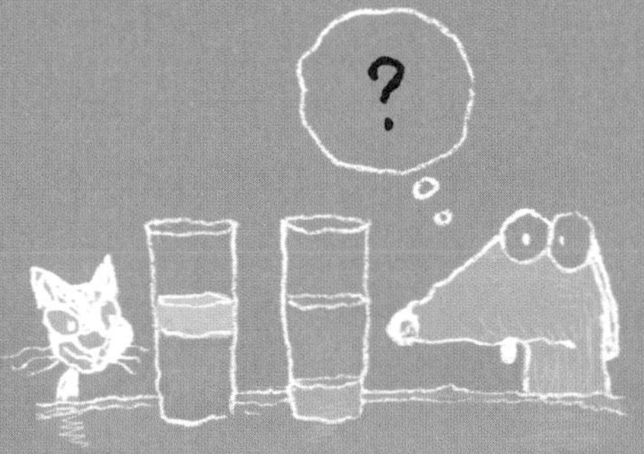

Η πρώτη μου Εγκυκλοπαίδεια για τις **ΕΠΙΣΤΗΜΕΣ** Larousse

Η **ΖΩΗ** ΚΑΙ Η **ΓΗ**

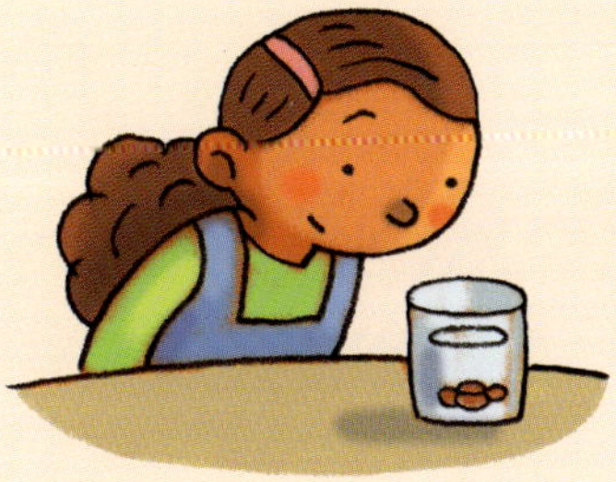

ΕΙΚΟΝΟΓΡΑΦΗΣΕΙΣ

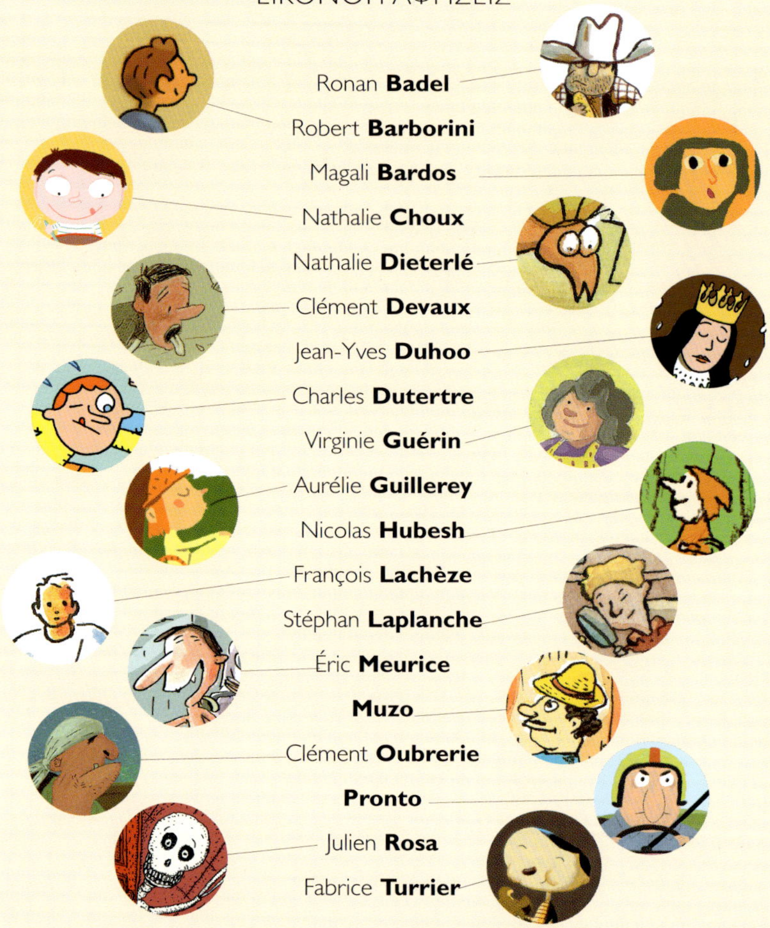

Ronan **Badel**
Robert **Barborini**
Magali **Bardos**
Nathalie **Choux**
Nathalie **Dieterlé**
Clément **Devaux**
Jean-Yves **Duhoo**
Charles **Dutertre**
Virginie **Guérin**
Aurélie **Guillerey**
Nicolas **Hubesh**
François **Lachèze**
Stéphan **Laplanche**
Éric **Meurice**
Muzo
Clément **Oubrerie**
Pronto
Julien **Rosa**
Fabrice **Turrier**

Εικονογράφηση εξωφύλλου: Émile **Bravo**

Σύνταξη: Pascal **Chauvel**
Επιστημονικός σύμβουλος: Éric **Mathivet**
Παιδαγωγικός σύμβουλος: Valérie **Faggiolo**
Καλλιτεχνική διεύθυνση: Frédéric **Houssin** & Cédric **Ramadier**
Γραφική σύλληψη και αναπαράσταση: **DOUBLE**
Χώρα παραγωγής: **Μαλαισία**

Η πρώτη μου Εγκυκλοπαίδεια για τις ΕΠΙΣΤΗΜΕΣ Larousse. Η ΖΩΗ ΚΑΙ Η ΓΗ
Πρώτη έκδοση Οκτώβριος 2005 – *Δεύτερη έκδοση* Μάρτιος 2009
Μετάφραση Εύη Γεροκώστα
Φιλολογική επιμέλεια και επιμέλεια μετάφρασης Εύη Παραδείση
ISBN 978-960-375-821-1 ΒΟΗΘ. ΚΩΔ. ΜΗΧ/ΣΗΣ 3821 Κ.Ε.Π. 1699 Κ.ΕΞ. 016/09

Εκδόσεις ΜΕΤΑΙΧΜΙΟ
Ιπποκράτους 118, 114 72 Αθήνα, τηλ.: 211 3003500, fax: 211 3003562, http://www.metaixmio.gr • e-mail: metaixmio@metaixmio.gr
Κεντρική διάθεση Ασκληπιού 18, 106 80 Αθήνα, τηλ.: 210 3647433, fax: 210 3610750
Υποκατάστημα Βόρειας Ελλάδας Ολύμπου 81, 546 31 Θεσσαλονίκη, τηλ.: 2310 250075, 2310 260085, fax: 2310 260085

Η πρώτη μου Εγκυκλοπαίδεια για τις ΕΠΙΣΤΗΜΕΣ Larousse

Η ΖΩΗ ΚΑΙ Η ΓΗ

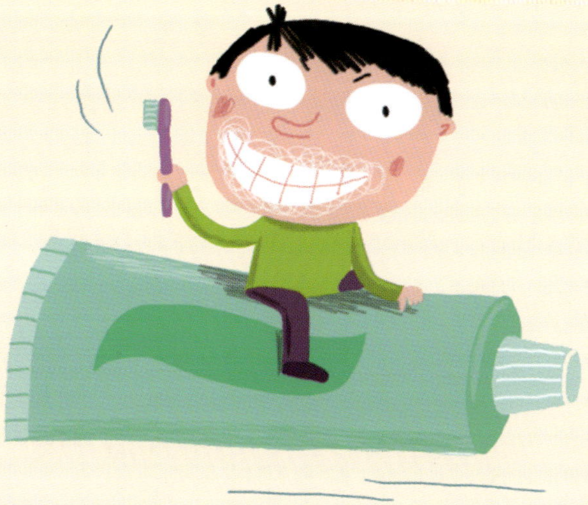

ΜΕΤΑΙΧΜΙΟ

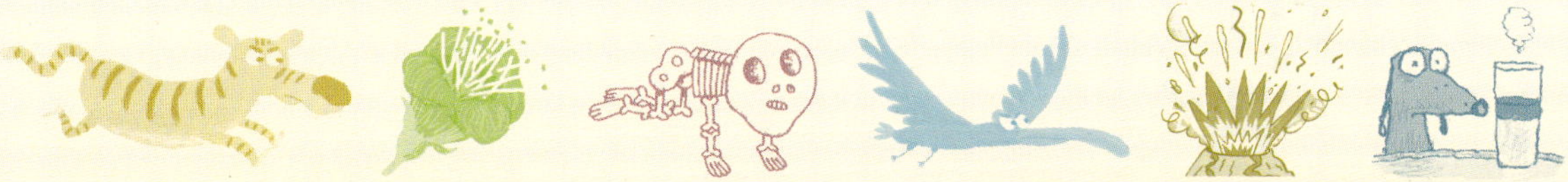

ΠΕΡΙΕΧΟΜΕΝΑ

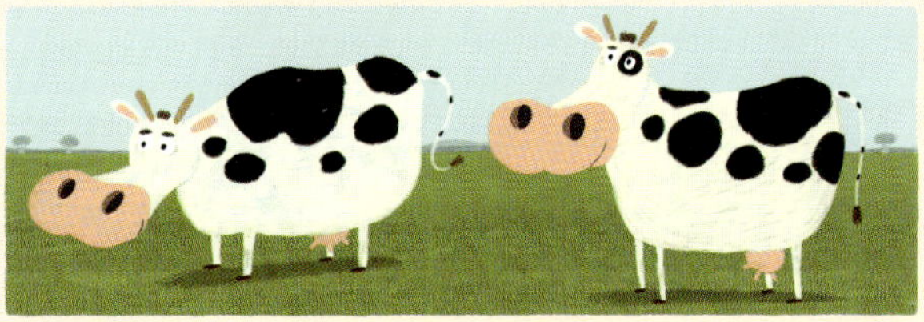

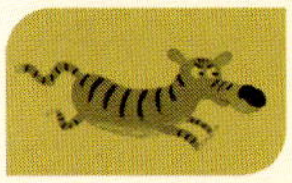

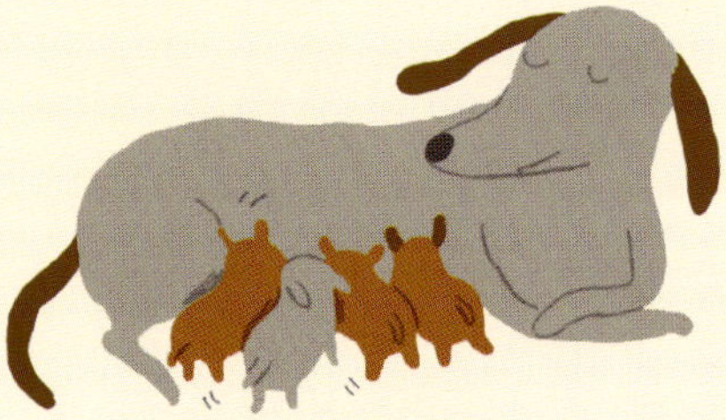

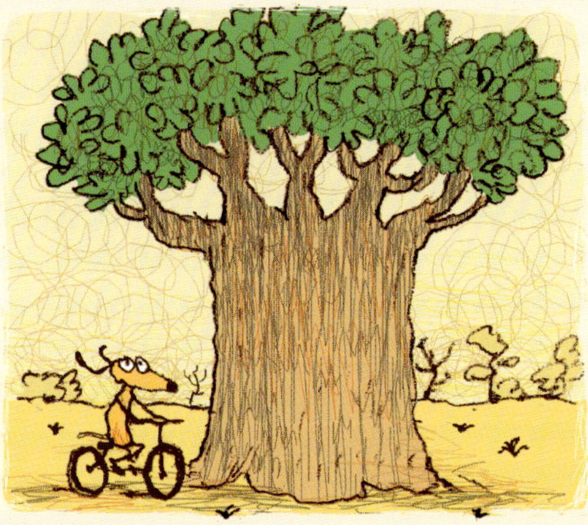

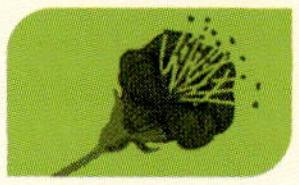

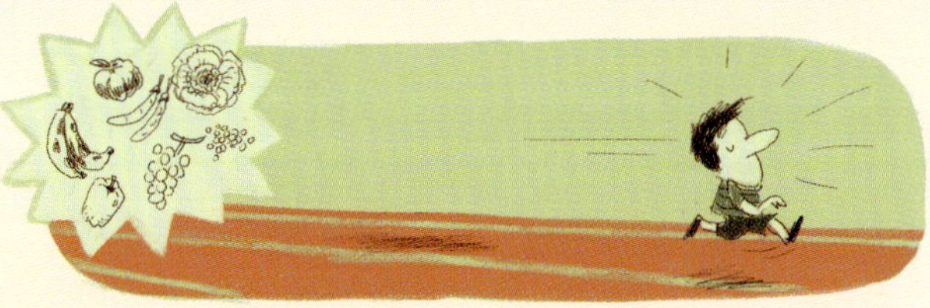

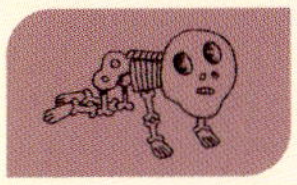

72-113
Η ΖΩΗ ΤΟΥ ΣΩΜΑΤΟΣ

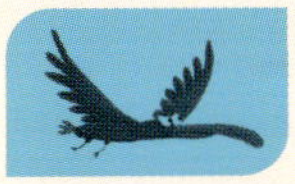

114-123
Η ΟΙΚΟΛΟΓΙΑ

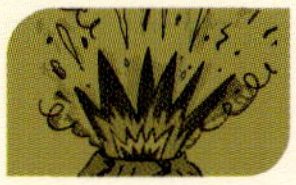

124-145
Η ΓΕΩΛΟΓΙΑ

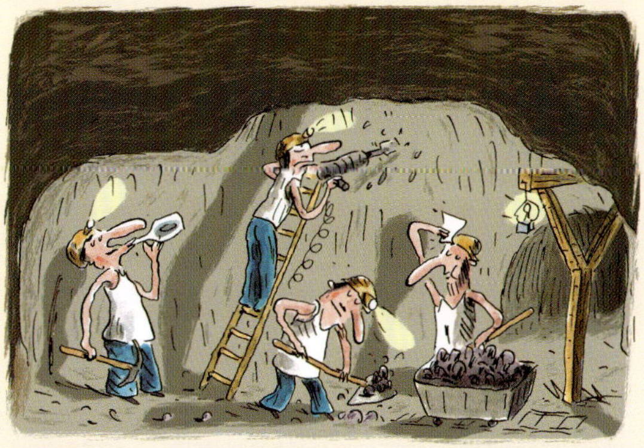

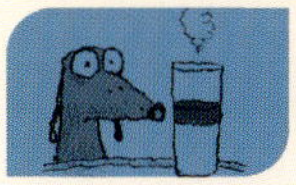

146-155
ΤΟ ΝΕΡΟ

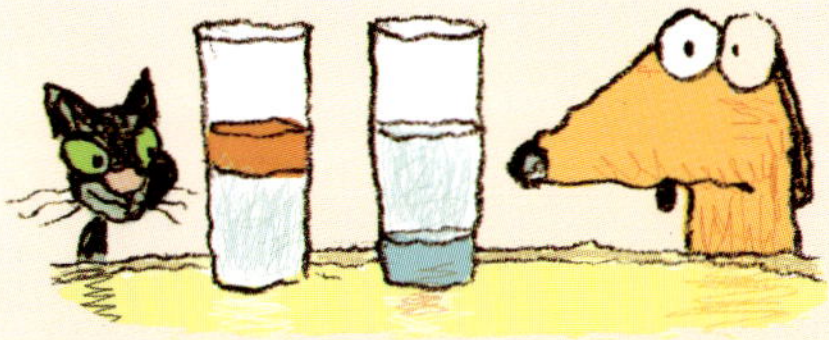

Η επιστήμη της ζωής

Η επιστήμη της ζωής είναι η βιολογία. Η βιολογία μελετά όλους τους ζωντανούς οργανισμούς: τα ζώα, τα φυτά, το ανθρώπινο σώμα.

Ό,τι κινείται δεν είναι απαραίτητα ζωντανό: ένα ρομπότ, ένα μόμπιλο, ένα αυτοκίνητο κινούνται, όμως δεν είναι ζωντανοί οργανισμοί· αντίθετα, ένα δέντρο είναι ζωντανός οργανισμός, παρόλο που δεν κινείται.

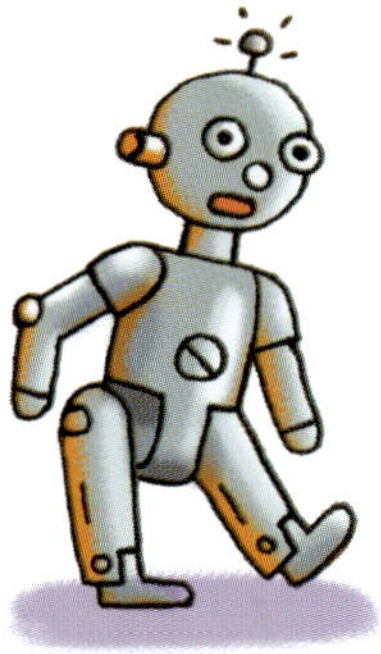
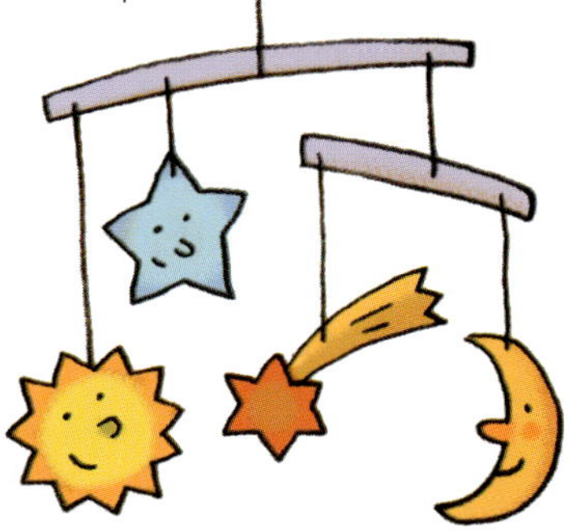
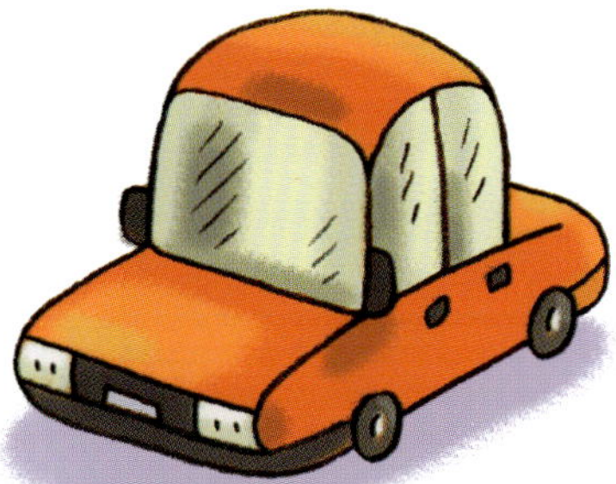

Ένα **ρομπότ**, ένα **μόμπιλο**, ένα **αυτοκίνητο**, παρόλο που **κινούνται**, δεν είναι ζωντανοί οργανισμοί.

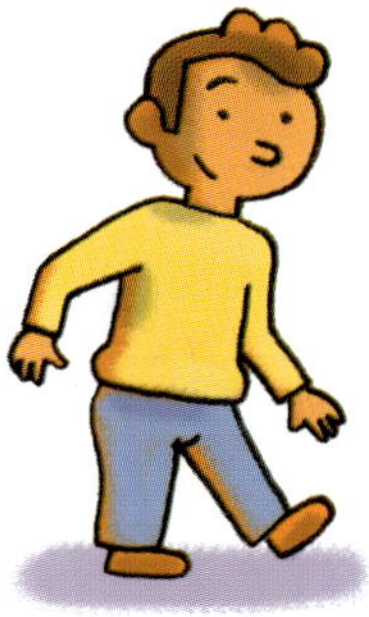
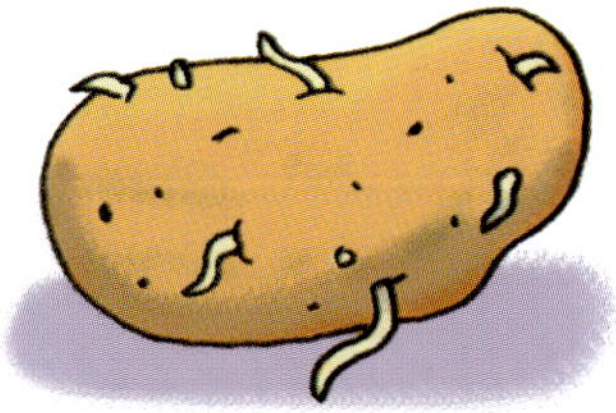
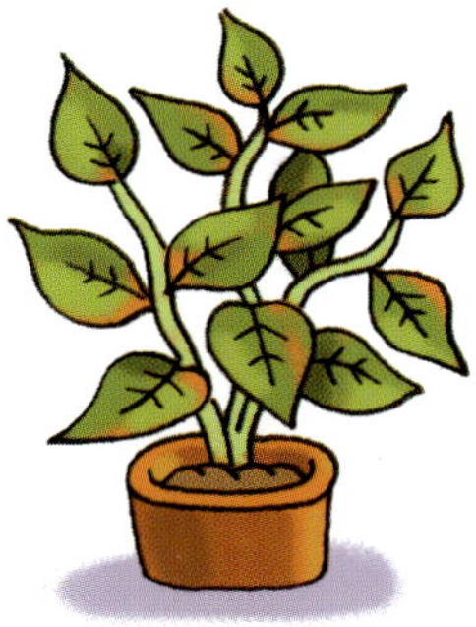

Όπως αυτό το **αγοράκι**, έτσι και μια **πατάτα** και ένα **πράσινο φυτό** είναι ζωντανοί οργανισμοί, παρόλο που **δεν κινούνται**.

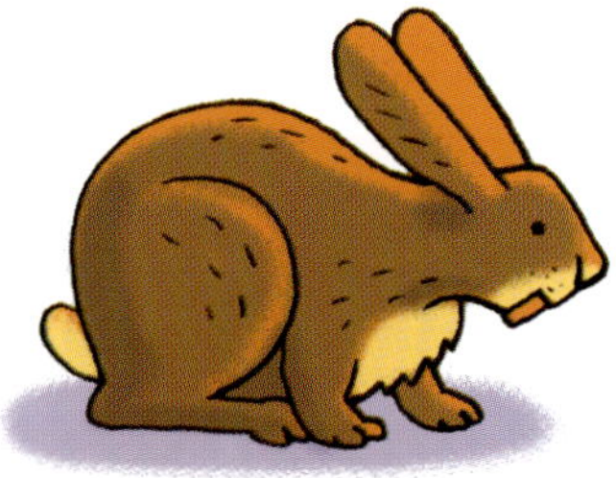
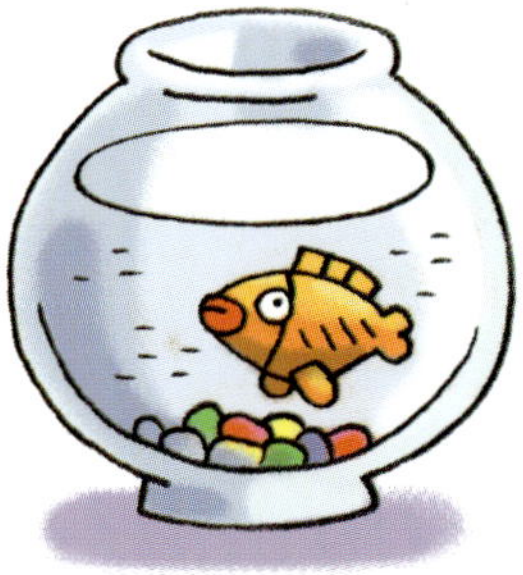
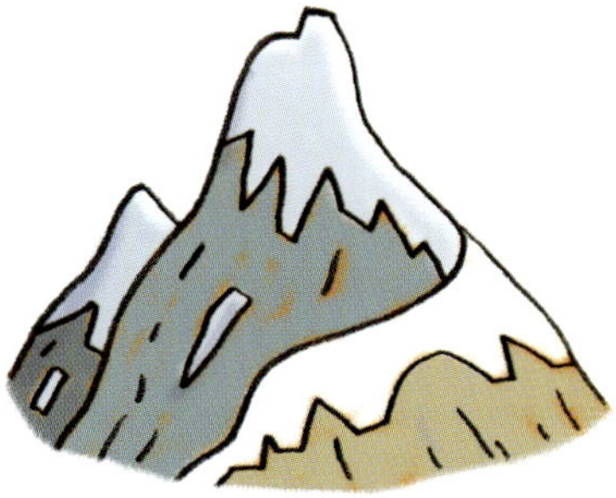

Ο **λαγός**, το **χρυσόψαρο** είναι **ζωντανοί οργανισμοί**... **όχι** όμως **το βουνό**.

Όπως οι **άνθρωποι**, τα **ζώα** και τα **φυτά** είναι και αυτά **ζωντανοί οργανισμοί**.
Τρέφονται, μεγαλώνουν και αναπαράγονται.

Οι ζωντανοί οργανισμοί

αναπνέουν
Για να ζήσουν, τα φυτά, τα ζώα και οι άνθρωποι πρέπει να αναπνέουν.

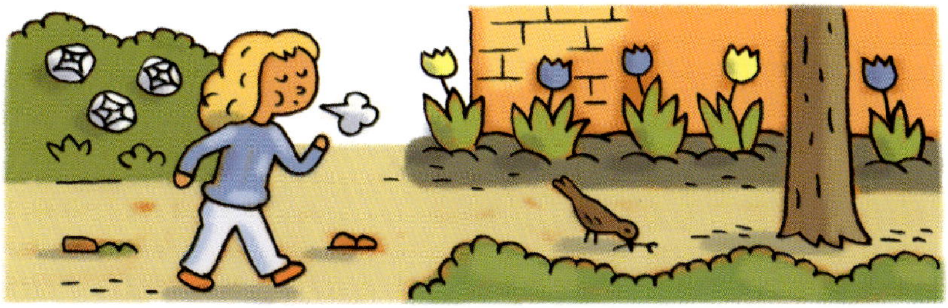

τρέφονται
Για να ζήσουν, τα φυτά, τα ζώα και οι άνθρωποι χρειάζονται ενέργεια. Αυτή την ενέργεια τους τη δίνει η τροφή.

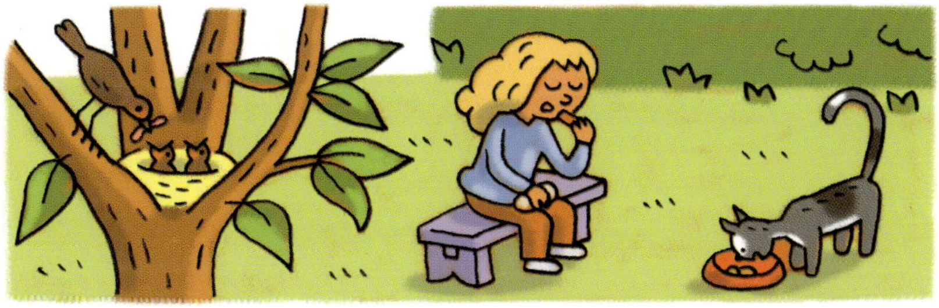

αναπαράγονται
Τα ζώα γεννούν μικρά. Τα φυτά γεννούν άλλα φυτά.

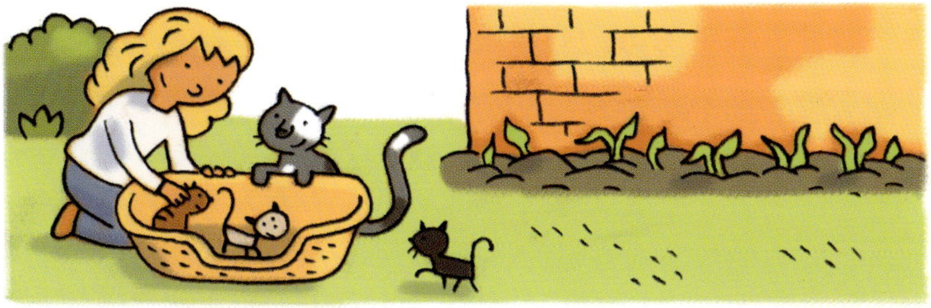

μεγαλώνουν
Στη διάρκεια της ζωής τους, οι ζωντανοί οργανισμοί μεγαλώνουν και αλλάζουν.

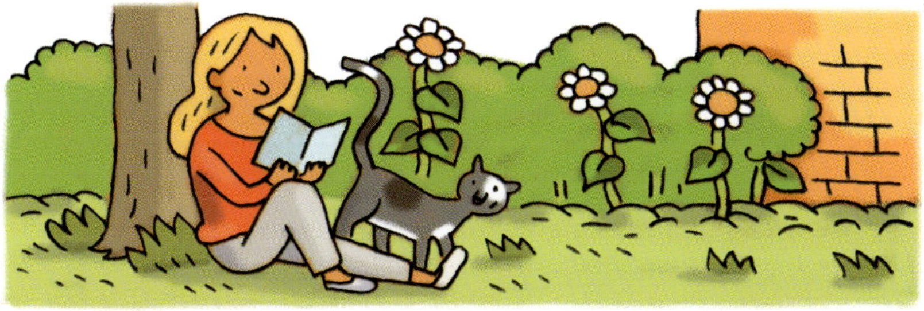

και πεθαίνουν
Άλλοι οργανισμοί ζουν λιγότερο και άλλοι περισσότερο. Όταν πεθαίνουν, τους αντικαθιστούν άλλοι.

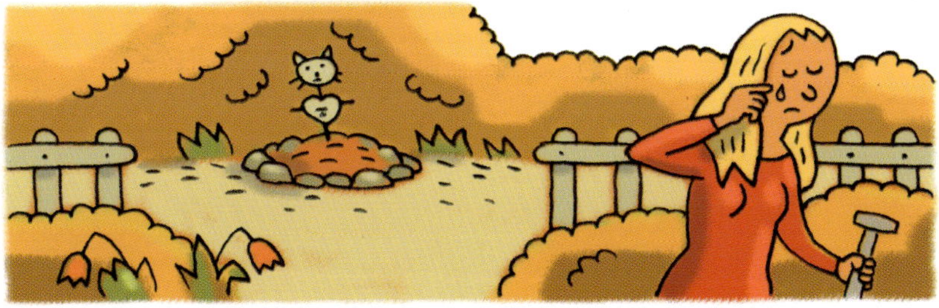

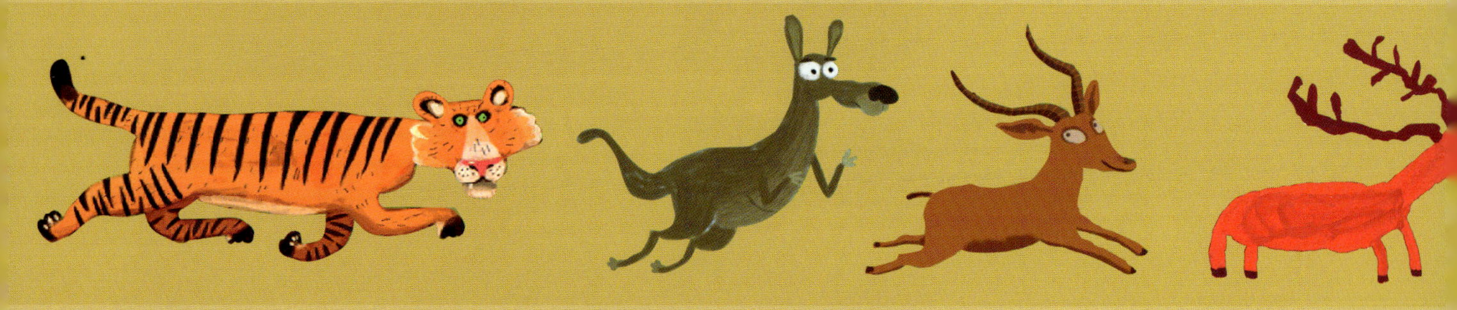

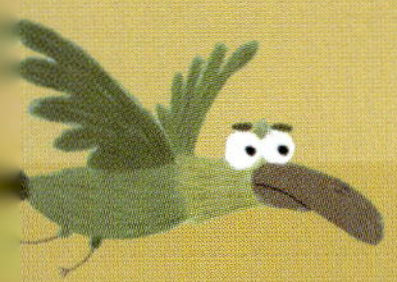

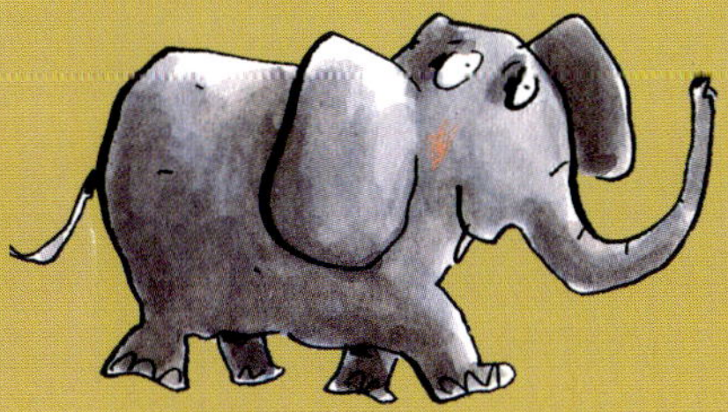

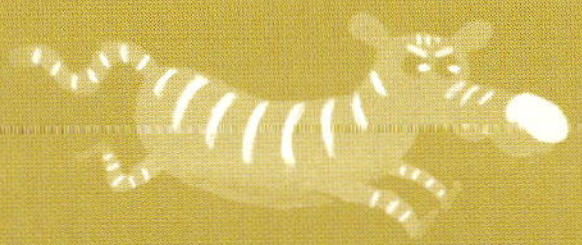

Η ΖΩΗ ΤΩΝ ΖΩΩΝ

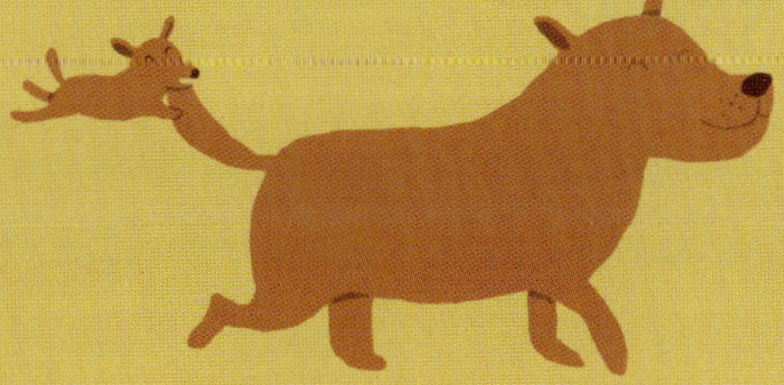

Πολλά και διαφορετικά ζώα

Τα ζώα διαφέρουν στην εμφάνιση.

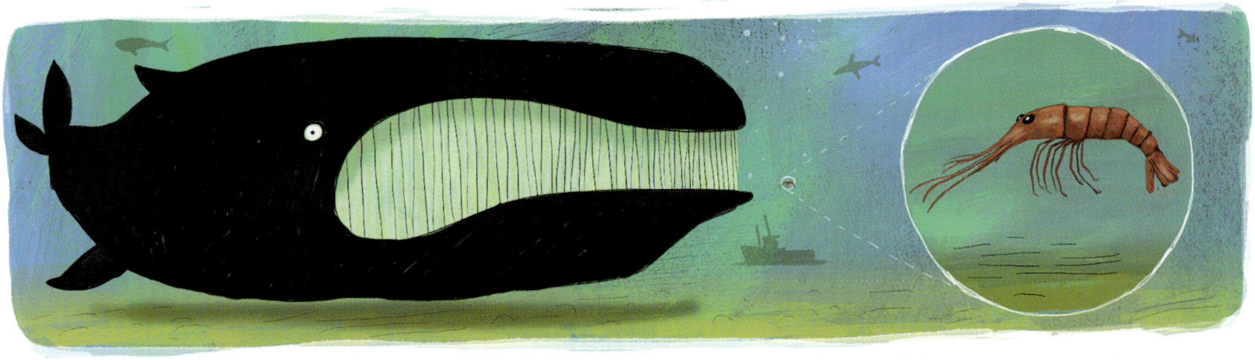

Υπάρχουν ζώα κάθε **μεγέθους**. Κάποια είναι τεράστια, κάποια άλλα μικροσκοπικά.

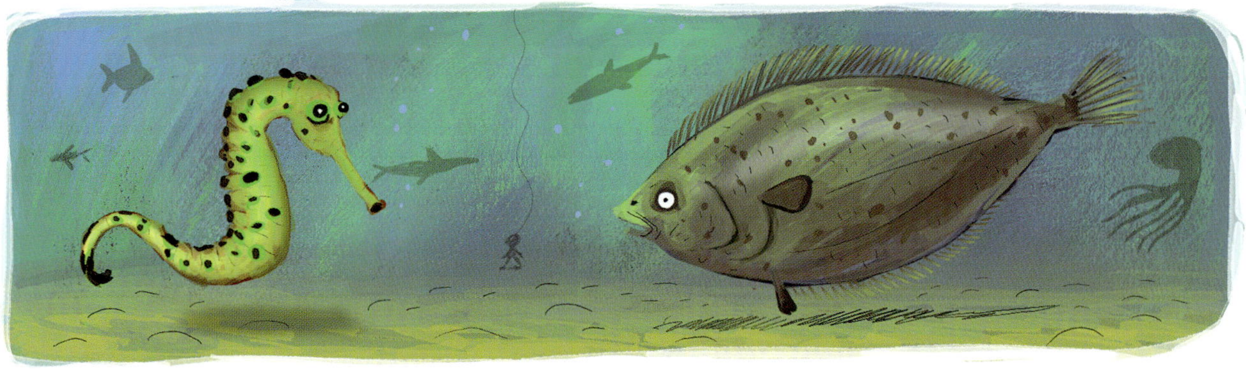

Υπάρχουν ζώα κάθε **σχήματος**. Άλλα είναι ολοστρόγγυλα, άλλα μακρόστενα...

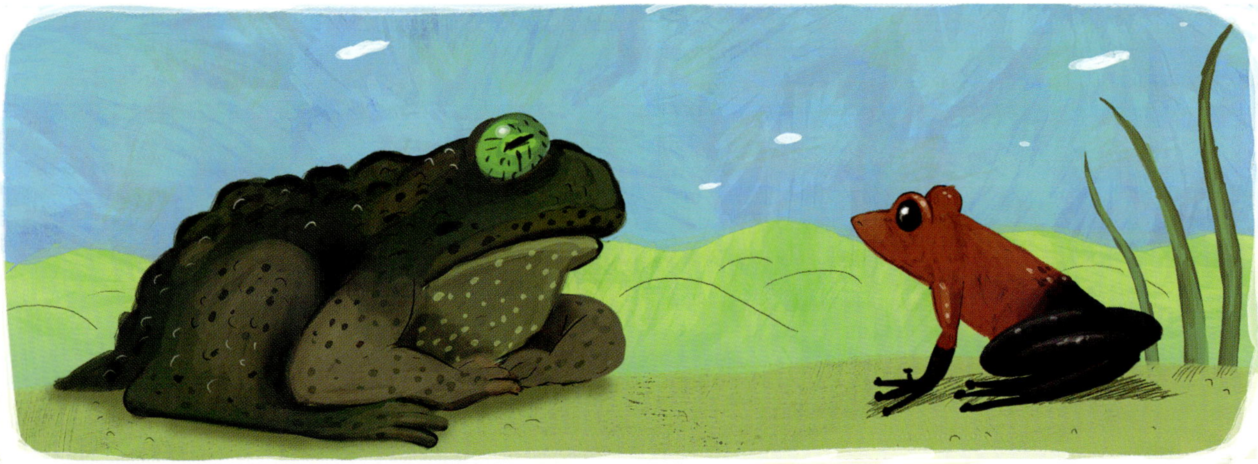

Τέλος, υπάρχουν ζώα κάθε **χρώματος**.

Διαφέρουν στον τρόπο ζωής τους.

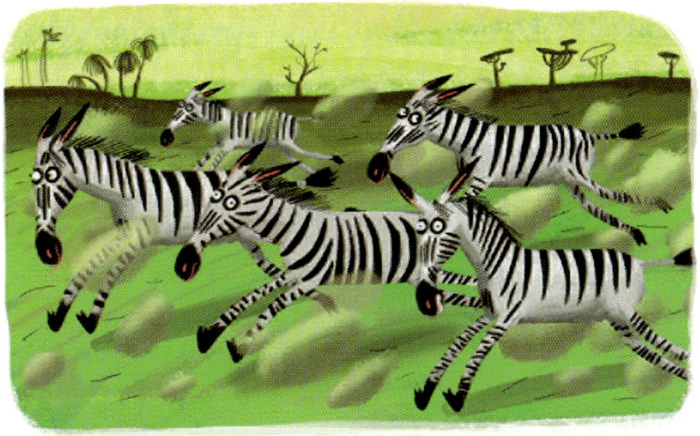

Κάποια ζώα ζουν σε **αγέλες**...

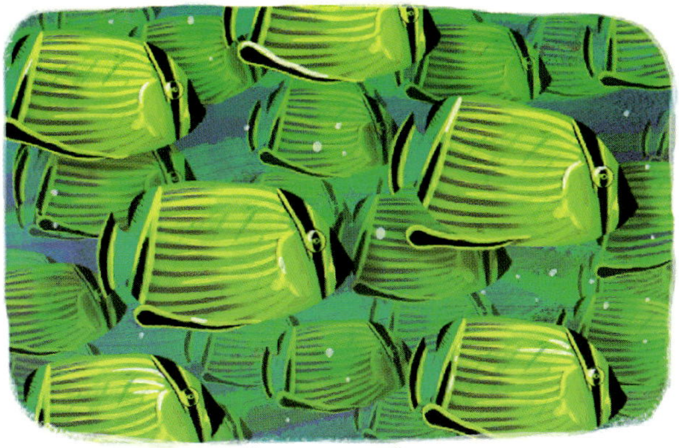

...ή σε **κοπάδια**.

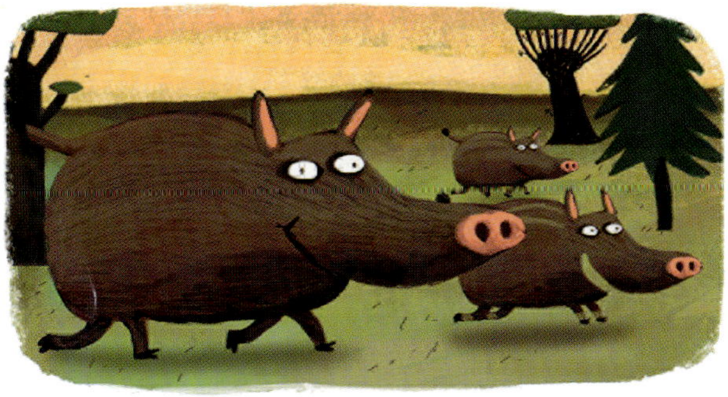

Κάποια ζουν σε **οικογένειες**...

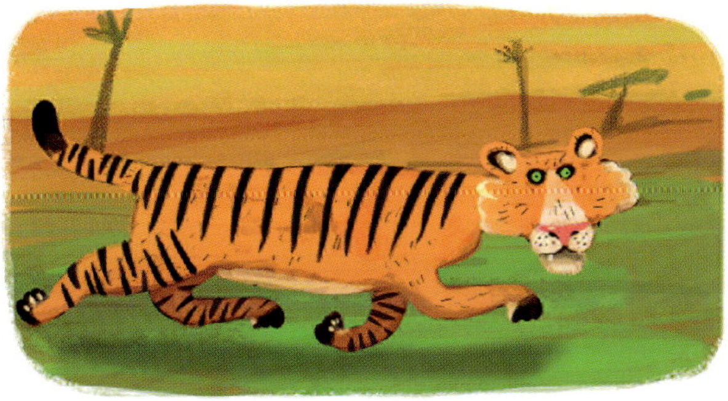

...κάποια άλλα **ολομόναχα**.

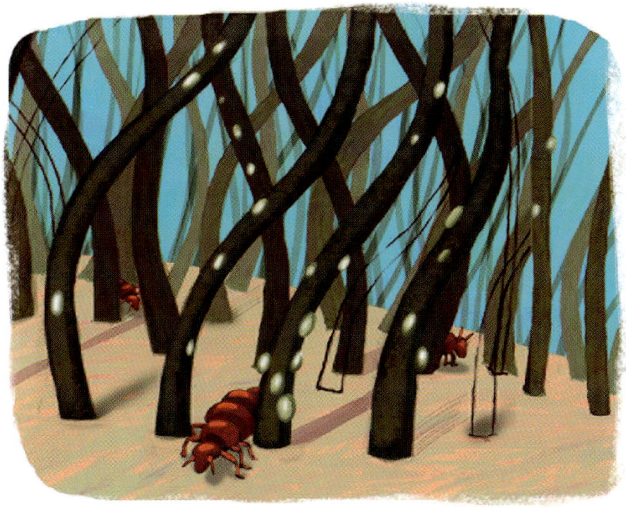

Τα ζώα που ζουν στο σώμα άλλων ζώων και τρέφονται από αυτό –όπως η **ψείρα** στα μαλλιά μας– ονομάζονται **παράσιτα**.

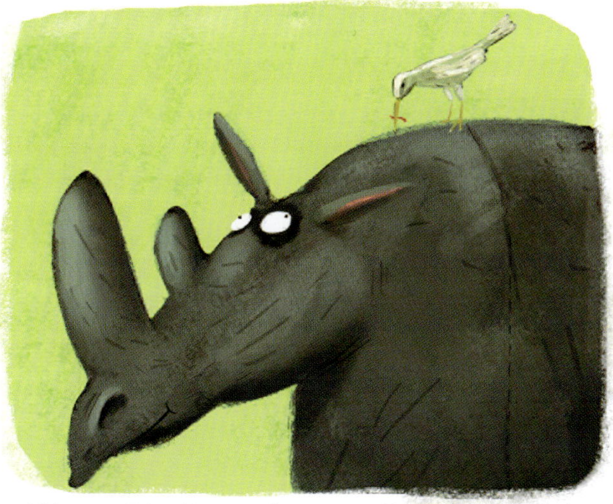

Κάποια ζώα ζουν πάντοτε **μαζί**. Ο **βουφάγος** μένει πάντα κοντά στο **ρινόκερο**. Τον απαλλάσσει από τα παράσιτα.

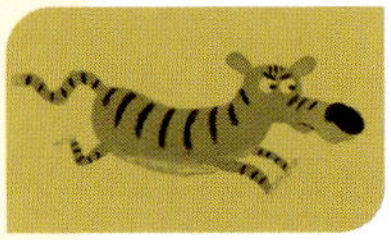

Με ή χωρίς σπονδυλική στήλη

ΤΑ ΣΠΟΝΔΥΛΩΤΑ

Τα ζώα που έχουν **σπονδυλική στήλη** ονομάζονται σπονδυλωτά.
Τα χωρίζουμε σε **5 μεγάλες ομάδες**.

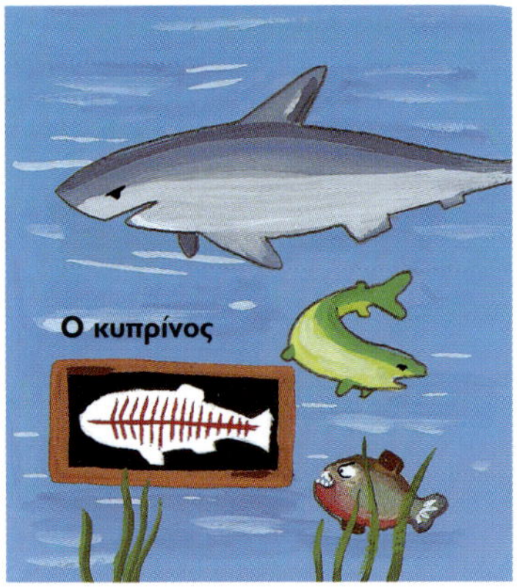

Τα ψάρια

Το δέρμα τους καλύπτεται από λέπια. Αναπνέουν μέσα στο νερό.

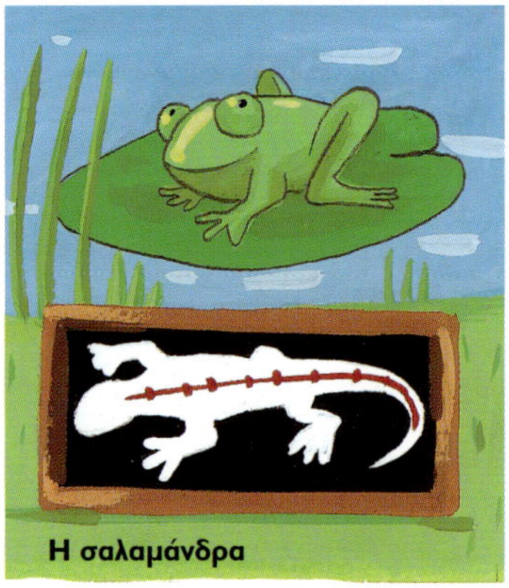

Τα αμφίβια

Το δέρμα τους είναι λείο και υγρό. Δεν έχουν τρίχωμα, ούτε φτερά ούτε λέπια.

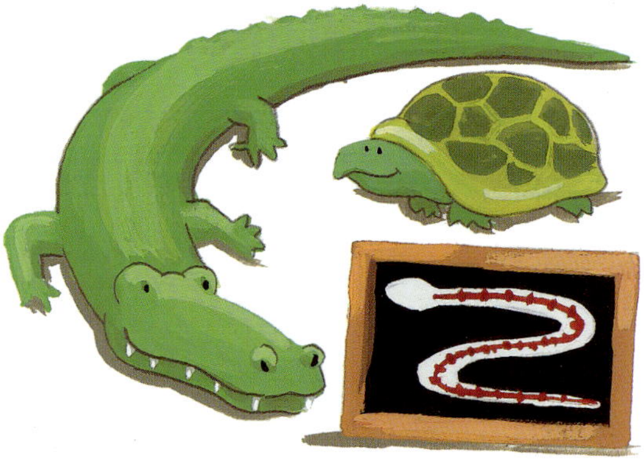

Τα ερπετά

Το δέρμα τους καλύπτεται από λέπια.

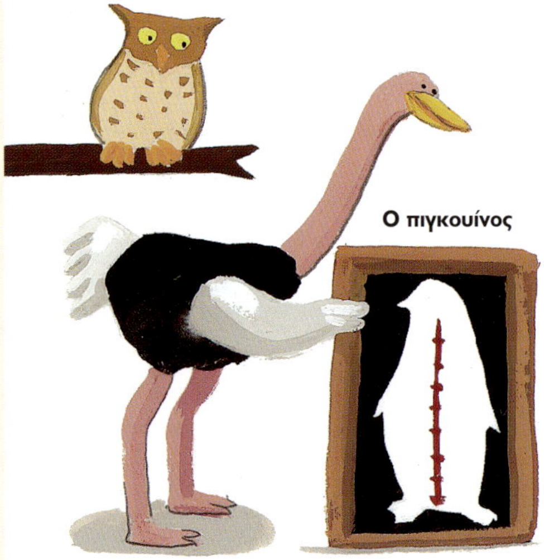

Τα πουλιά

Το δέρμα τους καλύπτεται από φτέρωμα. Έχουν πόδια και φτερά.

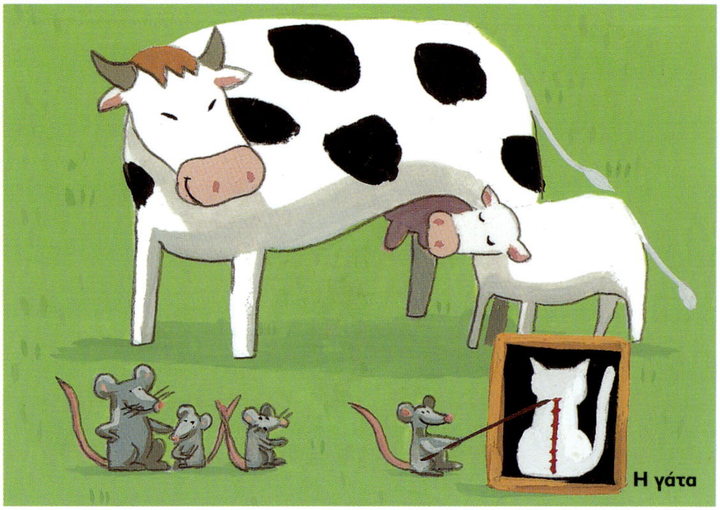

Τα θηλαστικά

Συνήθως το δέρμα τους καλύπτεται από τρίχωμα. Το θηλυκό τρέφει τα μικρά του με το γάλα του.

ΤΑ ΑΣΠΟΝΔΥΛΑ

Τα ζώα που **δεν έχουν σπονδυλική στήλη** ονομάζονται ασπόνδυλα.

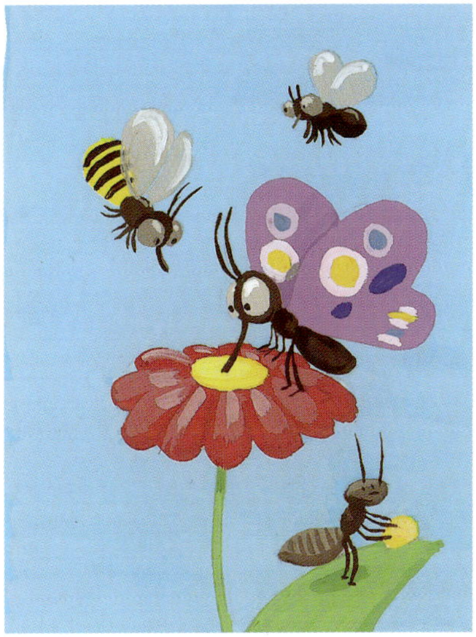

Τα έντομα
Έχουν 6 πόδια.

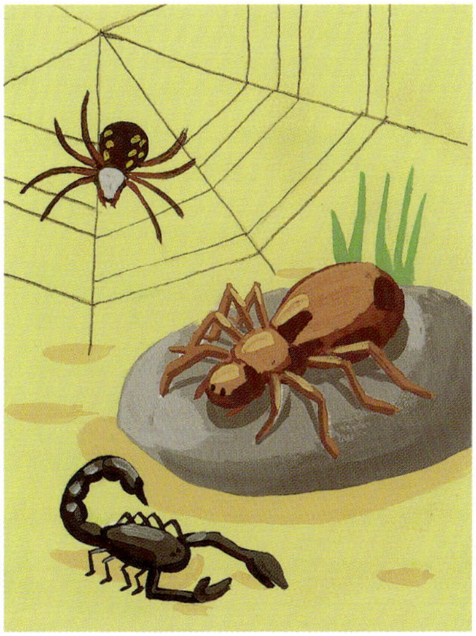

Τα αραχνοειδή
Έχουν 8 πόδια.

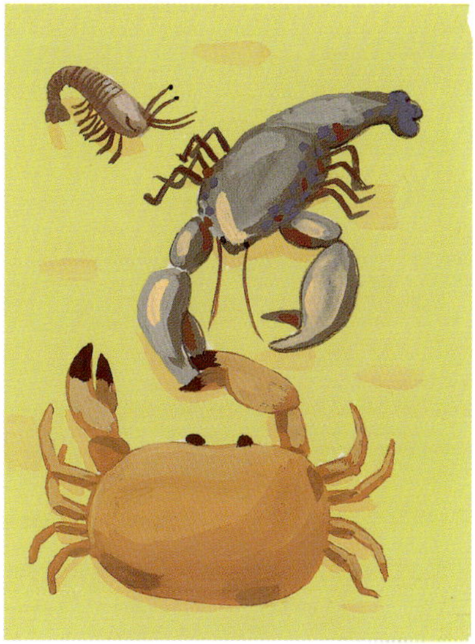

Τα οστρακοειδή
Έχουν από 8 έως 14 πόδια και πολλές φορές δαγκάνες.

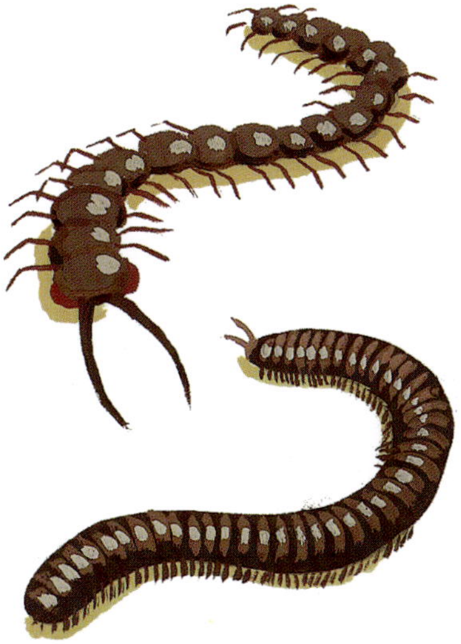

Τα μυριάποδα
Έχουν πολλά πόδια, όχι όμως και 1.000!

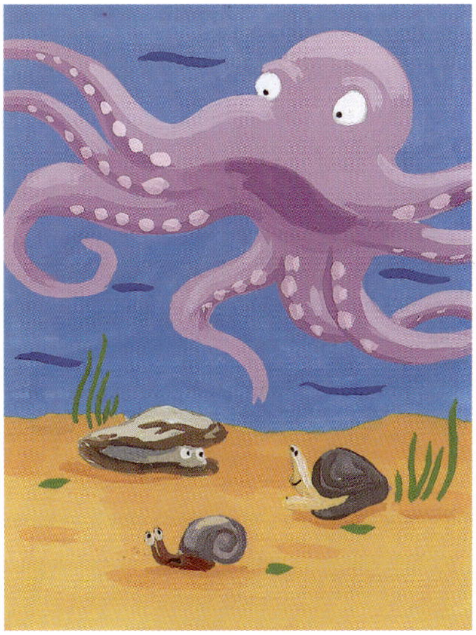

Τα μαλάκια
Έχουν μαλακό σώμα και πολλές φορές κέλυφος.

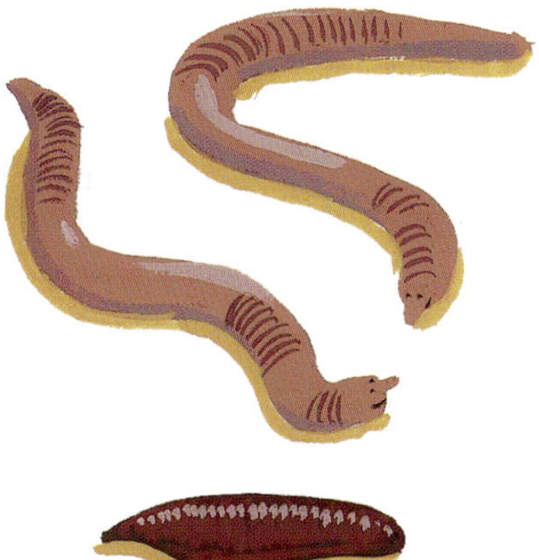

Τα σκουλήκια
Έχουν μαλακό σώμα, κυλινδρικό ή επίπεδο.

Τα έντομα

Τα πιο πολυάριθμα ζώα είναι τα έντομα.

Υπάρχουν πάνω από ένα εκατομμύριο είδη εντόμων.
Το σώμα τους αποτελείται από **3 μέρη**: το κεφάλι, το θώρακα και την κοιλιά.

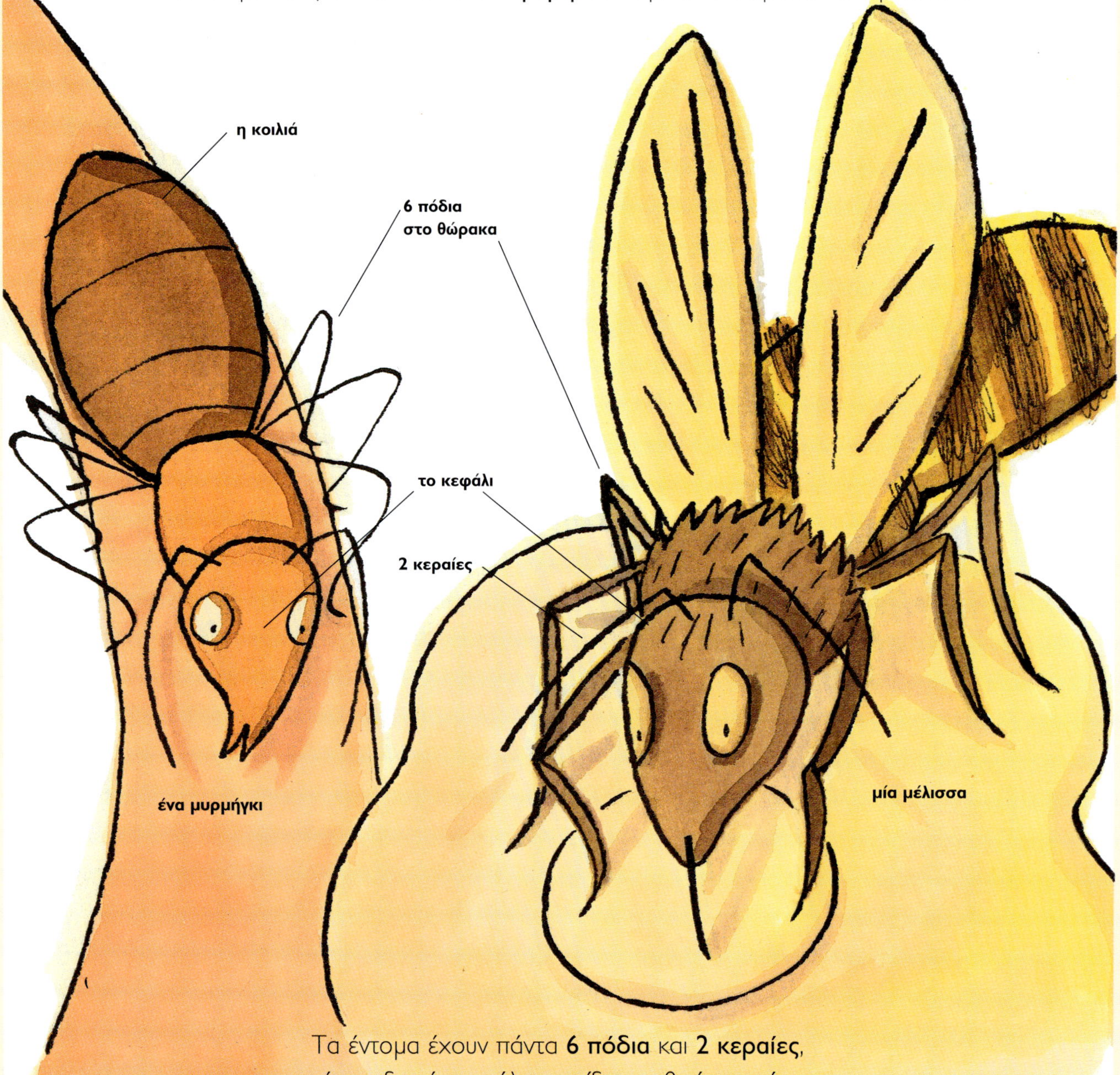

Τα έντομα έχουν πάντα **6 πόδια** και **2 κεραίες**,
όμως δεν έχουν όλα τον ίδιο αριθμό φτερών.

ΣειΡΑ σΟΥ νΑ ΠαίΞεις!

Ανάμεσα σε αυτά τα ζωάκια, **δύο δεν είναι έντομα**. Παρατήρησε καλά τα πόδια τους!

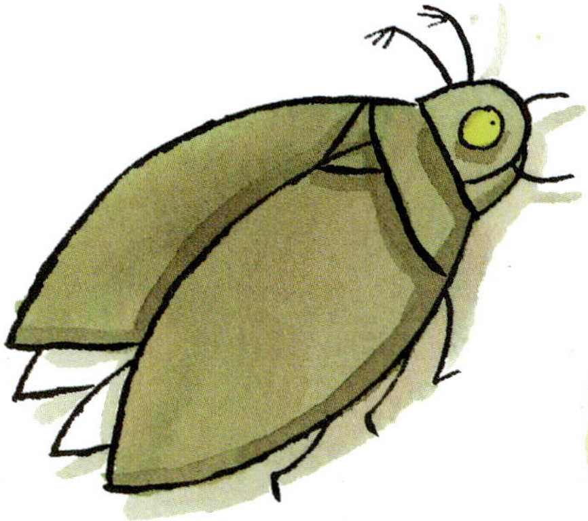

ένας **σκαραβαίος**

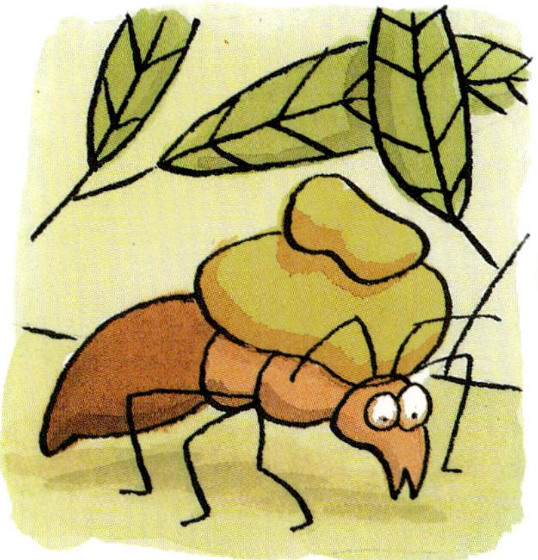

ένα **μυρμήγκι**

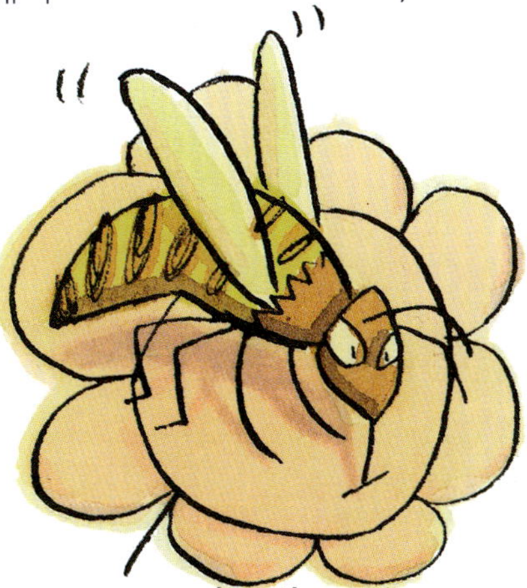

μία **μέλισσα**

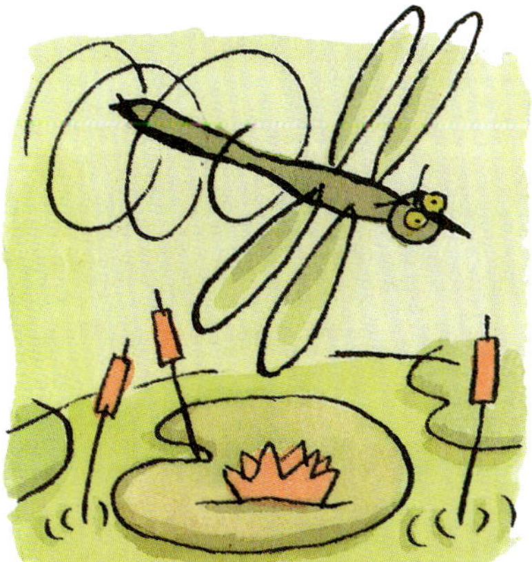

μία **λιβελούλα**

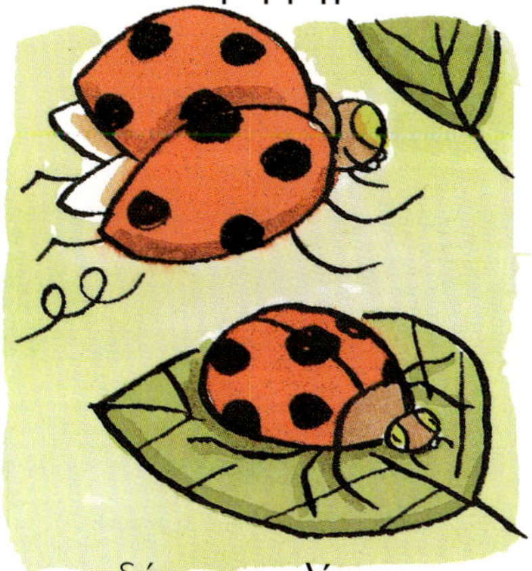

δύο **πασχαλίτσες**

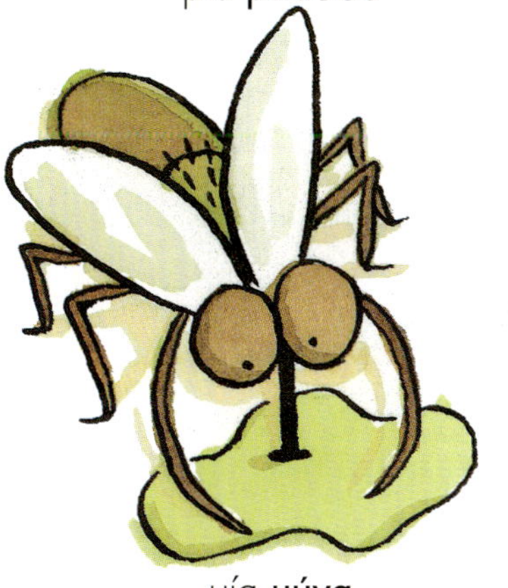

μία **μύγα**

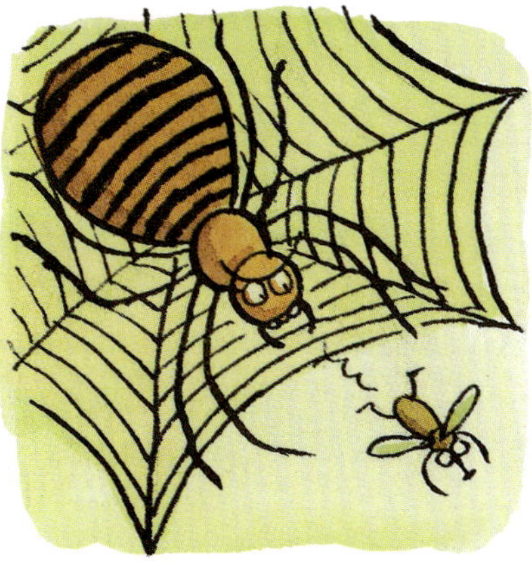

μία **αράχνη**

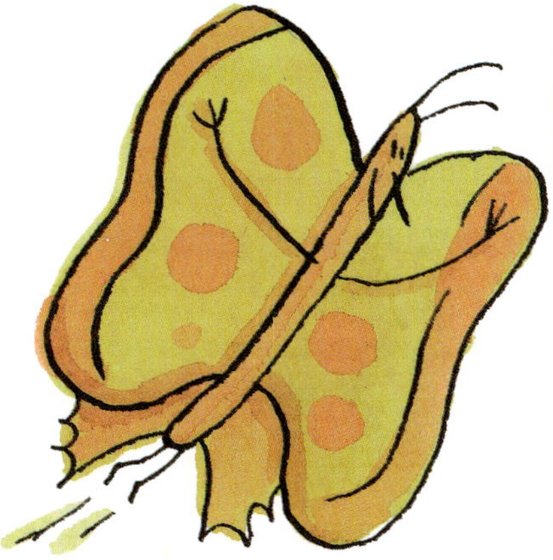

μία **πεταλούδα**

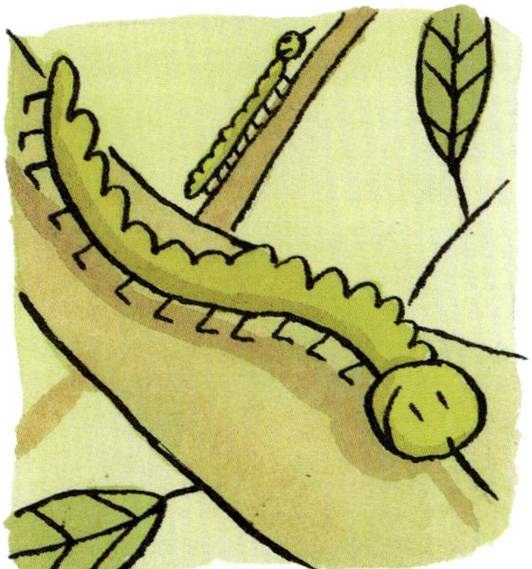

ένα **μυριάποδο**

Λύση: το μυριάποδο και η αράχνη έχουν πάνω από 6 πόδια, δεν είναι λοιπόν έντομα.

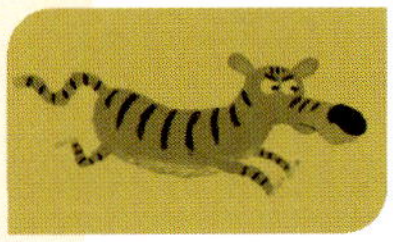

Τα ζώα μετακινούνται

Τα ζώα μετακινούνται με πολλούς τρόπους.

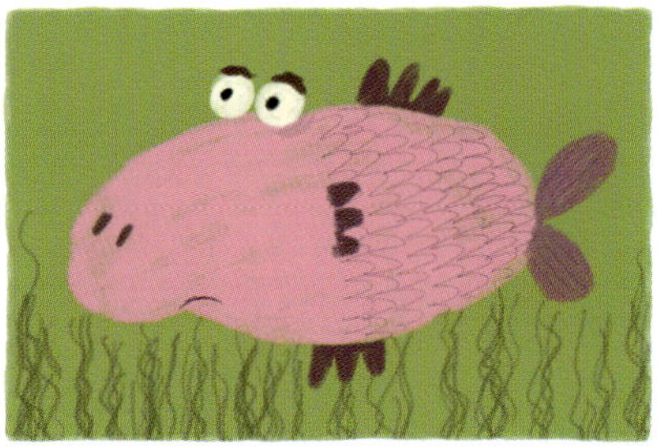

Κολυμπούν.

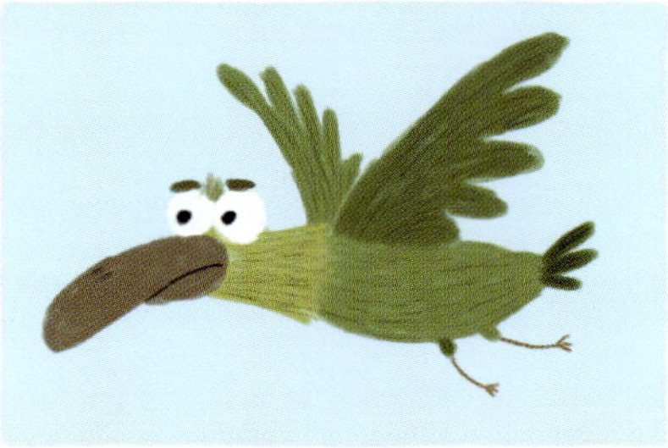

Πετούν.

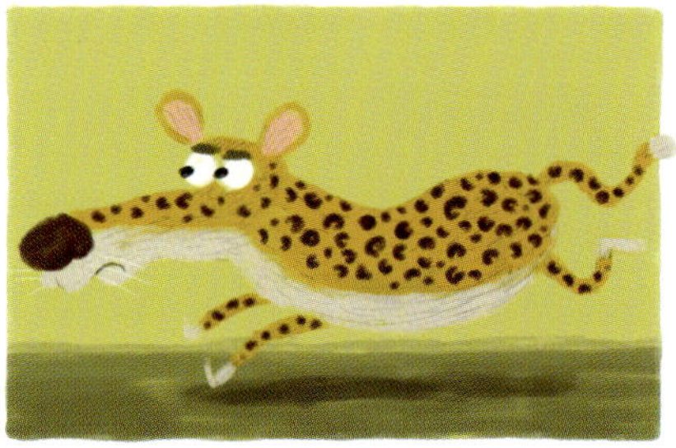

Τρέχουν.

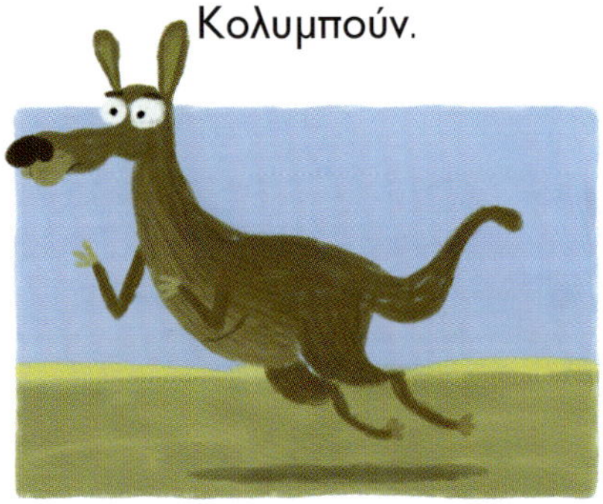

Πηδούν.

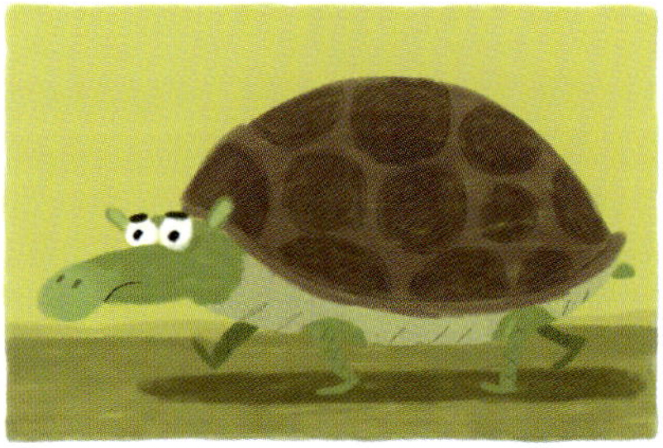

Περπατούν.

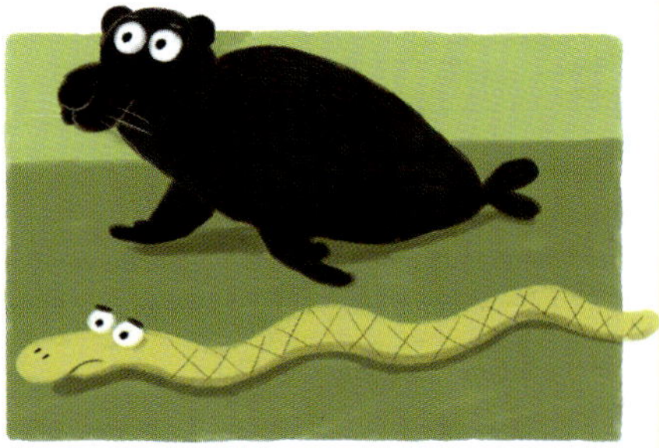

Έρπουν.

Κάποια ζώα είναι παράξενα.

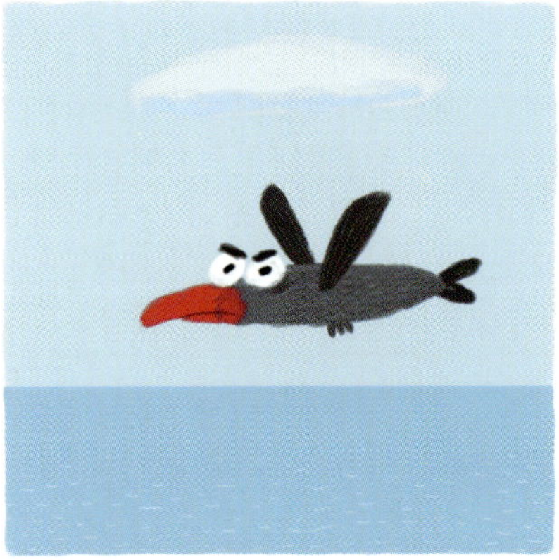

Το **χελιδονόψαρο** είναι ψάρι, όμως μπορεί και να πετάξει, όταν πρέπει να ξεφύγει από κάποιο θηρευτή.

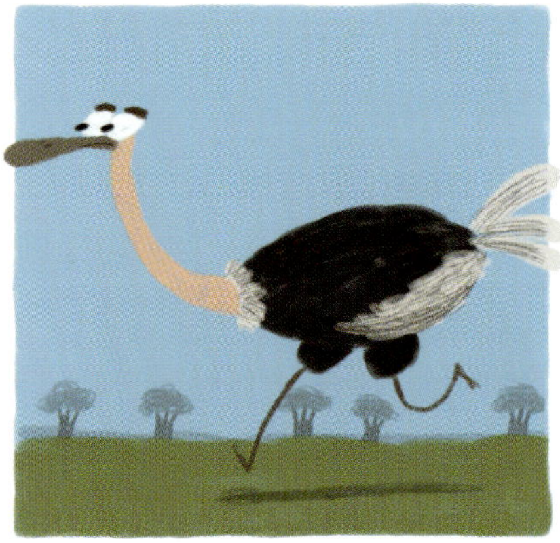

Η **στρουθοκάμηλος** είναι ένα πουλί... που δεν πετάει. Όμως τρέχει πολύ γρήγορα.

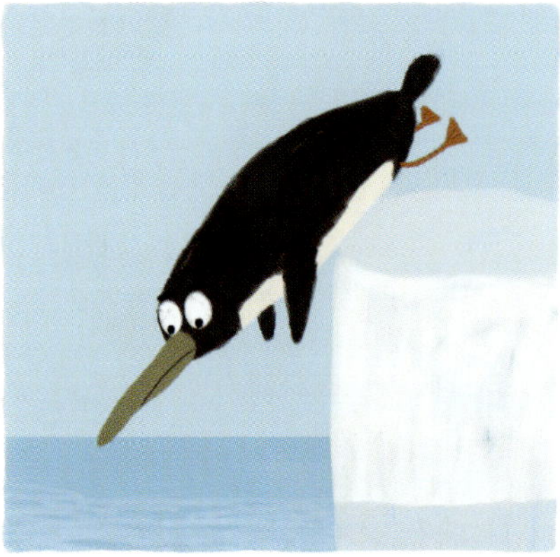

Ο **πιγκουίνος** είναι πουλί. Δεν πετά στον ουρανό, αλλά μέσα στο νερό!

ΑΠΟ ΤΟ ΠΙΟ ΓΡΗΓΟΡΟ ΣΤΟ ΠΙΟ ΑΡΓΟ

Το **γεράκι** είναι το γρηγορότερο ζώο στον ουρανό. 250 χλμ./ώρα

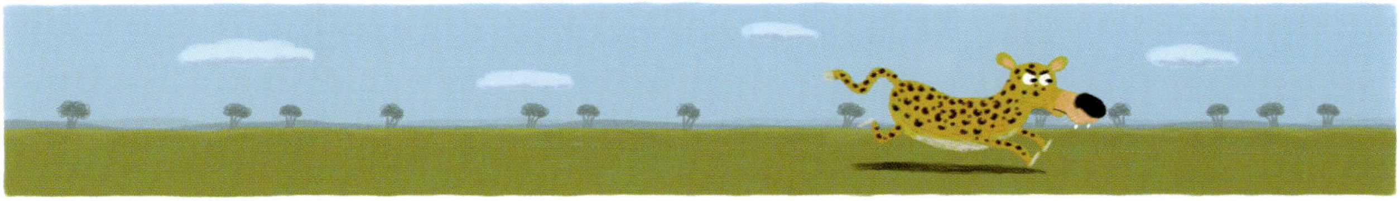

Το **τσιτάχ** είναι το γρηγορότερο ζώο στη γη. Τρέχει πολύ γρήγορα αλλά όχι για πολλή ώρα. 110 χλμ./ώρα

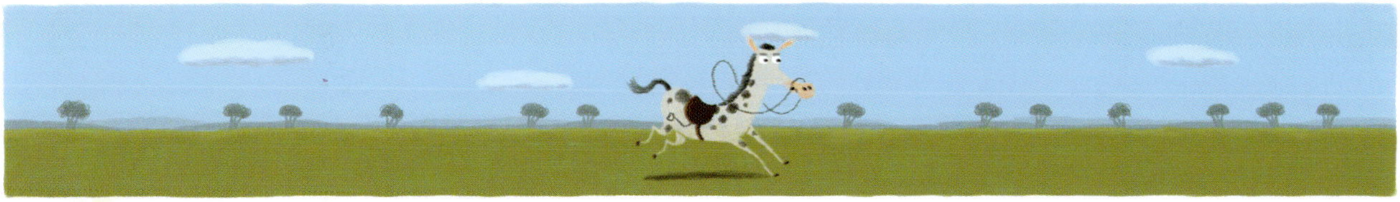

Το **άλογο** μπορεί να τρέχει γρήγορα και για πολλή ώρα. 70 χλμ./ώρα

Ένας **πρωταθλητής** στίβου μπορεί να τρέχει με ταχύτητα. 36 χλμ./ώρα

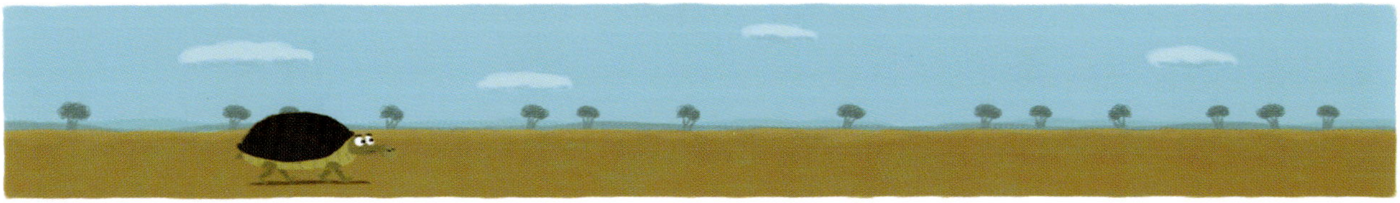

Η **χελώνα** προχωρά με τα χοντρά πόδια της. 2,8 χλμ./ώρα

Το **σαλιγκάρι** κινείται έρποντας. 5 μ./ώρα

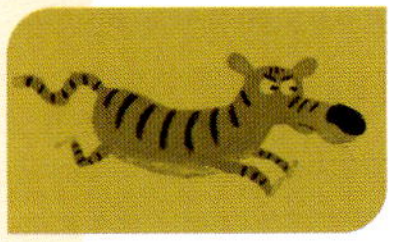

Τα ζώα κυνηγούν

Τα ζώα-θηρευτές, αυτά δηλαδή που τρέφονται με άλλα ζώα, κυνηγούν ή στήνουν παγίδα στις λείες τους.

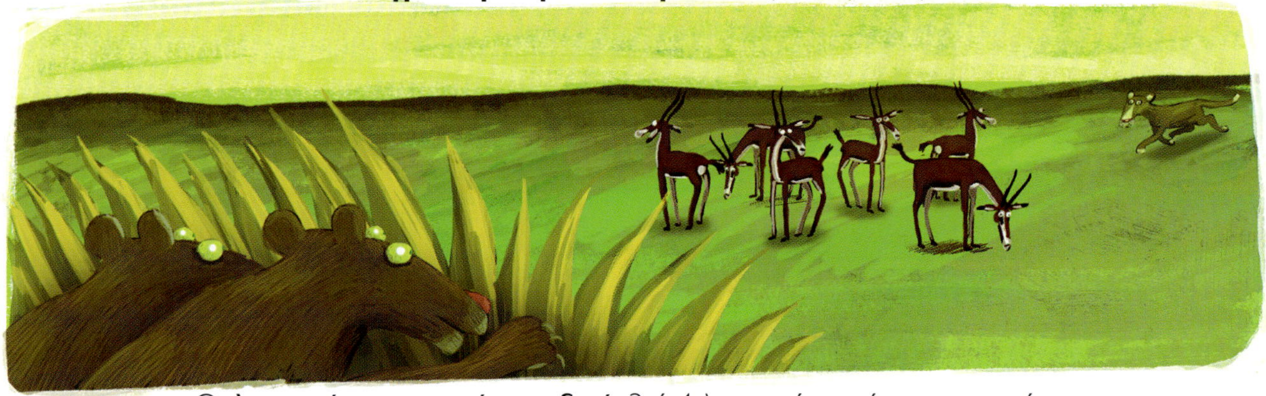

Οι **λιονταρίνες κυνηγούν ομαδικά**. 3 ή 4 λιονταρίνες μένουν κρυμμένες. Μια άλλη περιτριγυρίζει το κοπάδι και φαίνεται.

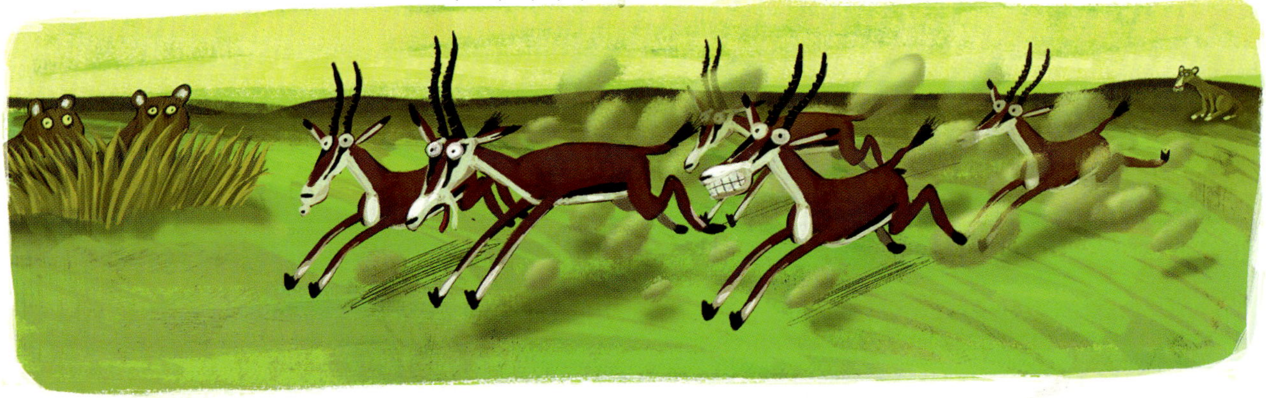

Μόλις τη δουν οι **γαζέλες**, φοβισμένες, τρέχουν μακριά...

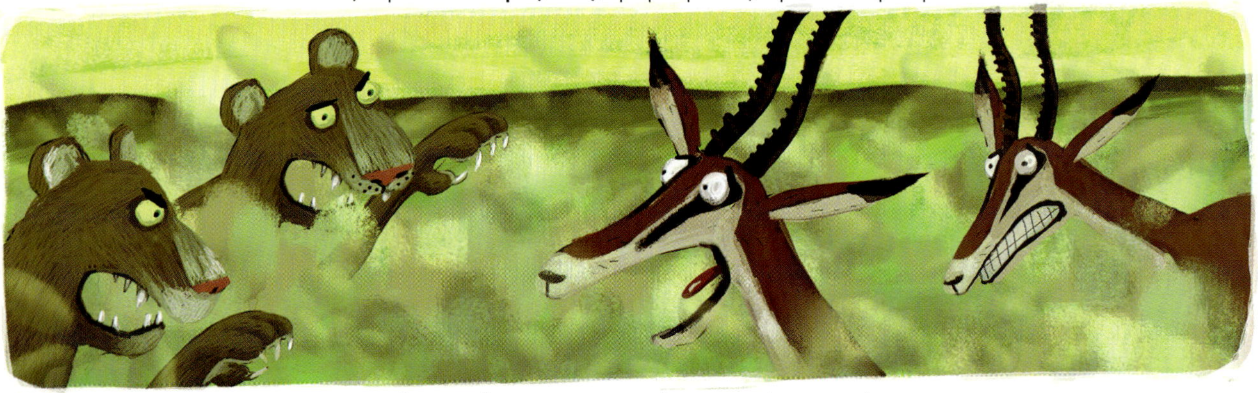

...απέναντι όμως τις περιμένουν οι **λιονταρίνες**.

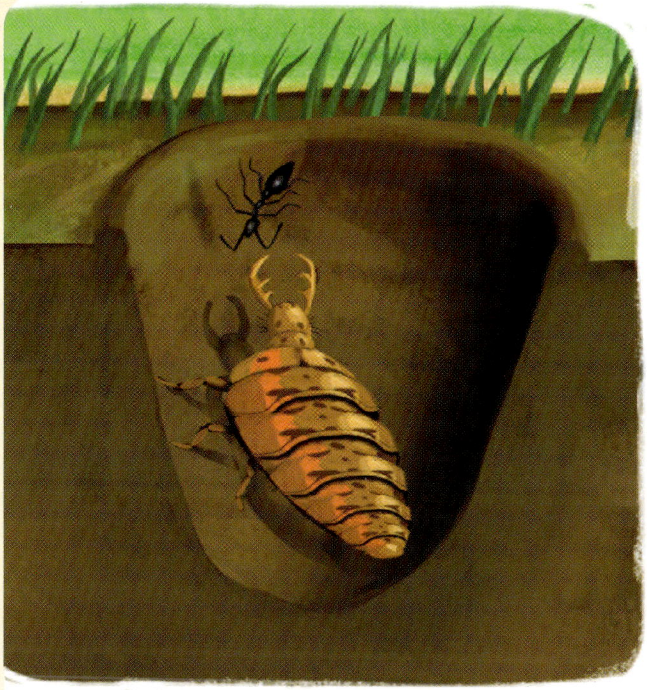

Για να πιάσει τα μυρμήγκια, η κάμπια του **μυρμηγκο-λέοντα** σκάβει μια τρύπα. Εκεί πέφτει το μυρμήγκι.

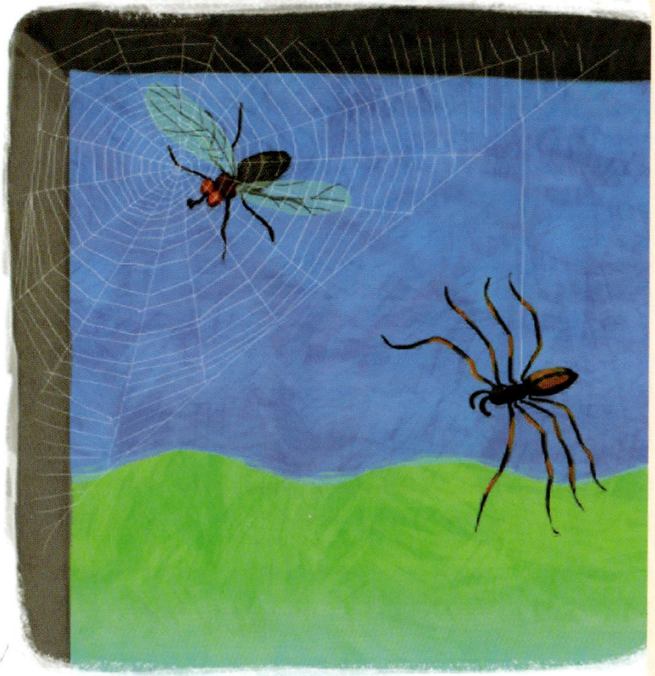

Για να πιάσει τα έντομα, η **αράχνη** υφαίνει έναν ιστό και, κρεμασμένη σε μια κλωστή, παραμονεύει.

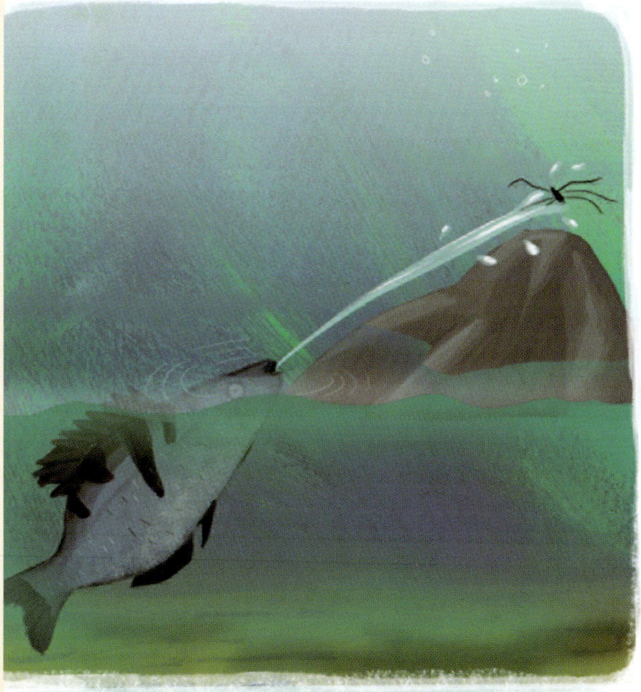

Το **ψάρι-τοξότης** φτύνει απότομα μια μεγάλη γουλιά νερό για να ρίξει κάτω τη λεία του.

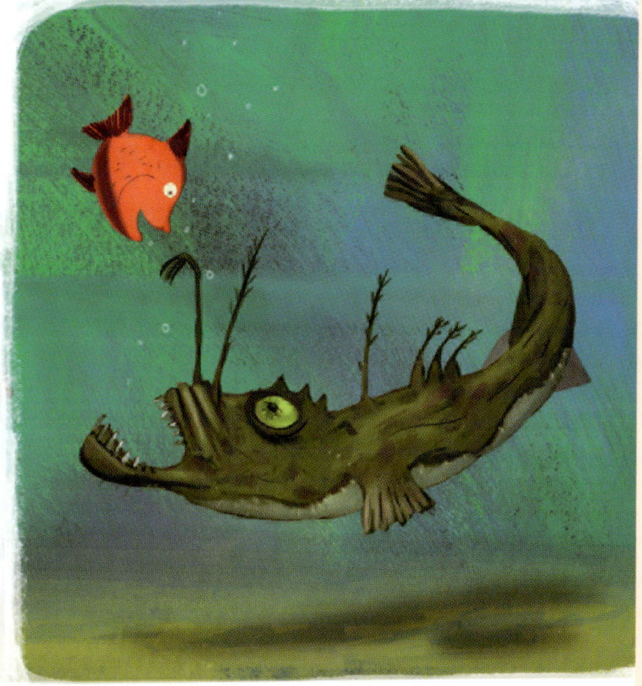

Το **βατραχόψαρο** «ψαρεύει με το καλάμι»: έχει για **δόλωμα** μια μικρή κλωστή πάνω στο κεφάλι του.

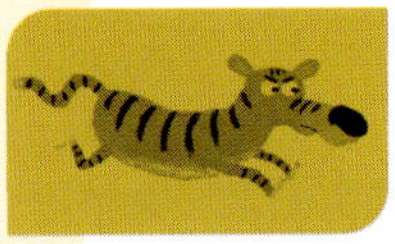

Τα ζώα προστατεύουν τον εαυτό τους

Οι λείες, τα ζώα που κυνηγιούνται από άλλα ζώα, πρέπει να προστατεύουν τον εαυτό τους. Για να το καταφέρουν, έχουν διάφορους τρόπους.

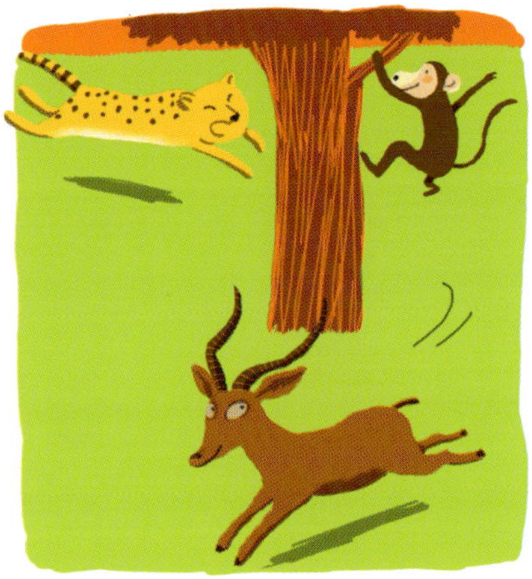

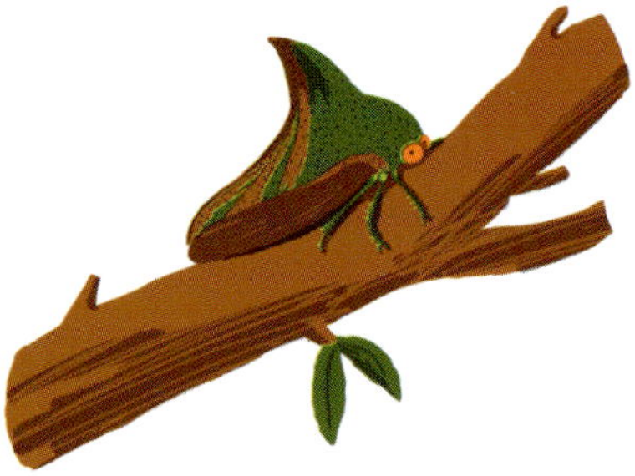

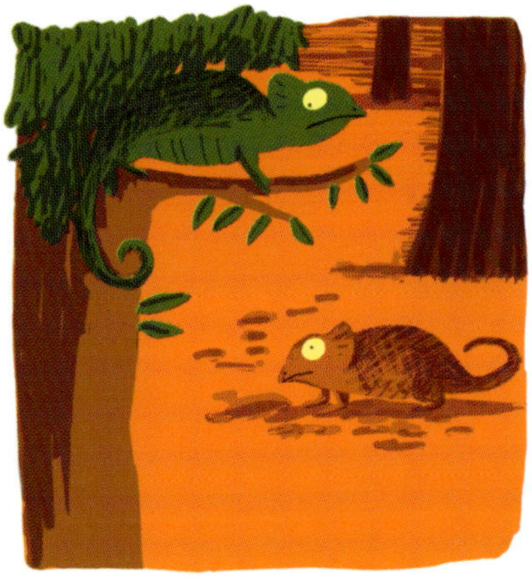

Η φυγή

Η **γαζέλα** μπορεί να τρέχει περισσότερη ώρα από το τσιτάχ. Έτσι, πολλές φορές καταφέρνει να του ξεφύγει.

Το καμουφλάζ

Κάποια **έντομα** μοιάζουν με αγκάθια, για να μη φαίνονται.

Ο **χαμαιλέοντας** αλλάζει χρώμα ανάλογα με το περιβάλλον στο οποίο βρίσκεται.

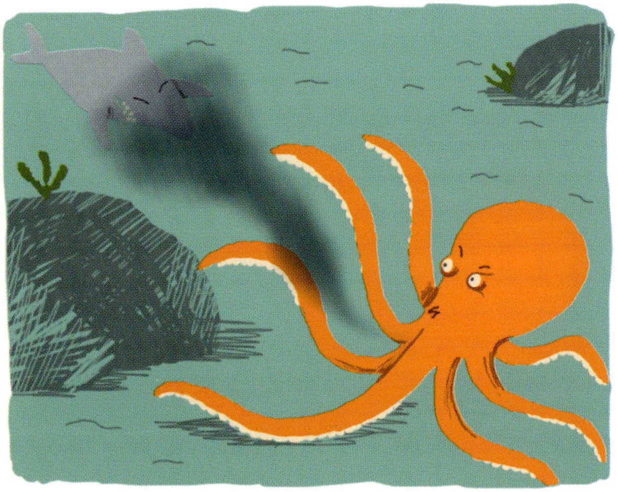

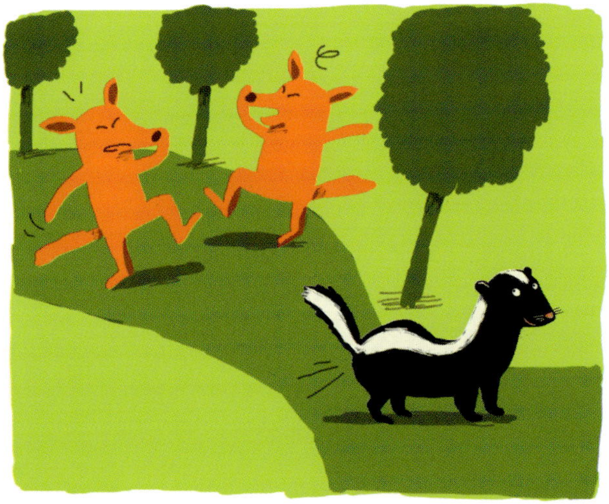

Ο αιφνιδιασμός

Το **χταπόδι** πετάει μελάνι, για να κρυφτεί μέχρι ν' απομακρυνθεί.

Όταν κινδυνεύει, το **κουνάβι** βγάζει μια πολύ δυσάρεστη μυρωδιά.

Η πονηριά

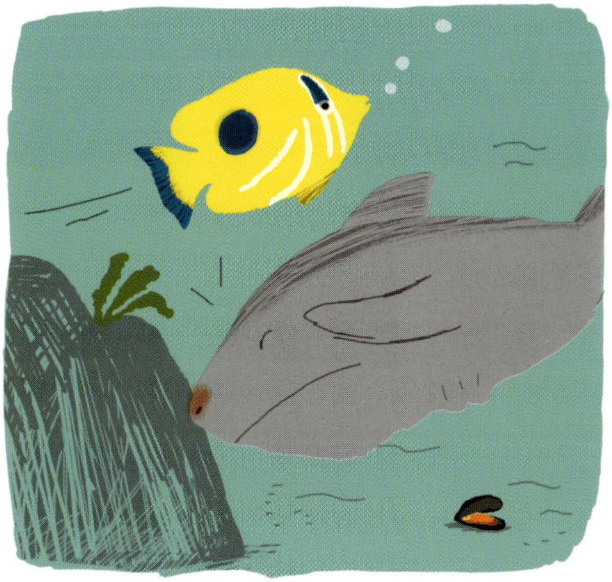

Αυτό το ψάρι έχει ένα «ψεύτικο μάτι» στο πίσω μέρος του σώματός του, για να ξεγελάει το θηρευτή του.

Το δηλητήριο

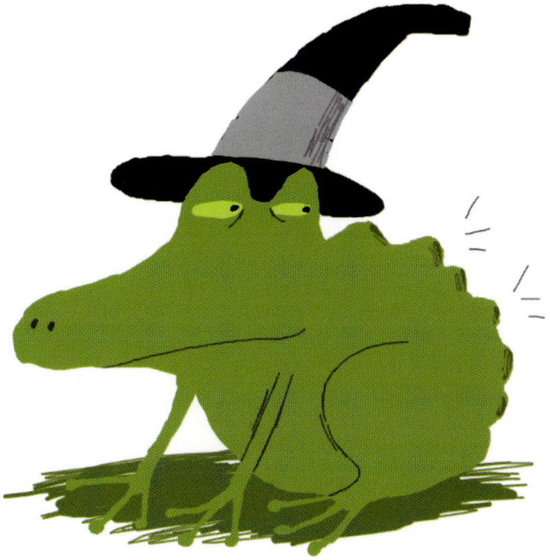

Ο **φρύνος** έχει χοντρές ελιές πάνω στο σώμα του· όταν τις αγγίζουμε, βγάζουν δηλητήριο.

Οι πανοπλίες

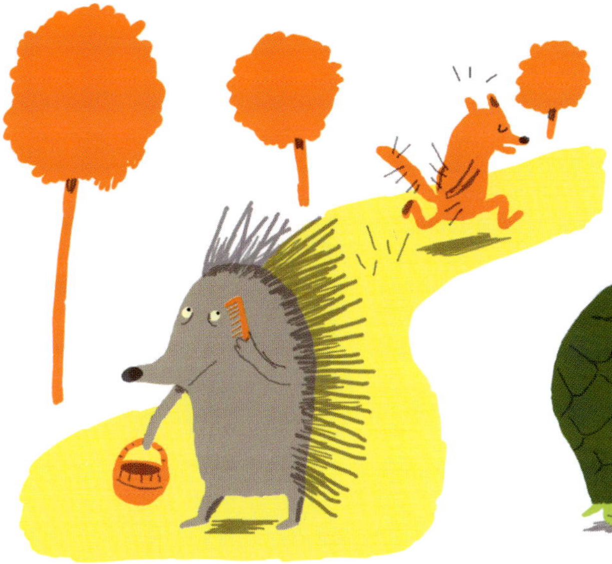

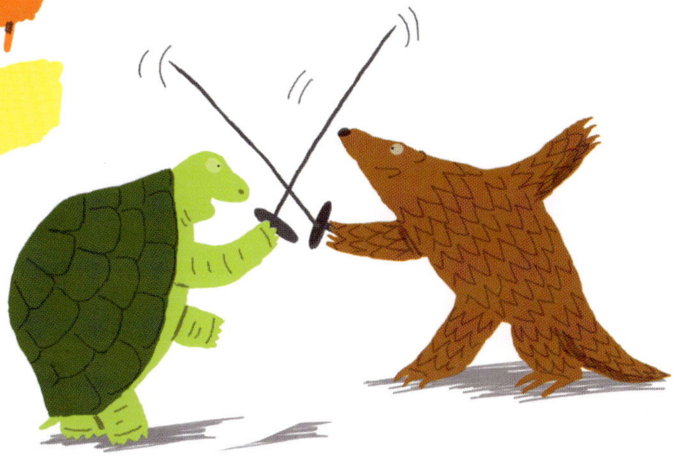

Η πλάτη του **σκαντζόχοιρου** είναι καλυμμένη με αγκάθια.

Το σώμα της **χελώνας** προστατεύεται από ένα καβούκι.

Ο **παγκολίνος** είναι ένα θηλαστικό που καλύπτεται με λέπια.

ΣειΡΑ σΟΥ νΑ ΠαίΞεις!

Το πέταγμα, το τρέξιμο, το κολύμπι, το πήδημα... Ξέρεις **πώς κινούνται αυτά τα ζώα**;
Μην ξεχνάς, μερικά από αυτά έχουν περισσότερους από έναν τρόπους!

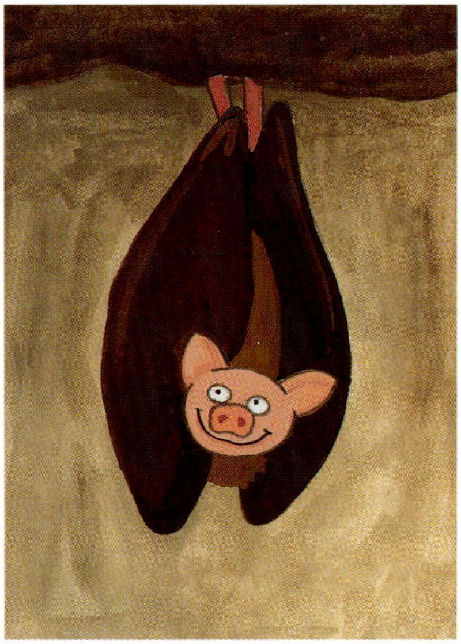

η **νυχτερίδα**

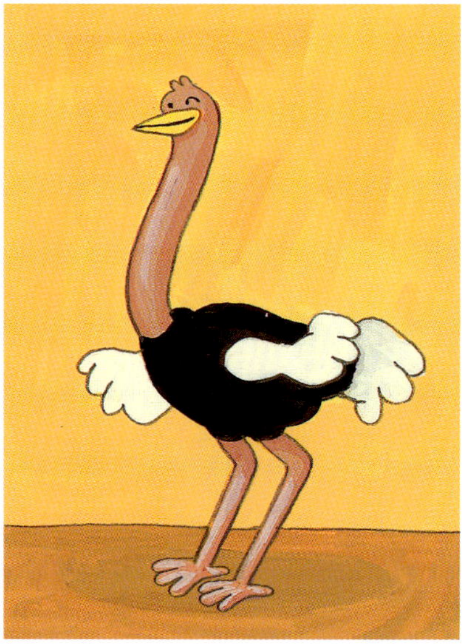

η **στρουθοκάμηλος**

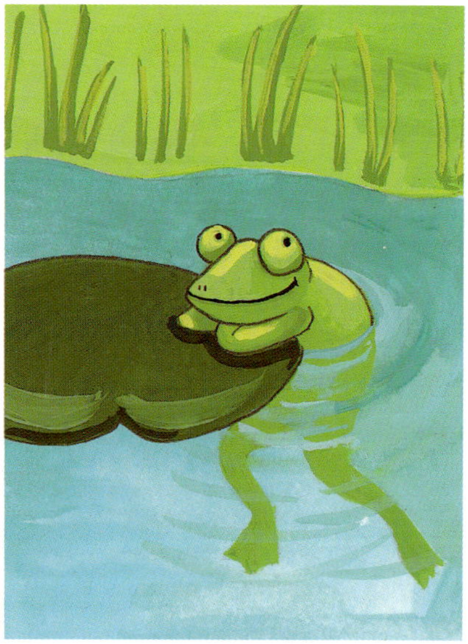

ο **βάτραχος**

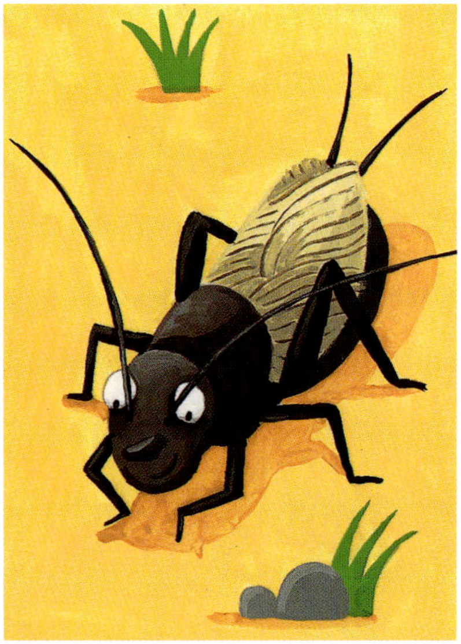

ο **γρύλος**

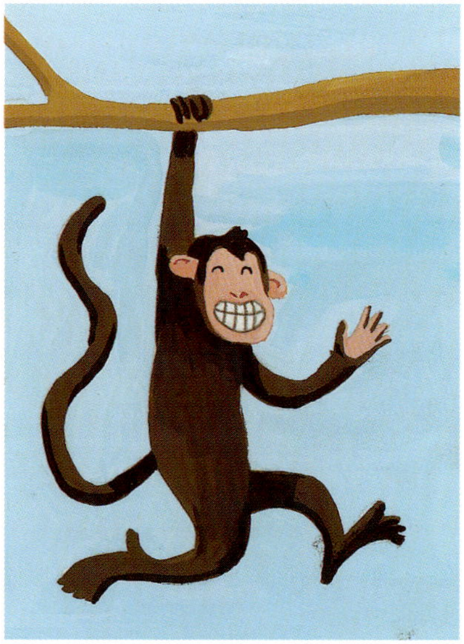

ο **πίθηκος**

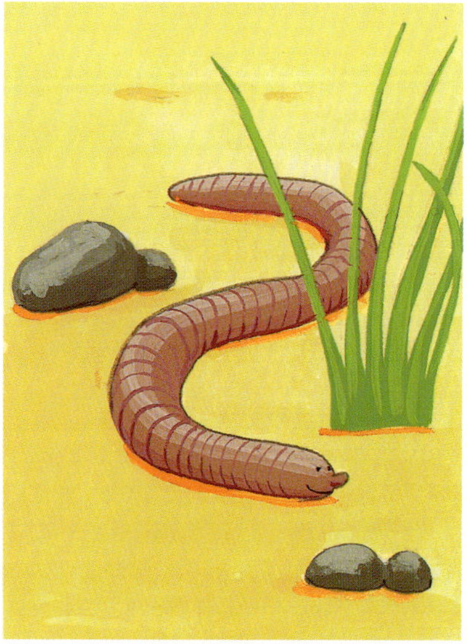

το **σκουλήκι**

Λύση: η νυχτερίδα πετάει· η στρουθοκάμηλος τρέχει· ο βάτραχος πηδάει και κολυμπάει· ο γρύλος πηδάει, πετάει και περπατάει· ο πίθηκος γαντζώνεται, περπατάει, πηδάει και τρέχει· το σκουλήκι έρπει.

Σ' αυτό το σχέδιο **κρύβονται 7 ζώα**. Μπορείς να τα βρεις;

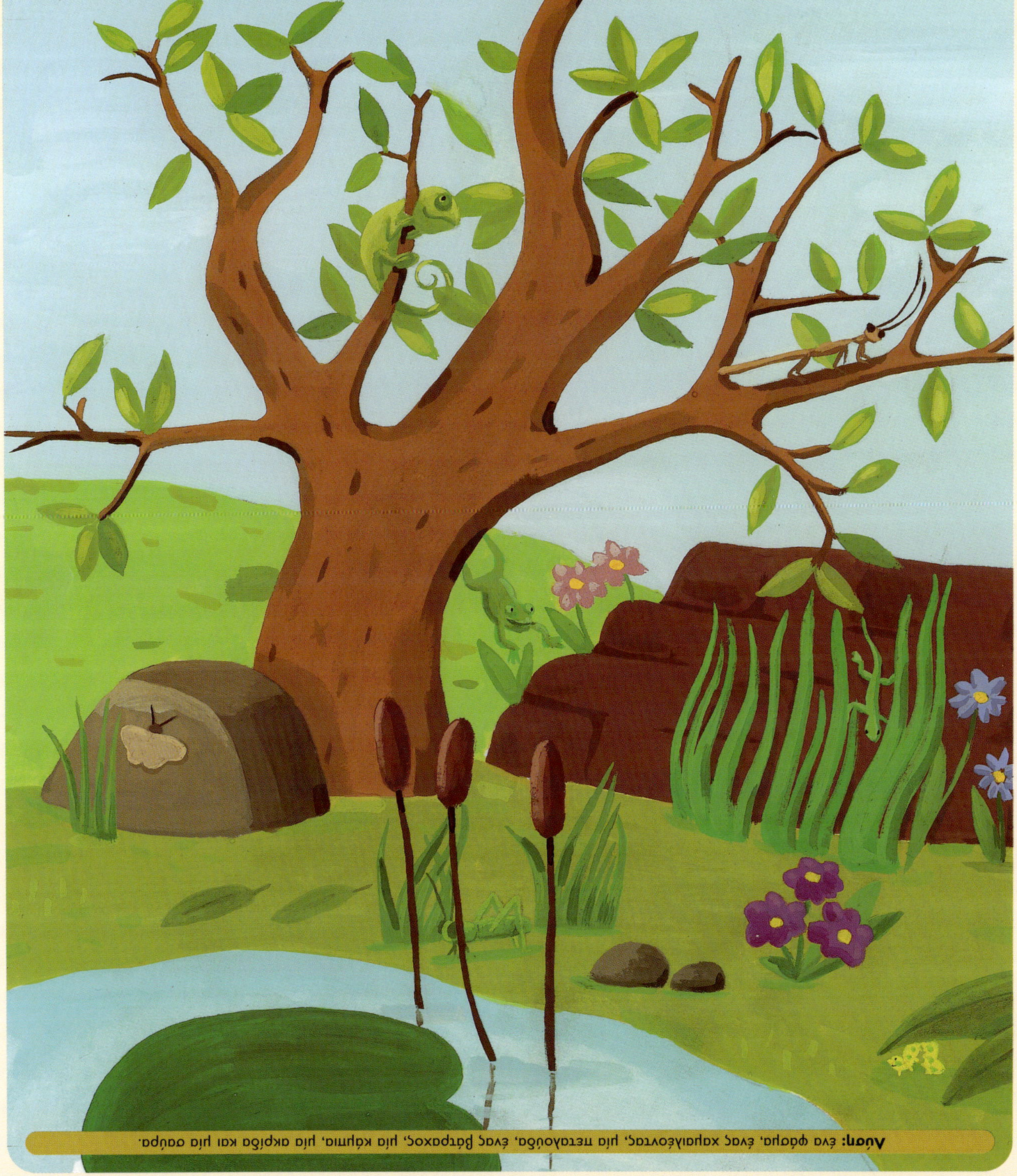

Λύση: ένα φάσμα, ένας χαμαιλέοντας, μια πεταλούδα, ένας βάτραχος, μια κάμπια, μια ακρίδα και μια σαύρα.

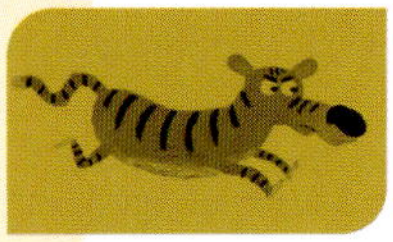

Η τροφή των ζώων

ΤΑ ΖΩΑ ΠΟΥ ΤΡΕΦΟΝΤΑΙ ΜΕ ΦΥΤΑ

Είναι τα περισσότερα ζώα.

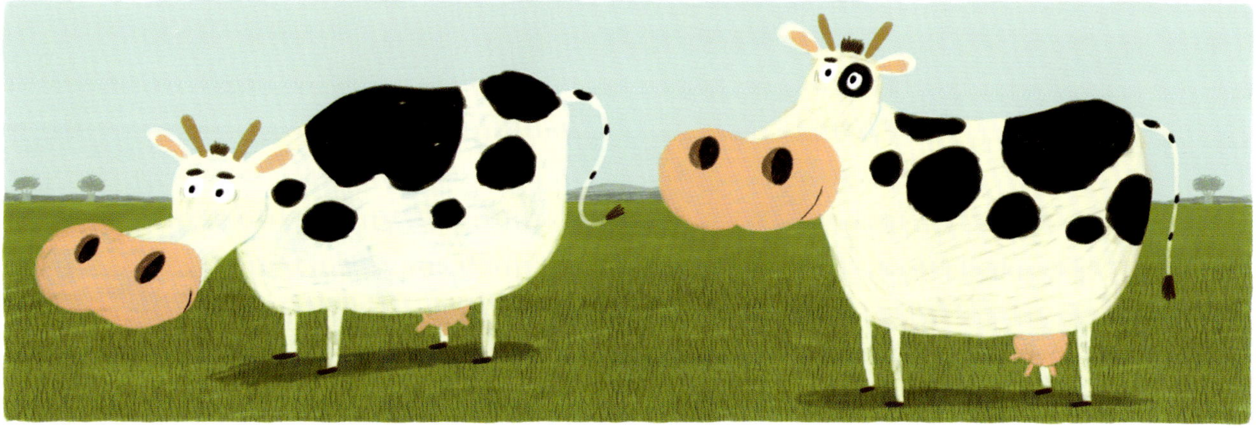

Η **αγελάδα** τρώει χορτάρι: είναι ένα **φυτοφάγο** ζώο.

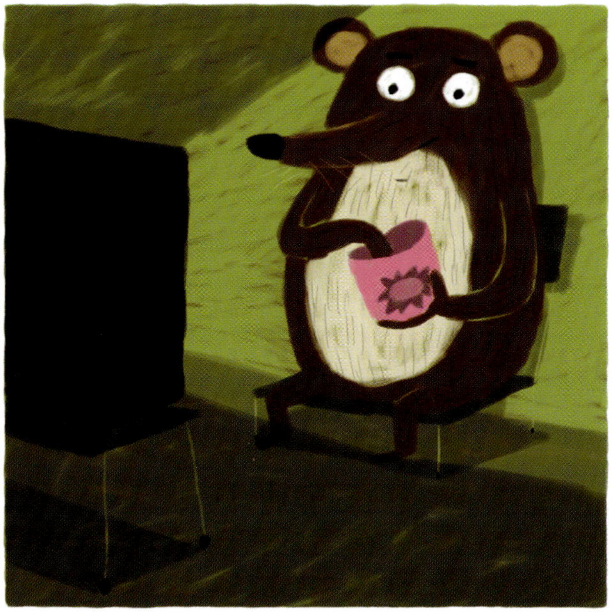

Ο **αρουραίος** τρώει κυρίως σπόρους.
Είναι **σποροφάγος**.

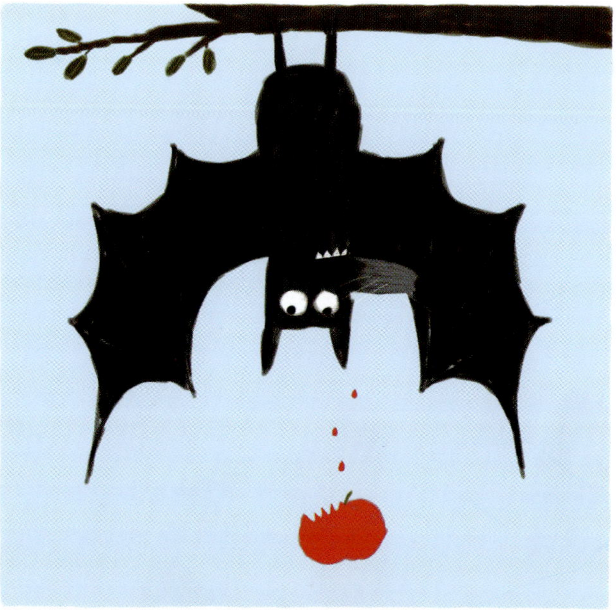

Μερικές **νυχτερίδες** τρώνε μόνο καρπούς.
Είναι **καρποφάγοι**.

ΤΑ ΖΩΑ ΠΟΥ ΤΡΕΦΟΝΤΑΙ ΜΕ ΑΛΛΑ ΖΩΑ

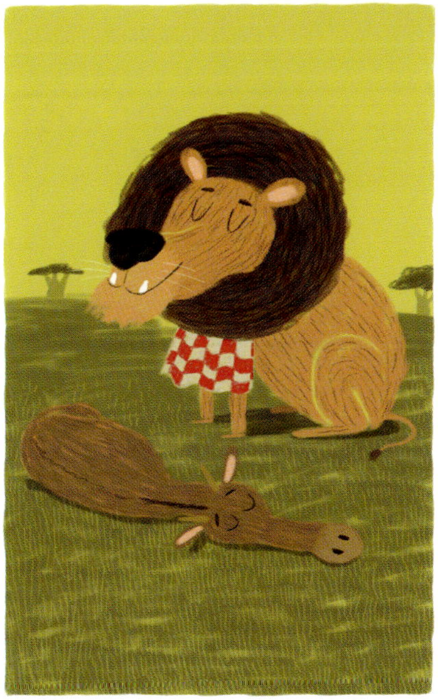

Το **λιοντάρι** τρέφεται με κρέας. Είναι **σαρκοφάγο**.

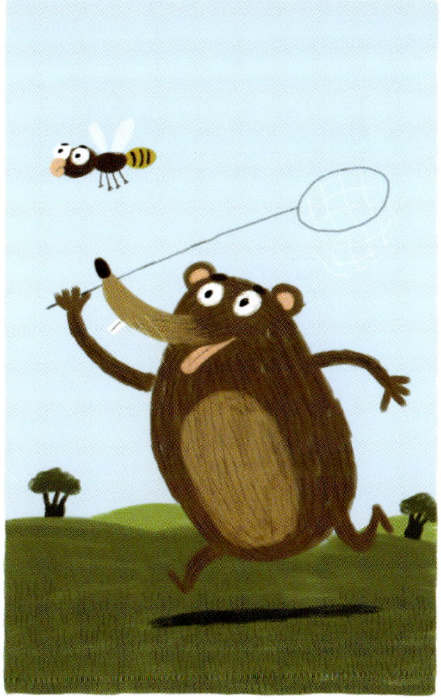

Η **μυγαλή** τρέφεται με έντομα. Είναι **εντομοφάγος**.

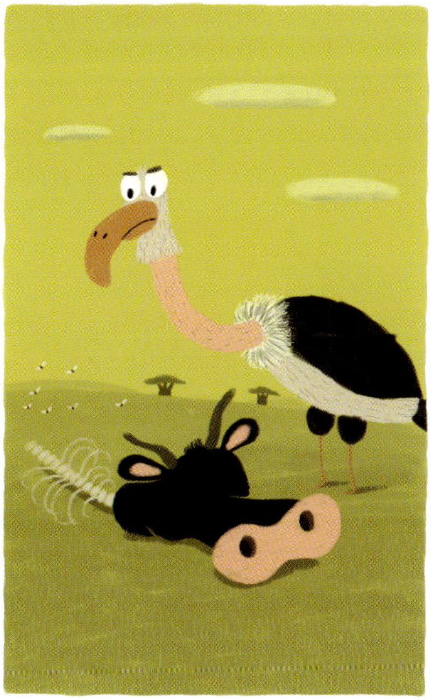

Ο **γύπας** τρέφεται με πτώματα. Είναι **όρνιο**.

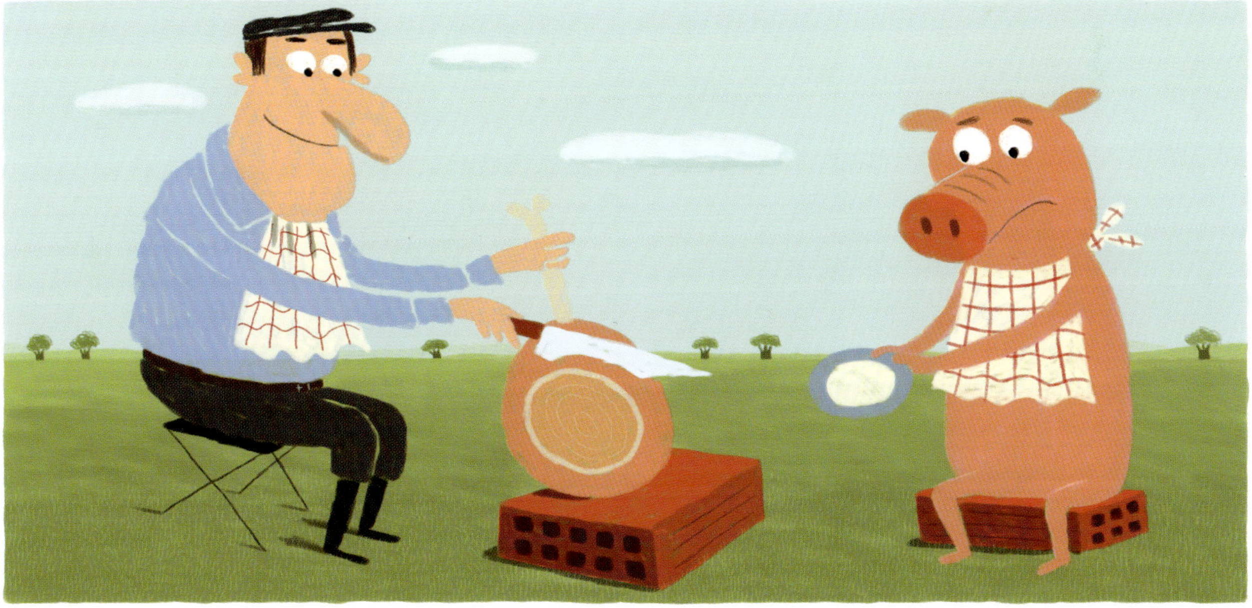

Η **αρκούδα**, το **γουρούνι**.... (και ο άνθρωπος!) τρώνε τα πάντα: κρέας, φρούτα, φυτά, σπόρους... Είναι **παμφάγα**.

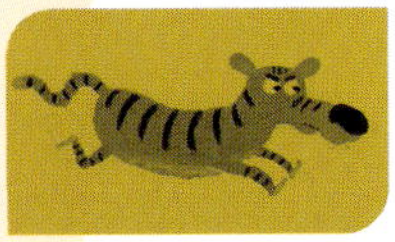

Οι τροφικές αλυσίδες

Πολλά είδη ζώων μπορούν να ζουν στο ίδιο μέρος, γιατί δεν τρώνε όλα τα ίδια πράγματα. Κάθε είδος τρέφεται με κάποιο άλλο είδος. Αυτή τη διαδικασία την ονομάζουμε τροφική αλυσίδα.

Στην αρχή τρώγεται πάντα ένα **φυτό**.

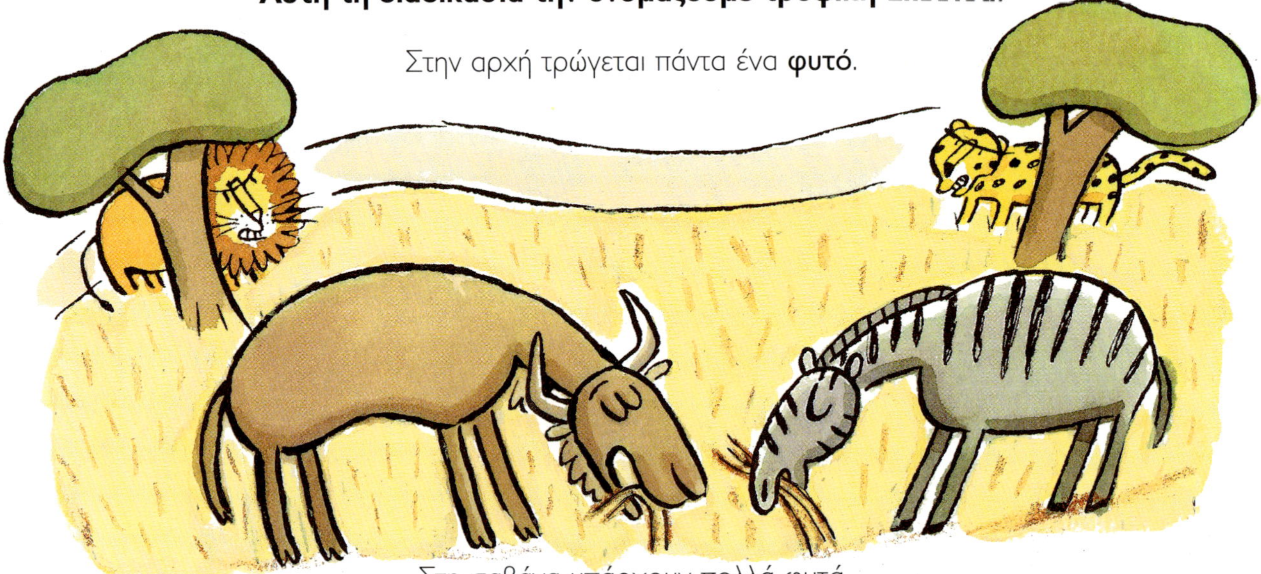

Στη σαβάνα υπάρχουν πολλά φυτά.
Εκεί ζουν **φυτοφάγα** ζώα, όπως η αντιλόπη και η ζέβρα.

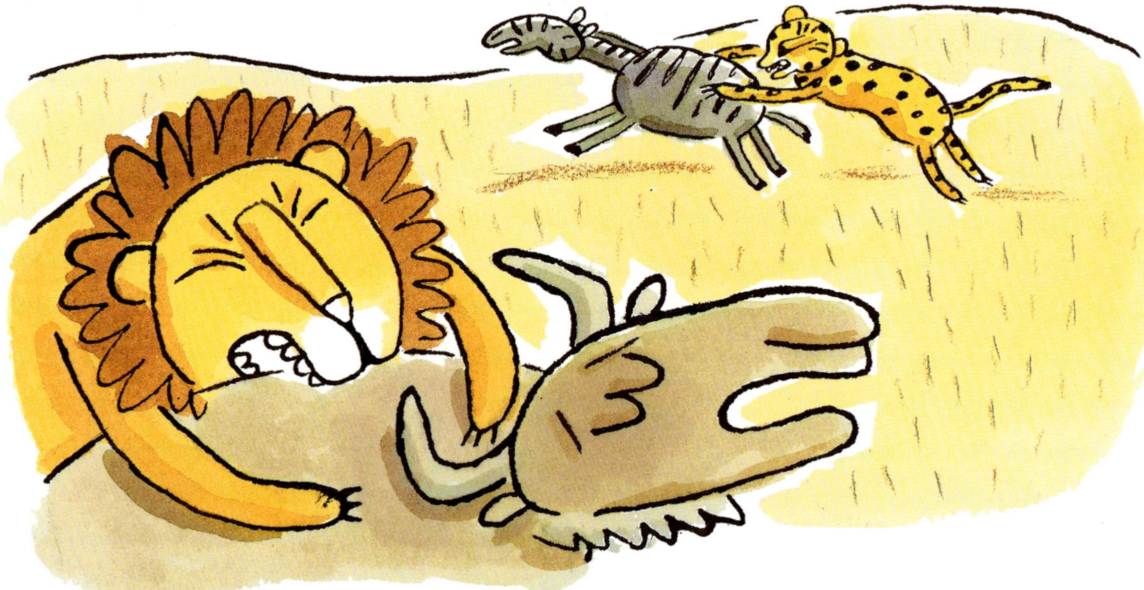

Τα **σαρκοφάγα** ζώα, όπως τα λιοντάρια και τα τσιτάχ, κυνηγούν τα φυτοφάγα.

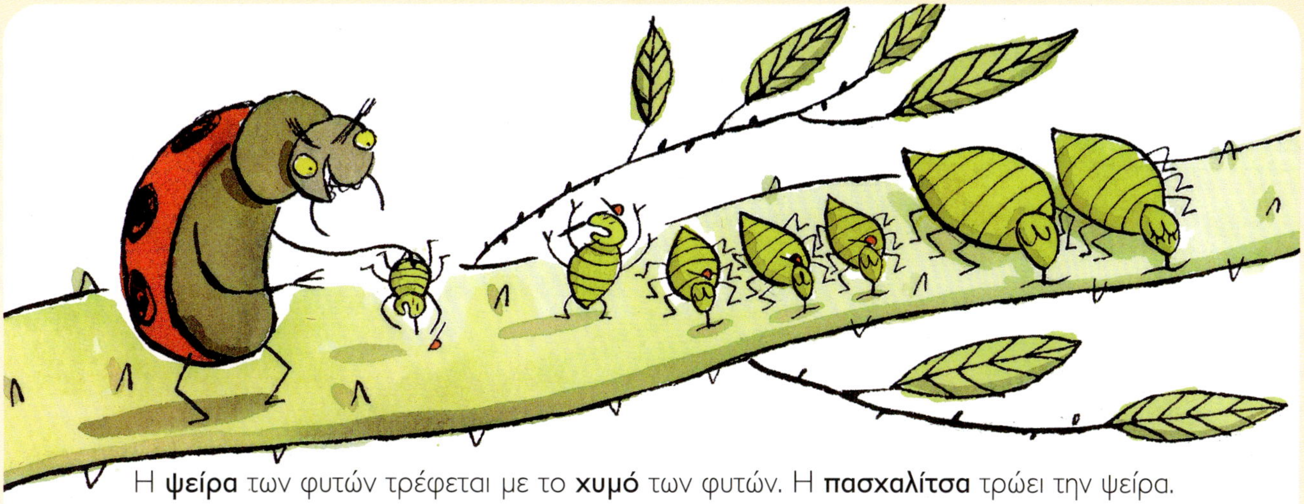

Η **ψείρα** των φυτών τρέφεται με το **χυμό** των φυτών. Η **πασχαλίτσα** τρώει την ψείρα.

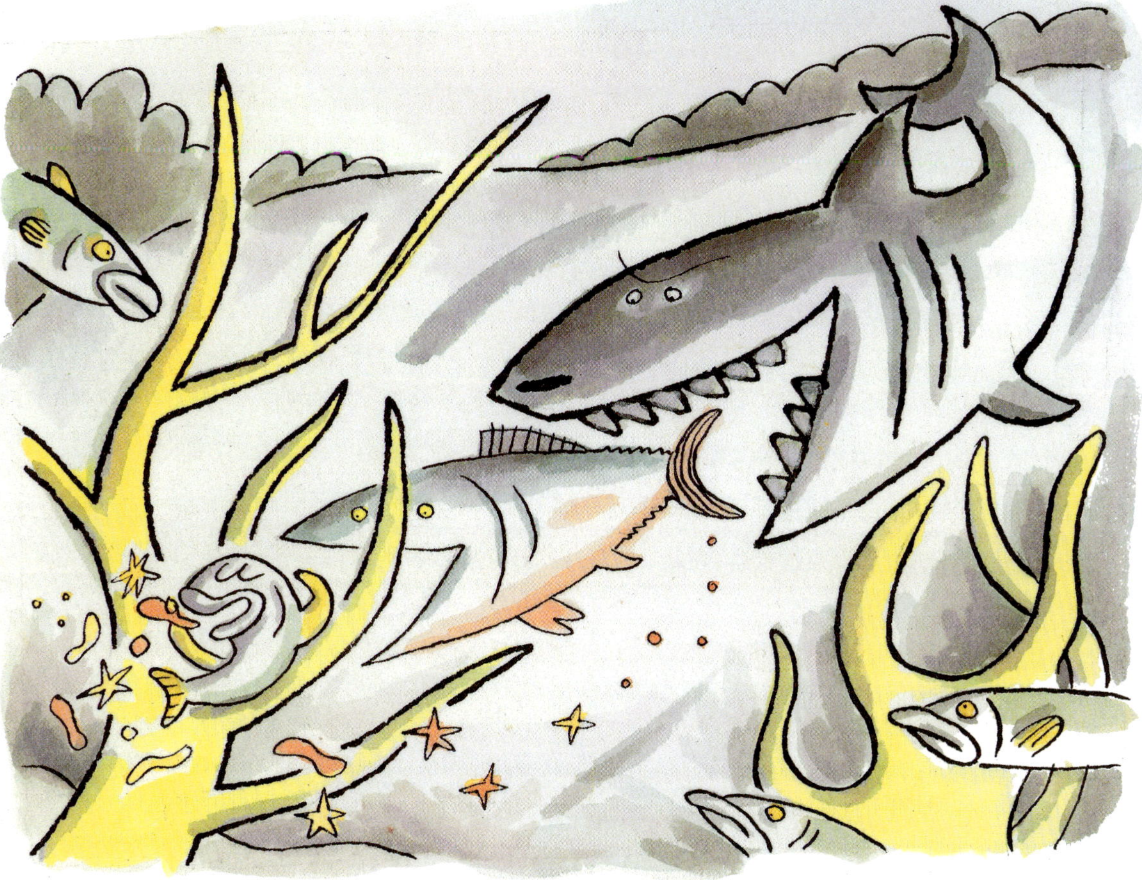

Μέσα στη θάλασσα, στην αρχή της τροφικής αλυσίδας, υπάρχει το **πλαγκτόν**, δηλαδή φυτά ή μικροσκοπικά ζώα που επιπλέουν μέσα στο νερό. Το σκουμπρί τρώει το πλαγκτόν. Ο τόνος τρώει το σκουμπρί. Ο καρχαρίας τρώει τον τόνο.

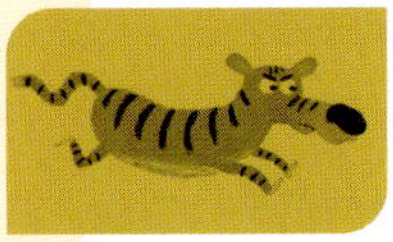

Η αποβολή της περιττής τροφής

Οι κουκουβάγιες αποβάλλουν ό,τι δε χωνεύουν.

Τρώνε μικρά ζώα. Όμως το στομάχι τους **δεν μπορεί να χωνέψει** τα σκληρά μέρη τους. Φτιάχνουν λοιπόν ένα **κουβαράκι** από κόκαλα και τρίχες και το φτύνουν.

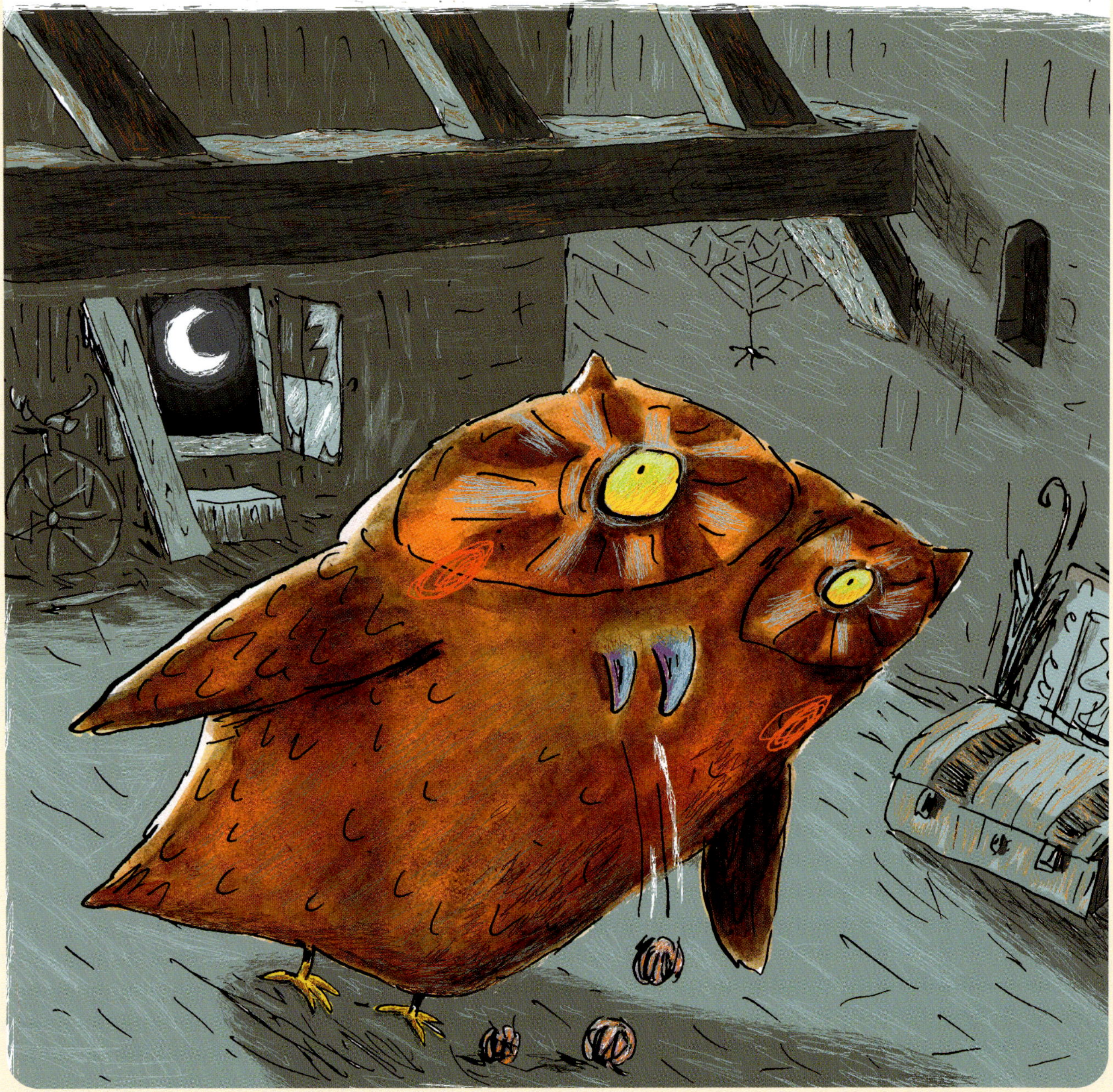

ΣειΡΑ σΟΥ νΑ Παίξεις!

Σ' αυτά τα κουβαράκια βρίσκουμε υπολείμματα ζώων που έχουν φαγωθεί από τις κουκουβάγιες. Παρατήρησε προσεκτικά τη μεγάλη εικόνα και **βρες τι έφαγε η κουκουβάγια**

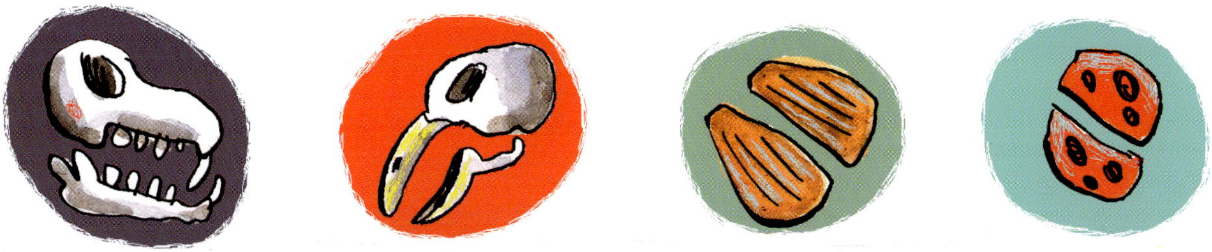

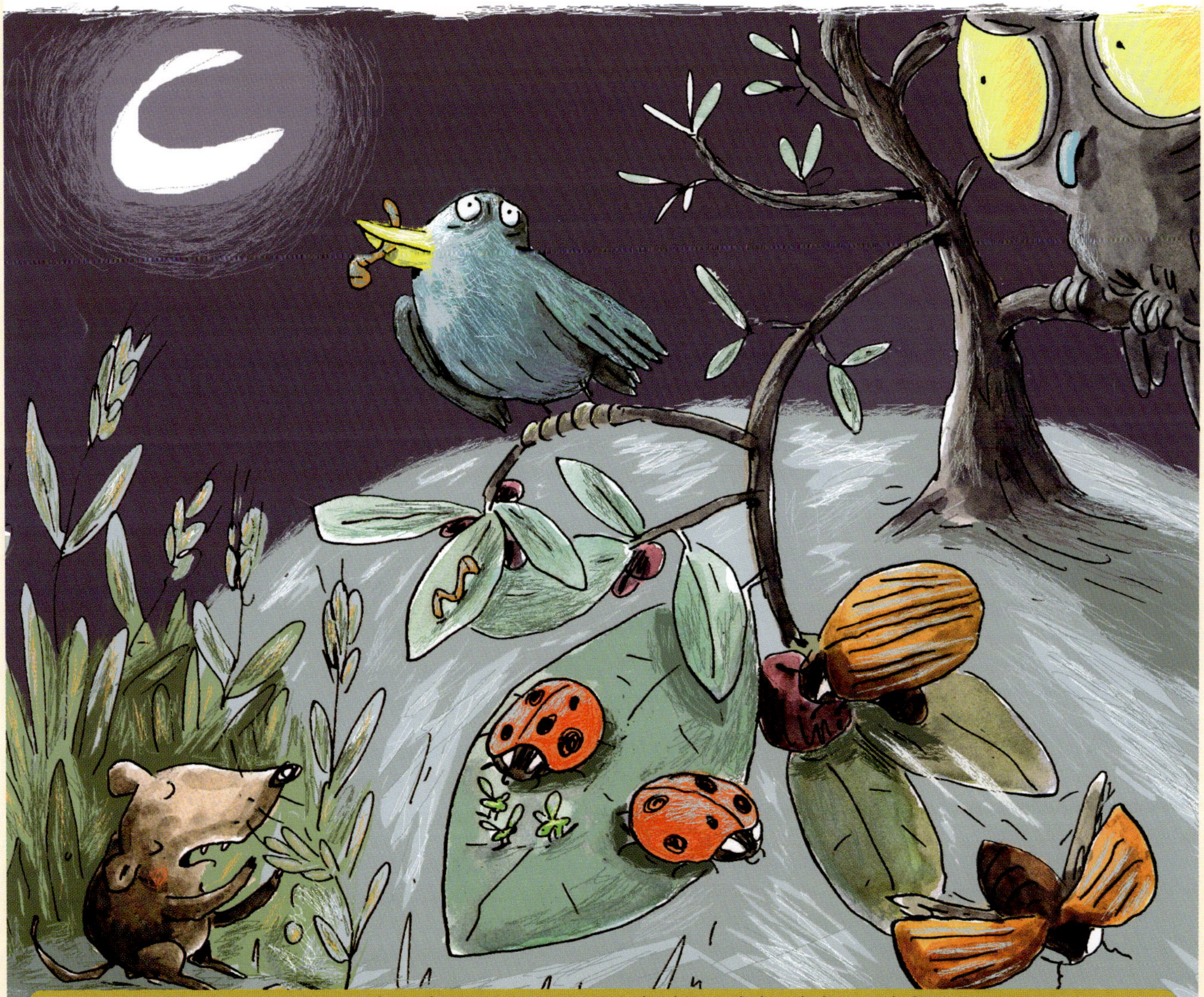

Λύση: η κουκουβάγια έφαγε τον αρουραίο, το πουλί, ένα σκαθάρι και μία πασχαλίτσα.

Ειδικά δόντια

Τα ζώα δεν τρώνε όλα τα ίδια πράγματα.
Δε χρησιμοποιούν τα δόντια τους με τον ίδιο τρόπο.

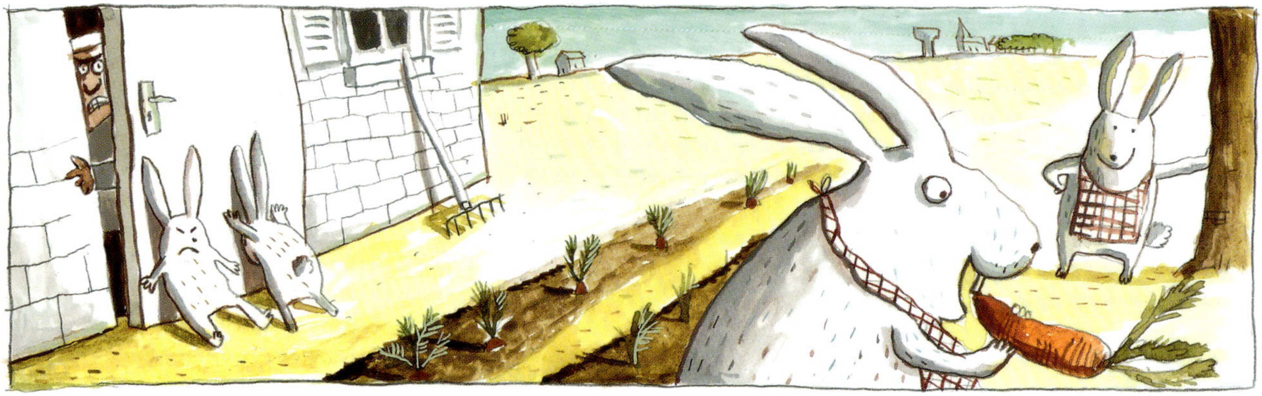

Οι **κοπτήρες** είναι λεπτά και κοφτερά δόντια. **Κόβουν** σαν ψαλίδια.

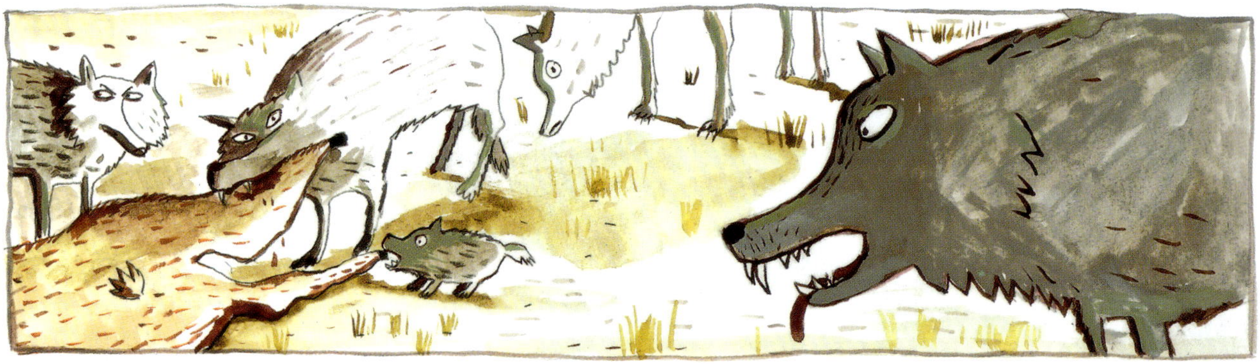

Οι **κυνόδοντες** είναι μυτερά δόντια. **Σκίζουν** και ξεκοκαλίζουν το κρέας.

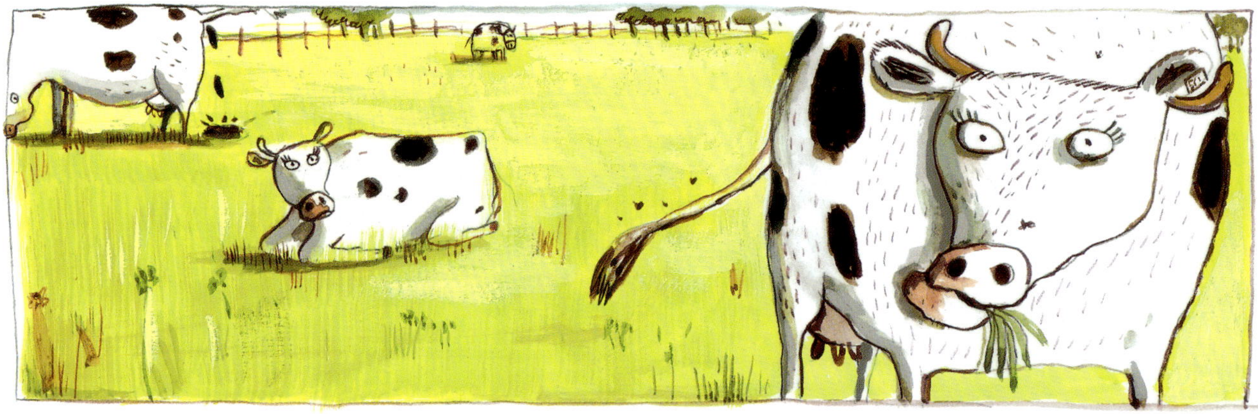

Οι **τραπεζίτες** είναι μεγάλα δόντια. **Αλέθουν** την τροφή με μια συνεχή κίνηση πηγαινέλα.

Όταν ξέρουμε τι τρώει ένα ζώο, μπορούμε να μαντέψουμε ποια δόντια του είναι πιο αναπτυγμένα.

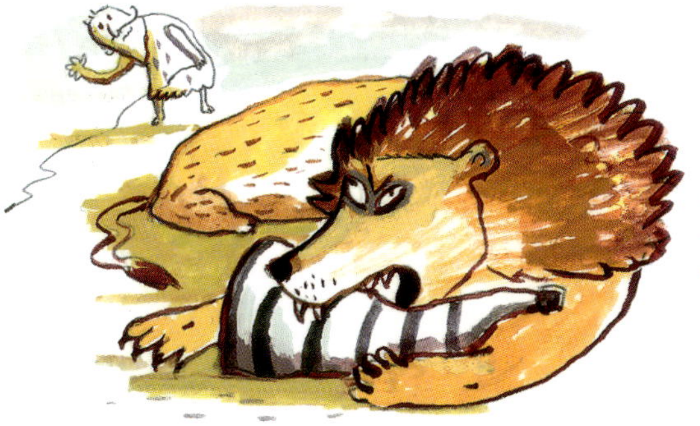

Το λιοντάρι είναι **σαρκοφάγο**.

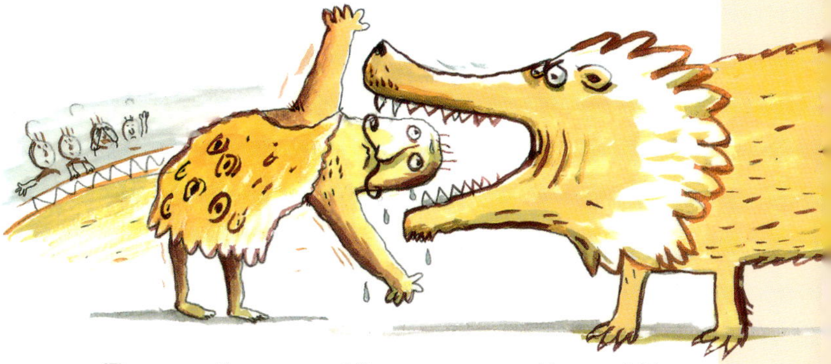

Έχει μεγάλους **κυνόδοντες**, για να ξεκοκαλίζει τη λεία του.

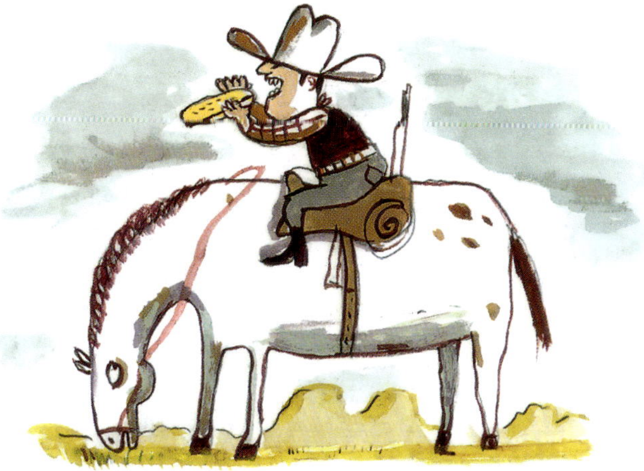

Το άλογο είναι **φυτοφάγο**.

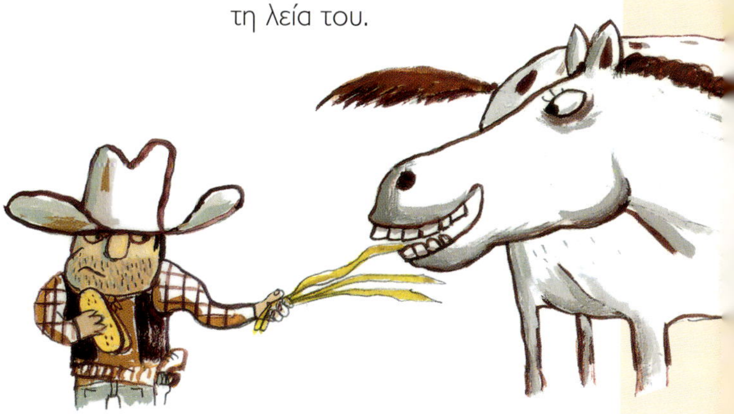

Έχει μεγάλους **κοπτήρες**, για να κόβει το χορτάρι, και μεγάλους **τραπεζίτες**, για να το αλέθει. Δεν έχει κυνόδοντες.

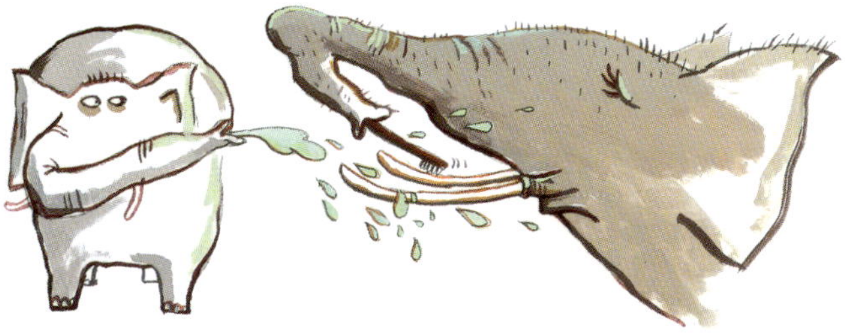

Οι **χαυλιόδοντες** του ελέφαντα είναι πολύ αναπτυγμένοι **κοπτήρες**.

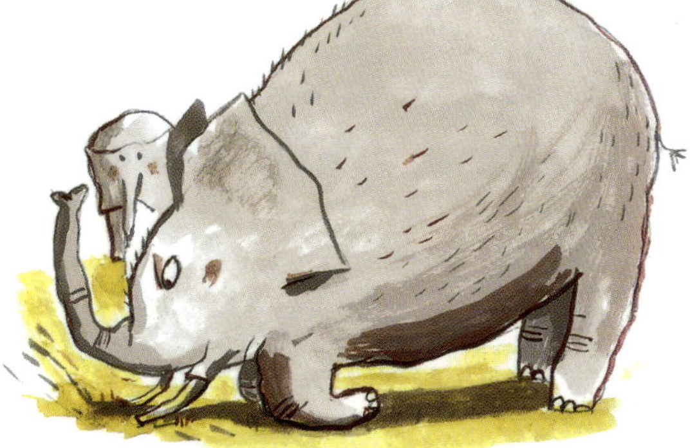

Με τους χαυλιόδοντές του, ο ελέφαντας μπορεί να **σκάβει** το χώμα, να **ξεριζώνει** ρίζες...

Αρσενικά και θηλυκά

Για να γεννηθούν μικρά, πρέπει να ζευγαρώσει ένα αρσενικό με ένα θηλυκό. Για να σαγηνεύσει το θηλυκό, το αρσενικό πρέπει να δείξει ότι είναι πιο δυνατό και πιο όμορφο από τα υπόλοιπα.

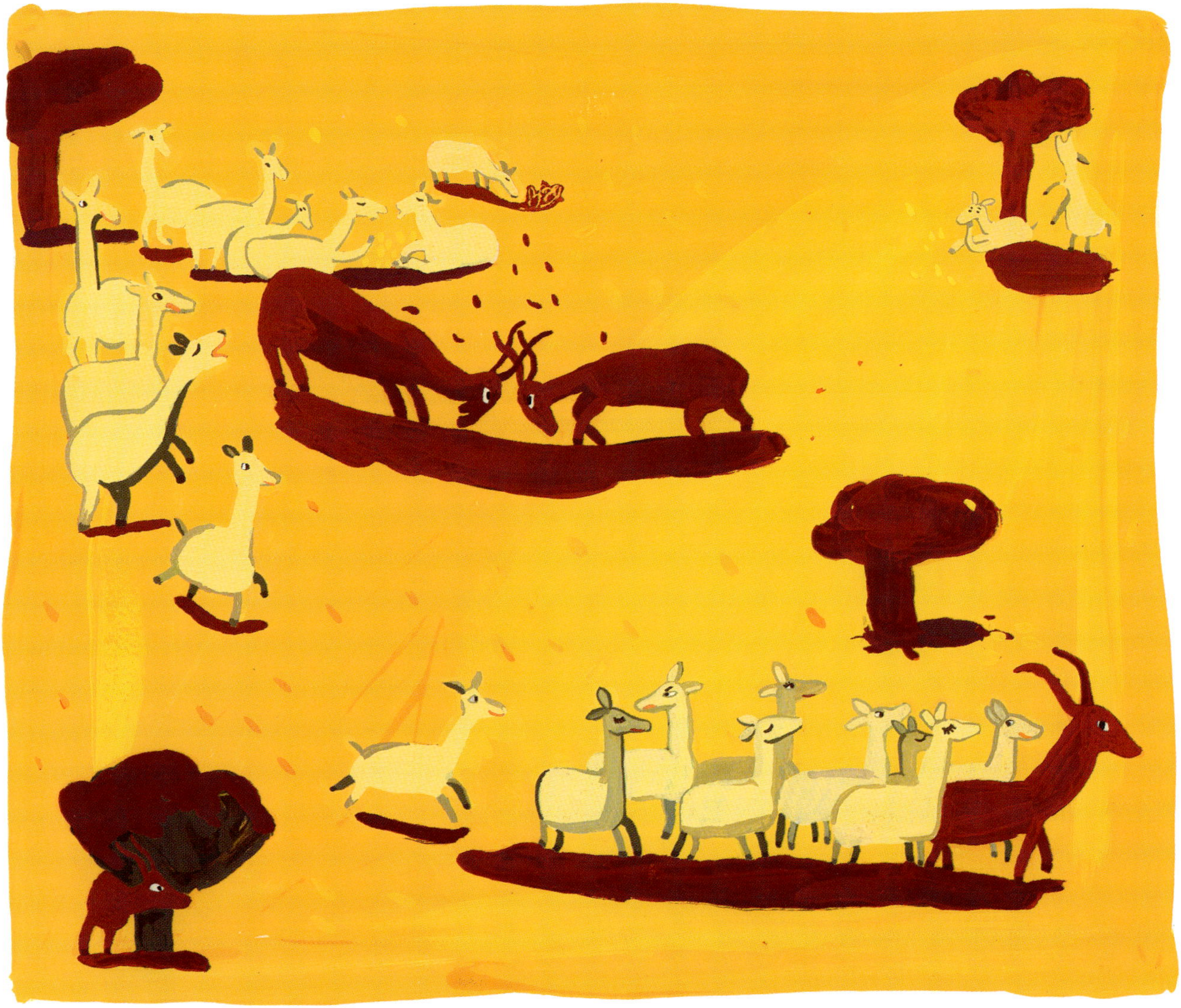

Πολλές φορές τα αρσενικά **μαλώνουν** για να κατακτήσουν μια ομάδα θηλυκών. Στο τέλος της μάχης, το δυνατότερο αρσενικό οδηγεί στο εξής το σύνολο του κοπαδιού.

Ο **κόκορας**
έχει ένα κατακόκκινο
λειρί και ωραία φτερά,
για να σαγηνεύει
τις κότες.

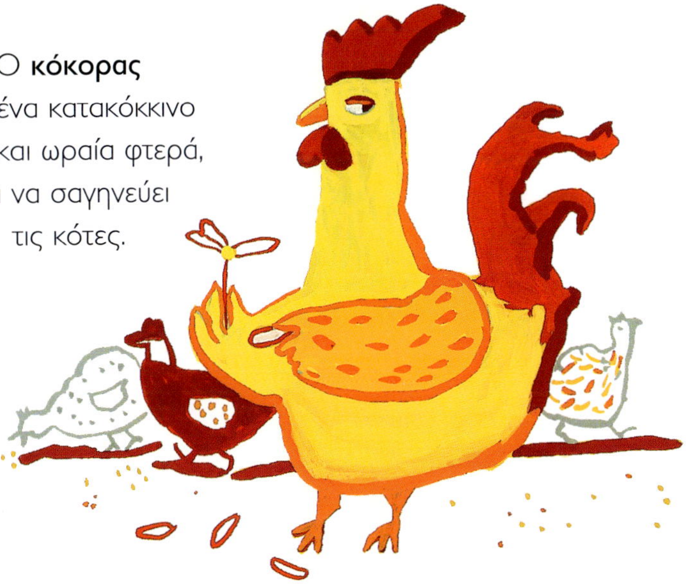

Το **παγόνι** ανοίγει τα
φτερά της ουράς του
μπροστά στα θηλυκά.
Καμαρώνει.

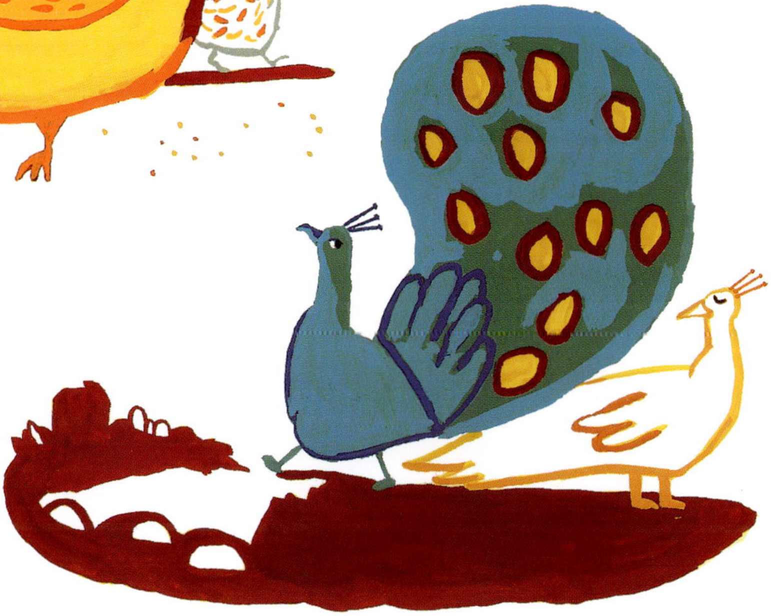

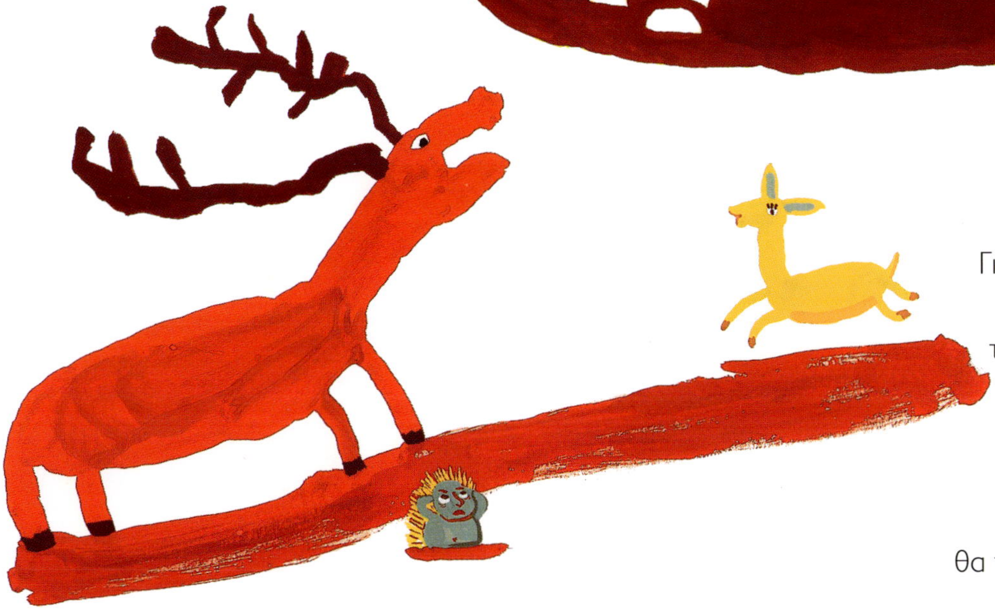

Για να προσελκύσει
τις ελαφίνες,
το **ελάφι** σκούζει.
Είναι σίγουρο
ότι τα μακριά
και γυαλιστερά
κέρατά του
θα τους αρέσουν πολύ!

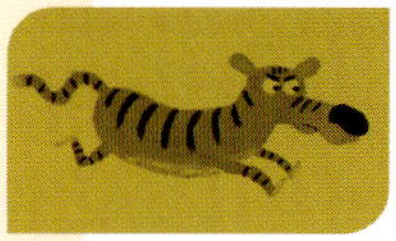

Διάφορα είδη αυγών

Πολλά ζώα προέρχονται από τα αυγά που γεννάει το θηλυκό.

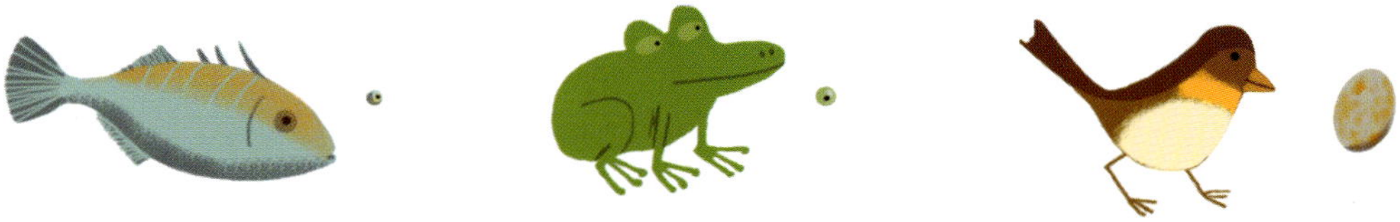

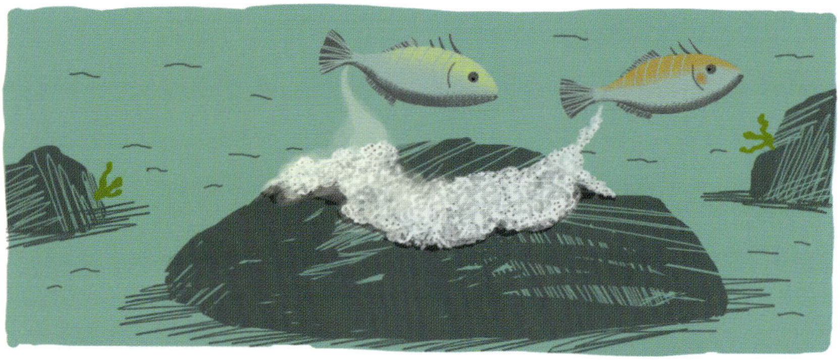

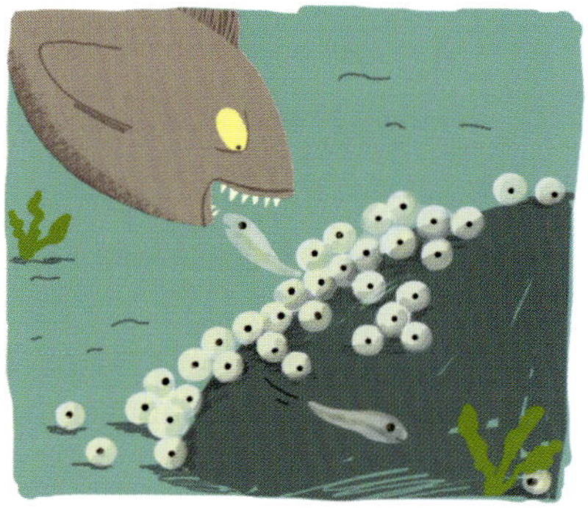

Το θηλυκό ψάρι **γεννάει** εκατομμύρια αυγά. Είναι πολύ μαλακά.

Το αρσενικό **γονιμοποιεί** αμέσως τα αυγά με το σπέρμα του. Τα **αυγά παρασύρονται** από το ρεύμα.

Πολλά αυγά **τρώγονται**, τα υπόλοιπα όμως δίνουν γόνους.

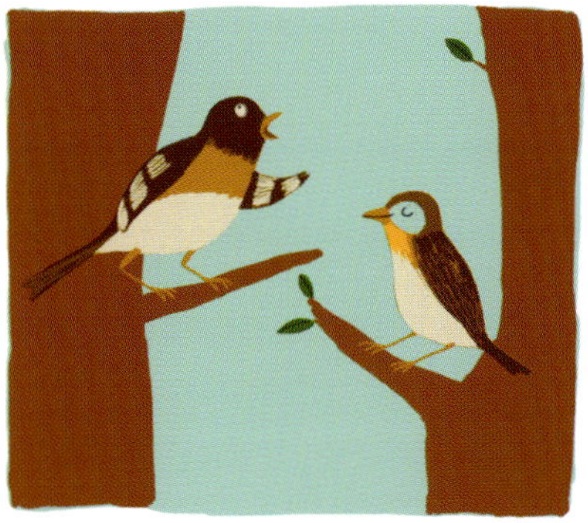

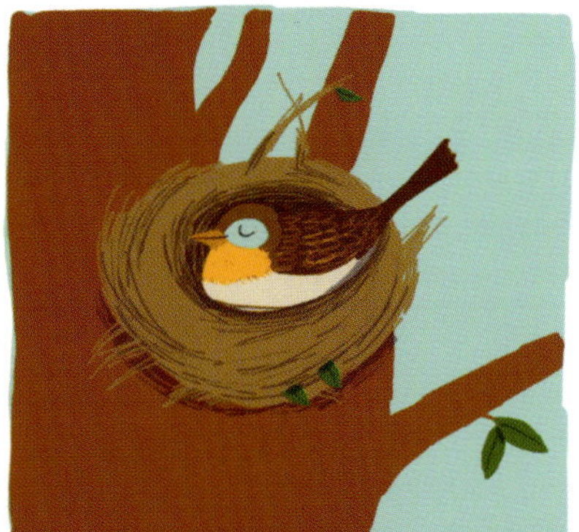

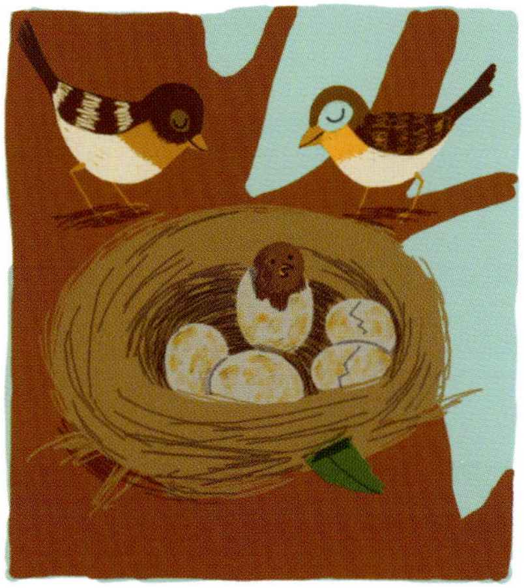

Το θηλυκό και το αρσενικό πουλί ζευγαρώνουν. Το θηλυκό **γεννά** 4-5 αυγά στη **φωλιά** που ετοίμασαν μαζί.

Το θηλυκό **κλωσά** τα αυγά. Τα μικρά μεγαλώνουν μέσα στο σκληρό τσόφλι, καλά προστατευμένα.

Όταν οι νεοσσοί είναι έτοιμοι, **σπάνε το τσόφλι**.

Στα θηλαστικά, τα μικρά μεγαλώνουν μέσα στην κοιλιά της μαμάς τους.

Οι άνθρωποι είναι και αυτοί θηλαστικά.

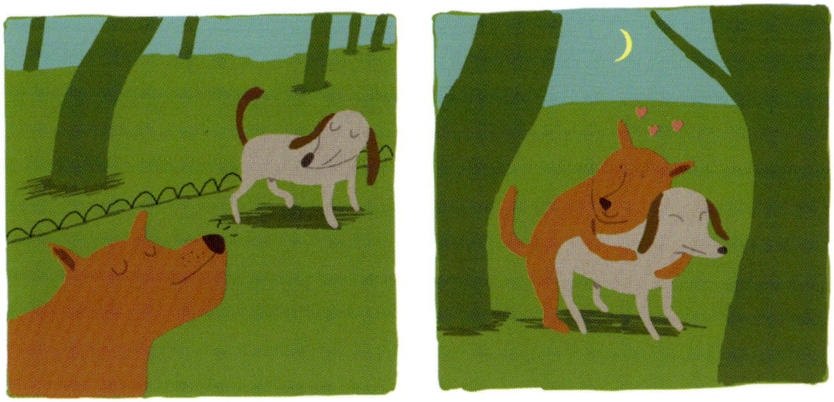

Ο σκύλος και η σκύλα **ζευγαρώνουν**.

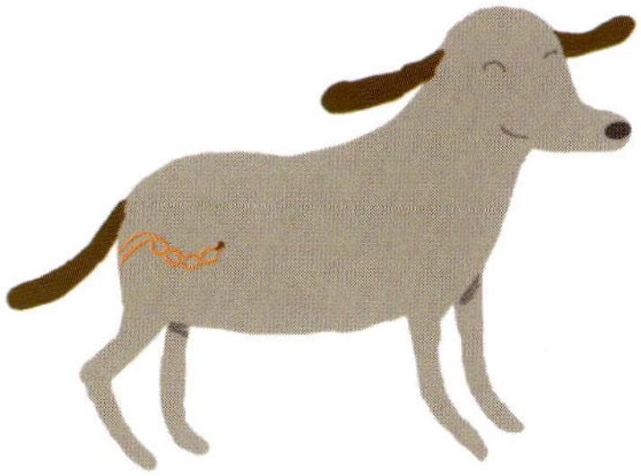

Τα μικρά σχηματίζονται **μέσα στην κοιλιά** της μητέρας.

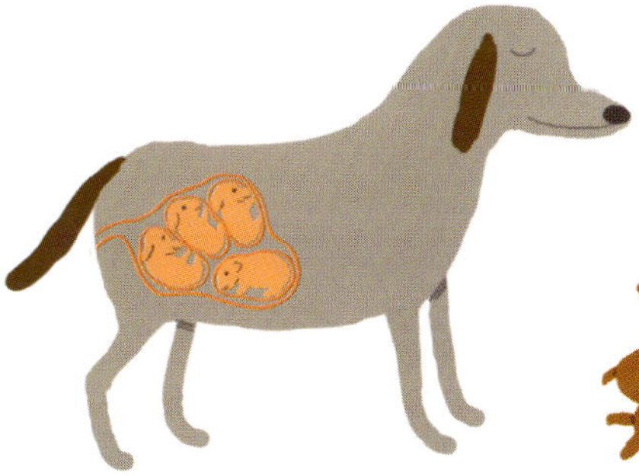

Μεγαλώνουν.

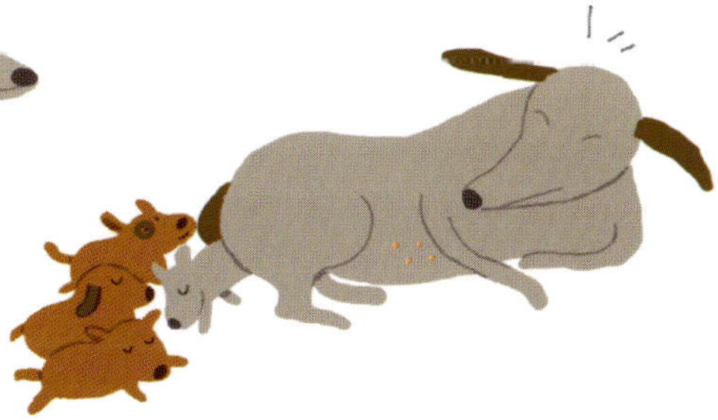

Γεννιούνται ύστερα από **9 εβδομάδες**.

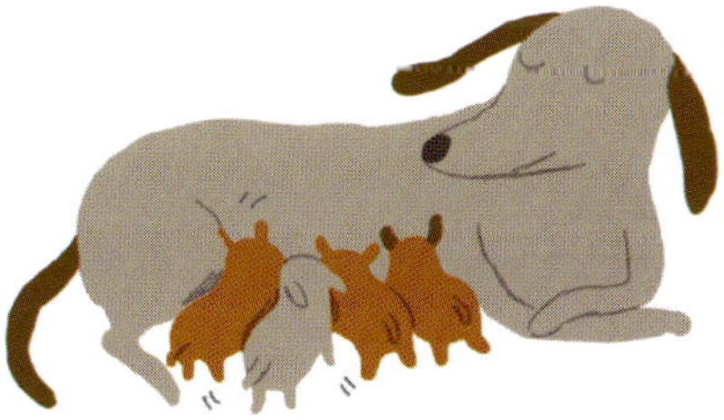

Θηλάζουν τη μητέρα τους.

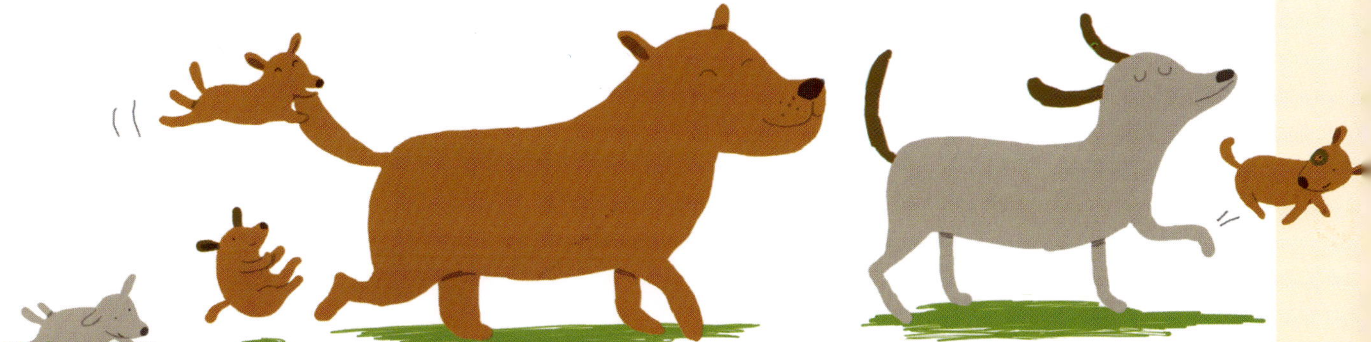

Η σκύλα φροντίζει τα σκυλάκια της μόνο για **μερικές εβδομάδες**.

Από τη γέννηση στην ενηλικίωση

Στα περισσότερα σπονδυλωτά (θηλαστικά, πουλιά και ερπετά), τα μικρά μεγαλώνουν πολύ εύκολα.

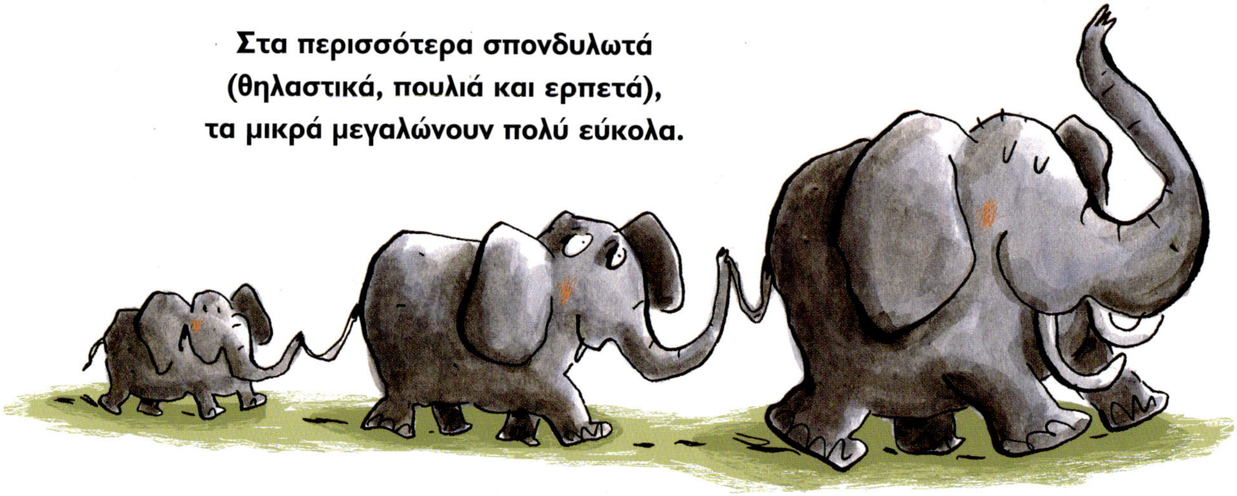

Μεγαλώνουν και παχαίνουν. Για κάποια άλλα όμως, τα πράγματα είναι **πιο περίπλοκα**.

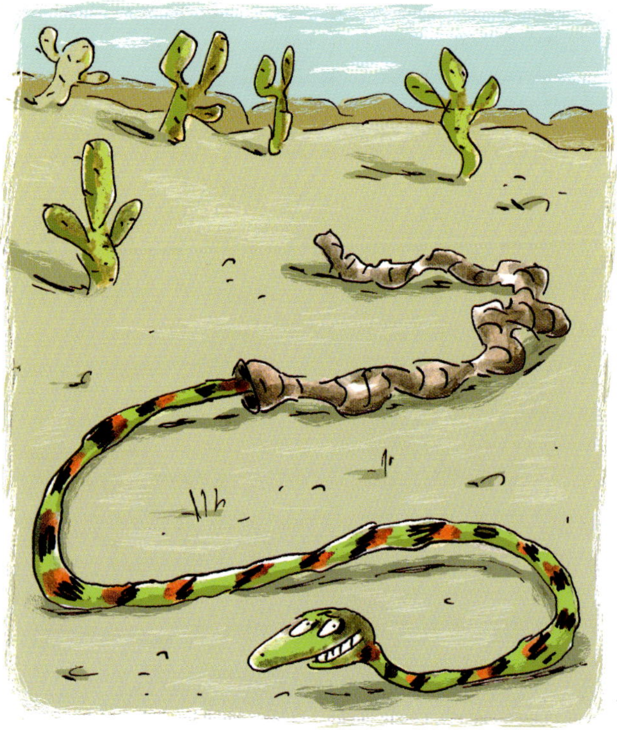

Όσο μεγαλώνει, το **φίδι** αλλάζει πολλές φορές δέρμα: βγάζει καινούριο και πετάει το παλιό.

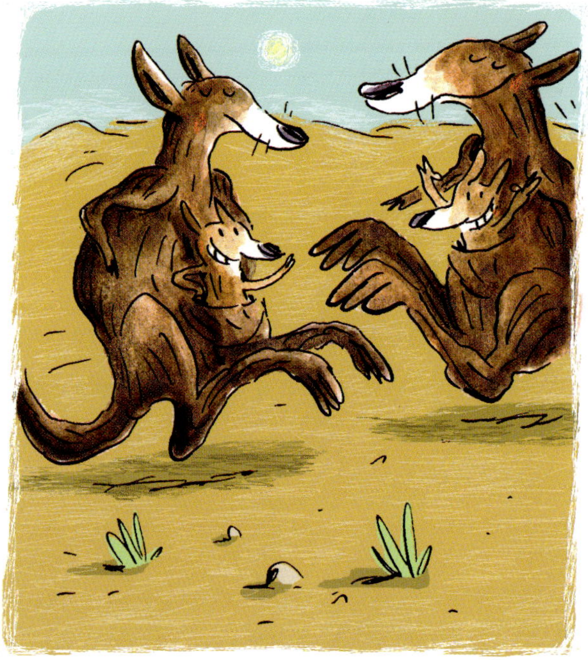

Όταν γεννιούνται, τα **καγκουρό** είναι μικροσκοπικά. Πρέπει να φτάσουν μέχρι την **τσέπη** της μαμάς τους, για να μεγαλώσουν στα ζεστά. Θα βγουν από την τσέπη σε 8 μήνες.

Για να γίνει **βάτραχος**, ο γυρίνος πρέπει ν' αλλάξει μορφή: αυτό ονομάζεται **μεταμόρφωση**.
Μόλις βγουν από το αυγό τους, οι γυρίνοι είναι μικροσκοπικοί·
έχουν μόνο ένα μεγάλο κεφάλι και ουρά. Αναπνέουν μέσα στο νερό.

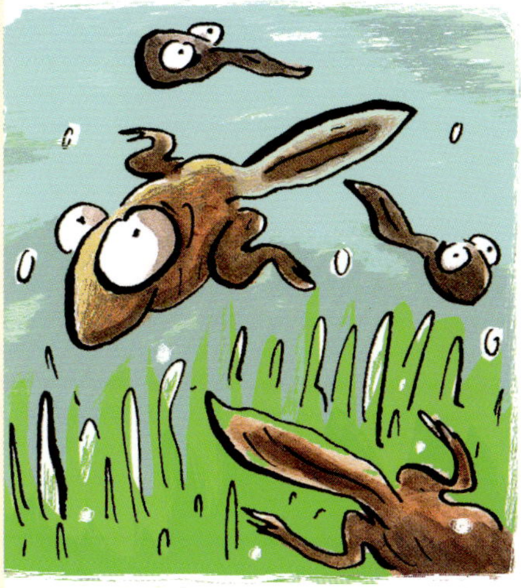

Πρώτα εμφανίζονται
τα **πίσω πόδια**,

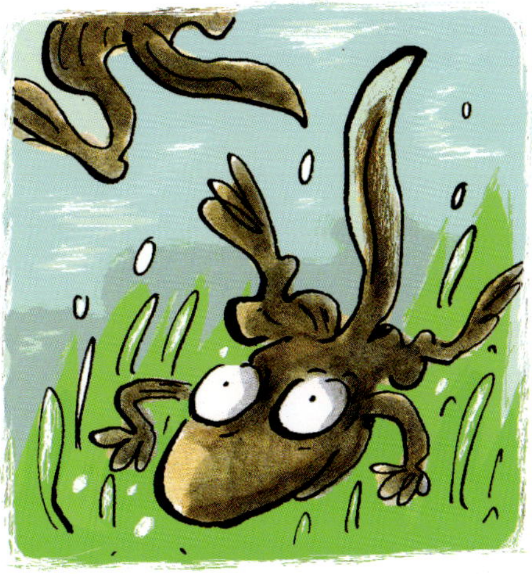

έπειτα τα **μπροστινά**.
Τέλος, η **ουρά** εξαφανίζεται.

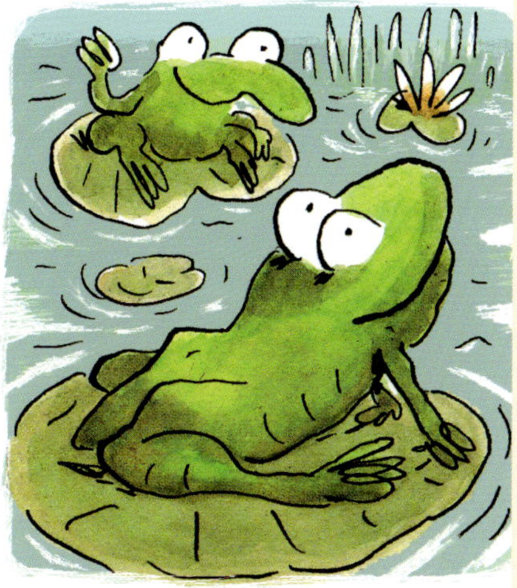

Ο **βάτραχος** μπορεί τώρα
να αναπνέει έξω από το νερό.

Για κάποια έντομα, όπως η πεταλούδα, η μεταμόρφωση είναι ακόμα πιο περίπλοκη.

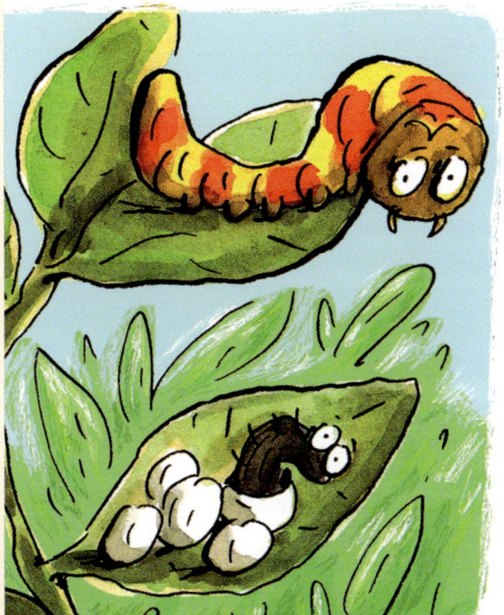

Μόλις σκάσει
το αυγό της πεταλούδας,
βγαίνει μια **κάμπια**.

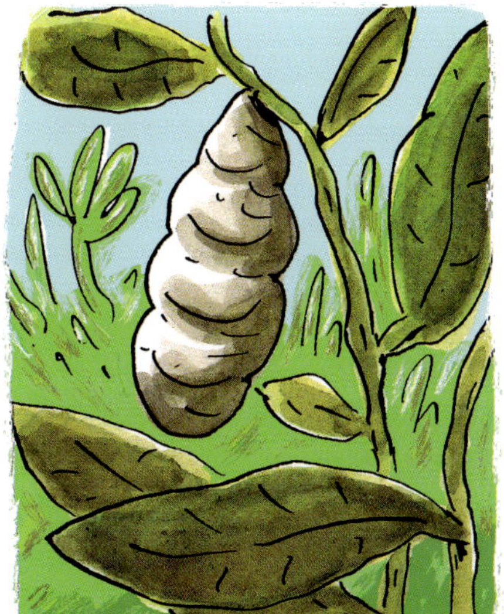

Η κάμπια μεγαλώνει
πολύ γρήγορα. Κρέμεται
και μετατρέπεται σε **χρυσαλλίδα**.

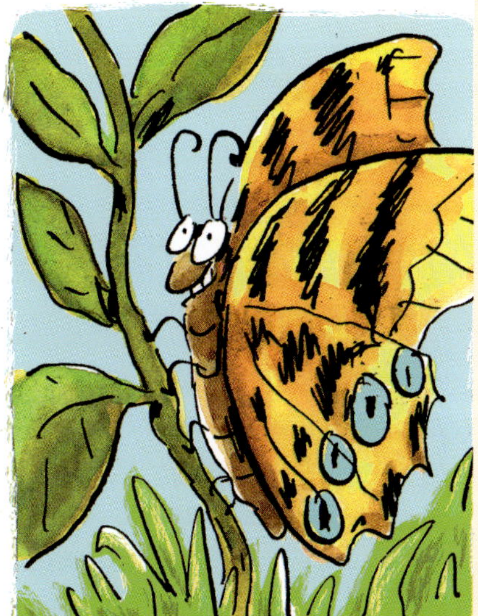

Στο τέλος η χρυσαλλίδα
γίνεται **πεταλούδα**.

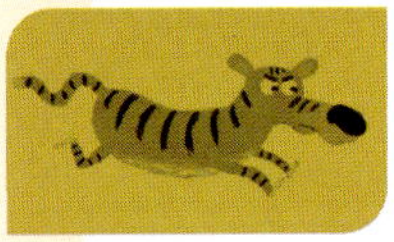

Δουλεύοντας με τα ζώα

Ο **κτηνίατρος** είναι ο γιατρός των ζώων της πόλης και της εξοχής.

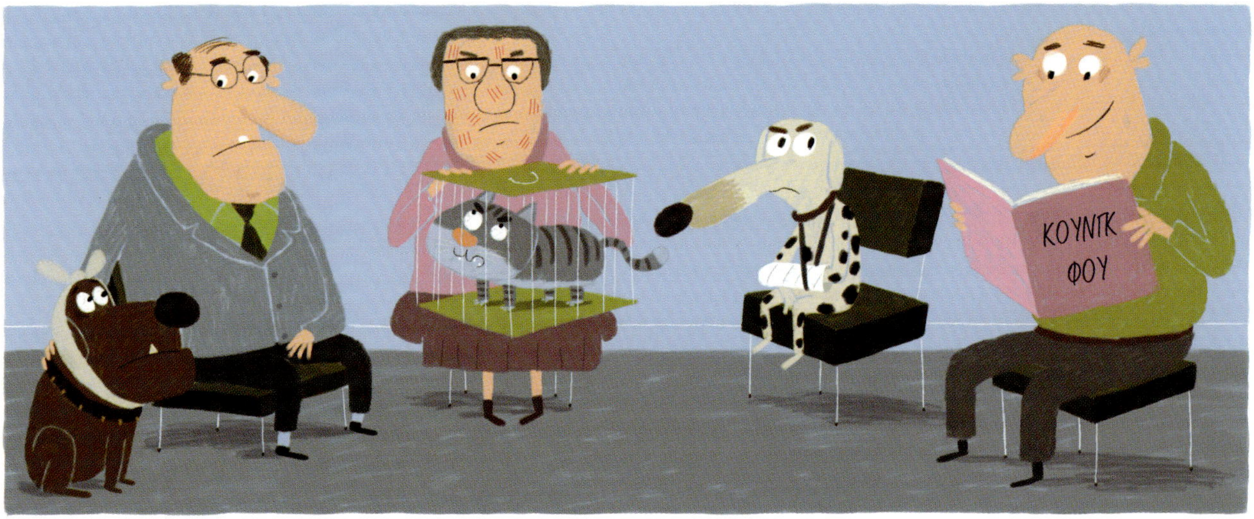

Στην πόλη, ο **κτηνίατρος** θεραπεύει τα σοβαρά ή τα ασήμαντα «βαβά» των γάτων, των σκύλων, των πουλιών που ζουν σε διαμερίσματα με τα αφεντικά τους.

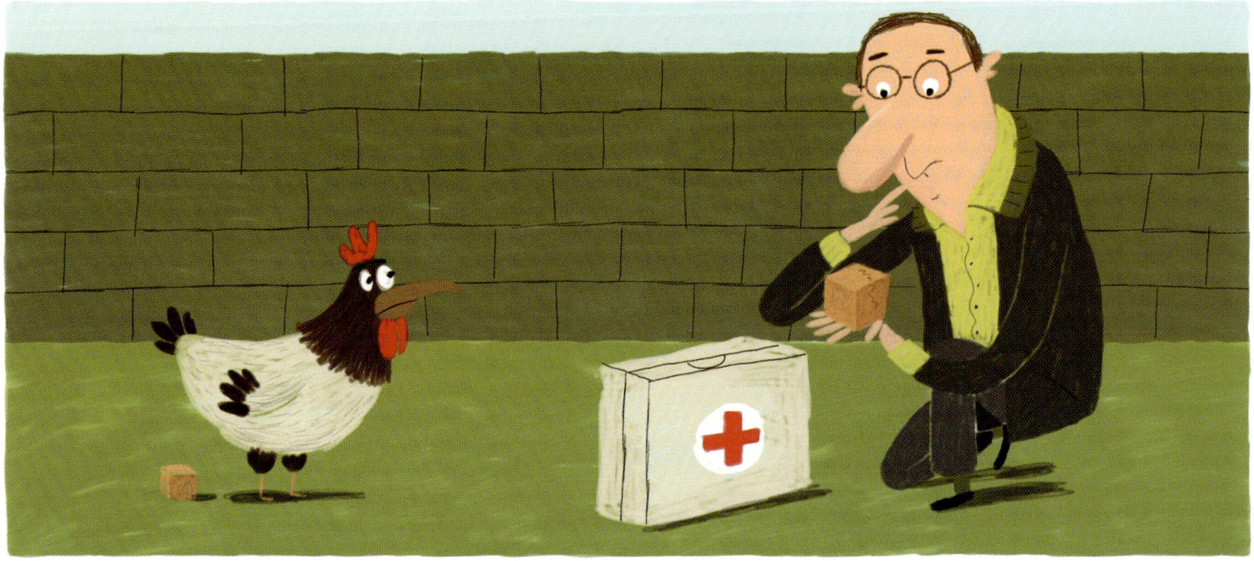

Στην εξοχή, ο **κτηνίατρος** γιατρεύει τα ζώα του αγροκτήματος. Τα βοηθάει να γεννήσουν τα μικρά τους.

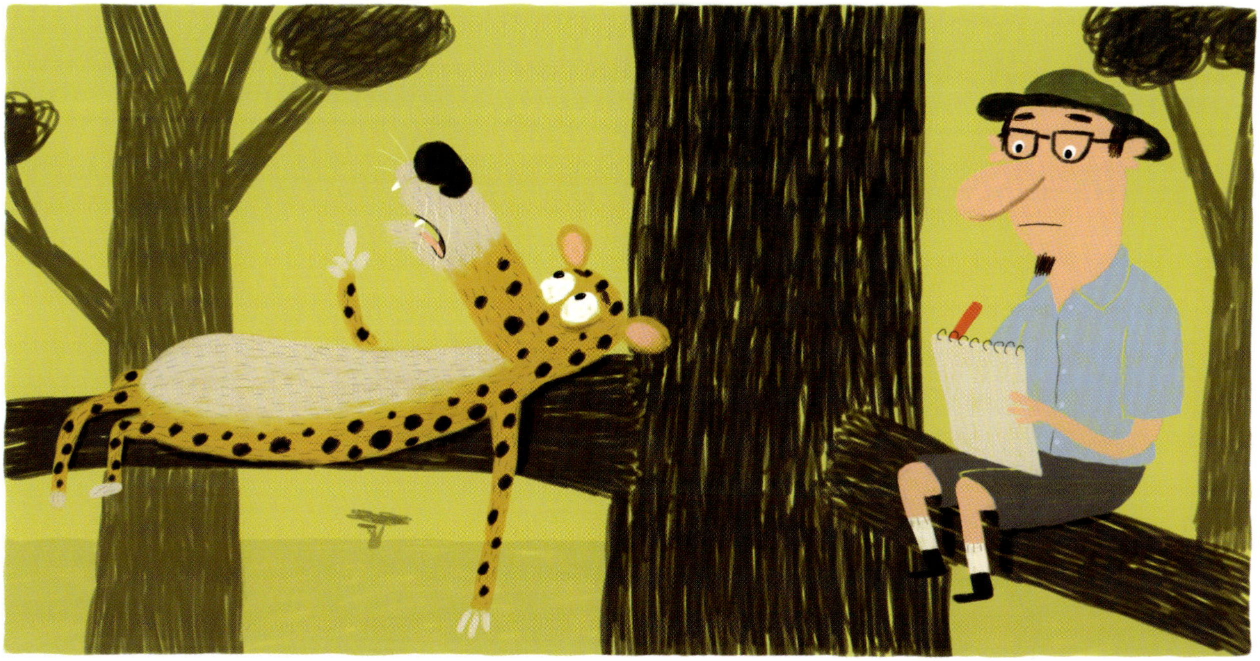

Οι **ζωολόγοι** μελετούν τη ζωή των ζώων, για να τα καταλάβουν καλύτερα και να ξέρουν πώς να τα προστατεύσουν.

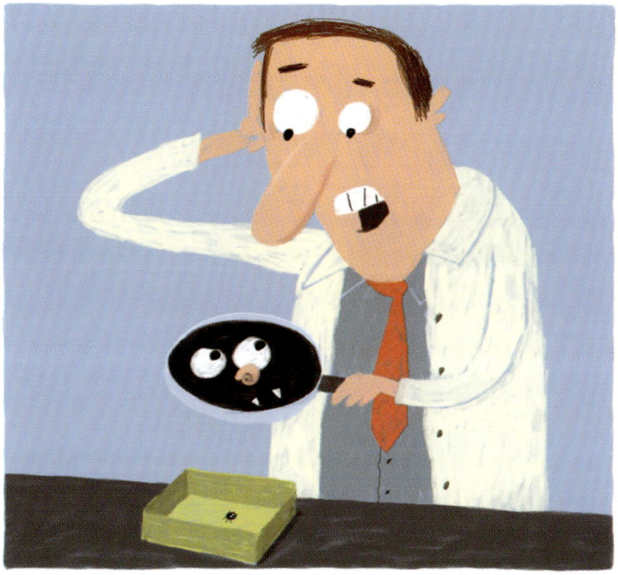

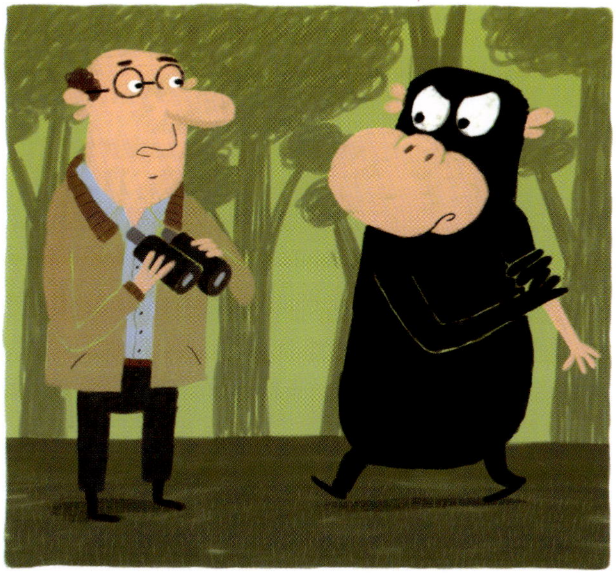

Κάποιοι **ζωολόγοι** μελετούν τη συμπεριφορά ενός συγκεκριμένου είδους για όλη τους τη ζωή. Κάποιοι παρατηρούν τις αράχνες, άλλοι τους γορίλλες... Προσπαθούν να καταλάβουν τον τρόπο ζωής τους.

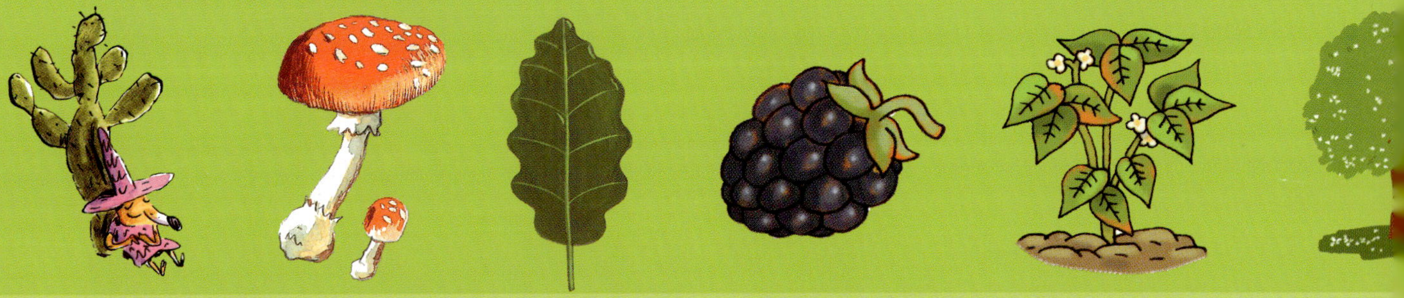

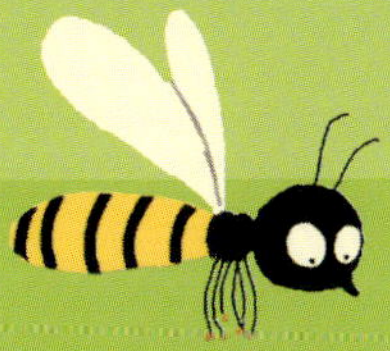
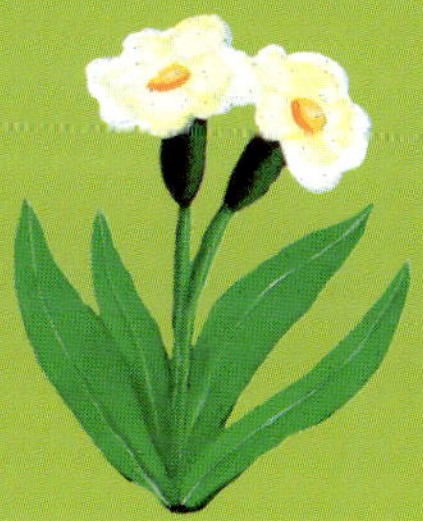
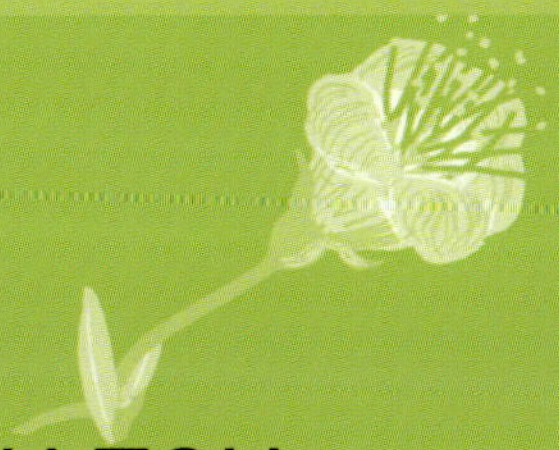

Η ΖΩΗ ΤΩΝ ΦΥΤΩΝ

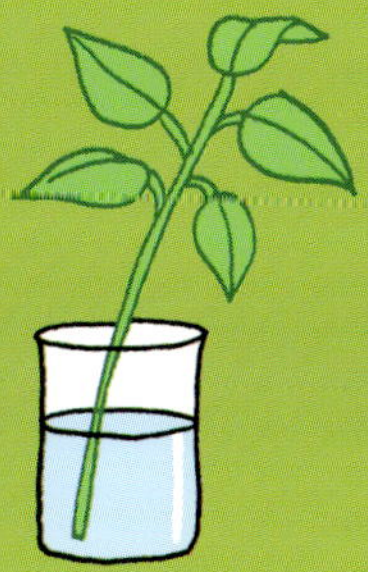
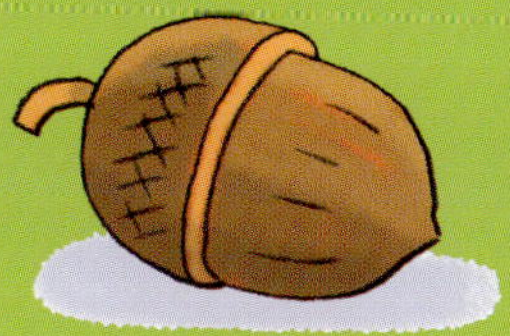

Ένας άλλος τρόπος να τρέφεσαι

Η διαφορά μεταξύ ζώων και φυτών είναι ο τρόπος με τον οποίο τρέφονται.

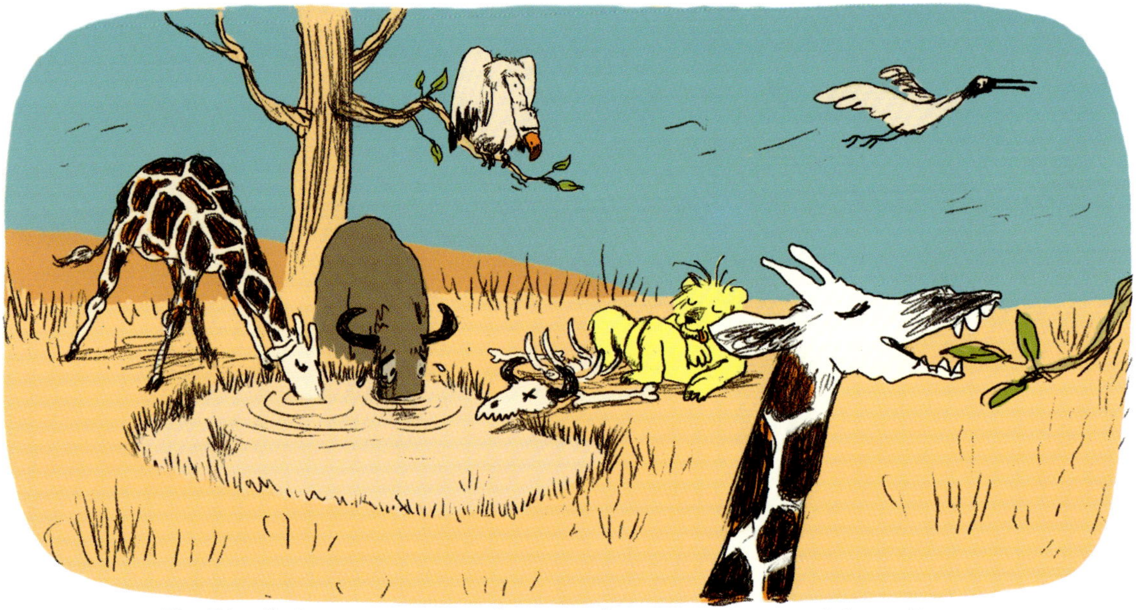

Τα **ζώα** βρίσκουν την τροφή τους μέσα στη φύση, εκεί όπου ζουν.

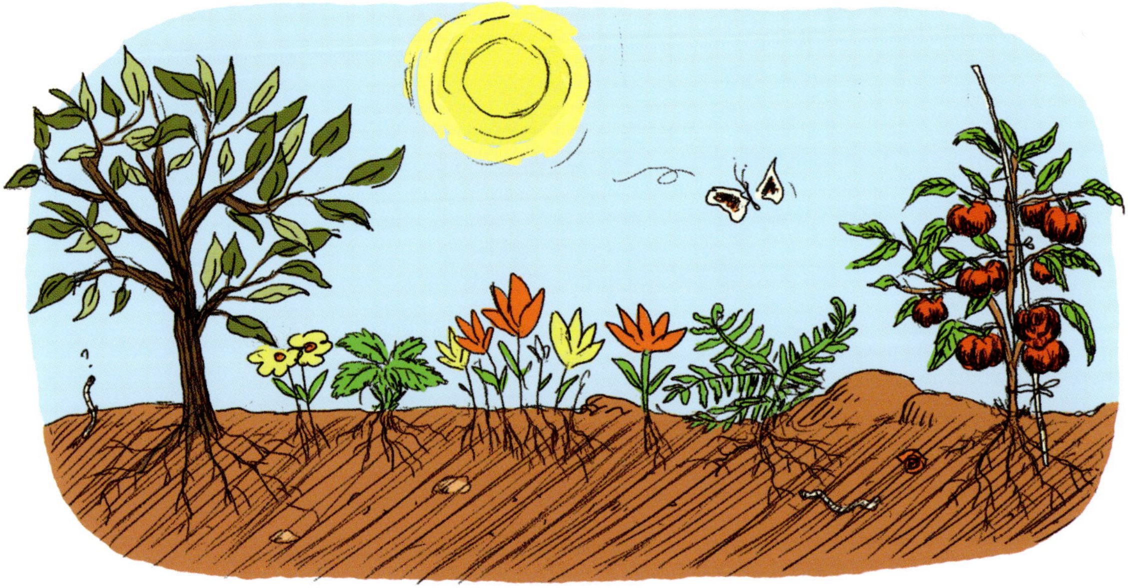

Τα **φυτά** δεν τρώνε. Τρέφονται από τις **ρίζες** τους και αιχμαλωτίζουν με τα **φύλλα** τους την ενέργεια του ήλιου.

ΣειΡΑ σΟΥ νΑ Παίξεις!

Κάποια ζώα μοιάζουν πολύ με φυτά.

Παρατήρησε αυτά τα σχέδια και μάντεψε ποια είναι **ζώα** και ποια **φυτά**.

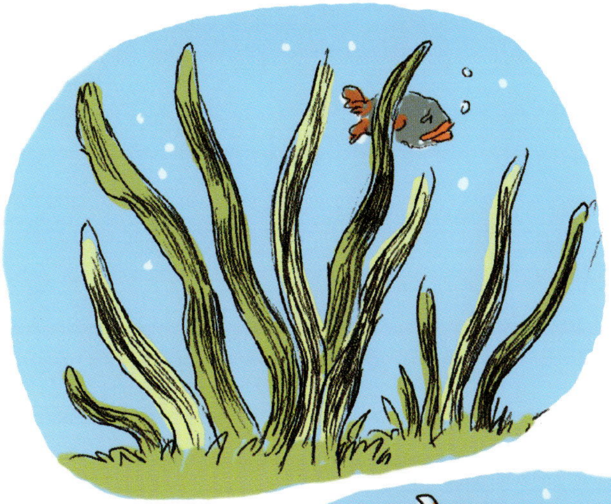

φύκια

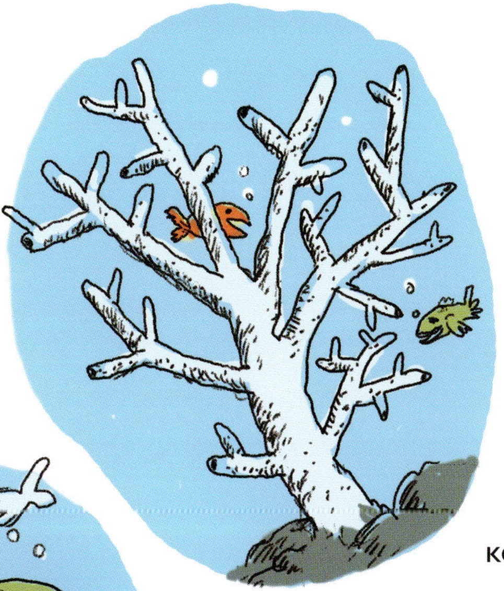

κοράλλια

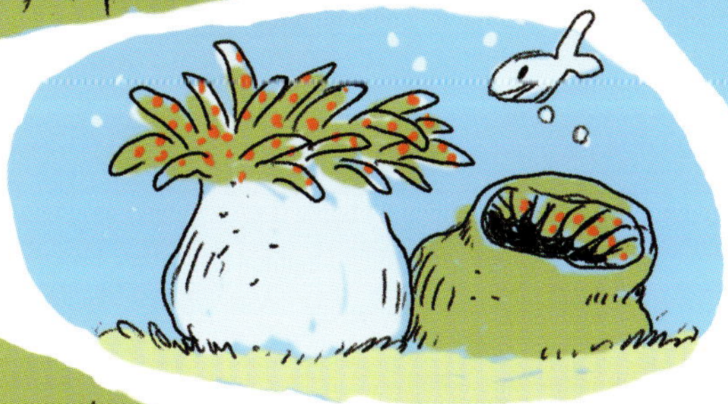

ανεμώνες της θάλασσας

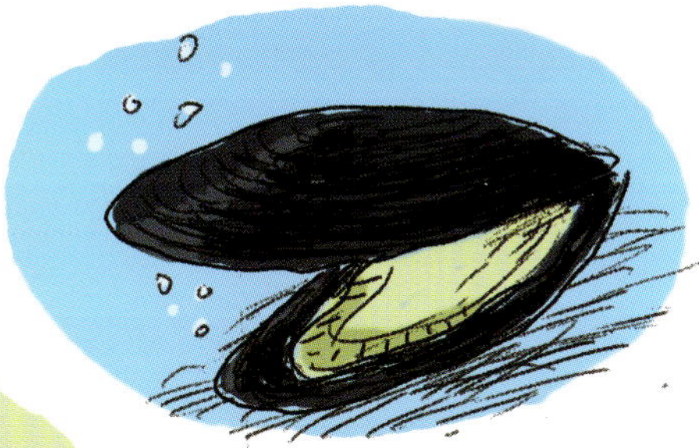

ένα μύδι

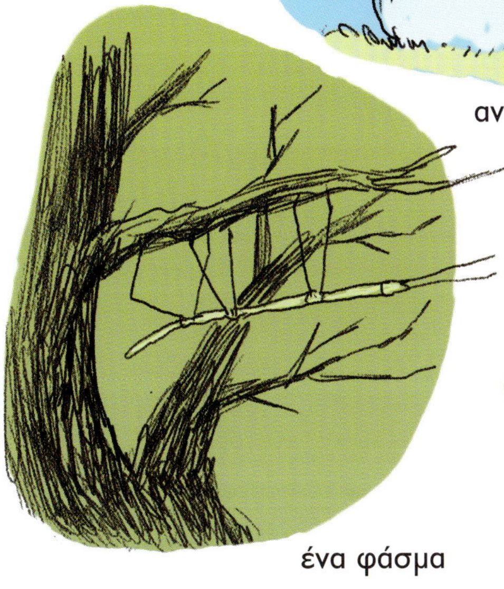

ένα φάσμα

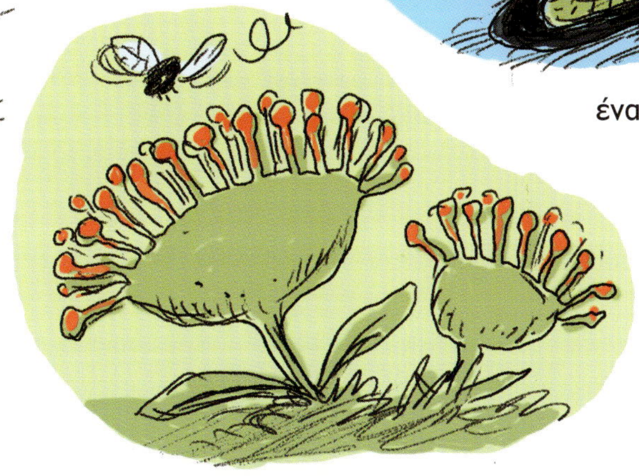

δροσέρες

Λύση: το φύκι είναι φυτό. το κοράλλι, η ανεμώνη της θάλασσας και το μύδι είναι ζώα που τρέφονται με άλλα μικροσκοπικά ζώα της θάλασσας. το φάσμα είναι ένα έντομο που μοιάζει με κλαδάκι. η δροσέρα καταπίνει έντομα, αλλά είναι επίσης ένα σαρκοφάγο φυτό.

Πολλά και διαφορετικά φυτά

Υπάρχουν φυτά κάθε μεγέθους.

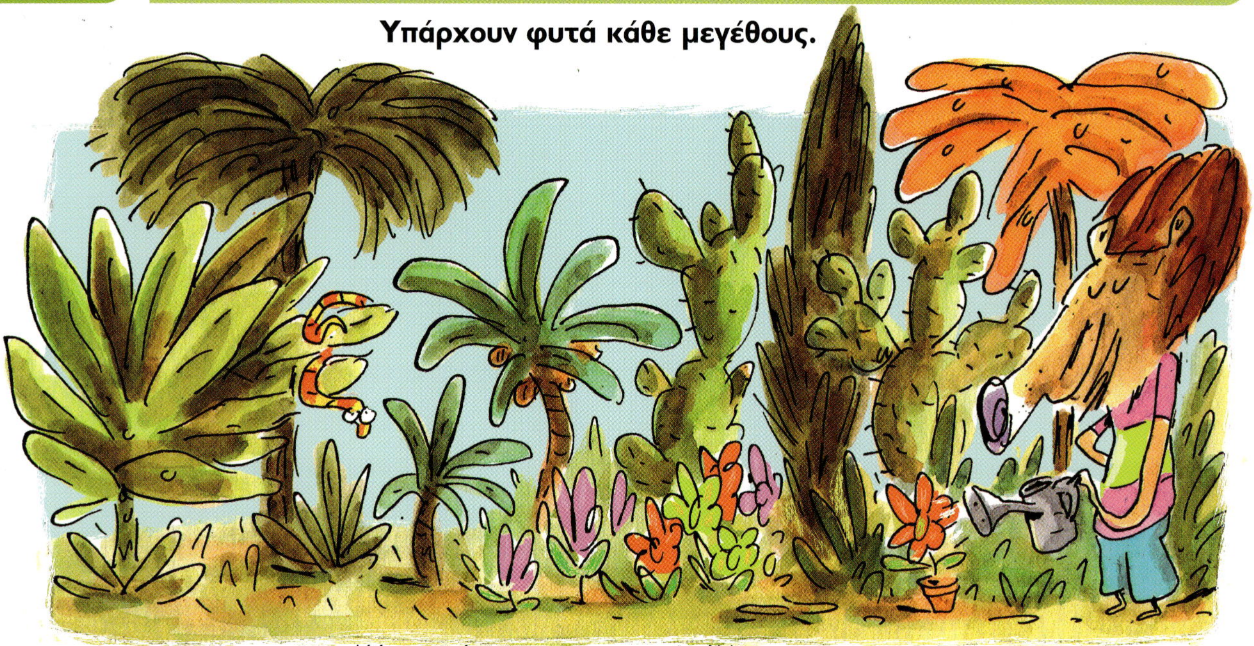

Κάποια είναι **μικροσκοπικά**, άλλα **τεράστια**.

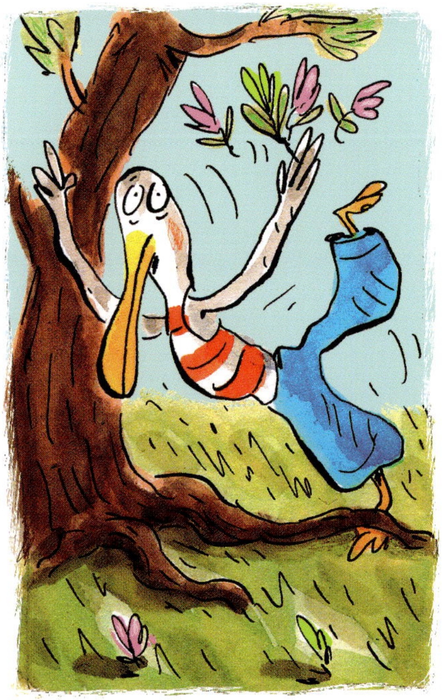

Τα φυτά στερεώνονται στο χώμα με τις **ρίζες** τους.

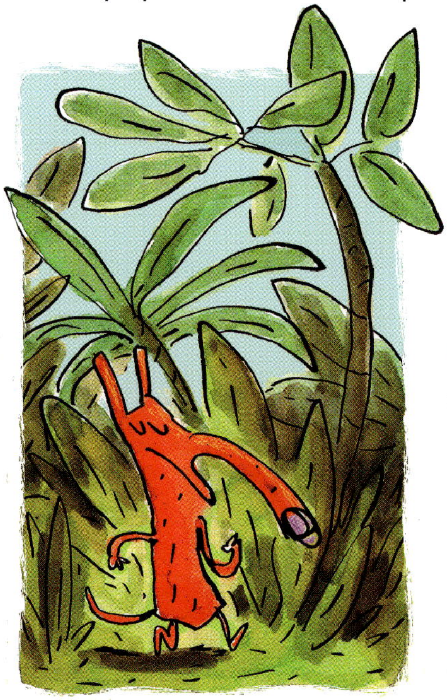

Τις περισσότερες φορές είναι **πράσινα**.

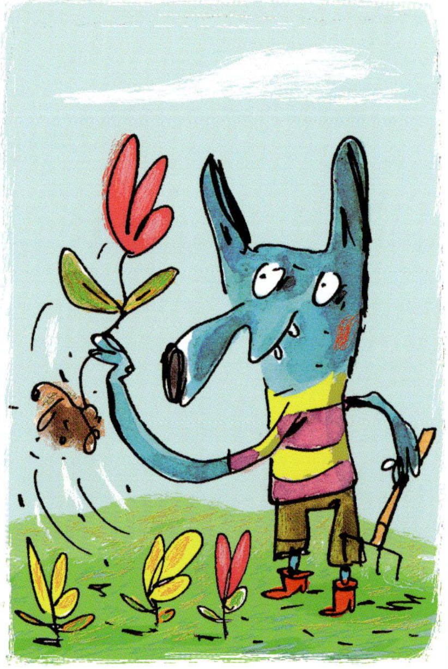

Πολλά φυτά έχουν **λουλούδια**.

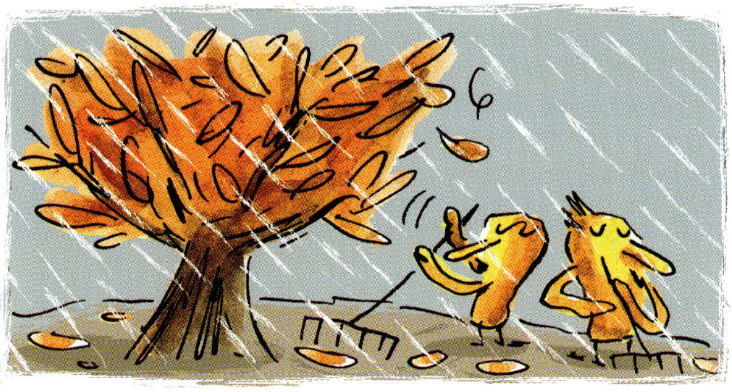

Ένα οπωροφόρο δέντρο έχει **φύλλα** από την άνοιξη μέχρι το φθινόπωρο.

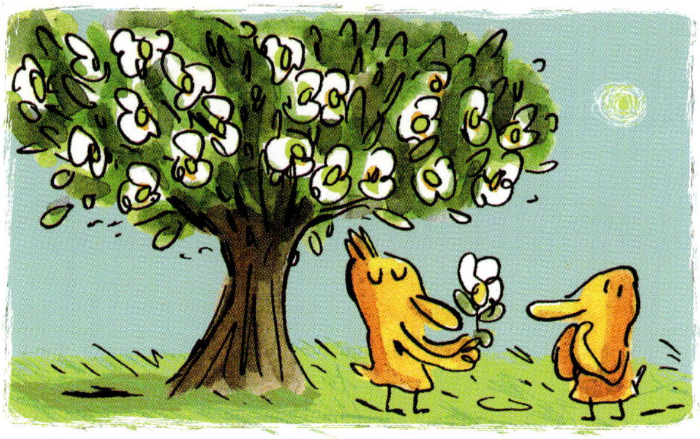

Την άνοιξη έχει **λουλούδια**.

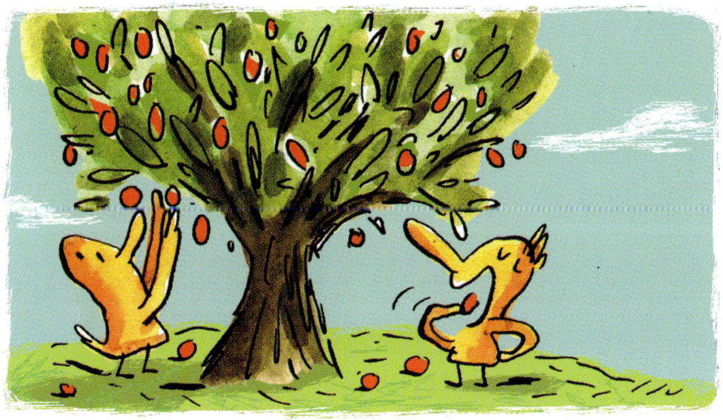

Το καλοκαίρι έχει **φρούτα**.

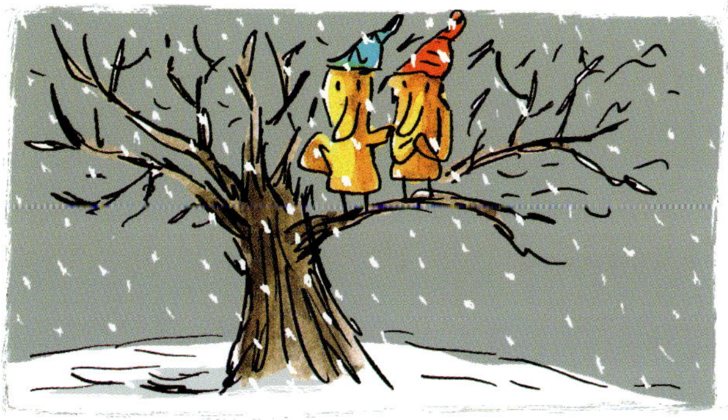

Το χειμώνα **δεν έχει φύλλα**.

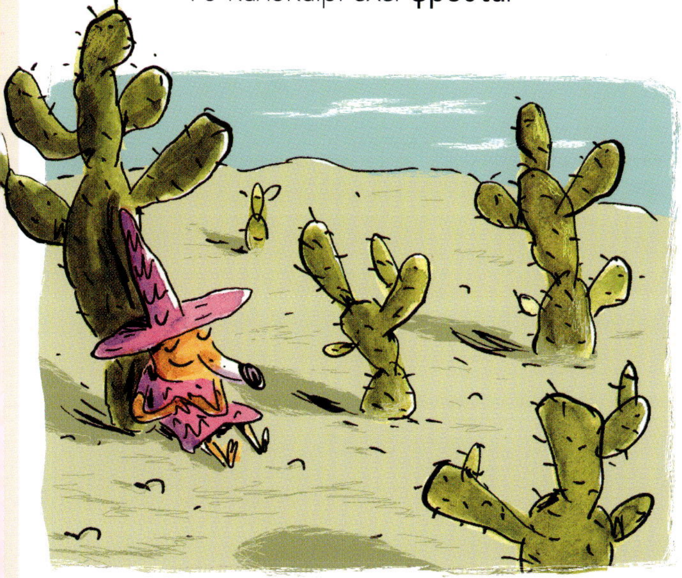

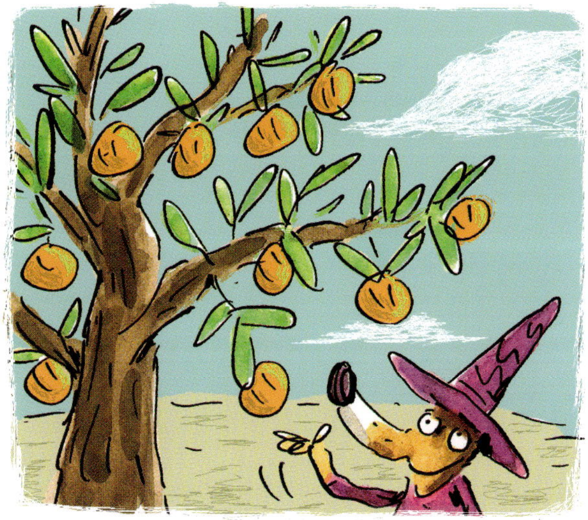

Στις **θερμές χώρες** τα φυτά έχουν φύλλα όλο το χρόνο.

Τα φυτά φυτρώνουν παντού

Στη Γη υπάρχουν παντού φυτά, ακόμα και στα ποτάμια και τις θάλασσες, στην έρημο ή στις παγωμένες βουνοκορφές.

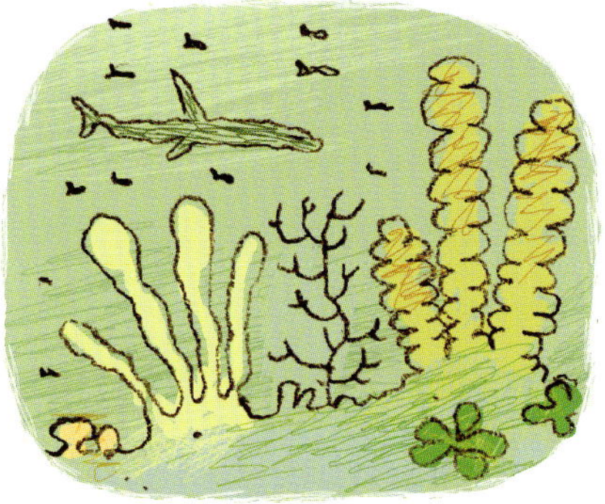

Τις περισσότερες φορές τα **φύκια** ζουν μέσα στο νερό.

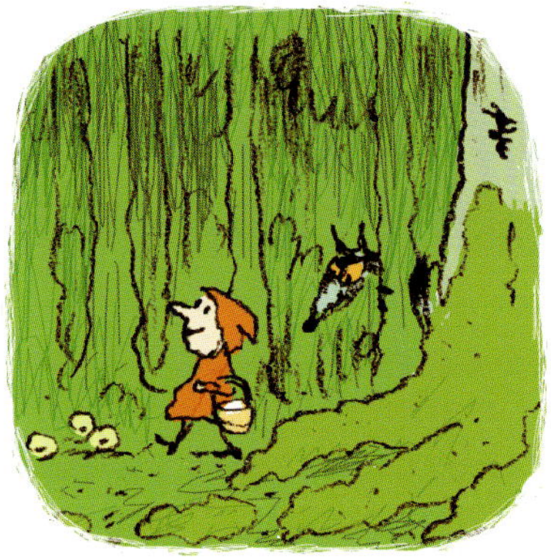

Τα **βρύα** ζουν σε υγρές περιοχές, πολλές φορές χαμηλά στον κορμό των δέντρων. Δεν τους αρέσει ο ήλιος.

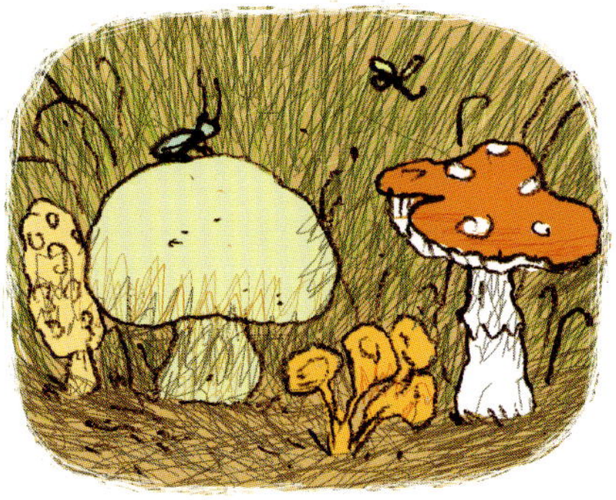

Τα **μανιτάρια** ζουν στα δάση. Κάποια τα τρώμε, κάποια άλλα είναι δηλητηριώδη: δεν πρέπει ούτε να τ' αγγίζουμε!

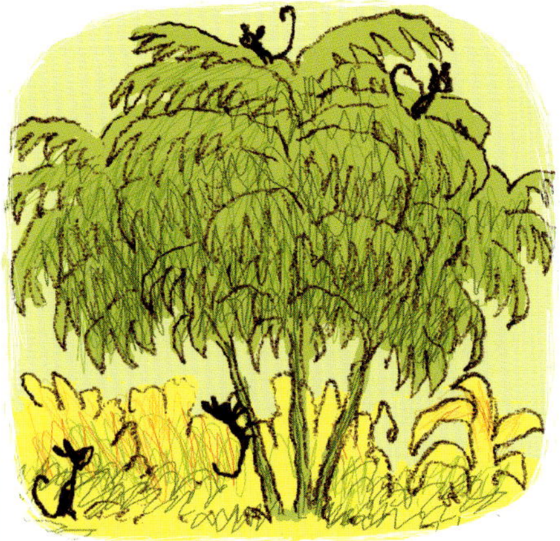

Στις θερμές χώρες οι **φτέρες** μπορούν να φτάσουν το ύψος ενός πολυώροφου κτιρίου.

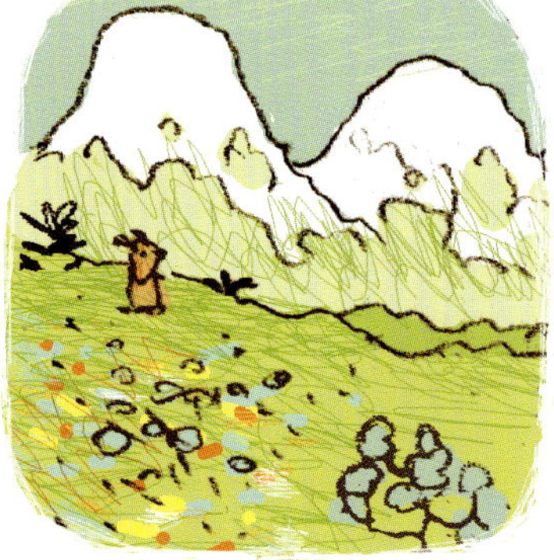

Τα **λουλούδια των βουνών** αντέχουν στο κρύο και το χιόνι.

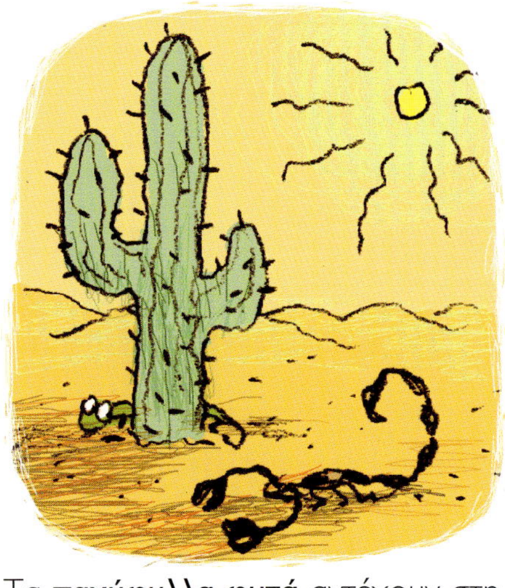

Τα **παχύφυλλα φυτά** αντέχουν στη ζέστη και την ξηρασία της ερήμου.

ΤΑ ΔΕΝΤΡΑ

Τα δέντρα χαρακτηρίζονται από τη μορφή και το φύλλωμά τους.

Τα **φυλλοβόλα** είναι δέντρα με επίπεδα φύλλα.

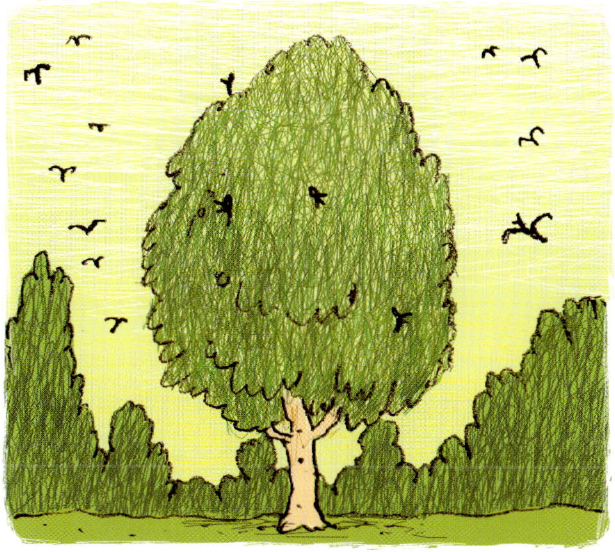

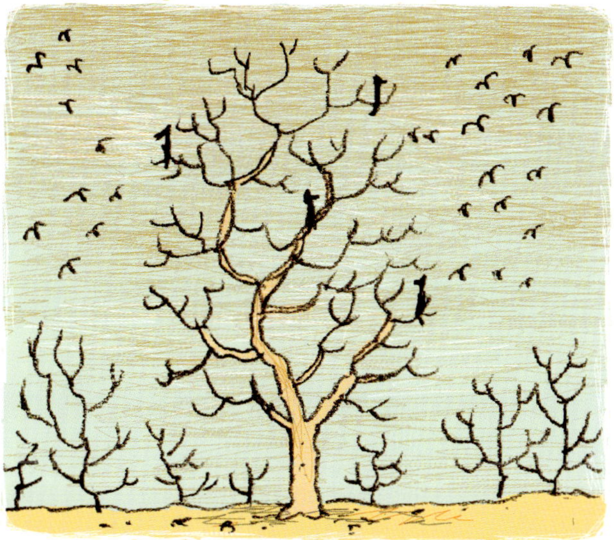

Το φθινόπωρο **πέφτουν**, στις περιοχές όπου δεν υπάρχει πολύς ήλιος το χειμώνα.

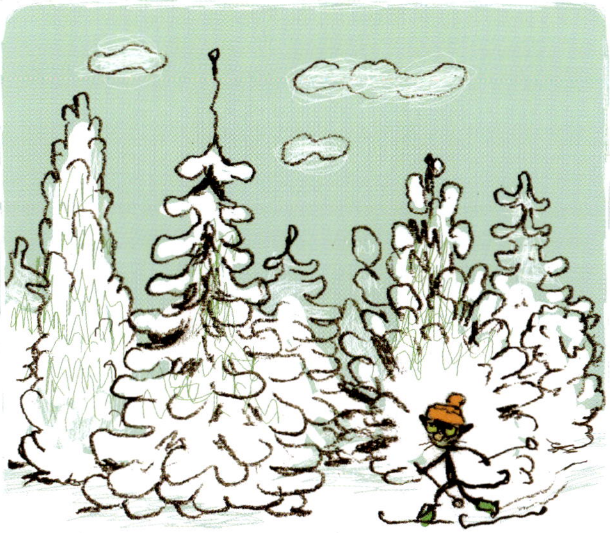

Τα **κωνοφόρα** έχουν φύλλα σε σχήμα **βελόνας**, που αντέχουν πολύ στο κρύο.

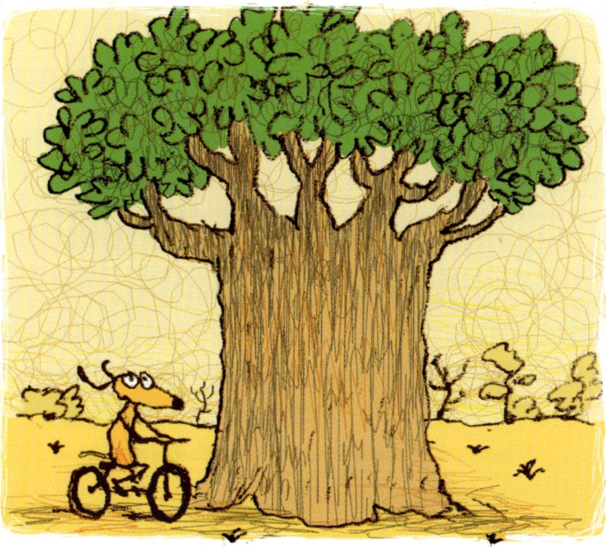

Το **μπαομπάμπ** έχει τεράστιο κορμό. Δε χάνει τα φύλλα του. Λέμε ότι τα φύλλα του είναι πολύ **ανθεκτικά**.

Η κατάταξη των φυτών

Όπως τα ζώα, έτσι και τα φυτά κατατάσσονται σε διάφορες ομάδες. Για να τα κατατάξουμε, βλέπουμε αν έχουν ρίζες, φύλλα ή λουλούδια.

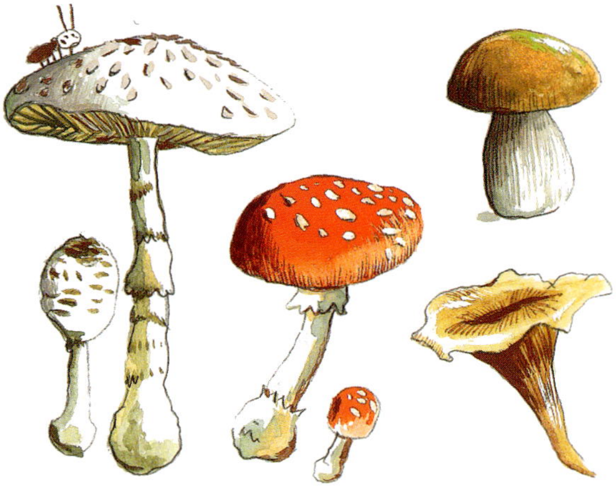

Τα μανιτάρια δεν είναι φυτά σαν όλα τα υπόλοιπα: δεν έχουν ούτε φύλλα ούτε ρίζες ούτε λουλούδια.

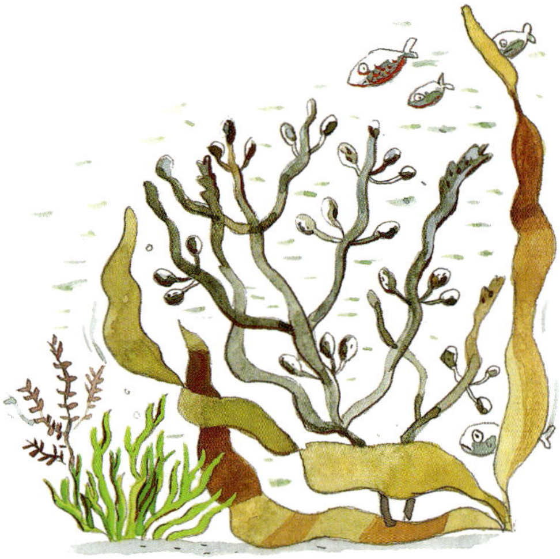

Τα φύκια έχουν φύλλα, όμως δεν έχουν ρίζες ούτε λουλούδια.

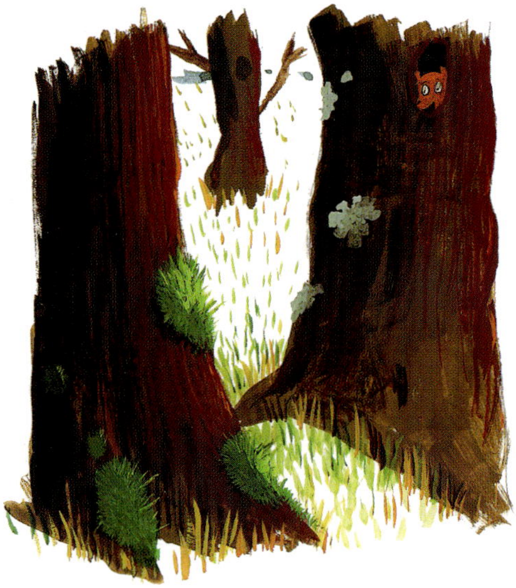

Τα βρύα έχουν πολλά φυλλαράκια, όμως δεν έχουν ρίζες ούτε λουλούδια.

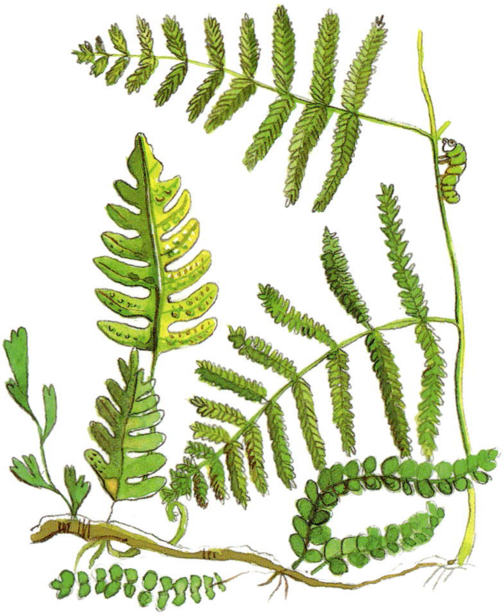

Οι φτέρες έχουν φύλλα και ρίζες, όχι όμως λουλούδια.

Τα φυτά με λουλούδια είναι τα πιο πολυάριθμα φυτά: έχουν ρίζες, φύλλα και λουλούδια. Σ' αυτή την ομάδα ανήκουν τα **δέντρα** και οι **πόες**.

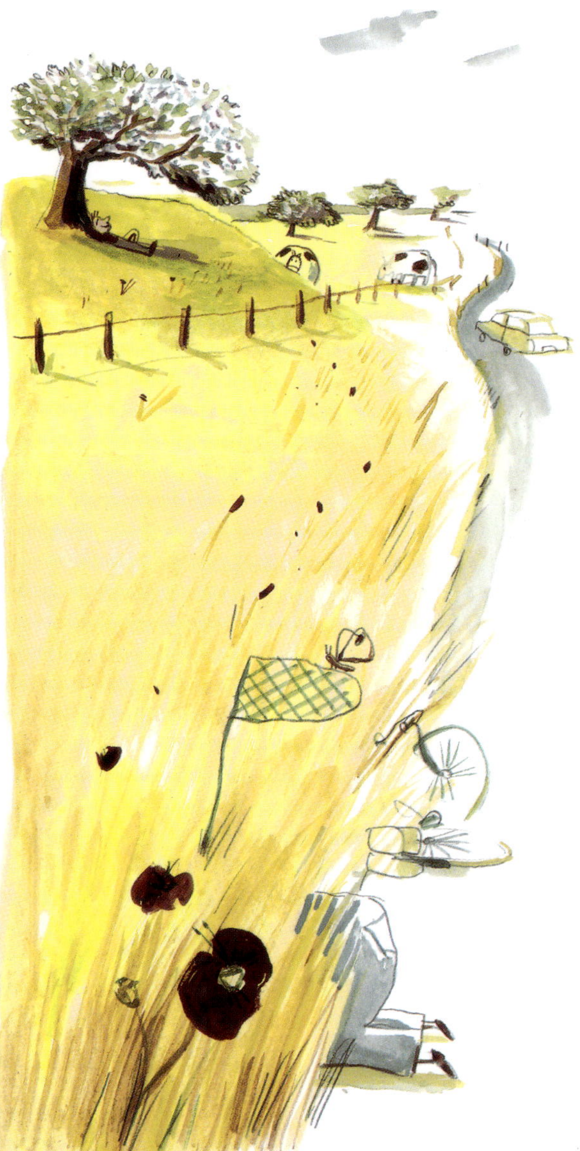

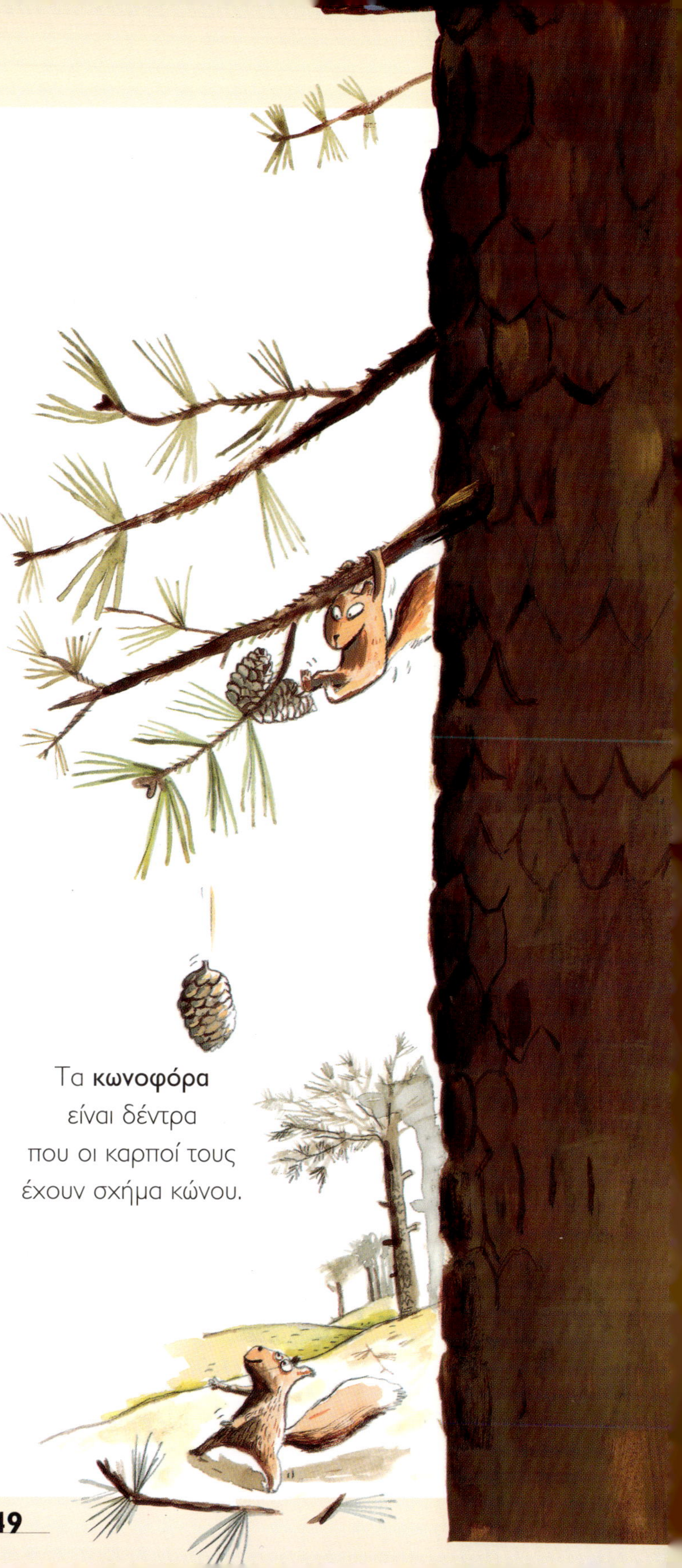

Τα **κωνοφόρα** είναι δέντρα που οι καρποί τους έχουν σχήμα κώνου.

Οι πόες είναι μικρά φυτά. Ο μίσχος τους είναι μαλακός σαν τα **λουλούδια** των κήπων και των αγρών.

ΣειΡΑ σΟΥ νΑ ΠαίΞεις!

Σ' αυτό το **τοπίο** υπάρχουν φυτά όλων των ειδών: φυτά με λουλούδια, βρύα, φτέρες, μανιτάρια, κωνοφόρα. Τ' αναγνωρίζεις;

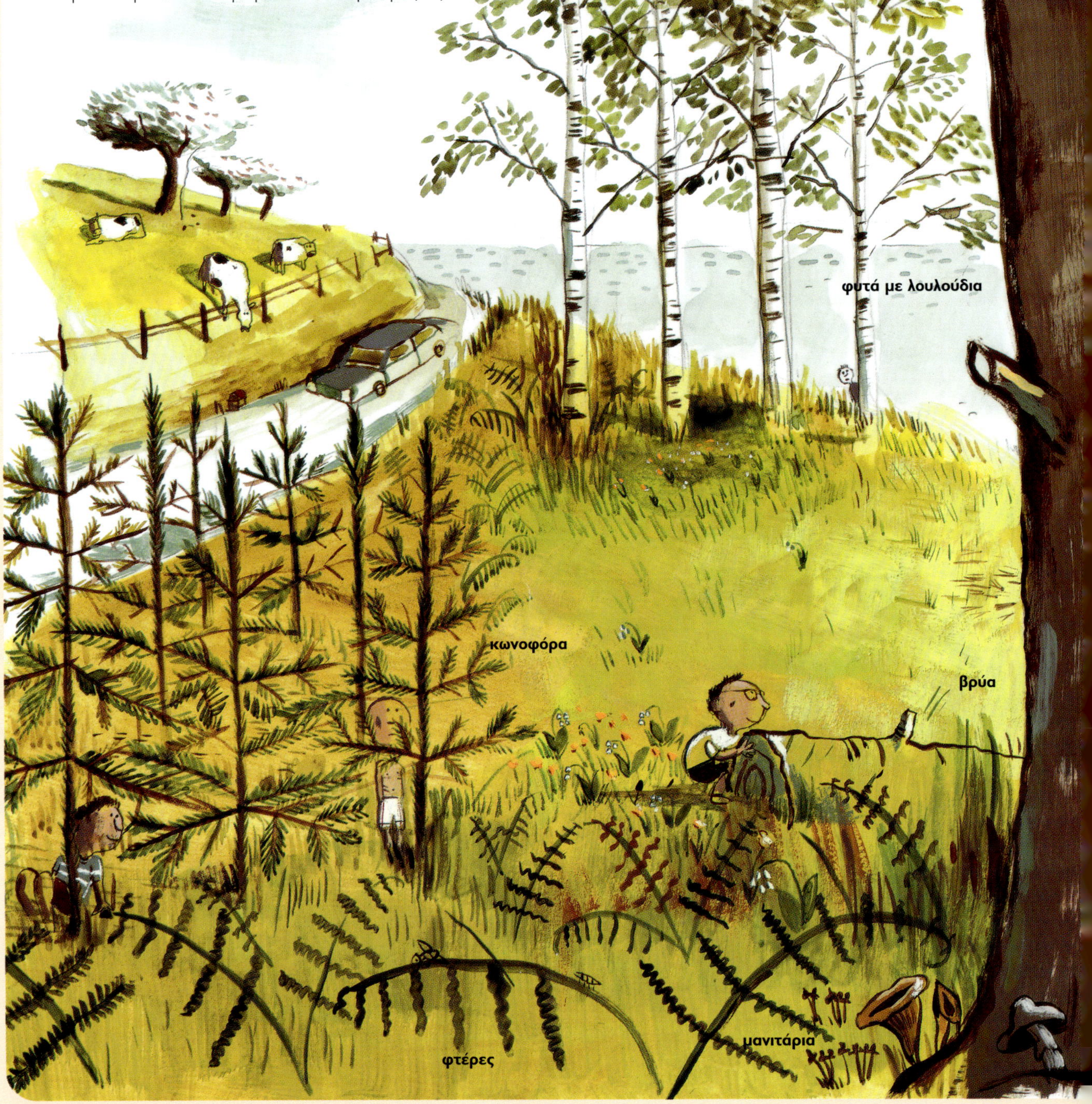

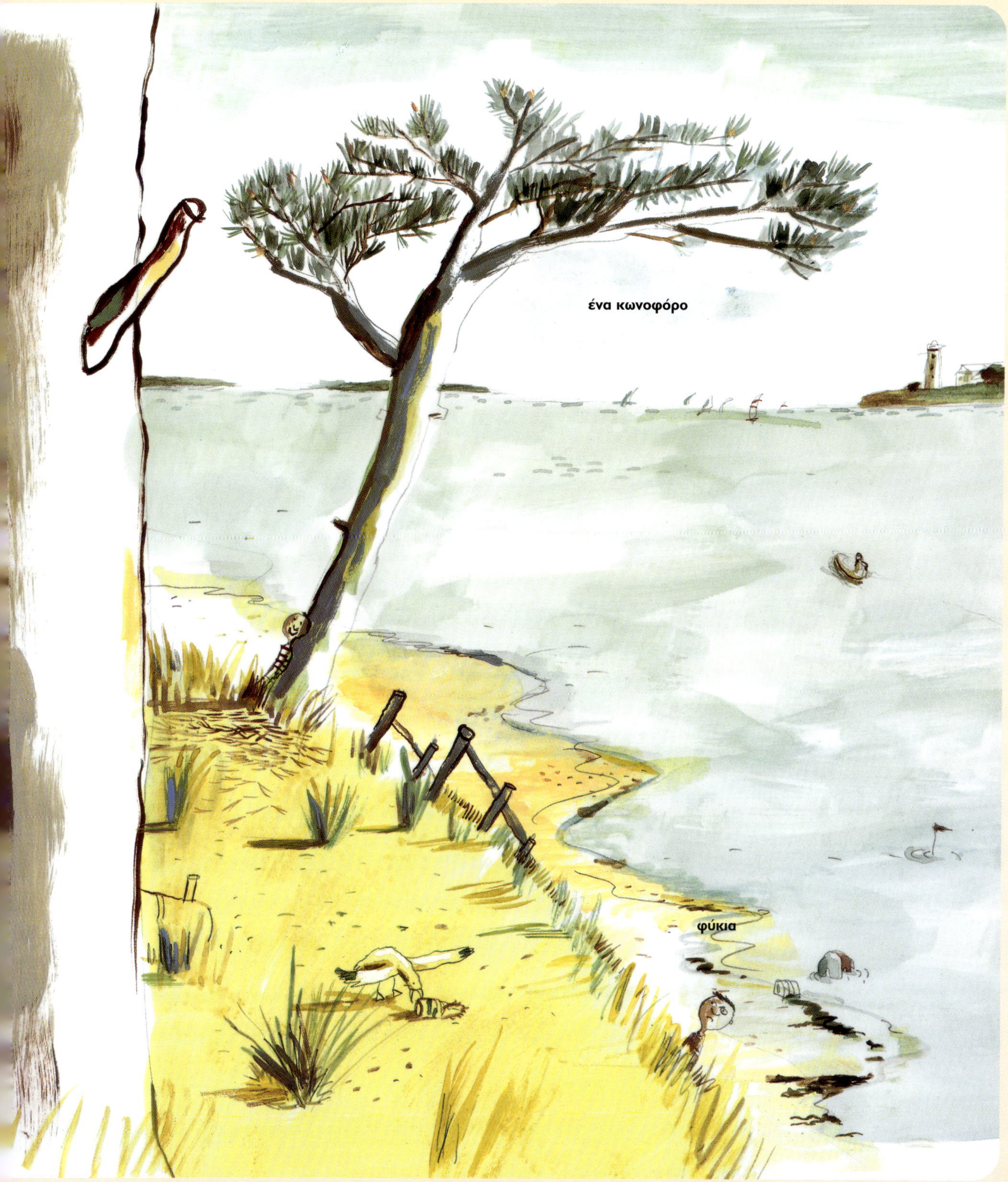
ένα κωνοφόρο
φύκια

Τα μέρη ενός φυτού

Μικρά ή μεγαλύτερα,
τα φυτά έχουν:
ρίζες (1)
μίσχο ή κορμό (2)
φύλλα (3)
και πολλές φορές
λουλούδια ή καρπούς.

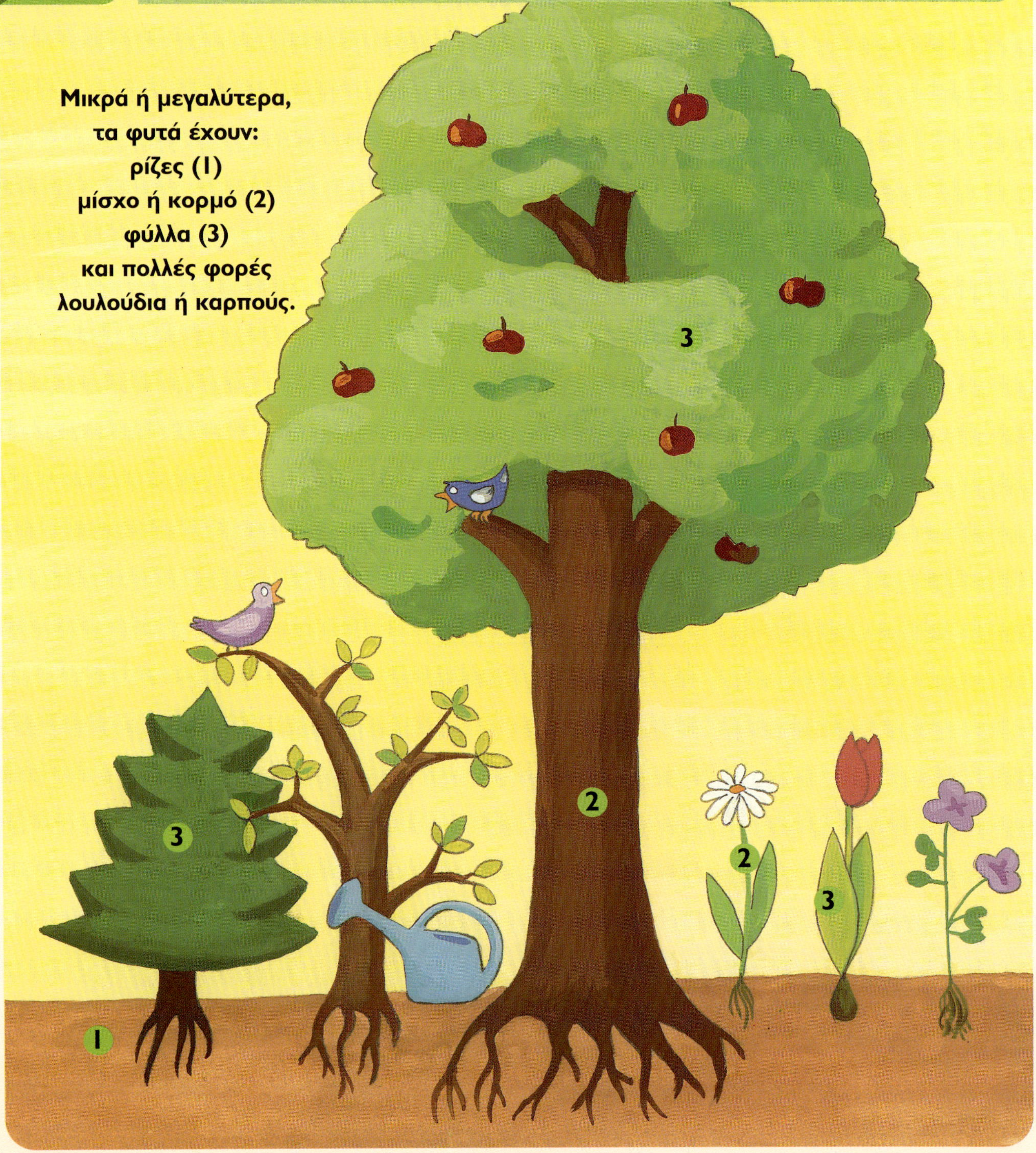

ΤΑ ΦΥΛΛΑ ΤΩΝ ΔΕΝΤΡΩΝ

Για να αναγνωρίσουμε ένα δέντρο, παρατηρούμε προσεκτικά τα φύλλα του.

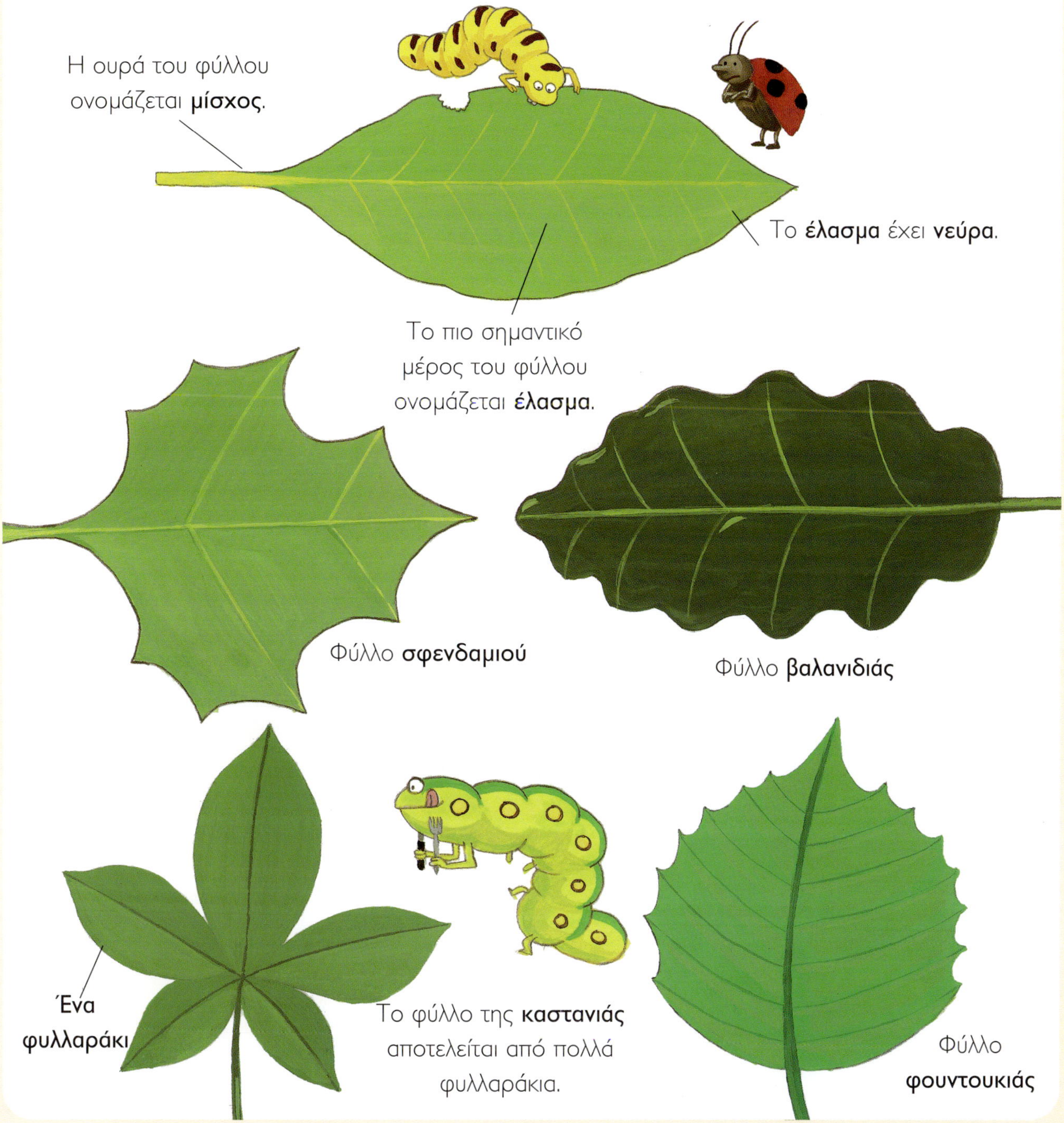

Τα φυτά ζουν

Τα φυτά παράγουν μόνα τους τη ζωντανή ύλη που χρειάζονται για να μεγαλώσουν.

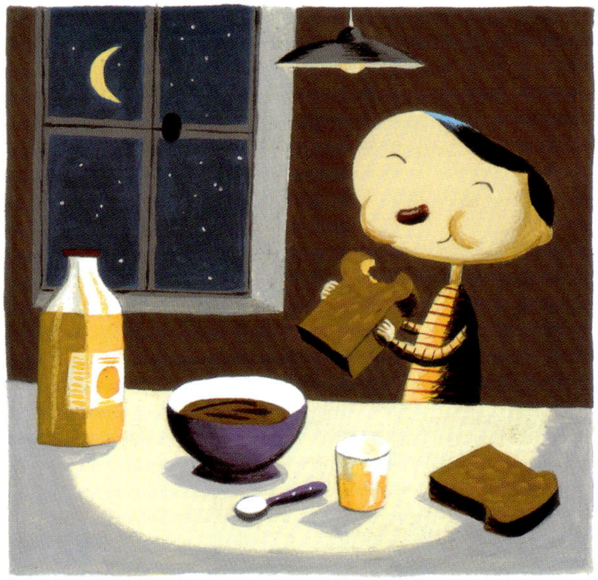

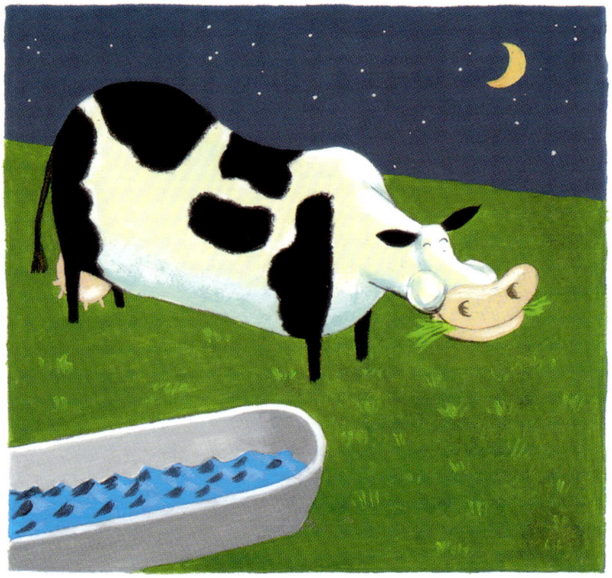

Όλοι οι ζωντανοί οργανισμοί χρειάζονται **ενέργεια** για να ζήσουν. Αυτό που δίνει ενέργεια στους ανθρώπους και τα ζώα είναι η **τροφή**.

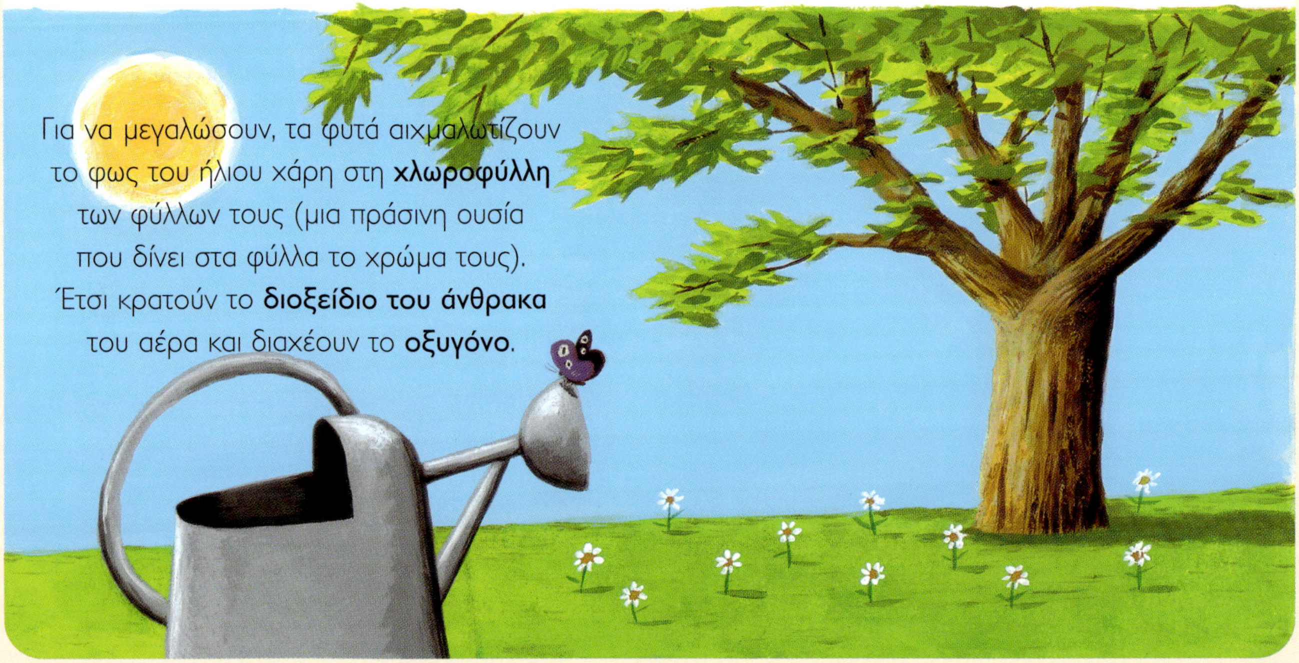

Για να μεγαλώσουν, τα φυτά αιχμαλωτίζουν το φως του ήλιου χάρη στη **χλωροφύλλη** των φύλλων τους (μια πράσινη ουσία που δίνει στα φύλλα το χρώμα τους). Έτσι κρατούν το **διοξείδιο του άνθρακα** του αέρα και διαχέουν το **οξυγόνο**.

Ένα φυτό **απορροφά** το νερό της γης με τις ρίζες του
και **παράγει** την τροφή του με το φως.

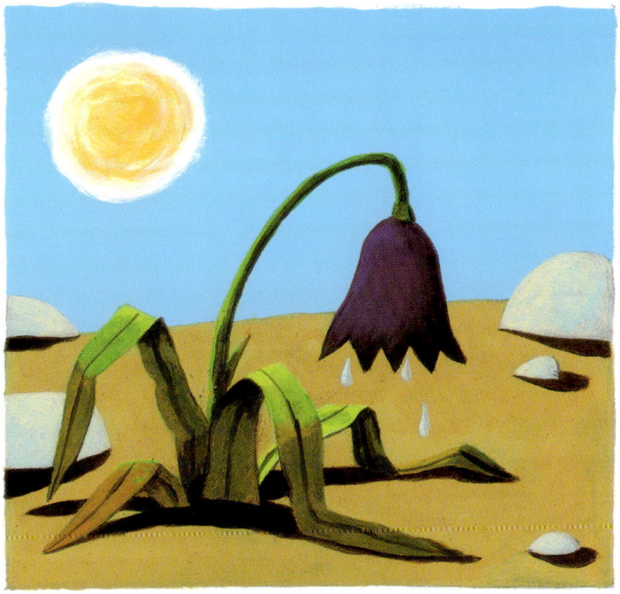

Ένα φυτό δεν μπορεί να ζήσει **χωρίς νερό**.

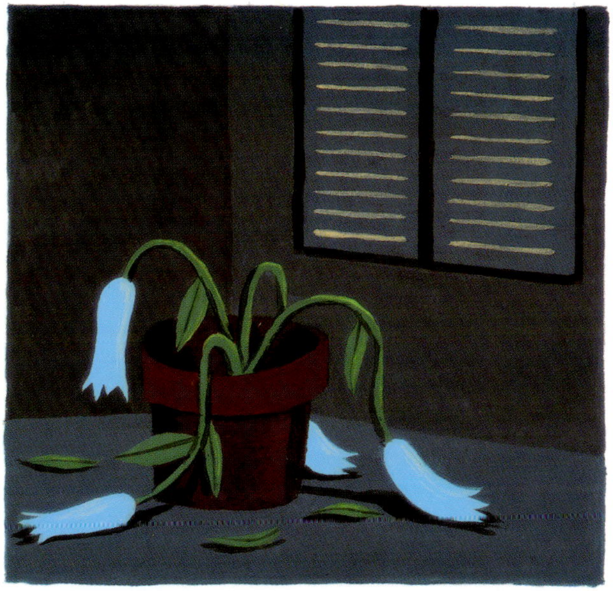

Ένα φυτό δεν μπορεί να ζήσει **χωρίς φως**.

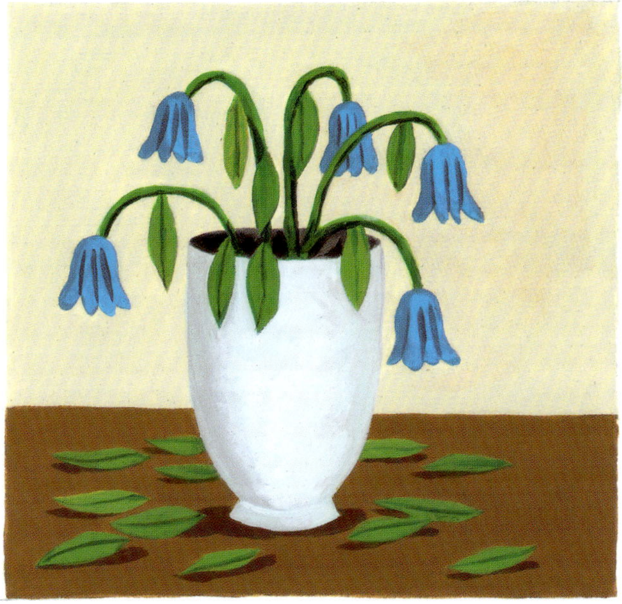

Ένα φυτό δεν μπορεί να ζήσει πολύ καιρό **κομμένο** από τις ρίζες του.

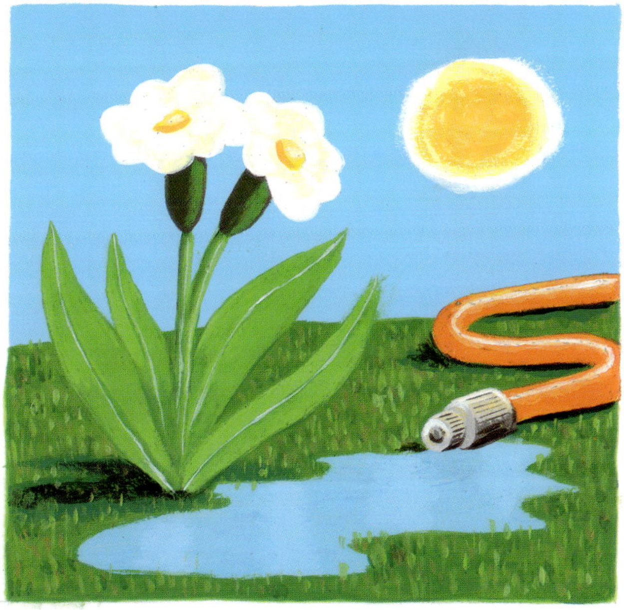

Για να ζήσει, ένα φυτό χρειάζεται **χώμα**, **νερό** και **φως**.

Ο χυμός τρέφει το φυτό

Ο χυμός κυκλοφορεί σε όλο το φυτό μέσα από μικροσκοπικούς «σωλήνες».

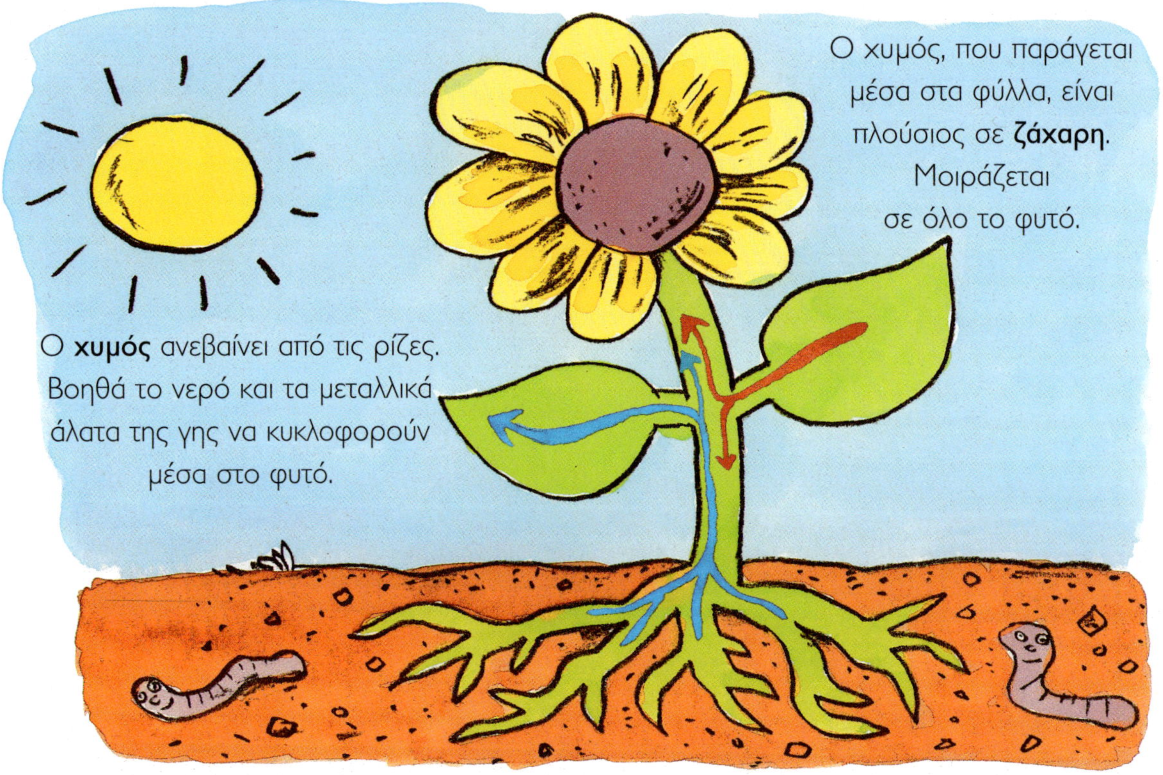

ΕΝΑ ΠΕΙΡΑΜΑ ΓΙΑ ΝΑ ΤΟ ΚΑΤΑΛΑΒΕΙΣ ΚΑΛΥΤΕΡΑ

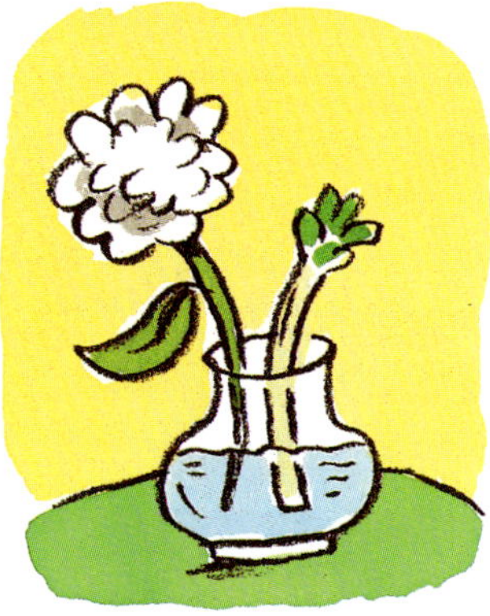

Βάλε μέσα σε ένα διάφανο βάζο ένα άσπρο **γαρίφαλο** και ένα κλαδάκι **σέλινο**.

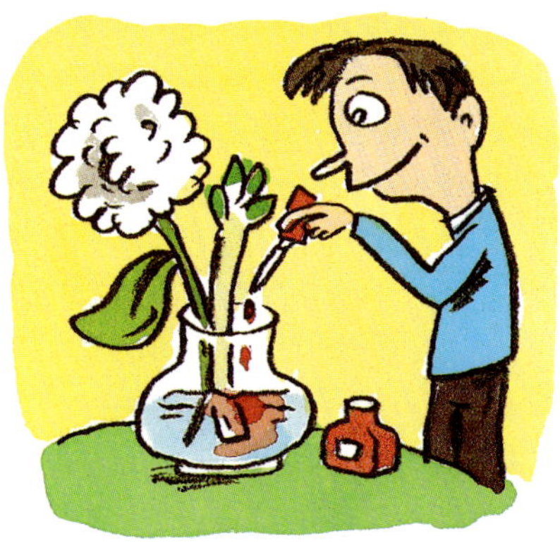

Ρίξε μέσα στο νερό μερικές σταγόνες **χρωματιστού μελανιού**.

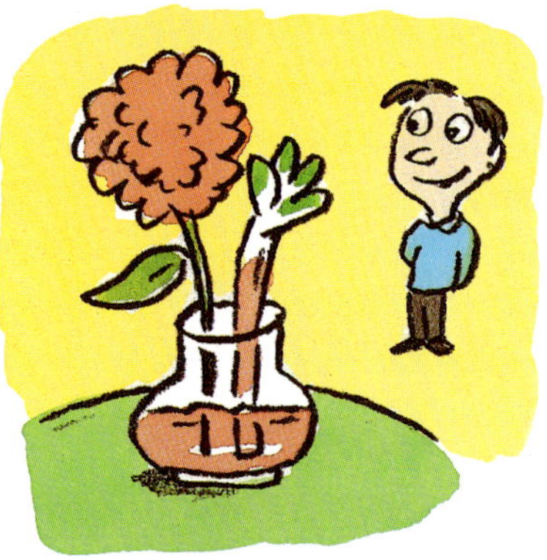

Παρατήρησε την αλλαγή στο χρώμα. Αυτή είναι η διαδρομή του **χυμού**.

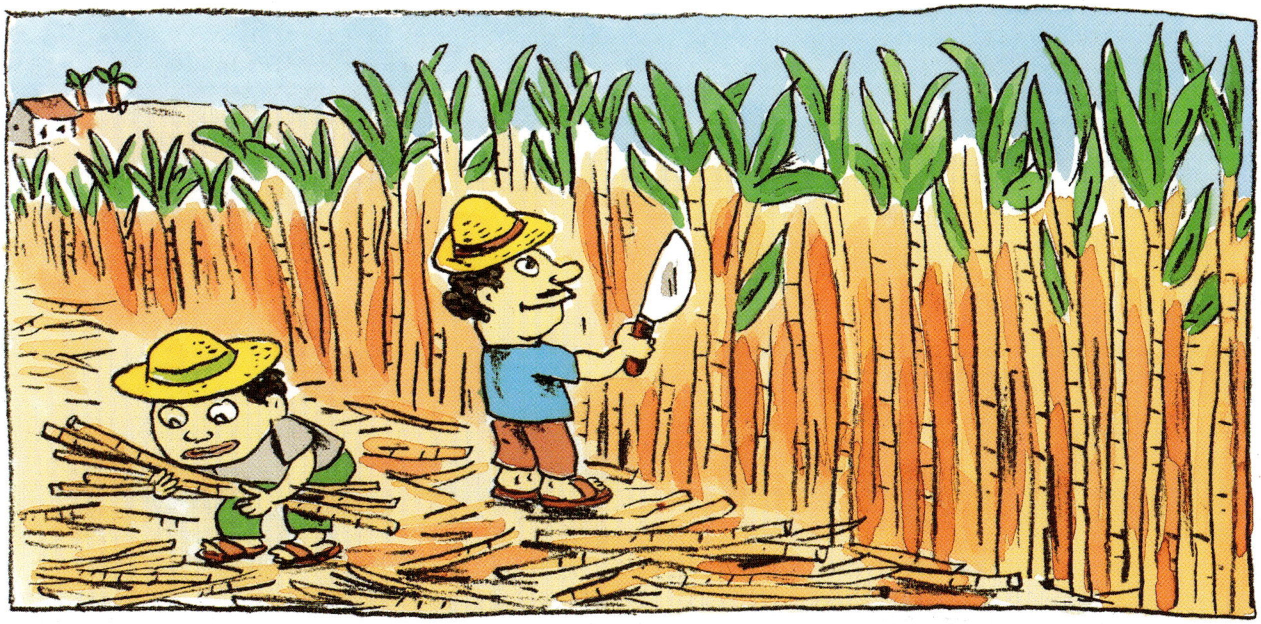

Ο **χυμός** κάποιων φυτών, όπως του **ζαχαροκάλαμου**, είναι πολύ **γλυκός**. Αν στύψουμε τους μίσχους του ζαχαροκάλαμου, παίρνουμε ένα υγρό που μας επιτρέπει να φτιάξουμε ζάχαρη.

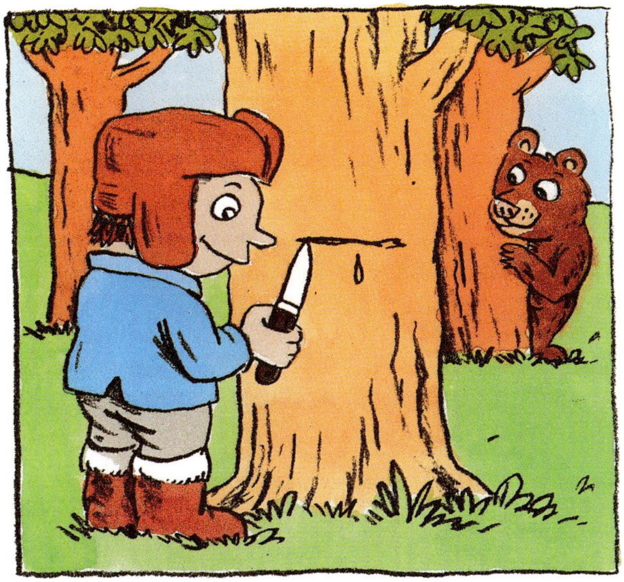

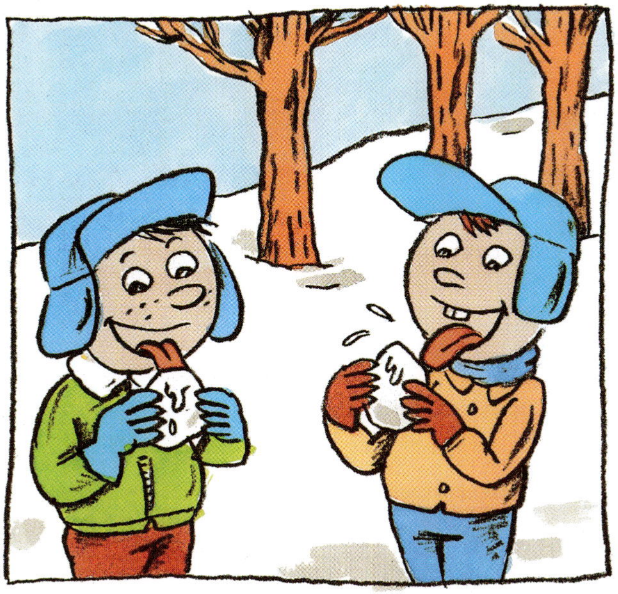

Το σιρόπι του **σφενδαμιού** φτιάχνεται από τον πολύ γλυκό χυμό του σφενδαμιού. Οι Καναδοί κάνουν μικρές σχισμές στον **κορμό** των σφενδαμιών για να τον μαζέψουν. Το χειμώνα, τα παιδιά αφήνουν λίγο χυμό να τρέξει πάνω στο χιόνι και στη συνέχεια τον απολαμβάνουν!

Η ζωή ενός δέντρου

Η ζωή ενός δέντρου αρχίζει με την ανάπτυξη του σπέρματος που περιέχεται στο σπόρο που έπεσε από κάποιο άλλο δέντρο.

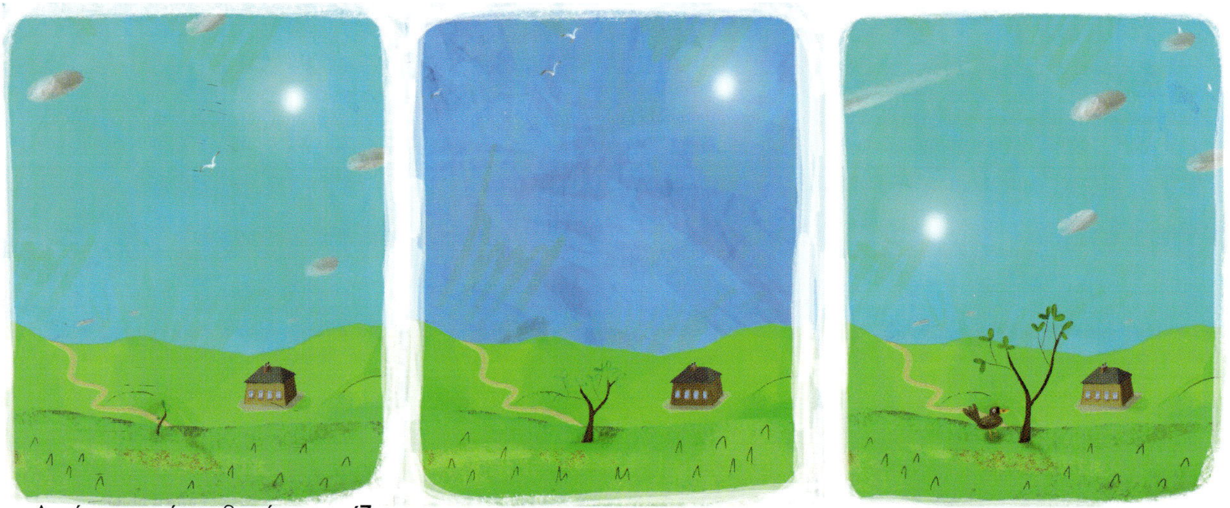

Από το σπόρο βγαίνουν **ρίζες** που βυθίζονται στο χώμα. Έπειτα μέσα από το χώμα βγαίνει ένας μίσχος.

Ο **μίσχος** απλώνεται προς το φως και βγάζει μικρά **φύλλα**. Έτσι, τα δέντρα μεγαλώνουν σε όλη τους τη ζωή.

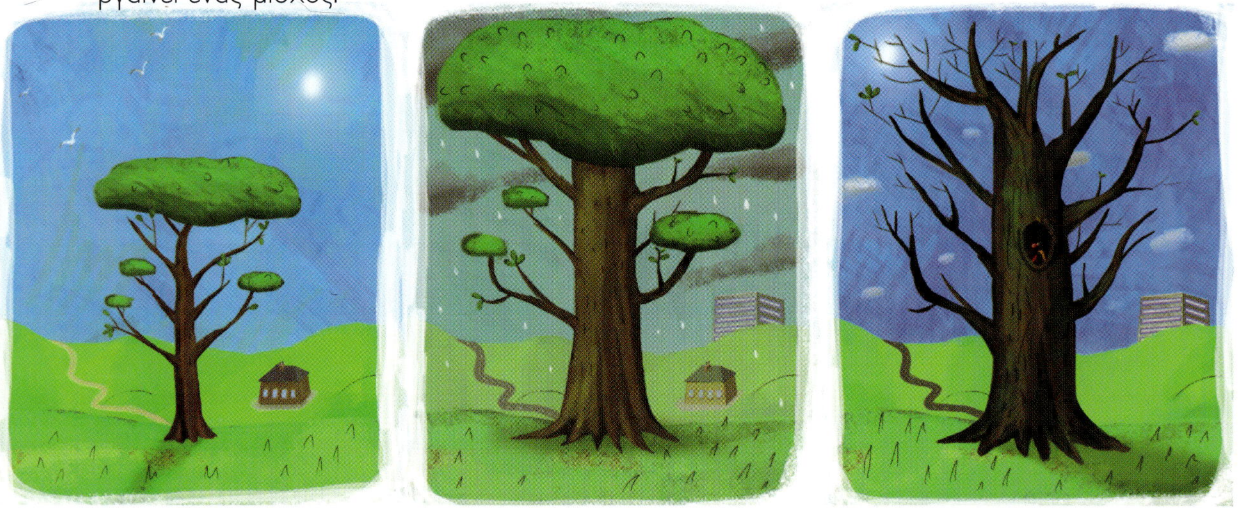

Κάθε άνοιξη ο **χυμός** κάνει να βγαίνουν καινούριες ρίζες και καινούρια φύλλα. Τα κλαδιά **μακραίνουν**, ο κορμός **χοντραίνει** και ψηλώνει.

Τα δέντρα **γερνούν** και πεθαίνουν κι αυτά. Κάποια βέβαια ζουν πάρα πολλά χρόνια.

Ο **φλοιός** προστατεύει το δέντρο. Σ' ένα νεαρό δέντρο είναι απαλός, ενώ σε ένα γέρικο δέντρο τραχύς. Ο **χυμός** κυλά κάτω από το φλοιό.

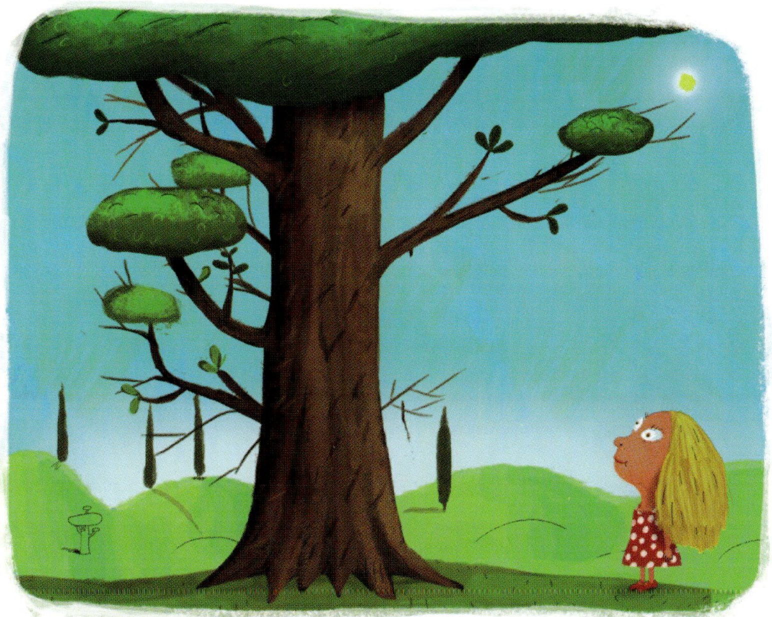

Κάθε καλοκαίρι στο ξύλο του κορμού σχηματίζεται ένας νέος **κύκλος ανάπτυξης**.

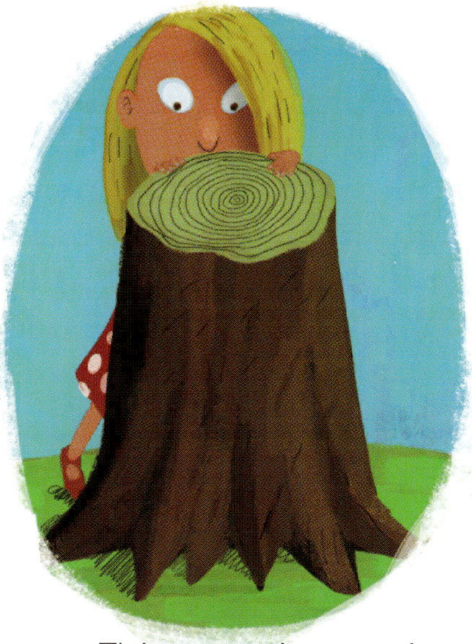

Σ' έναν κομμένο κορμό μπορούμε να δούμε τους κύκλους. Καθένας αντιστοιχεί σε ένα **χρόνο** ζωής.

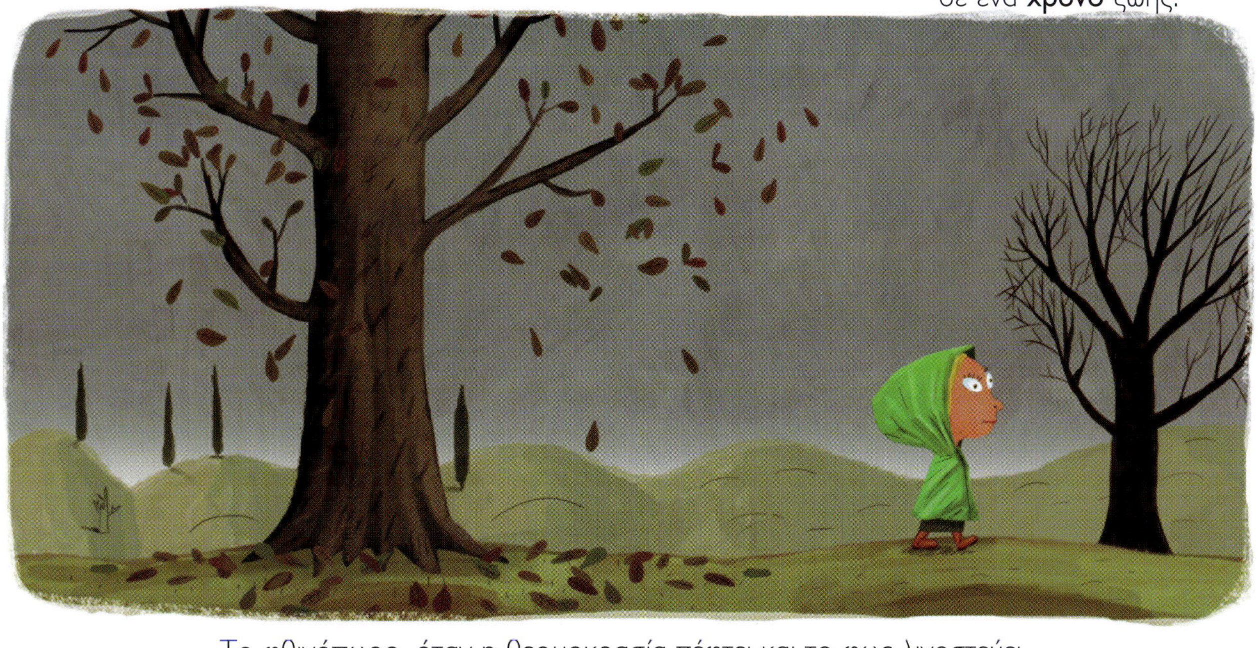

Το φθινόπωρο, όταν η θερμοκρασία πέφτει και το φως λιγοστεύει, η κυκλοφορία του χυμού **επιβραδύνεται**. Τα φύλλα πέφτουν.

Οι σπόροι μετακινούνται

Τα φυτά έχουν πολλούς τρόπους για να σκορπάνε τους σπόρους τους στη φύση και να βρίσκουν ένα κατάλληλο σημείο για να φυτρώσουν καλύτερα.

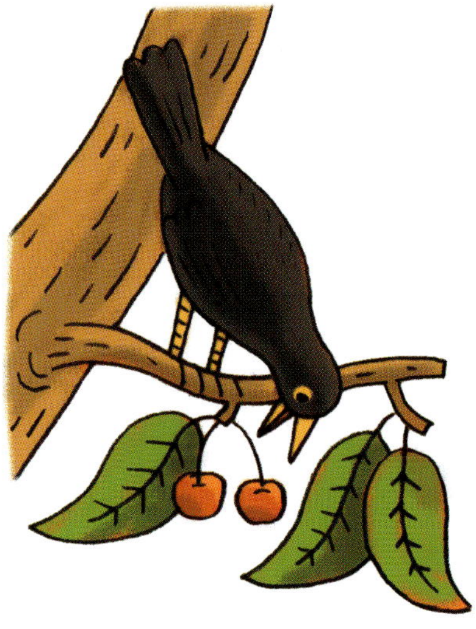

Όταν ένα πουλί τρώει ένα **κεράσι**, καταπίνει το κουκούτσι.

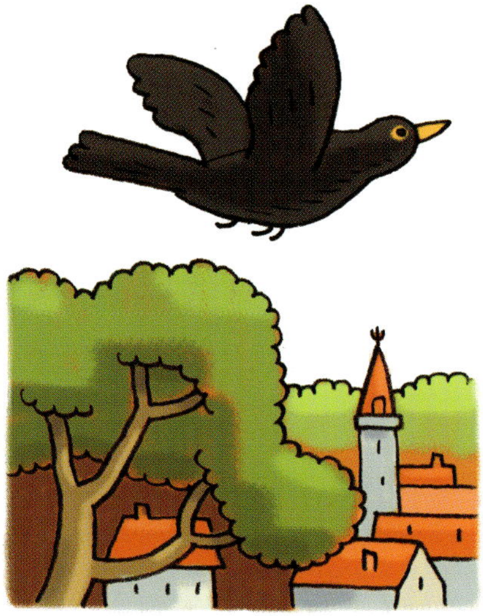

Μεταφέρει το **κουκούτσι** στην κοιλιά του.

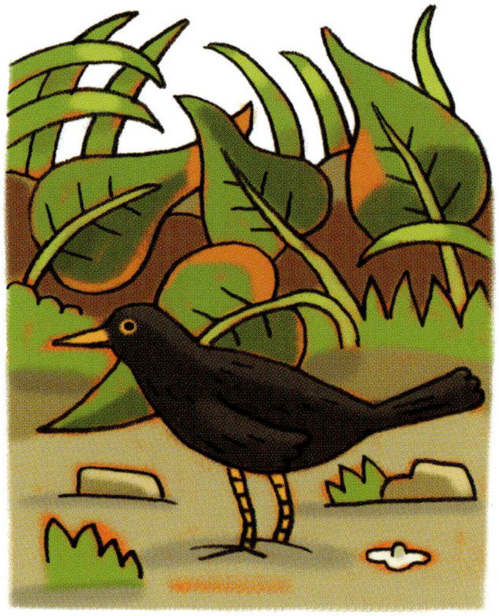

Αφήνει το κουκούτσι λίγο **πιο πέρα** με τα κακά του.

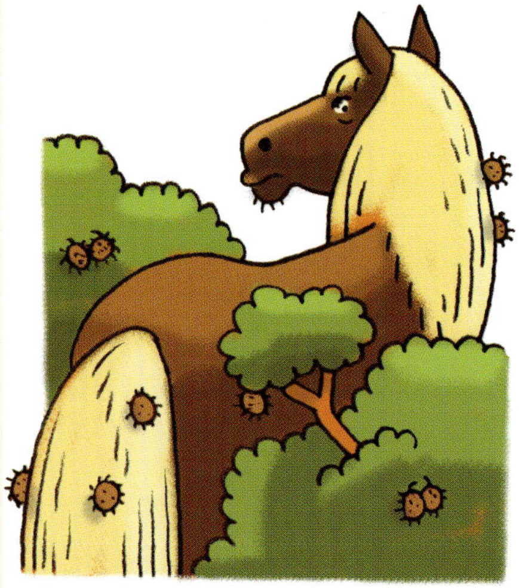

Ο σπόρος του **κολλησόχορτου** κρέμεται στις τρίχες των ζώων ή στα ρούχα των περιπατητών.

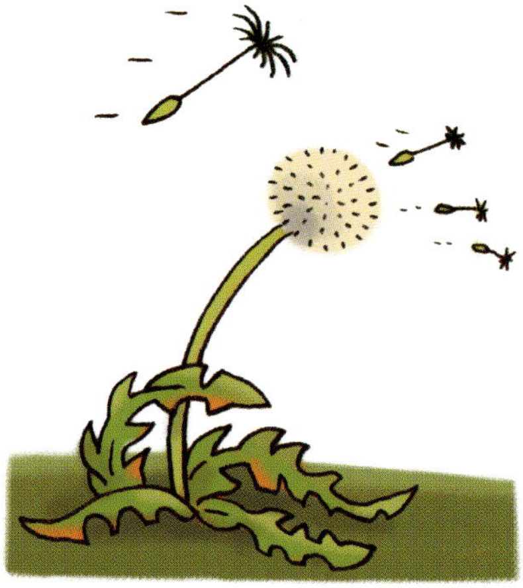

Ο σπόρος του **ραδικιού** μοιάζει με μικρό αλεξίπτωτο. Μεταφέρεται με τον άνεμο.

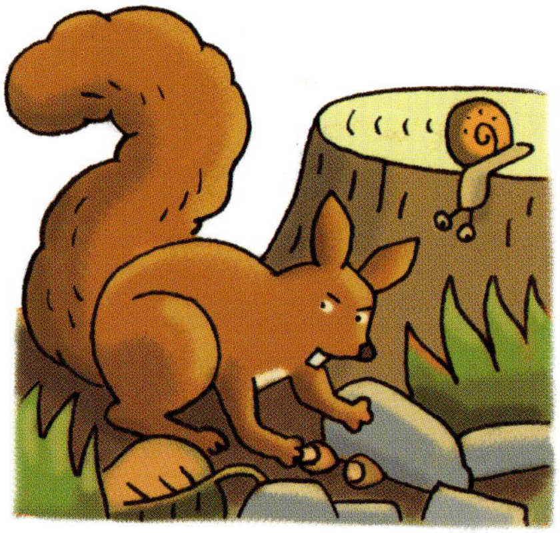

Ο **σκίουρος** κρύβει τα φουντούκια του μακριά από τη φουντουκιά που τα βρήκε. Πολλές φορές όμως τα ξεχνάει.

ΣειΡΑ σΟΥ νΑ Παίξεις!

Προσπάθησε να βρεις πώς κάθε καρπός θα καταφέρει να μετακινηθεί

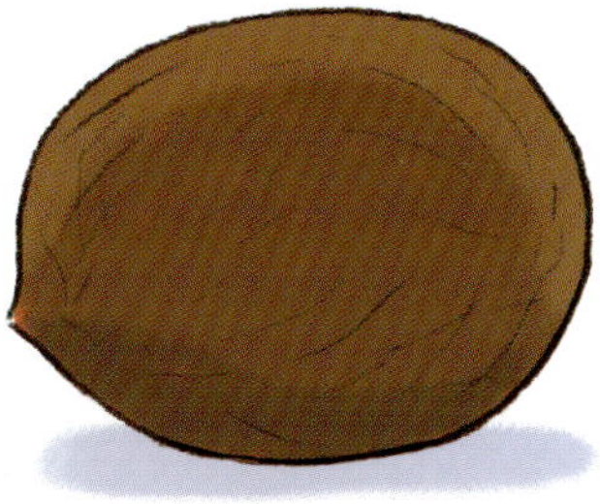

η **καρύδα**

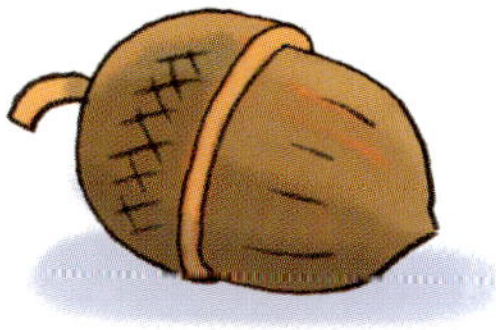

το **βαλανίδι**

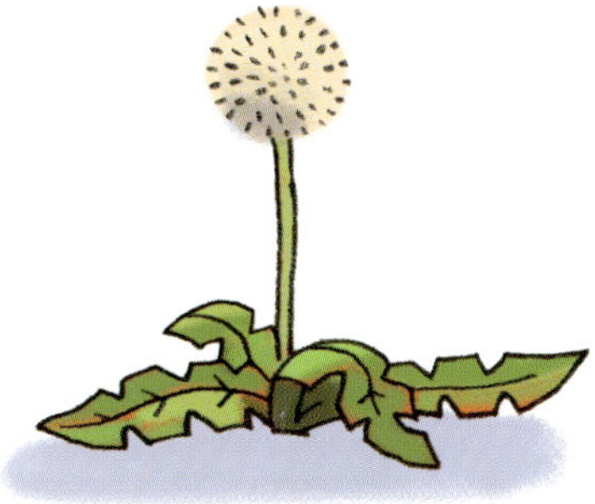

το **ραδίκι**

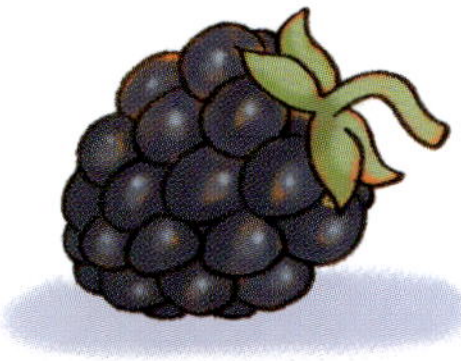

το **βατόμουρο**

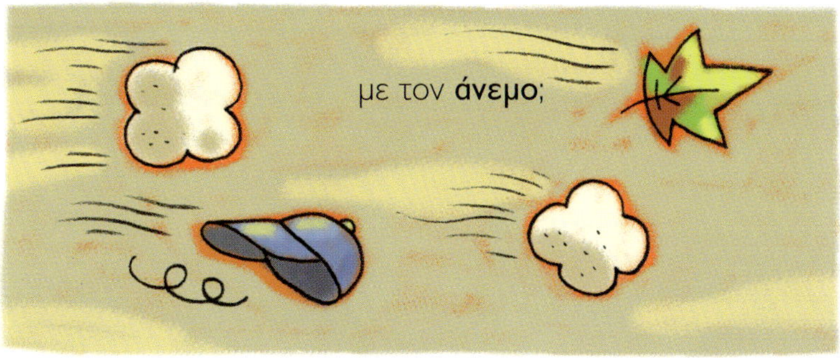

με τον **άνεμο**;

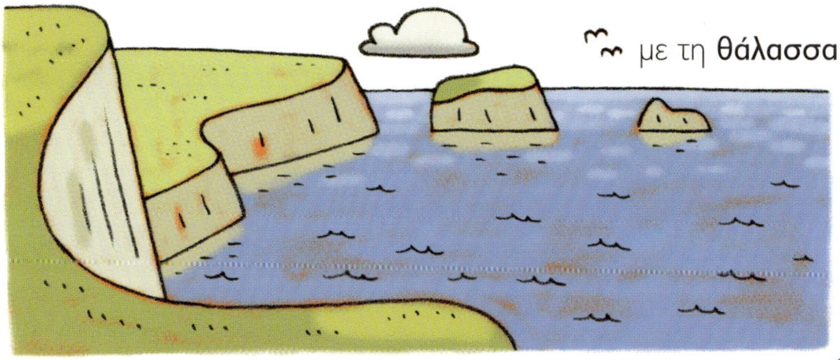

με τη **θάλασσα**;

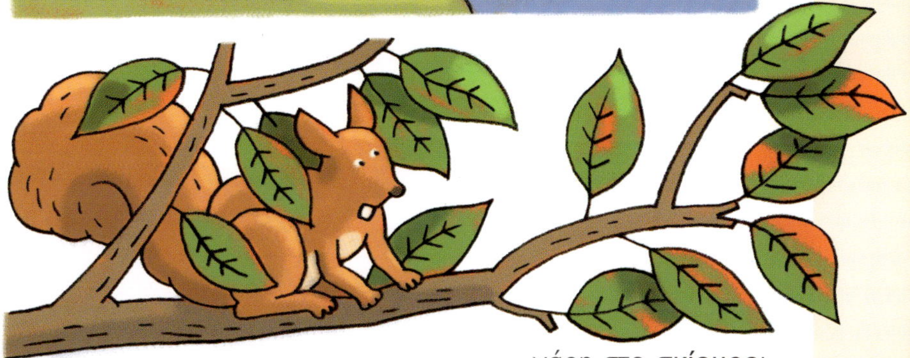

χάρη στο **σκίουρο**;

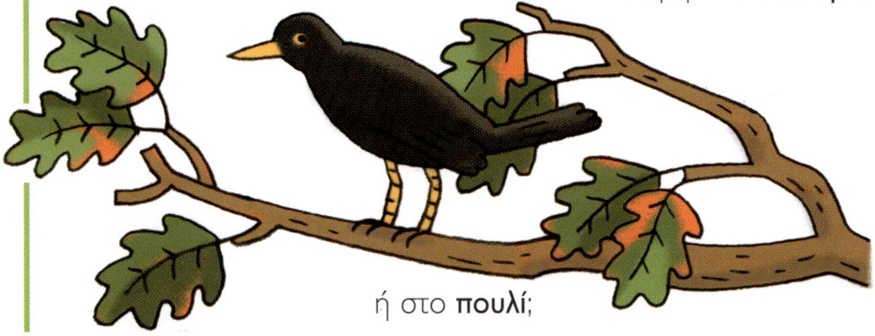

ή στο **πουλί**;

Λύση: η καρύδα μεταφέρεται με τη θάλασσα και αφήνεται σε μια παραλία. το βαλανίδι μεταφέρεται από το σκίουρο. το ραδίκι με τον αέρα. το βατόμουρο από ένα πουλί.

Λουλούδια για αναπαραγωγή

Τα περισσότερα φυτά αναπαράγονται χάρη στα λουλούδια.

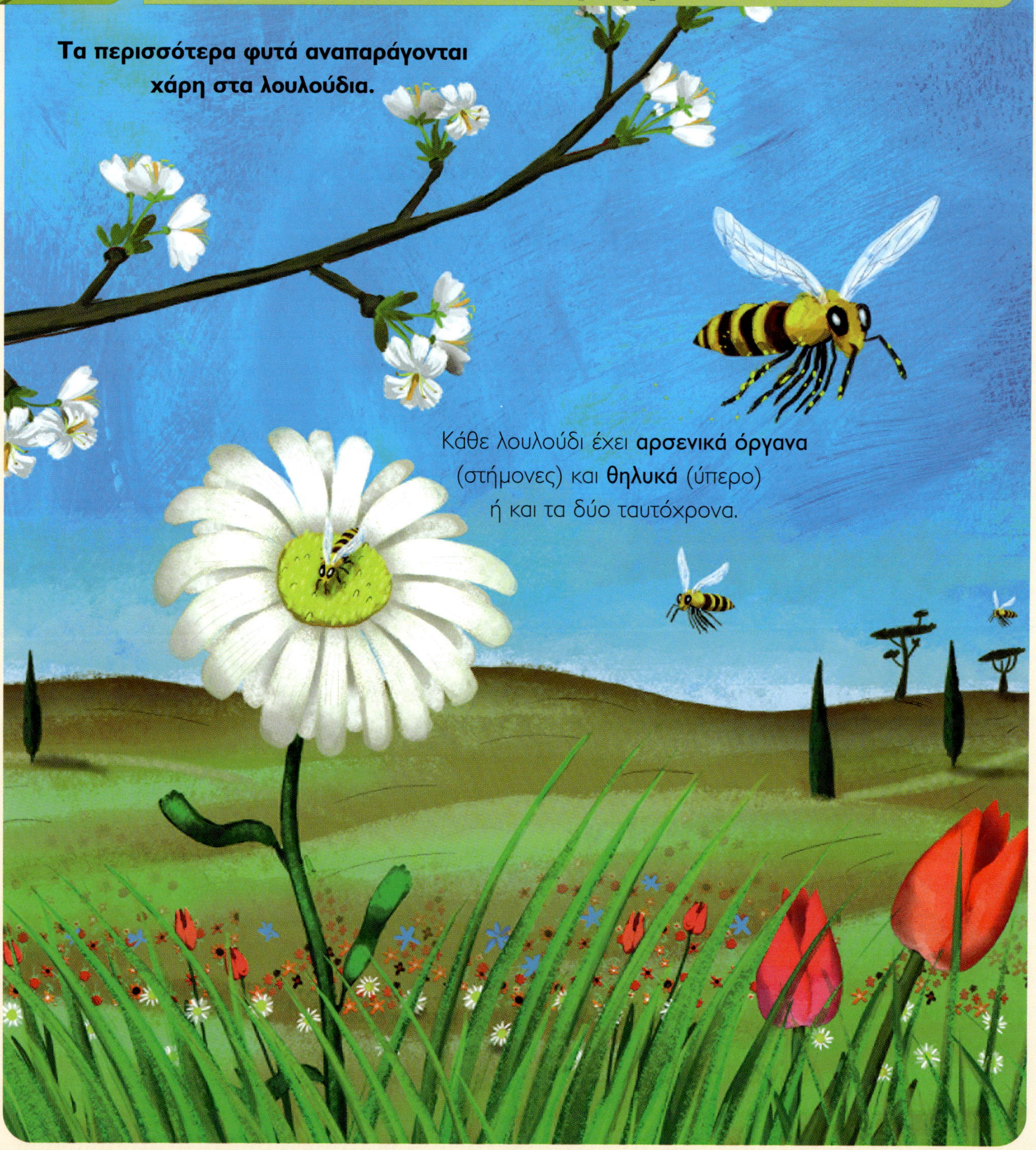

Κάθε λουλούδι έχει **αρσενικά όργανα** (στήμονες) και **θηλυκά** (ύπερο) ή και τα δύο ταυτόχρονα.

ΣΤΗΝ ΚΑΡΔΙΑ ΤΩΝ ΛΟΥΛΟΥΔΙΩΝ

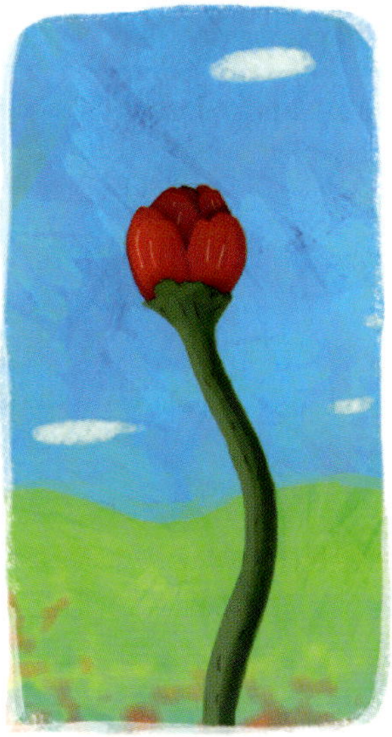

Τα **σέπαλα** είναι μικρά πράσινα φύλλα που προστατεύουν το μπουμπούκι του λουλουδιού.

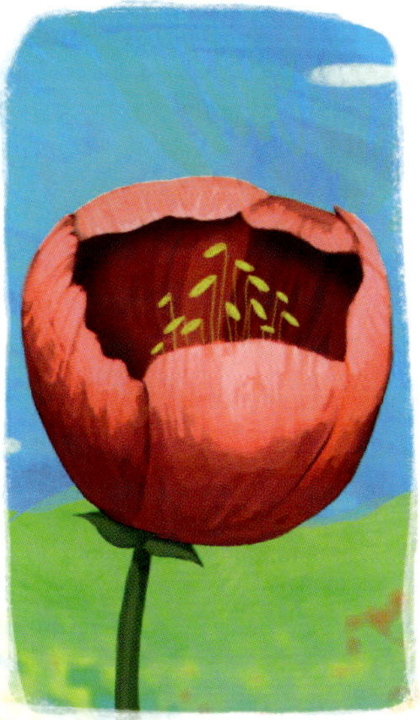

Οι **στήμονες** (που περιέχουν τη γύρη) και ο **ύπερος** συναντιούνται στο κέντρο του λουλουδιού και προστατεύονται από τα **πέταλα**.

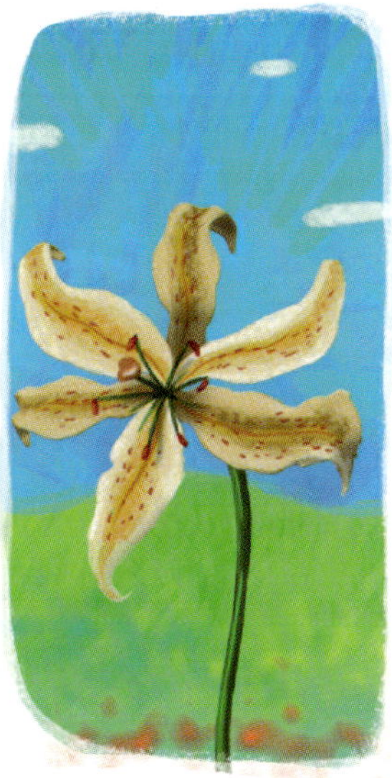

Ο **ύπερος** είναι το εξογκωμένο σημείο στη μέση των στημόνων.

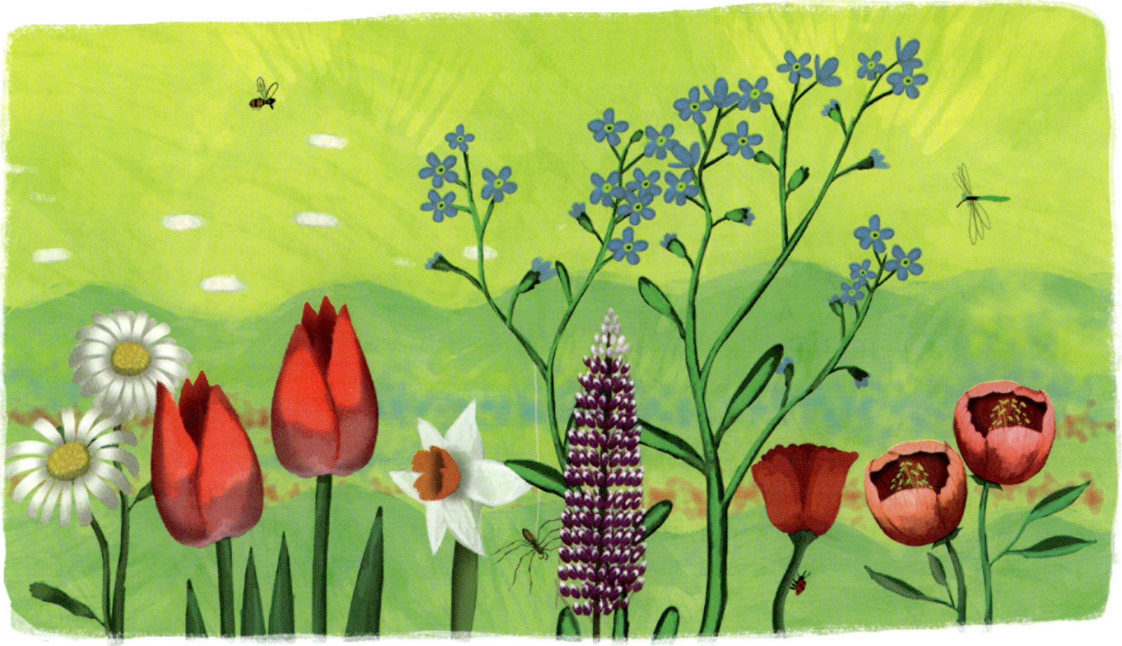

Τα περισσότερα φυτά με λουλούδια χρειάζονται **έντομα** για να σχηματίσουν τους σπόρους τους. Τα προσελκύουν με το **γλυκό νέκταρ** τους, τη **μυρωδιά** και τα **όμορφα χρώματά** τους.

Από το λουλούδι στο σπόρο

Για να σχηματιστεί ένας σπόρος, πρέπει ο σπόρος της γύρης ενός λουλουδιού να συναντήσει τον ύπερο ενός άλλου λουλουδιού του ίδιου είδους. Πολλές φορές σε αυτή τη διαδικασία βοηθάει ένα έντομο.

Τη στιγμή της αναπαραγωγής, οι στήμονες των λουλουδιών ανοίγουν και βγάζουν μια λεπτή σκόνη: είναι οι σπόροι της γύρης.

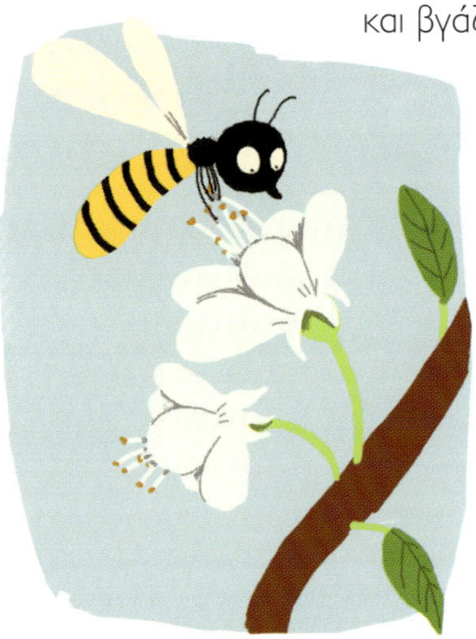

Οι **σπόροι** της γύρης γαντζώνονται στα πόδια των εντόμων...

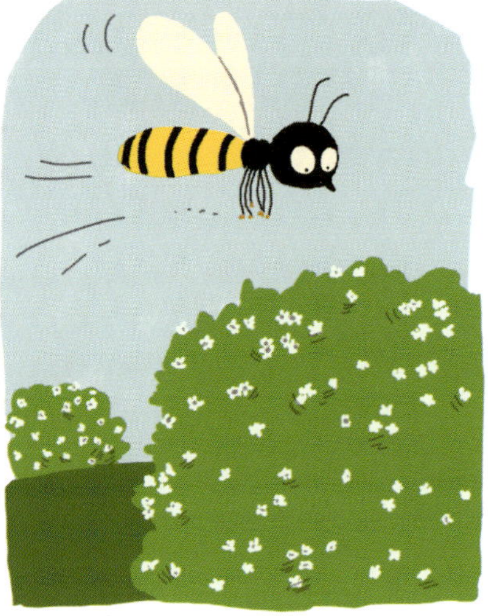

...τα έντομα τους μεταφέρουν **σε άλλα λουλούδια**...

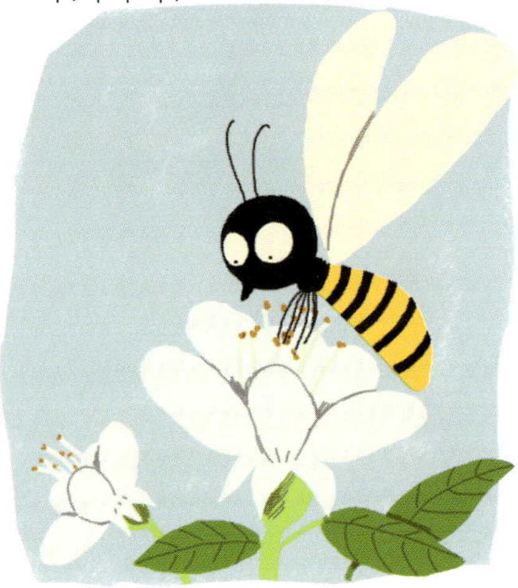

...και τους **αφήνουν** στον ύπερό τους.

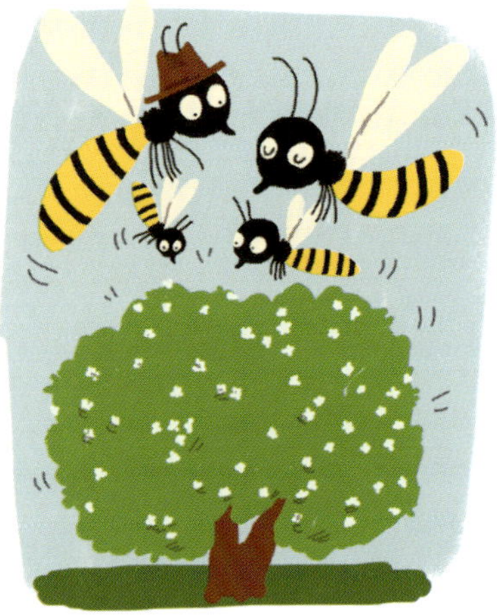

Τα ίδια έντομα πηγαίνουν πάντα στα **ίδια είδη** φυτών.

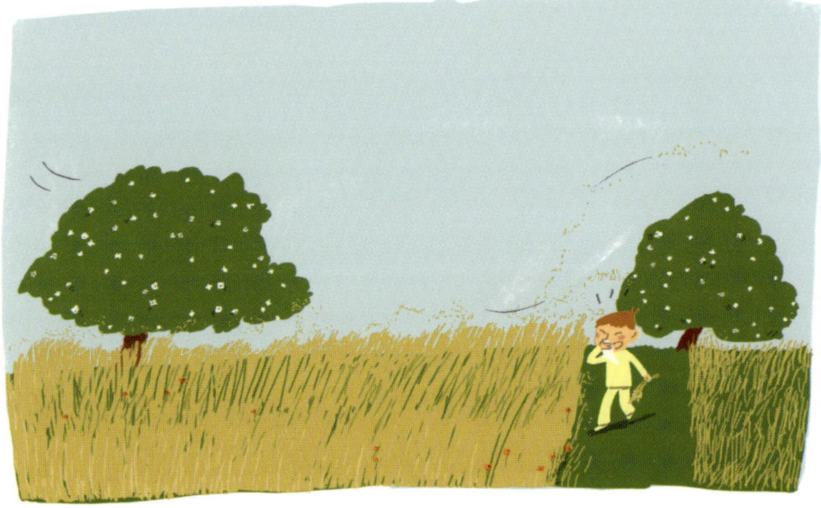

Η γύρη των λουλουδιών μπορεί επίσης να μεταφερθεί **με τον αέρα**, όπως συμβαίνει με τις βαλανιδιές.

ΑΠΟ ΤΟ ΣΠΟΡΟ ΣΤΟΝ ΚΑΡΠΟ

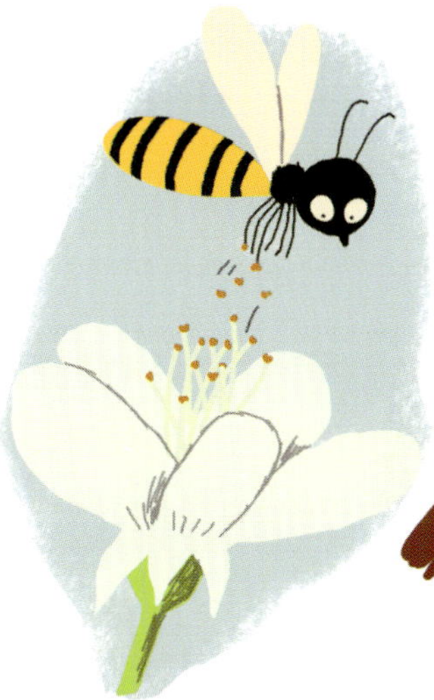

Οι σπόροι είναι αρσενικά μόρια. Διεισδύουν **στο εσωτερικό του ύπερου**, που περιέχει θηλυκά μόρια ή ωάρια.

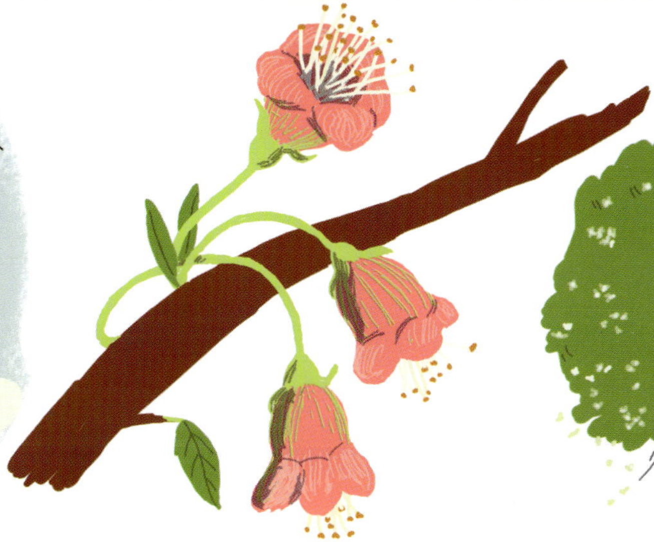

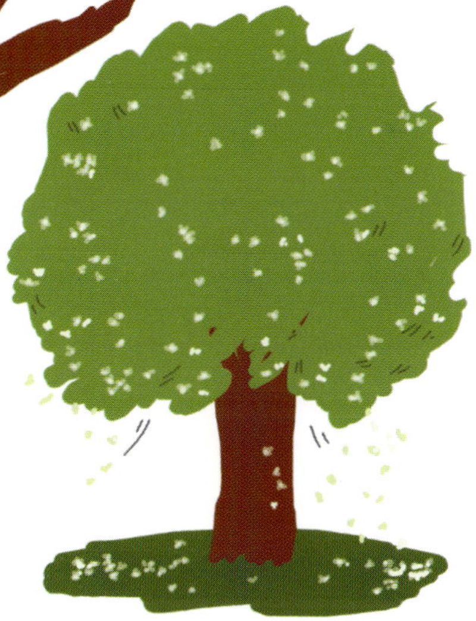

Όταν ο σπόρος συναντήσει ένα ωάριο, σχηματίζεται ο **καρπός**. Τα πέταλα πέφτουν.

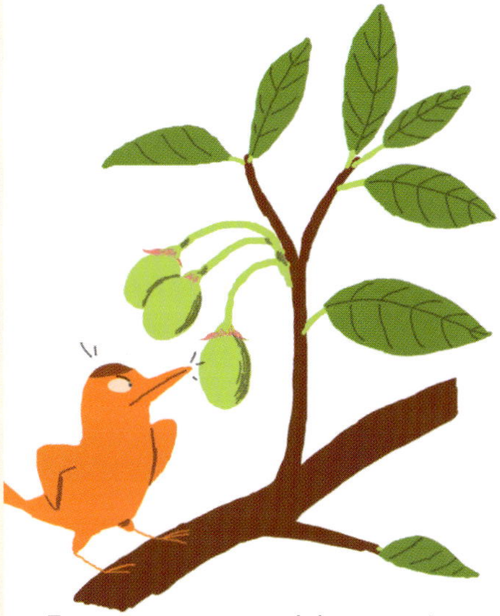

Για να σχηματιστεί ένα **κεράσι**, το ωάριο μετατρέπεται σε κουκούτσι και ο ύπερος σε καρπό.

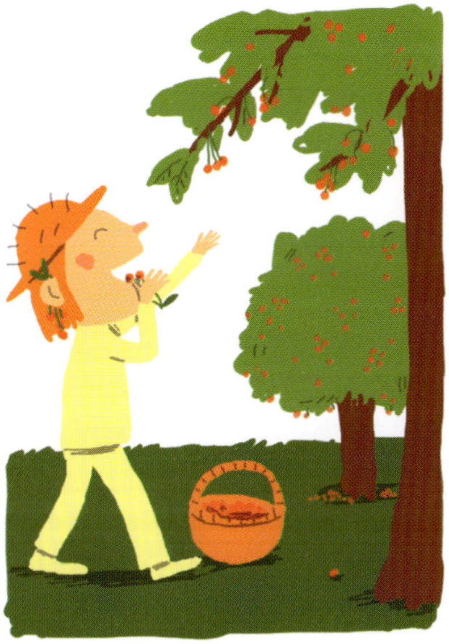

Στο κεράσι, **το μέρος που τρώμε** είναι ο ύπερος.

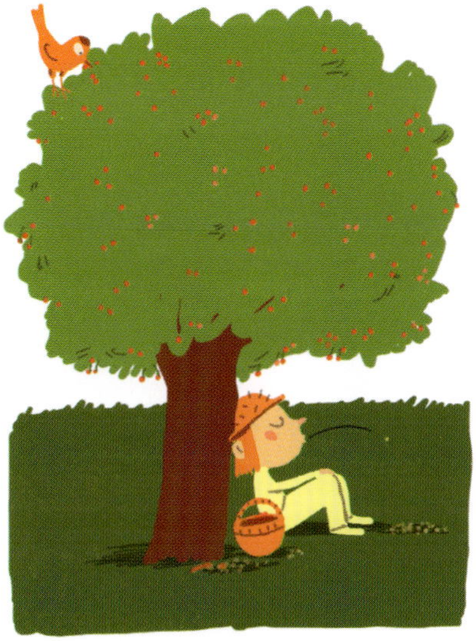

Το **κουκούτσι** περιέχει το σπόρο, που ίσως γεννήσει μια νέα κερασιά.

Άλλοι τρόποι αναπαραγωγής

Δε χρειάζονται όλα τα φυτά ένα λουλούδι για ν' αναπαραχθούν. Κάποια μπορούν να δημιουργήσουν ένα νέο φυτό με έναν απλό μίσχο: αυτό ονομάζεται φύτεμα.

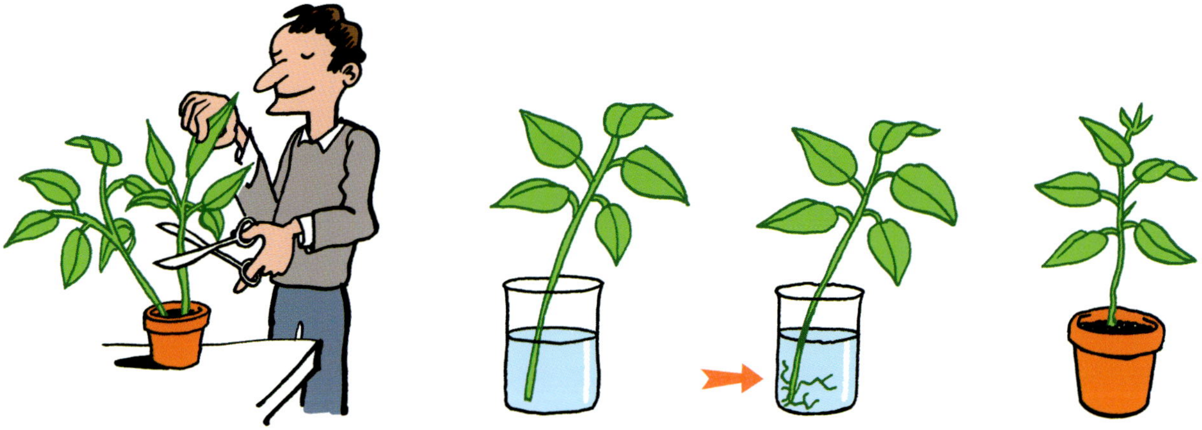

Κόβουμε το **μίσχο** ενός γερανιού.

Τον βάζουμε μέσα σ' ένα **ποτήρι νερό**.

Σχηματίζονται **ρίζες**.

Φυτρώνει ένα **νέο φυτό**.

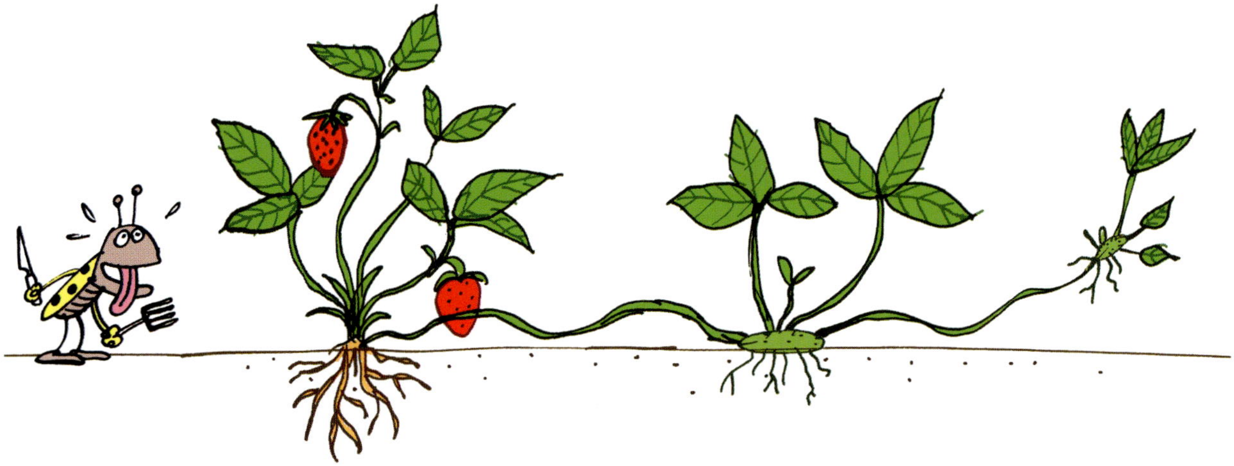

Κάποια φυτά, όπως η **φραουλιά**, φυτρώνουν μόνα τους στη φύση. Η φραουλιά έχει **μεγάλους μίσχους**, που από τη μια μεριά έχουν **φύλλα** και από την άλλη **ρίζες**. Οι ρίζες βυθίζονται στη γη και δίνουν μια νέα φραουλιά, διαφορετική από το φυτό «μαμά».

Η **πατάτα** είναι **βολβός**, δηλαδή ένα όργανο που περιέχει απόθεμα του φυτού και μπορεί να δημιουργήσει ένα νέο φυτό.
Δεν είναι σπόρος.

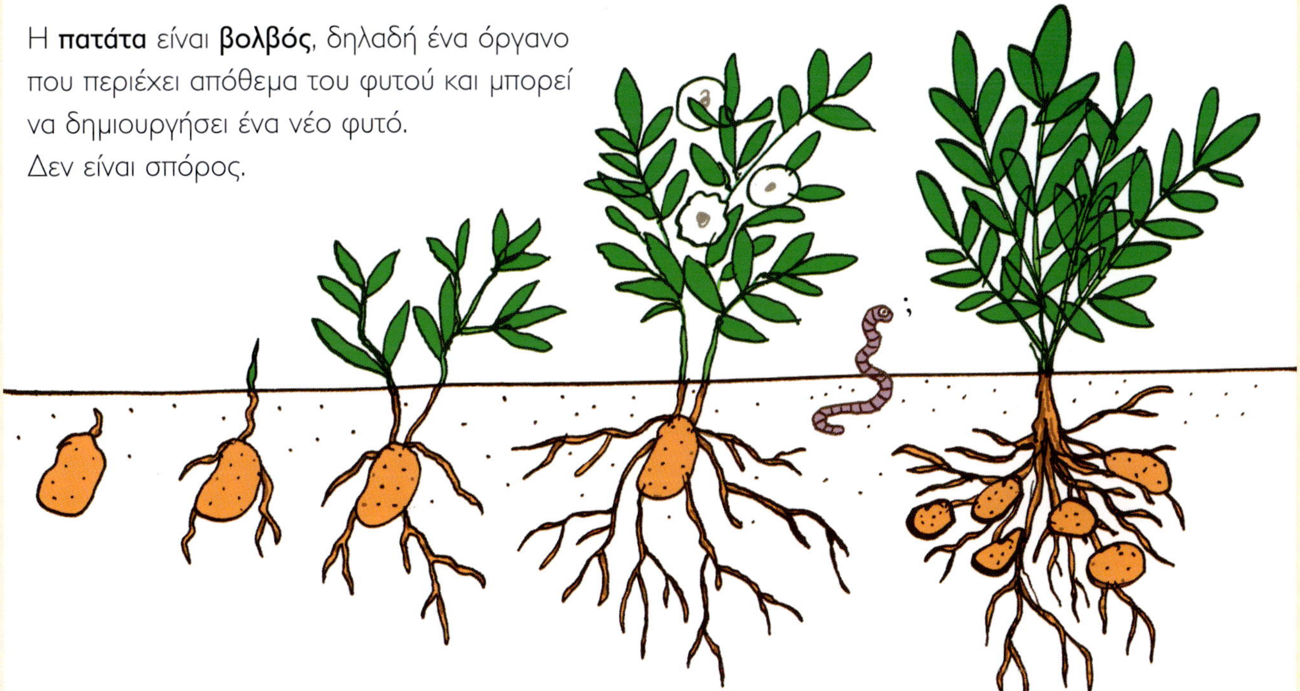

Όταν φυτεύουμε μια πατάτα, βγαίνουν μίσχοι που πρώτα βγάζουν **φύλλα** και μετά **λουλούδια**.
Οι **μίσχοι** φουσκώνουν κάτω από το χώμα: είναι οι καινούριες πατάτες.

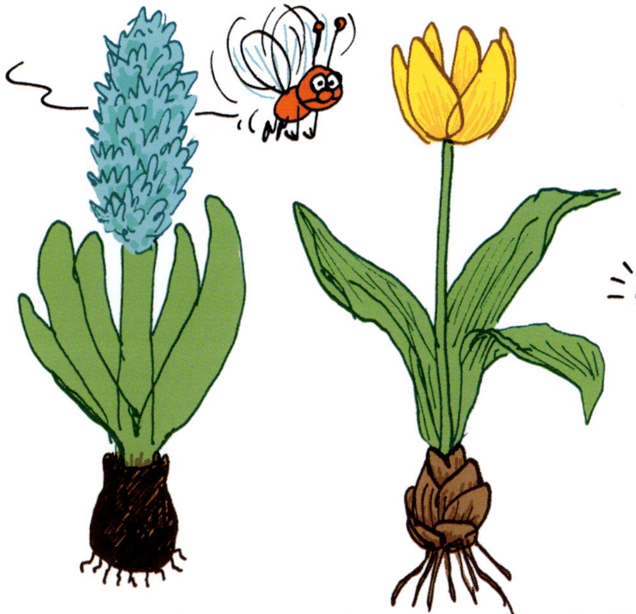

Ο **υάκινθος** και η **τουλίπα** είναι φυτά με **βολβούς**:
κάθε χρόνο δίνουν ένα καινούριο φυτό.

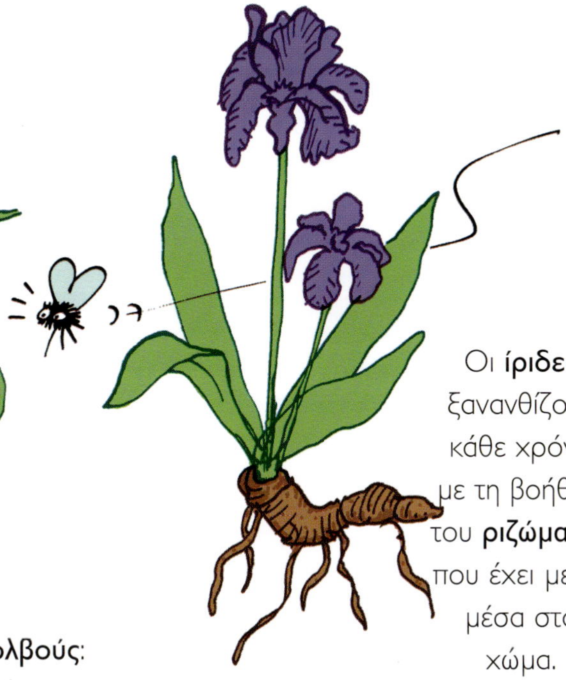

Οι **ίριδες** ξανανθίζουν κάθε χρόνο με τη βοήθεια του **ριζώματος** που έχει μείνει μέσα στο χώμα.

Παρατήρησε ένα σπόρο!

Για να καταλάβεις πώς σχηματίζεται ένας σπόρος, παρατήρησε ένα σπόρο φασολιάς.

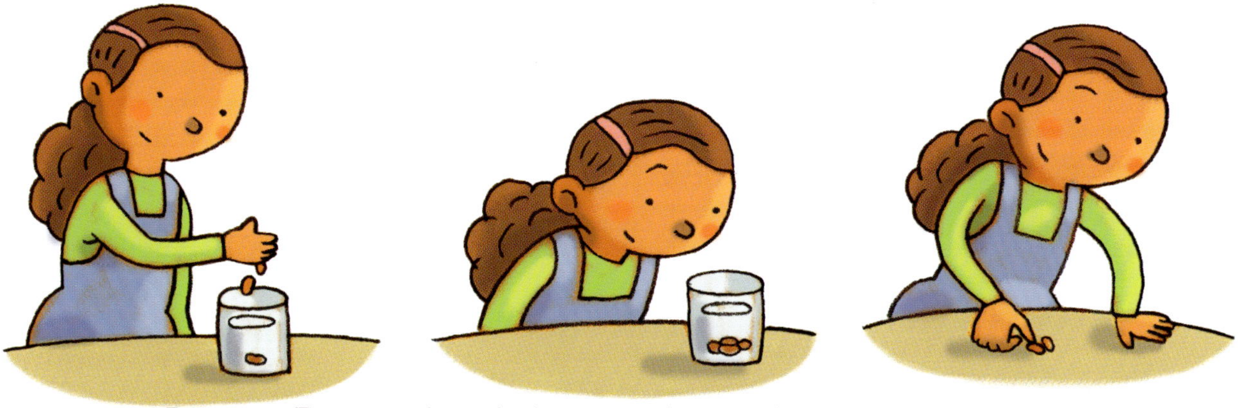

Για να ανοίξεις το σπόρο εύκολα με το νύχι σου, άφησε τον να μουσκέψει μερικές ώρες μέσα στο νερό.

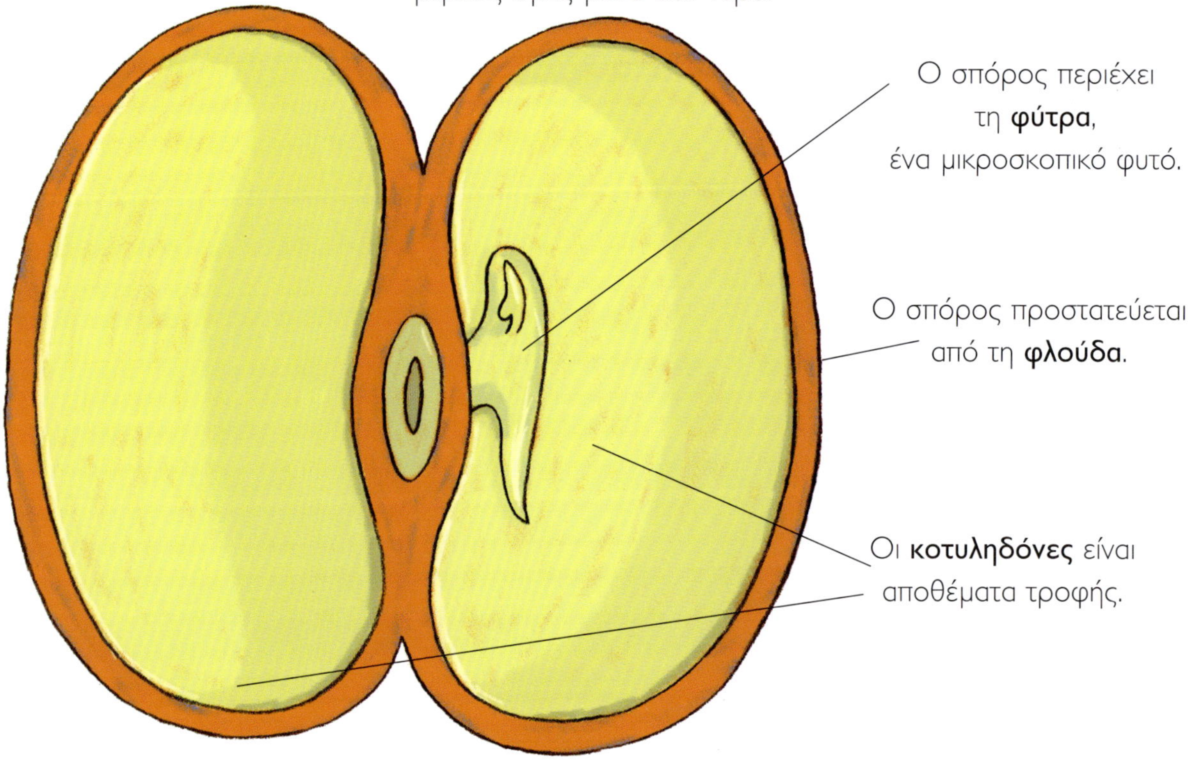

ΤΑ ΣΤΑΔΙΑ ΤΗΣ ΒΛΑΣΤΗΣΗΣ

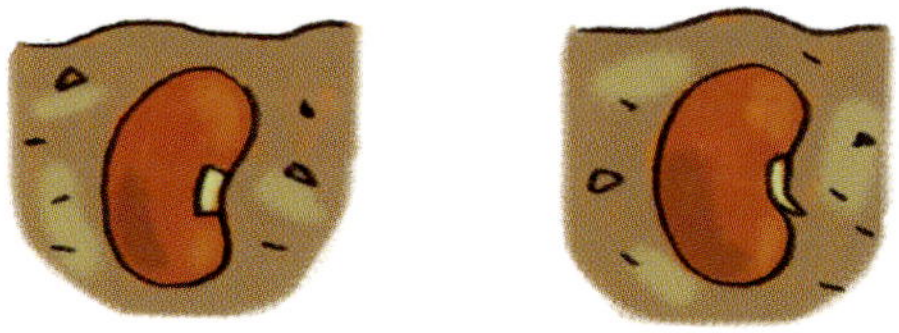

Αν **φυτέψουμε** το σπόρο ενός φασολιού, **φουσκώνει**: η φλούδα του σκίζεται.

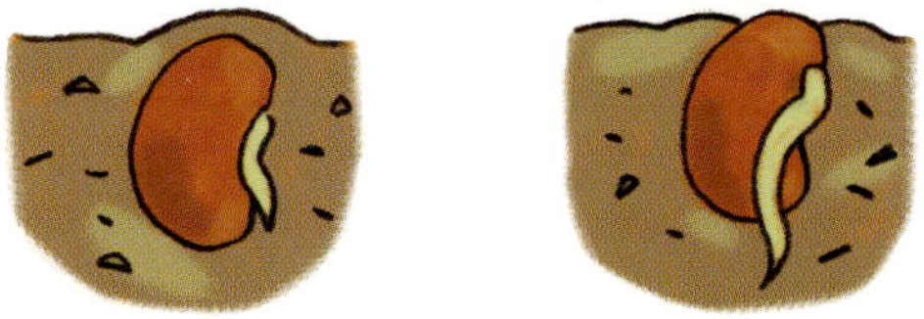

Εμφανίζεται μια **μικρή ρίζα**. Αυτό ονομάζεται **βλάστηση**.

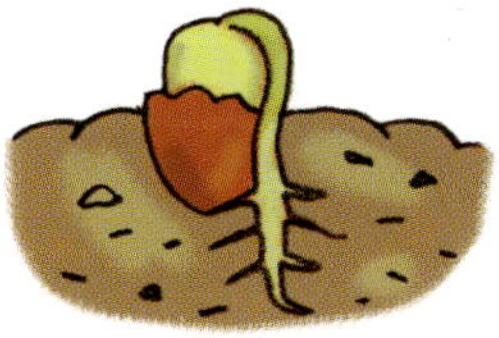

Όσο αναπτύσσεται, η ρίζα βοηθά τις δύο κοτυληδόνες να **βγουν** από το χώμα.

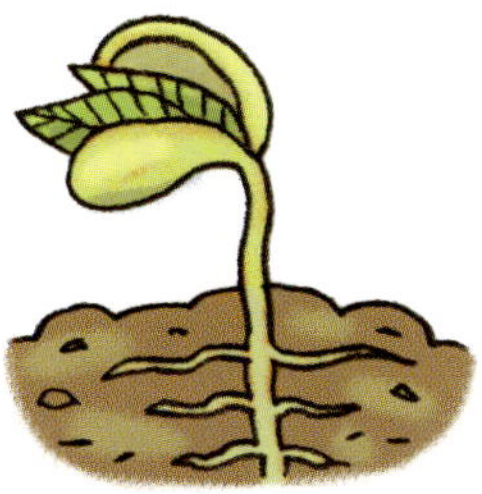

Τότε εμφανίζονται τα πρώτα **φύλλα**.

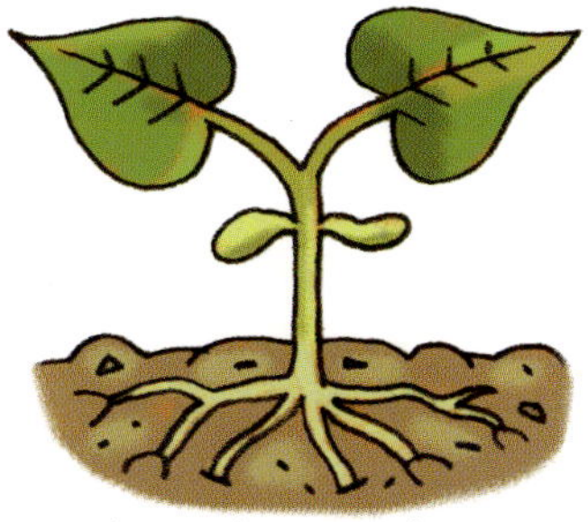

Το νεαρό φυτό μπορεί να **τραφεί** και οι κοτυληδόνες, εξαντλημένες, εξαφανίζονται.

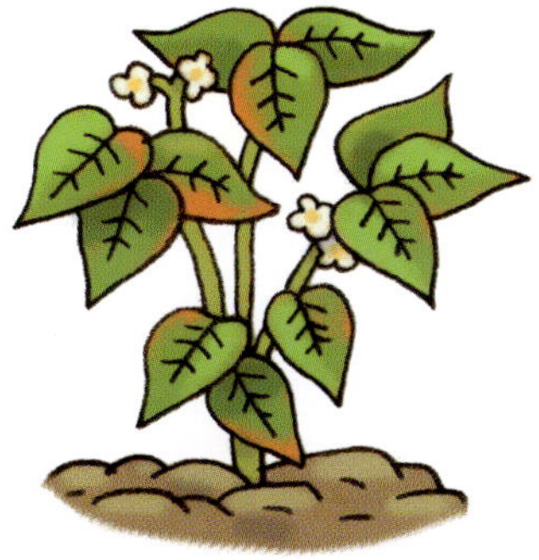

Μόλις γονιμοποιηθούν τα **λουλούδια**, σχηματίζονται σπόροι και καρποί.

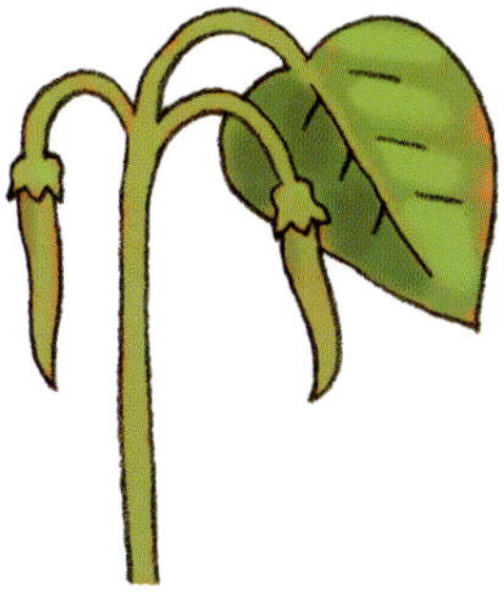

Ο ύπερος του λουλουδιού σχηματίζει τη **φλούδα** του φασολιού.

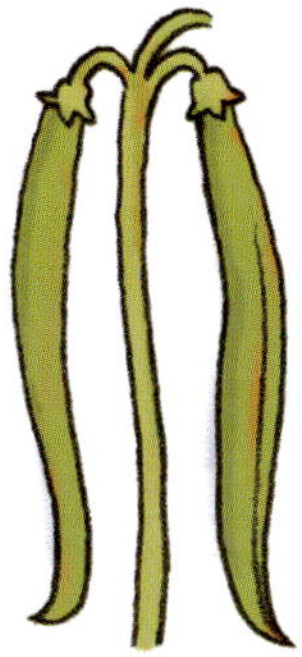

Είναι τα πράσινα φασολάκια που τρώμε.

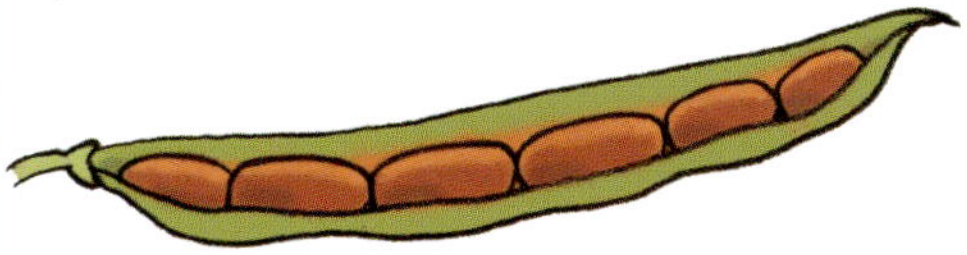

Οι σπόροι του φασολιού βρίσκονται μέσα στη φλούδα.

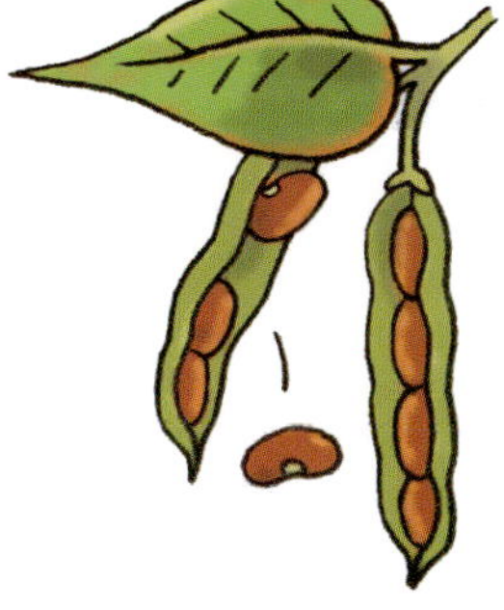

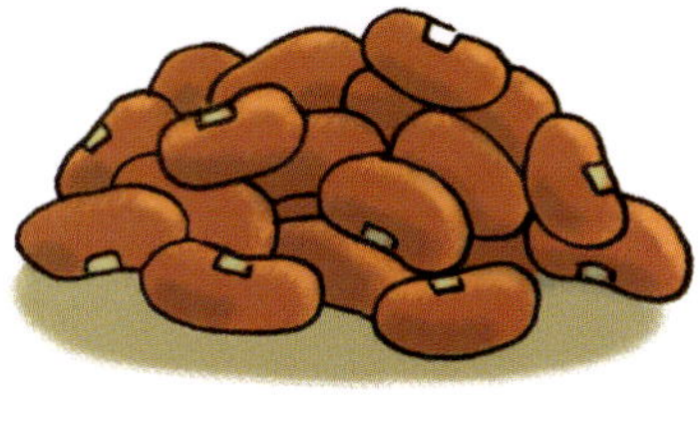

Μόλις φυτρώσουν, οι καρποί θα δημιουργήσουν νέα φυτά.

Δουλεύοντας με τα φυτά

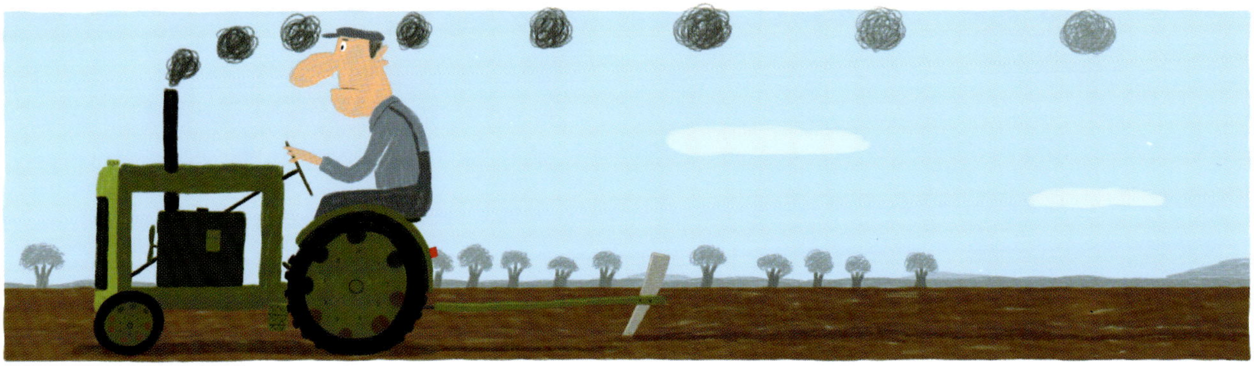

Ο **αγρότης** καλλιεργεί σιτάρι, καλαμπόκι, ηλιοτρόπια, ζαχαρότευτλα, φυτά που χρησιμεύουν στη διατροφή των ανθρώπων ή των ζώων που εκτρέφουν.

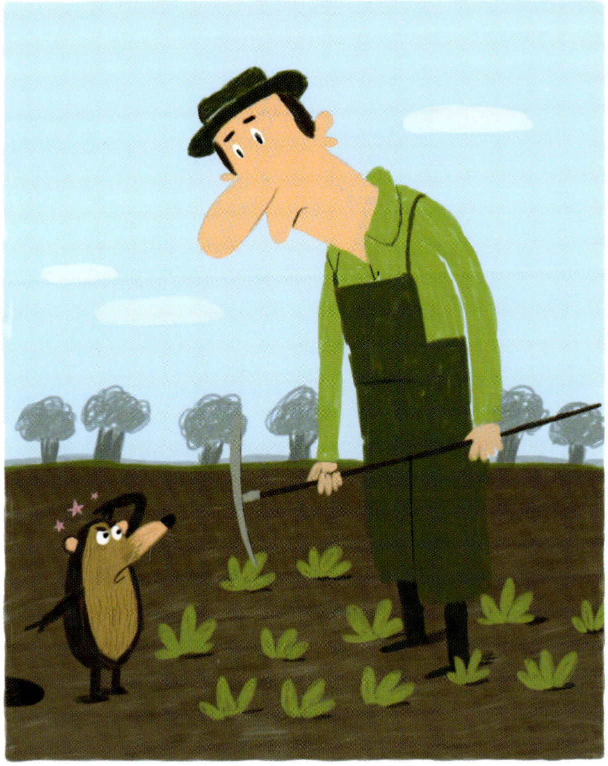

Ο **λαχανοκηπουρός** καλλιεργεί τα λαχανικά που αγοράζουμε στη λαϊκή.

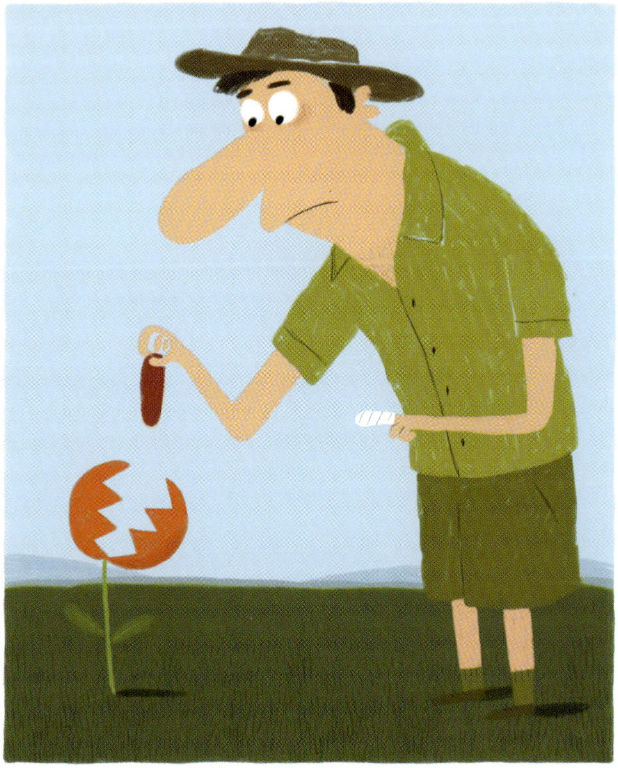

Οι **βοτανολόγοι** είναι ειδικοί στα φυτά. Κάποιοι γυρίζουν όλο τον κόσμο για να βρουν νέα είδη φυτών.

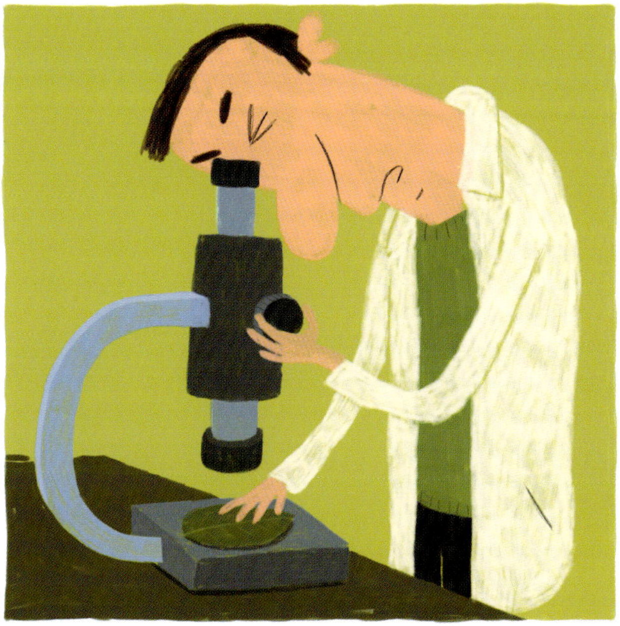

Κάποιοι βοτανολόγοι μελετούν την **ανατομία** των φυτών, δηλαδή τον τρόπο με τον οποίο είναι φτιαγμένα.

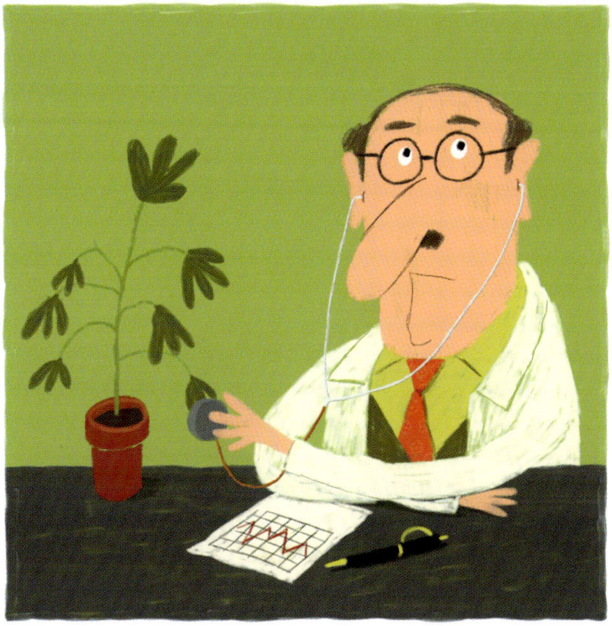

Άλλοι βοτανολόγοι μελετούν τη **φυσιολογία** των φυτών, δηλαδή τον τρόπο με τον οποίο ζουν.

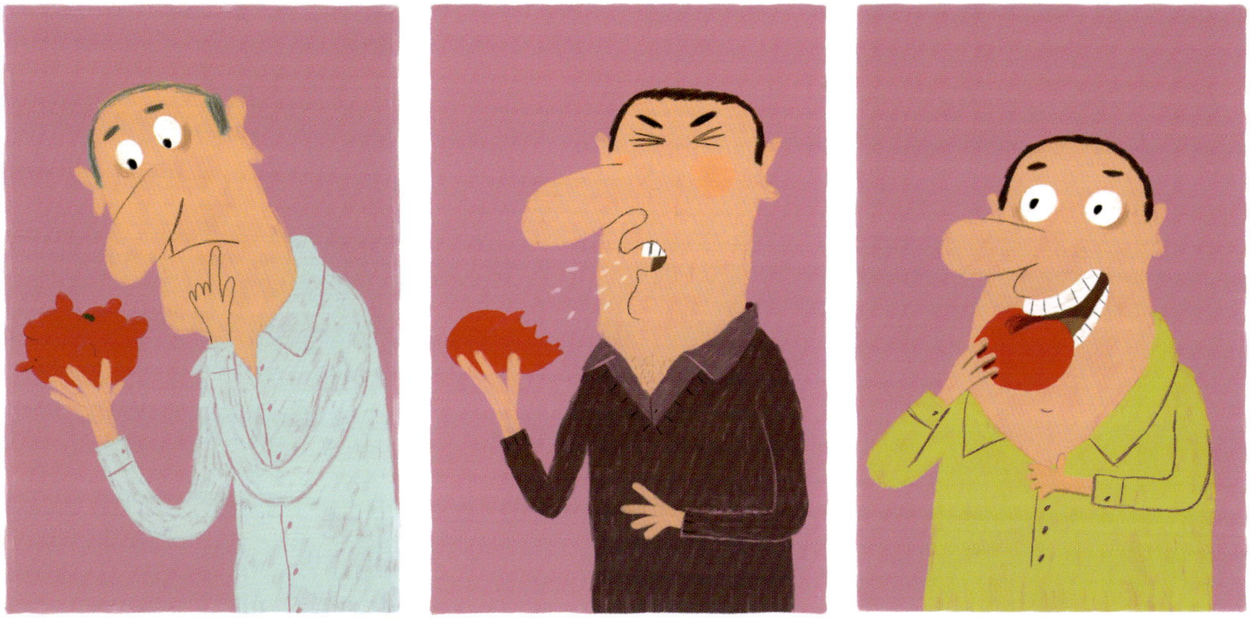

Ο **γενετιστής** μπορεί να δημιουργήσει νέα φυτά. «Ανακατεύει» τα φυτά μεταξύ τους, για να τα βελτιώσει: για παράδειγμα, μια γευστική αλλά όχι εμφανίσιμη ντομάτα με μια άγευστη αλλά κατακόκκινη ντομάτα... Φτιάχνει λοιπόν μια όμορφη και νοστιμότατη ντομάτα!

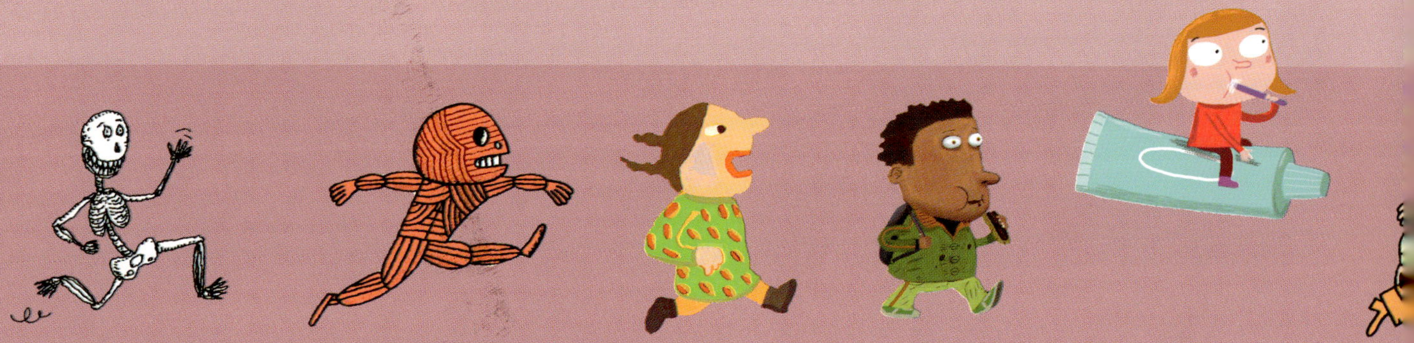

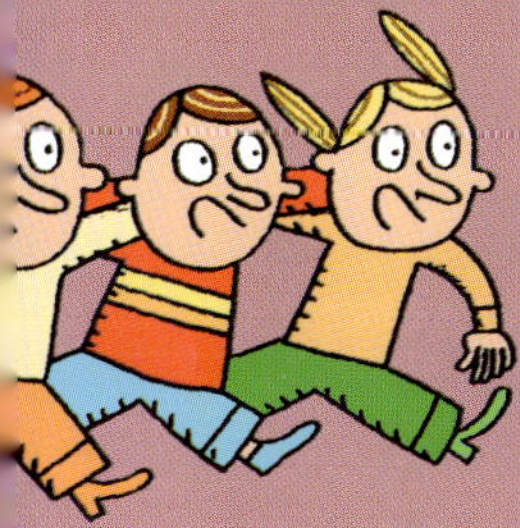
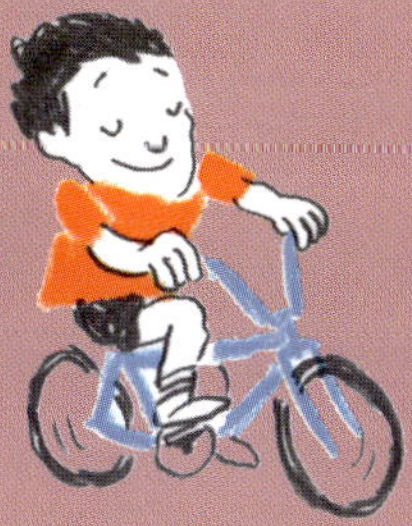
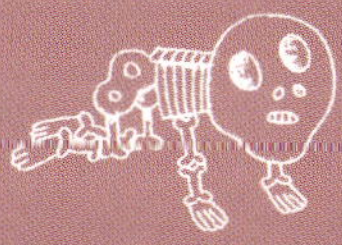

Η ΖΩΗ
ΤΟΥ ΣΩΜΑΤΟΣ

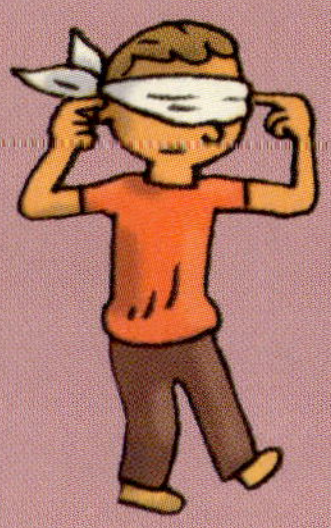
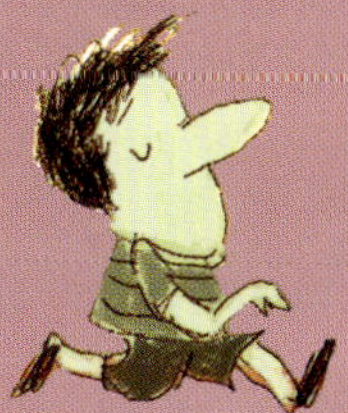

Τα μέρη του σώματος

Γνωρίζεις τα διάφορα μέρη του σώματος;

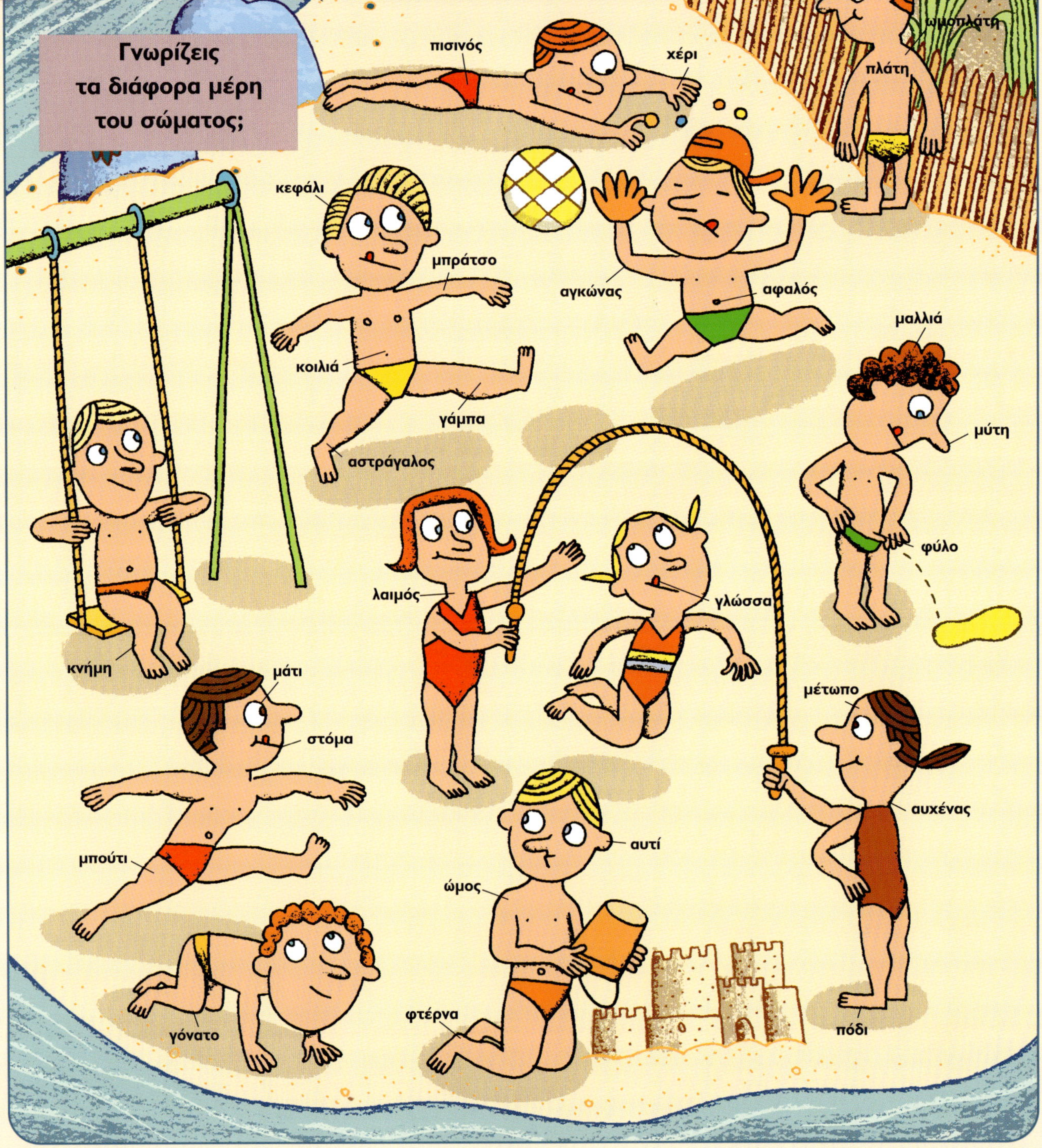

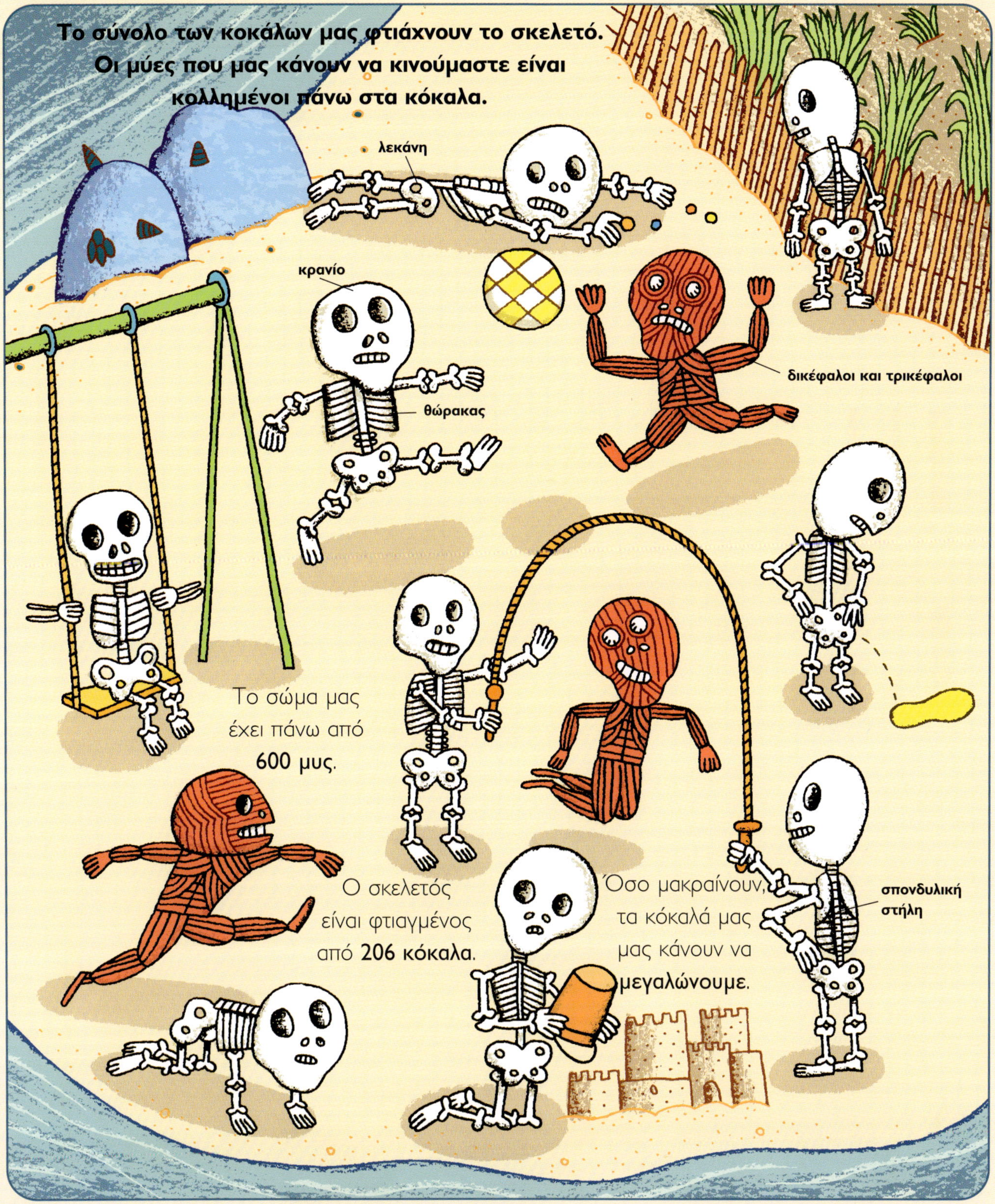

Το σύνολο των κοκάλων μας φτιάχνουν το σκελετό. Οι μύες που μας κάνουν να κινούμαστε είναι κολλημένοι πάνω στα κόκαλα.

Το σώμα μας έχει πάνω από **600 μυς**.

Ο σκελετός είναι φτιαγμένος από **206 κόκαλα**.

Όσο μακραίνουν, τα κόκαλά μας μας κάνουν να **μεγαλώνουμε**.

Τα κόκαλα και οι μύες

Τα κόκαλα είναι σκληρά. Στηρίζουν το σώμα και το βοηθούν να κινείται.

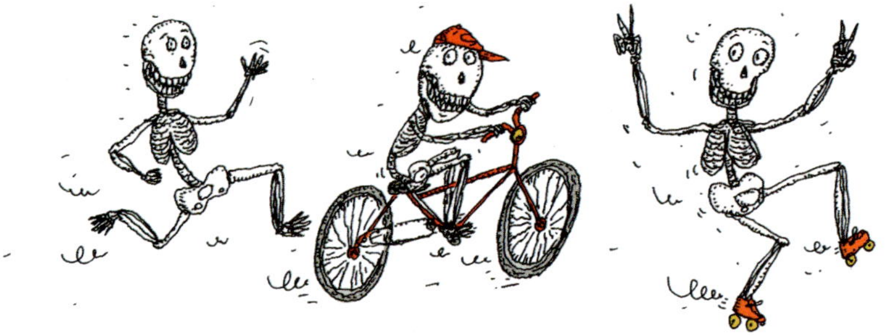

Χωρίς το **σκελετό**, το σώμα μας θα ήταν πολύ μαλακό, όπως του σκουληκιού ή του σαλιγκαριού.

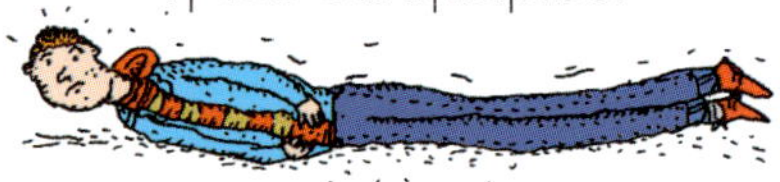

Τα κόκαλα του σκελετού μας δεν έχουν όλα το ίδιο σχήμα.

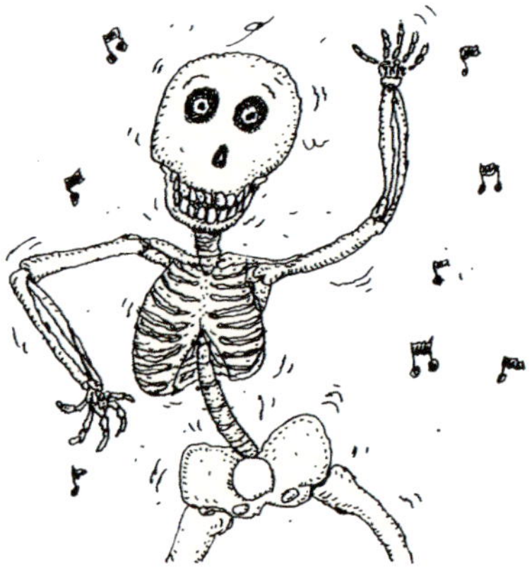

Οι **32 σπόνδυλοι** της σπονδυλικής στήλης στηρίζουν το πάνω μέρος του σώματός μας.

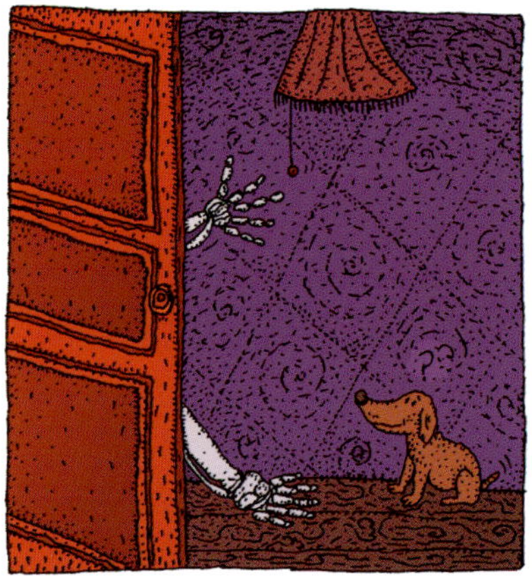

Το **χέρι** μας είναι σχηματισμένο από 27 μικρά κόκαλα. Το **πόδι** από 26 κόκαλα.

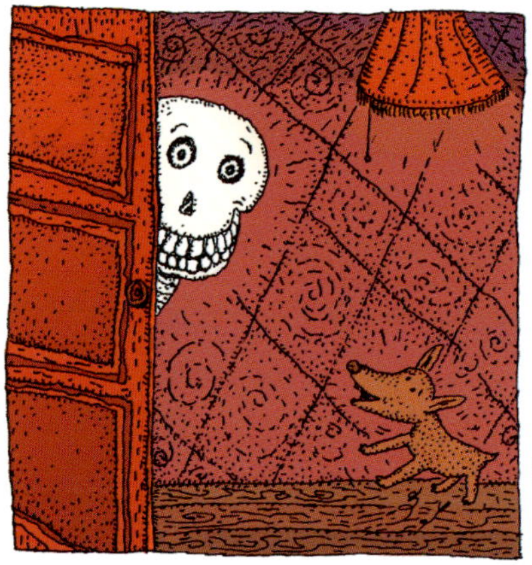

Τα κόκαλα του **κρανίου** είναι επίπεδα· σχηματίζουν ένα κουτί που προστατεύει τον εγκέφαλο.

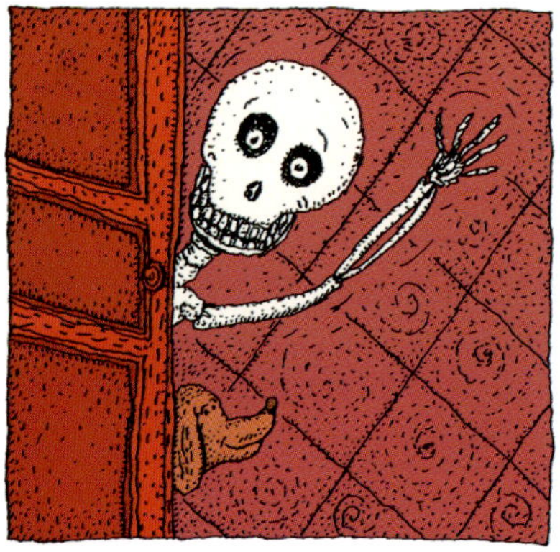

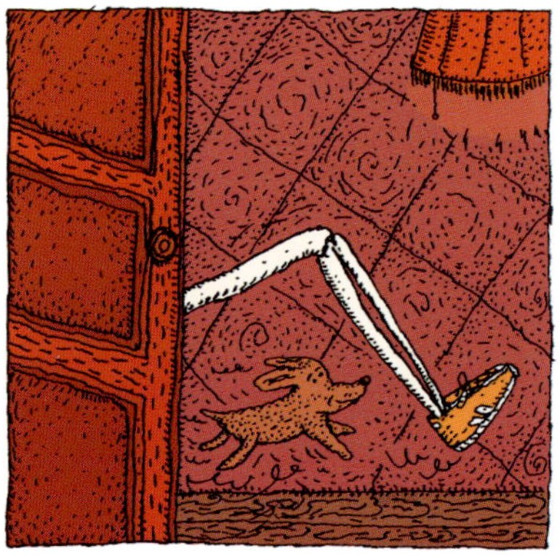

Τα κόκαλα των **χεριών** και των **ποδιών** είναι τα μακρύτερα.

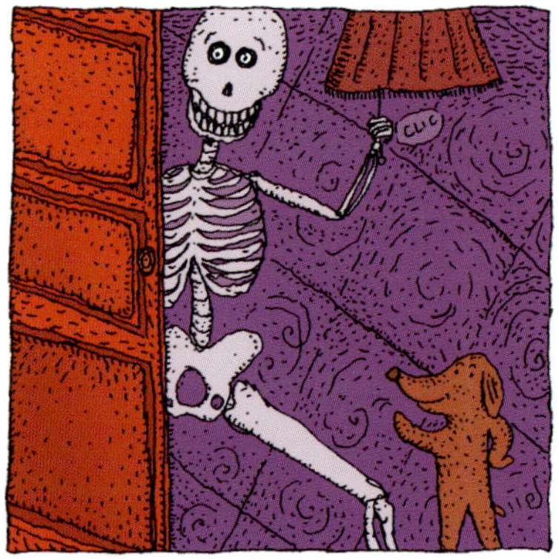

12 ζευγάρια **πλευρών** σχηματίζουν το **θώρακα**, που προστατεύει την καρδιά και τους πνεύμονές μας.

Τα κόκαλα κινούνται στο επίπεδο των αρθρώσεων: αρθρώσεις είναι οι αγκώνες, τα γόνατα, οι ώμοι...

Οι **μύες** κολλάνε στα κόκαλα με **τένοντες**. **Τραβιούνται** από τα κόκαλα για να τα κάνουν να κινηθούν.

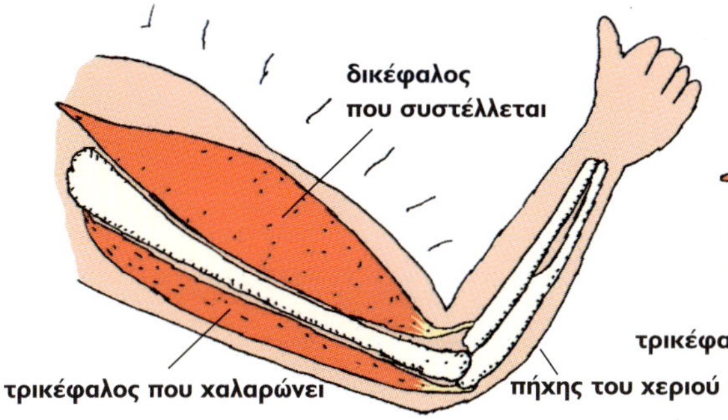

Όταν διπλώνουμε το χέρι μας, ο **δικέφαλος**, ο μυς του χεριού, φουσκώνει και μικραίνει. Τραβάει το κόκαλο του πήχη.

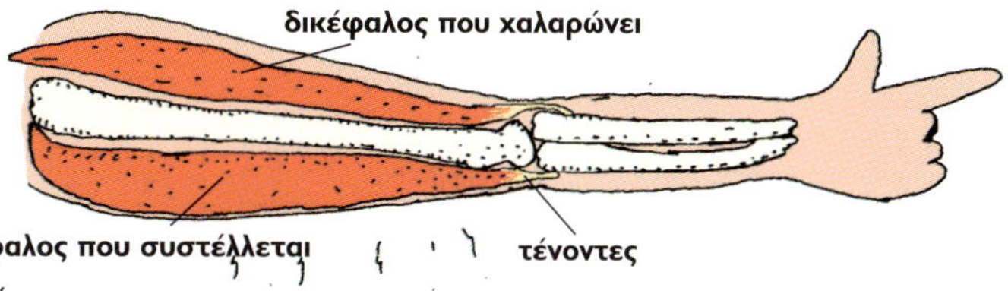

Όταν απλώνουμε το χέρι μας, ένας άλλος μυς αυτή τη φορά, ο **τρικέφαλος**, πρήζεται και συστέλλεται.

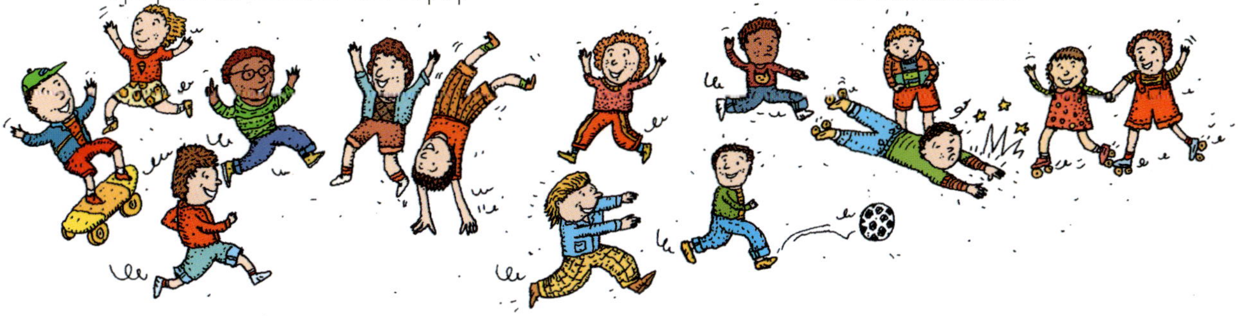

Όταν αθλούμαστε, οι μύες μας **δουλεύουν**: παχαίνουν και δυναμώνουν. Προσοχή όμως! Τα κόκαλα **σπάνε**.

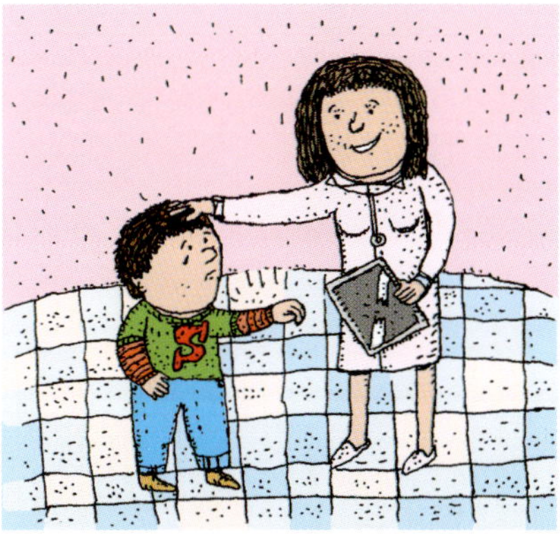

Πρέπει να κάνουμε **ακτινογραφία** στο νοσοκομείο, για να δούμε πού βρίσκεται το **ράγισμα**.

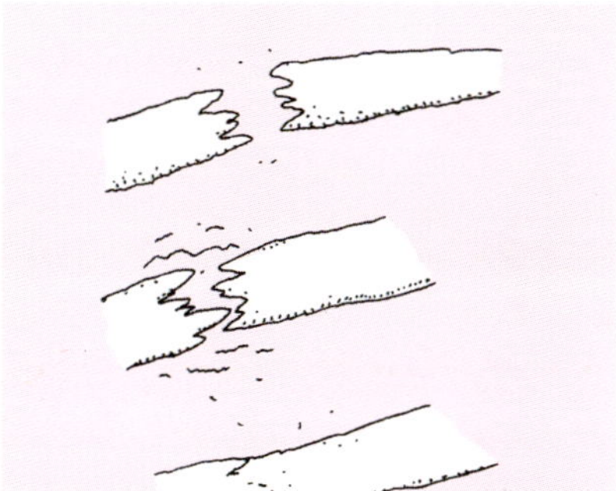

Ευτυχώς το κόκαλο είναι **ζωντανή ύλη**· θα ανασχηματιστεί μόνο του.

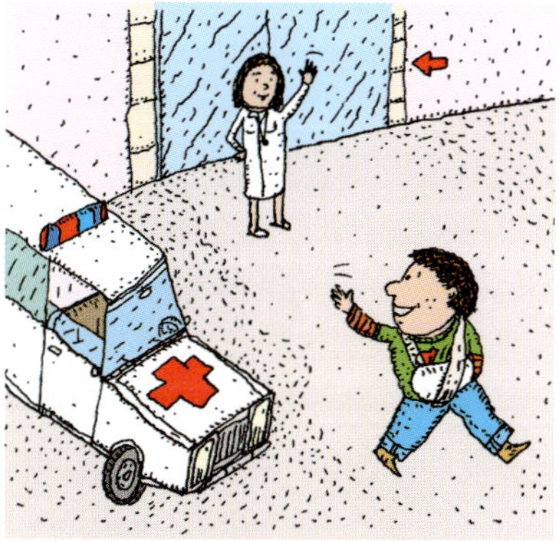

Για να μην κουνιέται όμως, πρέπει να βάλουμε το κόκαλο σε **γύψο**.

Ο εγκέφαλος

Τοποθετημένος μέσα στο κρανίο, ο εγκέφαλος είναι το όργανο που διατάζει το σώμα μας να κάνει ό,τι κάνει, ακόμα και να κοιμηθεί.

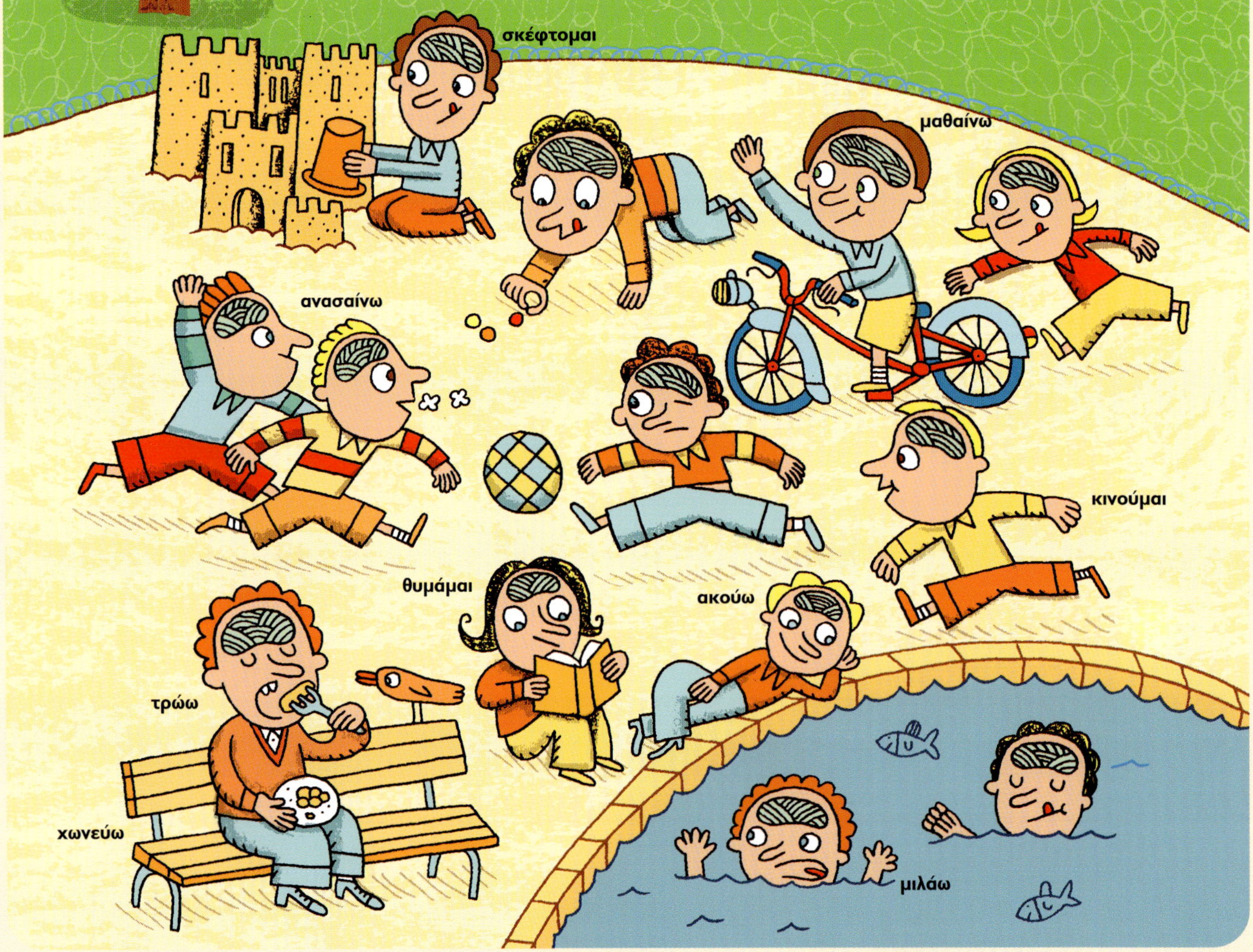

Οι 5 αισθήσεις μας ενημερώνουν τον εγκέφαλό μας για ό,τι συμβαίνει γύρω μας.

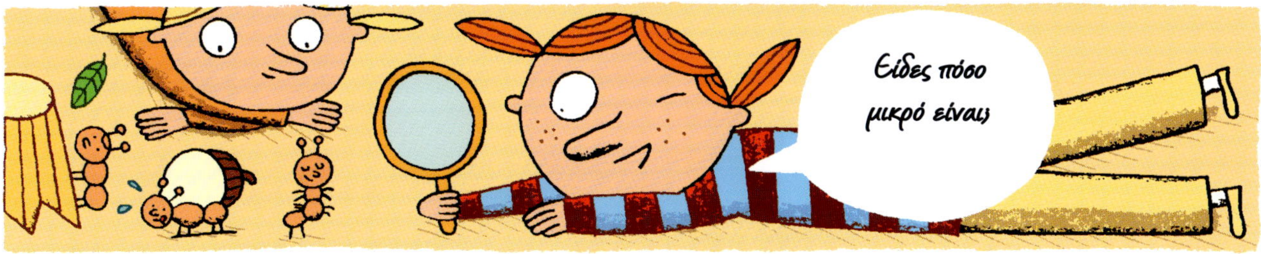

Η **όραση** μας επιτρέπει να βλέπουμε τα σχήματα, τα χρώματα…

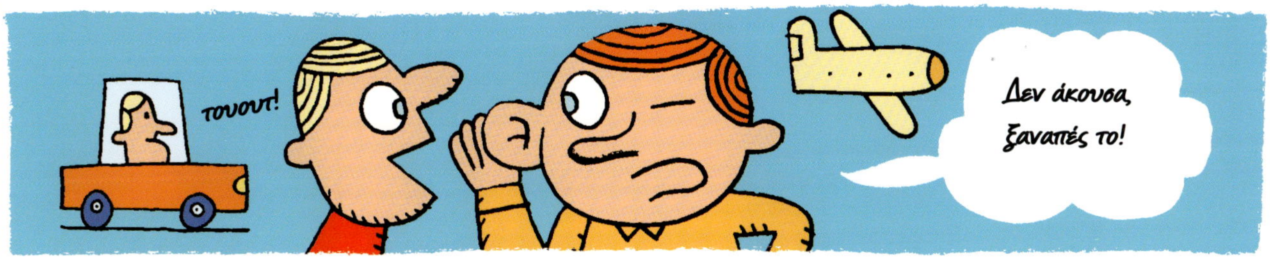

Η **ακοή** μάς επιτρέπει ν' ακούμε τους ήχους.

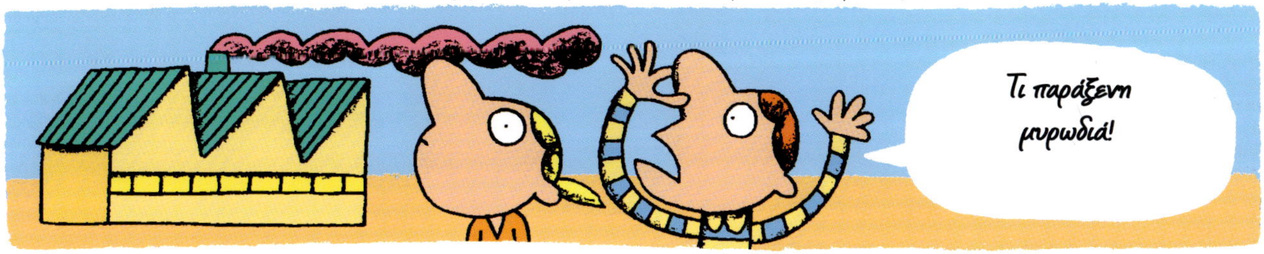

Η **οσμή** μάς επιτρέπει ν' αναγνωρίζουμε τις μυρωδιές.

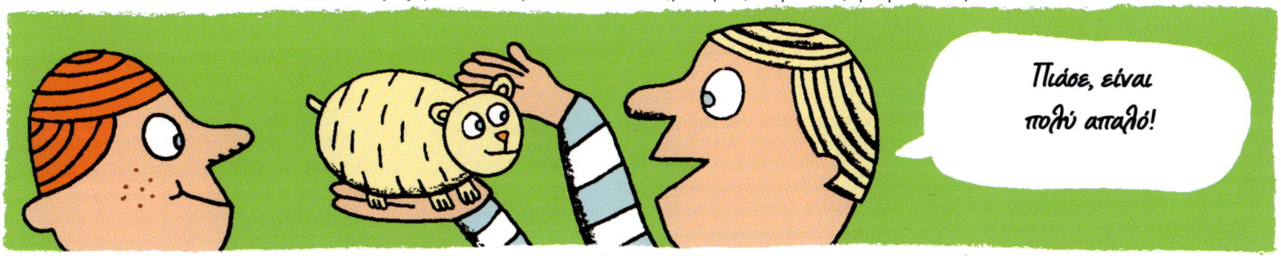

Η **αφή** μάς επιτρέπει να αναγνωρίζουμε το σχήμα, τη θερμοκρασία και την αίσθηση των πραγμάτων.

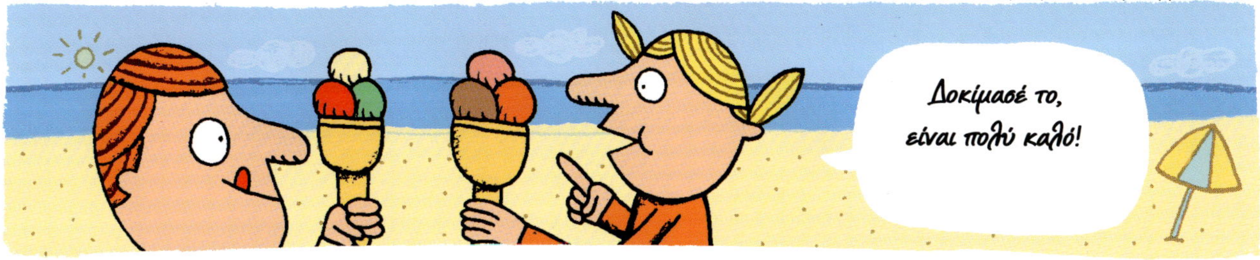

Η **γεύση** μάς επιτρέπει ν' αναγνωρίζουμε τις γεύσεις αυτών που τρώμε.

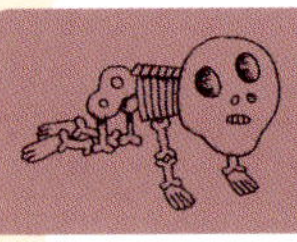

Η όραση και η ακοή

Το μάτι είναι το όργανο της όρασης.

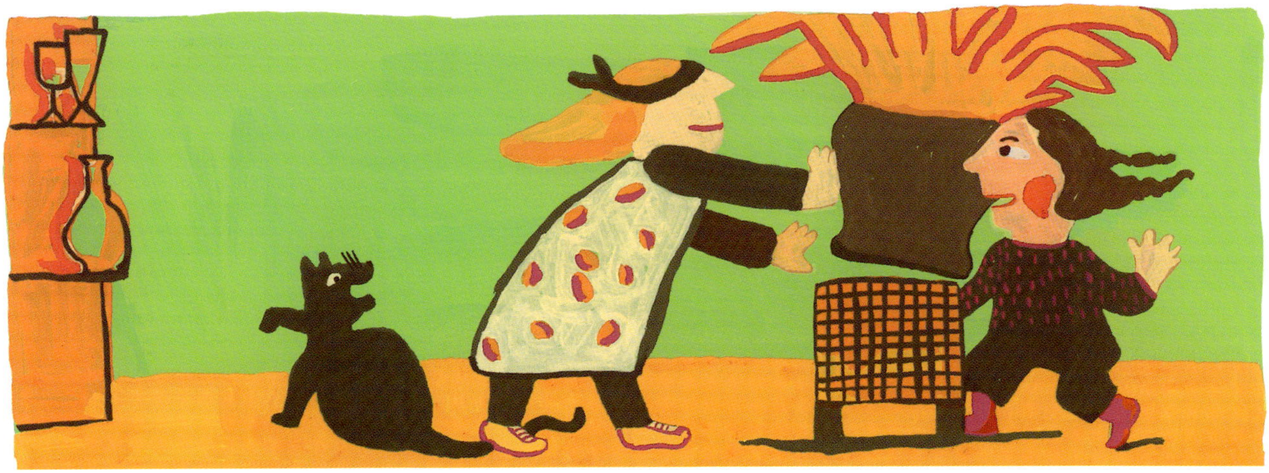

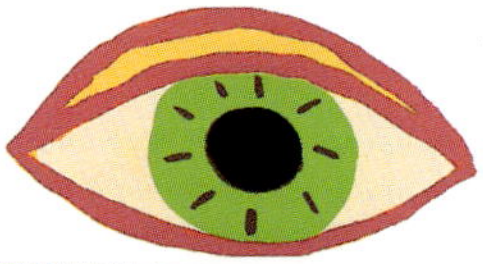

Το μικρό μαύρο στίγμα στη μέση του ματιού ονομάζεται **κόρη**.

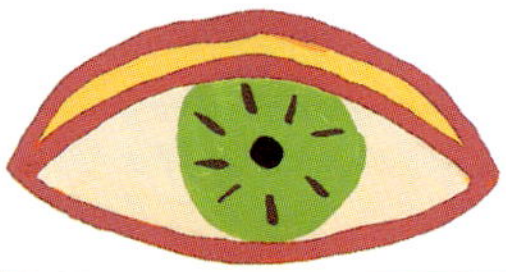

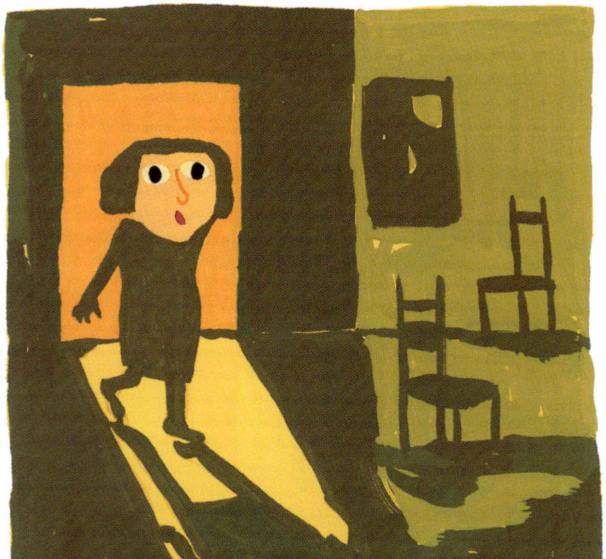

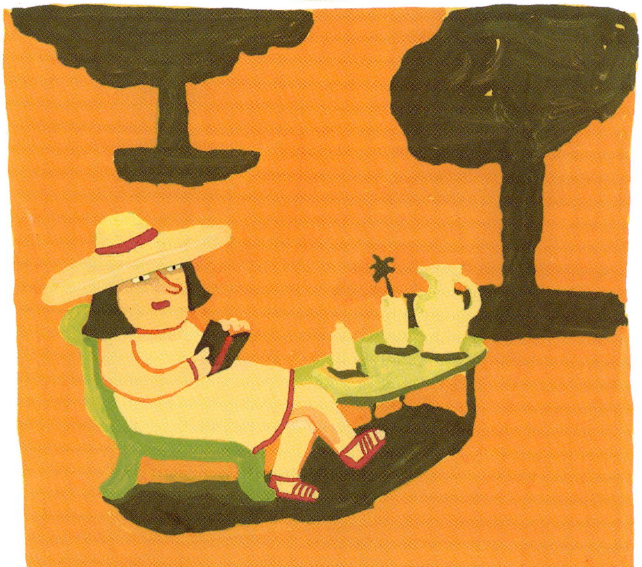

Όταν είμαστε στο σκοτάδι, **η κόρη μεγαλώνει**. Το μάτι έτσι αιχμαλωτίζει περισσότερο φως, για να βλέπουμε καλύτερα.

Όταν υπάρχει πολύ φως, που μας τυφλώνει, **η κόρη μικραίνει**.

Το αυτί είναι το όργανο της ακοής.

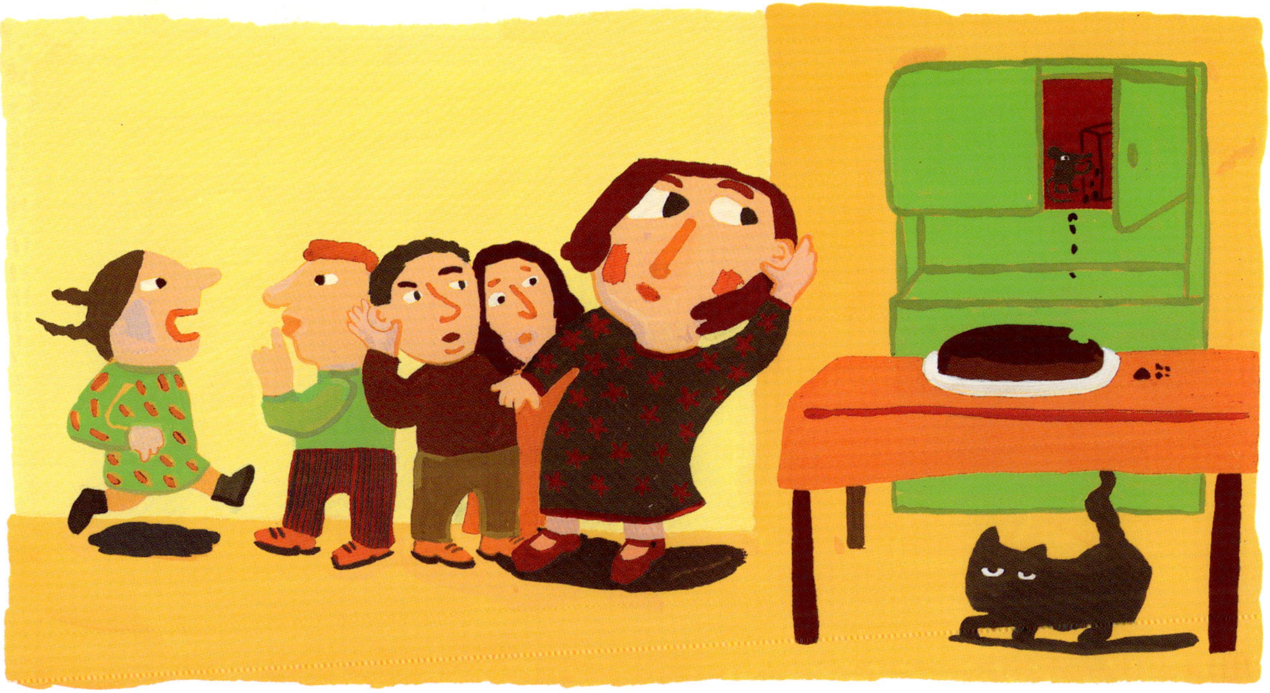

Μας επιτρέπει ν' ακούμε τους **ήχους**.

Ο ήχος μπαίνει **στο εσωτερικό του αυτιού** και χτυπά μια μικρή μεμβράνη: το **τύμπανο**.

ΠΡΩΤΑΘΛΗΤΕΣ, ΤΑ ΖΩΑ!

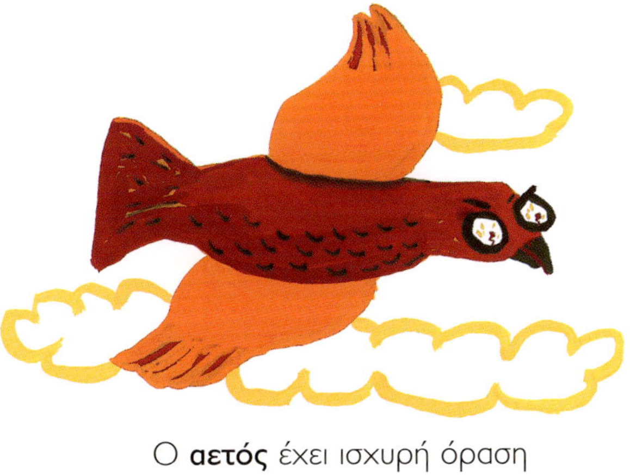

Ο **αετός** έχει ισχυρή όραση
και βλέπει τη λεία του από μακριά,
σαν να φοράει κιάλια... όμως μόνο τη μέρα.

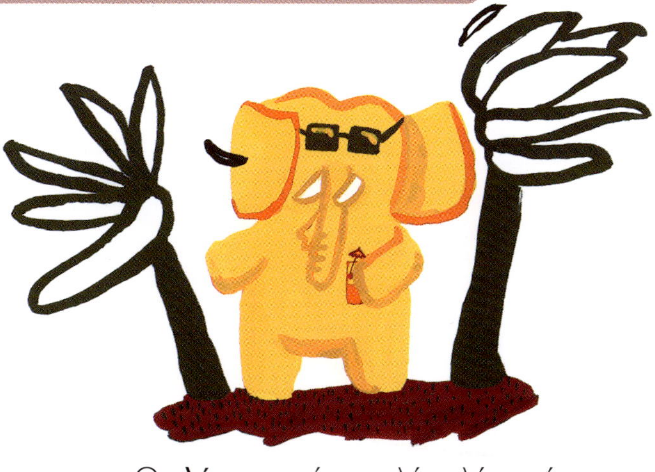

Ο **ελέφαντας** έχει πολύ καλή ακοή.
Τα μεγάλα αυτιά του του χρησιμεύουν ακόμα
σαν βεντάλια, για να δροσίζεται.

ΠαίΖΟΥμε μΕ την όΡΑση;

Για να διαπιστώσουμε αν έχεις καλή όραση, **παρατήρησε** αυτά τα σχέδια από μακριά (απομακρύνσου 8 βήματα).
Αν βλέπεις καλά όλα τα σχέδια στην τελευταία γραμμή, η όρασή σου είναι τέλεια!

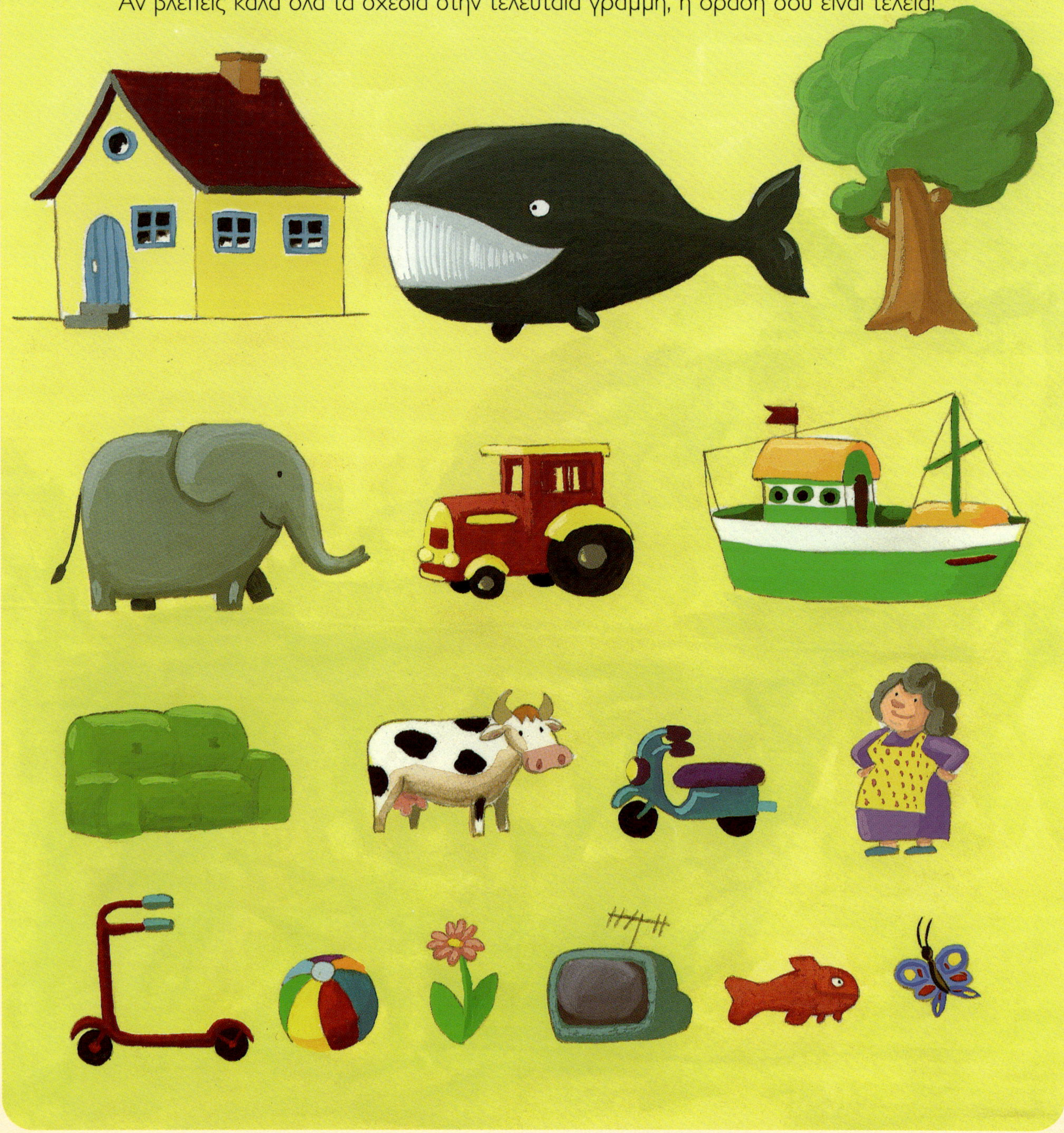

ΤΑ ΜΑΤΙΑ ΣΟΥ ΣΕ ΞΕΓΕΛΑΝΕ

Ποια είναι η πιο **μακριά γραμμή**;

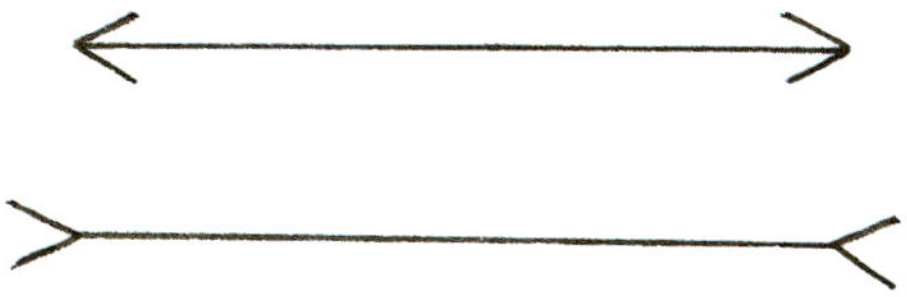

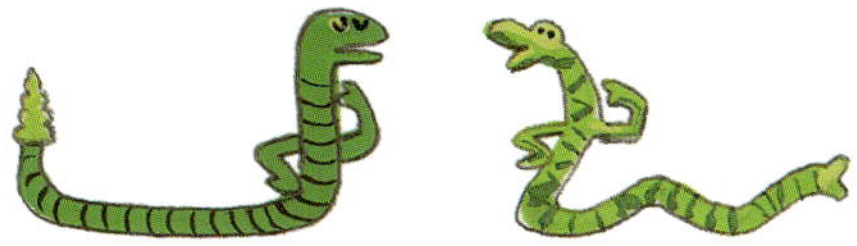

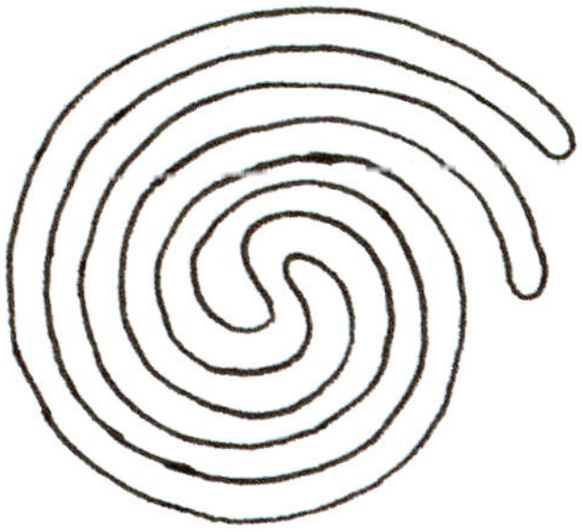

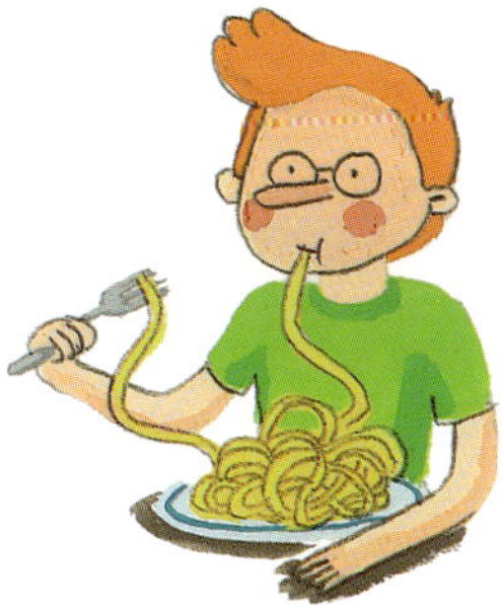

Τα **κορδόνια** είναι 1 ή 2;

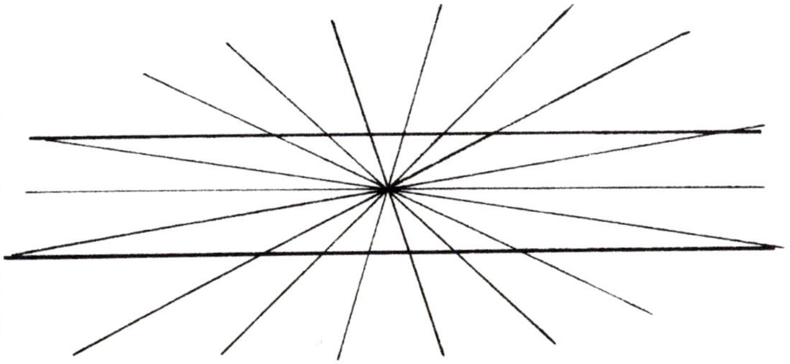

Οι 2 οριζόντιες **γραμμές** είναι ευθείες ή καμπύλες;

Ποιο είναι το πιο **μεγάλο τετραγωνάκι**;

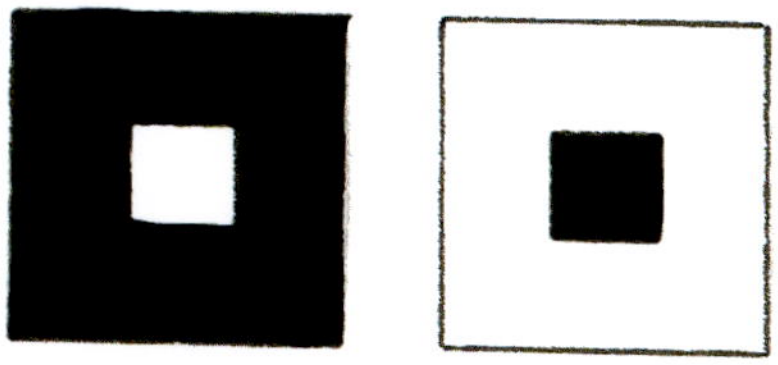

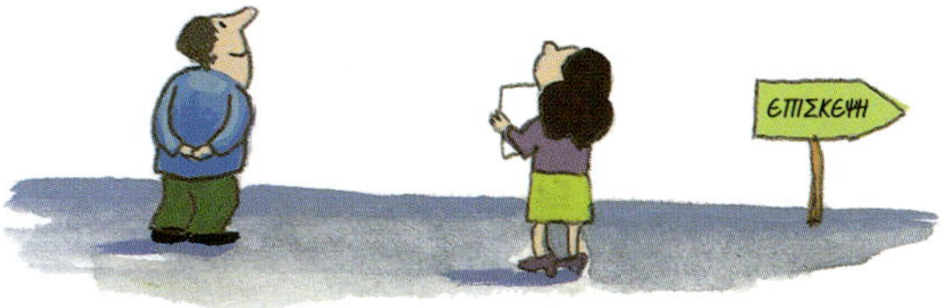

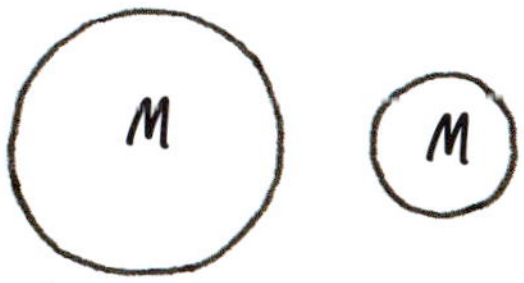

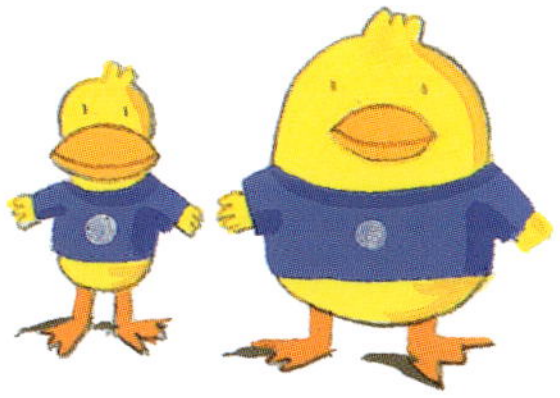

Ποιο είναι το **μεγαλύτερο Μ**;

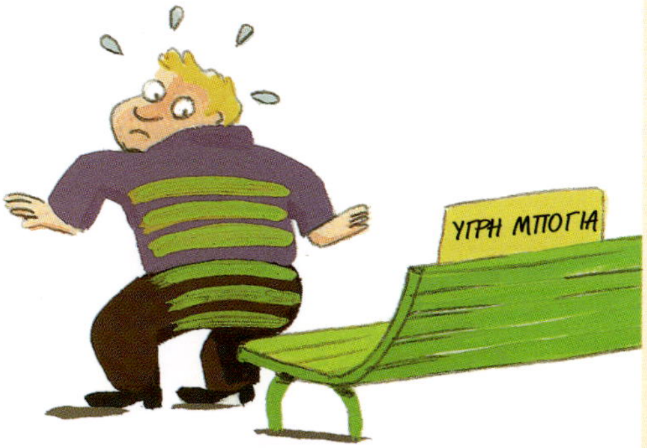

Λύση: Οι δύο γραμμές και τα δύο τετράγωνα έχουν το ίδιο μέγεθος. Το κορδόνι είναι μόνο ένα. Τα δύο Μ είναι ίδια. Οι δύο γραμμές είναι ευθείες.

Η οσμή, η γεύση και η αφή

Η μύτη είναι το όργανο της οσμής.

Αιχμαλωτίζει τις **μυρωδιές** στον αέρα.
Μπορεί ν' αναγνωρίζει πολλές και διαφορετικές μυρωδιές:

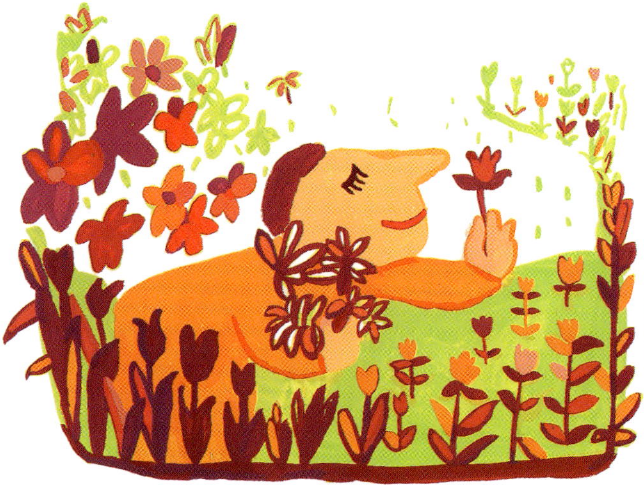

άλλες **ευχάριστες**...

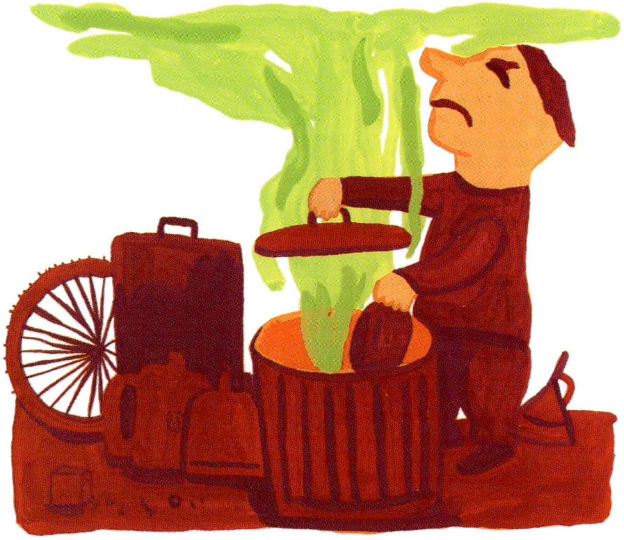

...άλλες **δυσάρεστες**.

Η γλώσσα είναι το όργανο της γεύσης.

Η γλώσσα αναγνωρίζει **τέσσερις γεύσεις**:

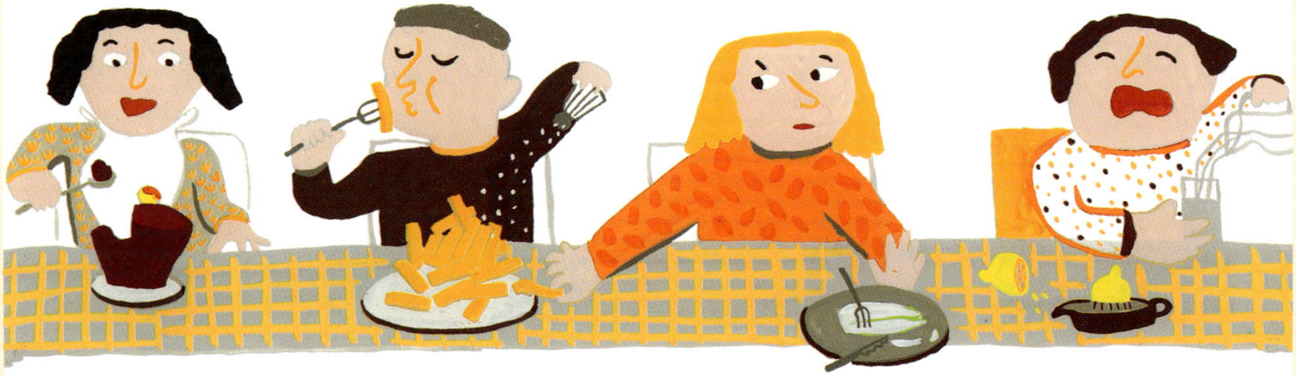

γλυκό **αλμυρό** **πικρό** **ξινό**

Το δέρμα είναι το όργανο της αφής.

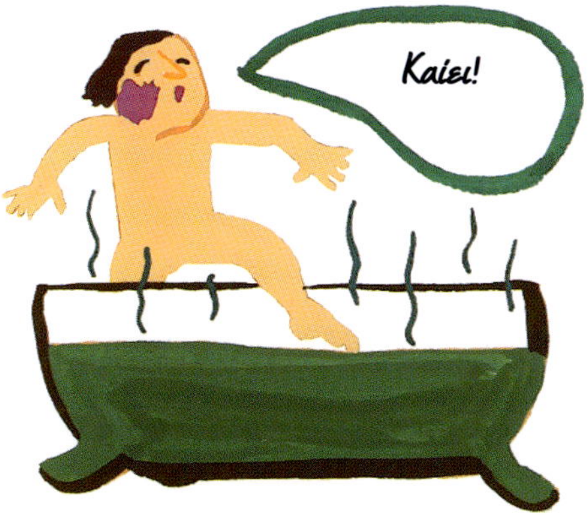

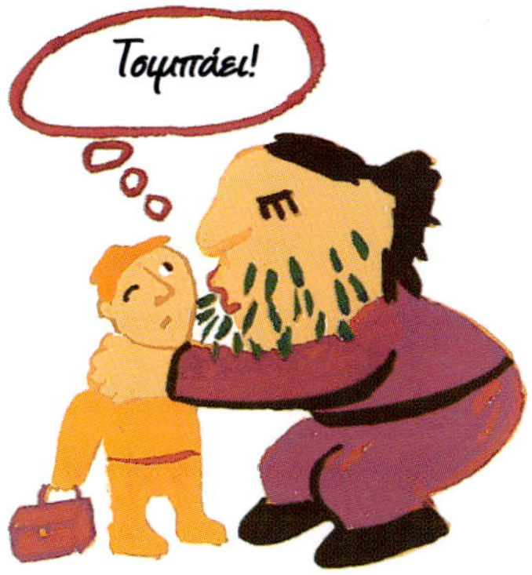

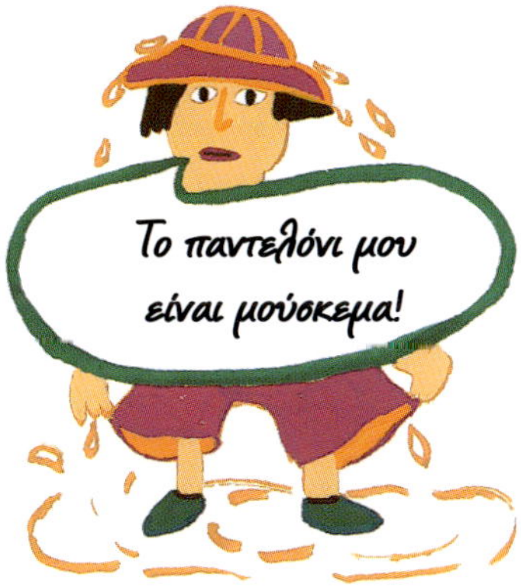

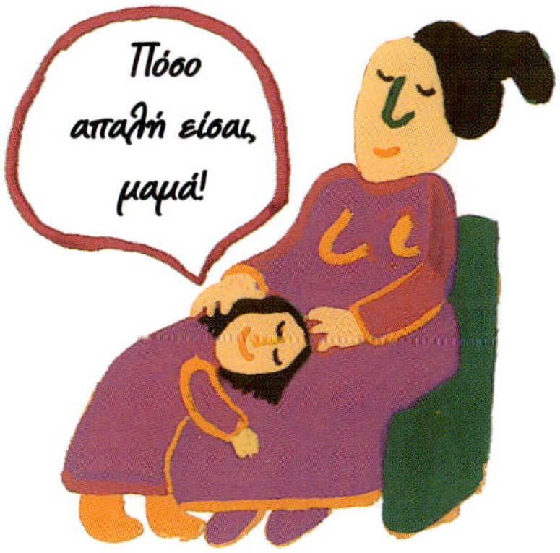

Τις περισσότερες φορές **αγγίζουμε** με τα **χέρια**.
Όμως όλο το **δέρμα** του σώματός μας μας επιτρέπει να αισθανόμαστε ό,τι αγγίζουμε.

ΠΡΩΤΑΘΛΗΤΕΣ, ΤΑ ΖΩΑ!

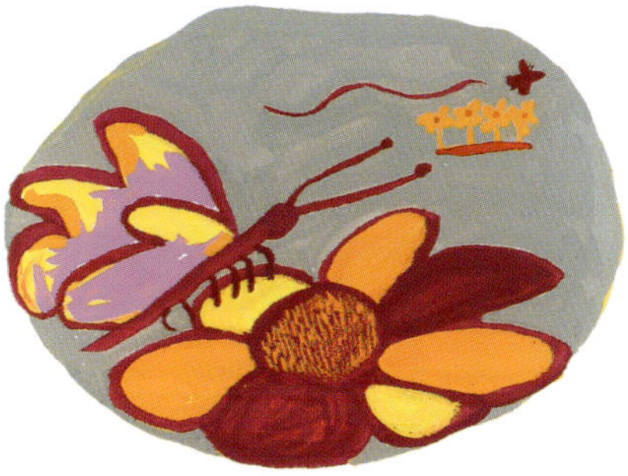

Με τις κεραίες της, η αρσενική **πεταλούδα** «μυρίζει» από πολύ μακριά το άρωμα της θηλυκής.

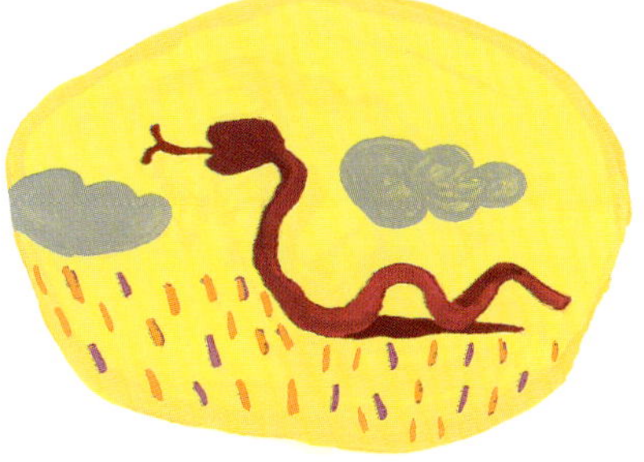

Το **φίδι** χρησιμοποιεί τη γλώσσα του για ν' αγγίζει ό,τι βρίσκεται γύρω του. Γι' αυτό βγάζει πολύ συχνά έξω τη γλώσσα του.

Οι άκρες των 2 μεγάλων κεραίων του είναι τα μάτια του **σαλιγκαριού**. Και μ' αυτά «αγγίζει».

Άκουσε τους ήχους!

Για ν' ακούμε, χρειαζόμαστε και τα δύο αυτιά μας.
Αν τα αυτιά μας είναι βουλωμένα, δεν ακούμε τίποτα. Μ' ένα βουλωμένο αυτί δεν καταλαβαίνουμε από πού έρχεται ο ήχος. Όμως με τα δύο αυτιά μας, ακόμα και με κλειστά μάτια, ακούμε μια χαρά!

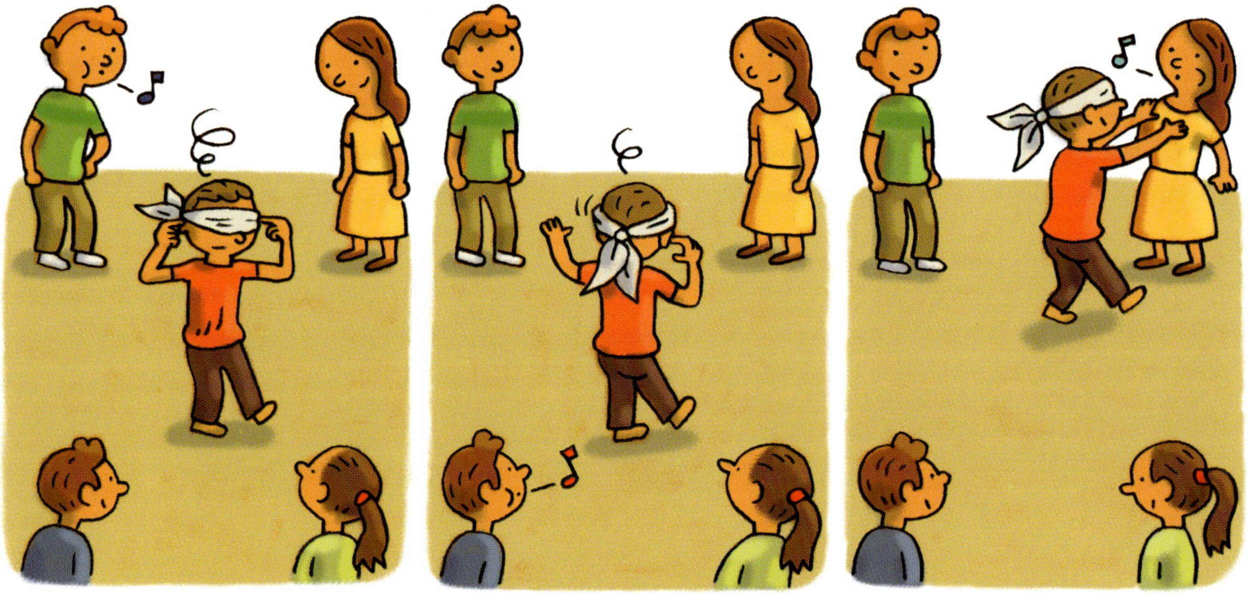

ΜΥΣΤΙΚΟ

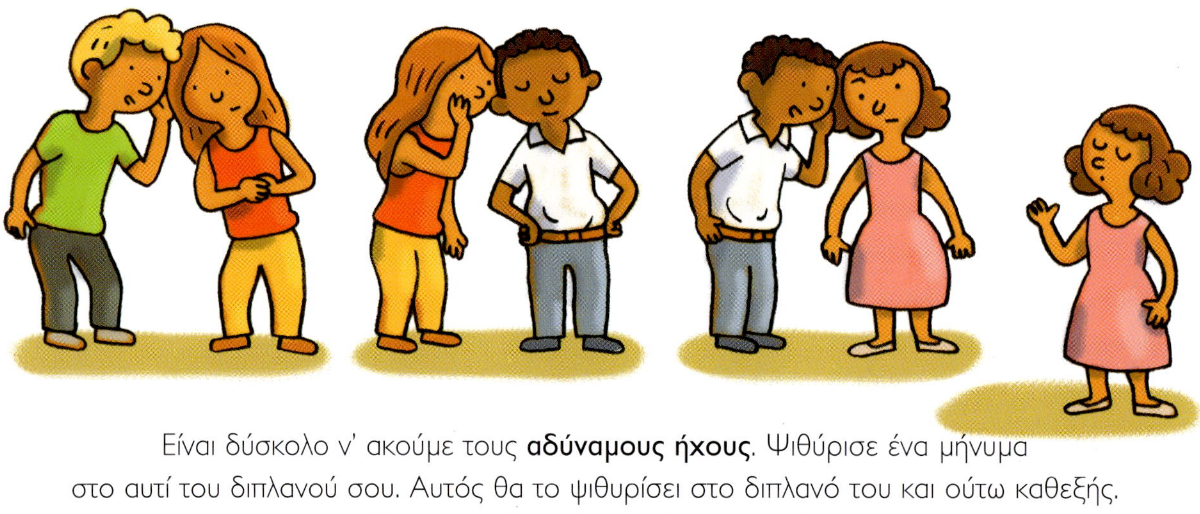

Είναι δύσκολο ν' ακούμε τους **αδύναμους ήχους**. Ψιθύρισε ένα μήνυμα στο αυτί του διπλανού σου. Αυτός θα το ψιθυρίσει στο διπλανό του και ούτω καθεξής. Άραγε ο τελευταίος το άκουσε καλά;

Η γλώσσα ή η μύτη;

Η γλώσσα καλύπτεται από μικρούς ανάγλυφους πόρους, τις θηλές, που μας επιτρέπουν να νιώθουμε τη γεύση των τροφών.

Κάθε σημείο της γλώσσας αναγνωρίζει μία από τις 4 γεύσεις.
Δοκίμασέ το με την άκρη της γλώσσας σου.

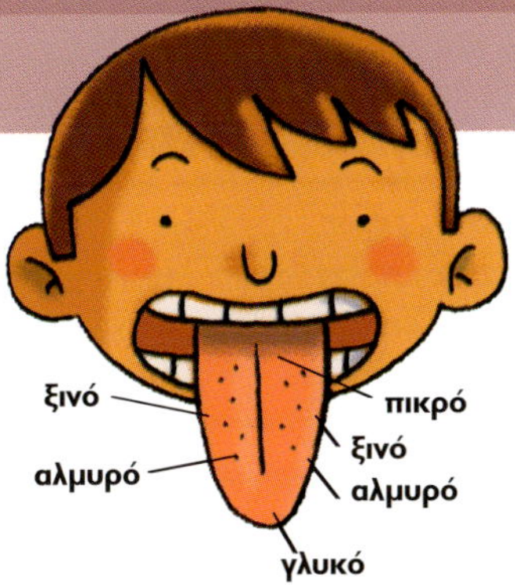

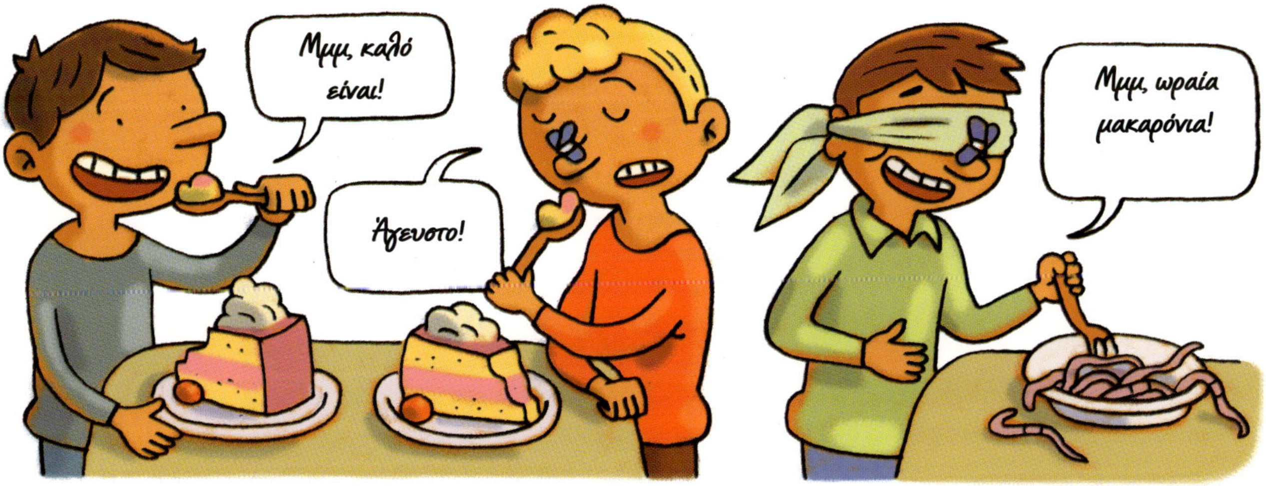

Χάρη στη **μύτη** «μυρίζουμε» τις γεύσεις αυτού που τρώμε.
Αν η **μύτη** μας είναι **βουλωμένη**, δεν μπορούμε να μυρίσουμε τίποτα και οι τροφές δεν έχουν γεύση.

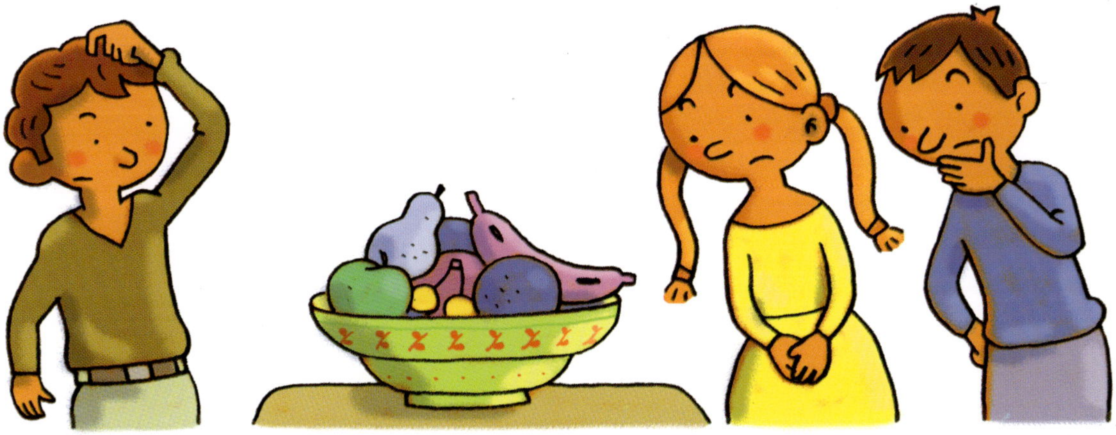

Είναι βέβαια σημαντικό και το τι **βλέπουμε**.
Θα σου άρεσε μια ροζ μπανάνα, ένα γαλάζιο πορτοκάλι ή μοβ τηγανητές πατάτες;

ΠαίΖΟΥμε ΜΕ τη γΕΥση;

Τι **γεύση** έχουν λοιπόν τα τρόφιμα;

Μπορείς να βρεις τη γεύση αυτού που τρώει κάθε παιδί; Προσοχή όμως! Κάποιες τροφές μπορεί να έχουν 2 γεύσεις.

ΓΛΥΚΟ	**ΑΛΜΥΡΟ**
ΠΙΚΡΟ	**ΞΙΝΟ**

ένα γλυκό

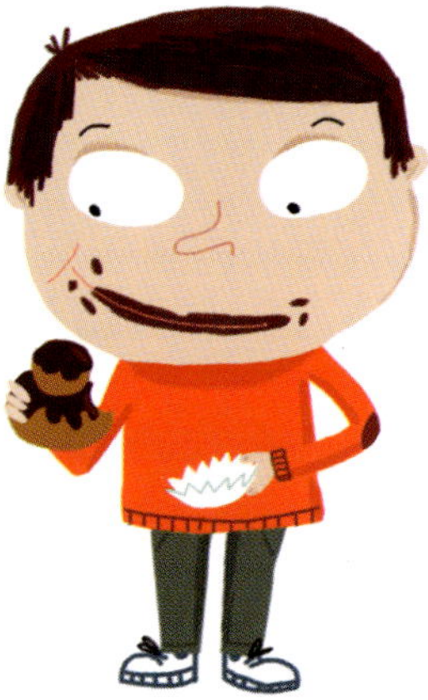

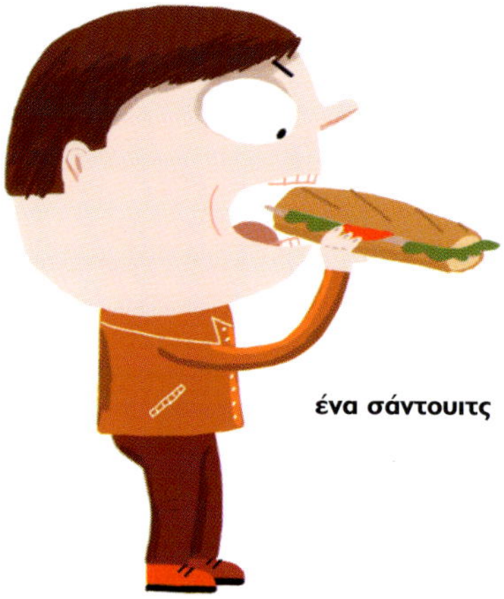

ένα σάντουιτς

φουντούκια

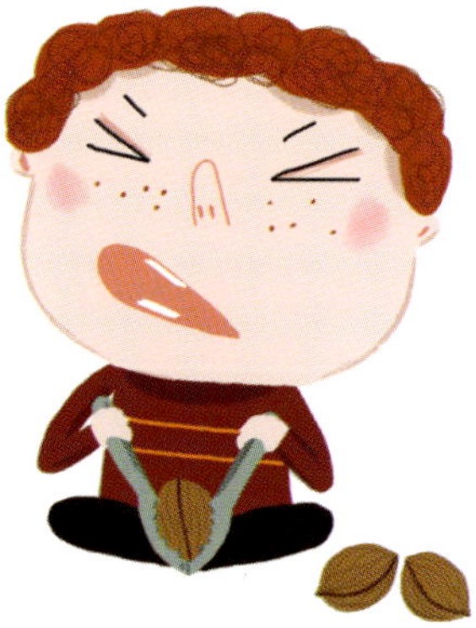

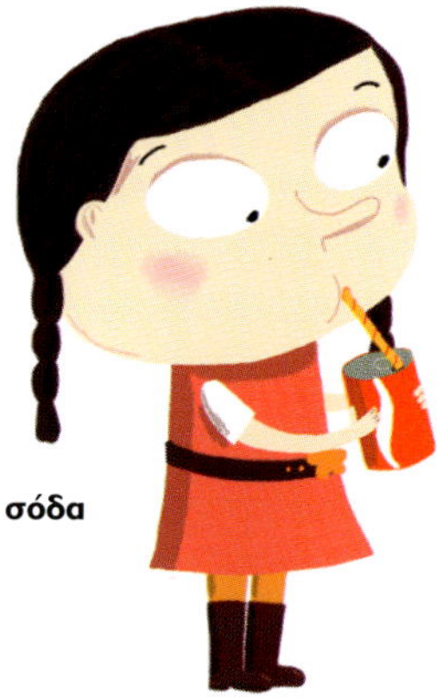

μία σόδα

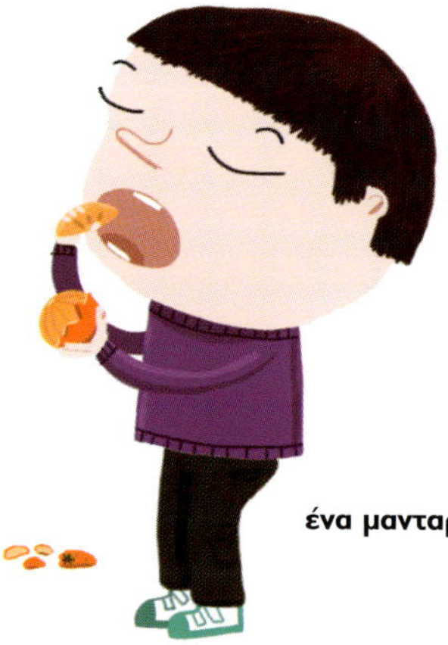

ένα μανταρίνι

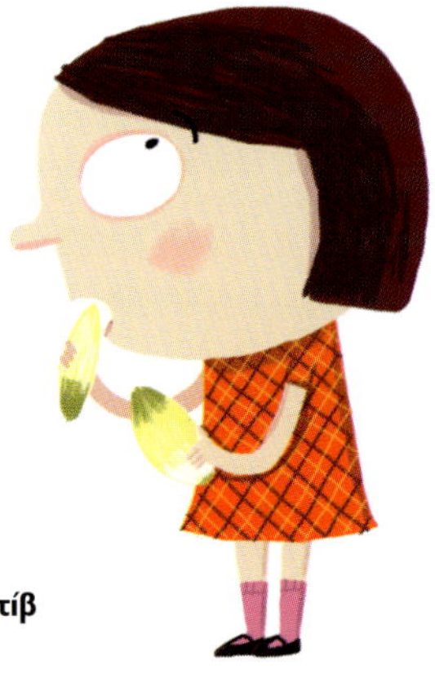

ένα αντίβ

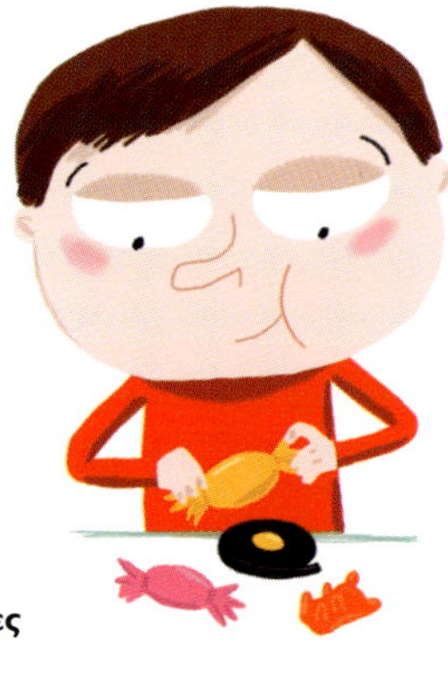

καραμέλες

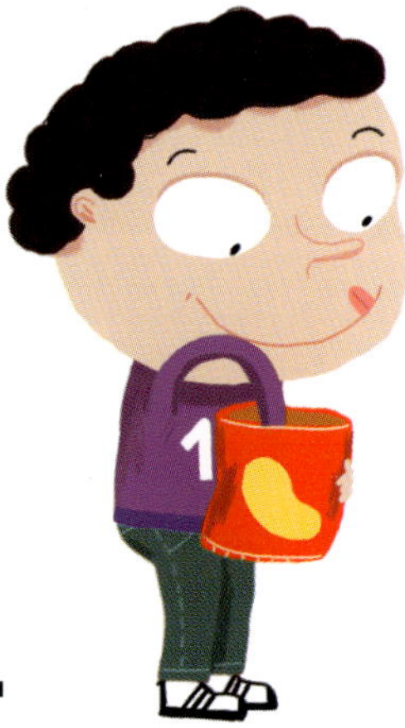

πατατάκια

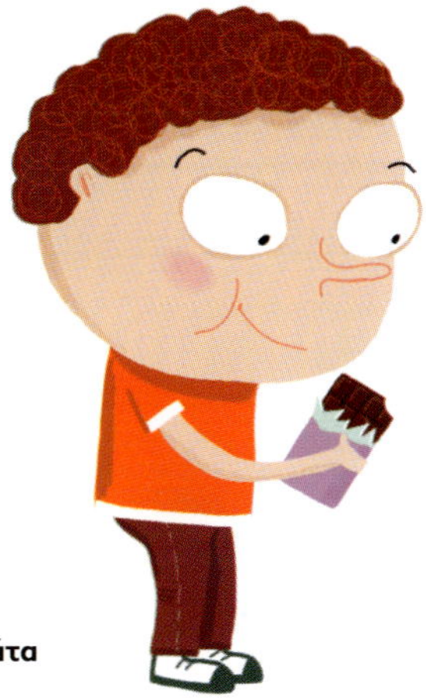

μαύρη σοκολάτα

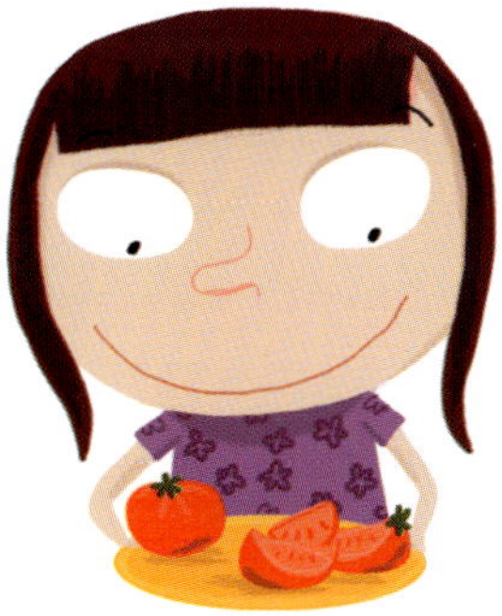

ντομάτες

ένα γκρέιπ φρουτ

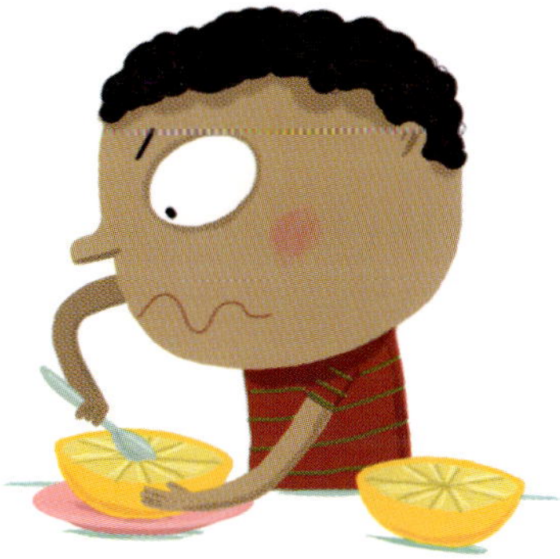

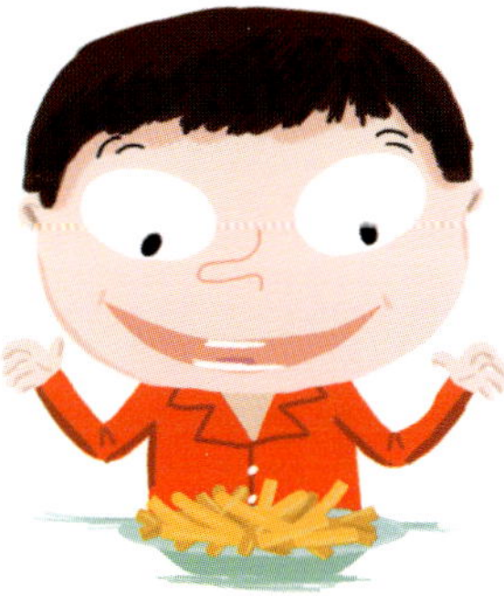

τηγανητές πατάτες

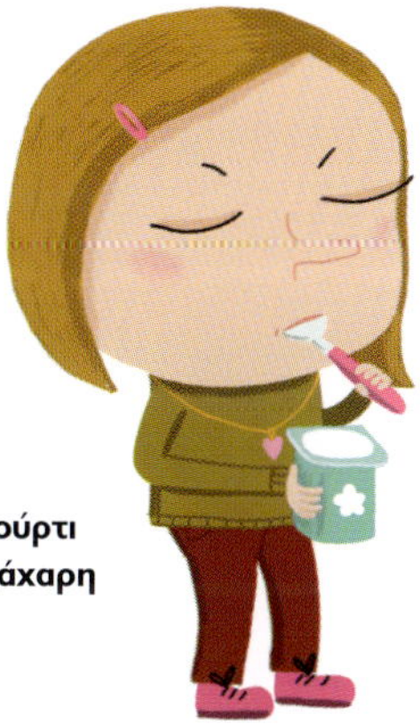

ένα γιαούρτι χωρίς ζάχαρη

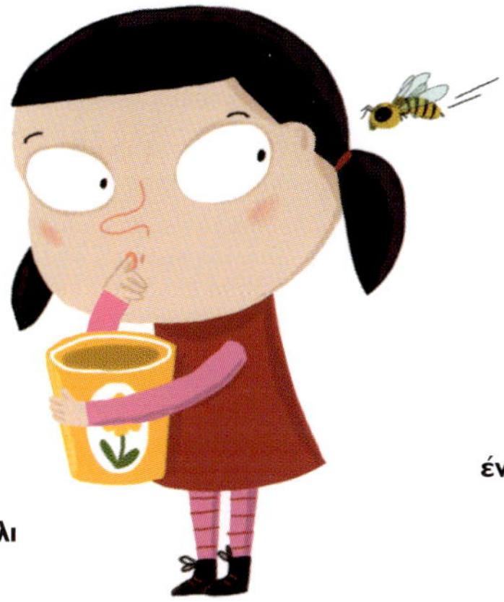

μέλι

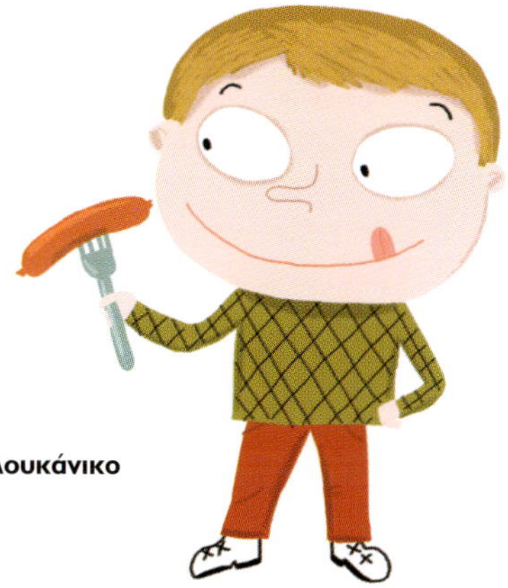

ένα λουκάνικο

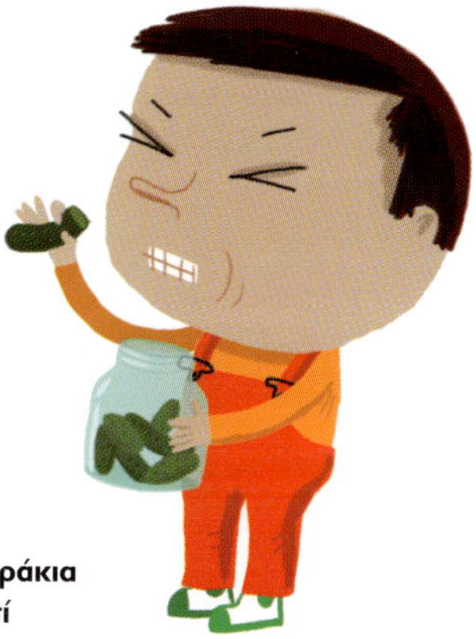

αγγουράκια τουρσί

Λύση: γλυκό: γλυκό, σόδα, καραμέλες, μέλι· **αλμυρό:** σάντουιτς, πατατάκια, πατάτες τηγανητές, λουκάνικο· **πικρό:** αντίβ, φουντούκια· **ξινό**: γιαούρτι χωρίς ζάχαρη, αγγουράκια τουρσί· **γλυκό και πικρό:** γκρέιπ φρουτ, μαύρη σοκολάτα· **ξινό και γλυκό:** ντομάτα, μανταρίνι.

ΠαίΖΟΥμε ΜΕ την αΦή;

Οι πιο ευαίσθητες ζώνες του σώματος είναι η γλώσσα και τα ακροδάχτυλα. Άλλες ζώνες του σώματος, όπως η πλάτη και το κάτω μέρος των ποδιών, είναι πολύ λιγότερο ευαίσθητες.

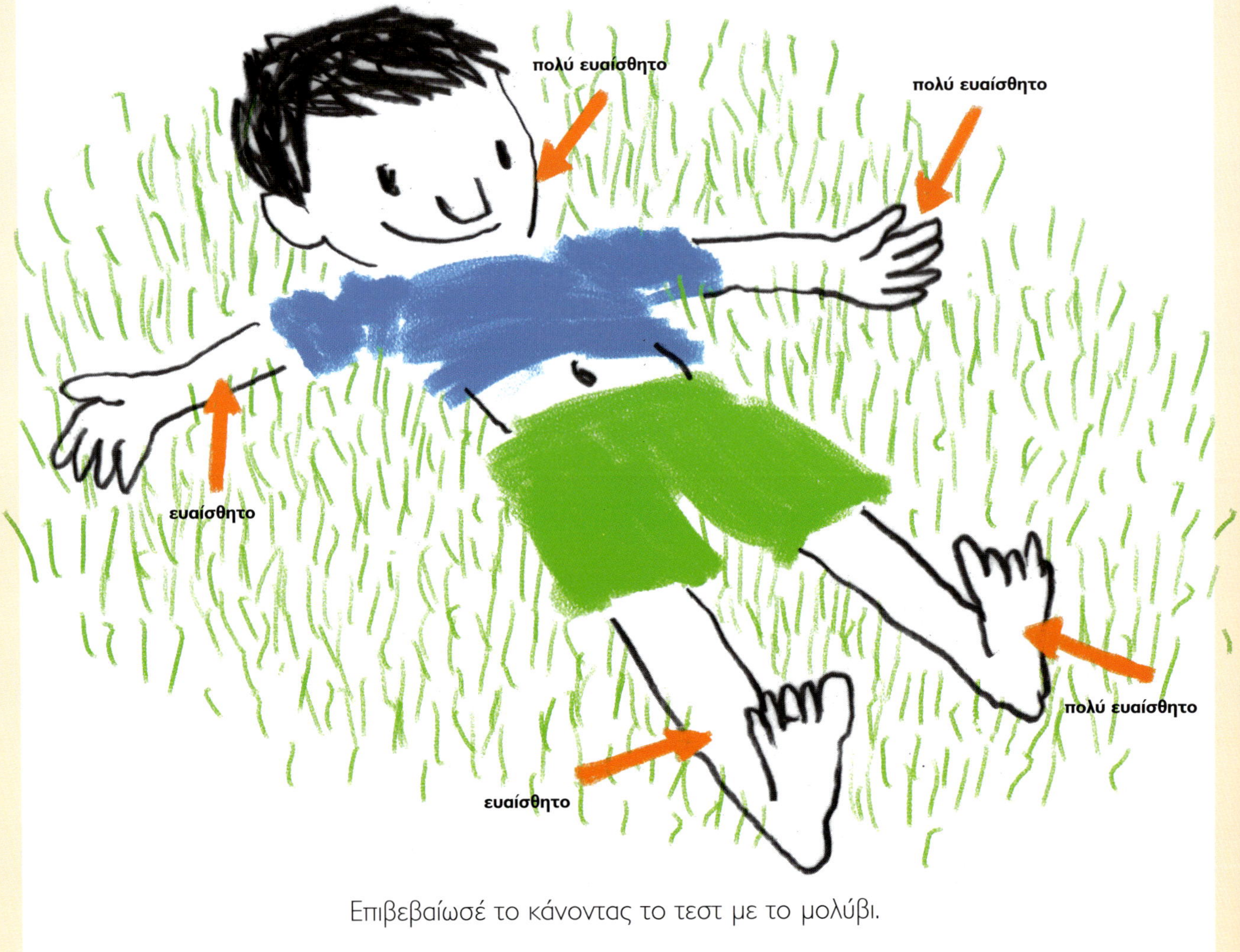

Επιβεβαίωσέ το κάνοντας το τεστ με το μολύβι.

ΤΟ ΤΕΣΤ ΜΕ ΤΟ ΜΟΛΥΒΙ

Πάρε **2** πολύ καλά ξυσμένα **μολύβια** και ένωσέ τα με σελοτέιπ.

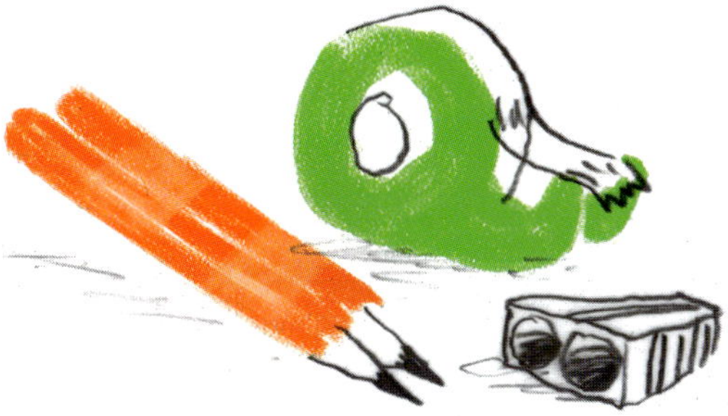

Τσίμπησε ελαφρά με τα μολύβια τα διάφορα μέρη του σώματός σου.

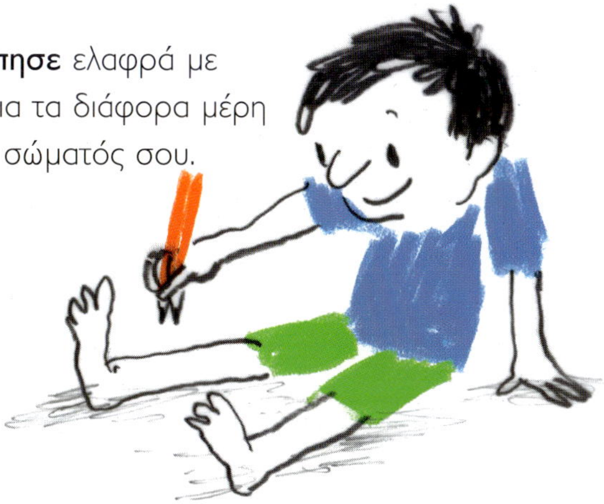

ψηλά στην πλάτη

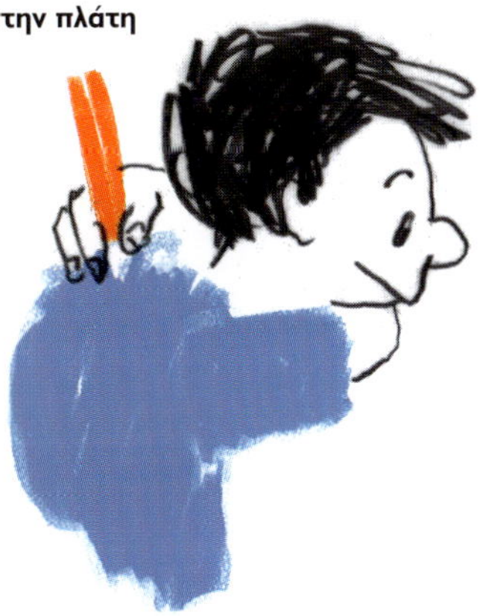

κάτω στα πόδια

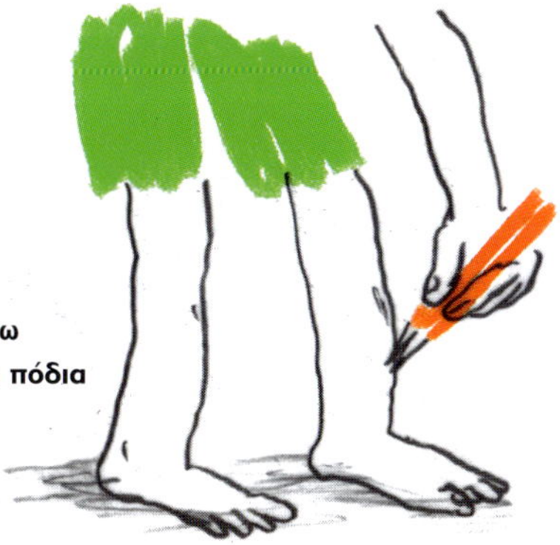

στο χέρι

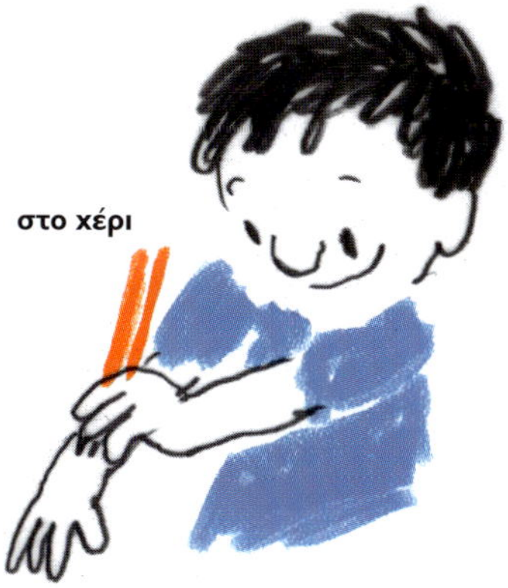

Πού αισθάνεσαι περισσότερο τις **2** μύτες;

στο μάγουλο

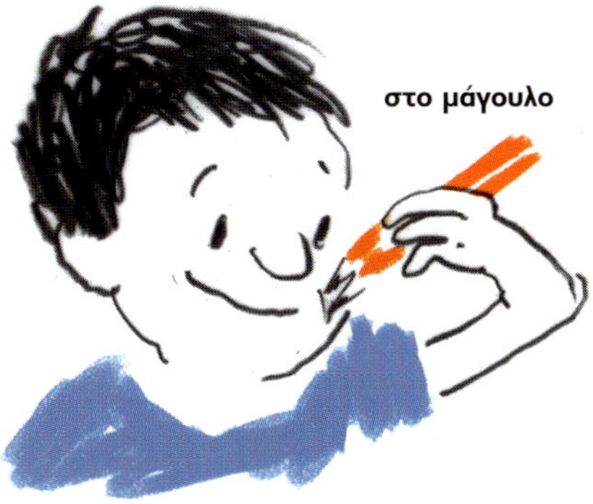

στο μπούτι

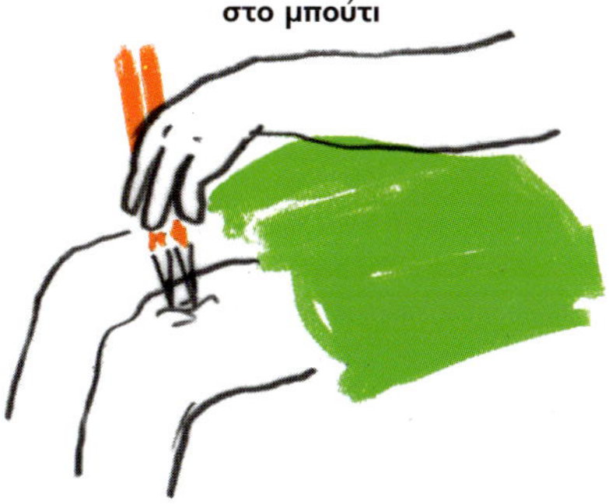

στην άκρη του ποδιού

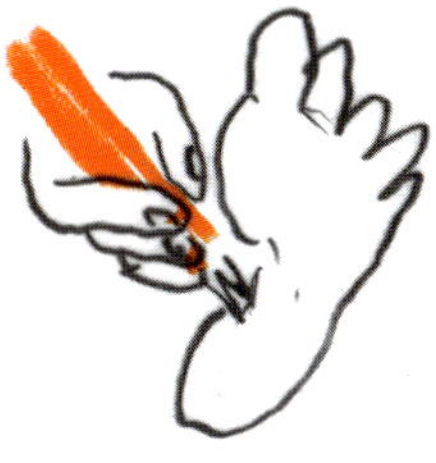

Εκεί όπου αισθάνεσαι μόνο τη μία μύτη, είναι μια **ευαίσθητη** ζώνη.
Εκεί όπου αισθάνεσαι και τις δύο μύτες, είναι μια **πολύ ευαίσθητη** ζώνη.

Η αναπνοή

Μέρα νύχτα, χωρίς να σταματάμε ποτέ, αναπνέουμε αέρα.

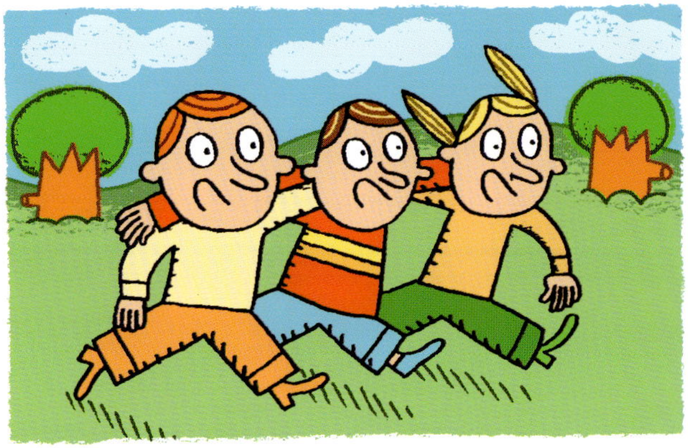

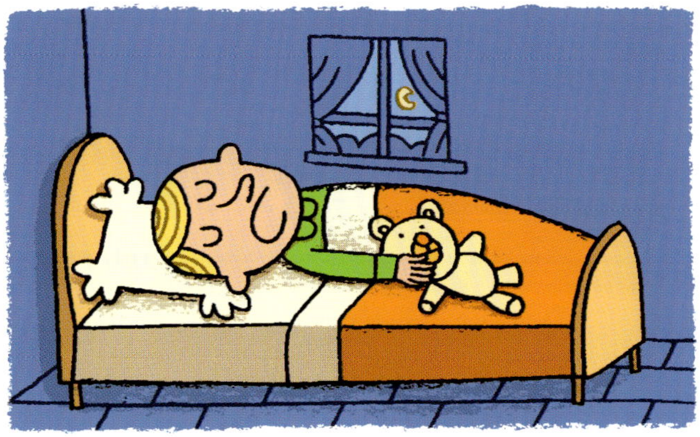

Γιατί στον αέρα υπάρχει ένα απαραίτητο αέριο για να ζει το σώμα μας: το **οξυγόνο**.

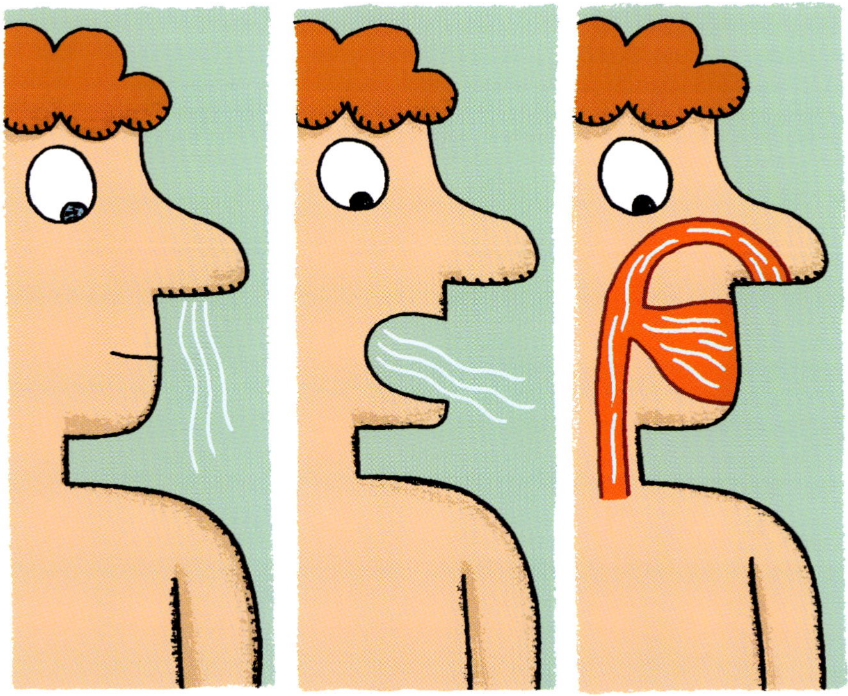

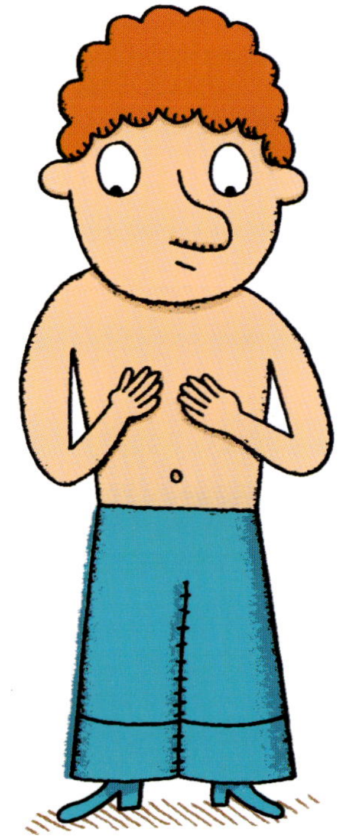

Ο αέρας μπαίνει στο σώμα μας από τη **μύτη** ή από το **στόμα**.
Κατεβαίνει από την **τραχεία** προς τους πνεύμονες.
Η τραχεία είναι ο μεγάλος σωλήνας που αισθανόμαστε μπροστά στο **λαιμό**.

Κάθε μέρα από τους **2 πνεύμονές** μας περνάνε σχεδόν **100.000 λίτρα αέρα!**

Η **τραχεία** χωρίζεται **στα δύο**, ένα μέρος για κάθε **πνεύμονα**.
Ο **αέρας** μπαίνει και βγαίνει από τους πνεύμονες.

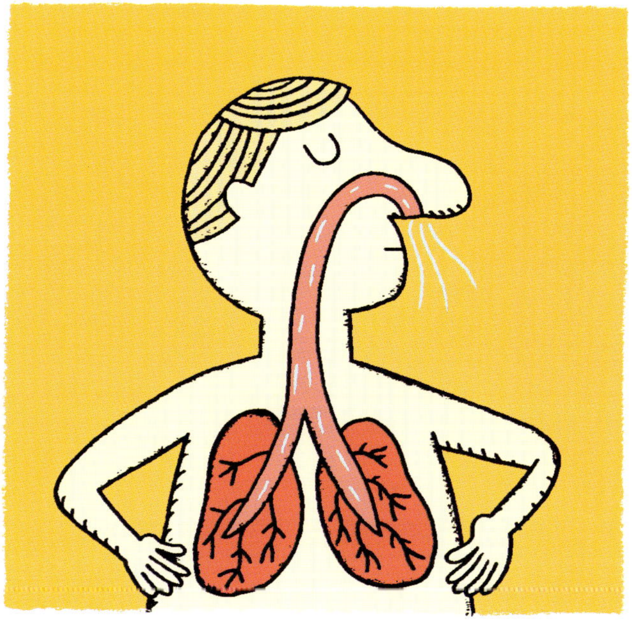

Όταν ο **αέρας**, γεμάτος οξυγόνο, **μπαίνει** στους πνεύμονες, φουσκώνουν. Αυτή η διαδικασία ονομάζεται **εισπνοή**.

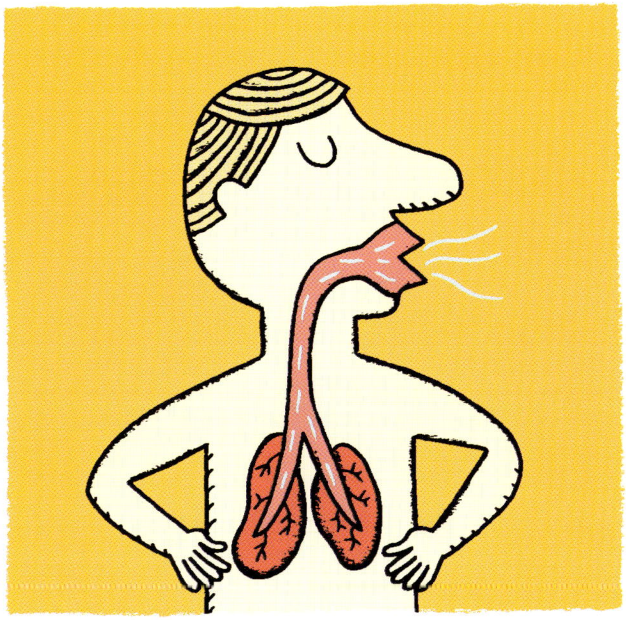

Όταν **βγαίνει ο αέρας**, οι πνεύμονες ξεφουσκώνουν. Αυτή η διαδικασία ονομάζεται **εκπνοή**.

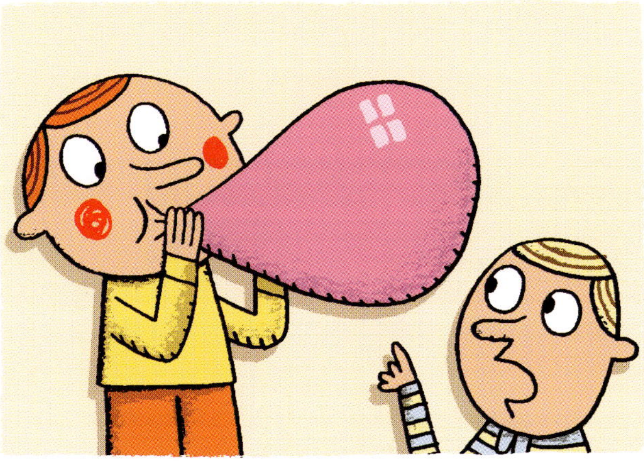

Όταν φυσάμε **βαθιά** μέσα σ' ένα μπαλόνι, ο **μισός** αέρας από τους πνεύμονες περνά μέσα στο μπαλόνι.

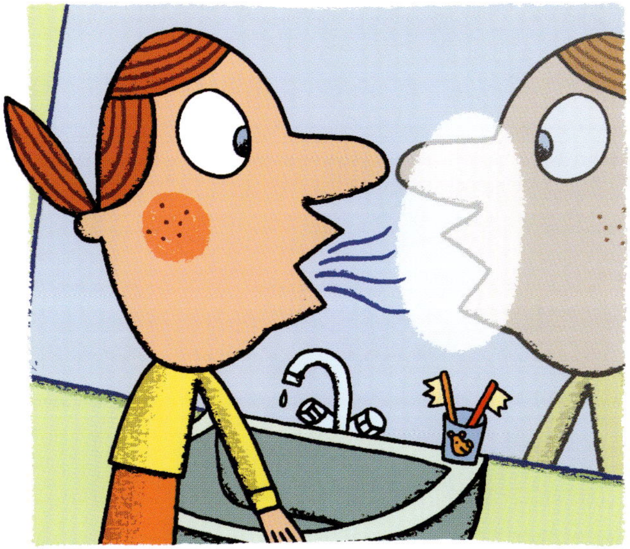

Ο **αέρας** που εκπνέουμε είναι **ζεστός** και **υγρός** και **θολώνει** τον καθρέφτη.

Η καρδιά βοηθά το αίμα να κυκλοφορεί

Για να φτάνει σε όλα τα σημεία του σώματός μας, το αίμα σπρώχνεται από τους χτύπους της καρδιάς μας.

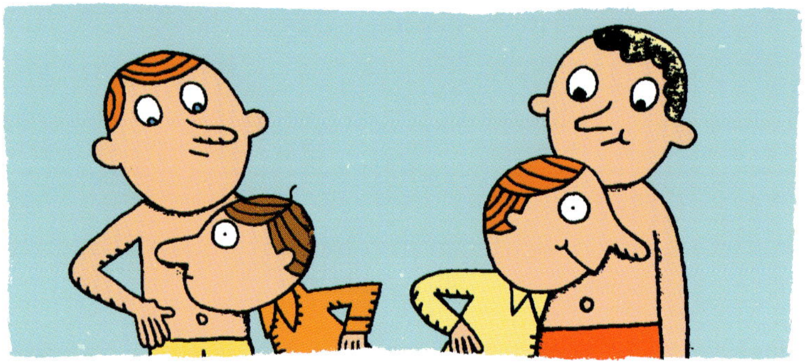

Η **καρδιά** είναι ένα είδος τρόμπας που βοηθά το αίμα να κυκλοφορεί στο σώμα μας: αυτή είναι η **κυκλοφορία του αίματος**.

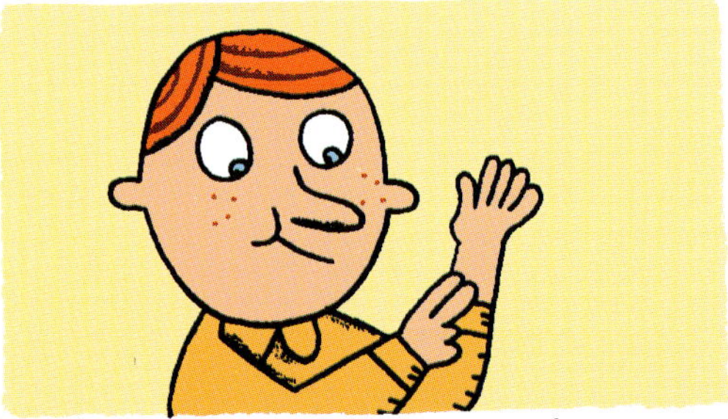

Νιώθουμε τους **χτύπους** του αίματος, που σπρώχνεται από την καρδιά, πιέζοντας τα δάχτυλα πάνω στις φλέβες της γροθιάς, του αστραγάλου ή του λαιμού μας.

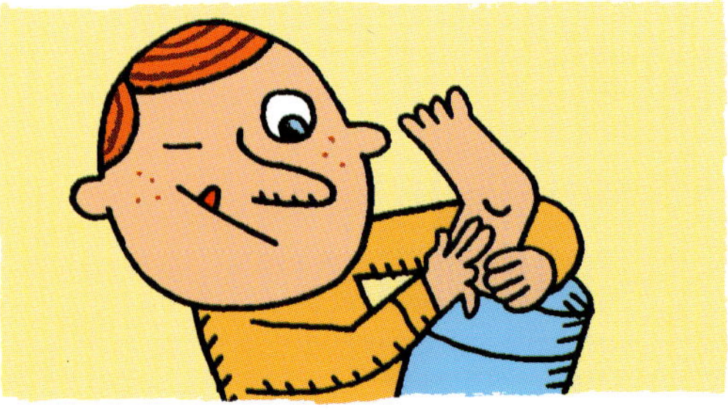

Τότε λέμε ότι παίρνουμε τους **σφυγμούς** μας. Έχουμε περίπου 72 σφυγμούς το λεπτό.

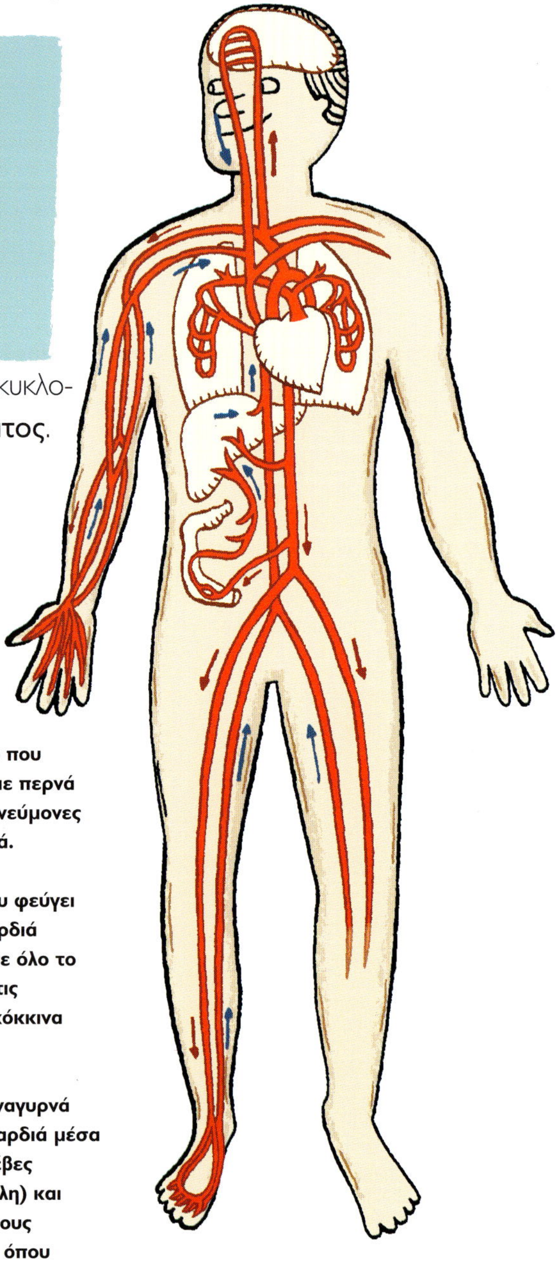

Το οξυγόνο που ανασαίνουμε περνά από τους πνεύμονες στην καρδιά.

Το αίμα που φεύγει από την καρδιά οδηγείται σε όλο το σώμα από τις αρτηρίες (κόκκινα βέλη).

Το αίμα ξαναγυρνά προς την καρδιά μέσα από τις φλέβες (γαλάζια βέλη) και πηγαίνει στους πνεύμονες, όπου ξαναπαίρνει οξυγόνο.

Η καρδιά δε χτυπά πάντα με τον ίδιο ρυθμό.

Η καρδιά χτυπά **γρηγορότερα**...

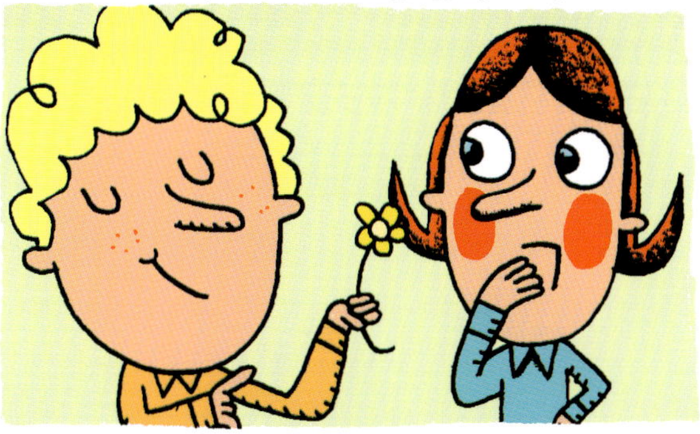

...όταν είμαστε **συγκινημένοι**.

Η καρδιά χτυπά **αργά**...

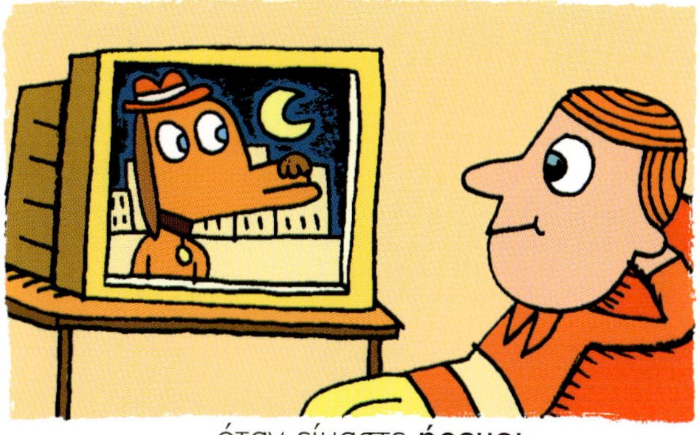

...όταν είμαστε **ήρεμοι**.

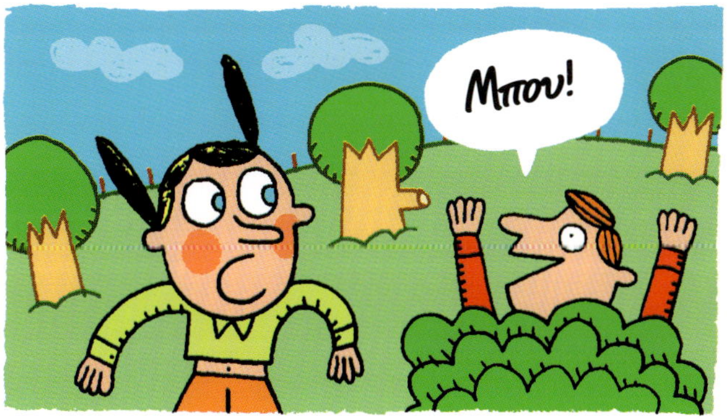

...όταν **φοβόμαστε**. Οι μύες χρειάζονται οξυγόνο, ώστε να αποφύγουμε τον κίνδυνο!

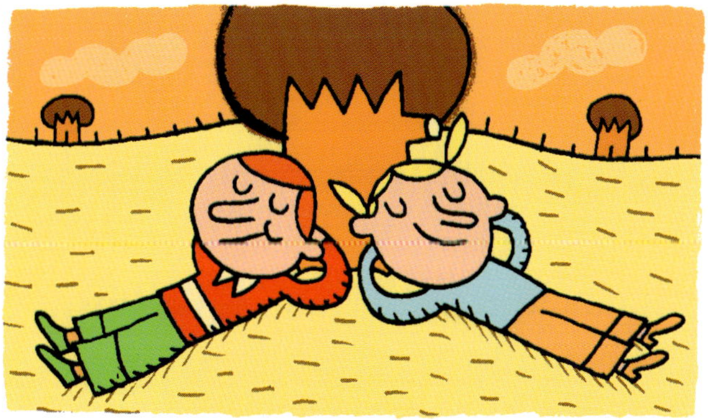

...όταν **ξεκουραζόμαστε**.

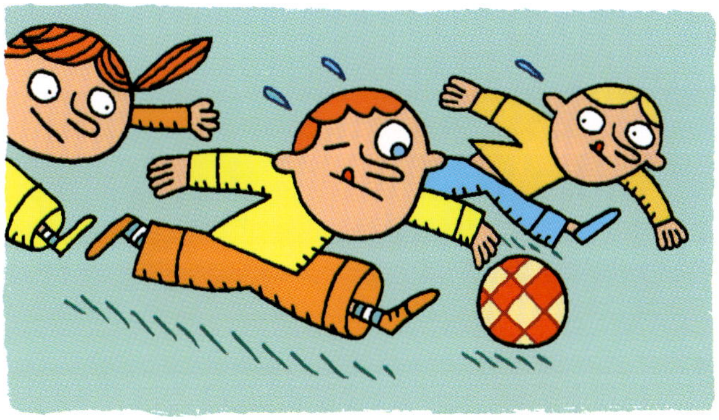

Οι μύες που δουλεύουν χρησιμοποιούν **περισσότερο οξυγόνο**. Το αίμα πρέπει να τους το φέρει γρήγορα.

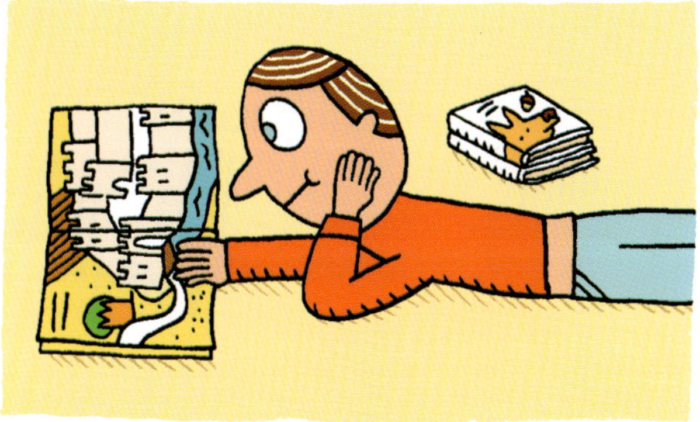

Οι μύες που δε δουλεύουν χρειάζονται **λιγότερο οξυγόνο**. Η καρδιά χτυπά πιο αργά.

Από τι φτιάχνεται το αίμα;

Αν τσιμπηθούμε ή πέσουμε, εμφανίζεται κόκκινο αίμα.

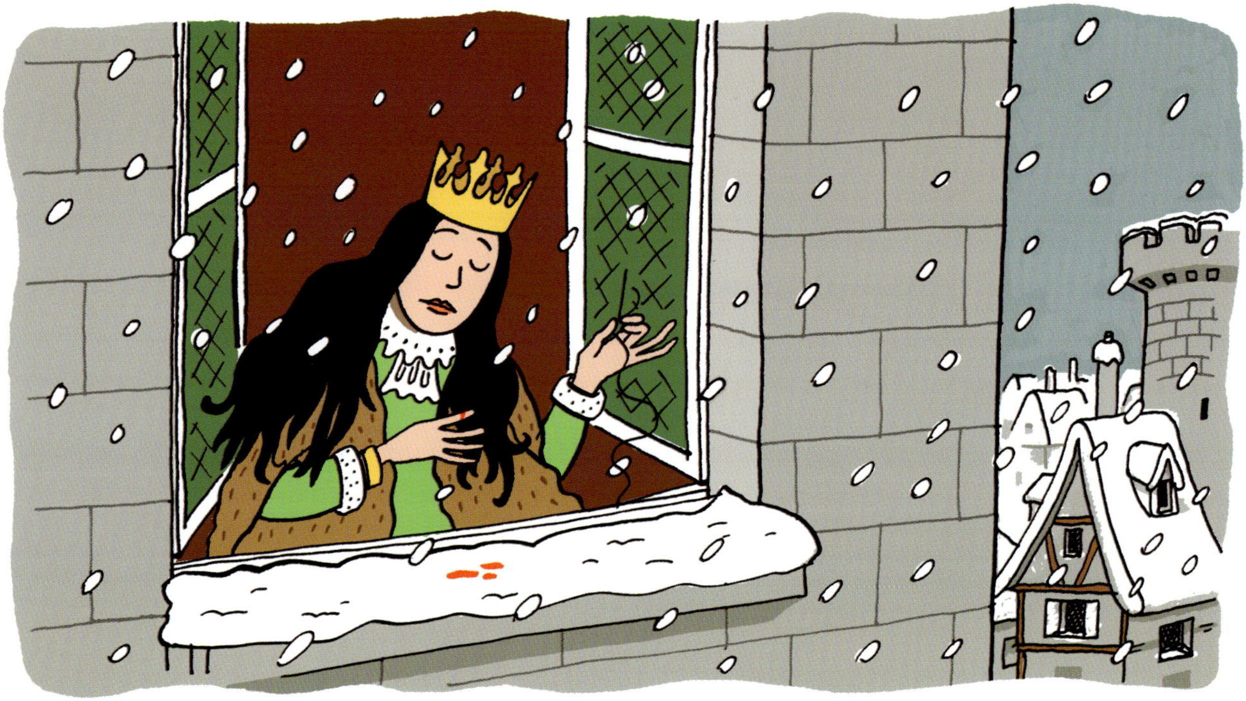

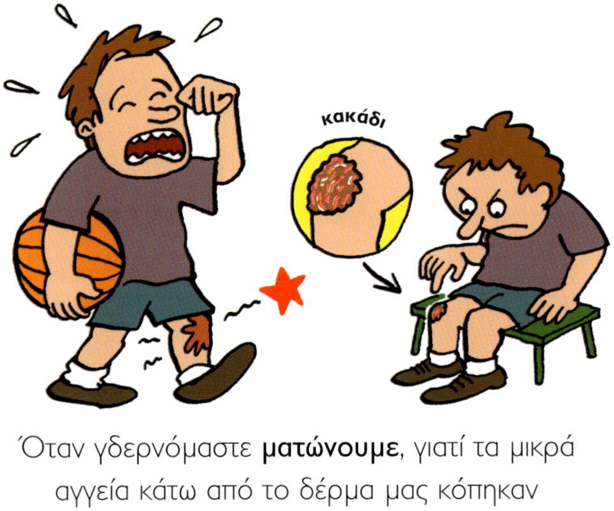

Όταν γδερνόμαστε **ματώνουμε**, γιατί τα μικρά αγγεία κάτω από το δέρμα μας κόπηκαν από τη γρατσουνιά. Για να τα διορθώσει, το αίμα σχηματίζει το **κακάδι**.

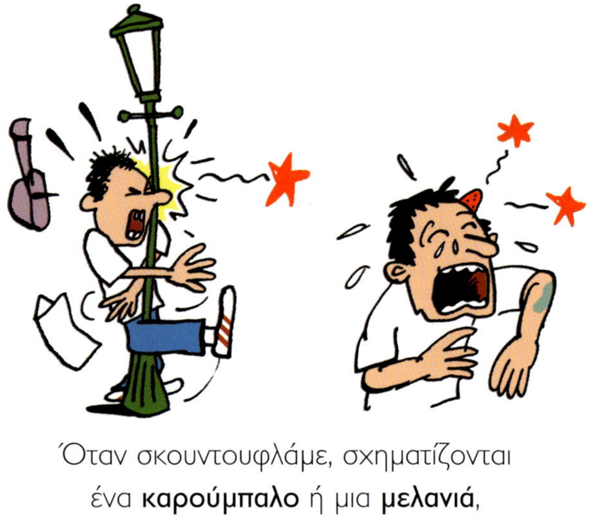

Όταν σκουντουφλάμε, σχηματίζονται ένα **καρούμπαλο** ή μια **μελανιά**, γιατί σ' εκείνο το σημείο βγήκε αίμα κάτω από το δέρμα.

Όμως τι υπάρχει μέσα στο αίμα;

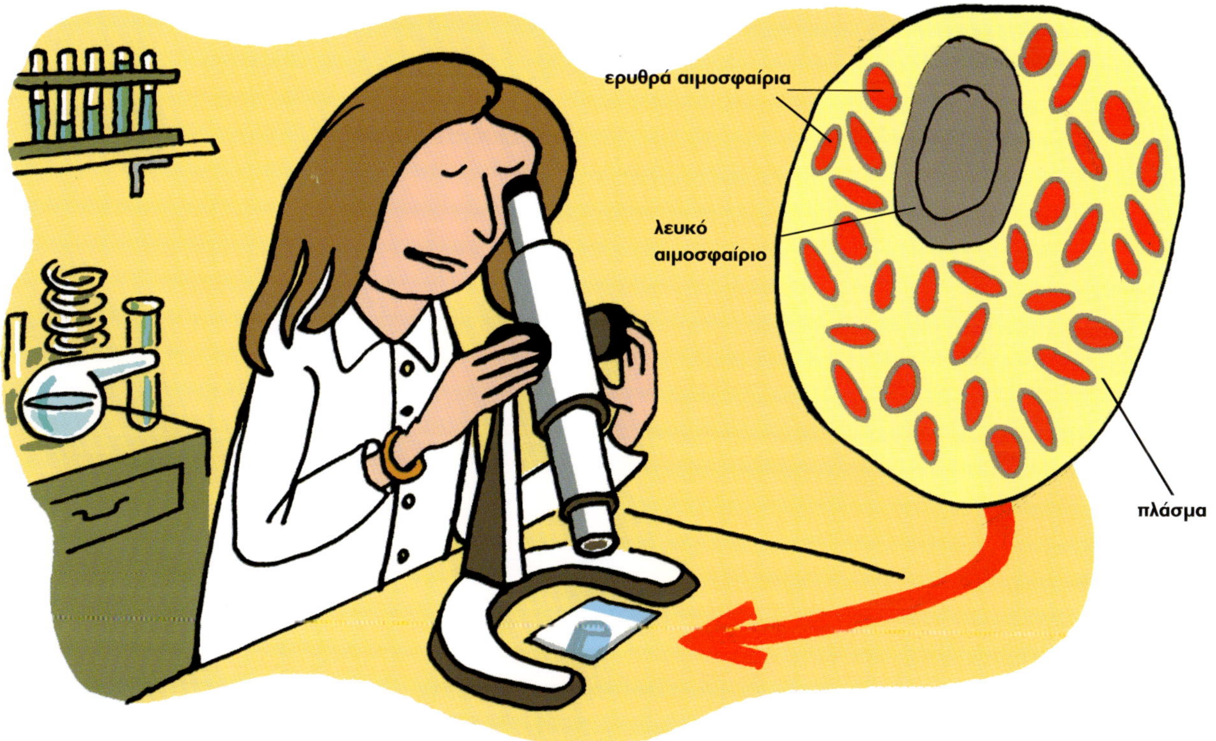

Όταν κοιτάζουμε στο μικροσκόπιο μια **σταγόνα αίμα**, βλέπουμε ότι το αίμα αποτελείται από διάφορα στοιχεία: τα ερυθρά αιμοσφαίρια, που του δίνουν το χρώμα του, τα λευκά αιμοσφαίρια και ένα υγρό: το πλάσμα του αίματος. Το σώμα μας έχει **5 λίτρα αίμα**, από τα οποία τα 3,5 είναι πλάσμα του αίματος.

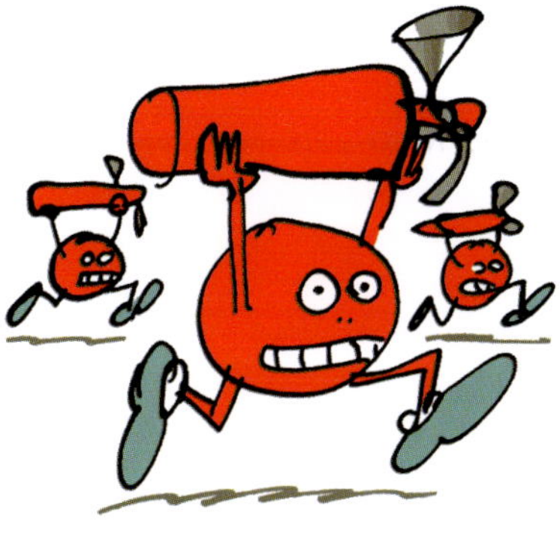

Τα **ερυθρά αιμοσφαίρια** μεταφέρουν το **οξυγόνο** σε όλο το σώμα. Γεμίζουν με οξυγόνο μέσα στους πνεύμονες.

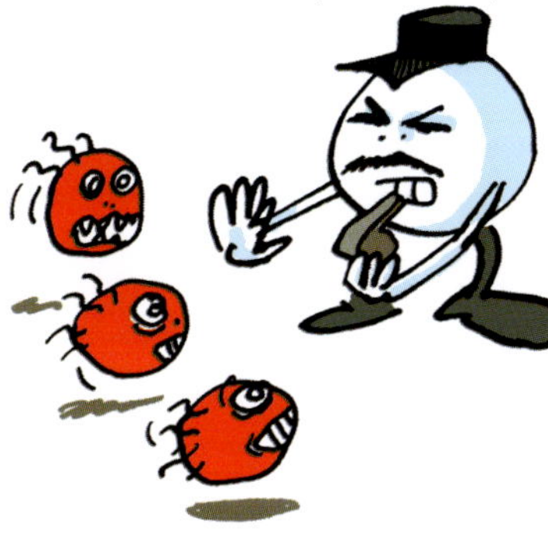

Τα **λευκά αιμοσφαίρια** είναι οι «φρουροί» του σώματος. Φροντίζουν να είναι όλα φυσιολογικά και καταστρέφουν τα **μικρόβια**.

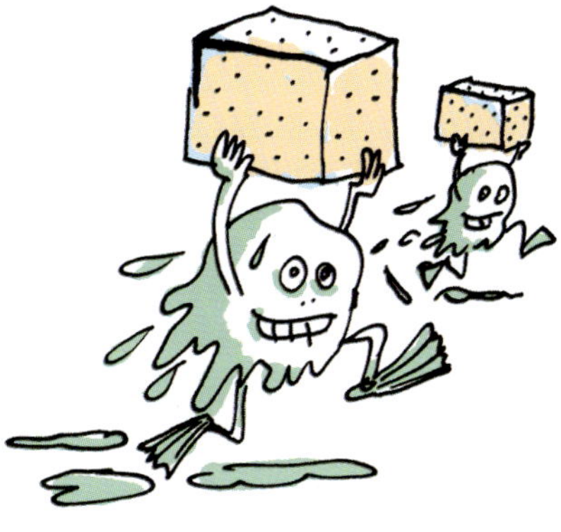

Το **πλάσμα του αίματος** είναι το υγρό μέρος του αίματος. Φέρνει τις **τροφές** στο σώμα μας.

Οι τροφές

Οι τροφές, δηλαδή ό,τι τρώμε, φέρνουν στο σώμα μας ό,τι χρειάζεται για να λειτουργεί σωστά.

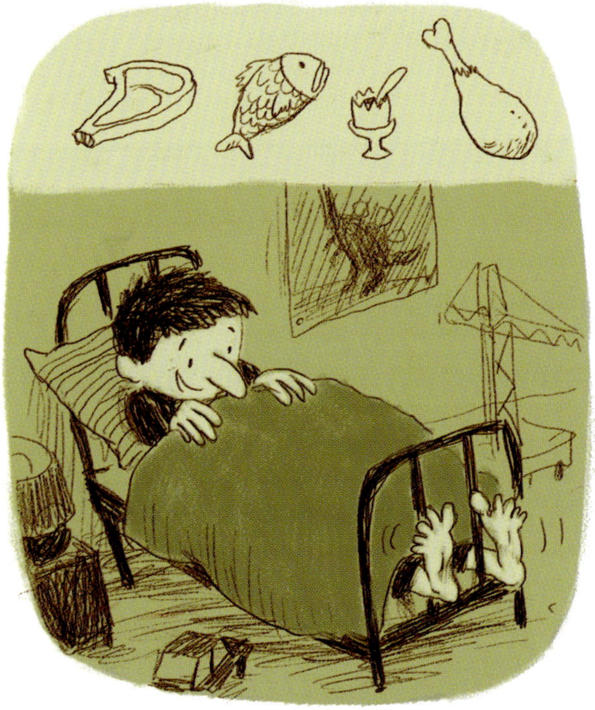

Το κρέας, το ψάρι, τα αυγά (τα πρωτίδια) είναι πλούσια σε **πρωτεΐνες**. Μας βοηθάνε να **μεγαλώσουμε**.

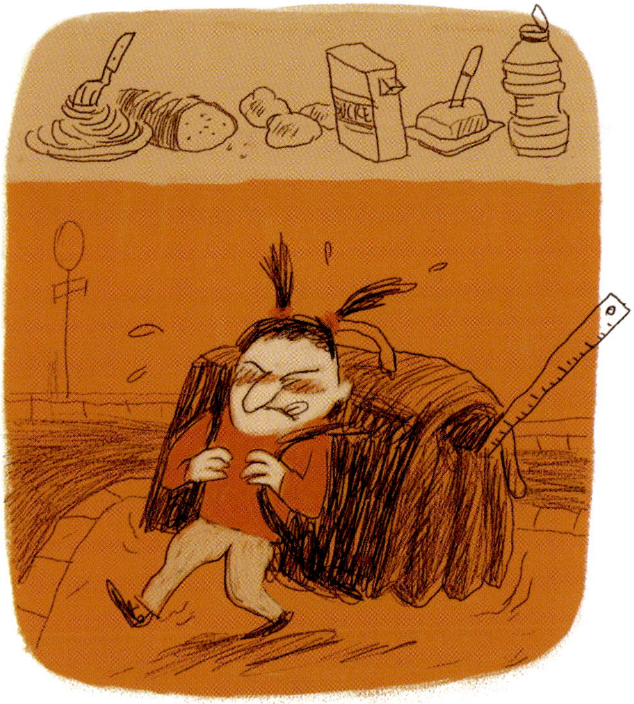

Τα τρόφιμα που είναι πλούσια σε **ζάχαρη** (τα γλυκίδια) ή σε **λίπος** (τα λιπίδια) δίνουν **ενέργεια** στους μυς.

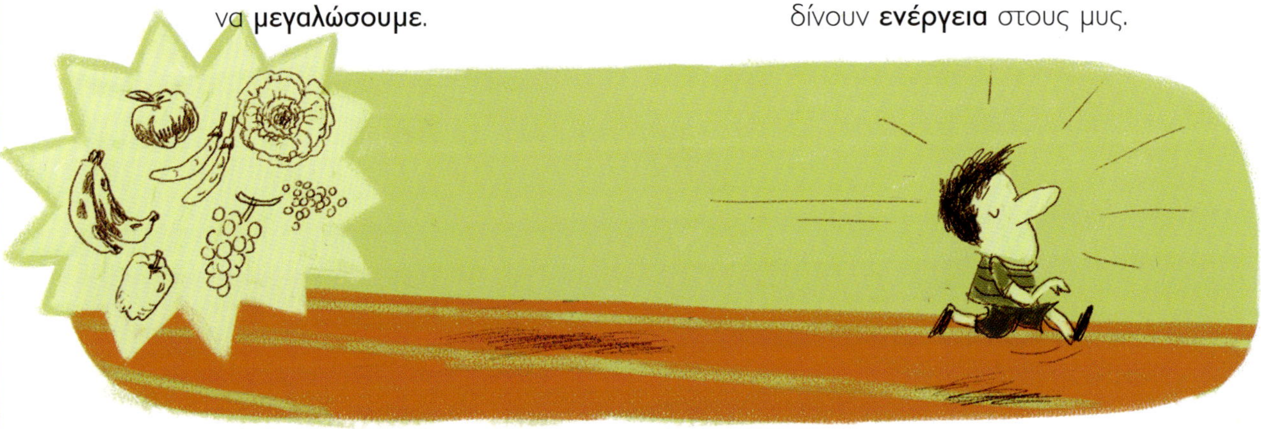

Τα φρούτα και τα λαχανικά είναι πλούσια σε **βιταμίνες**· είναι απαραίτητα για την υγεία μας.

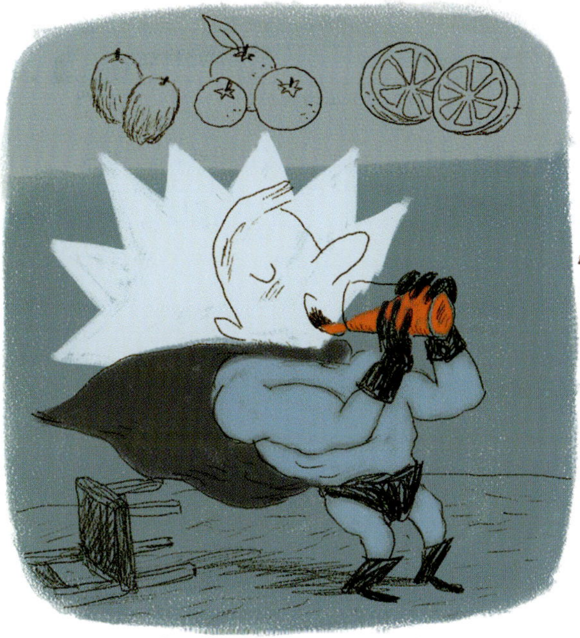

Η **βιταμίνη C** περιέχεται στα φρέσκα φρούτα. Βοηθάει το σώμα να αμύνεται ενάντια στις αρρώστιες.

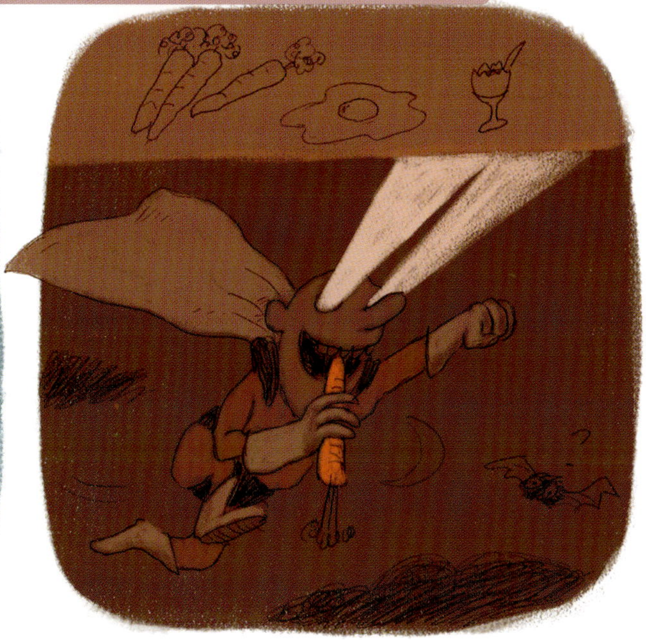

Η **βιταμίνη Α** περιέχεται στα καρότα, στα αυγά, στο συκώτι. Μας βοηθάει να μεγαλώνουμε και να βλέπουμε καλά.

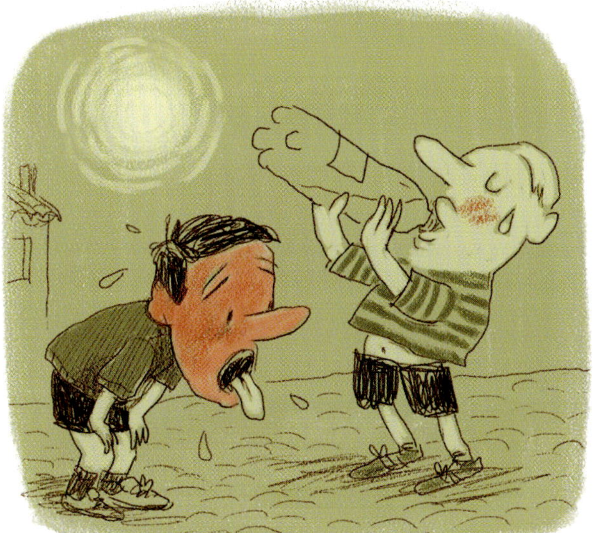

Περισσότερο από το μισό σώμα μας αποτελείται από **νερό**. Πρέπει να πίνουμε συχνά νερό, κυρίως ύστερα από μια προσπάθεια και όταν κάνει ζέστη.

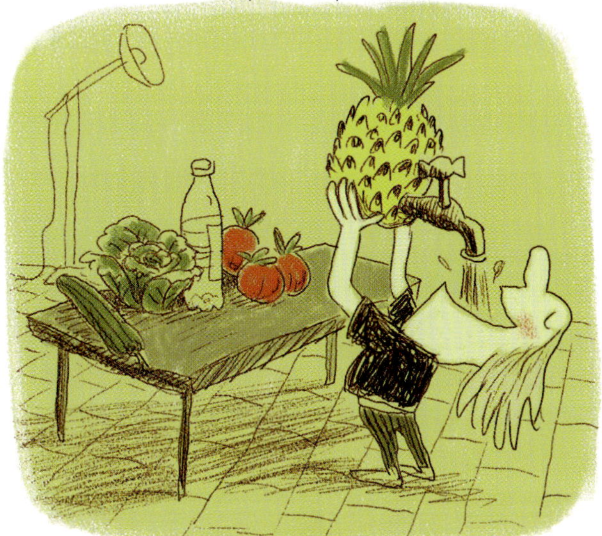

Χρειαζόμαστε περίπου **2 λίτρα** υγρά τη μέρα. Αυτά τα βρίσκουμε στα ποτά αλλά επίσης και σε ό,τι τρώμε.

Σε φόρμα

Για να λειτουργεί καλά το σώμα μας, πρέπει να το τρέφουμε καλά και να τρώμε λίγο απ' όλα: πρέπει δηλαδή να έχουμε μια ισορροπημένη διατροφή.

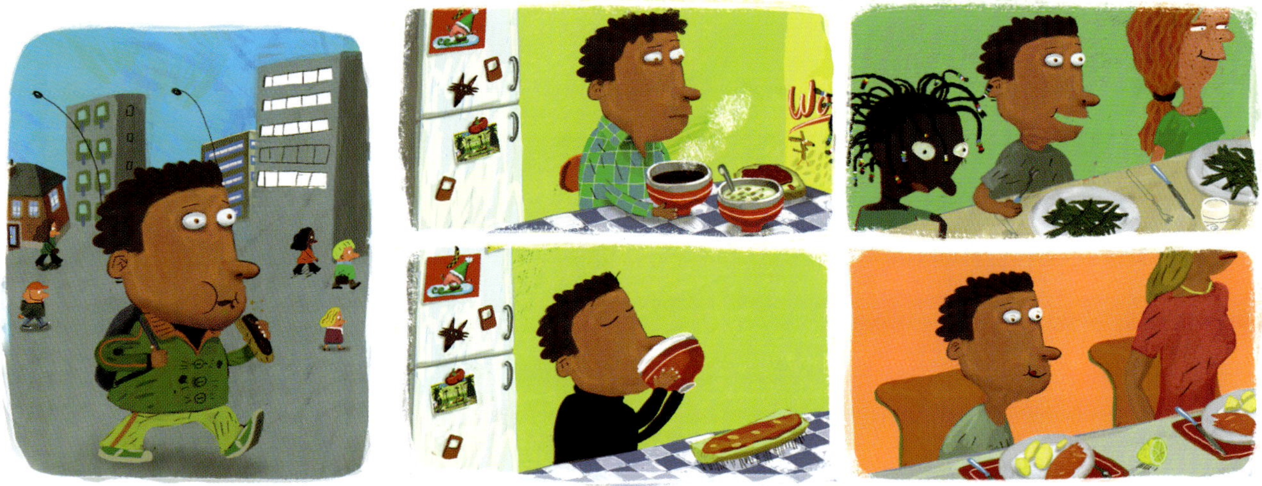

Δεν είναι καλό να τσιμπολογάμε πέρα από τα γεύματα. Τα **4 γεύματα** είναι αρκετά. Ένα καλό **πρωινό** είναι βασικό για να αρχίσουμε καλά τη μέρα μας!

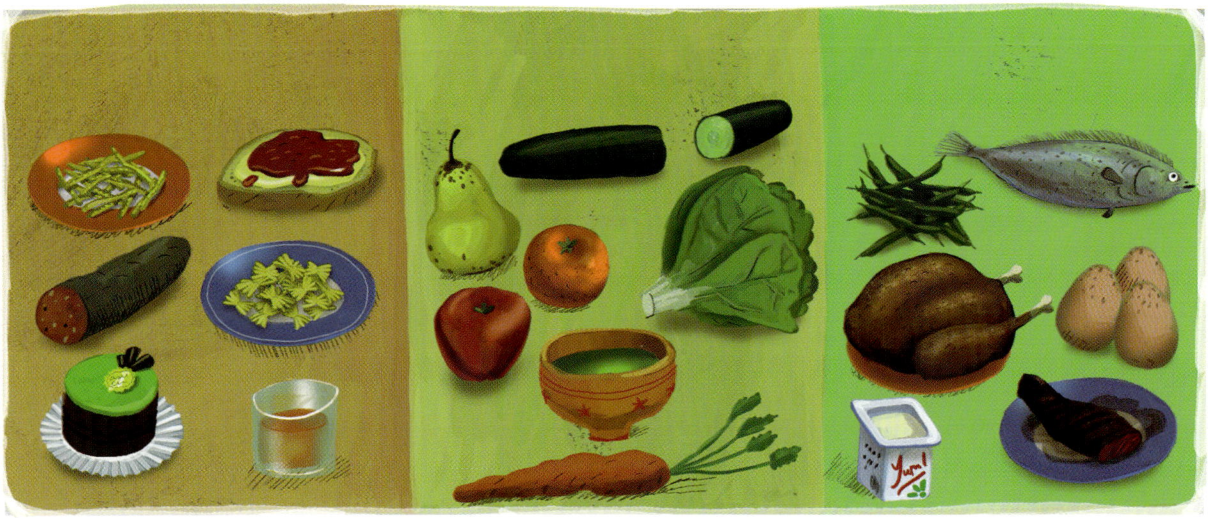

Για να τρεφόμαστε καλά, πρέπει να τρώμε **ένα τρόφιμο από κάθε ομάδα**: **κρέας** ή **ψάρι** ή **αυγό**, ένα **γαλακτοκομικό** (γιαούρτι, άσπρο τυρί), ένα **αμυλώδες** (μακαρόνια, πατάτες, ρύζι), ένα **λαχανικό** και ένα **φρούτο**.

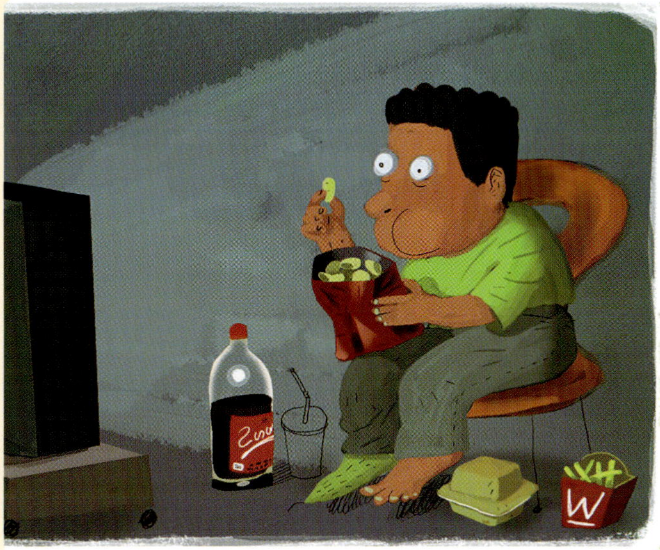

Αν **τρως πολύ**, χωρίς να αθλείσαι, κινδυνεύεις να **παχύνεις πολύ**. Μπορείς να τρως τηγανητές πατάτες, χάμπουργκερ και να πίνεις αναψυκτικά… αλλά σε μικρή ποσότητα!

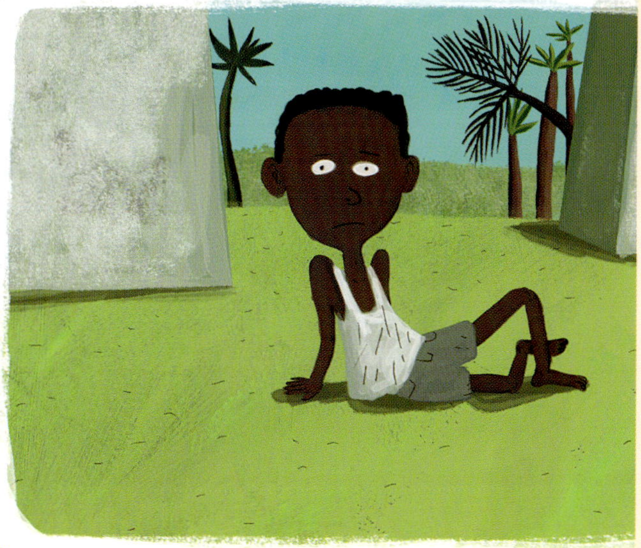

Σε κάποιες χώρες τα παιδιά δεν έχουν **αρκετή** τροφή καλής ποιότητας **για να φάνε**, είναι **ευαίσθητα** και θύματα κάθε είδους ασθένειας.

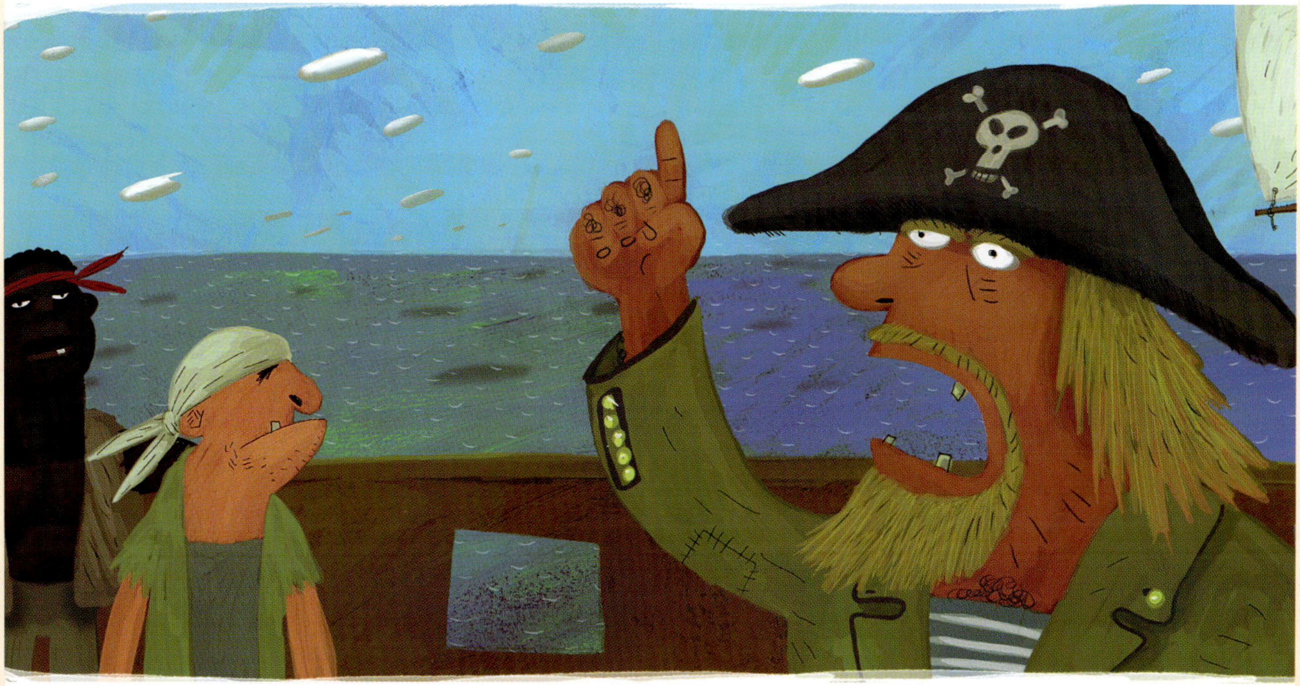

Άλλοτε, στα πλοία, οι ναυτικοί ή οι πειρατές δεν έτρωγαν **φρέσκα τρόφιμα**, που περιέχουν βιταμίνη C, και πάθαιναν **σκορβούτο**, μια αρρώστια που κάνει τα δόντια να πέφτουν.

Η πέψη

Πριν περάσουν στο αίμα, για να κάνουν το σώμα μας να λειτουργήσει, οι τροφές που τρώμε ακολουθούν ένα μακρύ δρόμο: είναι η πέψη.

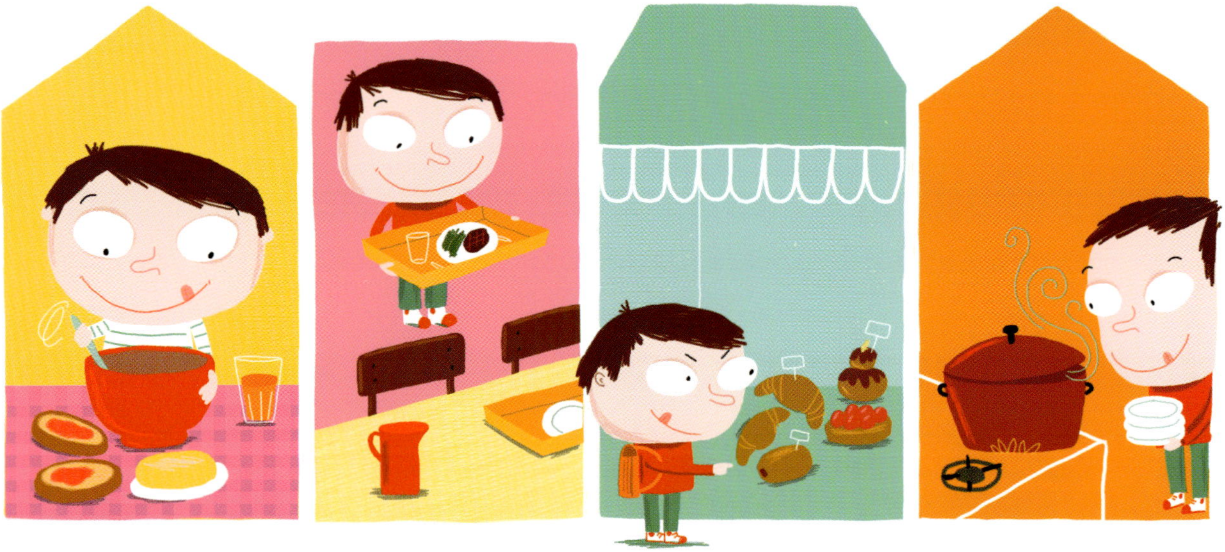

Ό,τι τρώμε σε κάθε γεύμα γίνεται κατά κάποιον τρόπο ένας **υγρός πουρές**.

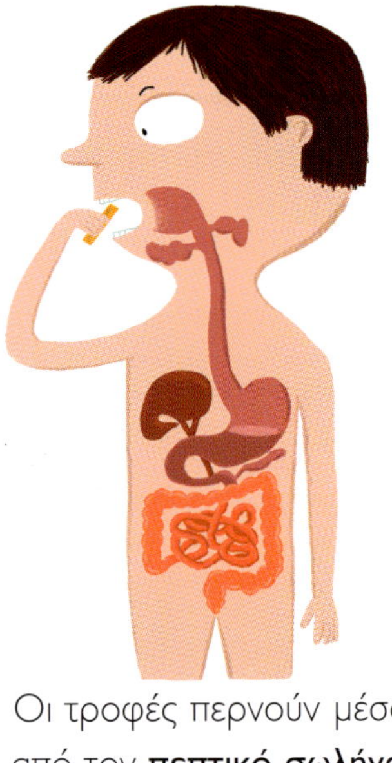

Οι τροφές περνούν μέσα από τον **πεπτικό σωλήνα**. Αυτός φτάνει από το στόμα μέχρι τον πρωκτό.

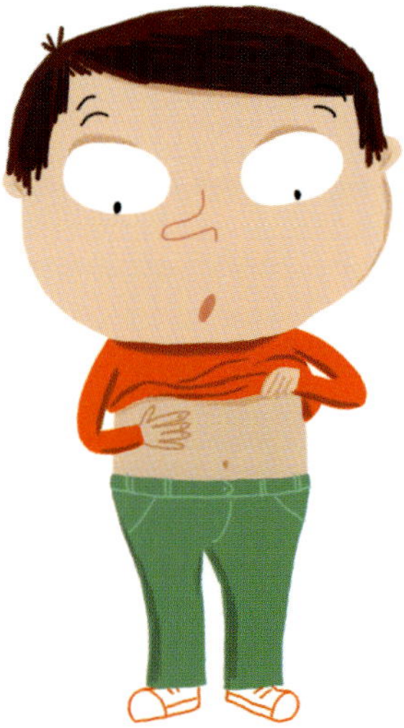

Τα **έντερα** είναι τυλιγμένα στην κοιλιά μας. Είναι 6 ή 7 μέτρα…

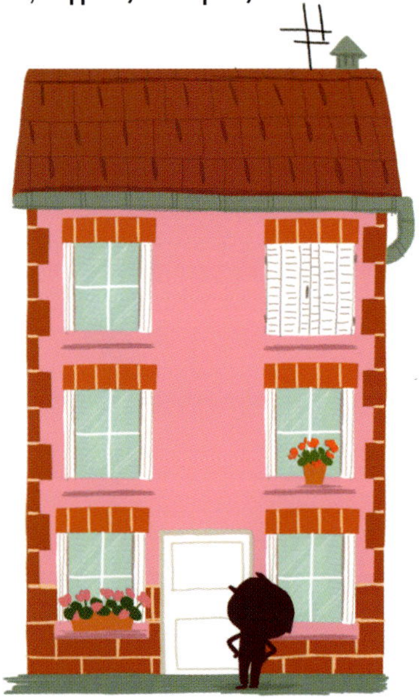

…όσο ύψος έχει δηλαδή ένα διώροφο σπίτι!

Χρειαζόμαστε περίπου **24 ώρες** για να χωνέψουμε ένα γεύμα.

15 δευτερόλεπτα μέσα στο στόμα

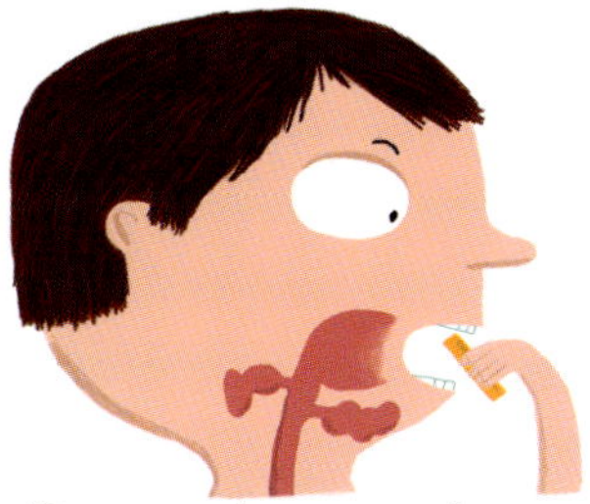

Οι τροφές **μασιούνται** με τα **δόντια** και μουσκεύονται με σάλιο.

5 ώρες μέσα στο στομάχι

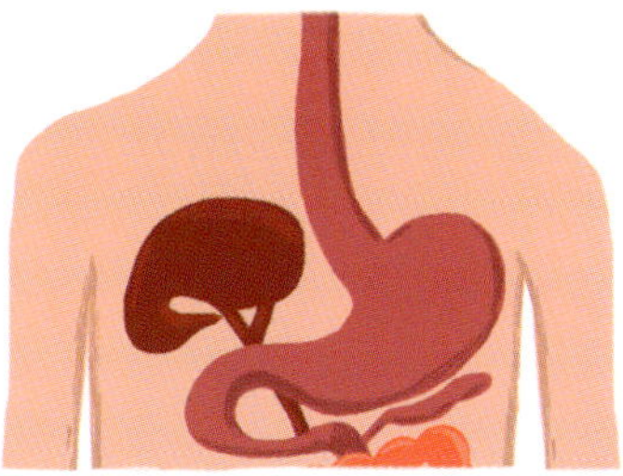

Έπειτα περνάνε στο **στομάχι**, ένα είδος μεγάλου σάκου, όπου μετατρέπονται σε πολτό.

18 ώρες μέσα στο έντερο

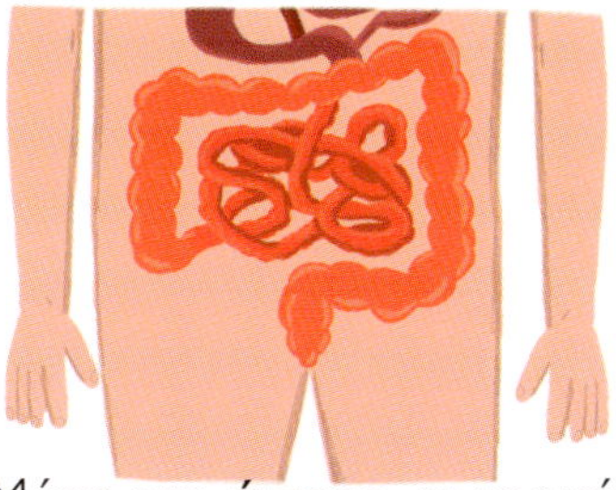

Μέσα στο **έντερο**, οι τροφές γίνονται τόσο λεπτές που μπορούν να περάσουν μέσα στο αίμα. Ό,τι μένει αποβάλλεται από τον πρωκτό.

Τα δόντια

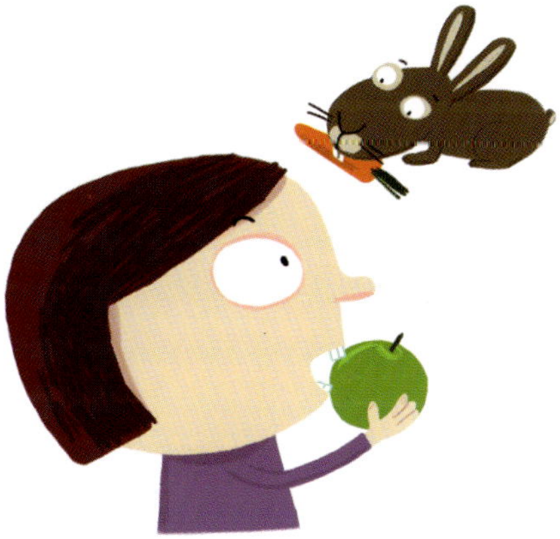

Τα δόντια που κόβουν την τροφή είναι οι **κοπτήρες**.

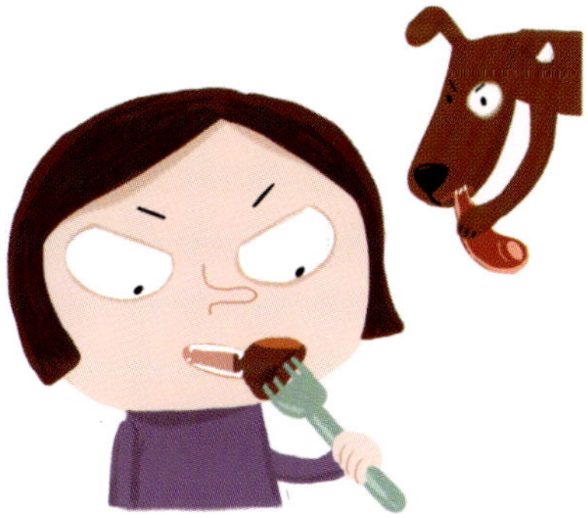

Τα δόντια που σκίζουν την τροφή είναι οι **κυνόδοντες**.

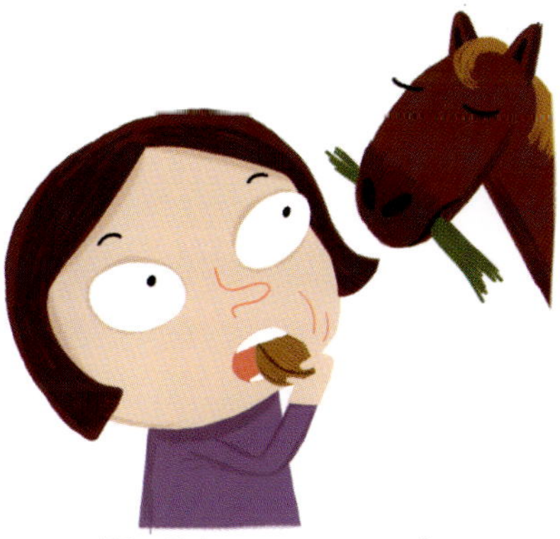

Τα δόντια που σπάνε την τροφή είναι οι **τραπεζίτες**.

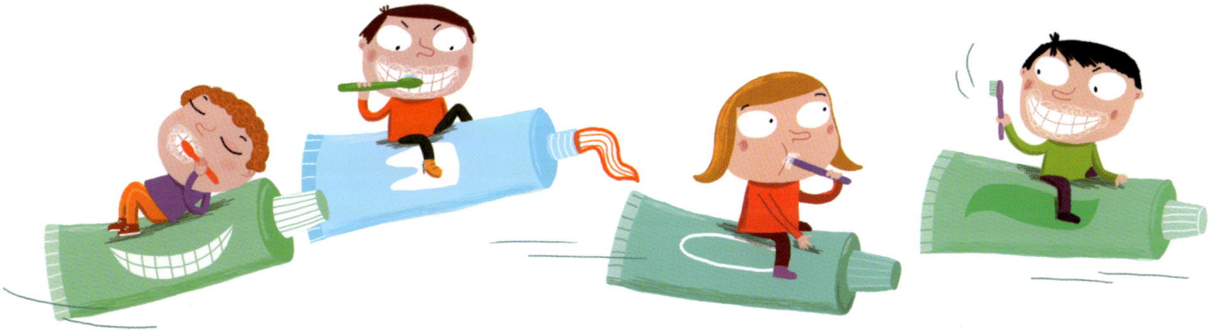

Πρέπει να **μασάμε** καλά πριν καταπιούμε και να **βουρτσίζουμε** προσεκτικά τα δόντια μας μετά τα γεύματα, γιατί τα κομματάκια που μένουν ανάμεσα στα δόντια γίνονται όξινα και, λόγω των βακτηρίων, κάνουν μικρές τρύπες στα δόντια και σχηματίζουν την **τερηδόνα**.

Το σώμα ζει

Για να λειτουργεί, το σώμα μας χρειάζεται τον αέρα που αναπνέουμε και ταυτόχρονα την τροφή που χωνεύουμε.

Ο αέρας τού φέρνει οξυγόνο και η **τροφή** τού φέρνει ενέργεια.

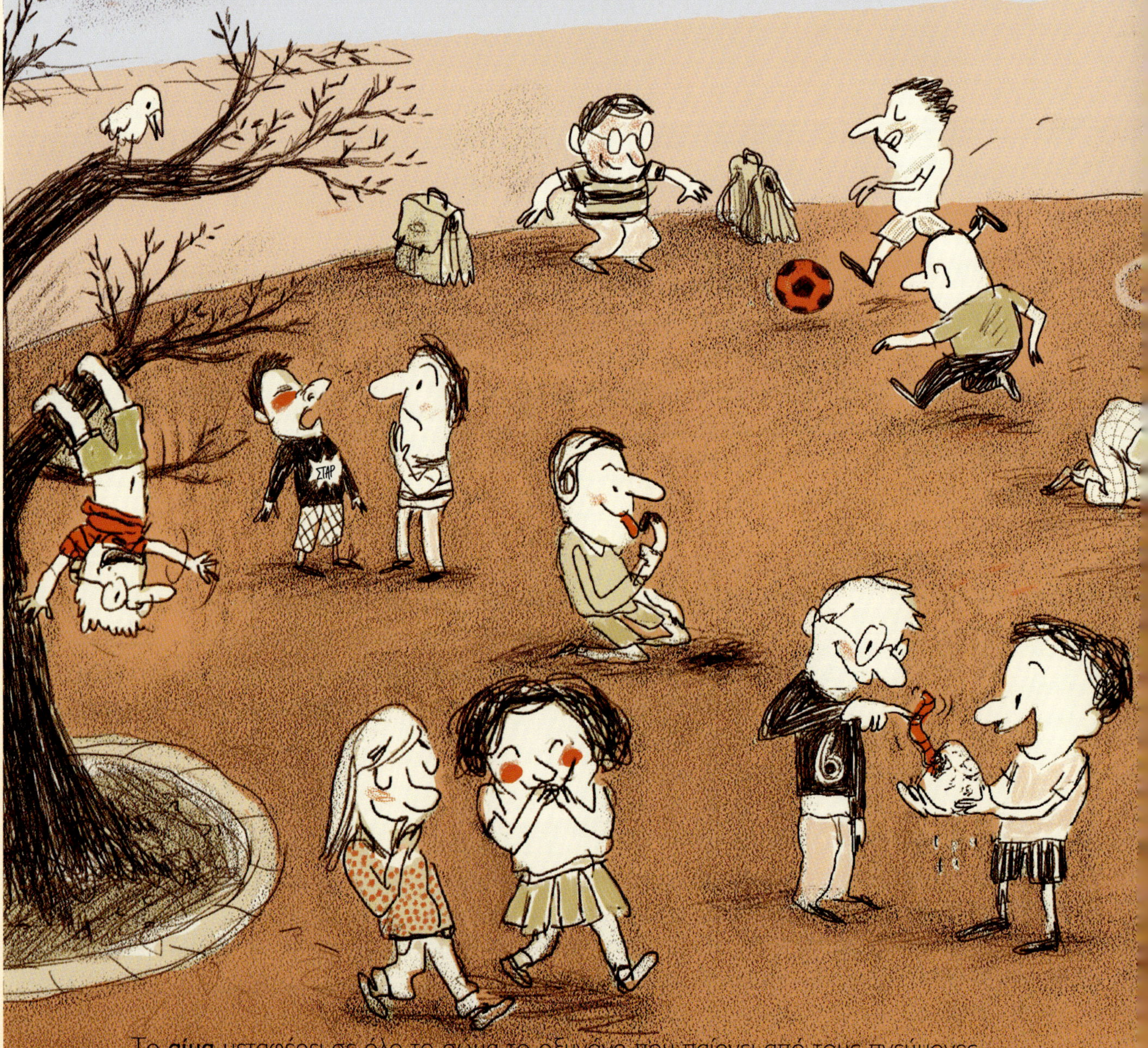

Το **αίμα** μεταφέρει σε όλο το σώμα το οξυγόνο που παίρνει από τους πνεύμονες και τα θρεπτικά στοιχεία που μεταφέρονται από το έντερο.

Για να λειτουργεί σωστά, το σώμα χρειάζεται επίσης **ύπνο**.
Για να είναι σε φόρμα, ένα παιδί πρέπει να κοιμάται τουλάχιστον **10 ώρες** κάθε νύχτα.

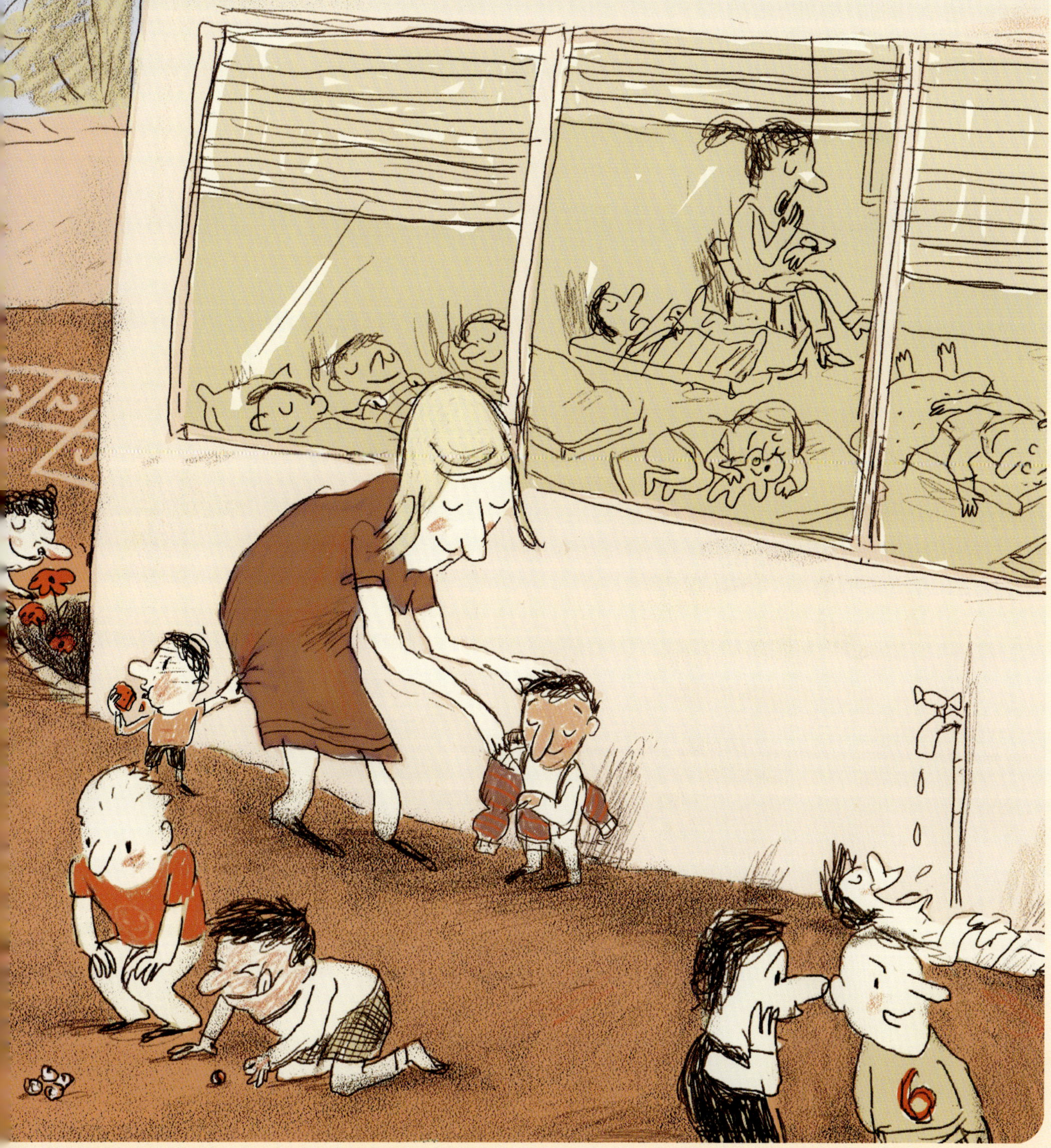

Και τα μωρά;

Για να γίνει ένα μωρό, χρειάζεται ένας μπαμπάς και μια μαμά που αγαπιούνται.

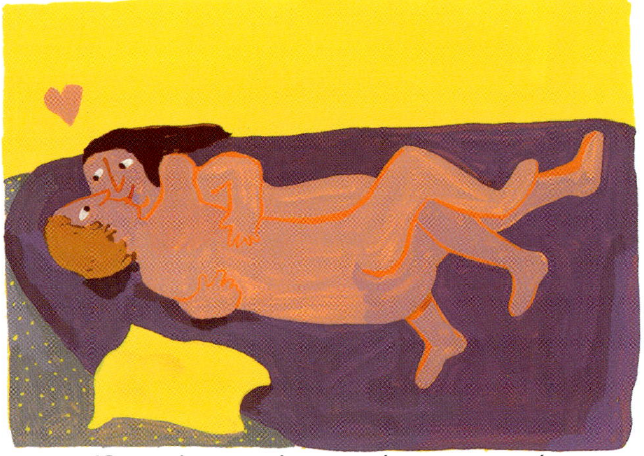

Όταν ένας σπόρος από τον μπαμπά (ένα σπερματοζωάριο) συναντά το σπόρο της μαμάς (το ωάριο), σχηματίζεται ένα **μικρό αυγό**. Αυτή η διαδικασία ονομάζεται **γονιμοποίηση**.

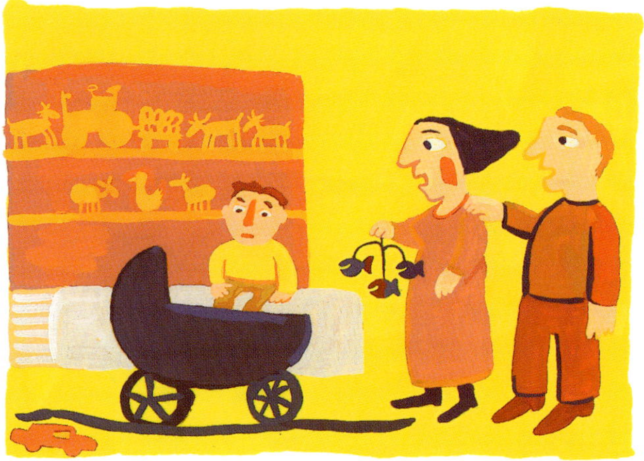

Αυτό το μικρό αυγό αναπτύσσεται **μέσα στην κοιλιά της μαμάς**. Γίνεται το έμβρυο του μωρού που θα γεννηθεί 9 μήνες αργότερα.

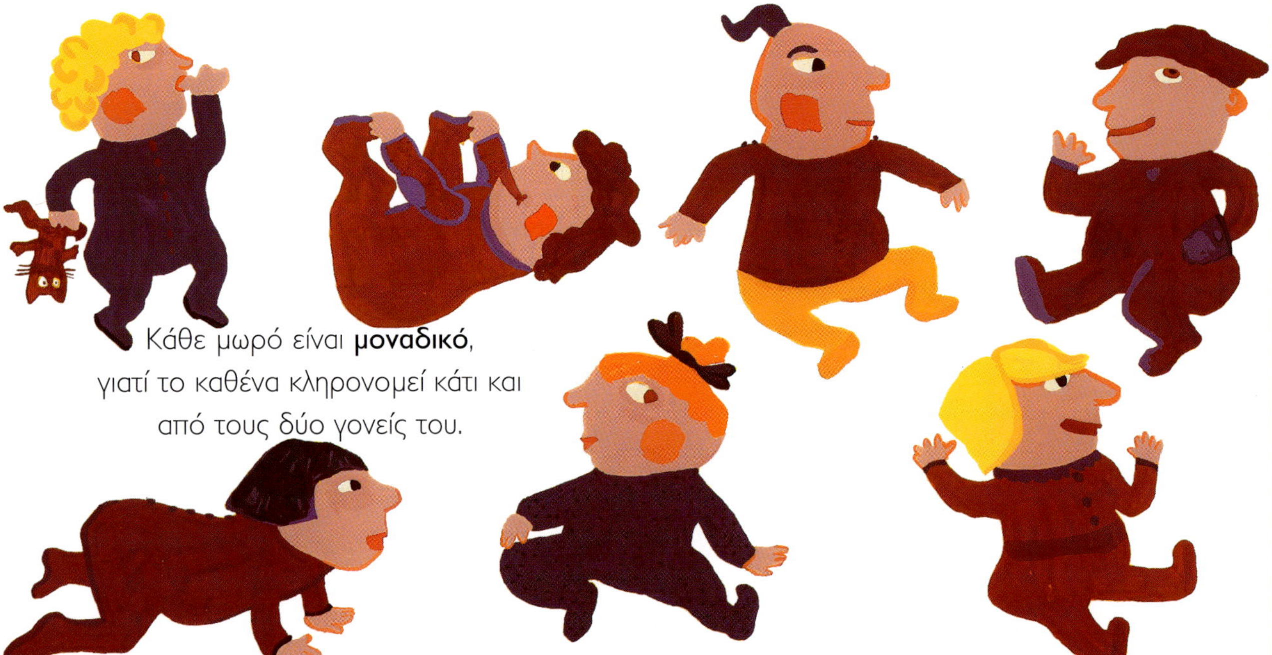

Κάθε μωρό είναι **μοναδικό**, γιατί το καθένα κληρονομεί κάτι και από τους δύο γονείς του.

Το μωρό μεγαλώνει σε μια ειδική **τσέπη** (τη μήτρα).
Αυτή η τσέπη είναι **ελαστική**. **Μεγαλώνει** μαζί με το μωρό.

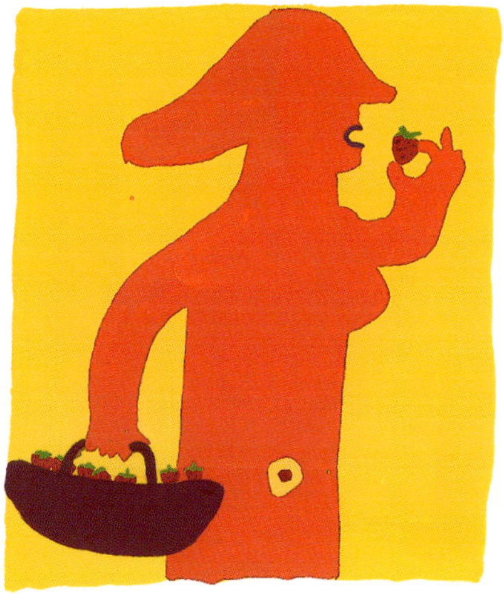

1ος μήνας:
το έμβρυο μοιάζει με κόκκο ρυζιού. Η **καρδιά** του έχει αρχίσει να χτυπά.

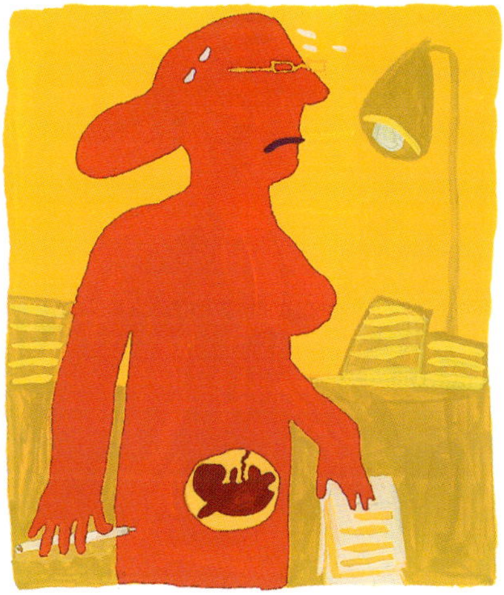

2ος μήνας:
εμφανίζονται το **κεφάλι**, τα **χέρια** και τα **πόδια**.

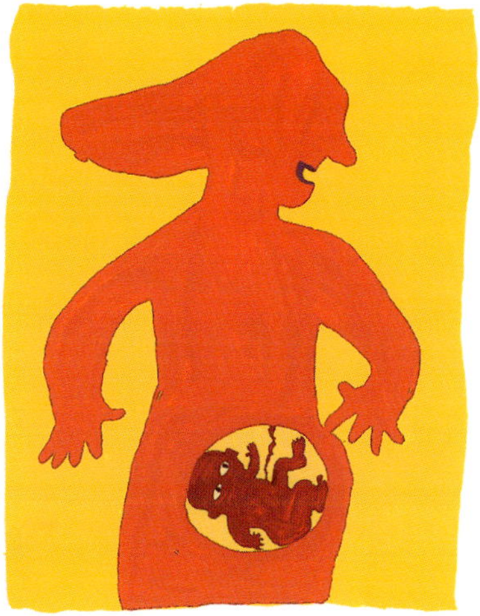

3ος μήνας:
είναι ήδη ένα **μωρό-μινιατούρα**.

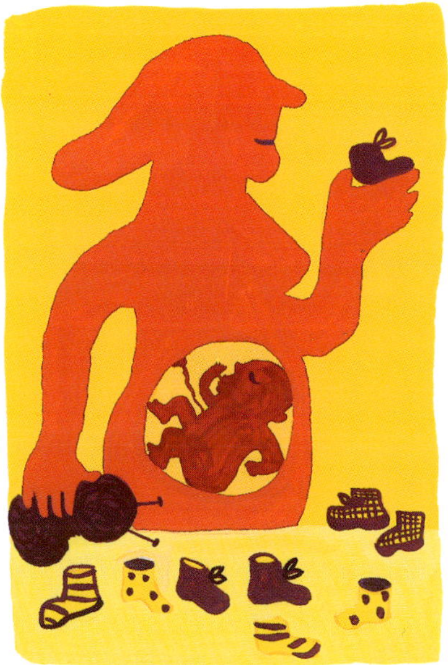

5ος μήνας:
η μαμά αισθάνεται το μωρό να **κινείται** μέσα στην κοιλιά της.

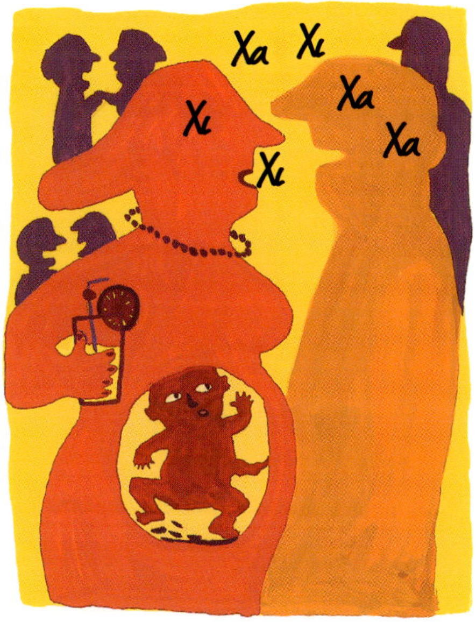

6ος μήνας:
το μωρό **ακούει** θορύβους και κινείται ολοένα και περισσότερο.

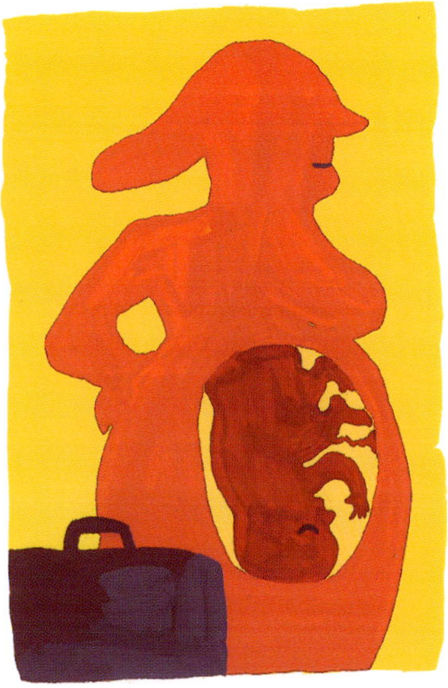

8ος μήνας:
το μωρό είναι σχεδόν έτοιμο να γεννηθεί.
Στρίβει με το κεφάλι κάτω.

Στην κοιλιά της μαμάς

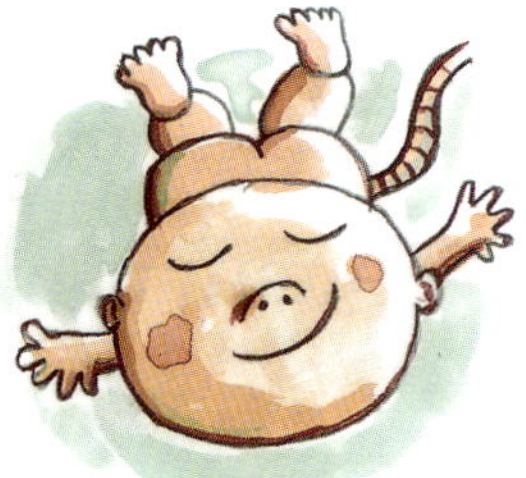

Το μωρό επιπλέει μέσα σε ένα υγρό που το προστατεύει, το **αμνιακό υγρό**.

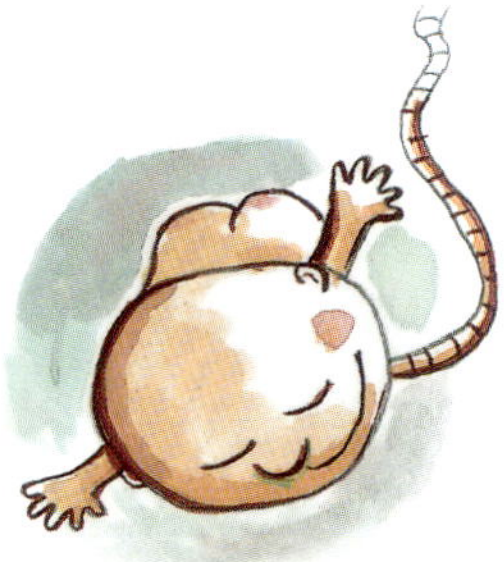

Το μωρό **κοιμάται** πολύ. Μερικές φορές **κινείται** και κάνει τούμπες.

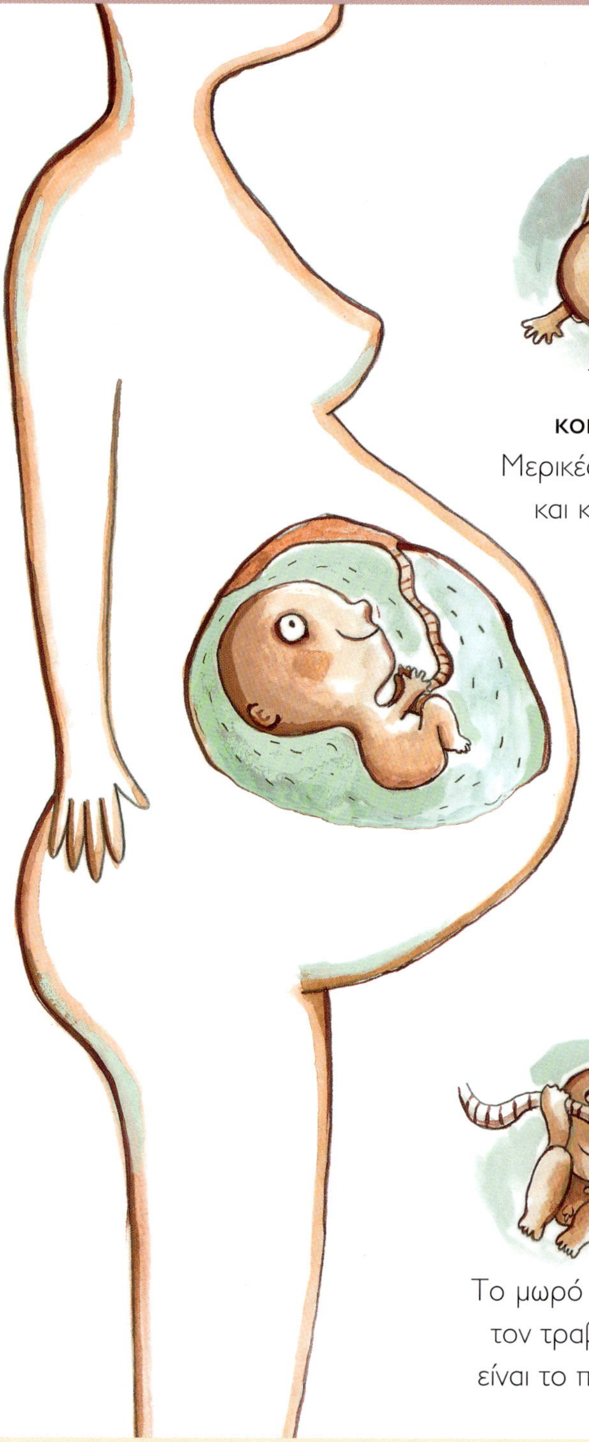

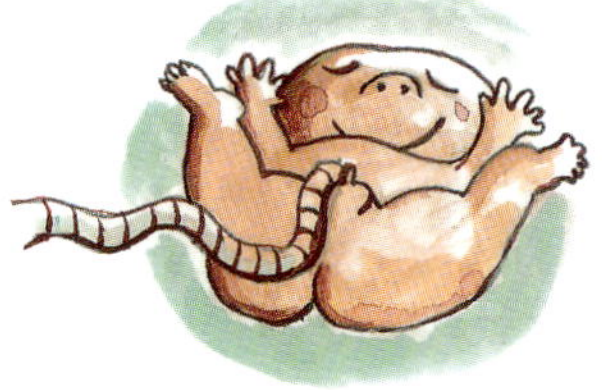

Ο **ομφάλιος λώρος** ενώνει το μωρό με τη μαμά του. Χάρη σ' αυτόν, η μαμά δίνει στο μωρό ό,τι χρειάζεται για να ζήσει, δηλαδή τροφή και οξυγόνο.

Το μωρό **παίζει** με το λώρο, τον τραβάει, τον πιπιλά… είναι το πρώτο του παιχνίδι!

Ύστερα από 9 μήνες, η μαμά νιώθει ότι το μωρό είναι έτοιμο να γεννηθεί. Αρχίζει η **γέννα**.

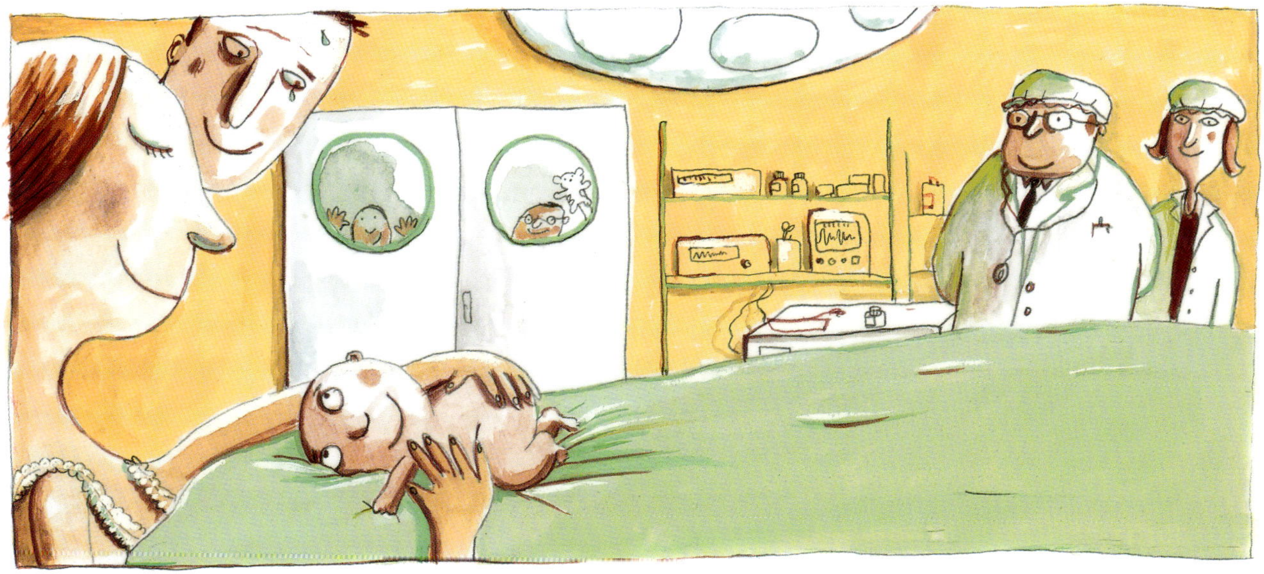

Στην **κλινική** βρίσκονται μια μαμή και ένας γιατρός, για να βοηθήσουν τη μαμά και το μωρό.

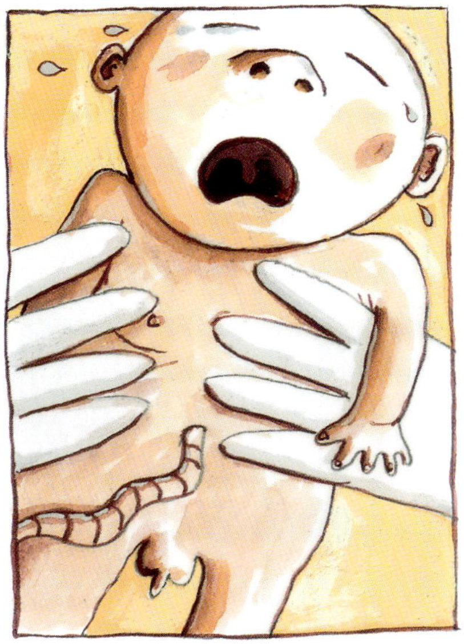

Όταν γεννιέται, το μωρό βγάζει την **πρώτη του φωνή**: είναι η πρώτη φορά που αναπνέει αέρα.

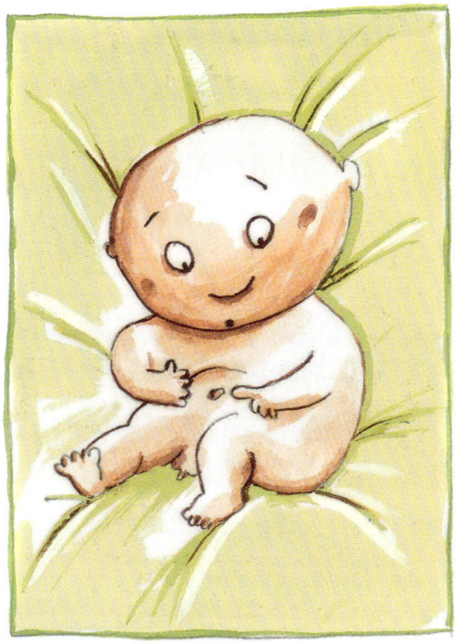

Ο γιατρός κόβει τον ομφάλιο λώρο. Η άκρη που μένει είναι ο **αφαλός**.

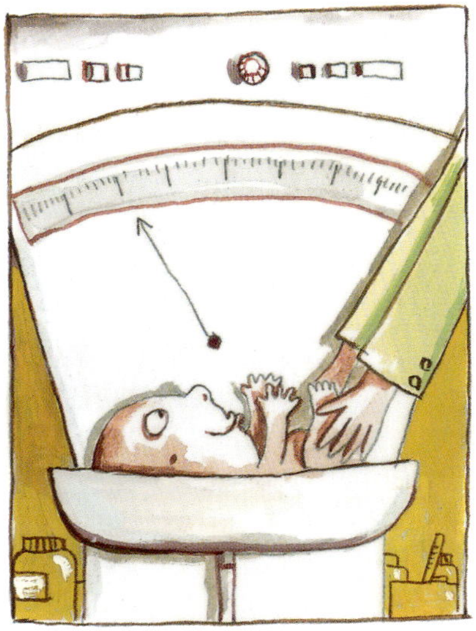

Το μωρό που γεννιέται έχει ύψος περίπου **50 εκατοστά** και ζυγίζει περίπου **3 κιλά**. Ρώτησε τη μαμά σου ποιο ήταν το βάρος και το ύψος σου όταν γεννήθηκες.

Αυτή είναι η ζωή!

Αφού γεννηθεί, το μωρό μεγαλώνει και το σώμα του αλλάζει.
Το μωρό κάνει πρόοδο κάθε μέρα· σιγά σιγά μαθαίνει να χρησιμοποιεί το σώμα του.

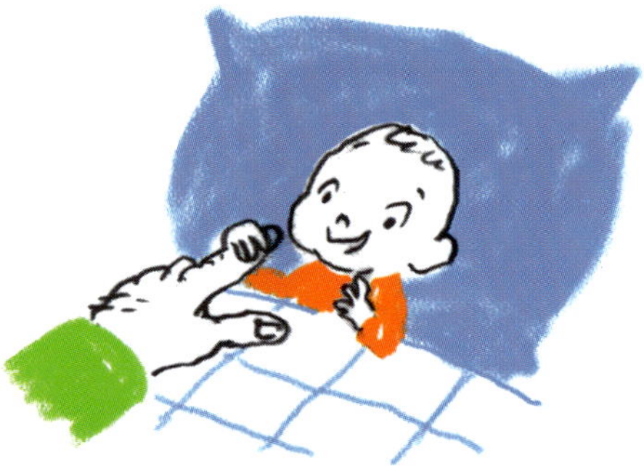

Στον **1 μήνα**, το μωρό **χαμογελάει**· σφίγγει πολύ δυνατά τα δάχτυλα.

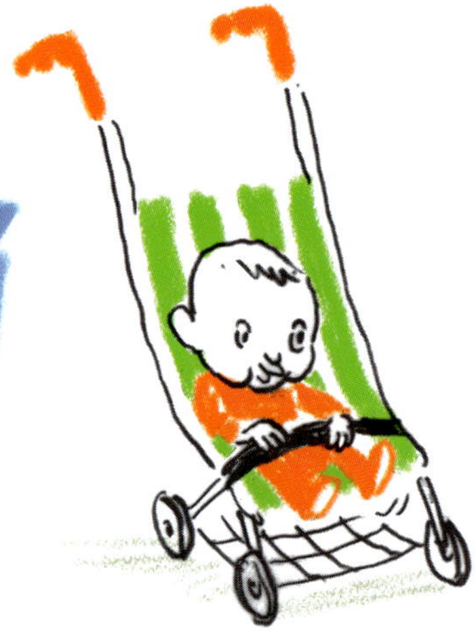

Γύρω στους **4 μήνες**, κρατάει όρθιο το κεφάλι του και λέει τις πρώτες του συλλαβές.

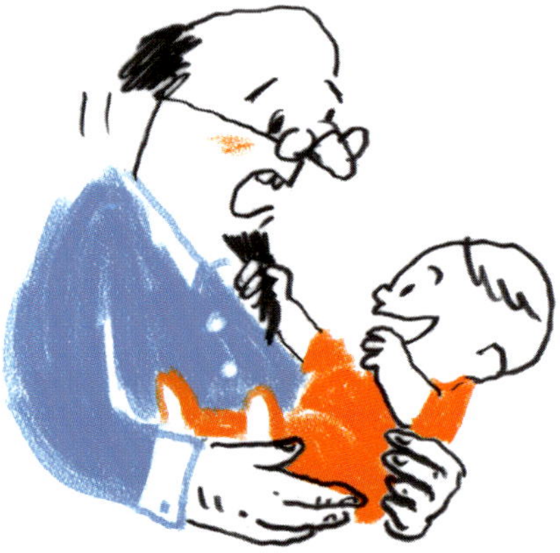

Γύρω στους **6 μήνες**, αρχίζει να αρπάζει τα πάντα!

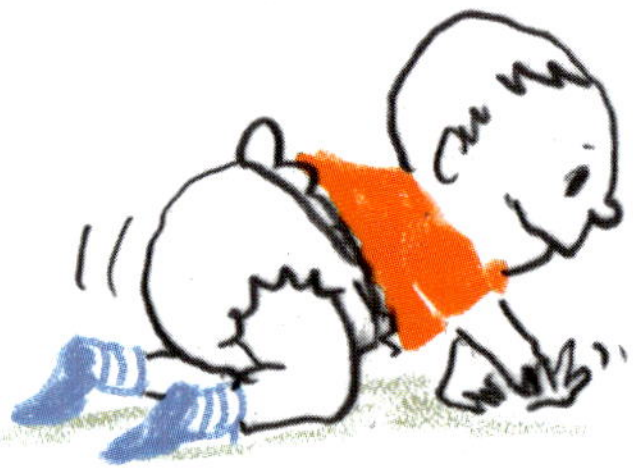

Γύρω στους **8 μήνες**, στέκεται καθιστό μόνο του και αρχίζει να μπουσουλάει.

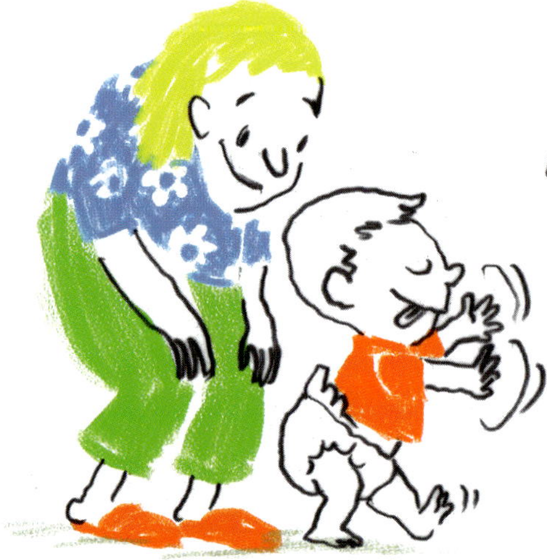

Στον **1 χρόνο**, κάνει τα πρώτα του βήματα και αρχίζει να εξερευνά τον κόσμο.

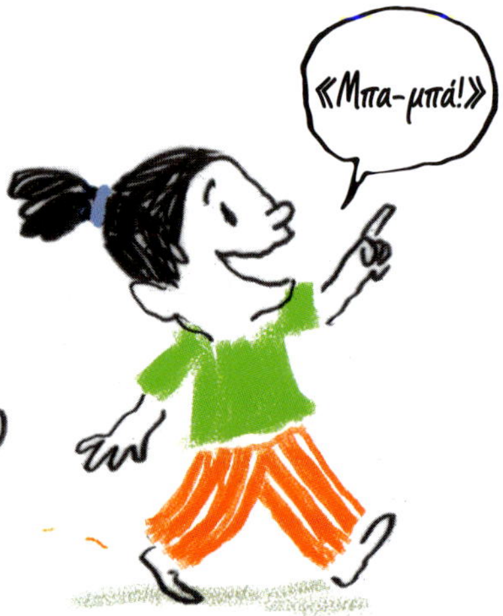

Στα **2 του χρόνια**, το παιδάκι περπατά, τρέχει και αρχίζει να μιλά.

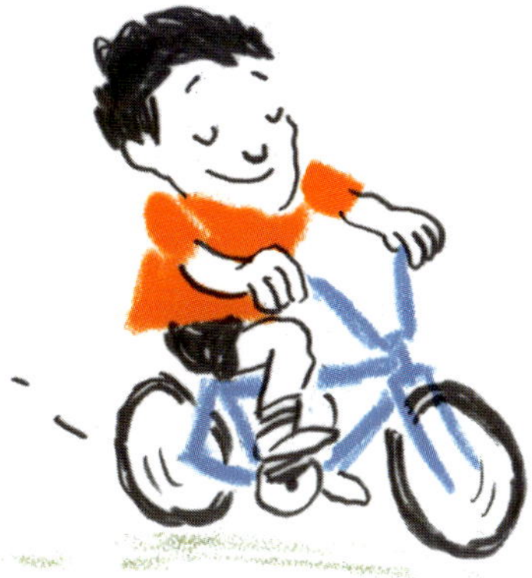

Στα **6 του χρόνια**, το **παιδί** μαθαίνει να διαβάζει, να γράφει, να κάνει ποδήλατο, να κολυμπά. Χάνει τα πρώτα του δόντια.

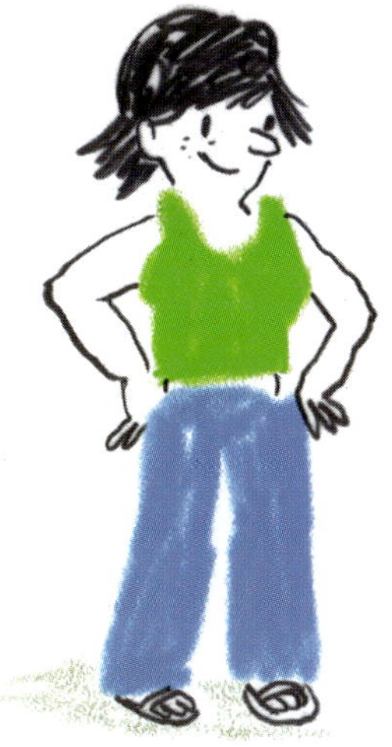

Γύρω στα **12 χρόνια**, το σώμα των **μικρών κοριτσιών** αρχίζει να γίνεται σώμα γυναίκας. **Μεγαλώνει** πολύ.

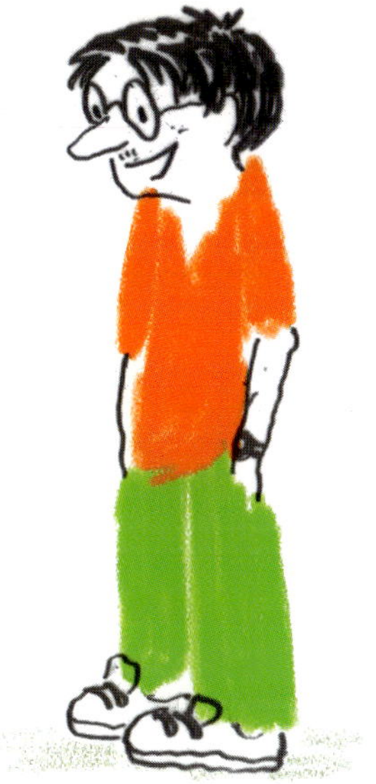

Στα **15 χρόνια**, η **φωνή** του **αγοριού** γίνεται πιο βαριά και βγάζει **γένια**.

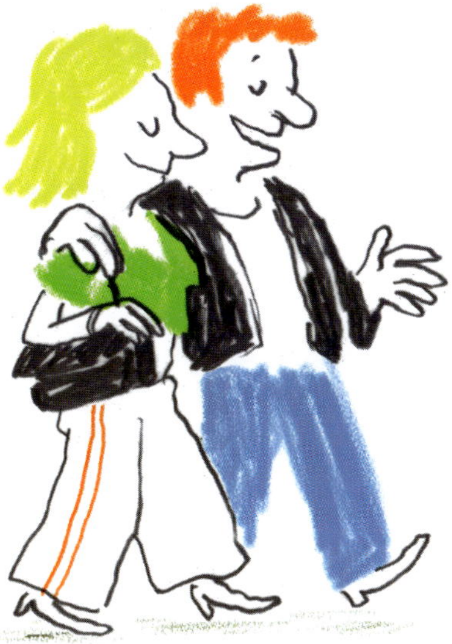

Στα **20**, τα κόκαλα σταματάνε να μεγαλώνουν. Τα αγόρια και τα κορίτσια γίνονται **ενήλικες**. Μπορούν να γίνουν τώρα κι αυτά γονείς!

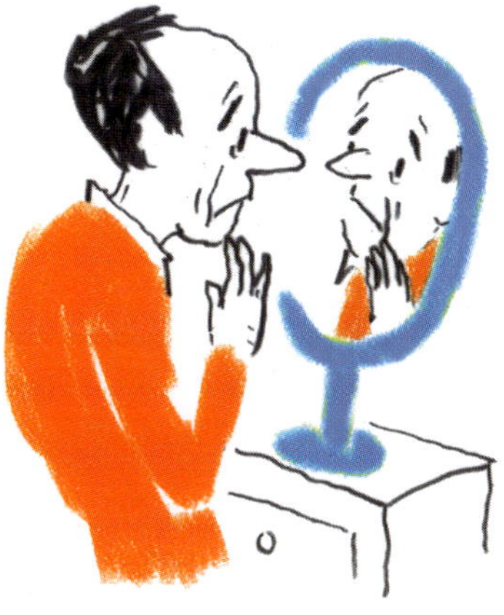

Στα **50**, το σώμα γίνεται λιγότερο ευλύγιστο και εμφανίζονται μικρές ρυτίδες στο πρόσωπο. Οι γονείς σύντομα θα γίνουν **παππούδες και γιαγιάδες**.

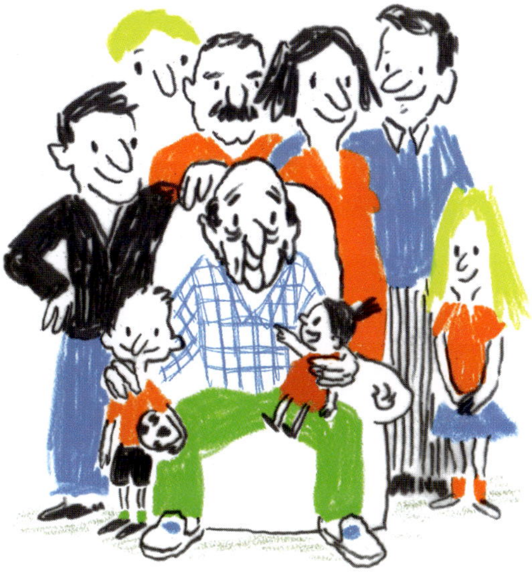

Στα **80**, είμαστε ηλικιωμένοι, το σώμα έχει **κουραστεί**. Όμως κάποιοι άνθρωποι μπορούν να ζήσουν 100 χρόνια, ίσως και περισσότερο!

Τα επαγγέλματα του σώματος

Ο γιατρός θεραπεύει τις αρρώστιες. Είναι ο ειδικός για το σώμα.

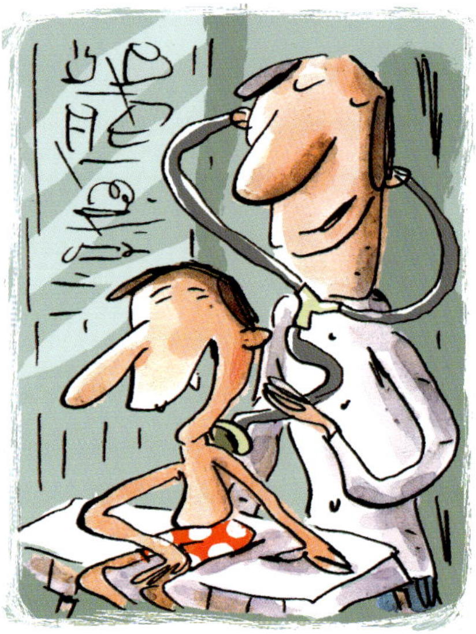

Ακούει την καρδιά
και τους πνεύμονες
με το **στηθοσκόπιο**.

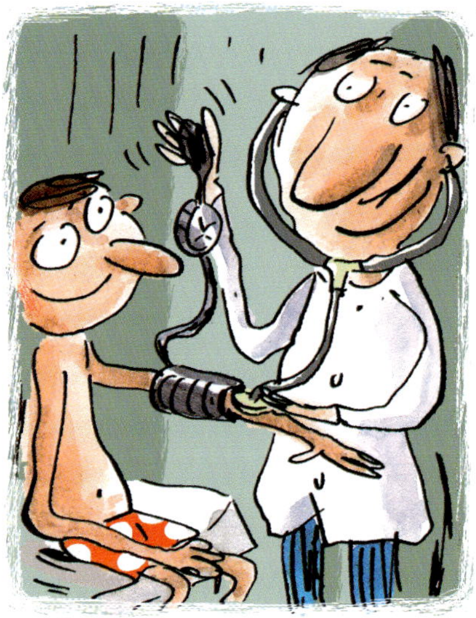

Μετρά την **πίεση**
με το **πιεσόμετρο**,
για να διαπιστώσει αν το αίμα
κυκλοφορεί καλά.

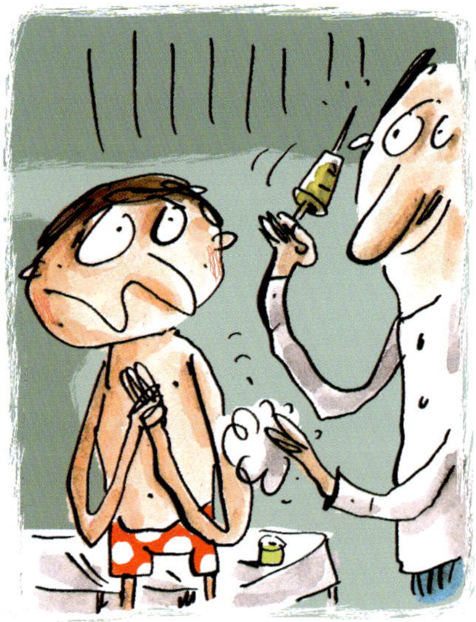

Κάνει **εμβόλια**.

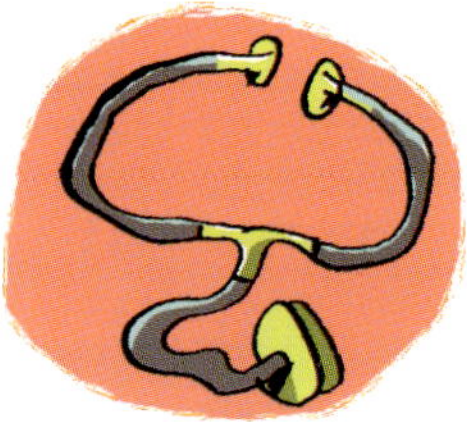

στηθοσκόπιο

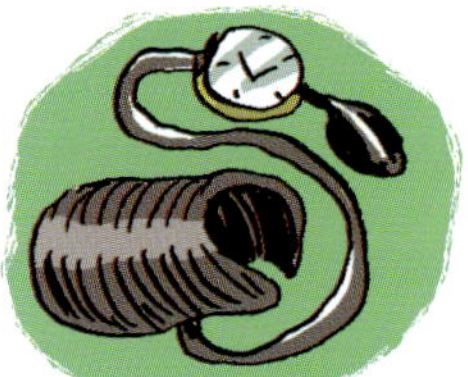

πιεσόμετρο

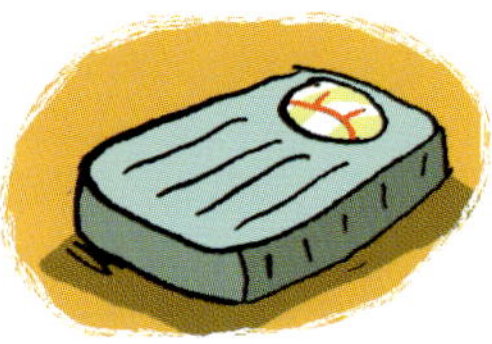

ζυγαριά

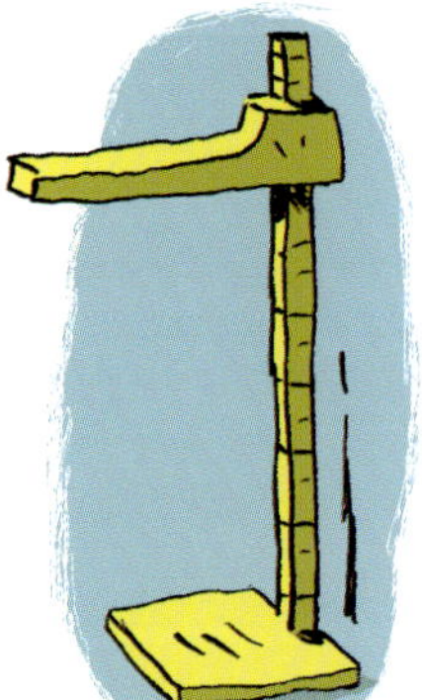

μέτρο

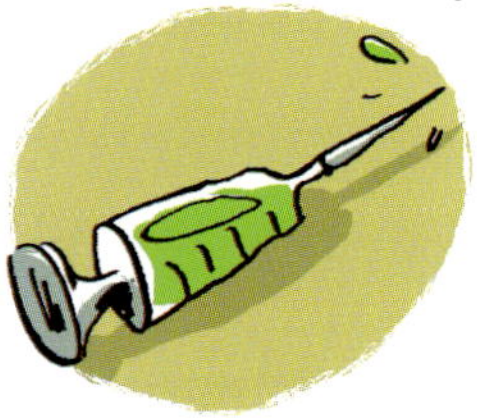

σύριγγα

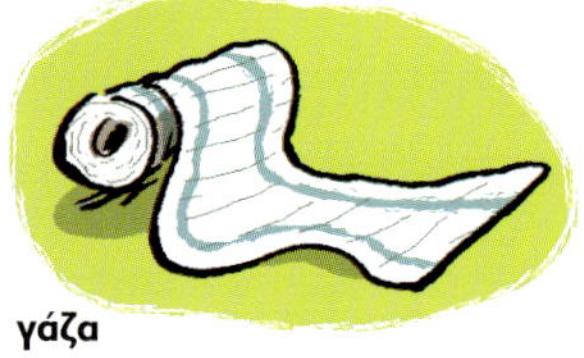

γάζα

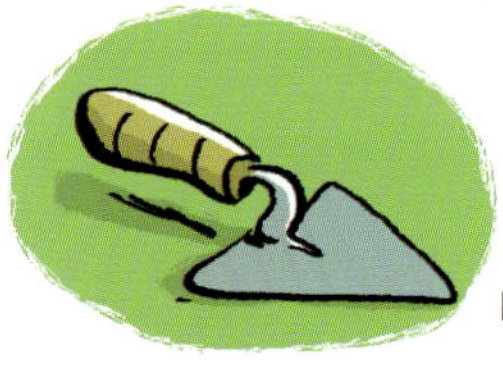

μυστρί

Μία από αυτές τις εικόνες δεν ανήκει στα εργαλεία του γιατρού. Ποια είναι;

Λύση: η παράταιρη εικόνα είναι το μυστρί.

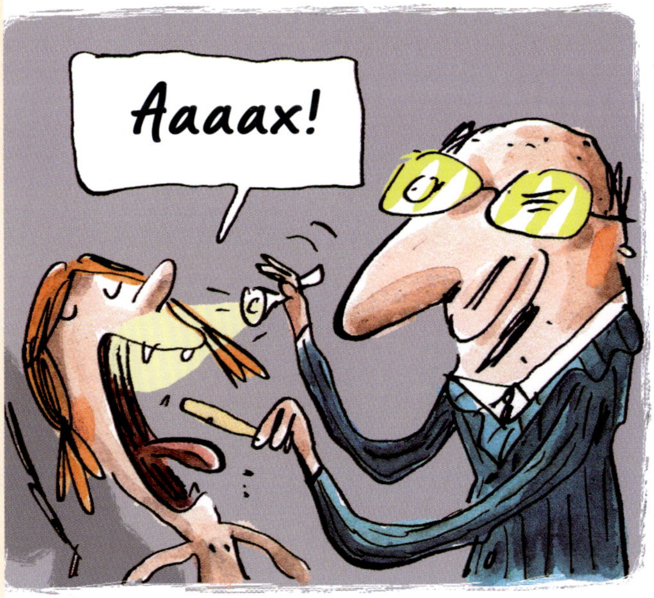

Ο **ωτορινολαρυγγολόγος** είναι ένας γιατρός που θεραπεύει τις αρρώστιες της **μύτης**, του **λαιμού** και των **αυτιών**. Για συντομία τον αποκαλούμε ω-ρι-λά.

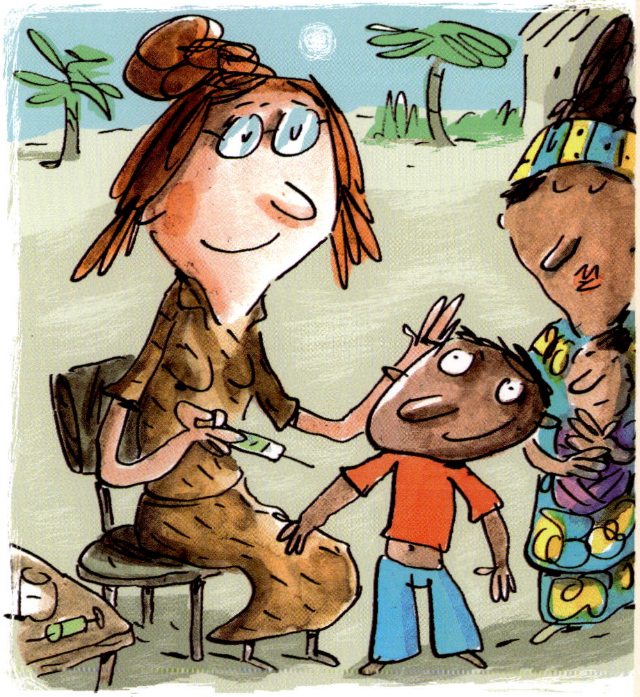

Για να θεραπεύουν τους αρρώστους στις χώρες που υπάρχει μεγάλη ανάγκη, κάποιοι γιατροί πηγαίνουν εκεί μερικές εβδομάδες το χρόνο. Αυτοί είναι οι **«γιατροί χωρίς σύνορα»**.

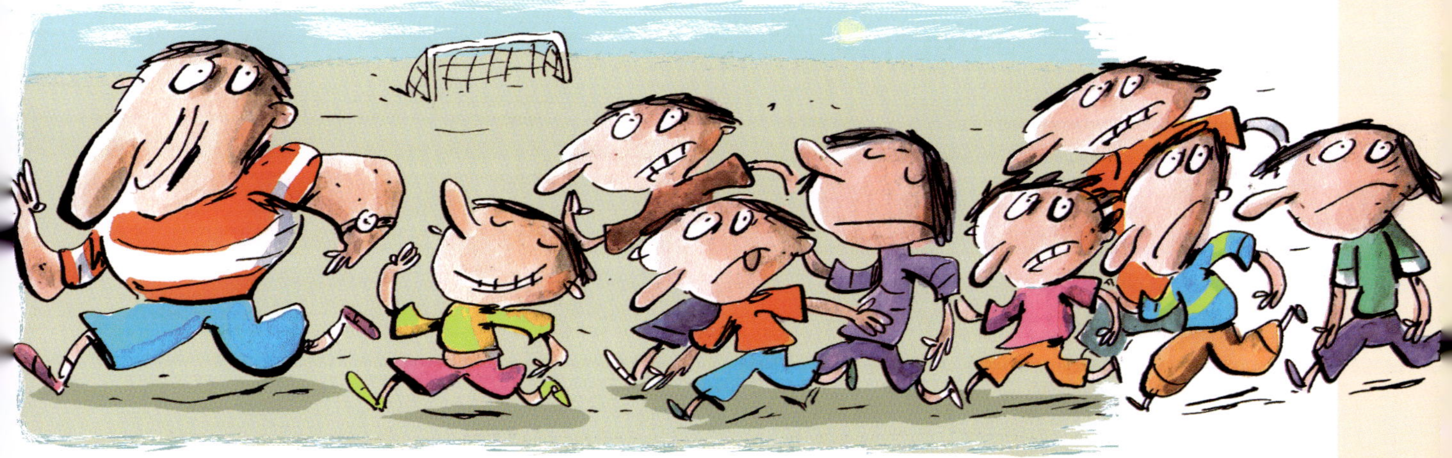

Ο **γυμναστής** μαθαίνει στα παιδιά να τρέχουν, να ξεφυσάνε, ν' αναπτύσσουν τους μυς τους, να **εξασκούν το σώμα τους**… Κάνει καλό στην υγεία, ακόμα κι αν μερικές φορές πονάει!

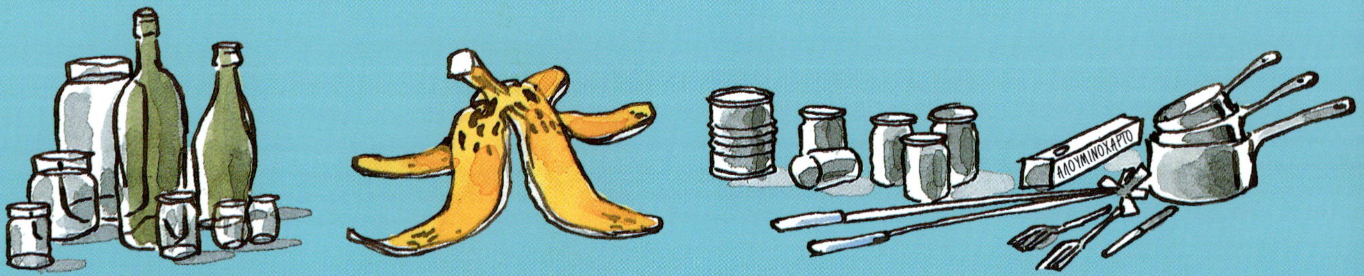
ΑΛΟΥΜΙΝΟΧΑΡΤΟ

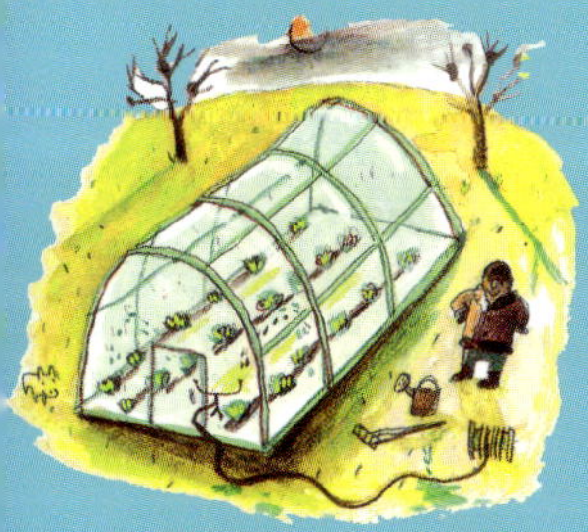

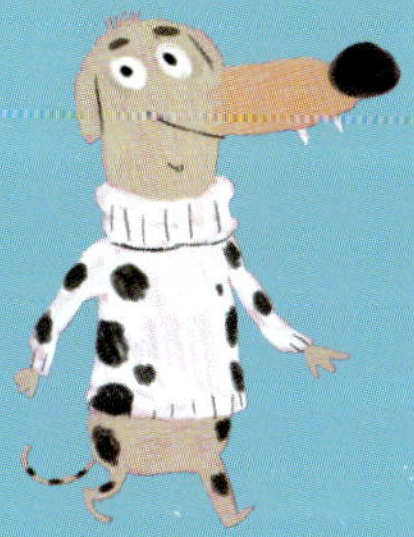

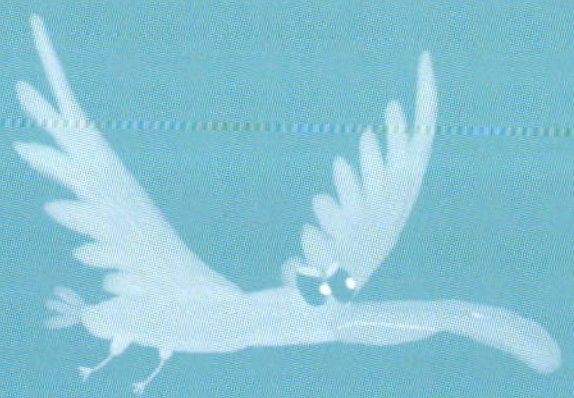

Η ΓΗ

Η ΟΙΚΟΛΟΓΙΑ

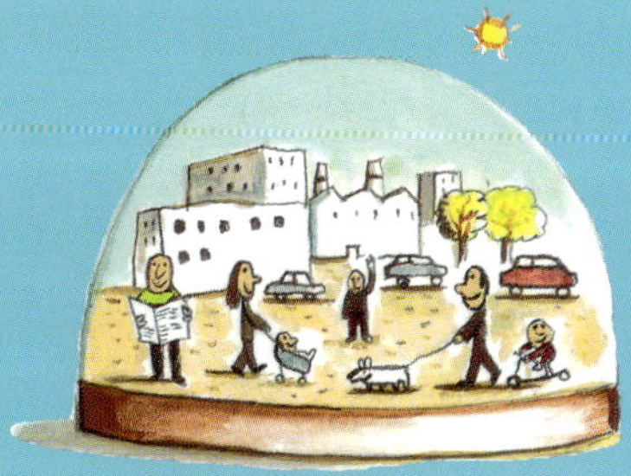

Η οικολογία, η επιστήμη του περιβάλλοντος

Η οικολογία είναι η επιστήμη που μελετά το περιβάλλον και ιδιαίτερα την επίδραση του ανθρώπου στη φύση.

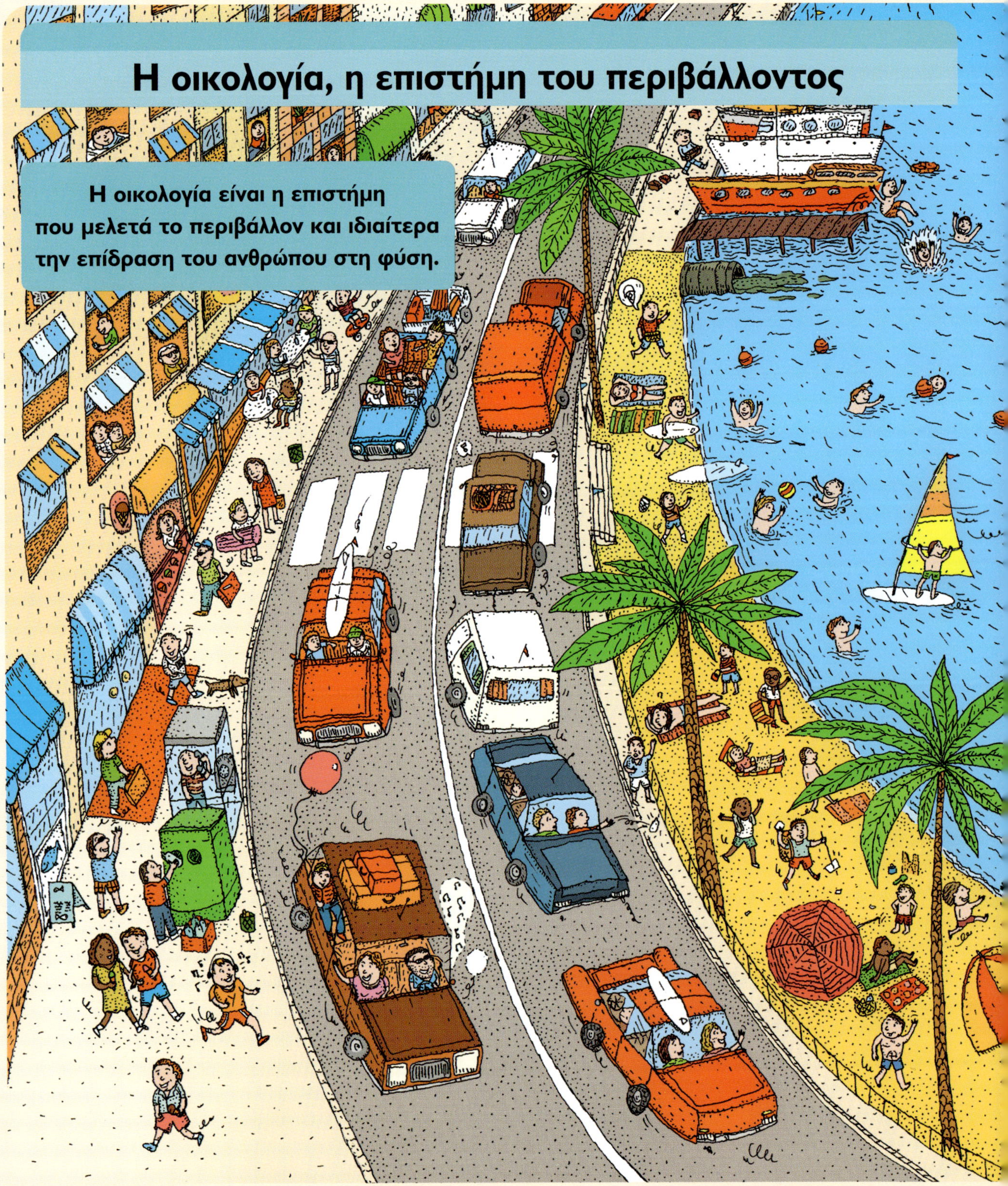

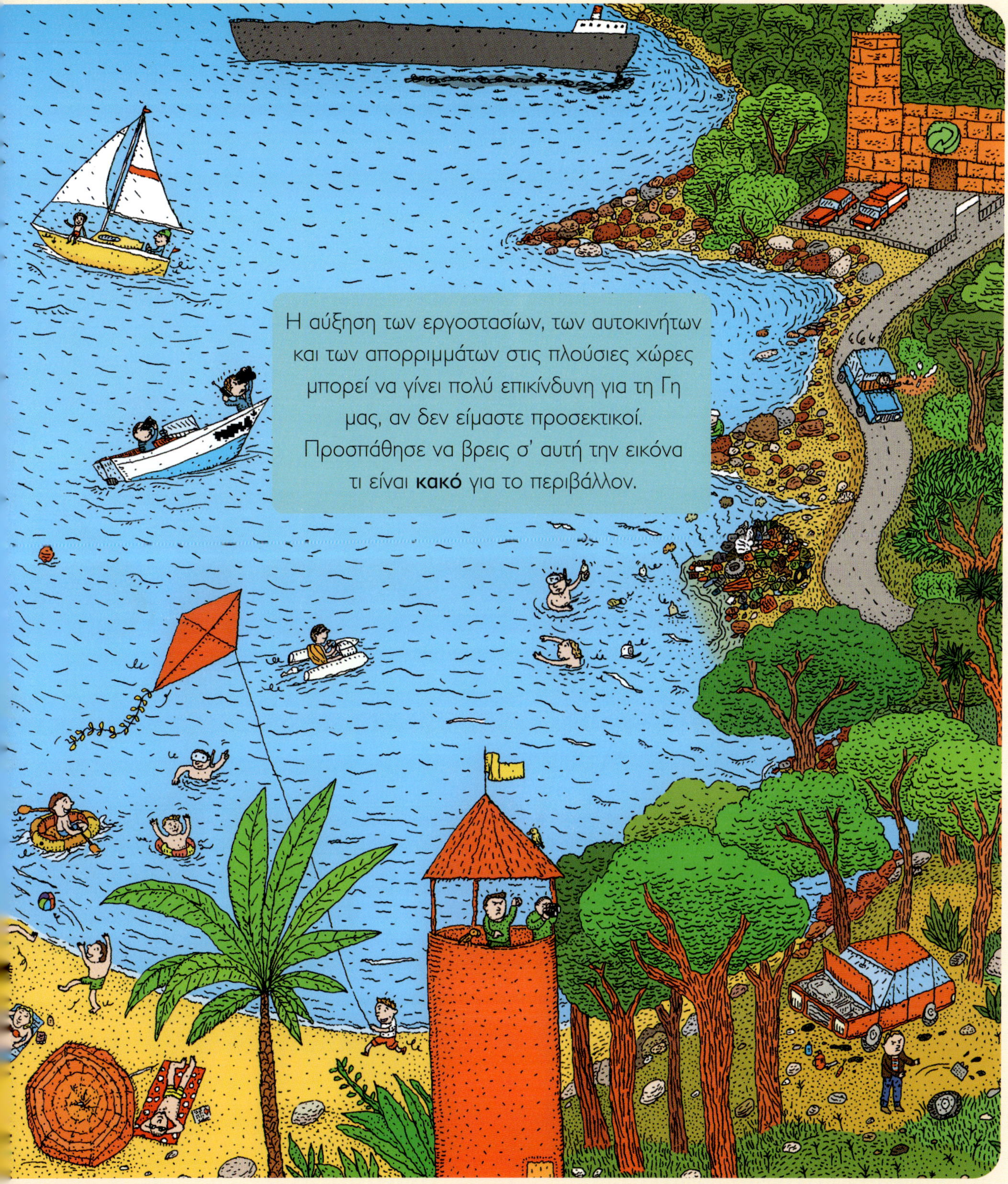

Η αύξηση των εργοστασίων, των αυτοκινήτων και των απορριμμάτων στις πλούσιες χώρες μπορεί να γίνει πολύ επικίνδυνη για τη Γη μας, αν δεν είμαστε προσεκτικοί. Προσπάθησε να βρεις σ' αυτή την εικόνα τι είναι **κακό** για το περιβάλλον.

Η Γη γίνεται όλο και πιο ζεστή

Εδώ και μερικά χρόνια διαπιστώνουμε ότι το κλίμα της Γης γίνεται όλο και πιο ζεστό.

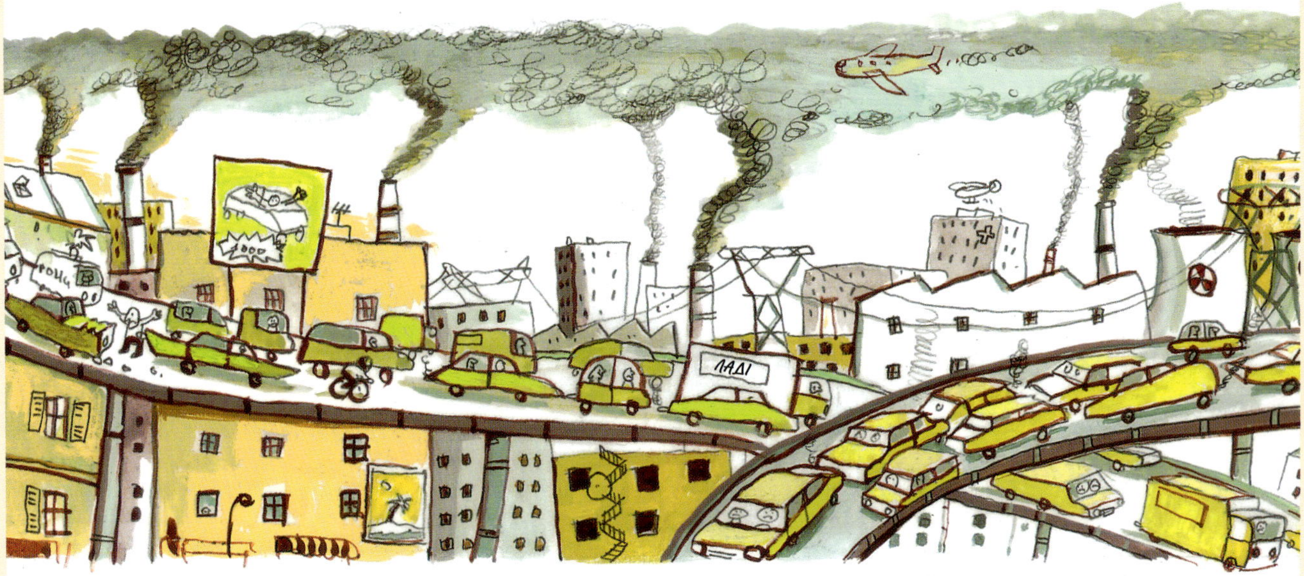

Τα **αέρια** που μεταφέρονται στην ατμόσφαιρα από τα εργοστάσια, τη θέρμανση, τον κλιματισμό και τα αυτοκίνητα είναι μία από τις αιτίες της αύξησης της θερμοκρασίας.

ΤΙ ΕΙΝΑΙ ΤΟ ΦΑΙΝΟΜΕΝΟ ΤΟΥ ΘΕΡΜΟΚΗΠΙΟΥ;

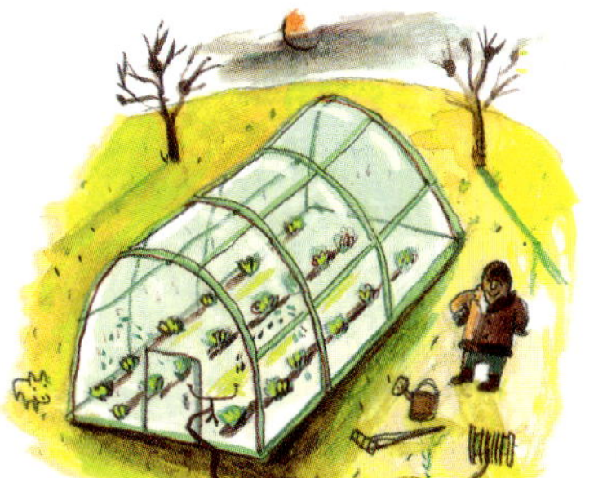

Τα **θερμοκήπια**, εκεί όπου οι άνθρωποι μεγαλώνουν τα φυτά, αφήνουν το φως του ήλιου να τα διαπερνά και συγκρατούν τη ζέστη.

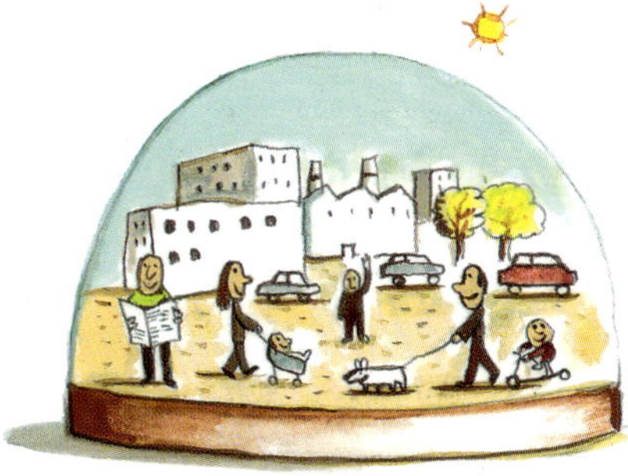

Η ατμόσφαιρα που περιβάλλει τη Γη λειτουργεί με τον ίδιο τρόπο, κρατά τον πλανήτη στη σωστή θερμοκρασία. Αυτό είναι το **φαινόμενο του θερμοκηπίου**.

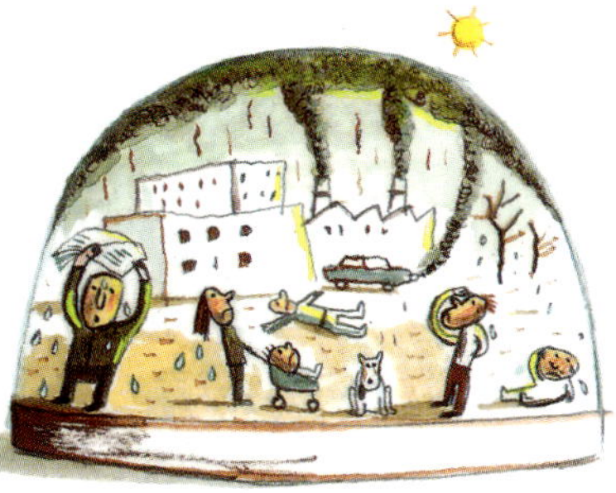

Όμως στην ατμόσφαιρα υπάρχουν όλο και περισσότερα αέρια που **εντείνουν** το φαινόμενο του θερμοκηπίου και ζεσταίνουν πολύ τη Γη.

Αν η θερμοκρασία της Γης αυξηθεί ακόμα περισσότερο, η ζωή στη Γη θ' αλλάξει.

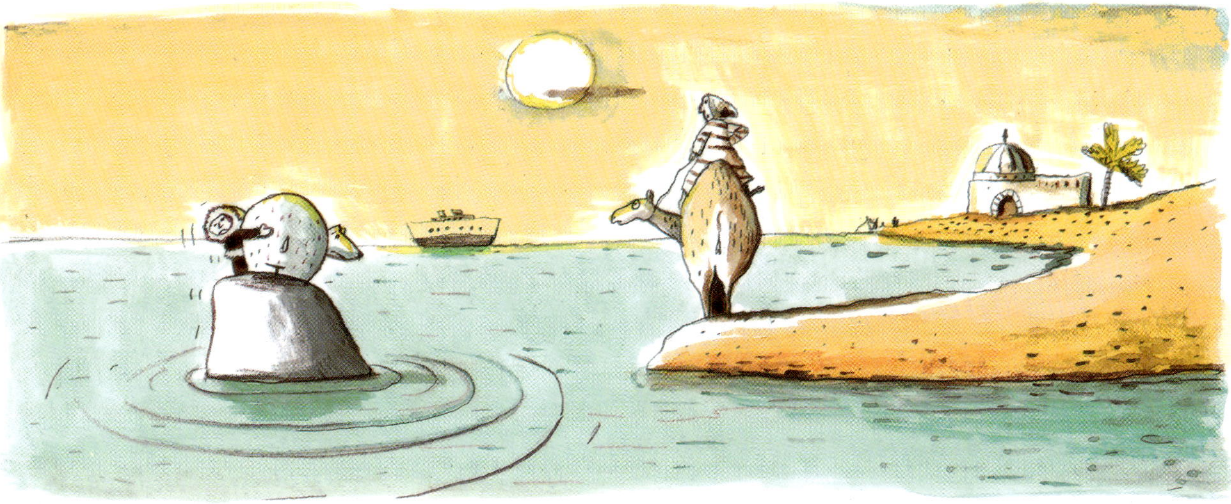

Οι **πάγοι** των πόλων και των βουνών θα λιώσουν και οι **έρημοι** θα απλωθούν περισσότερο.

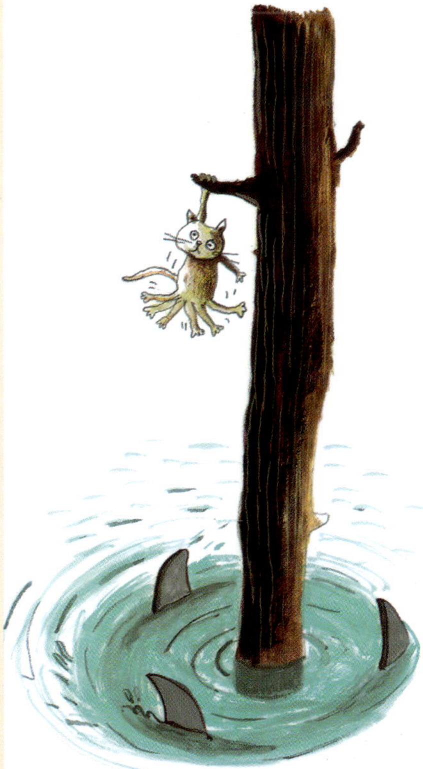

Η **στάθμη της θάλασσας** θα ανεβεί.

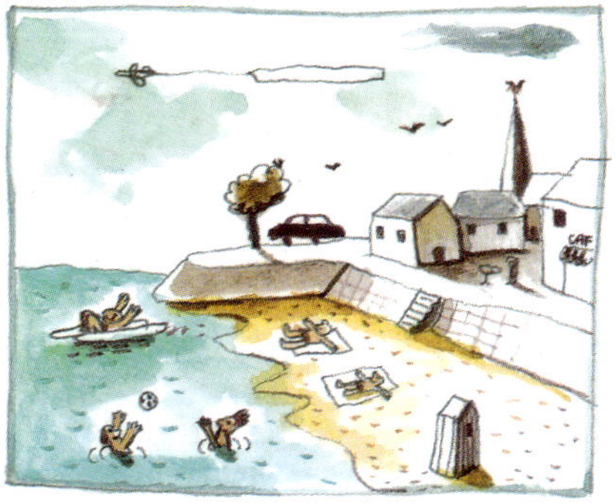

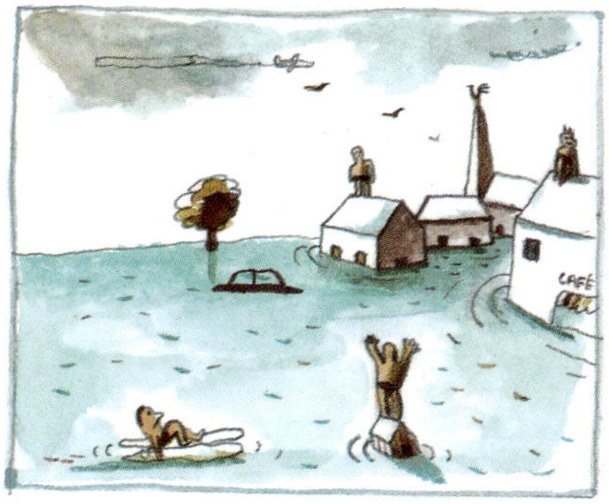

Κάποιες χώρες που βρίσκονται κοντά στη θάλασσα ή κάποια **νησιά** κινδυνεύουν να ξαναβρεθούν κάτω από το νερό.

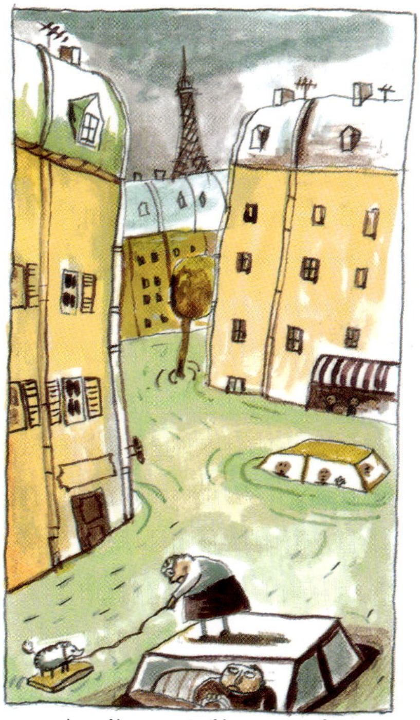

Αν έλιωναν όλοι οι πάγοι της Γης, η στάθμη της **θάλασσας** θα ανέβαινε κατά 80 μέτρα.

Πρέπει να προστατεύσουμε τη Γη μας!

Ο πλανήτης μας είναι το μόνο μέρος του σύμπαντος όπου μπορούν να ζήσουν άνθρωποι. Είναι πολύ ευαίσθητος, πρέπει λοιπόν να τον προστατεύσουμε. Για να περιοριστεί η μόλυνση, όλες οι χώρες πρέπει:

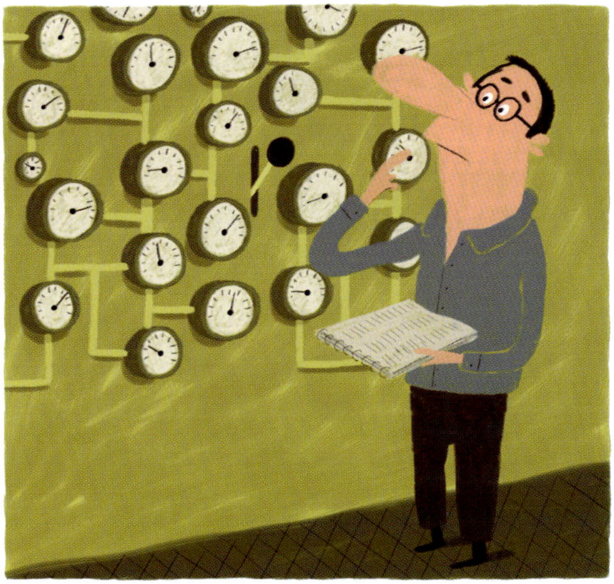

Να **ελέγχουν καλύτερα τις εγκαταστάσεις των εργοστασίων**, ώστε να μεταφέρονται λιγότερα αέρια στην ατμόσφαιρα.

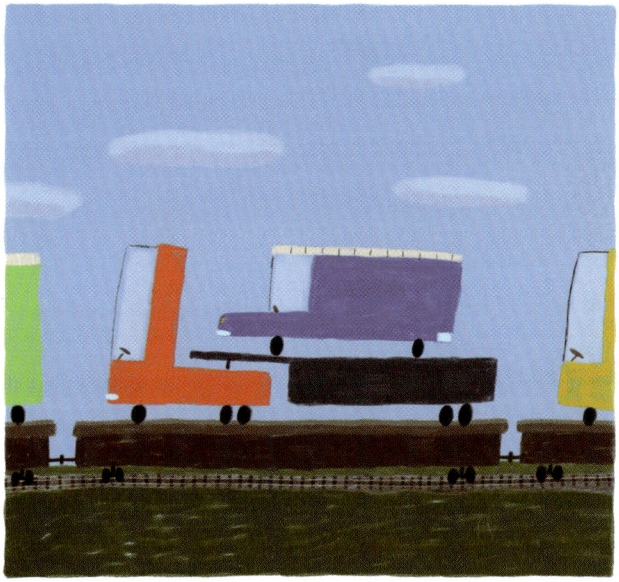

Να βελτιώσουν τις **μαζικές μεταφορές**, να προτιμούν τα τρένα από τα φορτηγά για τη μεταφορά των εμπορευμάτων.

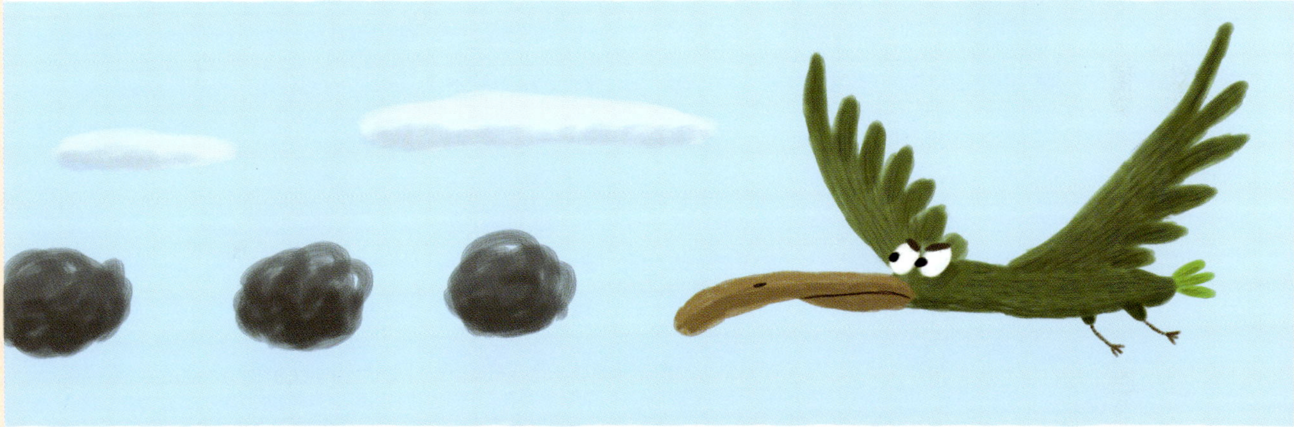

Να ζητήσουν από τους κατασκευαστές να **βελτιώσουν τις εξατμίσεις**, ώστε τα αεροπλάνα ή τα αυτοκίνητα να προκαλούν λιγότερη μόλυνση.

Όλοι μπορούμε να συμβάλουμε στην προστασία της Γης, ο καθένας με τον τρόπο του.

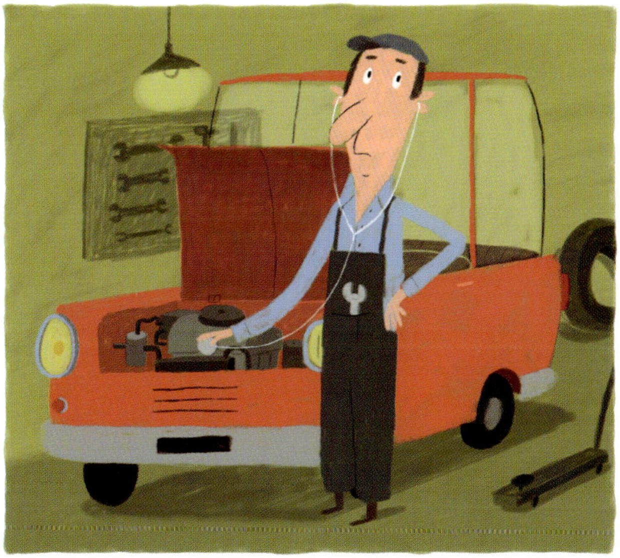

Να προσέχουμε για την **καλή κατάσταση του αυτοκινήτου μας**, κάνοντας συχνά σέρβις.

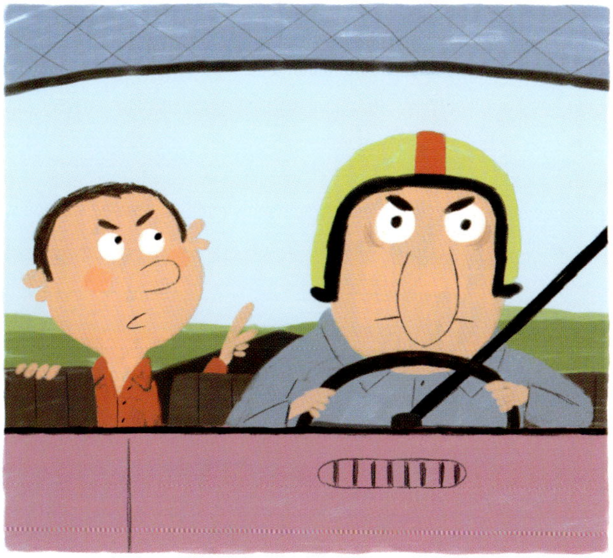

Να μειώνουμε την ταχύτητα όταν οδηγούμε, γιατί όσο πιο γρήγορα τρέχουμε τόσο περισσότερο μολύνουμε την ατμόσφαιρα.

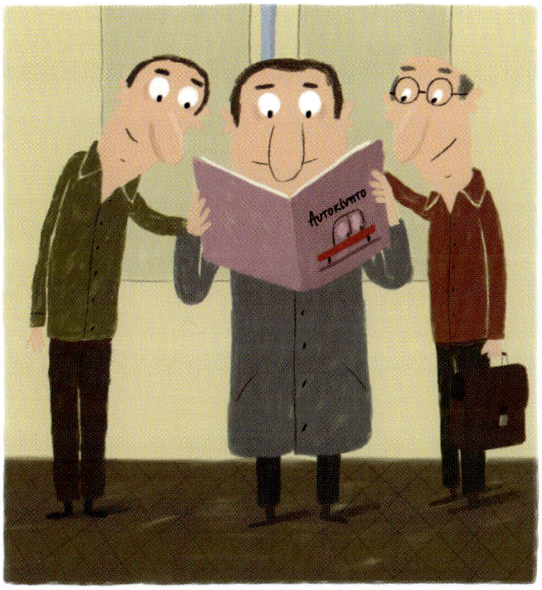

Να προτιμάμε τα **μέσα μαζικής μεταφοράς** ή το ποδήλατό μας!

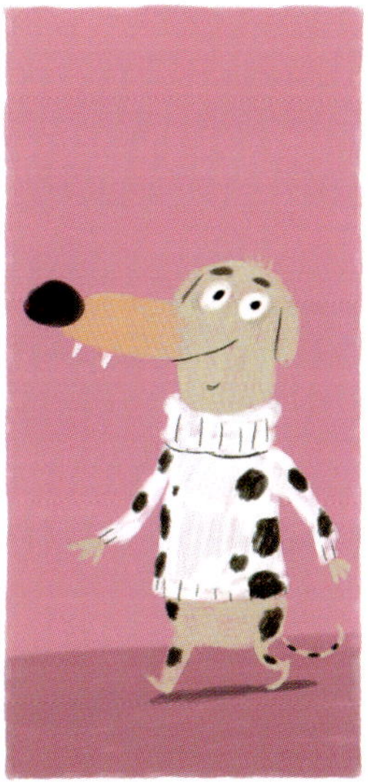

Να μειώνουμε τη θέρμανση μέσα στο σπίτι.

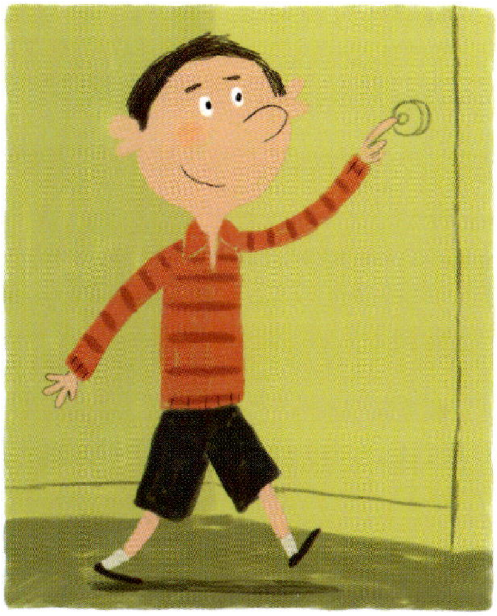

Πρέπει επίσης να σκεφτόμαστε να **σβήνουμε** τις ηλεκτρικές συσκευές ή το φως κάθε φορά που βγαίνουμε από ένα δωμάτιο.

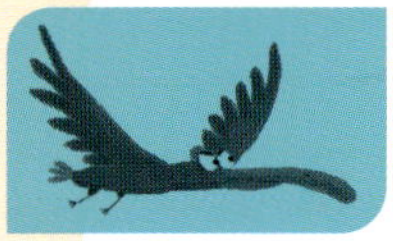

Ξεχωρίζω και ανακυκλώνω τα σκουπίδια

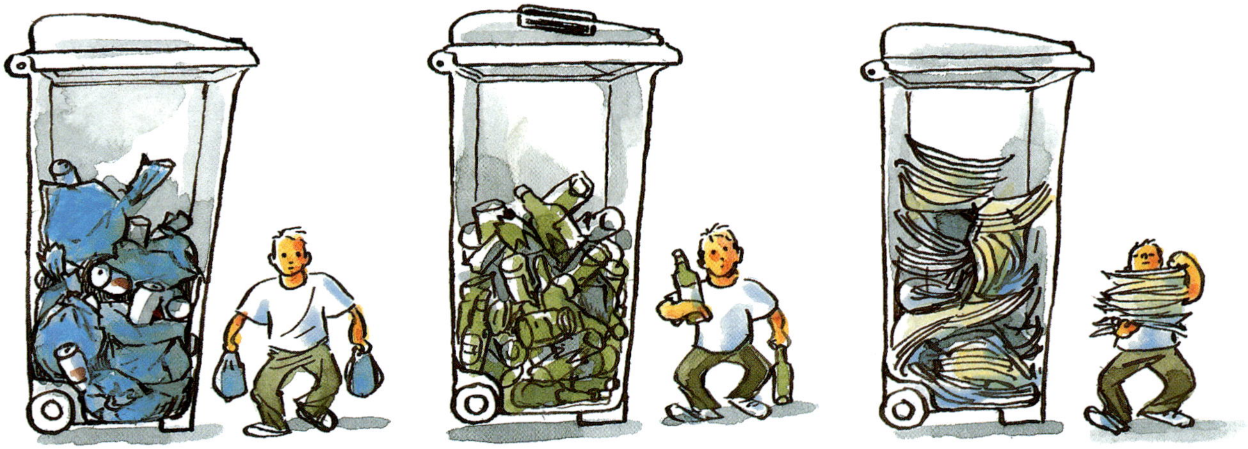

Κάθε μέρα χρησιμοποιούμε χαρτί, πλαστικά μπουκάλια, μεταλλικά κουτιά… που γίνονται σκουπίδια. Αυτά τα σκουπίδια πρέπει να τα **ξεχωρίζουμε**, γιατί πολλά από αυτά μπορούν να **ανακυκλωθούν**, δηλαδή να ξαναχρησιμοποιηθούν. Τα σκουπίδια που δεν ανακυκλώνονται καίγονται.

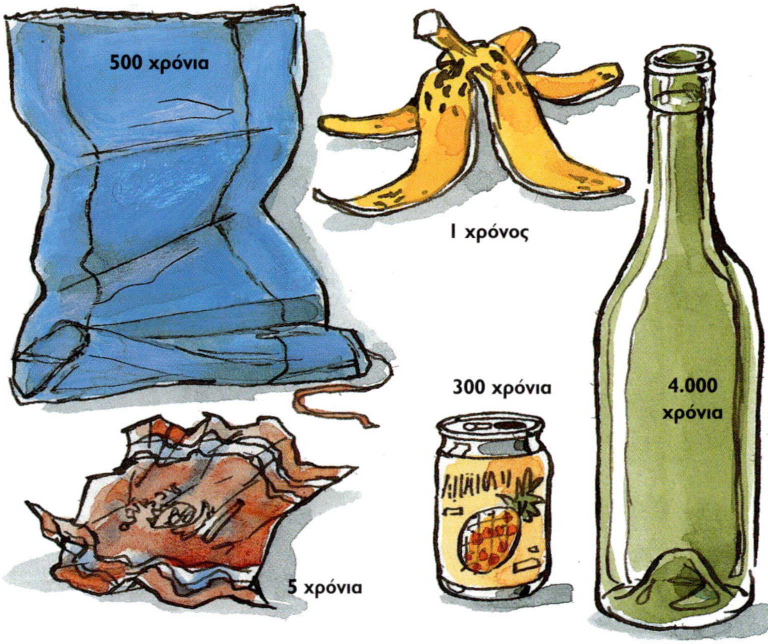

Δεν πρέπει **να πετάμε τίποτα** στη φύση, γιατί κάποια σκουπίδια χρειάζονται πολύ χρόνο για να εξαφανιστούν.

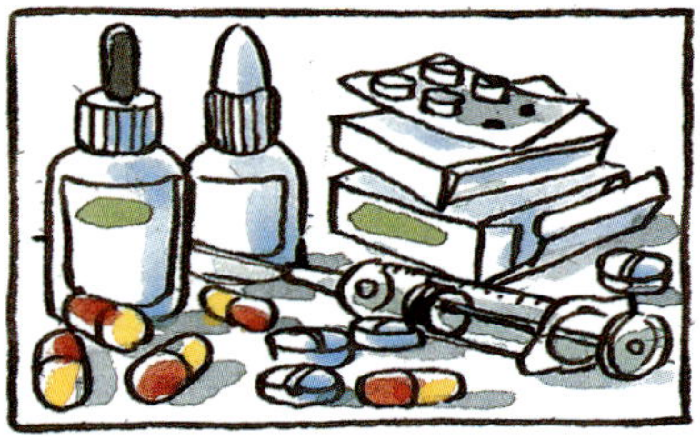

Οι **μπαταρίες μολύνουν** το νερό, πρέπει λοιπόν να τις βάζουμε σε ειδικά κουτιά. Τα **φάρμακα** μπορούμε να τα δίνουμε πίσω στο φαρμακείο.

Τα αντικείμενα για ανακύκλωση **ξεχωρίζονται**
με το χέρι στο εργοστάσιο ανακύκλωσης.
Γι' αυτό πρέπει να σεβόμαστε τις οδηγίες.

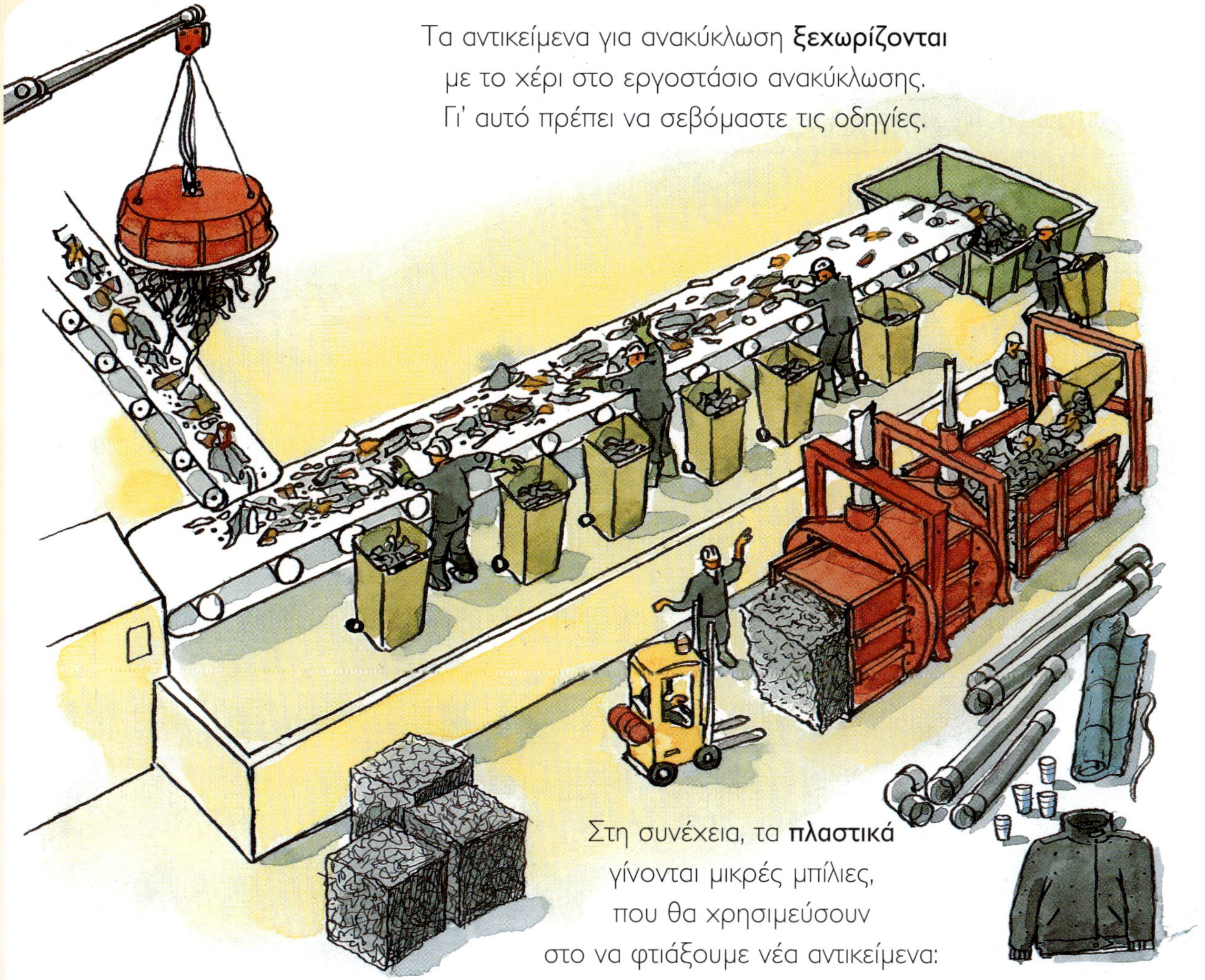

Στη συνέχεια, τα **πλαστικά**
γίνονται μικρές μπίλιες,
που θα χρησιμεύσουν
στο να φτιάξουμε νέα αντικείμενα:
ποτήρια, σακούλες σκουπιδιών,
ρούχα...

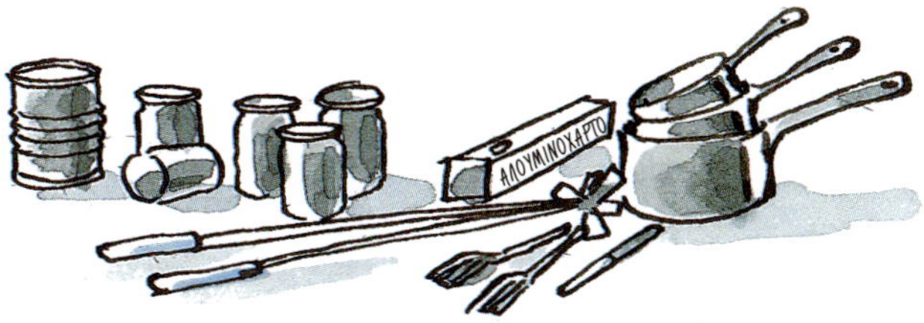

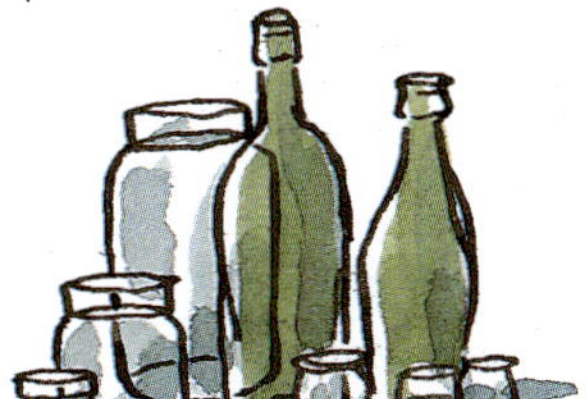

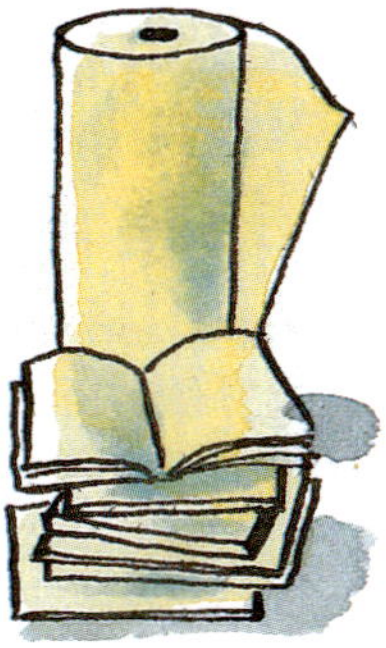

Τα **αλουμινένια κουτιά** θα χρησιμεύσουν
στο να φτιάξουμε νέα κουτιά κονσέρβας,
αλουμινόχαρτο, εργαλεία...

Το **γυαλί** αλέθεται, λιώνει
και χρησιμεύει στην παραγωγή
νέων μπουκαλιών, φιαλιδίων...

Το **χαρτί**
παράγει
ανακυκλωμένο
χαρτί.

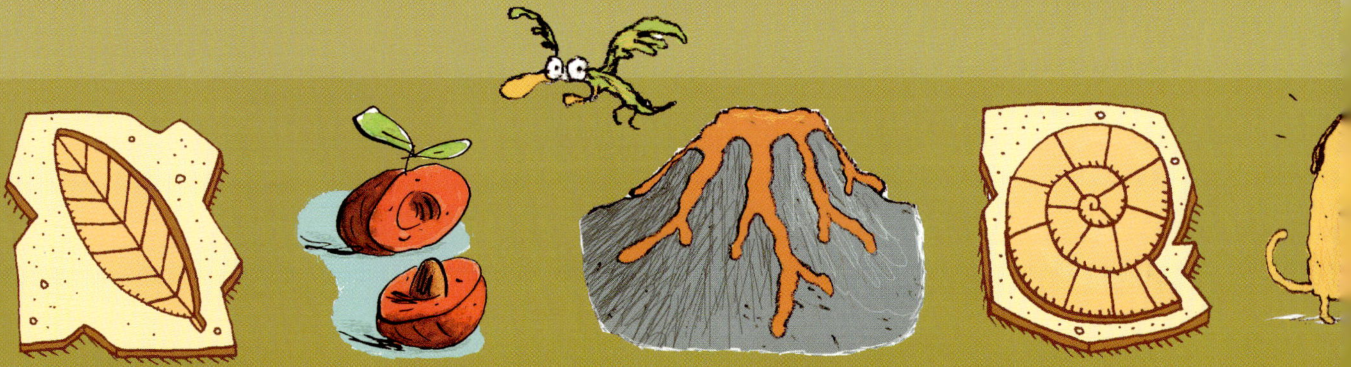

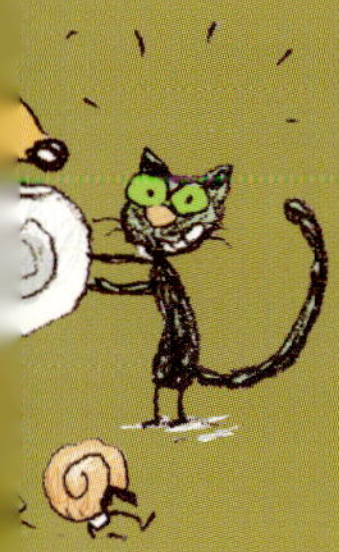

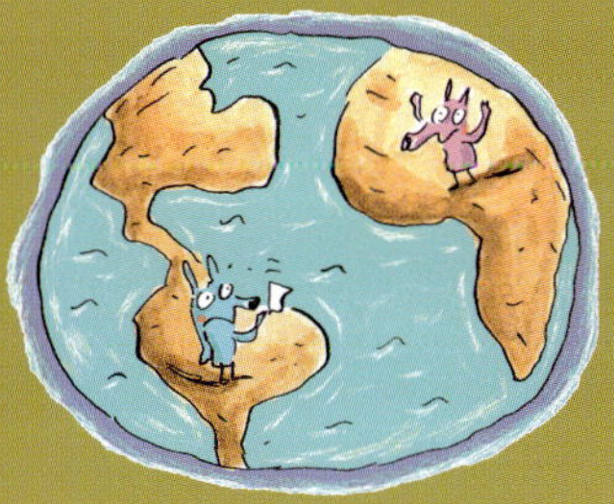

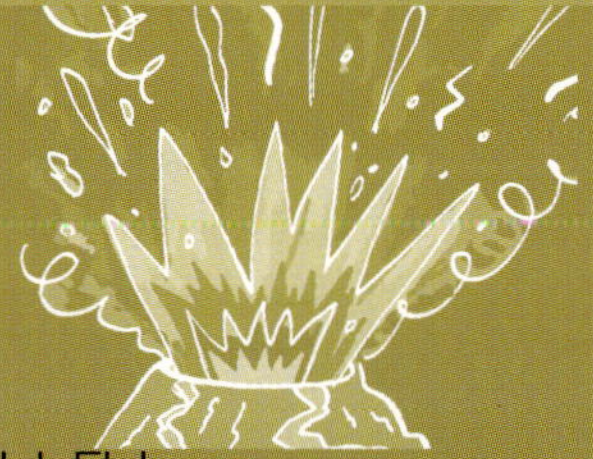

Η ΓΗ

Η ΓΕΩΛΟΓΙΑ

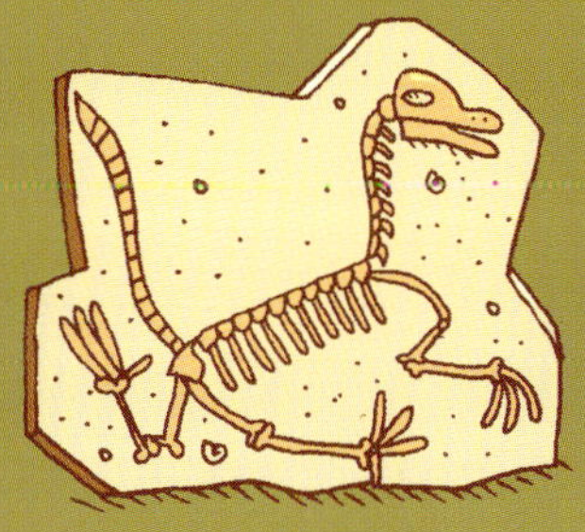

Στο εσωτερικό της Γης

Η Γη μοιάζει με κεράσι. Κάτω από τους ωκεανούς και τις ηπείρους όπου ζούμε, υπάρχουν πολλά στρώματα πετρωμάτων, διαφορετικών πυκνοτήτων.

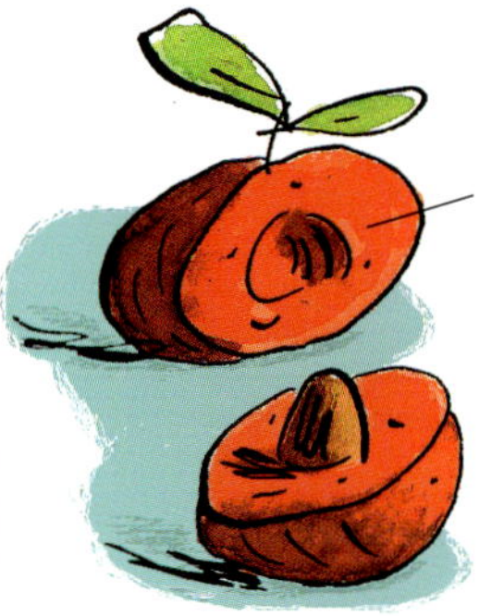

Το πρώτο στρώμα είναι πολύ λεπτό (όπως η φλούδα του κερασιού)· το ονομάζουμε **φλοιό της Γης**. Είναι στερεό.

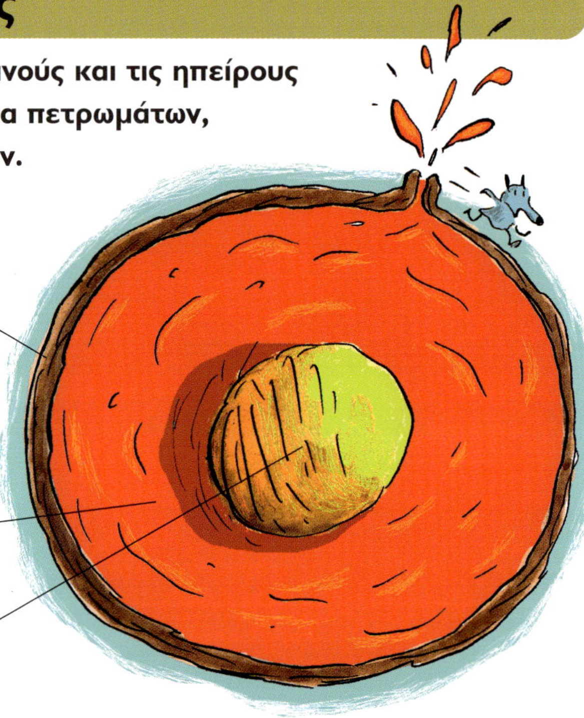

Ο **μανδύας** αποτελείται από ένα στρώμα καυτών πετρωμάτων. Κινείται.

Στο κέντρο της Γης υπάρχει ένας παχύς **πυρήνας**, που αποτελείται από μέταλλο.

Ο φλοιός της Γης δεν αποτελείται από ένα κομμάτι αλλά από **μεγάλες πλάκες**. Κάτω από το φλοιό, ο μανδύας κινείται αδιάκοπα και κάνει τις πλάκες να κινούνται. Έτσι, με το πέρασμα του χρόνου, οι ήπειροι άλλαξαν θέση.

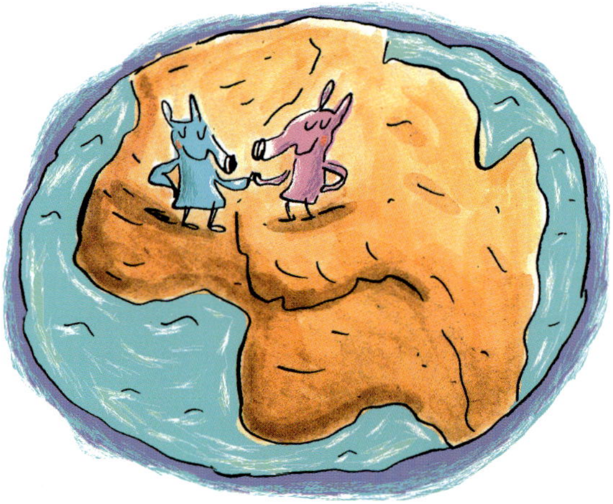

Τα πρώτα χρόνια της Γης, η **Αμερική** και η **Αφρική** ήταν κολλημένες.

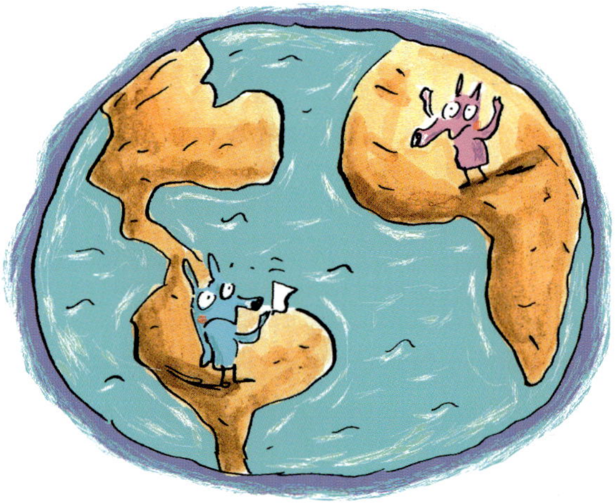

Σιγά σιγά οι ήπειροι **απομακρύνθηκαν**, μέχρι που πήραν τη σημερινή τους θέση.

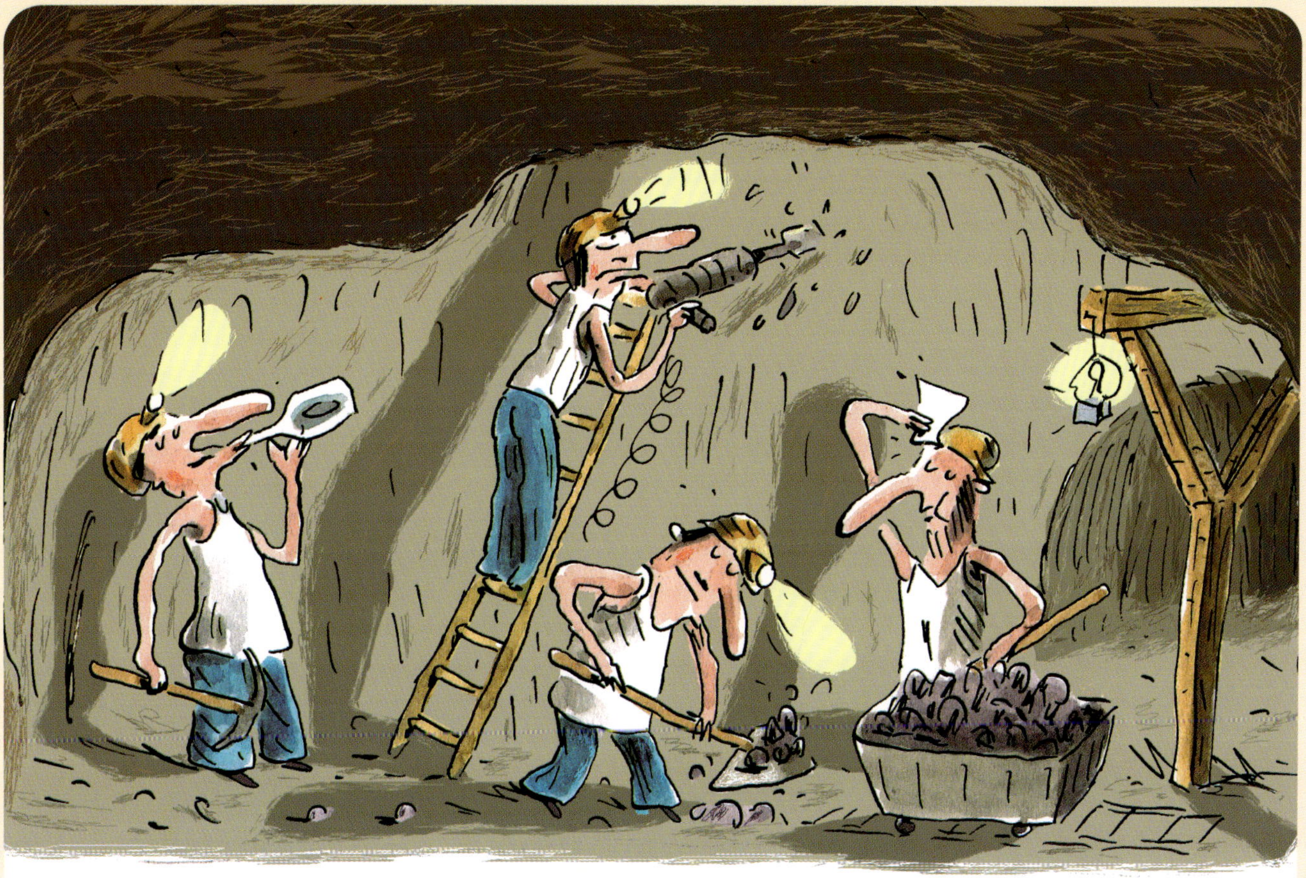

Το εσωτερικό της Γης **καίει**. Βαθιά στα ορυχεία, μόνο 3 χλμ. κάτω από τη γη, η θερμοκρασία του πετρώματος ξεπερνά τους 50 βαθμούς Κελσίου. Εκεί όπου αρχίζει ο μανδύας, η θερμοκρασία φτάνει τους 1.000 βαθμούς. Στο κέντρο του πυρήνα έχει 6.000 βαθμούς Κελσίου.

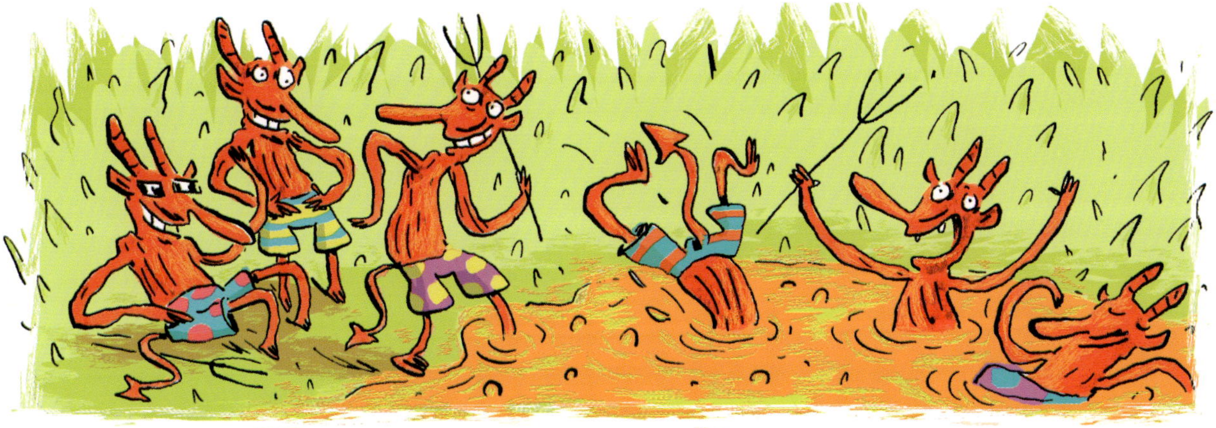

Το **κέντρο της Γης** βρίσκεται 6.000 χλμ. κάτω από τα πόδια μας. Η πιο βαθιά τρύπα που έχουν καταφέρει να σκάψουν οι άνθρωποι είναι 12 χλμ.

Τα ηφαίστεια

Τα ηφαίστεια είναι βουνά. Μερικές φορές ξυπνάνε και ξερνάνε καυτή λάβα, πετρώματα που καπνίζουν, αέρια και σκόνη: αυτή είναι η ηφαιστειακή έκρηξη.

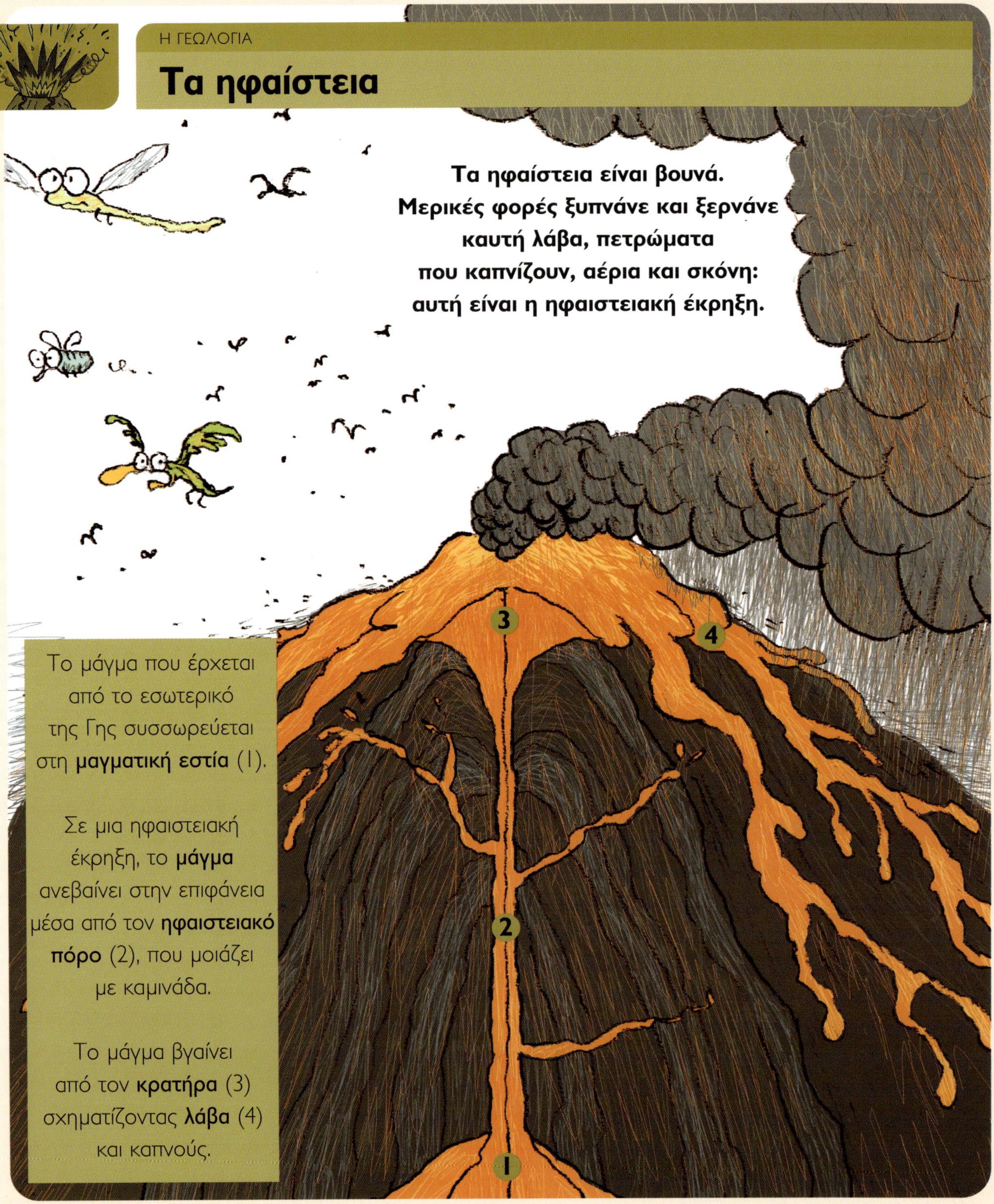

Το μάγμα που έρχεται από το εσωτερικό της Γης συσσωρεύεται στη **μαγματική εστία** (1).

Σε μια ηφαιστειακή έκρηξη, το **μάγμα** ανεβαίνει στην επιφάνεια μέσα από τον **ηφαιστειακό πόρο** (2), που μοιάζει με καμινάδα.

Το μάγμα βγαίνει από τον **κρατήρα** (3) σχηματίζοντας **λάβα** (4) και καπνούς.

Υπάρχουν τρία μεγάλα είδη ηφαιστειακών εκρήξεων.

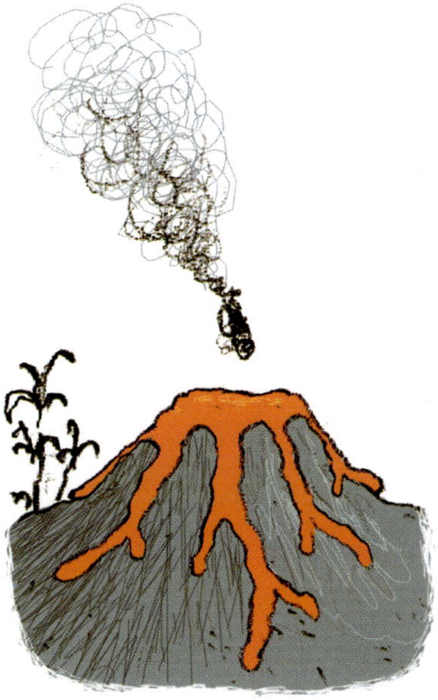

Αν η λάβα είναι **υγρή**, τρέχει γρήγορα. Δε γίνεται έκρηξη. Ο κόσμος προλαβαίνει να φύγει.

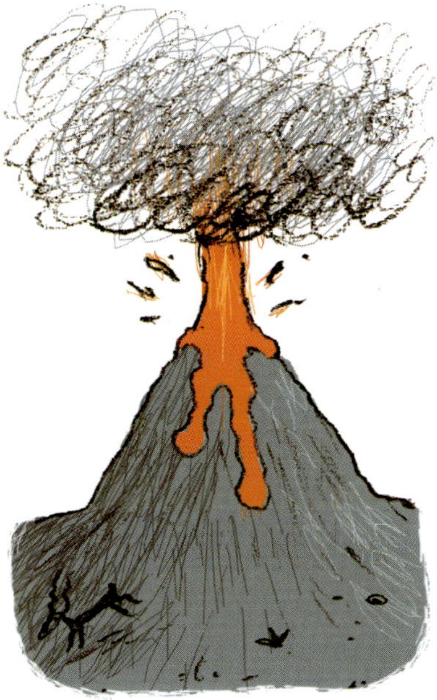

Αν η λάβα είναι **πιο πυκνή**, κυλά πιο αργά, όμως το σύννεφο αερίων και στάχτης μπορεί να γίνει επικίνδυνο.

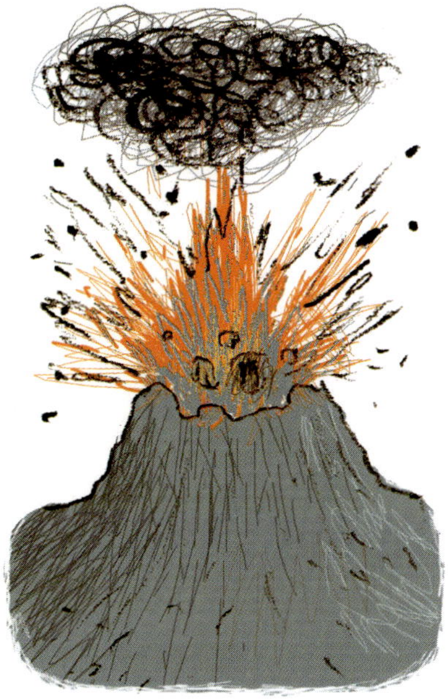

Αν η λάβα περιέχει **πολλά αέρια**, θα γίνει σίγουρα έκρηξη. Ο κόσμος δεν προλαβαίνει να φύγει.

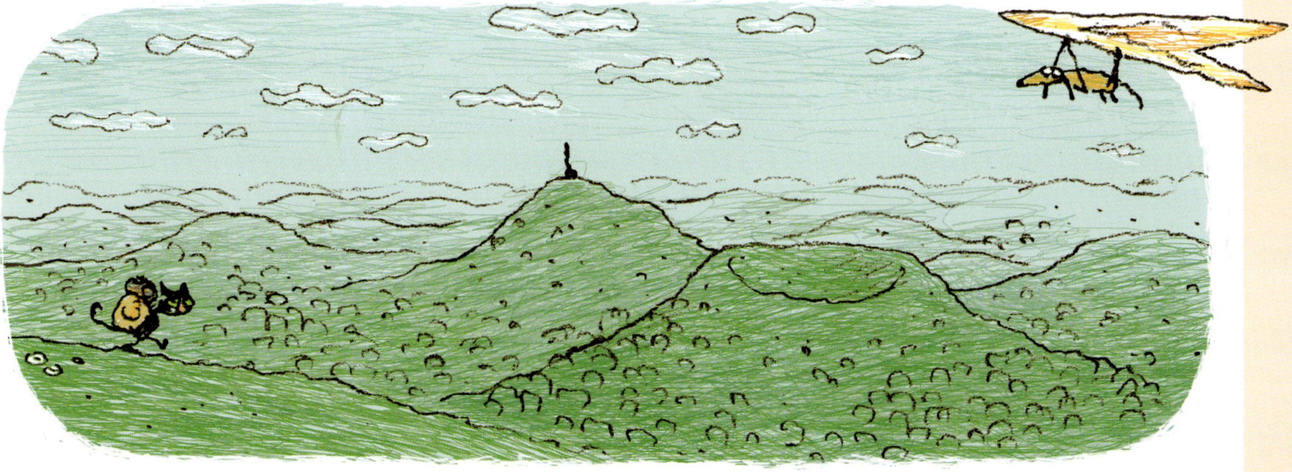

Τα ηφαίστεια που δεν έχουν εκραγεί εδώ και πολύ καιρό λέγονται **ενεργά**. Στην Ελλάδα υπάρχουν αρκετά ενεργά ηφαίστεια. Τα πιο γνωστά είναι της Σαντορίνης και της Νισύρου.

ΣειΡΑ σΟΥ νΑ ΠαίΞεις!

Για να καταλάβεις καλύτερα πώς γίνονται οι διάφορες ηφαιστειακές εκρήξεις, μπορείς να κάνεις **τρία πειράματα**. Καλύτερα να τα κάνεις στον κήπο με τη βοήθεια ενός μεγαλύτερου.

Για κάθε πείραμα θα χρειαστείς:

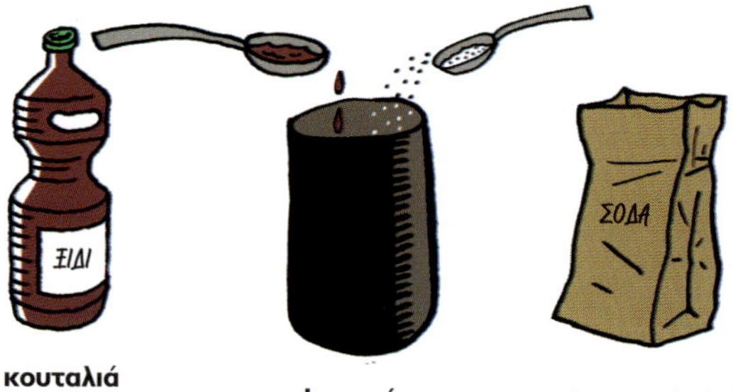

1 κουταλιά της σούπας ξίδι

1 κουτί από φιλμ

1 κουταλιά γλυκού δισανθρακική σόδα

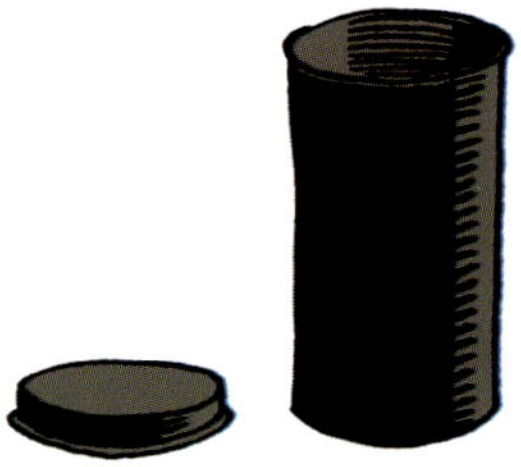

πείραμα χωρίς καπάκι

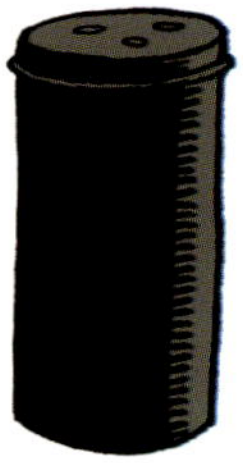

πείραμα με τρυπημένο καπάκι

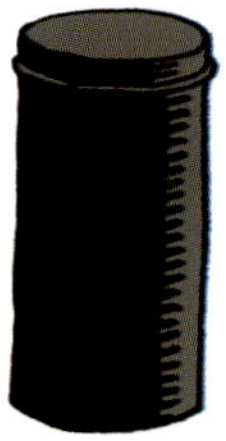

πείραμα με κλειστό καπάκι

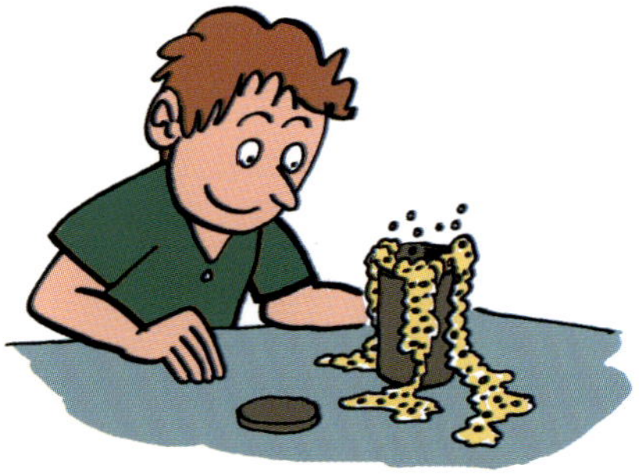

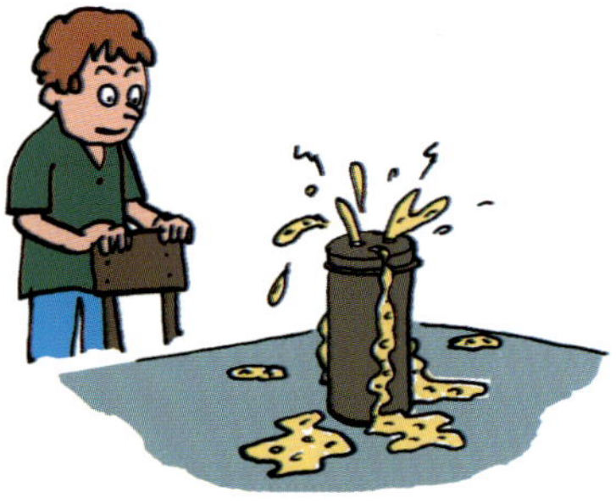

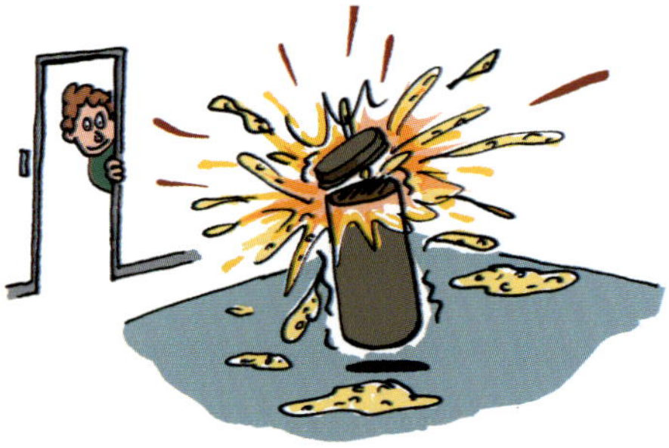

Το υγρό **ανεβαίνει αργά** και κυλά σιγά σιγά έξω από το κουτί.

Το υγρό **κυλά** από τις τρύπες με κάποιες μικρές εκρήξεις υγρού.

Το υγρό αρχίζει να τρέχει, πιέζει το καπάκι, το οποίο τελικά **πετάγεται** βίαια.

Διαπιστώνουμε λοιπόν ότι όσο πιο εύκολα κυλά το υγρό τόσο μικρότερη πιθανότητα έκρηξης υπάρχει. Αυτό ακριβώς συμβαίνει και με τις ηφαιστειακές εκρήξεις.

Αυτά τα τρία πειράματα αντιστοιχούν στις **τρεις μορφές ηφαιστειακής έκρηξης**.

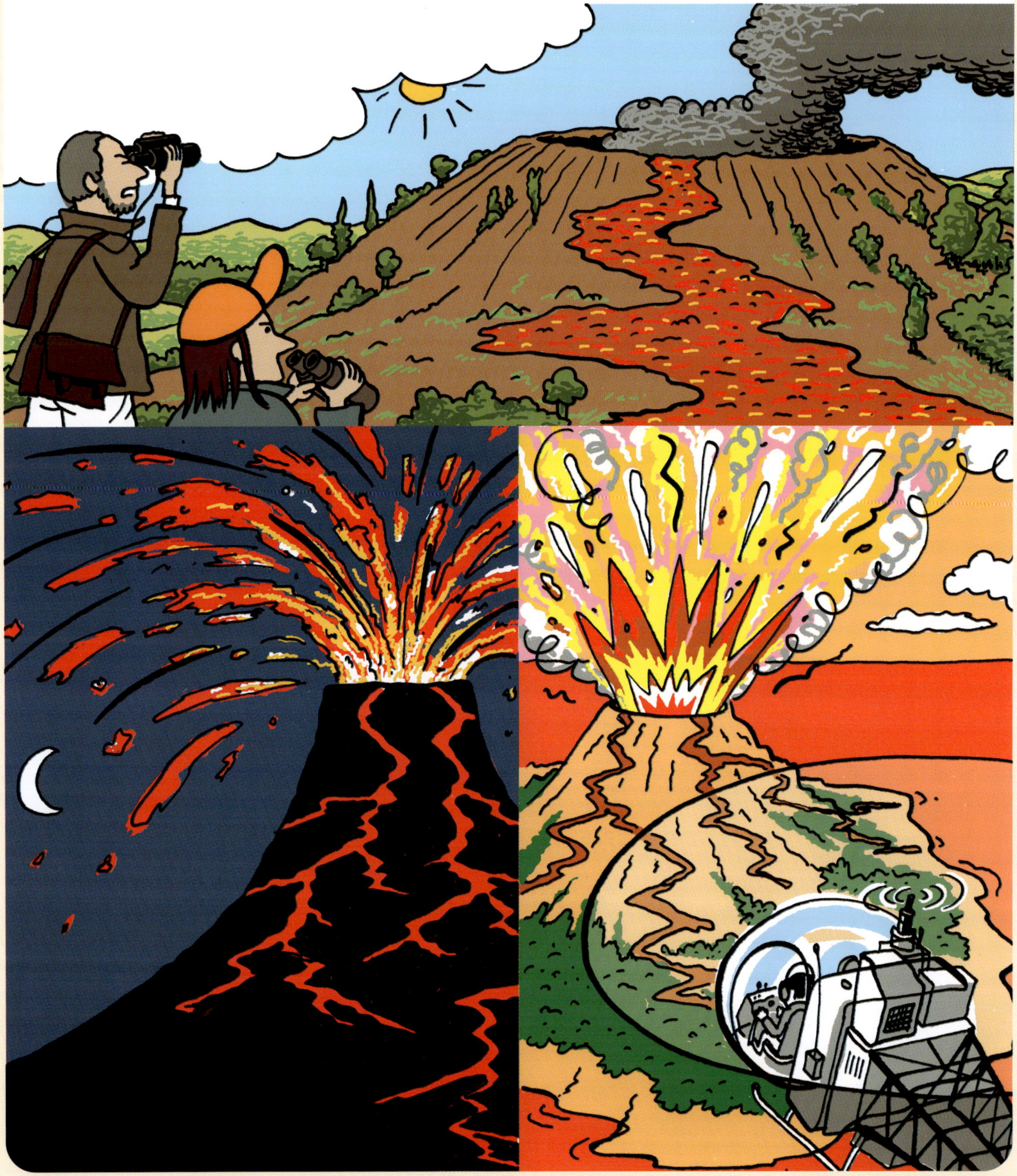

Οι σεισμοί

Σε όλο τον κόσμο η γη τρέμει πολλές φορές τη μέρα. Αυτό το τρέμουλο της γης οι επιστήμονες το ονομάζουν σεισμό.

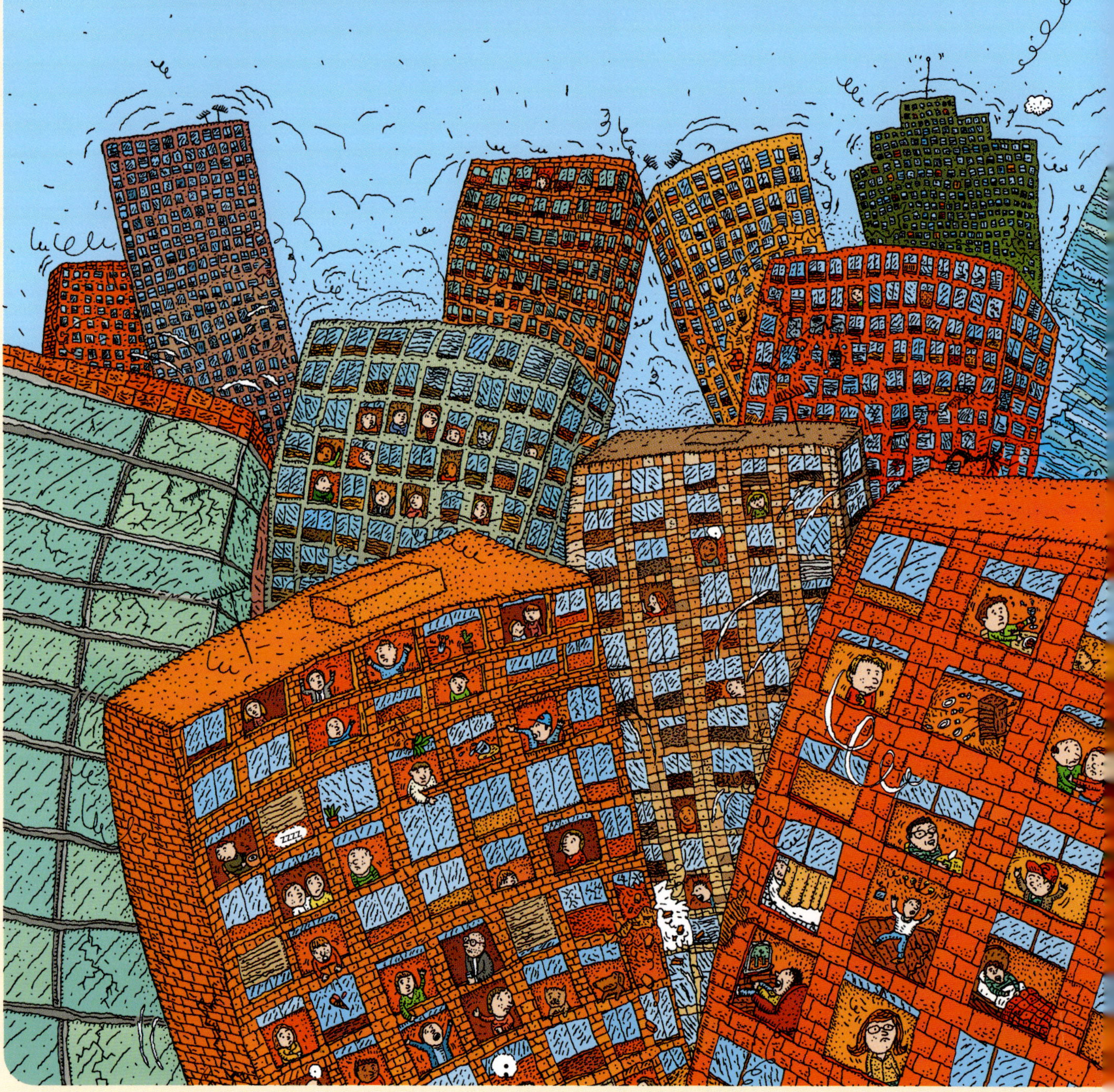

Τα περισσότερα κουνήματα είναι πολύ ελαφρά και δεν τα αισθάνεται κανείς, πολλές φορές όμως είναι ισχυρά και προκαλούν μεγάλες ζημιές.

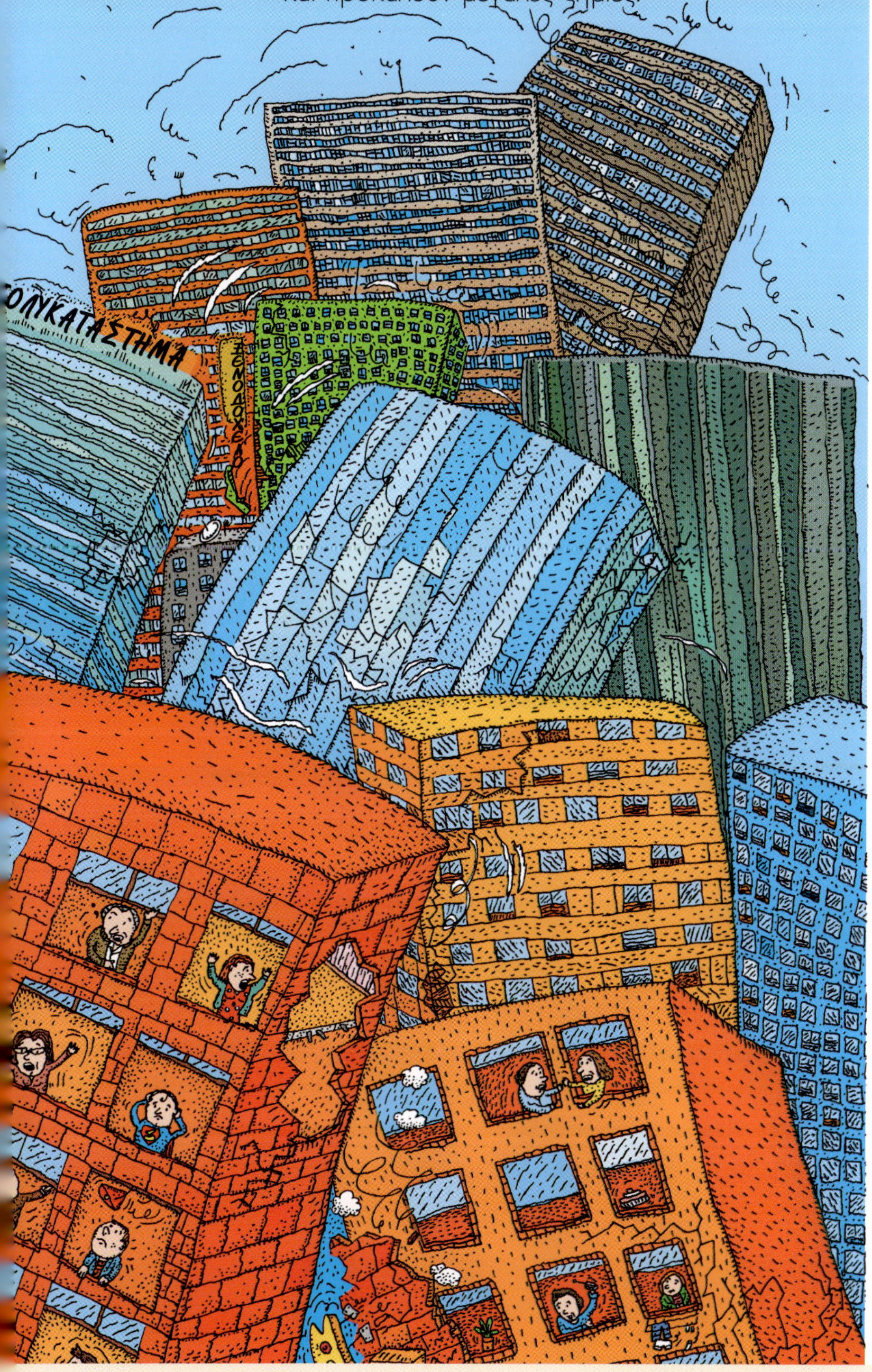

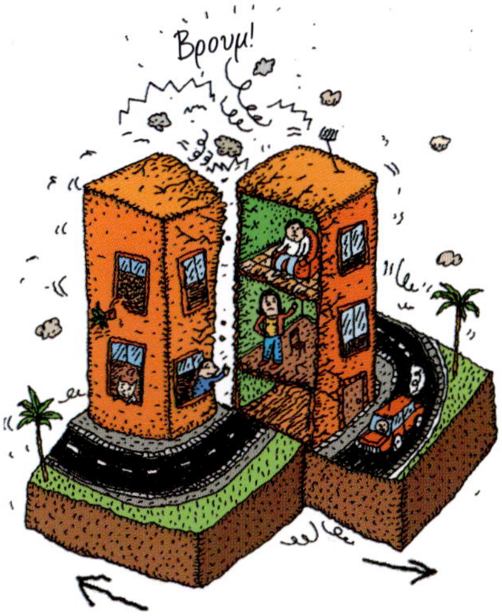

Σε ένα **σεισμό** οι πέτρες που αποτελούν το έδαφος μετακινούνται πλάγια…

…ή από πάνω προς τα κάτω.

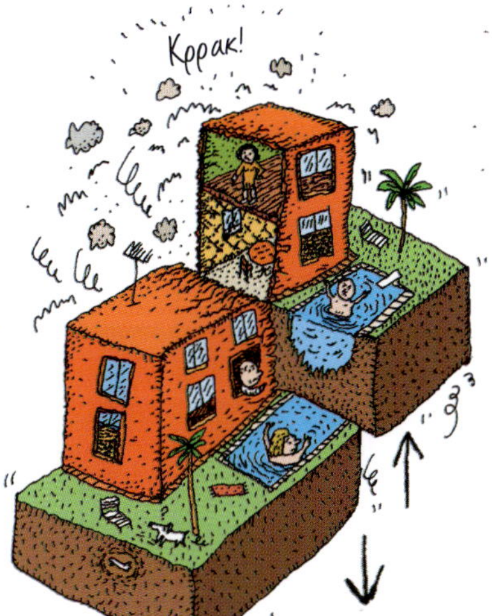

Οι ρωγμές προκαλούνται από τα **σεισμικά κύματα** που διαδίδονται στο έδαφος και κάνουν τα πάντα να τρέμουν.

Η κλίμακα Ρίχτερ

Οι σεισμοί δεν προκαλούν όλοι τις ίδιες «ζημιές». Για να αναγνωρίζουμε το βαθμό της σοβαρότητάς τους, χρησιμοποιούμε μια «κλίμακα», που τη δημιούργησε ένας αμερικανός γεωλόγος, ο Τσαρλς Ρίχτερ: είναι η κλίμακα Ρίχτερ. Έχει 10 επίπεδα.

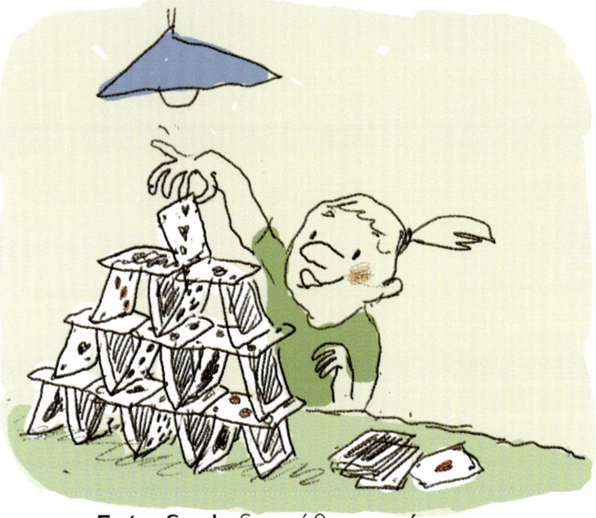

Επίπεδο 1: δε νιώθουμε **τίποτα**.

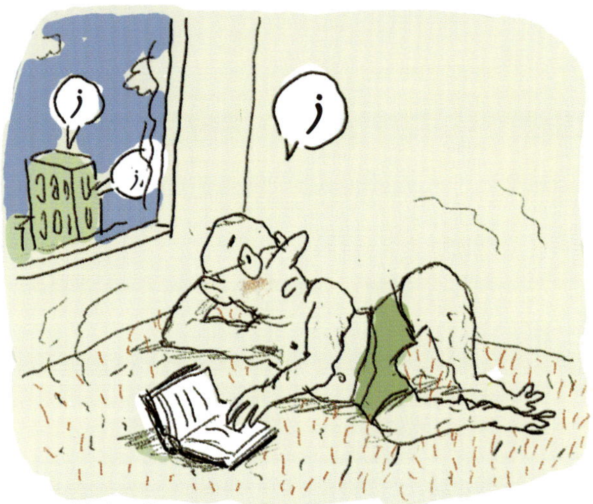

Επίπεδο 2: αισθανόμαστε κάτι στους **πάνω ορόφους**.

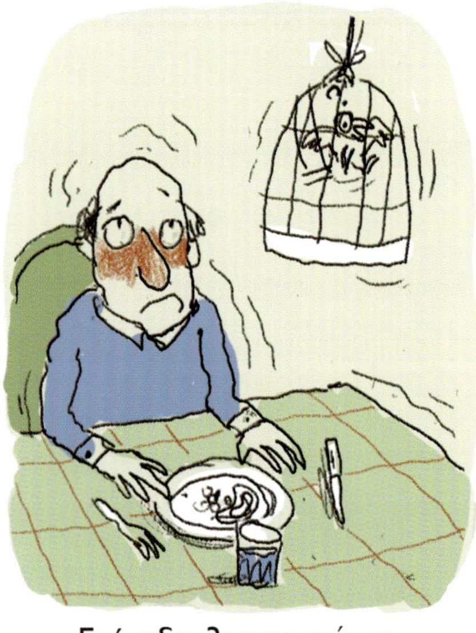

Επίπεδο 3: κουνιούνται τα **αντικείμενα που κρέμονται**.

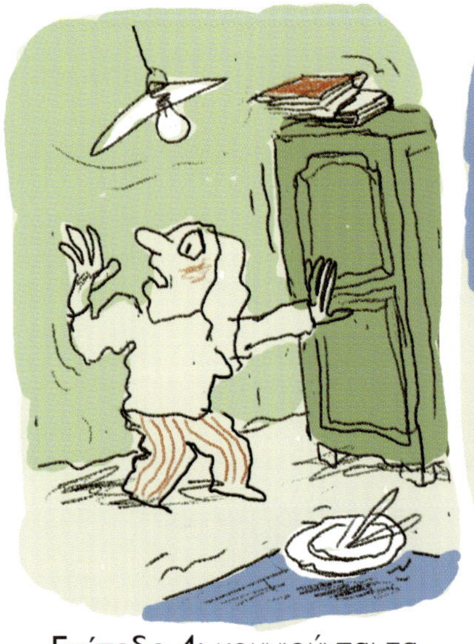

Επίπεδο 4: κουνιούνται τα **παράθυρα** και οι **πόρτες**.

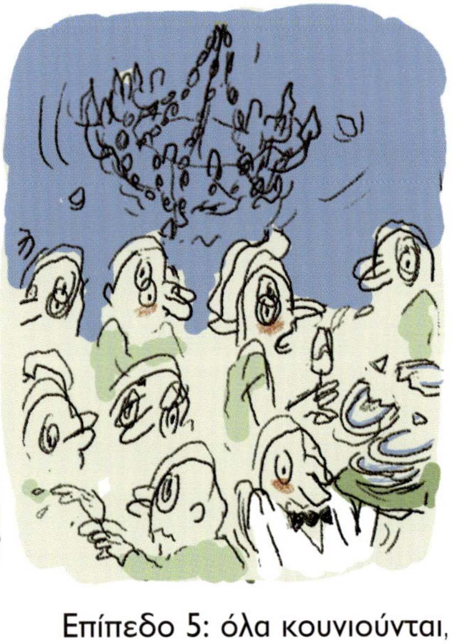

Επίπεδο 5: όλα κουνιούνται, όσοι κοιμούνται ξυπνούν.

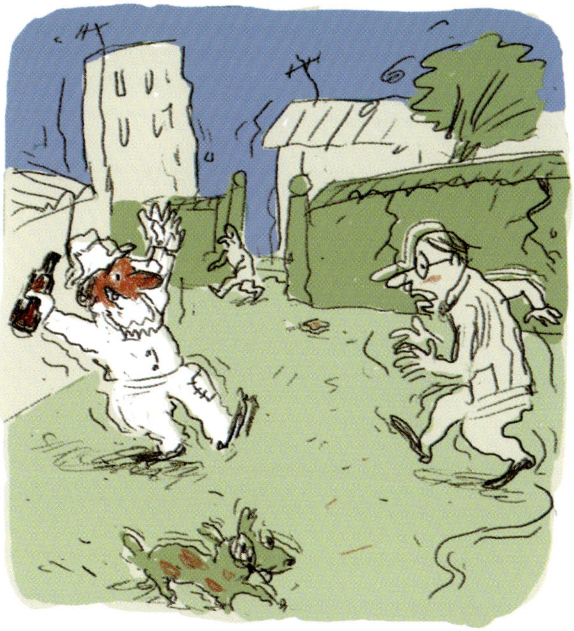

Επίπεδο 6: όλοι νιώθουν το **σεισμό**. Μπορεί να προκληθούν ζημιές.

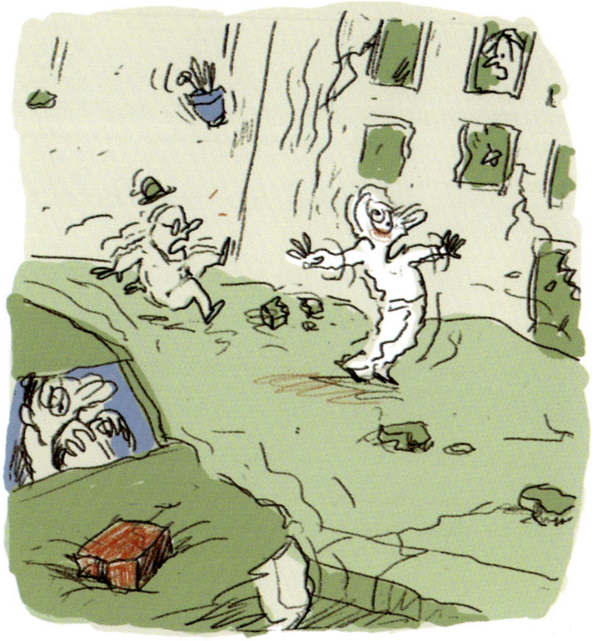

Επίπεδο 7: οι άνθρωποι δεν μπορούν να σταθούν **όρθιοι**. Οι ζημιές μπορεί να είναι πολύ σοβαρές.

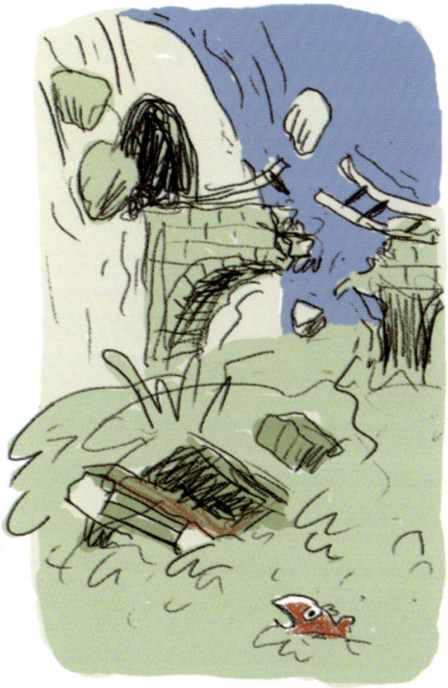

Επίπεδο 8: διαλύονται οι **ράγες**, ξεχειλίζουν τα **ποτάμια**.

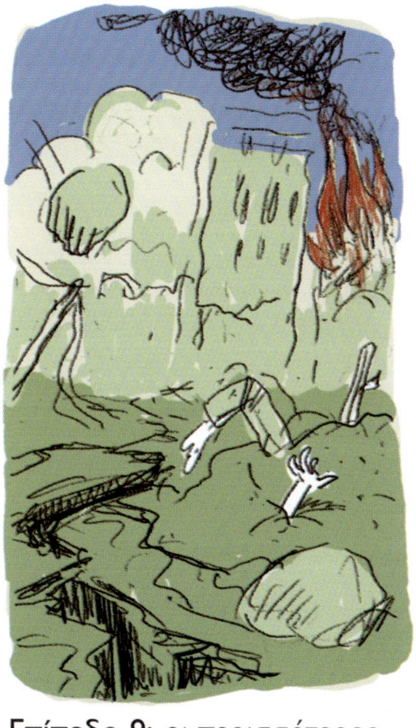

Επίπεδο 9: οι περισσότερες **κατασκευές καταρρέουν**.

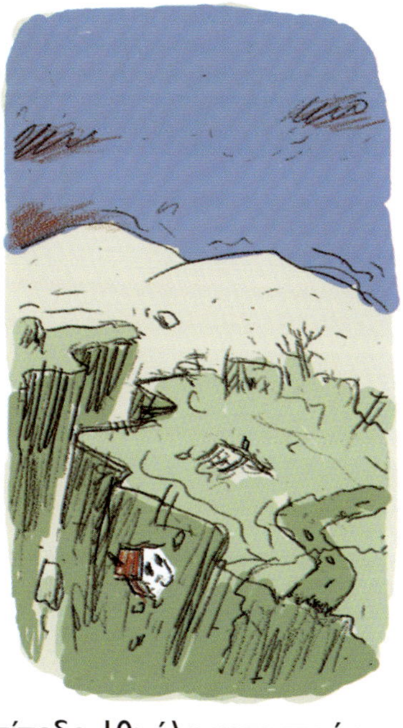

Επίπεδο 10: όλα καταστρέφονται. Το έδαφος δονείται ασταμάτητα.

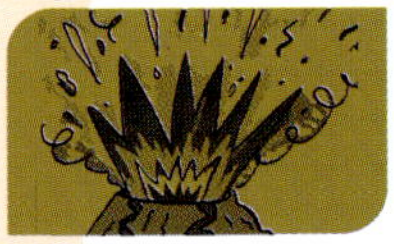

Τι είναι απολίθωμα;

Τα περισσότερα φυτά και ζώα που έζησαν στον πλανήτη μας στην αρχή της ιστορίας της Γης πέθαναν χωρίς ν' αφήσουν ίχνη. Ωστόσο, κάποια άφησαν απολιθώματα.

Τα απολιθώματα είναι τα κατάλοιπα ή τα αποτυπώματα φυτών ή ζώων που έχουν εξαφανιστεί. Υπάρχουν δύο είδη απολιθωμάτων: τα σκληρά μέρη των ζώων (κόκαλα, δόντια, καβούκια) που **μετατρέπονται σε πέτρα** και τα **αποτυπώματα** ενός φυτού ή ενός ζώου **πάνω στην πέτρα**.

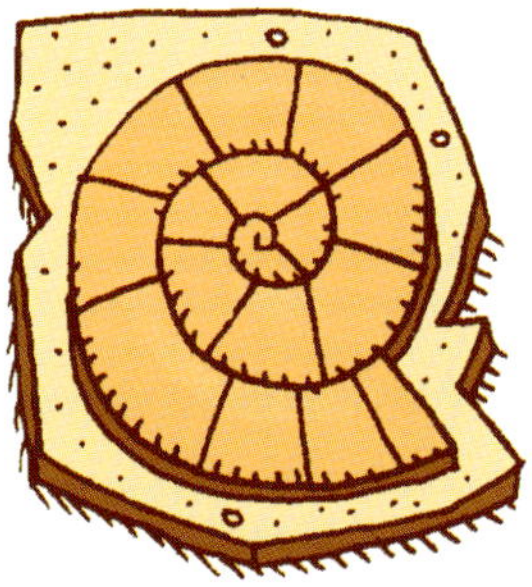

αποτύπωμα κοχυλιού

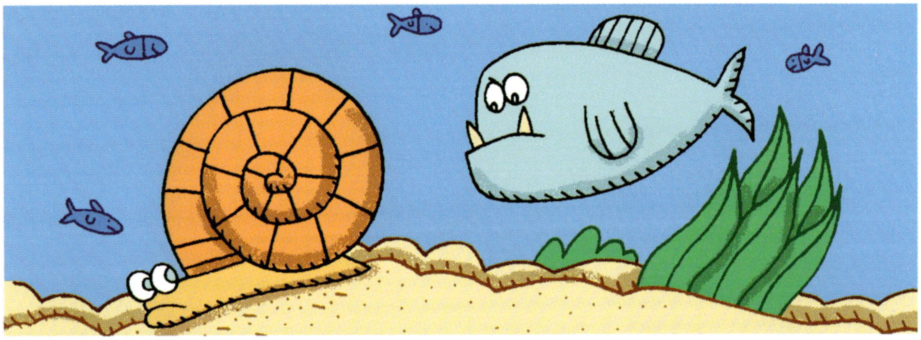

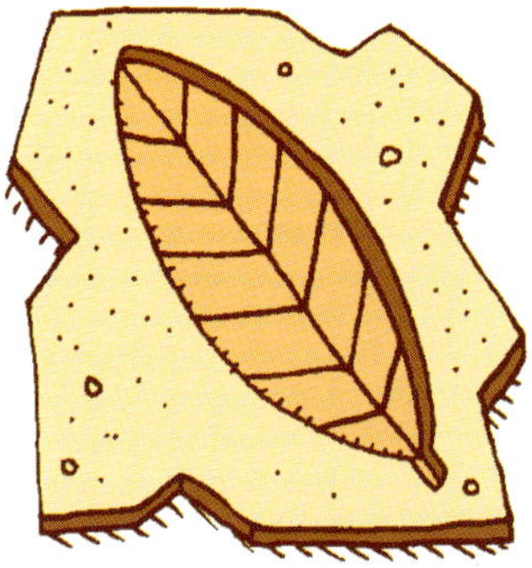

αποτύπωμα φυτού

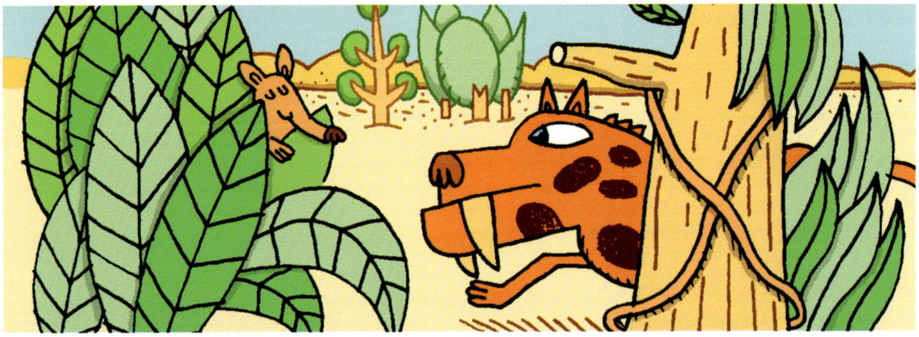

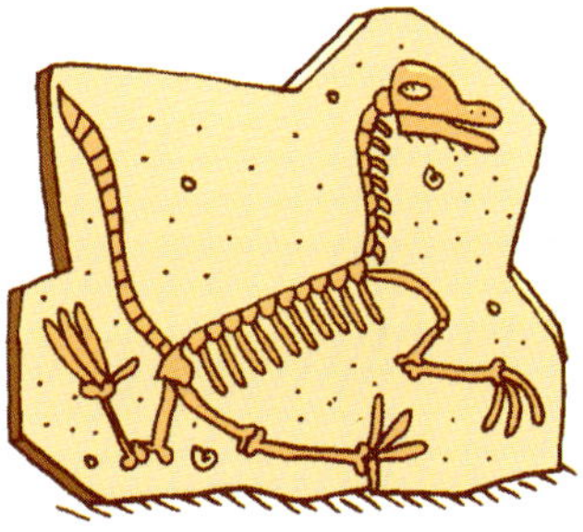

απολίθωμα σκελετού ενός πουλιού που έχει εξαφανιστεί: ο αρχαιοπτέρυξ.

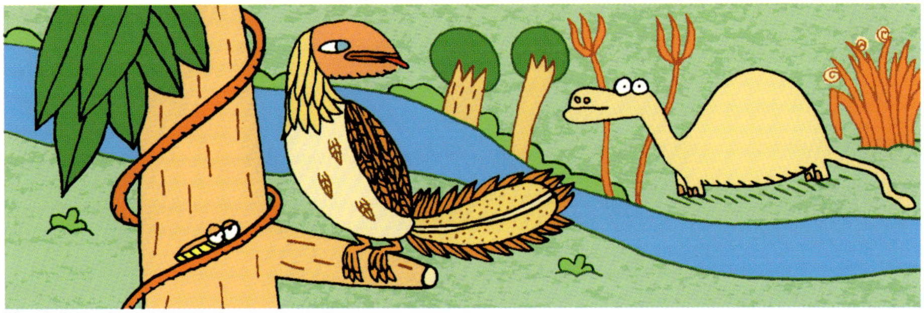

Η μελέτη των απολιθωμάτων μάς επιτρέπει να καταλάβουμε καλύτερα την ιστορία της ζωής στη Γη και ιδιαίτερα την **εξέλιξη** των φυτών και των ζώων.

Πολύ συχνά βρίσκουμε τα **κόκαλα** και τα **δόντια** από δεινόσαυρους ή μαμούθ.

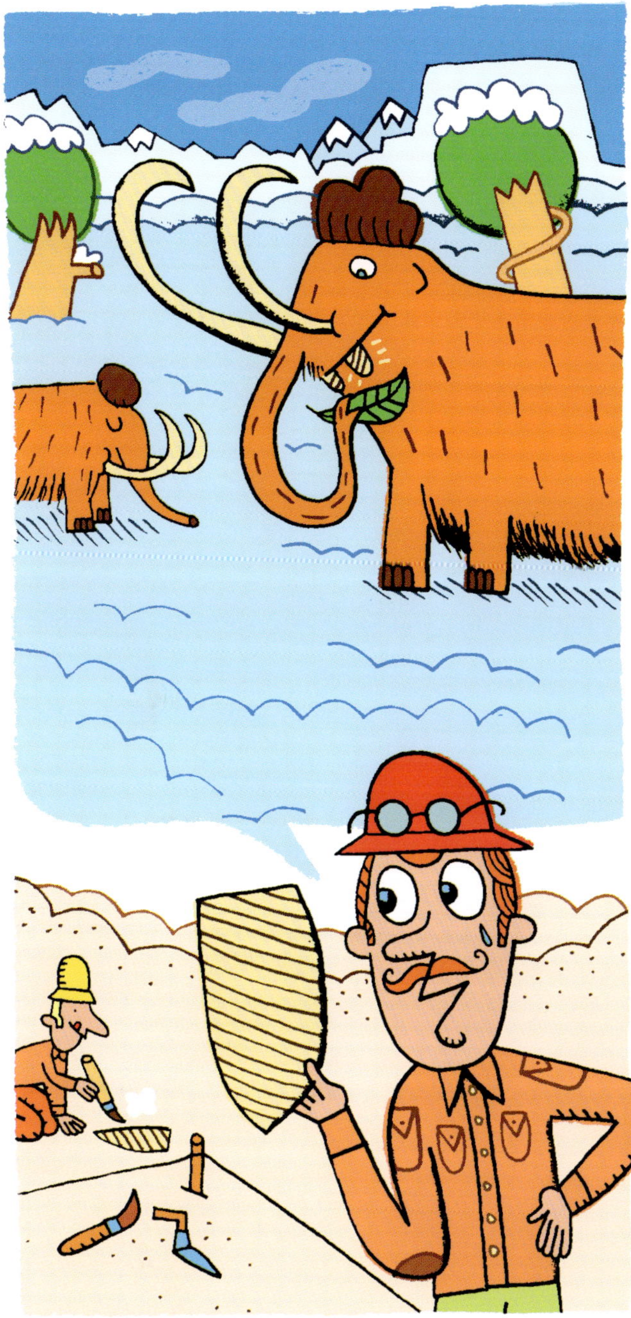

Στη Σιβηρία όμως έχουμε βρει και ολόκληρα μαμούθ, που διατηρήθηκαν μέσα στον πάγο.

Βρίσκουμε ακόμα **αποτυπώματα από βήματα** που άφησαν ζώα ή και προϊστορικοί άνθρωποι.

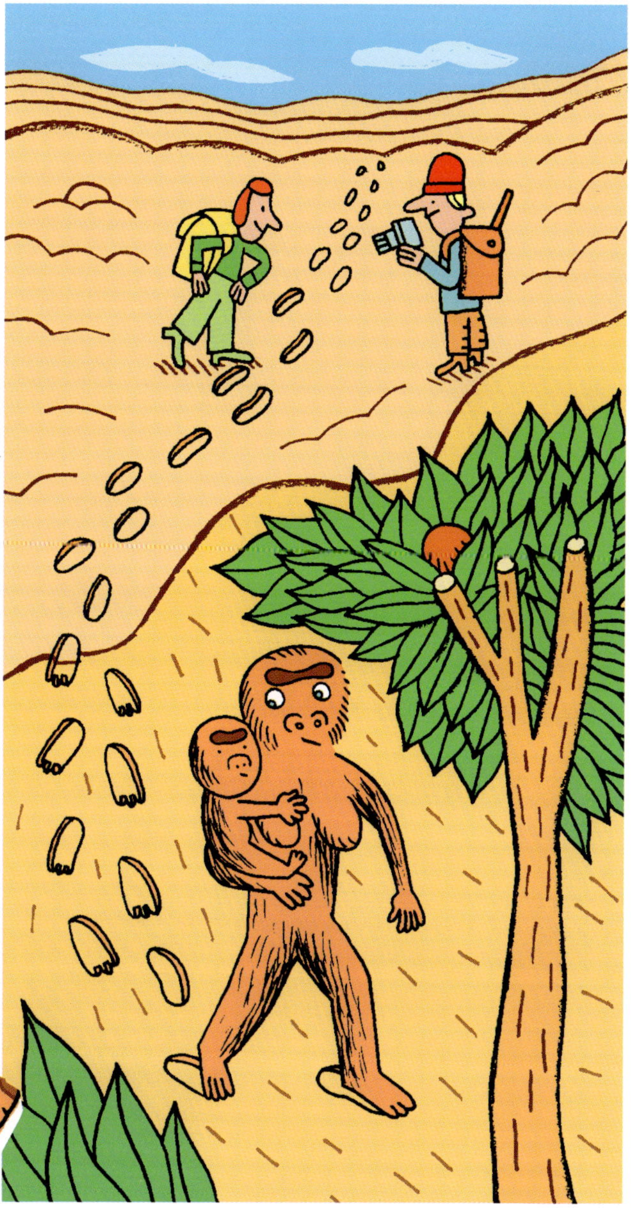

Στην Αφρική βρήκαμε **ίχνη** απολιθωμένων **βημάτων** από προγόνους των ανθρώπων που εξαφανίστηκαν πριν από πολύ πολύ καιρό, τους **αυστραλοπίθηκους**.

Πώς σχηματίζονται τα απολιθώματα;

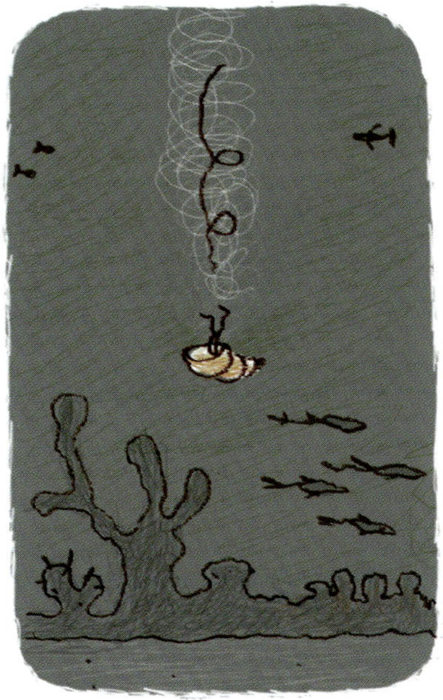

Ένα κοχύλι **πεθαίνει**.

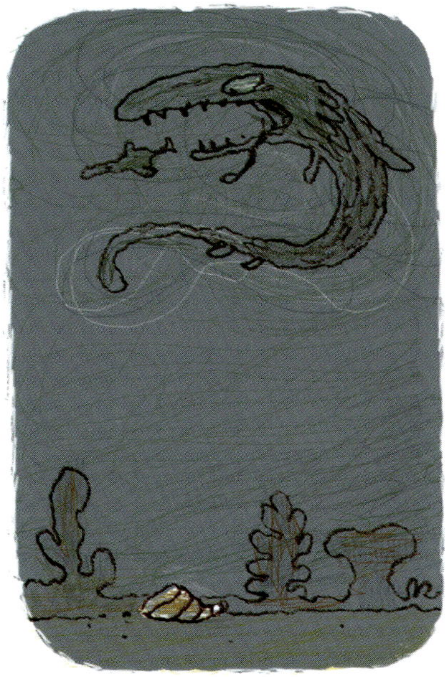

Πέφτει στο **βυθό του νερού**.

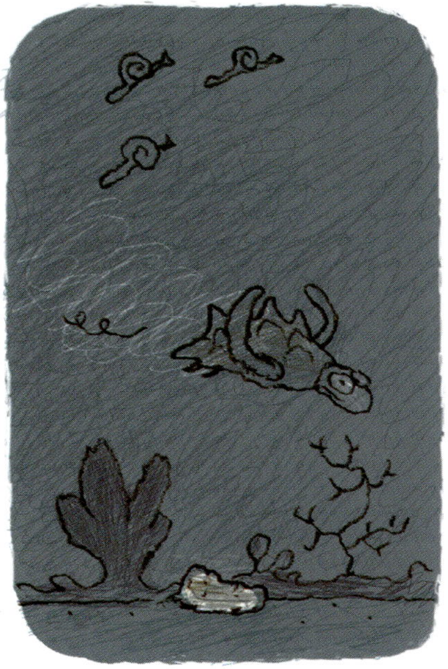

Το σώμα του αποσυντίθεται.
Μένει μόνο το **κέλυφος**.

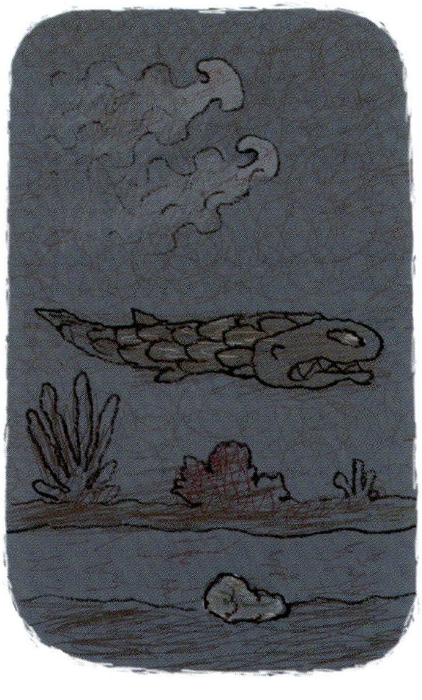

Σιγά σιγά καλύπτεται από **στρώματα λειψάνων** και **άμμου**.

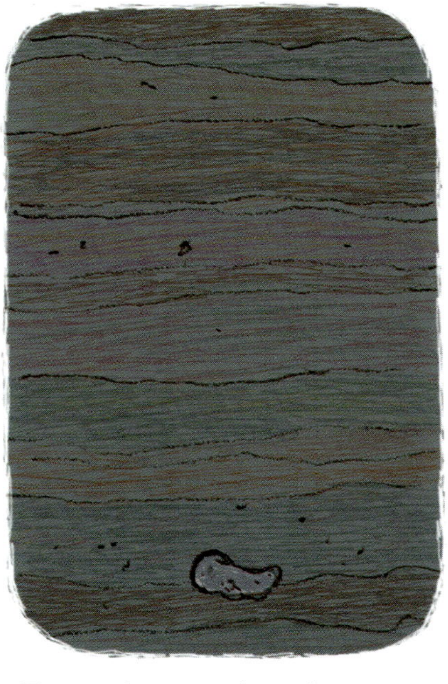

Τα στρώματα σκληραίνουν και μετατρέπονται σε **πετρώματα**.

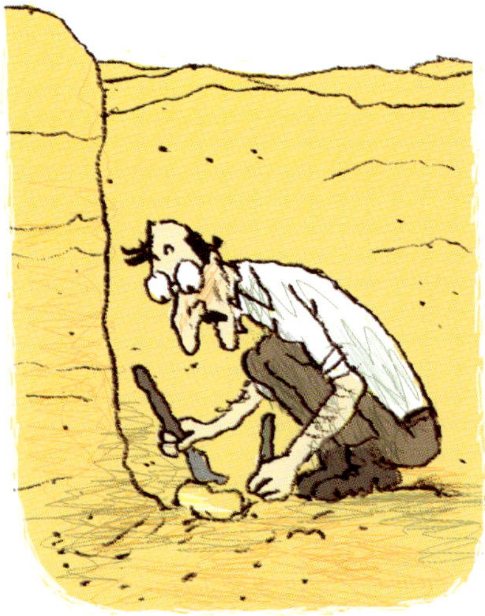

Εκατομμύρια χρόνια αργότερα, ο **γεωλόγος** ανακαλύπτει το **απολίθωμα**.

ΦΤιάΞΕ έΝα ΑποΛΙθωΜΑ

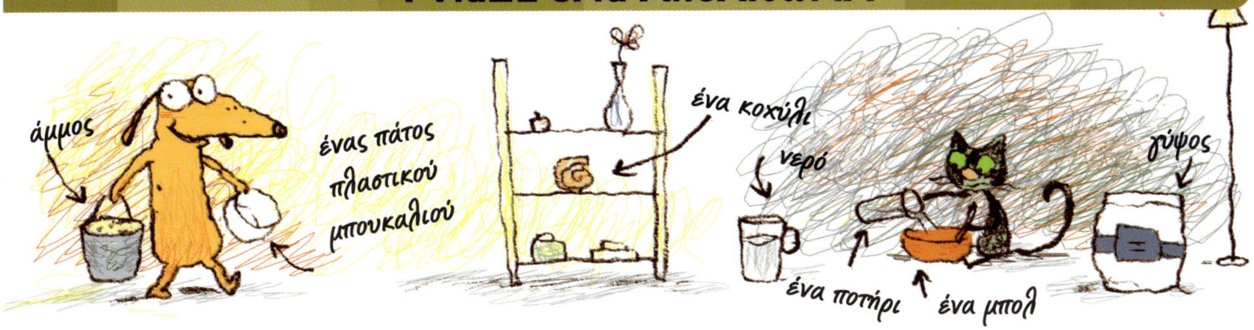

Φτιάξε πρώτα λίγο **γύψο**: βάλε μισό ποτήρι νερό μέσα σ' ένα μπολ, ρίξε ένα ποτήρι γύψο και ανακάτεψε καλά, μέχρι το μείγμα να γίνει πολύ λείο.

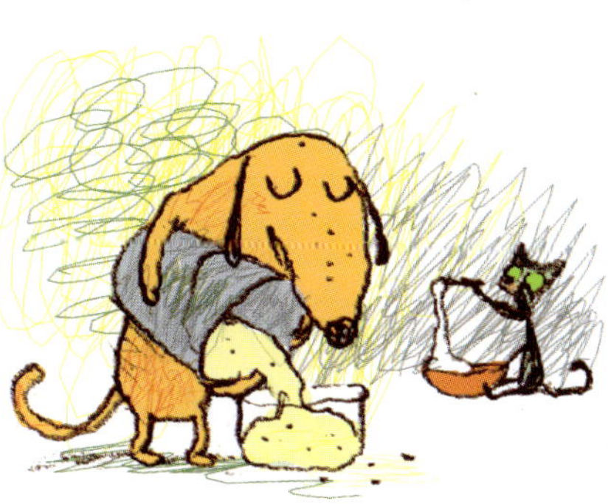

Ρίξε υγρή **άμμο** στον πάτο του μπουκαλιού.

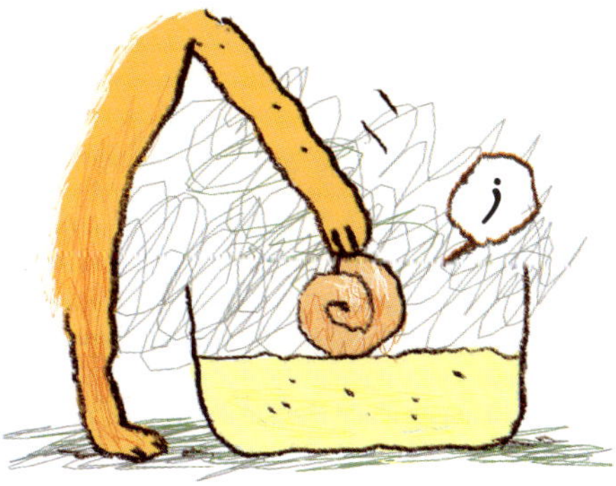

Βάλε το **κοχύλι** πάνω στην άμμο.

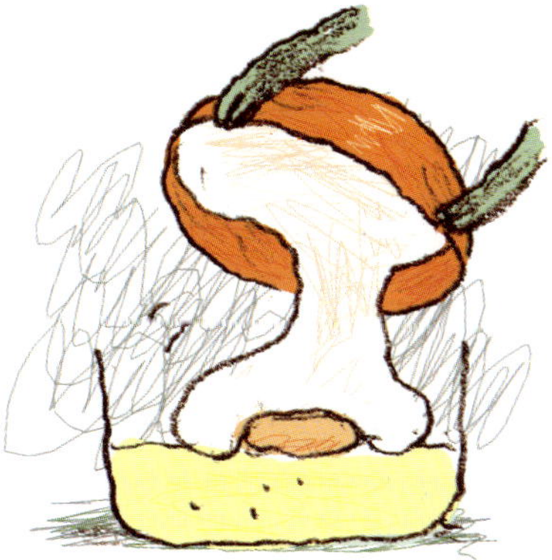

Πρόσθεσε το **γύψο**.

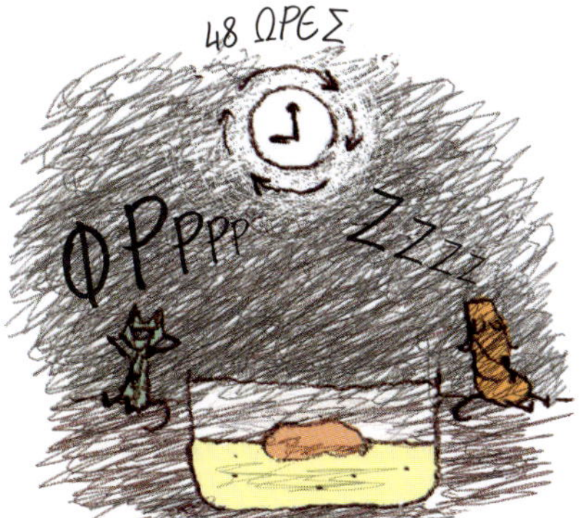

Άφησε να **στεγνώσει** για δύο μέρες.

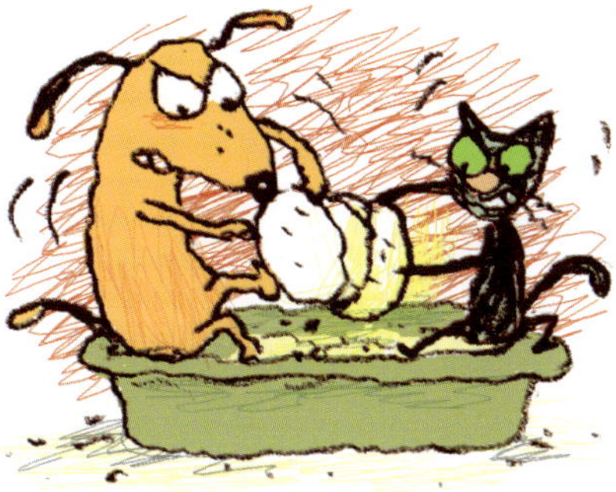

Για να **ξεκολλήσεις το απολίθωμά σου**, κόψε τον πλαστικό πάτο με το ψαλίδι. Μπορείς να τον κόψεις μέσα σε μια λεκάνη, για να μη γεμίσεις παντού άμμο.

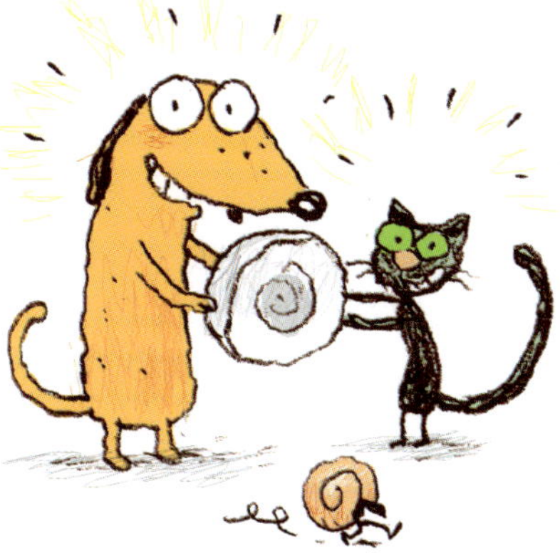

Το καλούπι σου μοιάζει με **απολίθωμα**.

Τα απολιθώματα των κοχυλιών

Τα απολιθώματα που βρίσκουμε συχνότερα είναι τα ίχνη των ζώων που έζησαν πριν από πολύ καιρό μέσα στη θάλασσα. Γιατί τα ξαναβρίσκουμε στη γη;

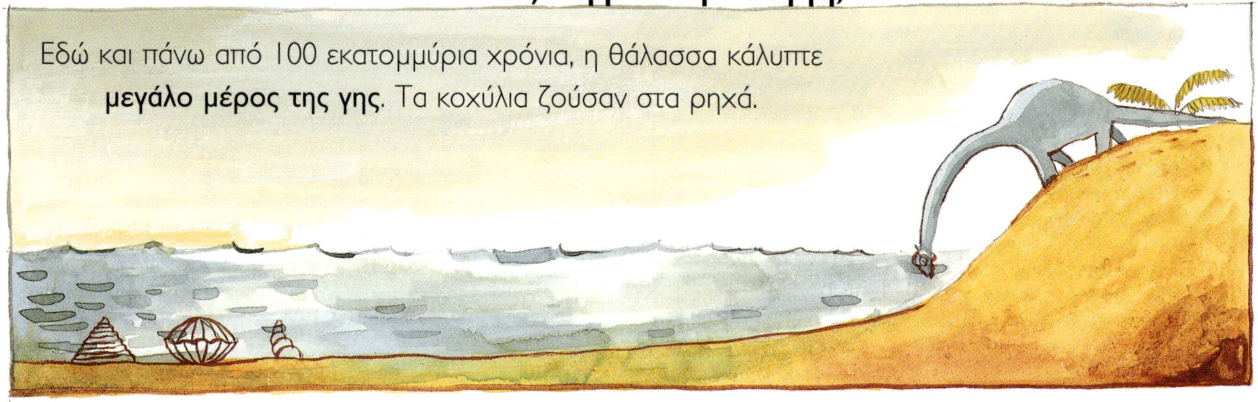

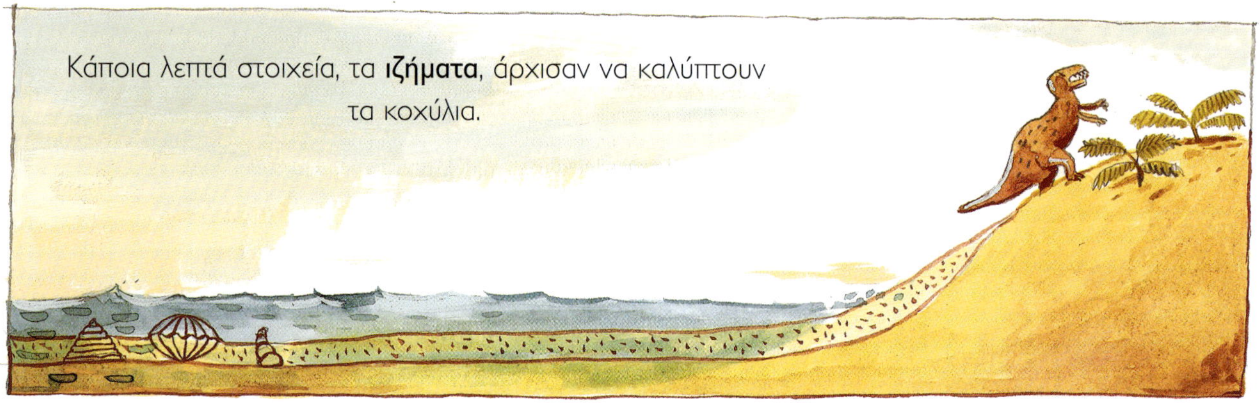

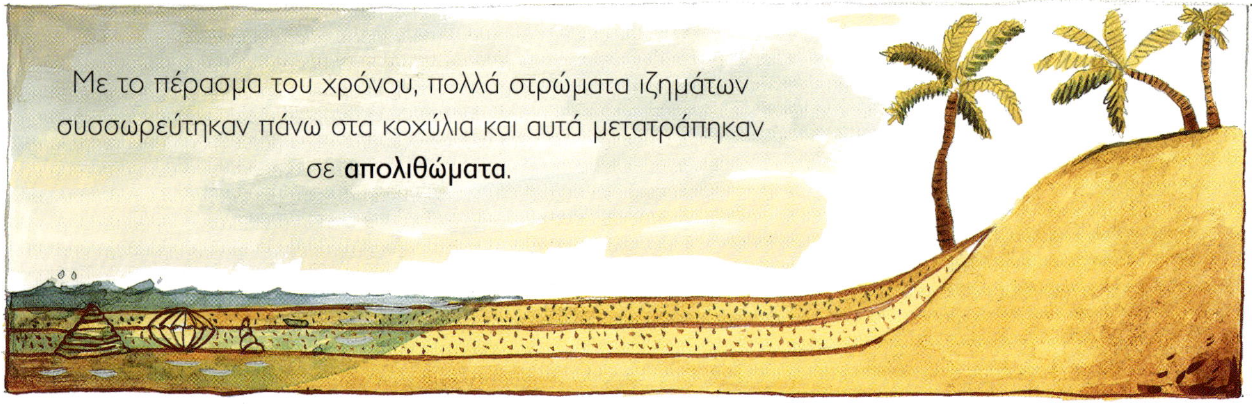

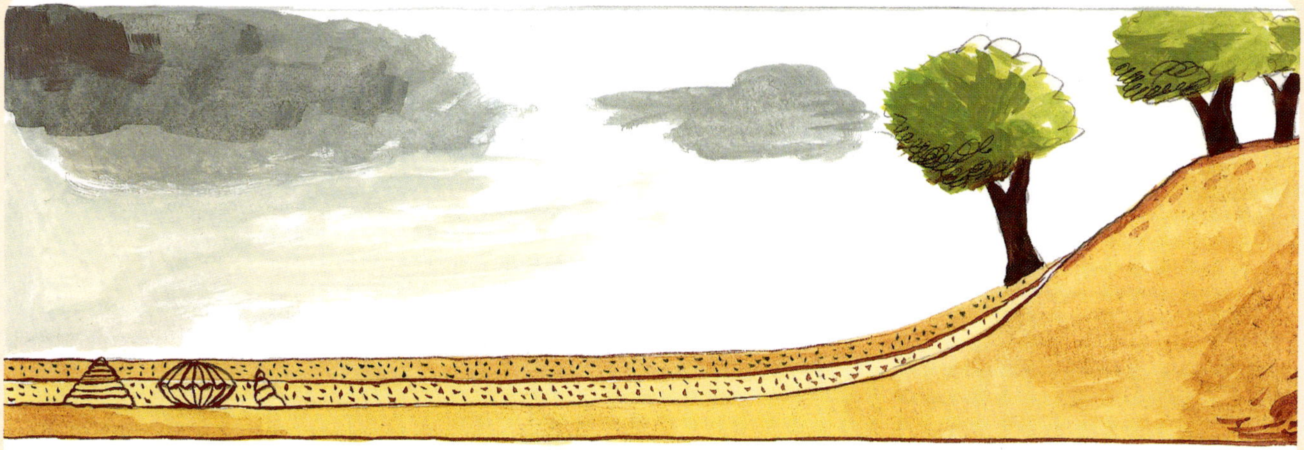

Στη συνέχεια, η θάλασσα **απομακρύνθηκε** από τη ζώνη όπου ζούσαν τα κοχύλια, αφήνοντας να εμφανιστούν τα στρώματα των ιζημάτων στα οποία ήταν κρυμμένα τα απολιθώματα.

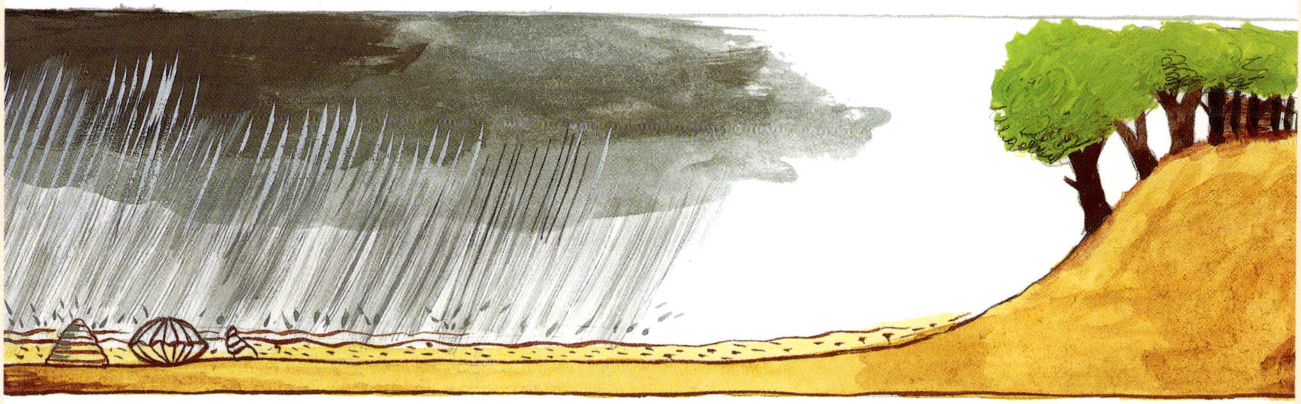

Σιγά σιγά το **νερό της βροχής** και ο **άνεμος** κατέστρεψαν τα στρώματα των ιζημάτων πάνω στα απολιθώματα.

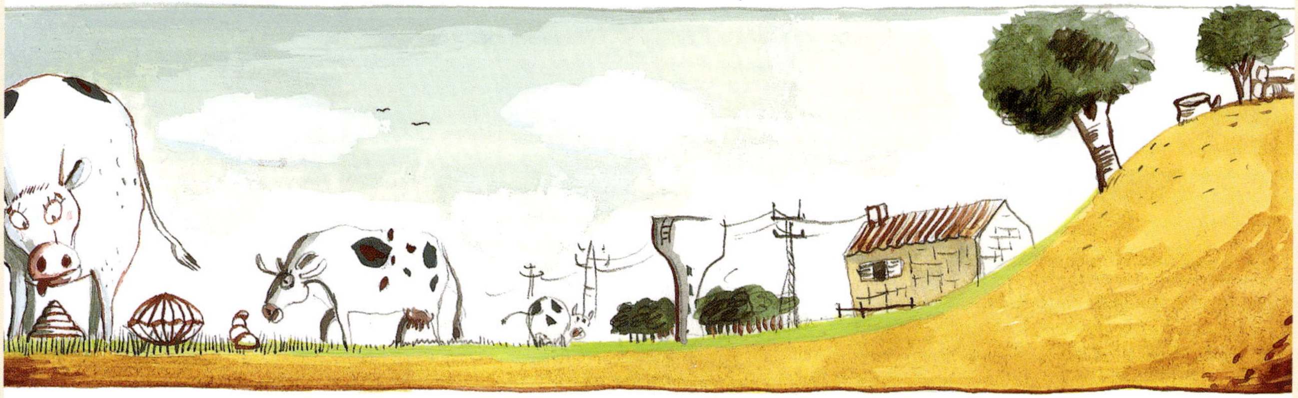

Τα απολιθώματα ξαναβρέθηκαν **στη στεριά**. Γι' αυτό σε πολλές περιοχές μπορούμε να ξαναβρούμε απολιθώματα στο έδαφος... χωρίς μάλιστα να χρειαστεί να σκάψουμε!

Τα πετρώματα

Το έδαφος της Γης είναι φτιαγμένο από κάθε είδους πέτρωμα. Κάποια είναι σκληρά, άλλα πιο μαλακά. Κάποια είναι πολύ όμορφα. Τα πετρώματα χρησιμεύουν σε πολλά πράγματα.

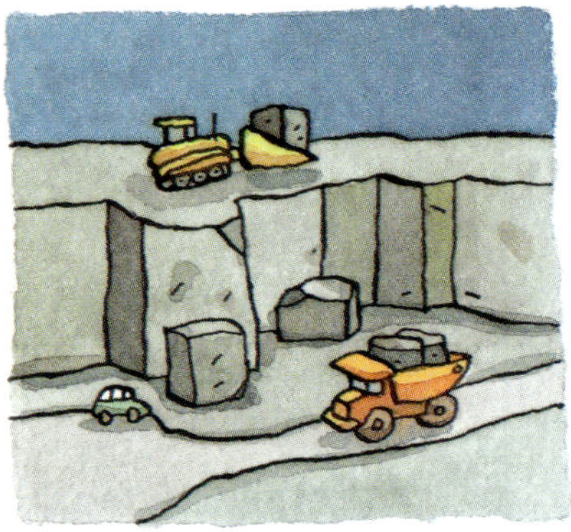

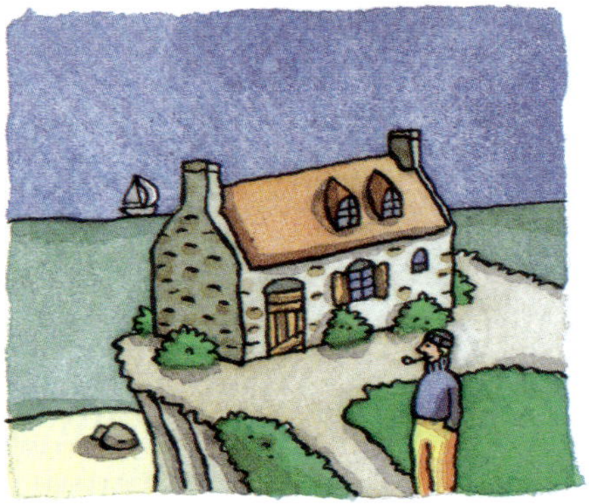

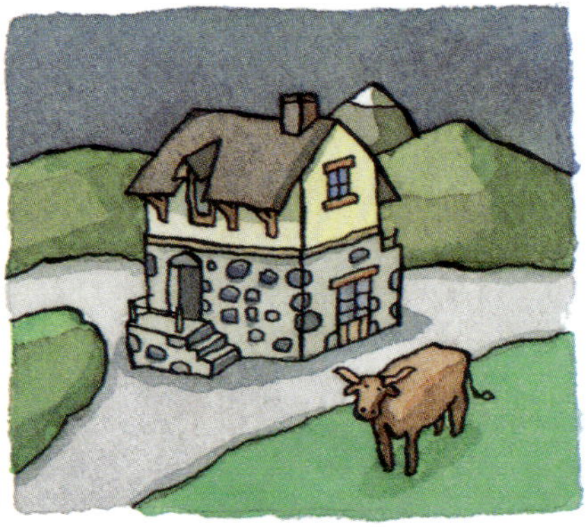

Ανάλογα με τις περιοχές, οι πέτρες με τις οποίες χτίζουμε διαφέρουν.

Για να χτίσουμε σπίτια, παίρνουμε πέτρες από τα **λατομεία**.

Πολλά σπίτια χτίζονται με **γρανίτη**, ένα γκρίζο πέτρωμα.

Άλλα χτίζονται με πετρώματα ηφαιστείων, δηλαδή με **βασάλτη**.

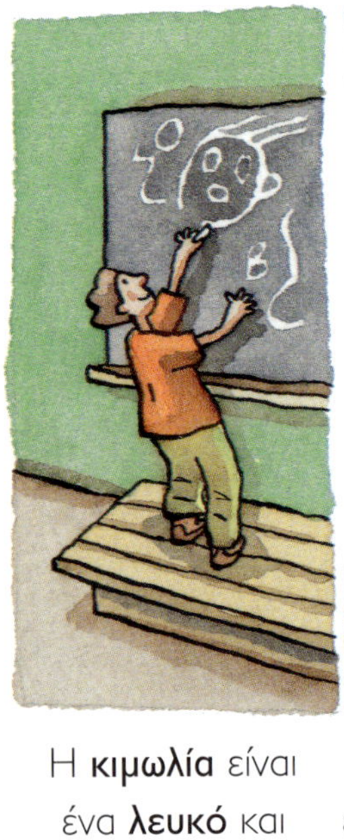

Η **κιμωλία** είναι ένα **λευκό** και πολύ μαλακό πέτρωμα.

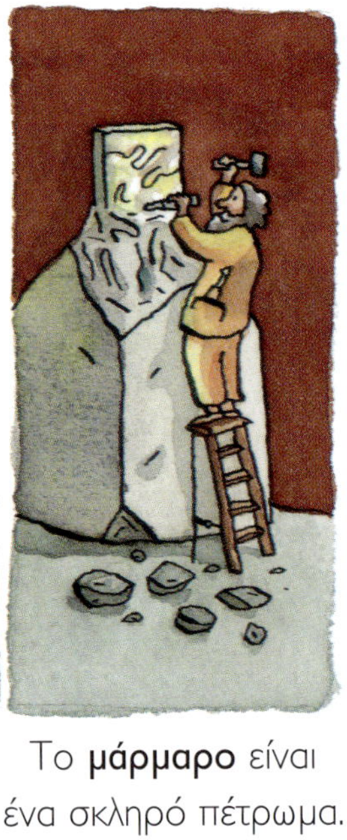

Το **μάρμαρο** είναι ένα σκληρό πέτρωμα. Με αυτό φτιάχνουμε τα **αγάλματα**.

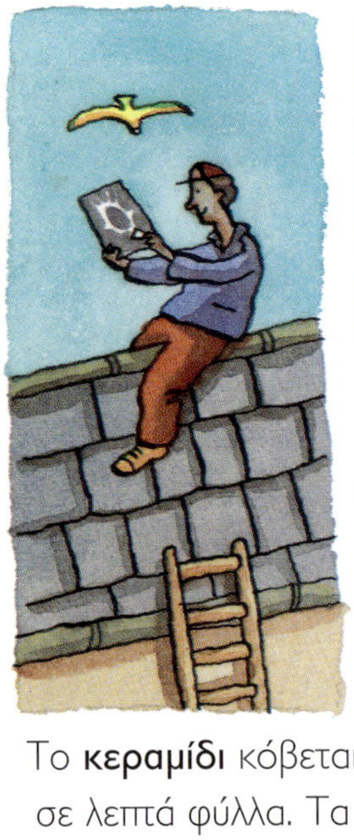

Το **κεραμίδι** κόβεται σε λεπτά φύλλα. Τα χρησιμοποιούμε για να φτιάξουμε **στέγες**.

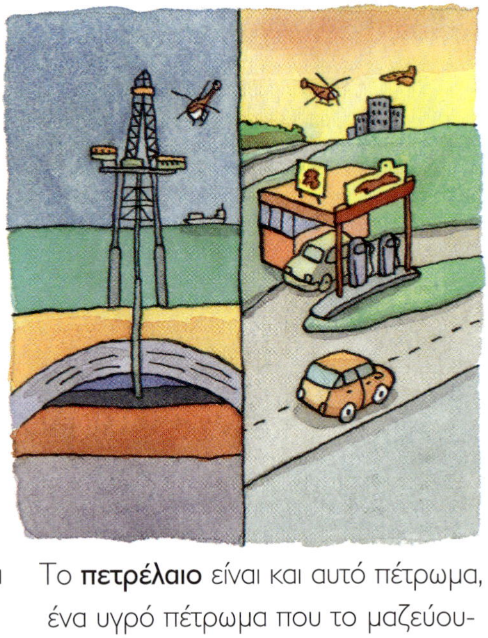

Το **πετρέλαιο** είναι και αυτό πέτρωμα, ένα υγρό πέτρωμα που το μαζεύουμε σκάβοντας μέσα στο έδαφος. Με αυτό φτιάχνουμε τη **βενζίνη**.

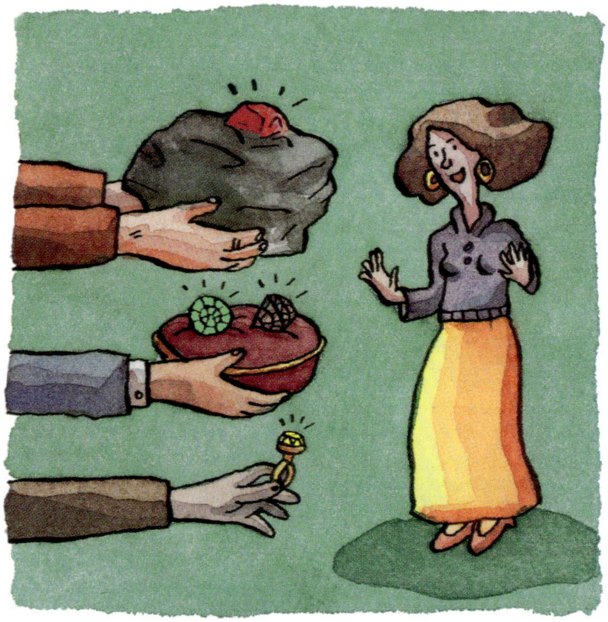

Οι **πολύτιμες πέτρες** είναι διαφανείς.
Το **διαμάντι** είναι το πιο σπάνιο· το **ρουμπίνι** είναι κόκκινο· το **σμαράγδι**, πράσινο· το **τοπάζι**, κίτρινο.

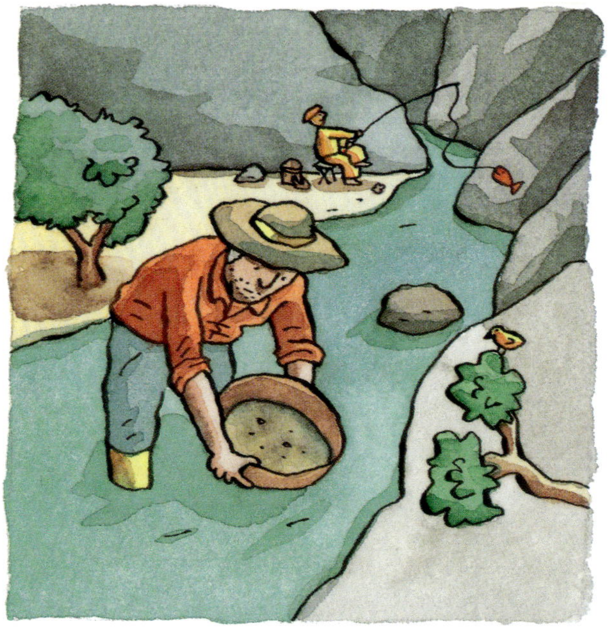

Στην άμμο και στα χαλίκια των ποταμών πολλές φορές βρίσκουμε **βόλους χρυσού**.
Ο χρυσός είναι ένα πολύτιμο μέταλλο.

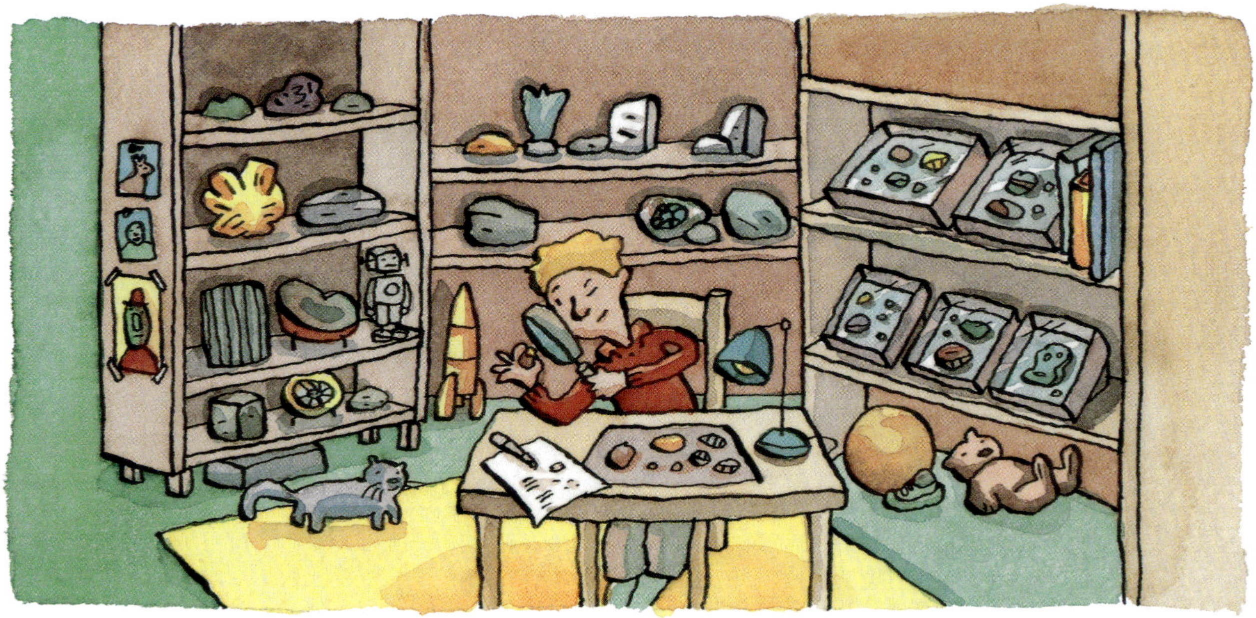

Αν σου αρέσει να μαζεύεις πέτρες, ψάξε απολιθώματα ή λαμπερούς κρυστάλλους. Βάλε τα σε κουτιά ανάλογα με τον τύπο τους, σημειώνοντας πάνω σε ετικέτες το σημείο όπου τα βρήκες.

Τα επαγγέλματα της Γης

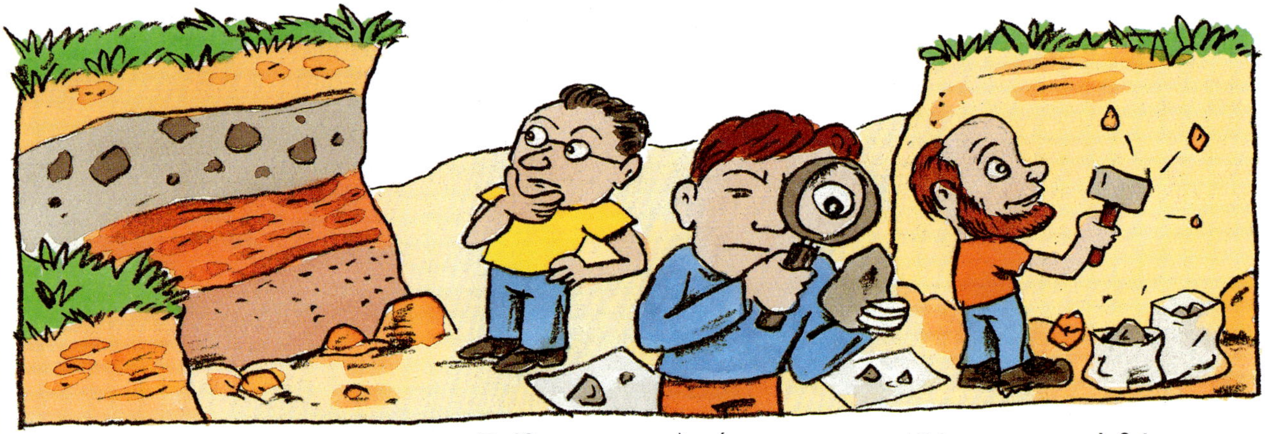

Ο **γεωλόγος** μελετά τα πετρώματα που σχηματίζουν το έδαφος και το υπέδαφος. Παρατηρεί τους διάφορους τύπους πετρωμάτων.

Σκάβει για να μελετήσει τη μορφή των **πετρωμάτων** στο πέρασμα του χρόνου.

Ψάχνει για **απολιθώματα**. Είναι εξοπλισμένος με ένα **μεγεθυντικό φακό**, για να παρατηρεί τις λεπτομέρειες των πετρωμάτων, με μια **πυξίδα**, για να βλέπει πώς είναι προσανατολισμένα, και με σακούλες, για να μαζεύει **δείγματα**...

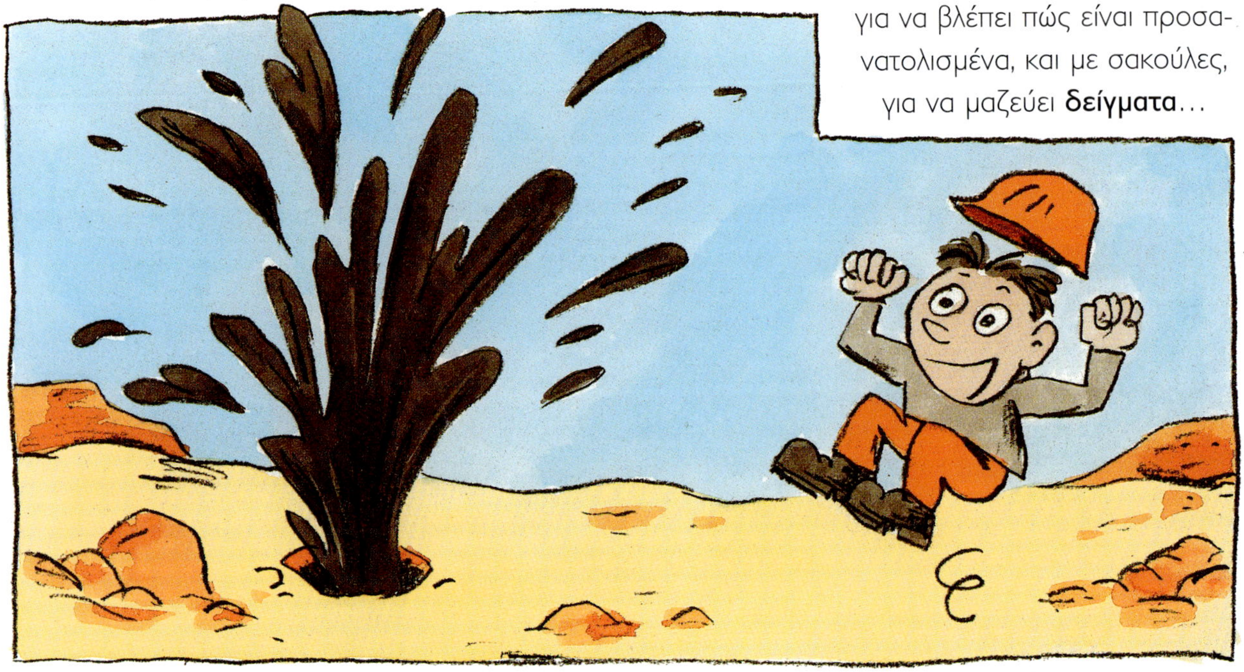

Οι γεωλόγοι είναι αυτοί που μελετούν το υπέδαφος, για να βρουν **πετρέλαιο**.

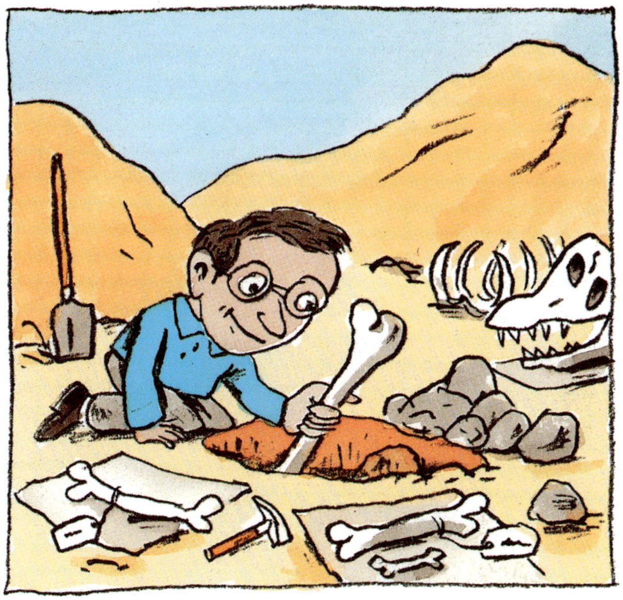

Ο **παλαιοντολόγος** ψάχνει και μελετά τα απολιθώματα και τα υπολείμματα των ζώων που έχουν εξαφανιστεί, όπως οι δεινόσαυροι ή τα μαμούθ, αλλά και τα ίχνη των προϊστορικών ανθρώπων.

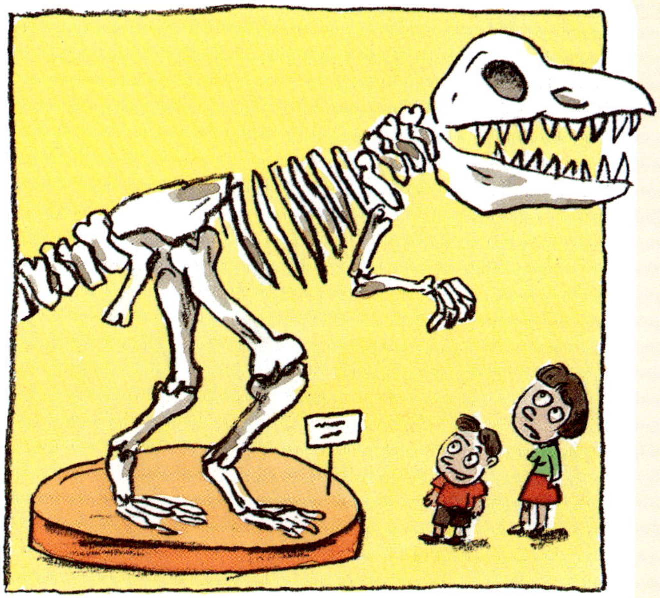

Χάρη στις έρευνες των παλαιοντολόγων μάθαμε ότι την εποχή των **δεινοσαύρων** ο άνθρωπος δεν υπήρχε ακόμη.

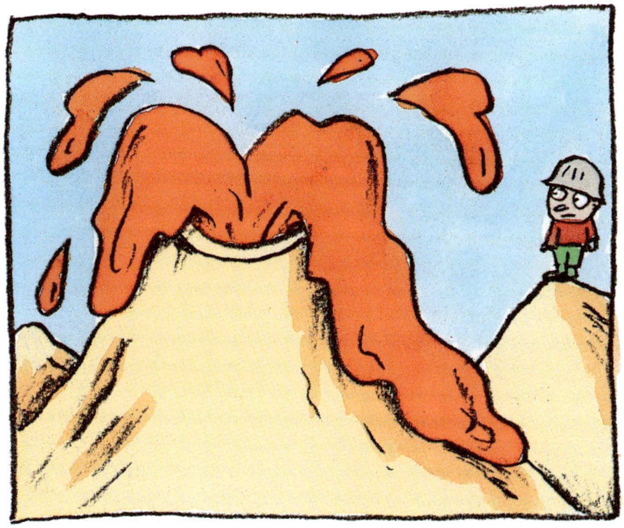

Ο **ηφαιστειολόγος** μελετά τα ηφαίστεια. Τα παρακολουθεί για να προβλέπει τις εκρήξεις που θα μπορούσαν να είναι επικίνδυνες.

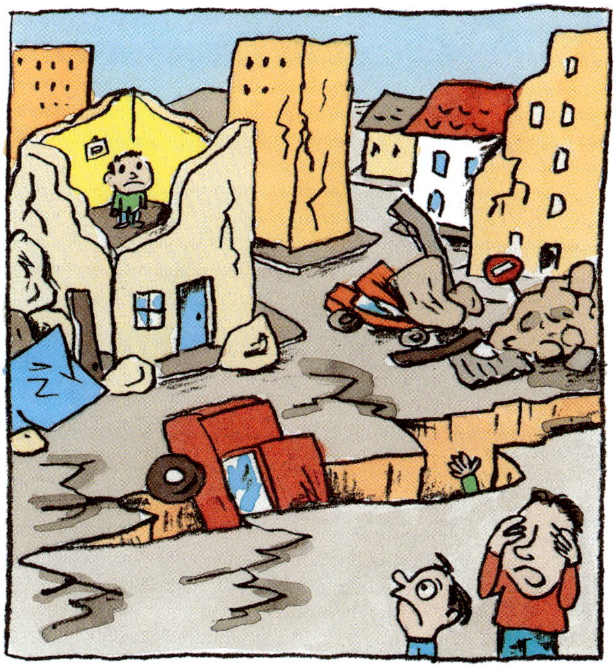

Ο **σεισμολόγος** μελετά τους σεισμούς.

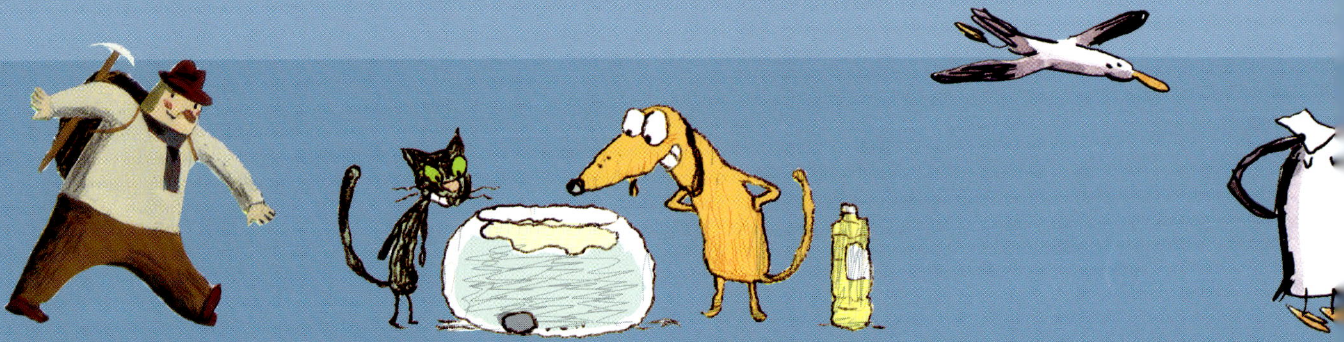

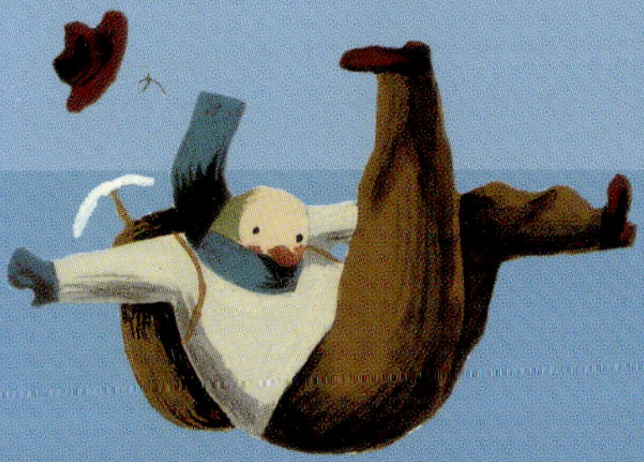

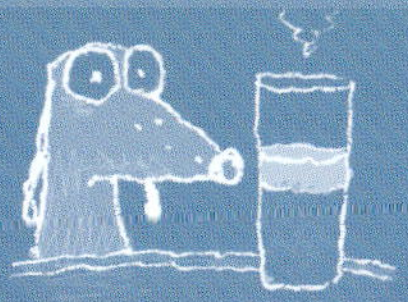

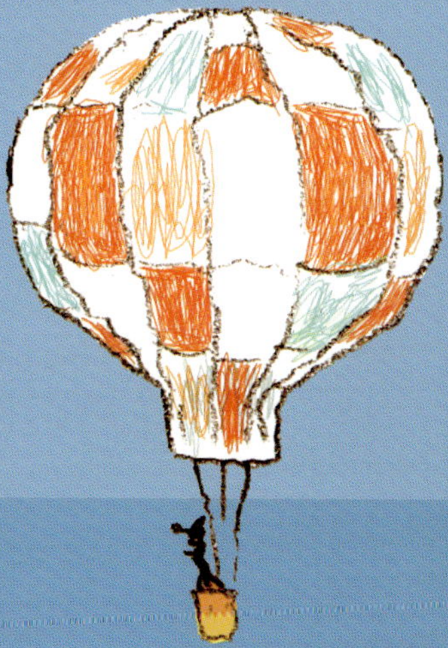

Η ΓΗ
ΤΟ ΝΕΡΟ

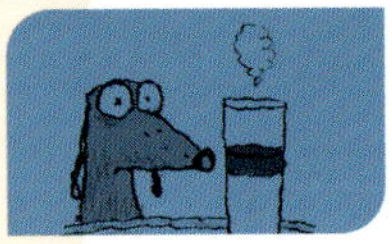

Το νερό σε όλες τις καταστάσεις του

Πάνω στη Γη το νερό υπάρχει σε τρεις μορφές, που τις ονομάζουμε καταστάσεις.

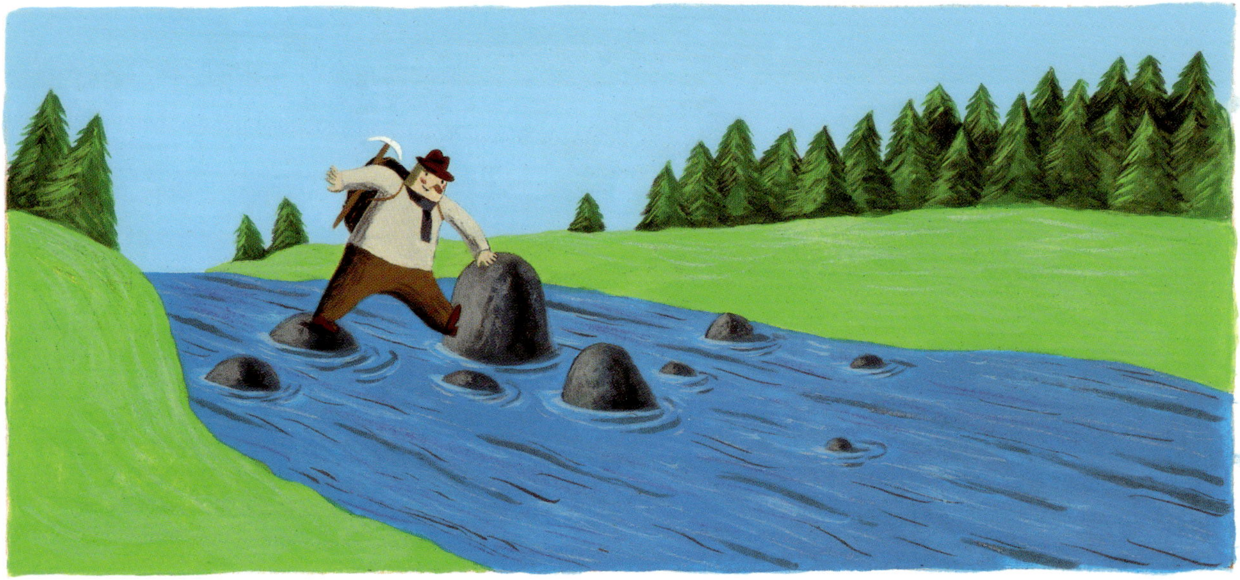

Η πιο συνηθισμένη κατάσταση του νερού είναι η **υγρή**: είναι το νερό των ποταμών και της θάλασσας.

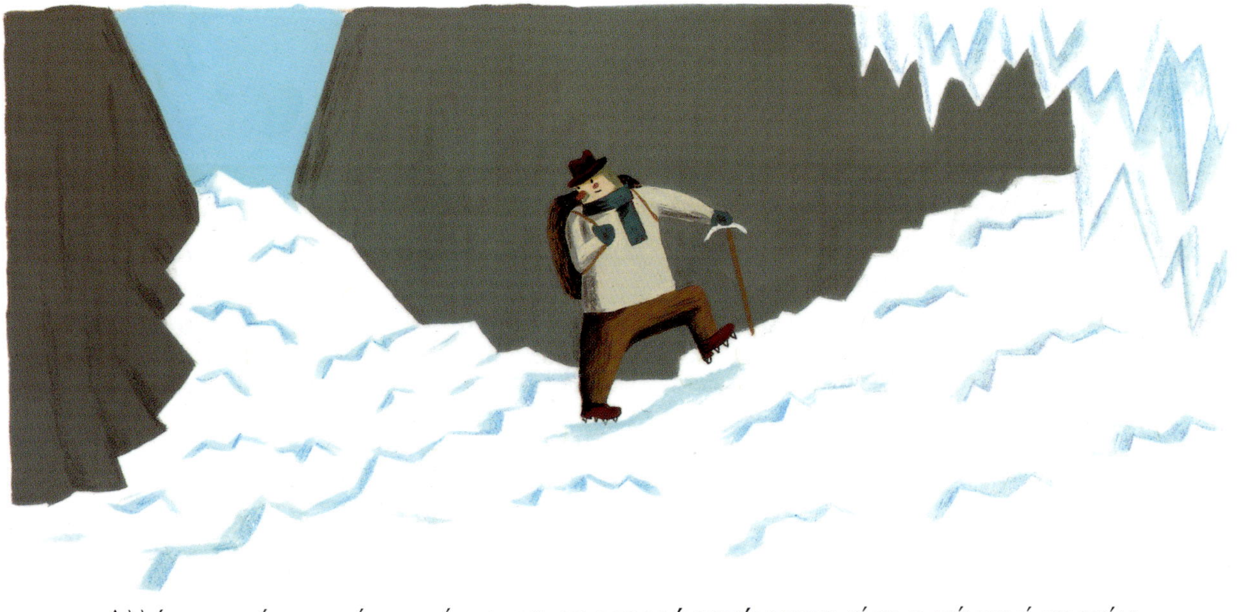

Αλλά το νερό μπορεί να υπάρχει και σε **στερεά κατάσταση**: είναι ο πάγος ή το χιόνι.

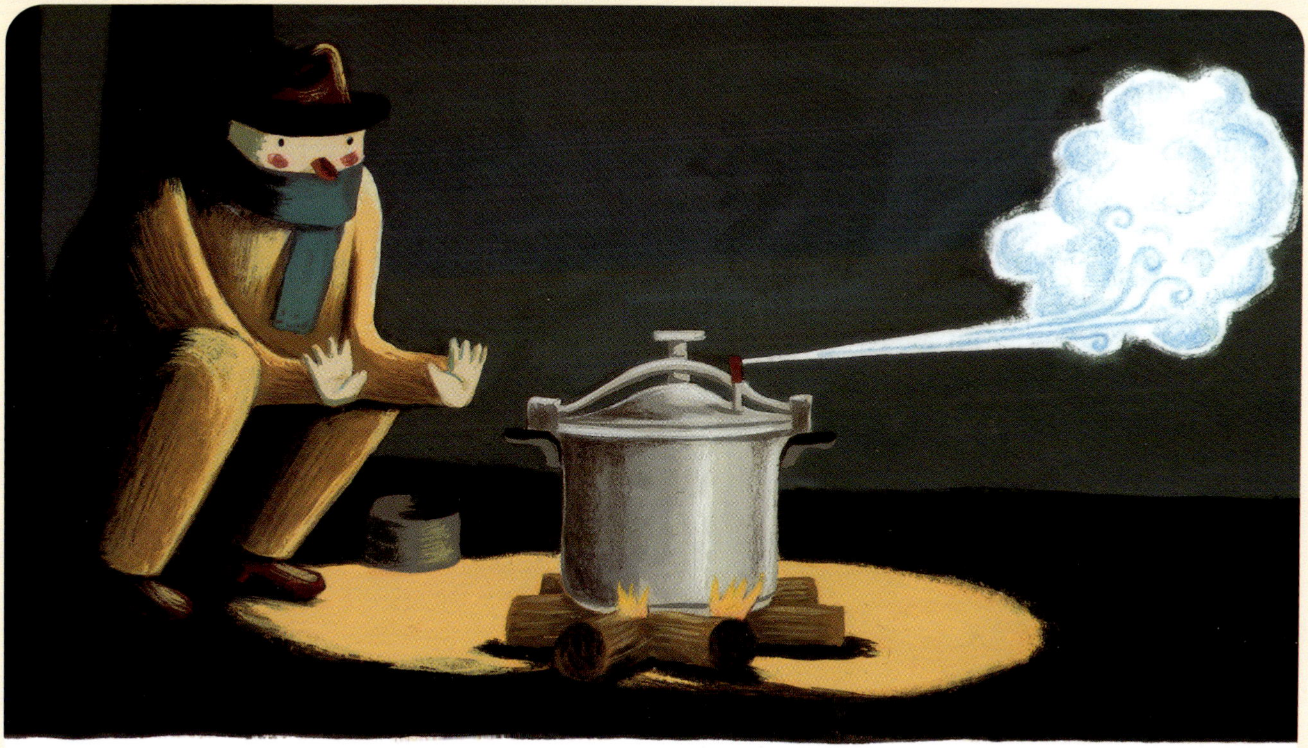

Το νερό μπορεί ακόμα να υπάρχει σε **αέρια κατάσταση**: είναι ο υδρατμός.

Η κατάσταση του νερού εξαρτάται από τη **θερμοκρασία**.

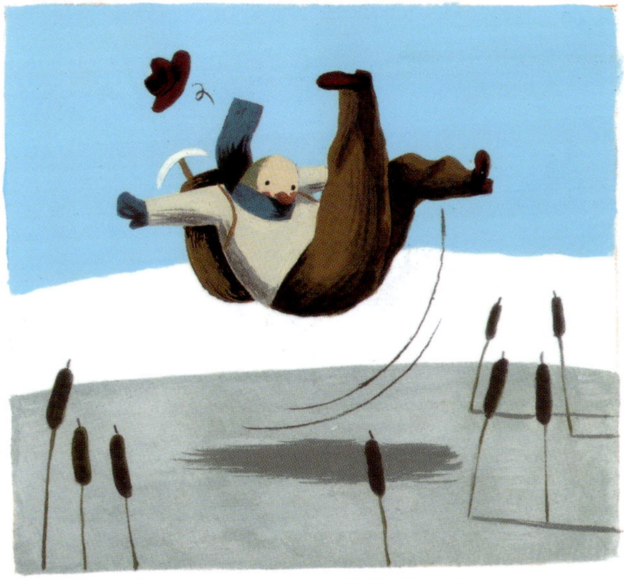

Το νερό **παγώνει** στους 0 βαθμούς Κελσίου: περνά από την υγρή στη στερεά κατάσταση.

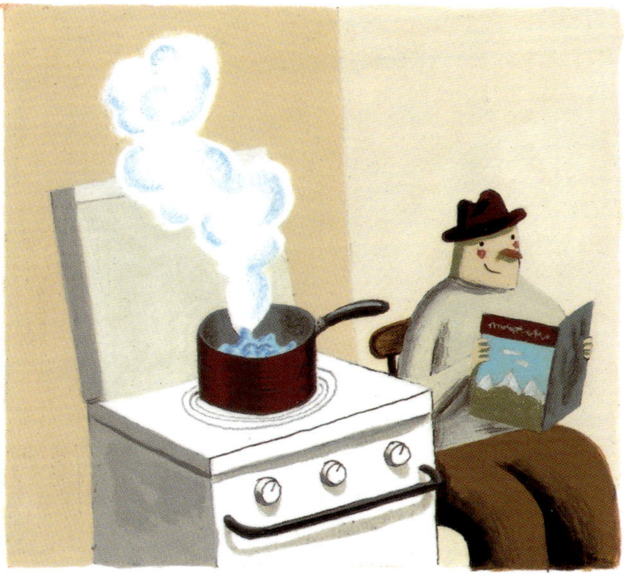

Το νερό **βράζει** στους 100 βαθμούς Κελσίου: τότε περνά από την υγρή στην αέρια κατάσταση.

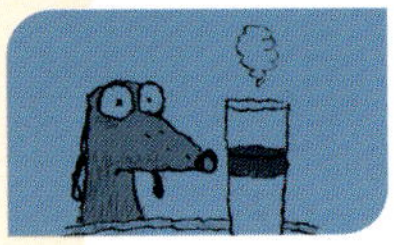

Δεν είναι όλα τα υγρά νερό

Το λάδι είναι ένα υγρό που δεν περιέχει νερό. Αλλά, όπως και το νερό, το λάδι μπορεί να είναι υγρό, αέριο ή στερεό.

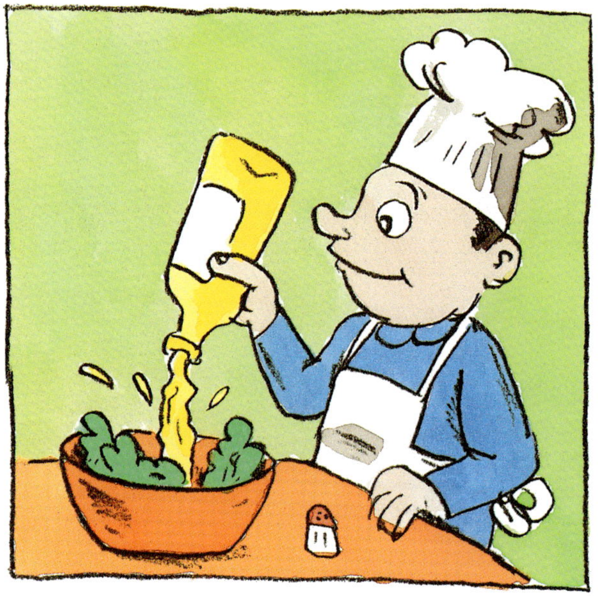

Το **λάδι** που ρίχνει ο μάγειρας στη σαλάτα είναι **υγρό**.

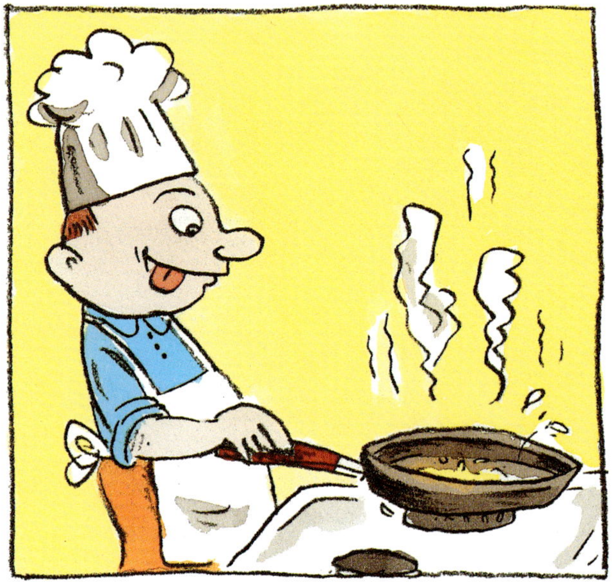

Το λάδι που **ζεσταίνει** ο μάγειρας στο τηγάνι «καπνίζει».

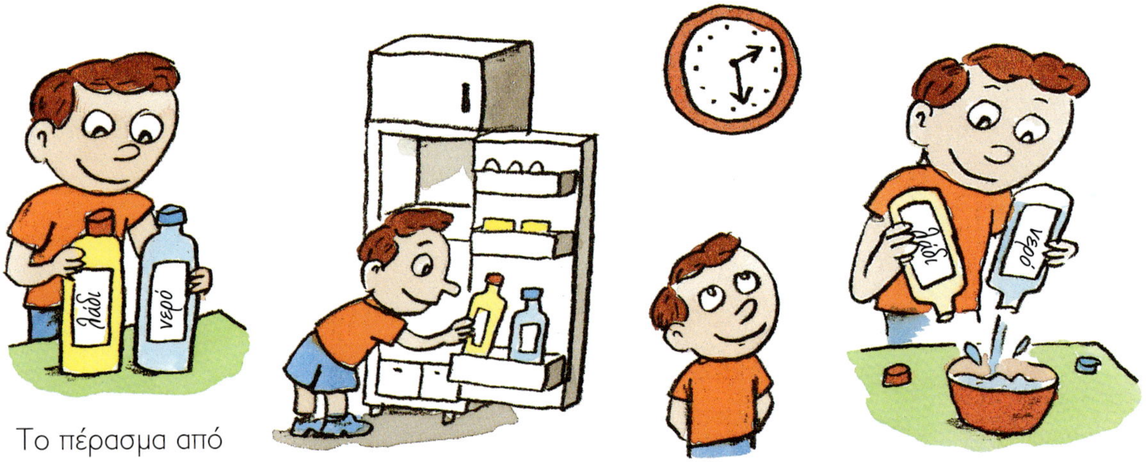

Το πέρασμα από την υγρή στη στερεά κατάσταση ονομάζεται **στερεοποίηση**.

Η **θερμοκρασία** της στερεοποίησης δεν είναι η ίδια για το νερό και το λάδι. Το λάδι στερεοποιείται σε 3 ώρες, στη θερμοκρασία του ψυγείου. Το νερό στερεοποιείται στην κατάψυξη.

Το πέρασμα από τη στερεά στην υγρή κατάσταση ονομάζεται **τήξη**.

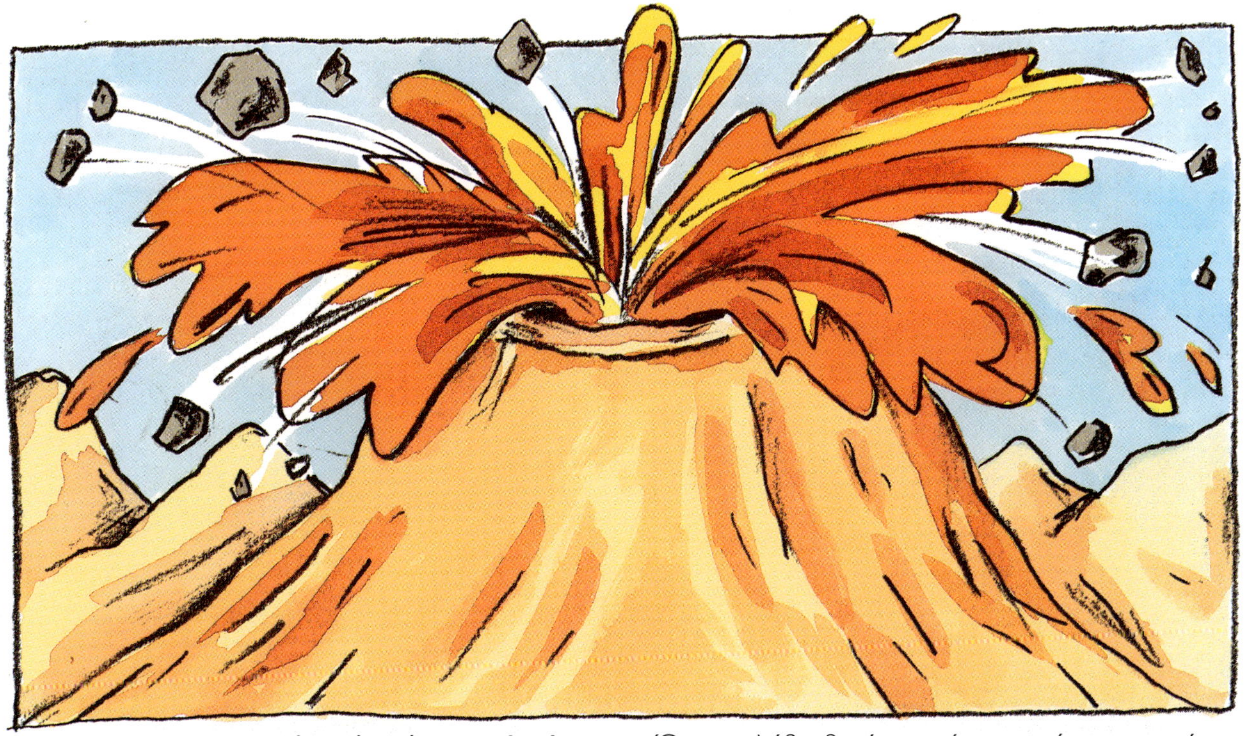

Η **λάβα** των ηφαιστείων είναι ένα **υγρό πέτρωμα**. Όταν η λάβα βγαίνει από το ηφαίστειο, παγώνει και στερεοποιείται, δηλαδή ξαναγίνεται στερεό πέτρωμα.

Το άρωμα περιέχει οινόπνευμα. Όταν ανοίγουμε το μπουκάλι, ένα μέρος αυτού του οινοπνεύματος γίνεται **αέριο** και μεταδίδει την ωραία μυρωδιά του αρώματος.

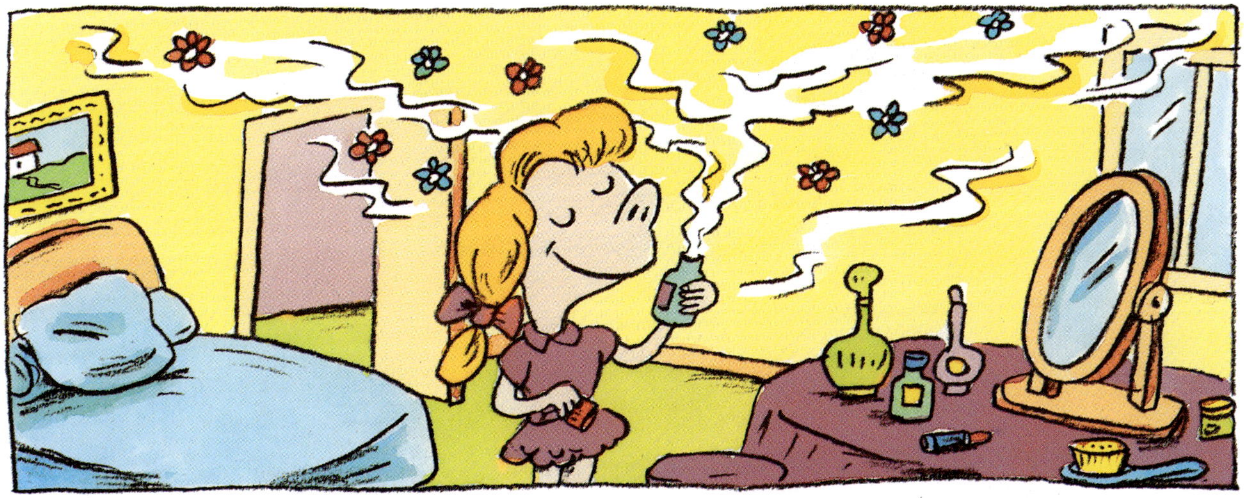

Το πέρασμα από την υγρή κατάσταση στην αέρια ονομάζεται **εξάτμιση**.

Πιο πυκνό, πιο αραιό

Το νερό, το λάδι ή ένα πέτρωμα δεν έχουν την ίδια πυκνότητα. Για τον ίδιο όγκο το νερό, το λάδι ή το πέτρωμα δεν έχουν το ίδιο βάρος.

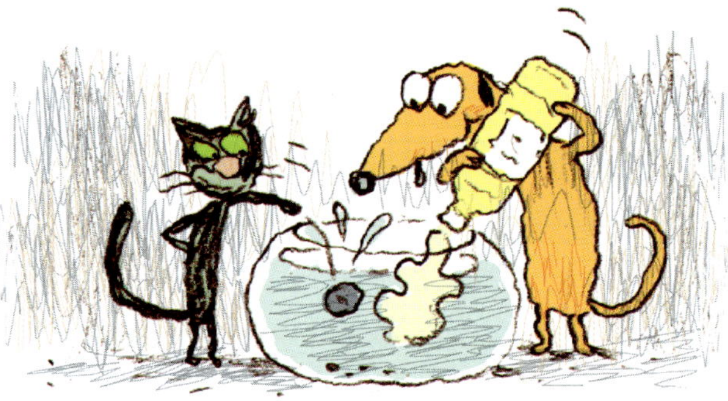

Αν βάλουμε **μέσα σ' ένα δοχείο** γεμάτο νερό λάδι και ένα χαλίκι,

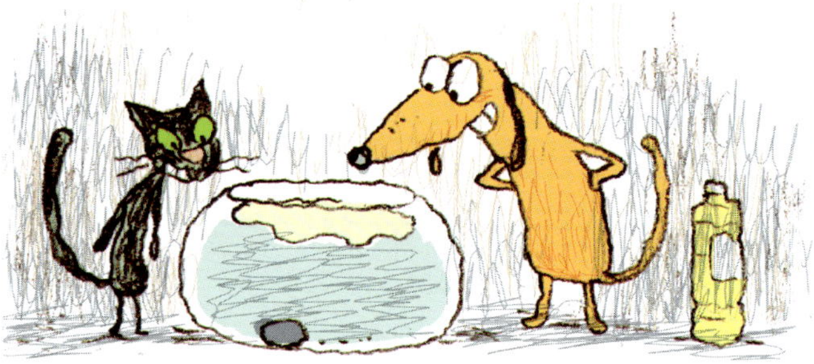

βλέπουμε ότι **το λάδι επιπλέει** πάνω από το νερό: το λάδι είναι λιγότερο πυκνό από το νερό. Το **χαλίκι πηγαίνει στον πάτο**: έχει μεγαλύτερη πυκνότητα.

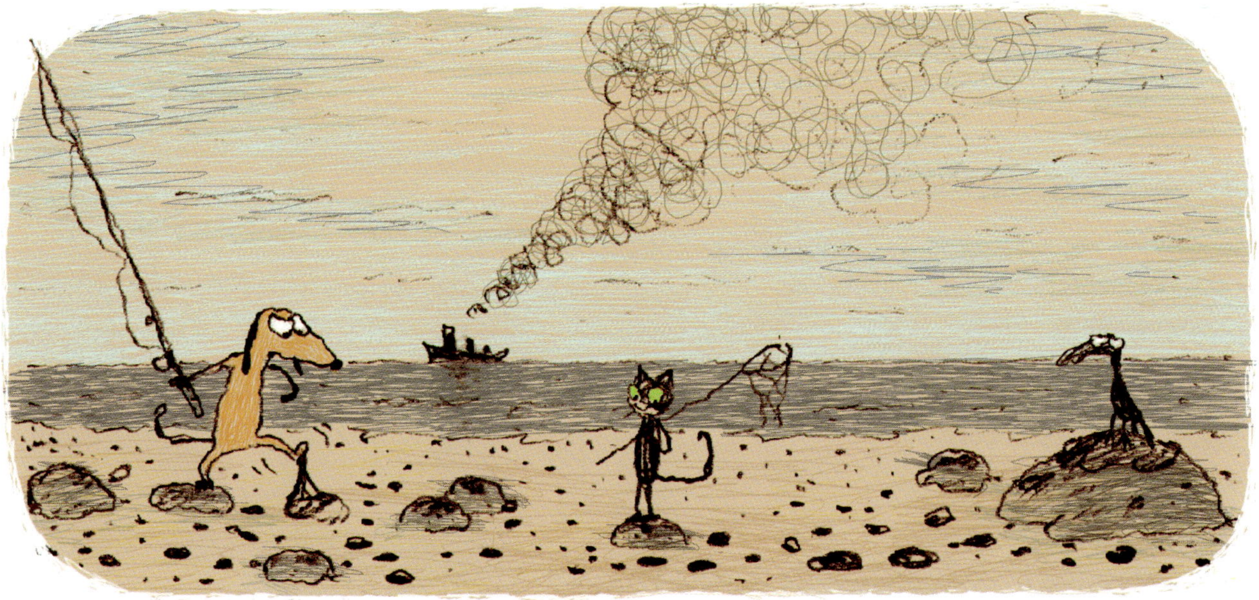

Όπως το λάδι, έτσι και το **πετρέλαιο** είναι λιγότερο πυκνό από το νερό: επιπλέει πάνω στο νερό. Αν ένα πετρελαιοφόρο χάσει το φορτίο του, το πετρέλαιο μένει **στην επιφάνεια της θάλασσας** και απλώνεται στις παραλίες: αυτή είναι η **πετρελαιοκηλίδα**.

ΕΝΑ πείΡαμα για ΝΑ το ΚΑΤαλάβεις ΚΑΛύτερα

Η **πυκνότητα** αλλάζει ανάλογα με τη **θερμοκρασία**.

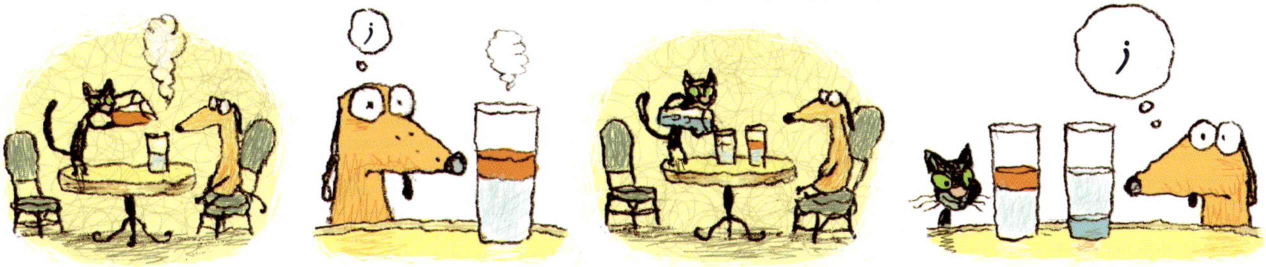

Ρίξε προσεκτικά **ζεστό χρωματισμένο νερό** σ' ένα ποτήρι κρύο νερό. Θα διαπιστώσεις ότι το ζεστό νερό μένει ψηλά: είναι λιγότερο πυκνό από το κρύο νερό.

Δοκίμασέ το ανάποδα. Ρίξε προσεκτικά **παγωμένο χρωματισμένο νερό** μέσα σε ζεστό νερό. Θα διαπιστώσεις ότι το παγωμένο νερό κατεβαίνει κάτω στο ποτήρι: έχει μεγαλύτερη πυκνότητα.

Το ίδιο συμβαίνει με τον **αέρα**. Ο ζεστός αέρας έχει μικρότερη πυκνότητα από τον παγωμένο αέρα. Έτσι ανεβάζουμε τα αερόστατα στον ουρανό.

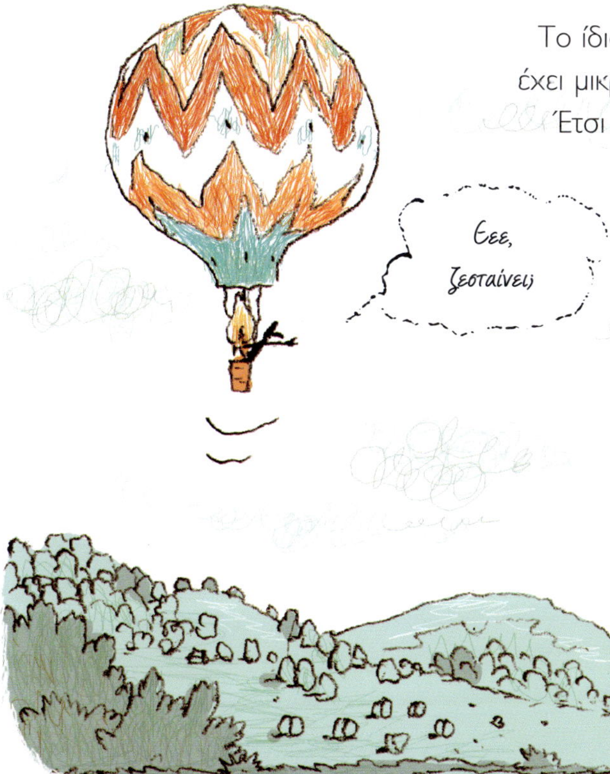

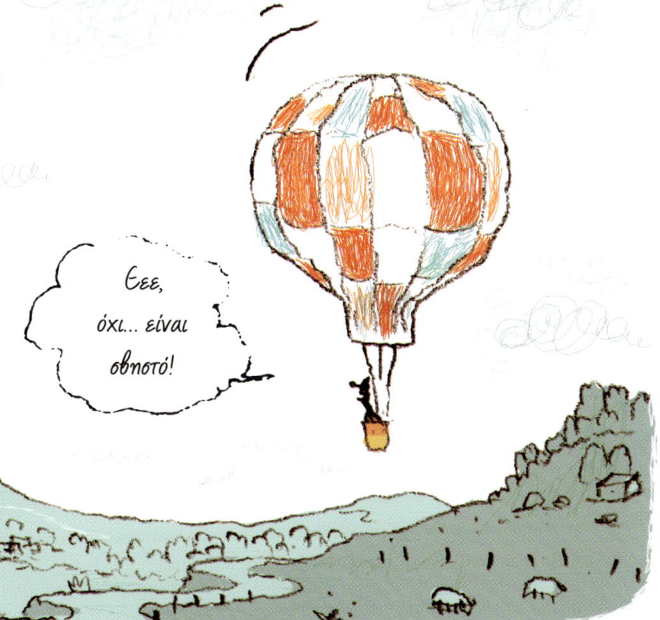

Όταν ο πιλότος **ζεσταίνει** τον αέρα, το **αερόστατο ανεβαίνει**, γιατί ο ζεστός αέρας έχει μικρότερη πυκνότητα από τον παγωμένο.

Για να ξανακατεβεί, αρκεί να αφήσει τον αέρα του αερόστατου να **παγώσει** σιγά σιγά, ώστε να γίνει πιο πυκνός και άρα πιο βαρύς.

Ο κύκλος του νερού

Στη Γη το νερό αλλάζει διαρκώς κατάσταση, μετατρέπεται σε βροχή, χιόνι, πάγο, σύννεφο… Αυτή τη διαδικασία την ονομάζουμε κύκλο του νερού.

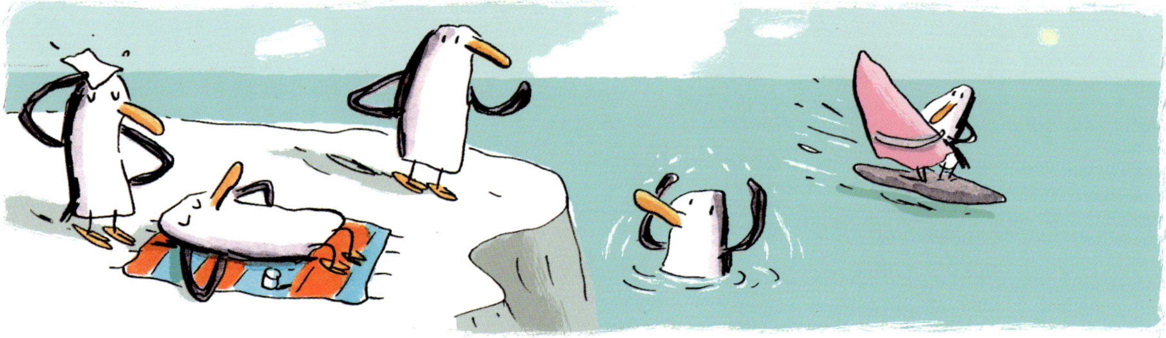

Όταν **ζεσταίνεται** από τον ήλιο, το **νερό** της θάλασσας **εξατμίζεται**.
Το νερό που βρίσκεται στη στεριά, στα ποτάμια και στις λίμνες, εξατμίζεται κι αυτό.

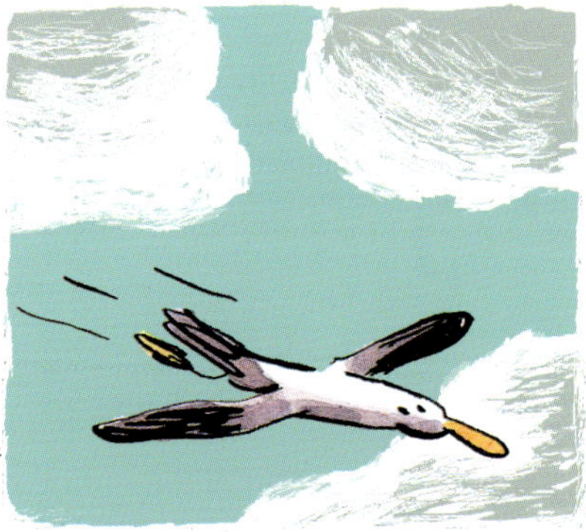

Ο ατμός σχηματίζει τα **σύννεφα**.

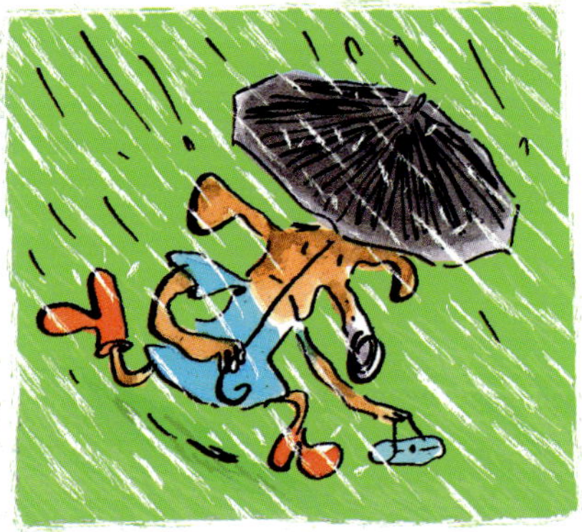

Το νερό ξαναπέφτει στο χώμα σαν **βροχή**

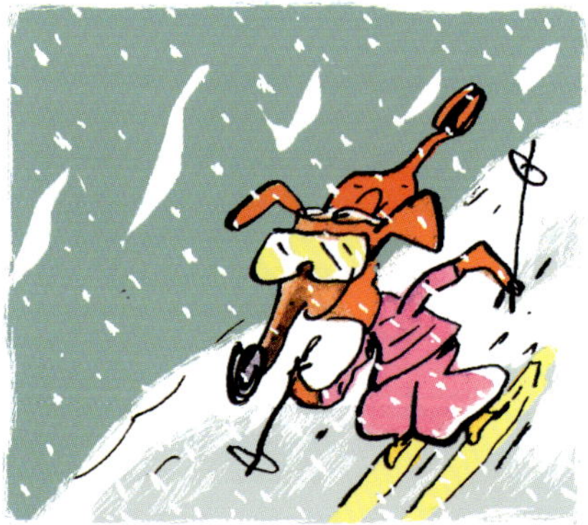

ή στα βουνά σαν **χιόνι**.

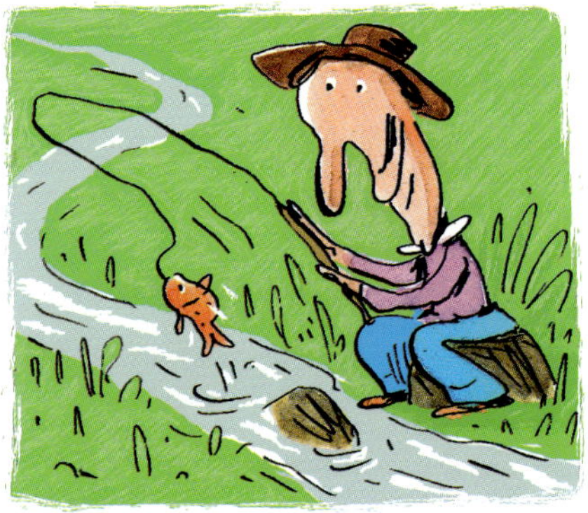

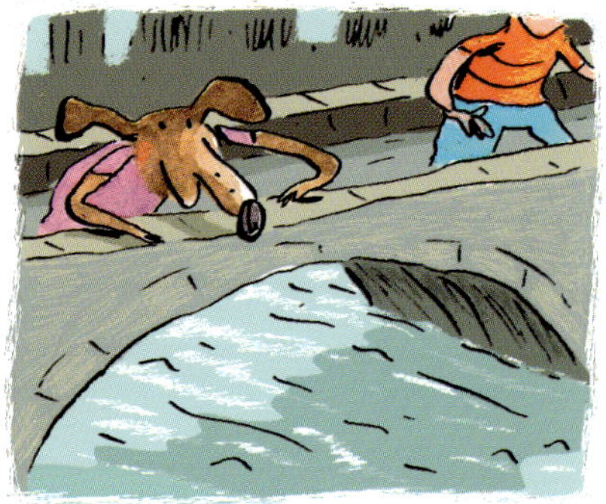

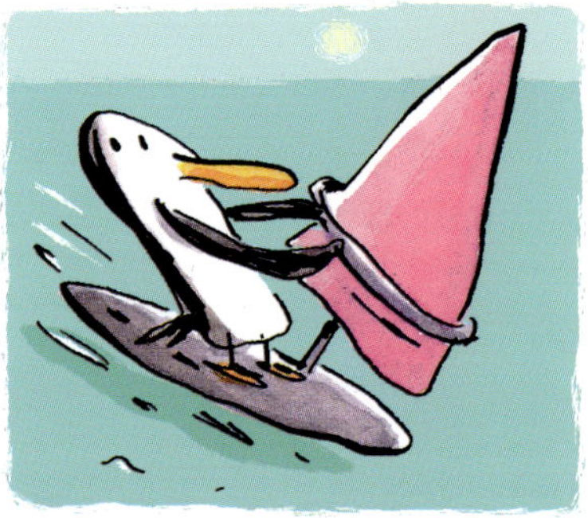

Η βροχή ή το λιωμένο χιόνι κατευθύνονται **προς τα ποτάμια** και επιστρέφουν στη θάλασσα.
Είναι ένας κύκλος που δε σταματά ποτέ!

ΔΥο ΠΕΙΡάματα για ΝΑ το ΚΑΤαλάβεις ΚΑΛύτερα

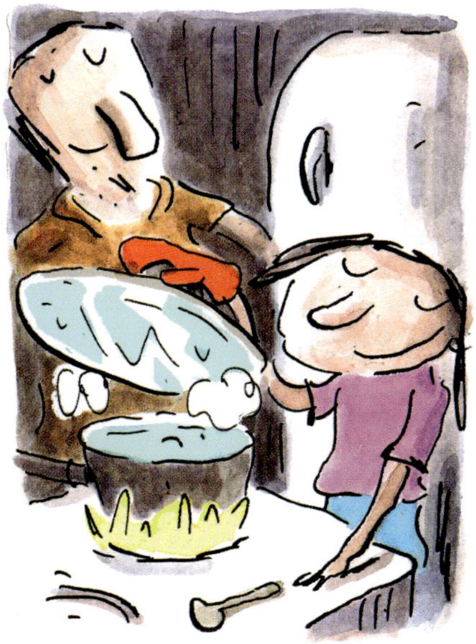

Άφησε ένα καπάκι στο **ψυγείο** για 1 ώρα. Βάλ' το πάνω σε μια κατσαρόλα με **νερό που βράζει**.

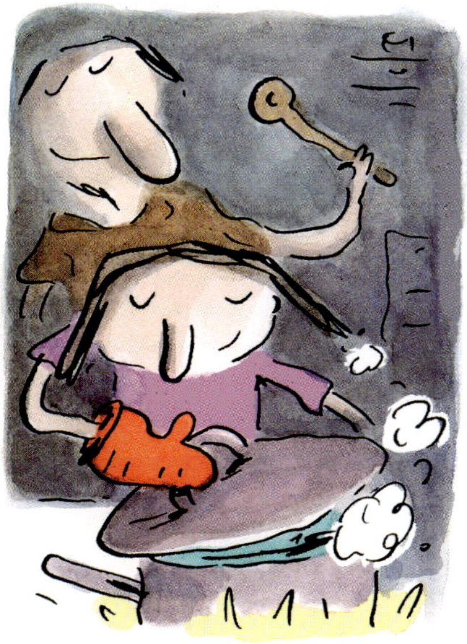

Όταν σηκώσεις το καπάκι, στην κατσαρόλα πέφτουν **σταγόνες νερού**.

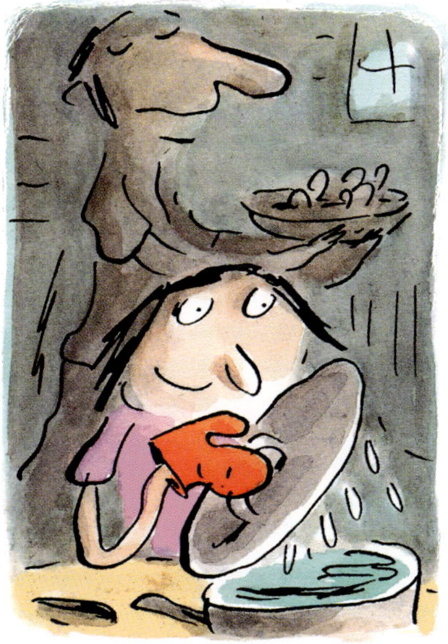

Ο ατμός του ζεστού νερού συμπυκνώνεται στο κρύο καπάκι. Έτσι σχηματίζεται η **βροχή**.

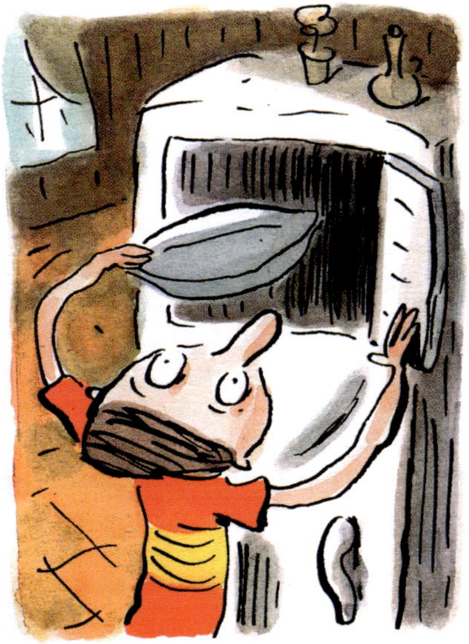

Βάλε ένα πιάτο **στην κατάψυξη** για 1 ώρα.

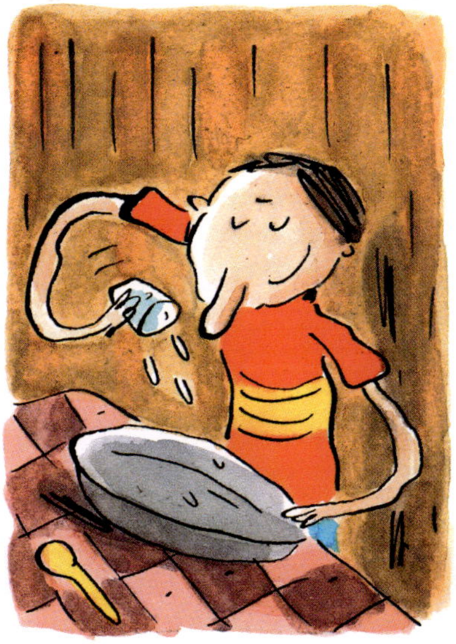

Βγάλ' το και ρίξε αμέσως **μερικές σταγόνες** παγωμένο νερό.

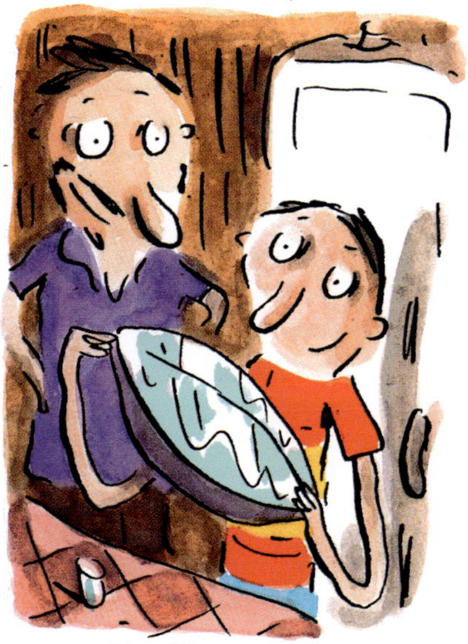

Η ψύξη του πιάτου μετατρέπει το νερό σε **λείο στρώμα πάγου**.

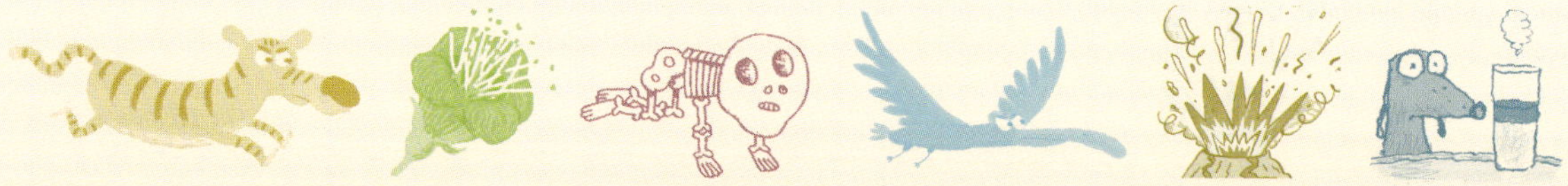

ΟΙ **ΟΡΟΙ** ΤΩΝ **ΕΠΙΣΤΗΜΩΝ**

Αιμοφόρο αγγείο: ένα μικρό κανάλι που χρησιμεύει στην κυκλοφορία του αίματος.

Αμφίβιο: αμφίβιο είναι ένα ζώο που ζει στη στεριά και στο νερό. Αμφίβιο είναι ο βάτραχος.

Αναπαράγομαι: δίνω ζωή σε άλλα πλάσματα του ίδιου είδους.

Ασπόνδυλο: ασπόνδυλο είναι το ζώο που δεν έχει σπονδυλική στήλη. Τα έντομα, τα σκουλήκια, τα οστρακοειδή είναι ασπόνδυλα.

Ατμόσφαιρα: το στρώμα αερίου που περιβάλλει τη Γη ονομάζεται ατμόσφαιρα.

Γεωλογία: η επιστήμη που μελετά το έδαφος και το υπέδαφος της Γης.

Γονιμοποίηση: γονιμοποίηση είναι η συνάντηση ενός αρσενικού κυττάρου με ένα θηλυκό κύτταρο, που καταλήγει στο σχηματισμό ενός νέου ζωντανού οργανισμού.

Εγκυμοσύνη: είναι η περίοδος των εννιά μηνών που η γυναίκα περιμένει ένα μωρό.

Είδος: ζωικό είδος είναι το σύνολο των ζώων που μοιάζουν και αναπαράγονται μεταξύ τους.

Έμβρυο: το μωρό ονομάζεται έμβρυο τους εννέα μήνες που βρίσκεται μέσα στην κοιλιά της μητέρας του.

Θηλαστικό: ζώο που το θηλυκό του έχει θηλές για να βυζαίνει τα μικρά του. Υπάρχουν θηλαστικά που ζουν στη γη και θηλαστικά που ζουν στη θάλασσα. Ο άνθρωπος και η φάλαινα είναι θηλαστικά.

Θηρευτής: θηρευτής είναι ένα ζώο που κυνηγά άλλα ζώα για να τραφεί.

Κάμπια: κάμπια είναι η μορφή που παίρνουν κάποια ζώα προτού ενηλικιωθούν.

Καρπός: ο καρπός περιέχει τους σπόρους και τους προστατεύει.

Κύτταρο: το κύτταρο είναι το μικρότερο στοιχείο που αποτελεί ένα ζωντανό οργανισμό. Τα φυτά, τα ζώα και οι άνθρωποι αποτελούνται από δισεκατομμύρια κύτταρα.

Λεία: ένα ζώο που έχει κυνηγηθεί και φαγωθεί από ένα άλλο ζώο ονομάζεται λεία.

Λουλούδι: το λουλούδι περιέχει όργανα που βοηθούν το φυτό να σχηματίζει τους σπόρους του και να αναπαράγεται.

Μαμή: η μαμή είναι μια γυναίκα που το επάγγελμά της είναι να συμπαραστέκεται στις γυναίκες στη διάρκεια της γέννας, πολλές φορές όμως τις παρακολουθεί και στη διάρκεια της εγκυμοσύνης τους.

Μαρσιποφόρο: θηλαστικό ζώο· το θηλυκό έχει μια τσέπη στην κοιλιά, που περιέχει τις θηλές του· εκεί μεγαλώνουν τα μικρά μετά τη γέννησή τους. Το καγκουρό και το κοάλα της Αυστραλίας είναι μαρσιποφόρα.

Μεταμορφώνομαι: αλλάζω εντελώς μορφή.

Μήτρα: στα θηλαστικά, το μωρό αναπτύσσεται μέσα στη μήτρα.

Οικολογία: η επιστήμη που μελετά το περιβάλλον, δηλαδή τις σχέσεις ανάμεσα στα ζωντανά όντα και το χώρο στον οποίο ζουν.

Οξυγόνο: το οξυγόνο είναι ένα αέριο πολύ εξαπλωμένο στη φύση, ιδιαίτερα στον αέρα που αναπνέουμε. Είναι απαραίτητο για τους περισσότερους ζωντανούς οργανισμούς.

Οργανισμός: το σύνολο των οργάνων ενός ζωντανού οργανισμού. Στον άνθρωπο είναι το σώμα.

Όργανο: το όργανο είναι ένα μέρος του σώματος με μια ιδιαίτερη λειτουργία. Το μάτι είναι το όργανο της όρασης.

Όρνιο: ζώο που τρέφεται με πτώματα ζώων σε αποσύνθεση. Ο γύπας είναι όρνιο.

Παμφάγο: τρέφεται με κρέας και φυτά. Ο άνθρωπος και η αρκούδα είναι παμφάγα.

Περιβάλλον: ο τόπος ζωής ενός ζωντανού οργανισμού.

Σαρκοφάγο: τρώει κυρίως κρέας. Ο λύκος είναι σαρκοφάγος.

Σπονδυλωτό: σπονδυλωτό είναι το ζώο που έχει σπονδυλική στήλη. Τα ψάρια και τα θηλαστικά είναι σπονδυλωτά.

Σπόρος: ο σπόρος επιτρέπει στο φυτό να αναπαράγεται.

Φυτοφάγο: τρέφεται με χόρτα και φύλλα. Η αγελάδα είναι φυτοφάγο ζώο.

Φωτοσύνθεση: το φαινόμενο με το οποίο τα φυτά αναπτύσσονται χρησιμοποιώντας το φως. Η φωτοσύνθεση είναι ένα από τα σημαντικότερα φαινόμενα της ζωής στη Γη.

Ψοφίμι: πτώμα ενός νεκρού ζώου, που έχει φαγωθεί από θηρευτές.

Χειμερία νάρκη: κάποια θηλαστικά, όπως η μαρμότα ή η αρκούδα, περνούν το χειμώνα σε χειμερία νάρκη. Ζουν με αργούς ρυθμούς, χωρίς να τρώνε, και κοιμούνται πολύ.

Χυμός: ο χυμός μοιράζει την τροφή σε όλο το φυτό. Υπάρχουν 2 είδη χυμών: ο χυμός που βοηθά το νερό και τα μεταλλικά άλατα των ριζών να κυκλοφορούν στα φύλλα και ο χυμός που ξεκινά από τα φύλλα και διανέμει σε όλο το φυτό τη ζάχαρη που παράγουν.

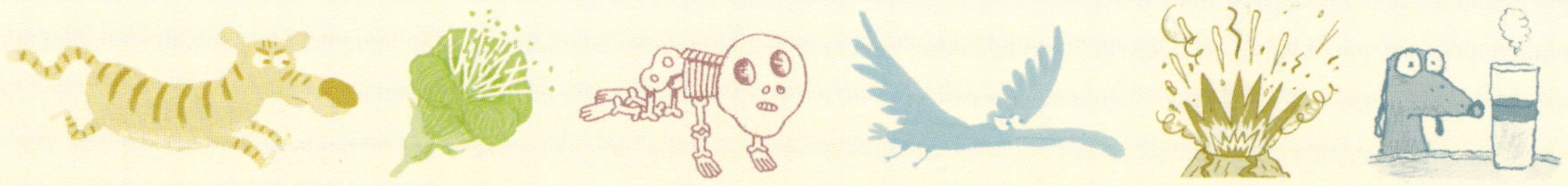

ΕΥΡΕΤΗΡΙΟ

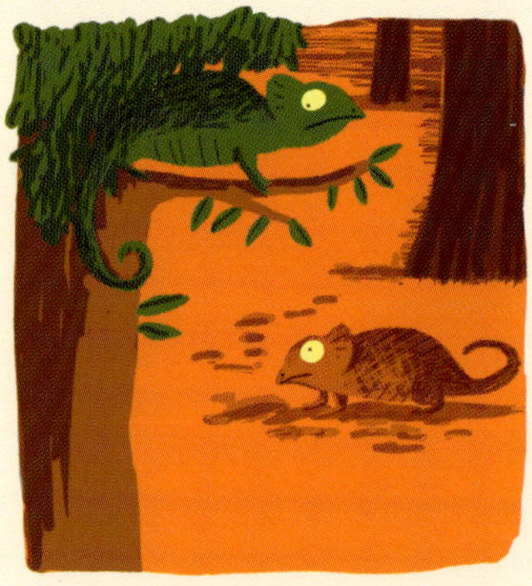

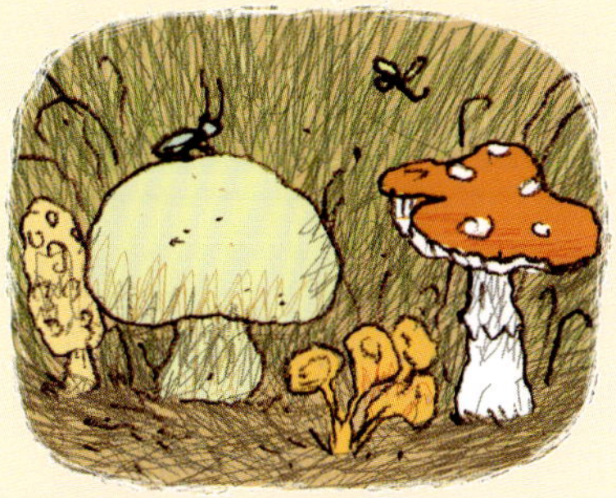

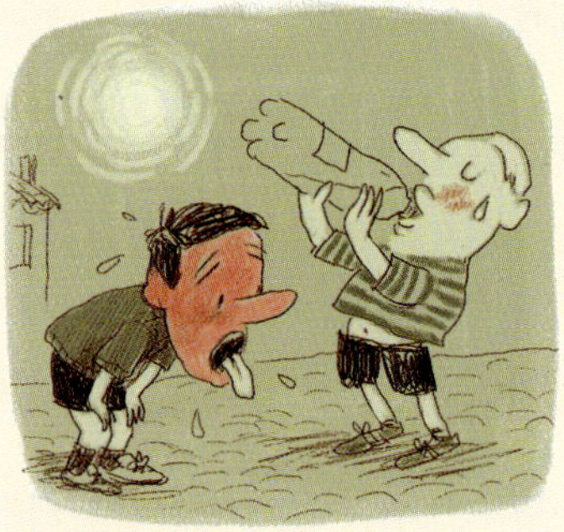

Ρ

Σ

Τ

Υ

Φ

Χ

Ψ

Ω

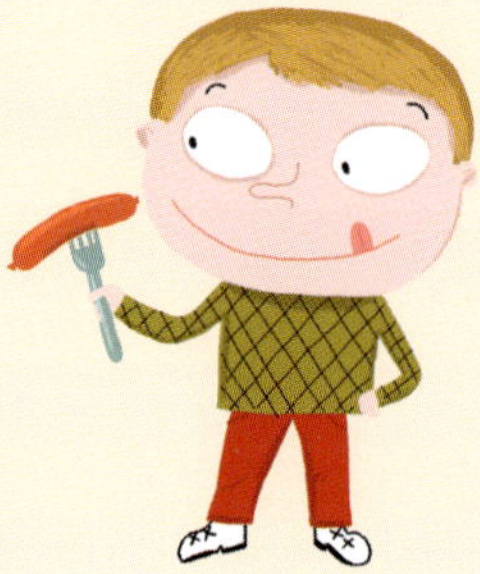

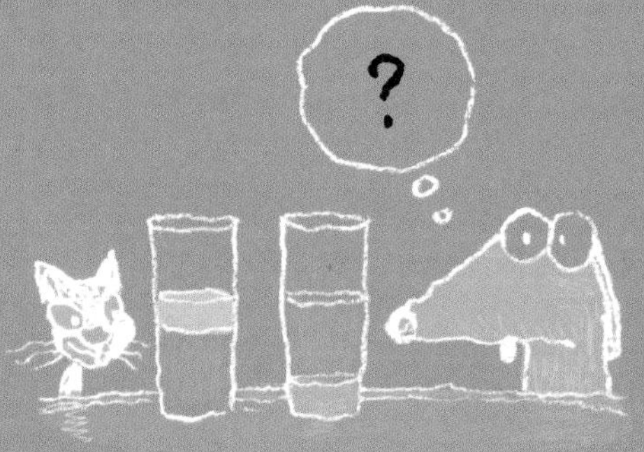